Strategy Game Programming with DirectX 9.0

Todd Barron

Wordware Publishing, Inc.

Library of Congress Cataloging-in-Publication Data

Barron, Todd.
   Strategy game programming with DirectX 9.0 / by Todd Barron.
     p. cm.
   ISBN 1-55622-922-4 (pbk.)
   1. Computer games--Programming.   2. DirectX. I. Title.
   QA76.76.C672B369 2003
   794.8'15268--dc21   2003012699
                                    CIP

ISBN 1-55622-922-4

10 9 8 7 6 5 4 3 2 1
0306

All inquiries for volume purchases of this book should be addressed to Wordware
Publishing, Inc., at the above address. Telephone inquiries may be made by calling:

(972) 423-0090

Dedication

For my best friend and the love of my life, my wife, Jennie.

In memory of Robert L. Brown Sr. and Ralph M. Davis Jr.

Contents

Contents

Part II

Building Blocks

Contents

Part III

Tool Development

Part IV

Advanced Topics

Acknowledgments

Jim Hill and Wes Beckwith at Wordware Publishing for publishing the book. Beth Kohler and Heather Hill at Wordware for editing the book and readying it for production. Gil Shif at Blizzard Entertainment for working with me to get the permissions to use their screen shots. Amy Farris at Westwood Entertainment for working with me to get the permissions to use their screen shots. Jeff Royle at ATI for setting me up with video cards to test compatibility. Sarah Davis at Discreet for setting me up with 3ds max to cover in the book. Susan Doering at Adobe for setting me up with Photoshop to cover in the book.

Introduction

Hello there, and welcome to the wonderful world of strategy game programming! One of my favorite genres of games has always been strategy. Nothing in the gaming world beats a long afternoon of playing a strategy game against a friend or foe.

As a beginner or intermediate game developer, you probably wonder how to put together such games. Although there are many components and game development is a long process, there are some key aspects to game programming that I cover in this book:

- Game mechanics
- Project planning
- Tile graphics
- Interface design and development
- Sound playback
- Unit control and management
- Tools development
- 3D animation
- Multiplayer

As you can see from this list of topics, I cover a wide range of strategy game development areas. You can think of this book as a development set of building blocks. Each topic, or block, can stand on its own. But when combined, the blocks truly shine.

The Audience

If you are a beginner or intermediate hobbyist game developer who wants to develop a foundation for strategy game production, this book should fit you just fine. Although I do cover some deep topics, I keep them accessible to the largest audience possible. If you are a veteran game developer with many titles under your belt, you probably should steer clear. After all, what are you doing reading a book! ;) Seriously though, most programmers with a background in game theory should be able to pick up the examples and be rolling in no time.

I do use C++ as the programming language for the examples, and everything has been compiled with Microsoft's Visual C++ version 6.0. Although I use C++, you will find that most of the code is very basic and I steer clear of templates and other features of C++ to keep the code as simple to read as possible.

As for the recommended operating system, I use Windows 2000, and most of the code has been checked out on Windows XP. Since the book is about DirectX, Linux is not supported.

 **Note**　　This book uses DirectX version 9 for all of the DirectX coverage.

What to Expect

You will find that most of the code examples in the book are very simple and straightforward. Do not expect to see optimized or very elegant code. I keep things simple so that they are easy to understand. Although the code is not optimized or elegant, it does work and it gets the point across.

Companion Files and Support

The companion files can be downloaded from www.wordware.com/files/ games and from my web site, www.lostlogic.com.

If you have any questions or problems with the book, you can reach me at my web site. I will also be posting new information and content for owners of the book. Be sure to sign up in my forums so I can give you access to the private "owners only" section!

The Beginning

Chapter 1

Learning from the Past

Prophets, seers, and historians have always said that you can learn about the present and even the future by studying the past. I, for one, do not discount their beliefs, so here is a brief history of strategy games. In this chapter, the following topics are covered:

- The early RTS games
- The first popular RTS games
- The future of RTS games
- The early strategy games

The Early RTS Games

Just as recorded history from long ago is not well recorded, the past of real-time strategy games are not that clear either. Many people claim that Westwood's Dune is the first RTS game, but I recall examples much sooner than that.

Intellivision's Utopia

In a land far, far away, two miles down the dirt road, past the old red dog, and left at the big oak tree, the Intellivision home game system populated several living rooms around the United States.

(Begin flashback sequence now.) It is a hot, summer afternoon and my brother, Eddie, and I are engaged in a heated battle. Several weeks of planning, maneuvers, and propaganda led to this moment. My PT boat fleet has encroached upon his waterways and destroyed his fishing fleet. His people are starving. Eddie's only hope is keeping his crops alive until the next rainfall. But, alas, I have supplied an army of rebels sympathetic to my cause to attack and destroy his crops. Bing, bong, beeng…. The turn is over. Arrrghhh, I now wait until the next turn to install my own puppet government on his island.

I spent many an afternoon playing Utopia with any victim — I mean, opponent — I could convince to play. Utopia was a rather original game in that you played out the game in real time, but turns were used to tally what had transpired and assign a score. You could play it in one-player mode, but playing against another human was where the true fun was had. Utopia is a mix of SimCity and Command & Conquer. You have to increase the welfare of your people but at the same time decrease your opponent's general well-being.

The Game Field

Figure 1.1 shows a representation of the Utopia game field. The world is divided into two distinct islands. There are a few elements that exist on the game field: land tiles, buildings, ocean tiles, ships, fish, and weather.

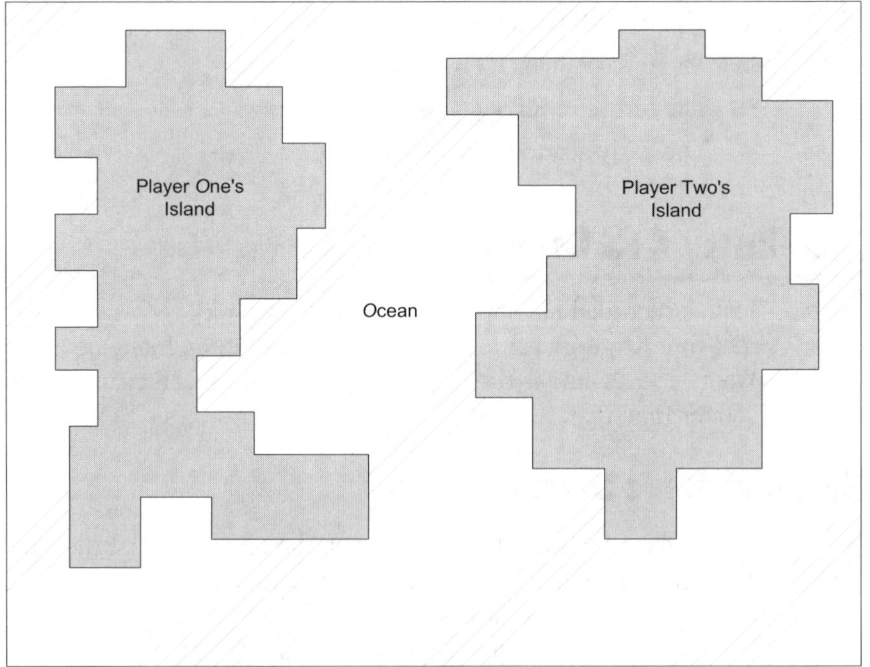

Figure 1.1: A representation of the Utopia game field.

Land Tiles

Land tiles make up the two islands. Each square of land can have one building or farm built upon it. The buildings provide infrastructure for your colony, while the farms provide food. Of course, nothing is free, so you can only build what you have enough money to pay for. Placement of items is key to the game, so you have to manage your land carefully.

Buildings

There are only a few buildings to choose from, but each one has a great impact upon your civilization's welfare. There are forts, factories, crops, schools, hospitals, housing projects, and rebel soldiers.

You may wonder how a rebel soldier can be a building. This may seem strange to you, but in the game, rebel soldiers can appear and occupy land tiles. The land they occupy cannot be used until the rebels are eradicated. The fort is used to prevent rebels from taking over your property. You see, rebels cannot appear on any tiles adjacent to a fort; therefore, if you have forts touching every building on your island, no rebels can attack. The forts also protect against pirates. A representation of the fort can be seen in Figure 1.2.

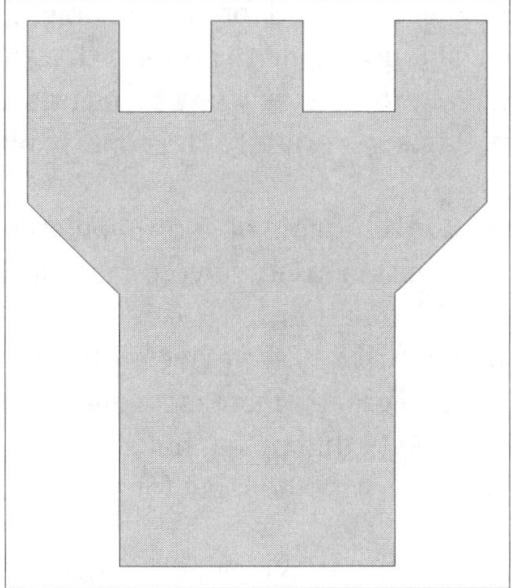

Figure 1.2: A representation of a fort in Utopia.

Factories are used to bring in revenue. Your total score is based on the amount of gold you produce, so factories are vital to victory. Each factory produces a minimum amount of gold per turn. The downside to factories is that they produce pollution that increases the death rate of your population. Another issue involving factories is your people's well-being. As it increases, so does the gold output of your factories. Keep your people happy and you will be rich! A representation of the factory can be seen in Figure 1.3.

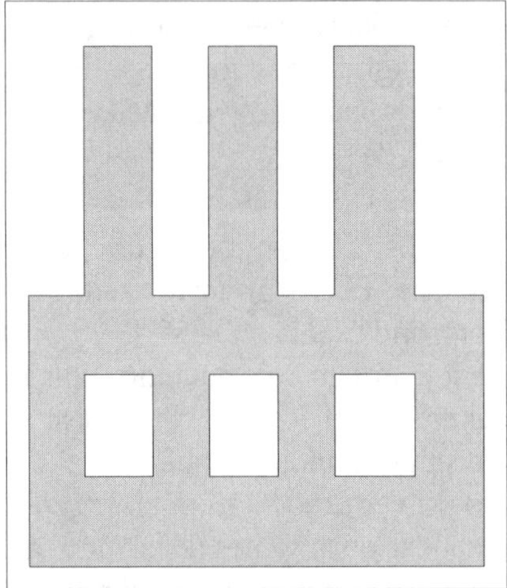

Figure 1.3: A representation of a factory in Utopia.

Crops are very simple in that they provide food for your people. Each crop sustains around 500 people. The downside to crops is that they have a limited lifetime. You have to replant them every few turns or so. The upside is that when rained upon, crops generate gold. Properly placed crops are gold mines.

Schools are used to increase the well-being of your population. As a side effect, well-being increases the productivity of your factories. An educated population is a productive population.

Hospitals increase your population. They are a necessity for having a large population base. Hospitals also greatly increase well-being. Basically, hospitals are some of the best buildings to have.

Housing projects are required to provide housing for your population. Each one holds 500 people.

Rebel soldiers aren't buildings but they do occupy a square of your opponent's land. You can buy rebels and they automatically appear on your foe's property. You have to keep in mind that rebels cannot invade areas protected by forts.

Ocean Tiles

A large portion of the game field consists of ocean. The ocean is free rein to all, as no one owns a particular ocean tile. You cannot build in the ocean, but you can build fishing boats or PT boats that sail around in it.

Ships

You can buy two types of ships in the game — fishing boats and PT boats. When you build a fishing boat, it appears in the next open tile by your base.

Fishing boats are controllable, as you can sail them around the ocean. When you park a fishing boat on a school of fish, it generates gold bars. Fishing boats also automatically feed 500 people. They are a necessity in the game.

PT boats help defend against pirates and your opponent's fleet of PT boats. You can also attack your enemy's fishing boats and send them to the bottom of the sea.

Fish, Weather, and Pirates

Players have a lot of control over the world, but there are things that are out of their control. Schools of fish and pirates randomly roam the ocean. Fish are good for earning gold, and pirates are bad in that they can sink your fishing fleet.

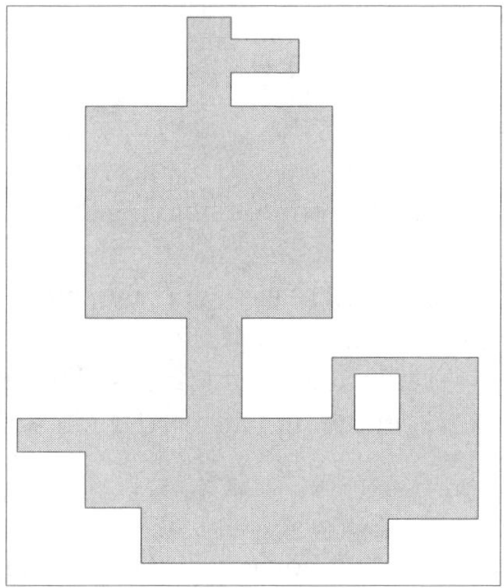

Figure 1.4: Dastardly pirates sail the oceans of Utopia.

There are a few types of weather — rainstorms, tropical storms, and hurricanes. Rainstorms are helpful because they generate gold for you when they move over your crops. Tropical storms also generate gold bars in the same manner, but they can destroy crops, sink ships, and sometimes even destroy a building. Hurricanes are the worst in that they lay waste to everything in their path. Be wary of hurricanes — they can destroy an entire fishing fleet if you are not quick to act.

Wrap-up

As you now know, Utopia has a very basic set of rules that guide it. Playing the game is fairly straightforward, as your only goal is to generate the most gold possible. The player with the most gold at the end of the game wins. It is very interesting that there are many strategies possible with such a short set of rules and play options.

I have discussed this game in detail to show you how a very simple game (by today's standards) can be so fun and complex to play. As you design and code games, you need to keep in mind that a simple set of base rules can make your game fun to play. Very complicated play systems are not a necessity. Having fun is what it is all about.

Bullfrog's Populous

A few years after Utopia made its debut, a company named Bullfrog released Populous. Populous is not your typical RTS game in that you do not directly produce military units. Instead, your houses "breed" more inhabitants. The more inhabitants you have, the greater your power.

The Hook

The first Populous game (there are at least three now) was the first popular game of its kind to let the player be a "god." This power allows the player to experience much more than just empire building. Not only do you get a larger civilization as a result of building more cities, but you also gain magical power. As your power increases, you gain more powerful spells to cast. Some of the spells are simple attacks, such as lightning strikes. Other spells are very powerful, such as volcanoes. There is nothing more fun then creating a volcano in the middle of your foe's city.

Terrain Building

Another unique feature of Populous is that you can deform the land your people inhabit. The tools in the game let you raise or lower land. By creating large areas of flat land, you provide your population with even terrain that can be built on. If you leave your land mountainous, your people are forced to live in small cottages. If you create wide-open plains, they can build castles and large buildings. Keep this unique form of play in mind when designing your game. Sometimes, the simplest ideas can make a game great fun to play.

As I mentioned earlier, there are multiple Populous games for sale. For the latest Populous news, visit http://www.populous.net.

The First Popular RTS Games

Most video game genres are defined by the advent of some popular game. Castle Wolfenstein and Doom made 3D shooters popular. SimCity made simulation-style games popular. Civilization defined turn-based strategy games. The road is not quite as clear for RTS games, as there are a couple of players who defined the genre.

Westwood's Command & Conquer

More than a decade after Utopia was released, a company named Westwood came out with the defining RTS game, Command & Conquer. C&C, as it soon became known, is not the first modern RTS to come about, but it really defines what a modern RTS is all about. Here you can see the title graphic for the game:

Figure 1.5: The Command & Conquer title screen. ©2002 Electronic Arts, All Rights Reserved.

It is all coming back to me now…My army stands ready, the APCs are loaded, my air force is fueled and ready to go, the nuclear weapon is armed. I send the "go" order to the decoy APC unit. It rushes the enemy's front defense system. While the enemy's defense system is busy attacking the decoy APC, I send in my fleet of helicopters to attack the construction center, the heart of the enemy's operation. Meanwhile, my 11th tank division slowly advances, destroying the outer wall of the enemy base. By this time, the helicopter squadron has breached the front-line air defense system and is attacking the nerve center. I give the green light to the APCs filled with engineers; they head off toward the enemy base. My helicopters have been destroyed, but they dealt a serious blow to the construction yard; it sits smoldering. Now is the time for my nuke. The code is sent, and the nuclear weapon soars up into the atmosphere, headed for the construction yard. When it hits, the enemy's nerve center is finished off. The combination of helicopter assault and nuclear power were too much for it. By this time, the tanks have formed a strong wedge in the enemy's base. The engineers arrive in the crater that once was a construction yard and disembark from the APC. They systematically place satchel charges on all remaining defenses. The charges explode and take down their targets. Once that is complete, the tanks move in and demolish all that is left of the base. Oh wait, does the clock really read 5 A.M.?

I can't count how many hours I spent playing C&C at my first office. My business partner and I invited a couple friends up to the office and played until the wee hours of the morning. My first office measured a tiny ten feet by ten feet. The Pentium-133s (top of the line at that time) generated so much heat that the office usually stood at a constant 89 degrees Fahrenheit. None of this was a deterrent though; all of us would cram into the office and play. Usually more than four people would show up, and everyone would take turns battling it out.

The Story

The background for Command & Conquer is that you control the United Nations Global Defense Initiative, or GDI, team. The GDI is at war with the evil Brotherhood of NOD, which is led by an evil being named Kane. You can see his mug in Figure 1.6. The general premise is that both factions are on a planet competing for Tiberium. Tiberium is the mineral that makes the "world go around." Tiberium is used to build any military unit or building in the game. Without it, you lose. Since Tiberium is a mineral, it has to be harvested. So, the general strategy in the game is to harvest as much Tiberium as possible, build up your army, and destroy the other player(s).

Figure 1.6: Kane, the evil commander (from Tiberian Sun). ©2002 Electronic Arts, All Rights Reserved.

The Interface

C&C had several elements brought over from Westwood's earlier game, Dune. The general interface can be seen in Figure 1.7.

As you can see in the figure, the interface has the following main elements: radar display, resource readouts, items to build, power level, and the game area.

Figure 1.7: The Command & Conquer interface. ©2002 Electronic Arts, All Rights Reserved.

Radar Display

The radar display shows you the terrain, buildings, and units on the game map. As the game starts out, the radar display is inactive. Players have to build certain buildings before it turns on. This adds a nice little element to the game in that you don't just start out with the technology. All the game engine has to do to draw the radar map is represent each map tile as a pixel. First, the terrain is drawn, followed by the buildings and then the units. Players are given different colors to distinguish them from one another.

Most RTS games of today utilize some sort of radar display. Games like Age of Empires by Ensemble Studios also use the radar display to show resources, people, terrain, and other items of interest. Considering Age of Empires is a medieval game, it is not really a radar display, but the same type of information is shown. Maybe some farmer developed a solid fuel rocket out of pig waste to launch spy satellites with. You decide.

Resource Readouts

Command & Conquer only has a single resource readout at the top that is used to display the amount of Tiberium the player owns. When planning your RTS game, think about where you place the readouts. You do not want text cluttering up the entire interface, so this is an important aspect of interface design.

Items to Build

On the bottom right of the interface are buttons representing buildings and units the player can build. When the game begins, players can only build a couple of items. As the game progresses, the player discovers new items to build, and they appear on the build bar. This is a good way to present to the player all items that are able to be built. Instead of having to navigate many menus, players only have to scroll to the unit or building they want and click on it. Figure 1.8 shows a picture of the GDI scout bike.

Figure 1.8: The GDI scout bike. ©2002 Electronic Arts, All Rights Reserved.

Power Level

Although Tiberium is the most important material in Command & Conquer, without energy your buildings do not operate. The power bar at the lower-right side of the interface represents the amount of energy used versus what is available. As the player builds power stations, the bar becomes greener and gets taller. As more buildings come online, the power bar turns redder. This style of readout gives the player a visual representation of power supply versus demand. It is rather ingenious in that the player doesn't have to read numbers to figure it out. This brings me to another point; keep your game from looking like a spreadsheet. You can do this by utilizing graphical representations for numeric values.

Game Area

What would a game be without a game area? Nothing more than the dashboard of a car would be without the windshield! The game area is used to present the game in action. The terrain, buildings, and units in the game are displayed on it. You may be reading this and thinking, "Duh, I know that." But before you jump to conclusions, think about all the games of yesteryear that lacked a game area. Text adventure games, MUDs, and BBS games mostly lacked a game area. I think it is interesting that many popular games of the past didn't even have graphical output. Keep this in mind when designing your games. You do not have to have flashy graphics and special effects to make a fun and challenging game.

Technology

As with most modern RTS games, Command & Conquer has two warring factions. Each faction has its own set of strengths and weaknesses. These strengths and weaknesses come in the form of units and weapons.

The evil Brotherhood of NOD has heavy and slow units with lots of firepower. They also have extremely strong defenses and special attacks. One such special attack is a nuclear missile. When NOD players build a Temple of NOD, they get the ability to launch a nuclear missile every so often. The ominous temple can be seen in Figure 1.9.

When a nuke is launched, the temple has to recharge. This keeps the game balanced, as NOD players cannot just sit back and launch missile after missile. The nuclear missile is particularly devastating when it hits ground zero. Most buildings in the game cannot withstand such an attack and easily succumb. In Figure 1.10 you can see the devastation wreaked by just such an attack.

As I mentioned earlier, NOD also has some nice defenses. One such defense is the Hand of NOD. The Hand of NOD is a laser tower that fires a beam that destroys most enemies with a single shot. The downside to the defense is that is consumes a lot of energy and is fairly weak versus swarms of enemies. You can see the weapon in action in Figure 1.11.

With all of the firepower available to NOD, you may be wondering what the GDI has going for them. As it turns out, the GDI has very fast units and a strong air force. For a special weapon, the GDI has the ion cannon, which fires an extremely powerful beam of energy at one target. Usually, it can destroy almost anything it hits.

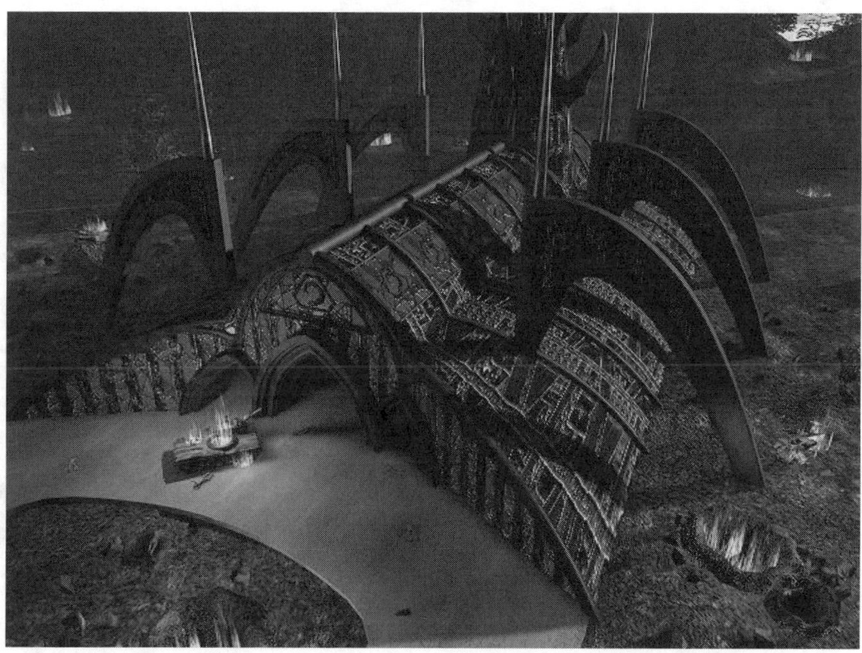

Figure 1.9: The Temple of NOD. ©2002 Electronic Arts, All Rights Reserved.

Figure 1.10: A nuclear missile attacks a GDI player. ©2002 Electronic Arts, All Rights Reserved.

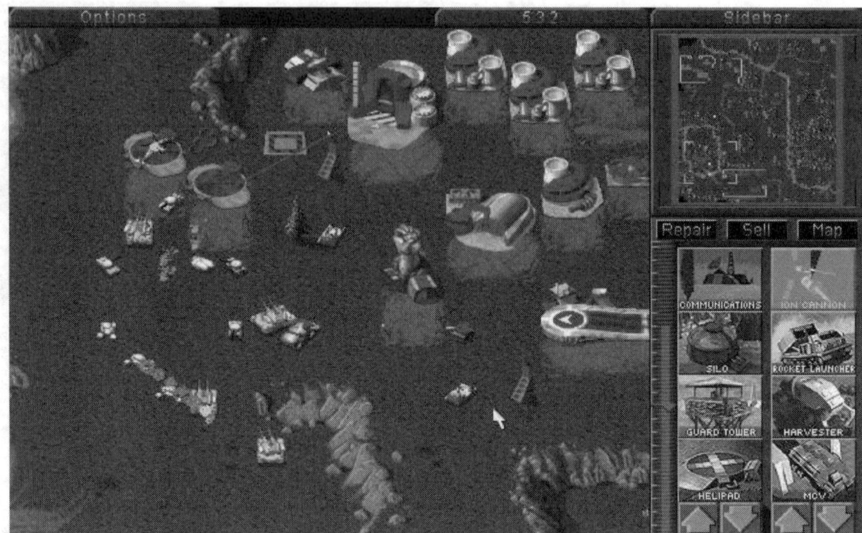

Figure 1.11: The Hand of NOD in action. ©2002 Electronic Arts, All Rights Reserved.

The air force is where the GDI really shines. Its attack helicopters are almost indestructible when flying in formation. One strategy I use in the game is to build fleets of Orca helicopters and then send them in a swarm to destroy the enemy. If you build enough of them, they overwhelm air defenses. The Orca helicopter can be seen in Figure 1.12.

Figure 1.12: GDI's Orca helicopter. ©2002 Electronic Arts, All Rights Reserved.

Game Balance

I believe that out of everything C&C offers, its sense of balance is what stands out. Command & Conquer is one of the most balanced games ever made, in my opinion. You can't just win the game with a single unit type or strategy. Everything in the game seems to have a nemesis.

Game balance is something you should strive for in all types of strategy game programming. If you have an imbalance, players will find it quickly and exploit it. This is very evident in games such as Total Annihilation by Cavedog Entertainment. In Total Annihilation, the first person to build a large air force wins. It's as easy as that. The aircraft move too quickly to be effectively shot down.

When designing your games, be sure to run combat simulations between the units. This allows you to test for strengths, weaknesses, and areas of extreme imbalance.

Warcraft: Orcs & Humans

Around the same time that C&C came out, another company released a very entertaining RTS game. The game, of course, is Warcraft by Blizzard Entertainment. Residing on the opposite end of the spectrum, Warcraft is a fantasy medieval game, while C&C is a futuristic war game.

In Warcraft, you play either the orcs or the humans. The game revolves around the battle for the land of Azeroth. Several scenarios are available, 12 per side I believe. Playing the single-player game was fun and all, but I got the most pleasure from beating the snot out of my friends in multiplayer mode. Warcraft is another one of those games that used to take up hours and hours of my time. We would play it until dawn and come back for more.

As with Command & Conquer, Warcraft is a very balanced game. Whether you play the orcs or the humans, you have an equal chance of winning against a well-matched foe. Later on, Warcraft II: Tides of Darkness was released, but I do not think it is nearly as well balanced. It may be due to the sheer number of units available. One thing to keep in mind is that more is not always better. A game with hundreds of unbalanced units is much worse than a game with a dozen perfectly balanced units.

Blizzard's StarCraft

Another popular title by Blizzard Entertainment is StarCraft. StarCraft is a lot like Warcraft: Orcs & Humans, but this time it is based in the future. The game features three distinct races, each with its own strengths and weaknesses. This feature alone made StarCraft stand out from its peers.

Before StarCraft, most RTS games featured similar races or sides pitted against each other. StarCraft was the first to introduce very different competitors. In Figure 1.13 you can see the race called the Zurg attacking the Humans.

Figure 1.13: The Zurg attacking the Humans in StarCraft. ©2002 Blizzard Entertainment, All Rights Reserved.

The Future of RTS Games

Now that you have seen the RTS past, I have the future to show you. Of course, I am no fortuneteller, but I can take a stab at it.

Massively Multiplayer RTS Games

I predict that RTS games of the future will be played on a massive scale. Currently, there are a few massively multiplayer games in the works, but I bet you will see many more in the coming years. I, for one, would like to see a war game that could be played by thousands of players at the same time. Sure, there are a few games that claim to do that now, but none of them truly deliver in my opinion.

Imagine how fun it would be to command a small unit of soldiers in such a game. Every decision you make could have an effect on the outcome of the battle or war. Everything from supply stations to command and control would be modeled. The options are limitless given enough CPU power and bandwidth.

Smart Computers

Face it: Computer opponents are really dumb. There isn't a real-time strategy game made today that poses a really hard challenge without cheating. All you have to do is play a game of Empire Earth to see cheating AI in action. The game gives the computer opponent tons more resources to use, and I suspect their production queues are shorter as well. Sure, some games are difficult at first, but how long does it take to see the patterns? Not long. In the future, enough CPU power will be available to create phenomenal artificial intelligence algorithms. The problem coders face today is that AI takes up huge amounts of processing time. With the constant hunger for tons of frames per second with special visual effects, not much is left for AI. Perhaps, sometime down the line enough cycles will be available for our silicon enemies.

The Early Strategy Games

Unlike real-time strategy games, general strategy games have been around for a very long time. I can't begin to claim I know which ones were first, but there are a few that I remember catching my attention.

Warlords

Way back when, I used to play a game called Warlords on my Amiga computer. Several friends would come over to my house and we would take turns making our moves in the game. These sessions usually lasted 12 hours or more since each of us had to take our turn independently. Eventually one of us would win, and it really was a lot of fun.

Warlords is a turn-based strategy game by Strategic Studies Group where you command fantasy troops and lead them against opponents. There are castles strewn about the countryside that allow you to build the armies necessary for conquest. The twist to the game is the fact that the castles produce different armies. Some castles produce dragons, where other castles product elves. You can also obtain heroes that make a huge difference. The heroes can travel the land and find special combat artifacts in old temples and ruins. The heroes are really important to the game since their bonuses affect the armies traveling with them.

Over the years, SSG has released a few new versions of Warlords, including a real-time strategy game named Warlords: Battlecry, of which there is even a second version. The appeal of Warlords comes from its great artificial intelligence. The AI in the series has always been second to none and provides for a rewarding single-player experience.

Empire

Around 1987, a company named Interstel released a game called Empire. Empire is a 2D turn-based strategy game in which you take over cities in an effort to dominate the world. Each time you take over a city, you are allowed to produce new armies in it. You can choose which army to build from a list of eight different military units. Some units take longer to produce than others, and some units are only available to cities next to the ocean. For example, the aircraft carrier is only available to cities with a harbor.

Empire is a strangely addictive game that keeps you busy for hours on end. I'm not even sure why it is so addictive. Maybe it is because the more cities you take over, the more units you can produce? Or maybe it is because the maps are very large and take a long time to explore? The key thing to keep in mind here is that the game is simple, but it is a ton of fun to play. This should be the goal of most game programmers.

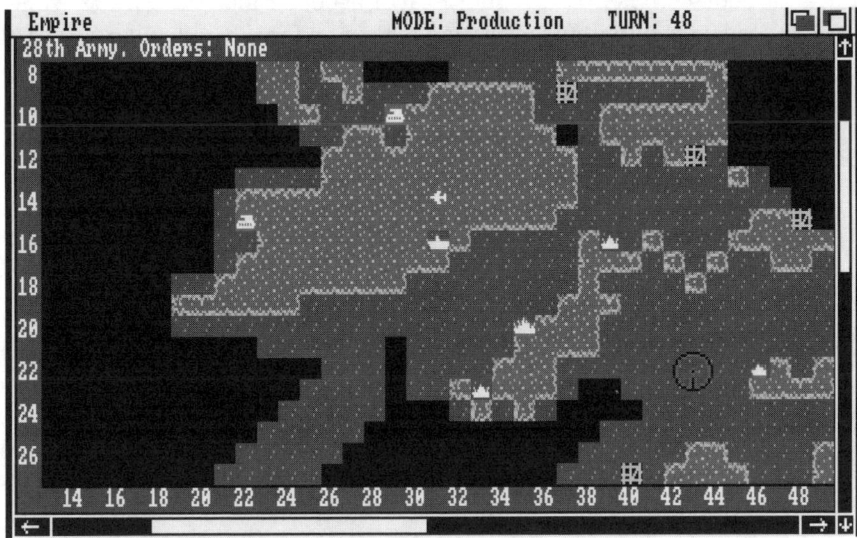

Figure 1.14: Classic Empire. ©2003 Killer Bee Software, All Rights Reserved.

If you are interested in Empire, check out Killer Bee Software. Mark Kinkead of Killer Bee Software bought the rights to the Empire series and is planning a restoration release of Empire and an updated version.

Command H.Q.

Another one of my favorite old strategy games is Command H.Q. Ozark Softscape, a small development house based in Arkansas, developed it. Owing to the world being such a small place, a developer named Mark Botner who worked for Ozark actually works with me now. (Hi, Mark!)

In Command H.Q. you fought battles one on one with another player or against the computer. The game is very similar to Empire in that you take over cities, build units, and raid the other player's territory. The twist comes in that you get to choose the time period of the game. If you choose a time in the past, such as 1918, you play with old technology. If you choose the future, say 2023, you play with futuristic units. The game even supports multiplayer play over a modem or serial link cable.

Command H.Q. has a couple of hooks to keep players happy. The first is resource management. This game is one of the first that I ever played to bring economy into the picture. Taking over an oil field has strategic value just as taking over an important outpost does. The second hook comes from the multiplayer aspect. Since the game's AI is pretty weak, the multiplayer action makes up for it by allowing you to play against a friend.

The Seven Cities of Gold

If you ever owned a Commodore 64 or an Atari 800 computer, you probably owned The Seven Cities of Gold. This is yet another great strategy game by Ozark Softscape. It was published around 1987 and was a great success. In this game you explore the New World as Christopher Columbus or the Spanish conquistadors.

The game is very fun and addictive since you have to explore the New World one bulky pixel at a time. You start by buying supplies and men to help on your voyage. Once you are ready to go, you set sail for the New World. This in itself is interesting since you can miss the new world completely and die of starvation! Assuming you find the New World, you must land and set up missions with the local natives. This adds another twist since you can either meet natives peacefully or ransack their villages for gold. If you meet them peacefully, then word of your honor will spread and other villages are apt to respond in kind. If you kill the natives, then word of your treachery will spread even faster and future meetings with natives will most likely end in bloodshed.

There are many levels of strategy to this game that I have not even come close to touching. All I can say is it was a lot of fun and a good model for future games. I suggest that you study it and learn what you can from it.

X-COM: UFO Defense

No classic strategy game list is complete without a mention of X-COM. X-COM is a very entertaining game in which you defend the earth from alien invasion. The main part of the game takes place in an isometric view of squad combat. You control a squad of troops against aliens in various combat scenarios. The cool part of the game comes from the technology. You start out with low-tech equipment, á là terrestrial equipment and then upgrade it as you recover alien technology. With each battle, your soldiers become better and better, and eventually you are evenly gunned with the aliens. There is nothing more satisfying then firing a guided missile around the corner, down the hallway, and through the door to the right to dispatch an enemy.

X-COM combined resource management and tactical strategy as well by giving you control over the world's defenses. You have to intercept enemy fighters, build defense bases, and engage the enemy on the ground. All of this makes for a very rewarding experience.

The only downside to X-COM is the sequels. The original game is a ton of fun, but the follow-ups are not so hot.

That ends my list of early strategy games. I could go on and on for a long time about other ones, but I think you have a good sampling now. Why do I list these games? To give you ideas for your own strategy games. I can hardly think of a better way to start designing a game than to look to the past and see what people have written before you. History is a great teacher.

Recap

At the end of each chapter is a compilation of the tips and tricks I present throughout the chapter. Without further ado, here they are for Chapter 1:

- A simple set of base rules can make your game fun to play. Very complicated play systems are not a necessity. Having fun is what it is all about.

- Sometimes, the simplest ideas can make a game great fun to play.

- When planning your RTS game, think about where you place the readouts. You do not want text cluttering up the entire interface, so this is an important aspect of interface design.

- Keep your game from looking like a spreadsheet. You can do this by utilizing graphical representations for numeric values.

- You do not have to have flashy graphics and special effects to make a fun and challenging game.

- When designing your games, be sure to run combat simulations between the units. This allows you to test for strengths, weaknesses, and areas of extreme imbalance.

- A game with hundreds of unbalanced units is much worse than a game with a dozen perfectly balanced units.

Chapter 2

Getting Started with Windows

We all know how most programmers like to get straight to the code. To make sure you stay entertained, I am now covering how to get started with your very first game shell. Since DirectX is Windows based, the first thing you have to learn is how to create a basic Windows application. In this chapter, I cover the following:

- Windows program architecture
- How to create a Windows program

If you are familiar with Windows programming, you may wish to skip this chapter. If not, sit back, relax, and enjoy the show.

Windows Program Architecture

If you come from another operating system, such as UNIX, Linux, or DOS, Windows programming may seem a little foreign. First of all, you no longer have the `main()` function. You now have a replacement called `WinMain()`. Just as the `main()` function is required for other operating systems, the `WinMain()` function is required for Windows programming.

Event-driven Processing

The next little tidbit of difference in Windows programming is that Windows programs are event driven. This means that instead of your program having to troll for information, it actually can sit back and wait for messages to come to it via a message queue. Messages received are processed in what is called the *message handler*. The items handled in the message handler are usually called *events*.

Events

You may be wondering what kinds of events are processed. There are hundreds, if not thousands, of possible events, some of which are described in Table 2.1.

Table 2.1: Windows event messages

Event	Action
WM_KEYDOWN	This event is triggered when a non-system key is pressed. Keyboard input is vital to most games, so this is an important message.
WM_KEYUP	This event is triggered when a non-system key is released. Not only do you need to know when a key is pressed, but you need to know when it is released. This is why this event is important.
WM_LBUTTONDOWN	This event is triggered when the user presses down on the left mouse button while the cursor is in the window.
WM_LBUTTONUP	This event is triggered when the user releases the left mouse button while the cursor is in the window.
WM_SETFOCUS	This event is triggered when the window has gained keyboard focus. For example, when a window is not active and you click on it, a WM_SETFOCUS event is triggered.
WM_SIZE	This event tells the window that it has been resized. This is important in situations where you need to modify the layout of your interface to fit the new size.

Tip   There are many other event messages. I suggest you use the help tool in Visual C++ and search for all WM_ messages.

Program Structure

If the message handler's purpose sounds a bit strange to you still, don't worry. I haven't shown how it fits into the big picture yet. Figure 2.1 helps make things more clear.

In Figure 2.1, there are a few key areas of interest. First of all, there is the Windows program. It is the graphic that has a keyboard under it. The keyboard represents possible input from the user.

The Event Queue

The second key area is labeled *event queue*. This is where things start to deviate from non-Windows programming. The events that I talked about earlier are received in the event queue. Almost every time a Windows program receives input or an event from the user or the operating system, it generates an event that is stored in the event queue. Programs

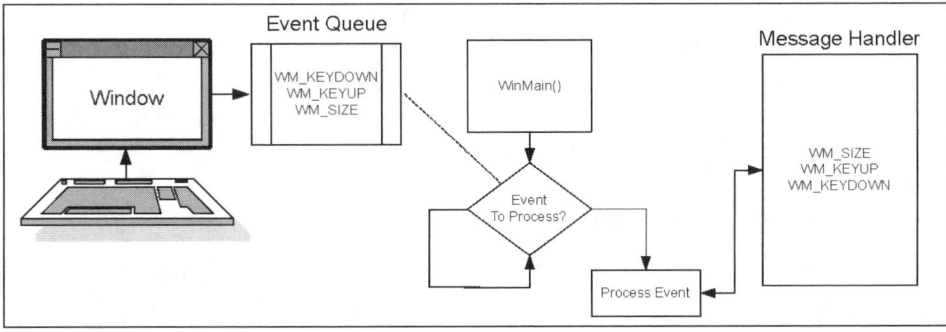

Figure 2.1: The Windows message handler structure.

use a queue system so that messages are never missed. Also, the event can sit in the queue for as long as the program needs.

If you are familiar with non-Windows programming, you know that if the program is busy and the user presses a key, the keypress is probably lost. This is because the program was busy doing something else and missed it. With Windows programming, the keyboard message is sent to the event queue for storage. It is safe until retrieved by the program. It's really kind of cool if you think about it; there is no more worrying about missed input.

Events in the event queue are processed on a FIFO, or first-in first-out, basis. This means that the first message to be put into the queue is the first message that is pulled when the program asks for the next event. There is nothing really earth shattering here; it's just a standard queue.

In Figure 2.1, the event queue has three messages in it: `WM_KEYDOWN`, `WM_KEYUP`, and `WM_SIZE`. To the informed developer, this represents three possible actions on the user's part. The user first pressed a key and then released it. Then the user sized the window.

The WinMain() Function

Next up to bat is the `WinMain()` function. As I said earlier, it is required for all Windows programs and is the first function called when your program is executed.

Underneath the `WinMain()` function in Figure 2.1 is a decision box with the title "Event To Process?" This represents the message loop that is standard in most Windows applications. Basically, once you have initialized your Windows program to display the window and assorted buttons, you then wait for events to happen. Usually, you have some sort of loop that sits there checking the message queue for events. This is why there is a dotted line to the event queue. The process events loop is sitting there checking the queue until something is present.

Once a message is found in the event queue, it is pulled from the queue and sent to the message handler for processing.

The Message Handler

When you create a window in your program, you specify the function that processes the messages for that window. The function is the actual message handler. So there you have it: The message handler is nothing more than a function that receives the messages sent to your program.

Normally, the message handler is one giant `switch` statement that checks through each type of message pertaining to your program and then acts on it. There are many types of messages that you will never even bother with. Most of my games only check a few key types.

Tip   Games only require a few types of events to check for because most input is handled through DirectX, not Windows events. When writing standard Windows applications, you tend to use more events than in games programming.

Writing Your First Windows Program

That ends my discussion of the theory behind Windows programming. Now it's time to write your first Windows program. In all of the examples I cover, I use Microsoft's Visual C++ 6.0 compiler. If you do not own this product, I suggest that you go out and buy it.

Tip   The last time I checked, Visual C++ 6.0 Standard cost around $100 USD. You probably can get it cheaper through a student discount program. It is well worth the money.

Setting Up Visual C++ 6.0

Go ahead now and launch your copy of Visual C++ 6.0. You should see a screen resembling Figure 2.2.

There is nothing very special about the interface shown in Figure 2.2. Your basic controls are at the top: File, Edit, View, Insert, and so on. In Visual C++, everything you do has to be associated with a *project*. The project is the highest level in the hierarchy of the development environment.

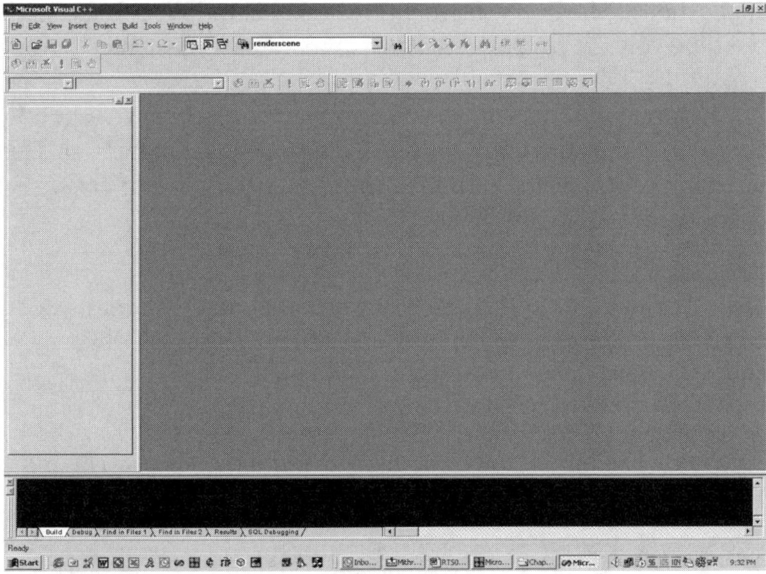

Figure 2.2: The Visual C++ 6.0 interface.

How to Create the Project

The best way to learn is by doing, so create a new project by going to the File menu and selecting New. You will be presented with a myriad of options, as shown in Figure 2.3.

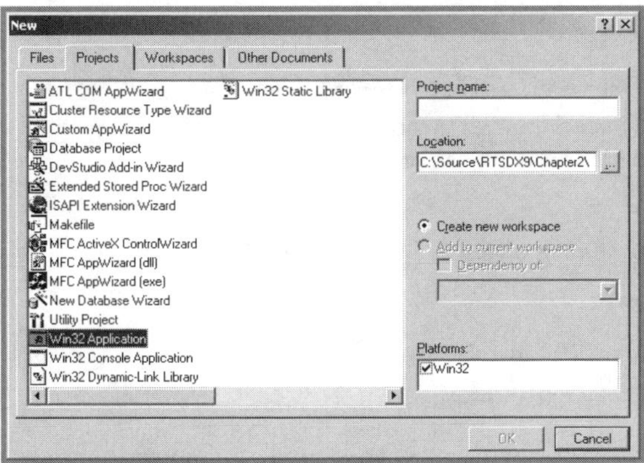

Figure 2.3: The new project dialog in Visual C++.

The dialog you see is used to set what type of project you want to create. You see, Visual C++ is used to make all sorts of programs, including ActiveX controls, COM objects, DevStudio add-ins, and even Windows applications. The one you are interested in is the Win32 Application. It is the type you use to create Windows programs. Select Win32 Application to pick that type.

Before you can go on your merry way, you now have to tell Visual C++ the name of your project and where you want it stored. This information is entered in the Project name and Location edit boxes. For this example, enter CreateWindow for the project name.

Tip   I store all of my source code in C:\Source\. I suggest you create a similar directory structure in which to store all of your code. It is best to have your code in a single location than scattered all over your hard drive.

Select the OK button once you have entered the appropriate information. You are now presented with the dialog shown in Figure 2.4.

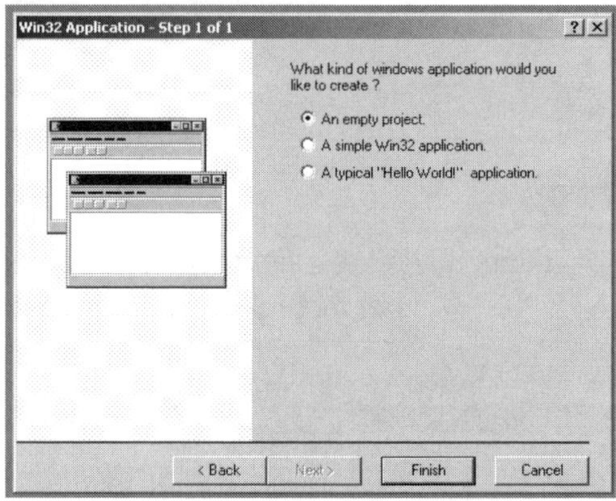

Figure 2.4: The dialog used to select what kind of Windows application you wish to

In Figure 2.4, the dialog presents three options:

■   An empty project

■   A simple Win32 application

■   A typical "Hello World!" application

The first option, an empty project, is the most typical type used. This creates an empty project with no objects included. Basically, it creates a blank canvas with which to work.

The second option, a simple Win32 application, is used rarely, as all it does is create a program that does nothing. It actually creates the source files for you; they just don't do very much.

The third option, a typical "Hello World!" application, does the most of the three options. It creates a complete Windows program that displays the text "Hello World!" I still don't use this one very often because the code looks a bit cluttered for my taste.

Select the first option and press the Finish button to open the dialog shown in Figure 2.5.

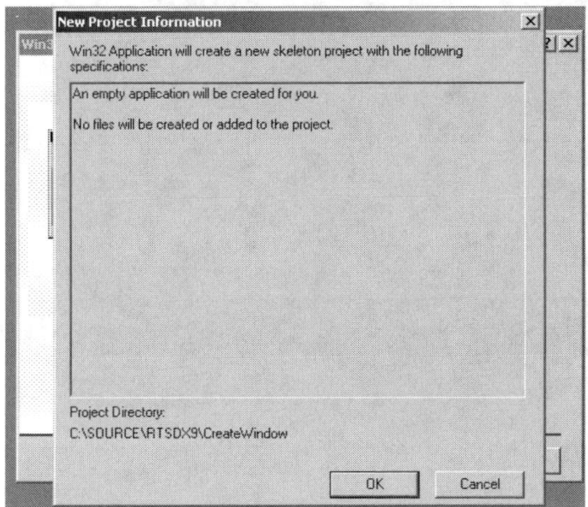

Figure 2.5: The dialog used to confirm the application type chosen.

The dialog presented to you is nothing special either. It is just there to make sure you are creating the type of project desired. Select OK to continue.

The Workspace

There it is in all its glory — your project! Now that you have a project created, it is time to browse around a little bit. Check out Figure 2.6 on the following page.

Take a look at the workspace, the area at the left that contains the name of your project with a + graphic next to it. Go ahead and expand the tree by clicking on the + icon. You are now presented with three sub-folders in the project files tree:

■ Source Files

■ Header Files

■ Resource Files

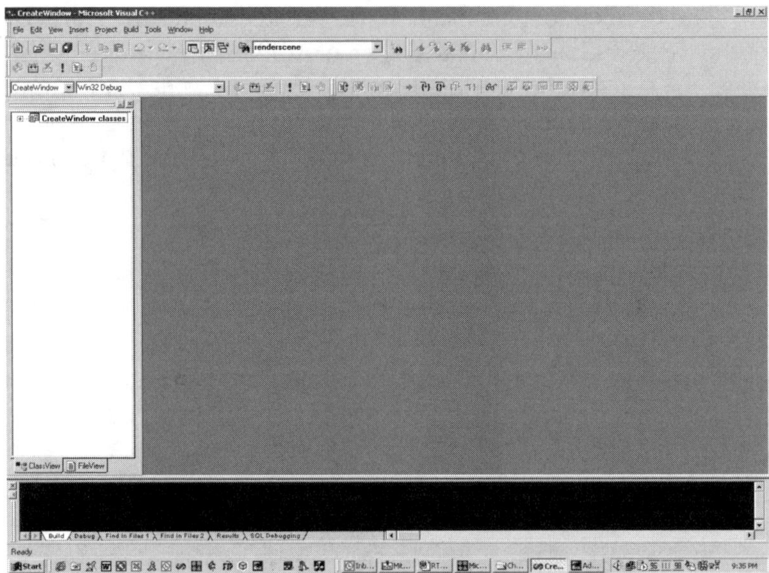

Figure 2.6: The empty project space for your new program.

Hopefully you know how to program in C or C++ and what source and header files are. If not, I suggest you go buy a book on C++ programming and learn it before continuing. Otherwise, you are in for a very rough ride.

Note   Workspaces are the second level of your environment's hierarchy. The project is at the top of the chain, followed by the workspace. The files in your project are at the bottom. You can have multiple workspaces in a single project, just as you can have multiple source files within a single workspace.

Resource Files

If you know how to program but are new to Windows programming, the Resource Files folder may puzzle you.

In Windows programming, *resources* are elements used to enhance or add to your application. Some examples of resources are icons, bitmaps, wave files, and text strings. The beauty of resources is that they are compiled into your program. You don't have to worry about installing them on the user's machine, as they are part of the executable file.

Tip   Resources are cool, but don't include tons of them in your programs. The executables you generate will be way too big if you do. This causes problems when releasing a simple executable update to your users. Instead of being able to download a small executable, they will have to download a huge one complete with the resources.

I don't want to get lost on a wild resource tangent, so let's move on. You have no files in your project yet; therefore, there is nothing listed under the folders. You can remedy this by adding a C++ source file to the project.

Adding Source Files to the Project

Go to the Project menu and select Project | Add To Project | New. Once you have done this, the dialog shown in Figure 2.7 appears.

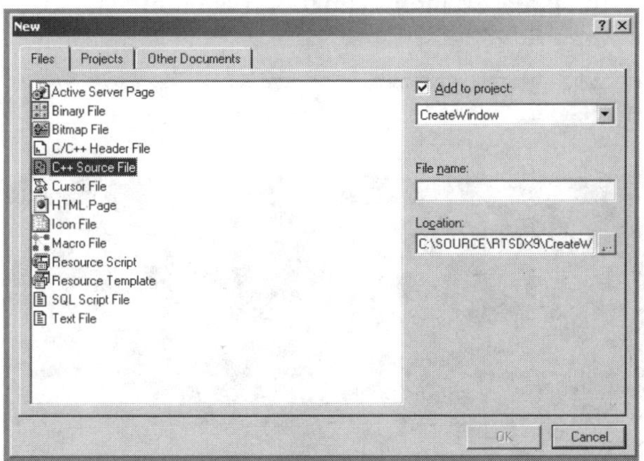

Figure 2.7: The dialog used to select what kind of file you want to add to your project.

This dialog is really the same one shown in Figure 2.3 but with a different tabbed area selected. Instead of selecting the type of project to create, now select the type of file to add. The types you are most interested in should be C/C++ Header File and C++ Source File. Select C++ Source File before moving on.

You are close now but not quite there yet. Before you can select OK, you must specify the name of the file to create. Enter CreateWindow as the filename and select OK.

Note   You don't have to give the source file and the project space the same name. I only did so to keep things organized. Feel free to name the source file whatever you wish. (Some people use Main.)

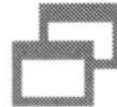

Tip   The proper extension is added when you create a new file for a project. You do not need to type it in. For example, if you created a C++ source file named Main, it would be saved as Main.cpp on the hard drive.

Now that the file is created and added to the project, you can see it in the workspace window. Check out Figure 2.8.

I had to expand the Source Files folder to see the CreateWindow.cpp that I just created. When you double-click on any file shown in the workspace window, it loads and displays in the edit area. In Figure 2.8 you can also see the CreateWindow.cpp file. It is empty and just waiting for you to type something into it.

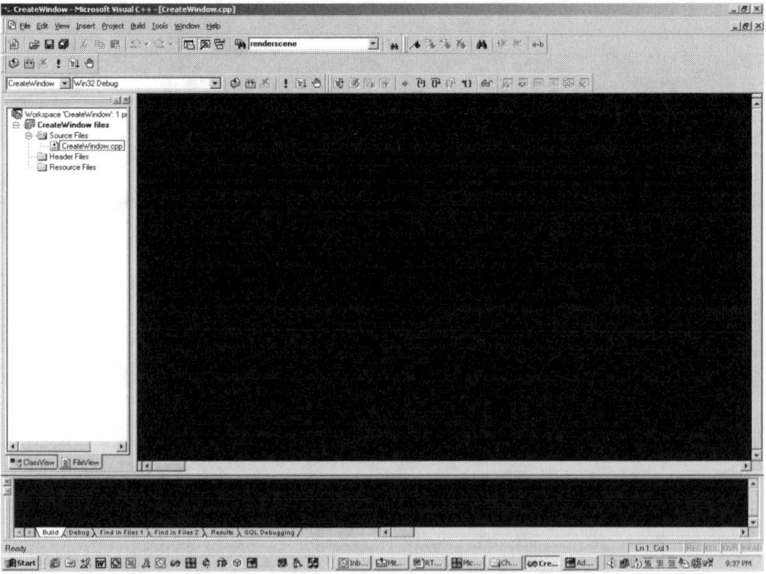

Figure 2.8: The workspace view with the source files visible.

Getting Down and Dirty with the Code

Now that you have a blank source file beckoning you, it is time to write
the actual Windows code. Don't worry too much; I am going to walk you
through each step. Check out the following code listing. It shows a complete working Windows program.

```c
// Standard windows include
#include <windows.h>

// Message Loop CallBack Function prototype
LRESULT CALLBACK fnMessageProcessor (HWND, UINT, WPARAM, LPARAM);
// Function called automatically when the program starts
int WINAPI WinMain (HINSTANCE hInstance, HINSTANCE hPrevInstance, PSTR szCmdLine,
                    int iCmdShow)
{
    HWND            hWnd;
    MSG             msg;
    WNDCLASSEX      wndclass;

    // Set up window class
    wndclass.cbSize         = sizeof(WNDCLASSEX);
    wndclass.style          = CS_HREDRAW | CS_VREDRAW;
    wndclass.lpfnWndProc    = fnMessageProcessor;
    wndclass.cbClsExtra     = 0;
    wndclass.cbWndExtra     = 0;
    wndclass.hInstance      = hInstance;
    wndclass.hIcon          = LoadIcon(NULL, IDI_APPLICATION);
    wndclass.hCursor        = LoadCursor(NULL, IDC_ARROW);
    wndclass.hbrBackground  = (HBRUSH) GetStockObject (WHITE_BRUSH);
    wndclass.lpszMenuName   = NULL;
    wndclass.lpszClassName  = "Window Class";
// Class Name
    wndclass.hIconSm        = LoadIcon(NULL, IDI_APPLICATION);

    // Register the window class
    if(RegisterClassEx(&wndclass) == 0)
    {
        // The program failed, exit
        exit(1);
    }

    // Create the window
    hWnd = CreateWindowEx(
        WS_EX_OVERLAPPEDWINDOW,
        "Window Class",             // Class name
        "Create Window Example",    // Title bar text
        WS_OVERLAPPEDWINDOW,
        0,
        0,
        320,
        200,
        NULL,
        NULL,
```

```
            hInstance,
            NULL);

        // Display the window
        ShowWindow(hWnd, iCmdShow);

        // Process messages until the program is terminated
        while(GetMessage (&msg, NULL, 0, 0))
        {
            TranslateMessage(&msg);
            DispatchMessage(&msg);
        }

        return (msg.wParam);
    }


// Message loop callBack function (REQUIRED FOR ALL WINDOWS PROGRAMS)
LRESULT CALLBACK fnMessageProcessor (HWND hWnd, UINT iMsg, WPARAM wParam, LPARAM lParam)
{
    switch(iMsg)
    {
        // Called when window is first created
        case WM_CREATE:
            return(0);
        // Called when the window is refreshed
        case WM_PAINT:
            return(0);
        // Called when the user closes the window
        case WM_DESTROY:
            PostQuitMessage(0);
            return(0);
        default:
            return DefWindowProc(hWnd, iMsg, wParam, lParam);

    }
}
```

The Include and Function Prototypes

The first few lines of code set up the header files to include and the function prototypes. The only header file required in Windows programming is the `windows.h` header.

The only function prototype required for this example is one for the message handler. Every Windows program must have a function that is called when messages are processed, and it has to follow this prototype:

```
LRESULT CALLBACK fnMessageProcessor (HWND, UINT, WPARAM, LPARAM);
```

The name can be different, but the parameters must stay intact. This is because Windows automatically calls this function and it won't act properly if you change it.

Inside the WinMain() Function

The first item of note in the `WinMain()` function is the object you use to create windows. The object is a structure of type `WNDCLASSEX` and is very important for creating windows in your program.

The WNDCLASSEX Data Structure

If you have programmed Windows programs in the past, you may have used the `WNDCLASS` structure. There are a couple of differences between it and the `WNDCLASSEX` object. The first difference is the inclusion of a size parameter that specifies the size of the structure. The second difference is the inclusion of a parameter that specifies the handle to a small icon for the window.

The following is the prototype of the `WNDCLASSEX` structure:

```
typedef struct _WNDCLASSEX {
    UINT     cbSize;
    UINT     style;
    WNDPROC  lpfnWndProc;
    int      cbClsExtra;
    int      cbWndExtra;
    HANDLE   hInstance;
    HICON    hIcon;
    HCURSOR  hCursor;
    HBRUSH   hbrBackground;
    LPCTSTR  lpszMenuName;
    LPCTSTR  lpszClassName;
    HICON    hIconSm;
} WNDCLASSEX;
```

Don't you just love it when you are presented with a structure full of members to memorize? Not! Well, at least Microsoft made the member variables easy to read. The first member is a `UINT` called `cbSize`. The `cbSize` member is used to set the size of the data structure. Always use `sizeof(WNDCLASSEX)` when setting this member. Take a look at the code listing above to see where I initialize this member.

Note   In case you are wondering, a `UINT` is an unsigned integer. This means that the number can only be positive.

The second member is a `UINT` called `style`. Just as the name indicates, the `style` member is used to specify the style of the window you are creating. The cool part about the style member is that you can specify several styles in combination with each other by using multiple flags separated by the bitwise OR (`|`) operator. Table 2.2 lists the available styles.

Table 2.2: Window styles

Value	Action
CS_BYTEALIGNCLIENT	Aligns the window's client area (content area) on the byte boundary in the x-axis direction. This has an effect on the window's horizontal position and its width. Personally, I have never had to use this.
CS_BYTEALIGNWINDOW	Aligns the window on the byte boundary in the x-axis direction. This has an effect on the window's horizontal position and its width. I haven't had to use this one either.
CS_CLASSDC	This style allocates a single device context to be used by all windows in the class structure. I haven't talked about device contexts yet, but I do later on, so don't worry too much. With Windows, it is possible to create multiple window classes of the same type in different threads. Since you can have multiple copies of the class out there, multiple threads can try to access the device context at the same time. This causes a lock to take place on all but one thread until that thread is done with the context.
CS_DBLCLKS	This one is real simple. When this style is indicated, Windows will send double-click messages to your window when the user double-clicks the mouse within the window's area. This may seem like a no-brainer, but many applications record the time of each mouse click to determine double-clicks. I simply use the double-click style to do it for me.
CS_GLOBALCLASS	This style allows for the creation of a global window class. I suggest you consult the documentation that comes with Microsoft's Visual C++ for more information. You do not need this style for game development.
CS_HREDRAW	This style forces a redraw of the entire window when the size of it is altered along its width.
CS_NOCLOSE	Disables the Close operation available on the menu bar.
CS_OWNDC	Allocates a unique device context for each window created using the class.
CS_PARENTDC	Sets it to where the child window shares the same clipping area as its parent. This allows the child window to paint on the parent window. This is not to mean that the child uses its parent's device context. In actuality, the child receives its own device context from the system's pool. One thing this flag does do is to enhance the performance of the application.
CS_SAVEBITS	Stores in memory a bitmap of the area underneath the window. This way, when the window is moved, the area underneath is blitted to the screen. This keeps from sending a `WM_PAINT` message to any windows obscured by the window.
CS_VREDRAW	Forces a redraw of the entire window when the size of it is altered along its height.

The third member is a `WNDPROC` function pointer named `lpfnWndProc`. The pointer set here points to the Windows message handler function that the window uses to receive messages. This is very important, and the function you reference here must follow the exact prototype listed in my code. Look at Figure 2.9 to see the relationship between the class and the message handler.

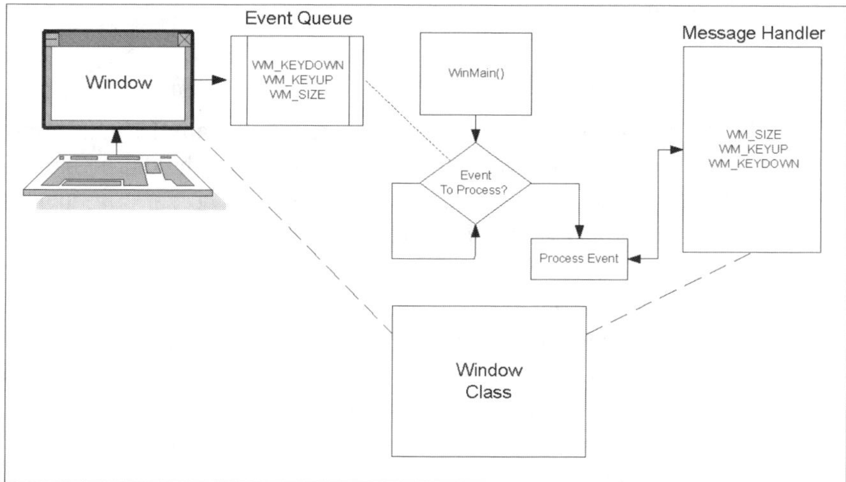

Figure 2.9: The relationship between the window class and the message handler.

The fourth member is an `int` named `cbClsExtra`. This integer sets the number of bytes to allocate following the window class data structure. I have no clue what this is used for, as every example I have seen sets it to 0. I suggest you do the same. If you wish, you can just ignore it as the system sets it to 0 as a default.

The fifth member is an `int` named `cbWndExtra`. This integer sets the number of bytes to allocate following the window instance. This one works just like the previous member in that the system defaults it to zero bytes.

The sixth member is a `HANDLE` named `hInstance`. The handle you specify here is the handle to the instance to which the window procedure of the class belongs. For most purposes, set this to the `hInstance` handle that is passed to the `WinMain()` function.

The seventh parameter is named `hIcon` and is of type `HICON`. The `HICON` type is nothing more than a `HANDLE` in disguise, so don't let it confuse you. This particular handle points to the icon class that the window uses. The icon class is actually an icon resource. Try not to set this to `NULL`, as the windows program has to redraw the icon graphic every time the window is minimized if you do.

As you look at the code for the seventh parameter, you see that I used the `LoadIcon()` function call.

The `LoadIcon()` function loads an icon resource from the executable program. Even though you have resources compiled into your Windows program, you still have to load them, which is why this function is necessary. Now on to the prototype:

```
HICON LoadIcon(
    HINSTANCE hInstance,
    LPCTSTR lpIconName
);
```

Luckily, this function only has two parameters, an `HINSTANCE` and an `LPCTSTR`. The first parameter, named `hInstance`, holds the handle of the instance to the module whose executable files contain the icon you wish to use. In my program example, I set this to `NULL`. When you do this, you are allowed to use built-in Windows icons, which are commonly referred to as *standard* icons.

The second parameter is a string pointer that points to the name of the icon to load. As you can see in the example I am covering, I have set this to `IDI_APPLICATION`. This value is the default application icon that you see in many Windows programs. The rest of the standard values can be seen in Table 2.3.

Table 2.3: Standard icon values

Value	Description
IDI_APPLICATION	This is the default application icon that my example uses. Most of the time you use this value if you do not want a custom icon.
IDI_ASTERISK	This value creates a little bubble with an "I" in it for your program icon.
IDI_ERROR	A red circle with an "X" in it.
IDI_EXCLAMATION	Can you guess what this one looks like? If you guessed an exclamation point, you are wrong! This one looks like the IDI_ASTERISK icon.
IDI_HAND	I have no idea why this one is duplicated, but it is exactly the same as the IDI_ERROR icon.
IDI_INFORMATION	Yet another duplication. This one is a little bubble icon just like the IDI_ASTERISK value.
IDI_QUESTION	This value gives your application a question mark icon.
IDI_WARNING	Oh, the joy of duplicated code. This is just like the IDI_EXCLAMATION value.
IDI_WINLOGO	This gives your application the cool little Windows logo for an icon.

That's it for the `LoadIcon()` function. Now back to our regularly scheduled program. Oh wait, before you go, Figure 2.10 illustrates the various icon graphics.

Figure 2.10: The graphics of various standard window icons. ©2002 Microsoft, All Rights Reserved.

The eighth member in the `WNDCLASSEX` data structure is very similar to the seventh, except this time you are setting the cursor that the window uses. It is of type `HCURSOR` and named `hCursor`. The `HCURSOR` data type is just another handle in disguise. Normally you set this value to the handle of the cursor class you want your program to use for a custom cursor. But instead of creating a custom cursor, I use the `LoadCursor()` function.

The `LoadCursor()` function is just like the `LoadIcon()` function, except it loads a cursor resource instead of an icon resource. Here is the prototype:

```
HCURSOR LoadCursor(
    HINSTANCE hInstance,
    LPCTSTR lpCursorName
);
```

The first parameter, named `hInstance`, holds the handle of the instance to the module whose executable files contain the cursor you wish to use. In my program example, I set this to `NULL`. When you do this, you are allowed to use built-in Windows cursors. The built-in cursors are commonly referred to as *standard* cursors. Are you experiencing déjà vu as well?

The second parameter is a string pointer that points to the name of the cursor to load. As you can see in the example I am covering, I have set this to `IDC_ARROW`. This value is the default cursor you see in many Windows programs. The rest of the standard values can be seen in Table 2.4.

Table 2.4: Standard cursor values

Value	Description
IDC_APPSTRING	This cursor is the standard arrow but with an hourglass attached to it. You normally set this cursor when your program is busy.
IDC_ARROW	The standard Windows cursor.
IDC_CROSS	Creates a cool cross-hair cursor.
IDC_HELP	This cursor is the standard arrow but with a question mark attached to it. This is a good cursor to use when presenting the user with a question to answer.
IDC_IBEAM	This is the I-beam cursor. Normally you use this when the user is in text edit mode.

Value	Description
IDC_NO	The circle-with-a-slash-through-it cursor. This is useful for when the user has the cursor over an area they are not allowed to click in.
IDC_SIZEALL	The size cursor. This is useful when the user is resizing a window or graphic element.
IDC_SIZENESW	This is another size cursor. Instead of having arrows point in all four directions, this one has arrows that point northeast and southwest.
IDC_SIZENS	This is like the previous cursor, except the arrows point north and south.
IDC_SIZENWSE	This is like the previous two cursors, except the arrows point northwest and southeast.
IDC_SIZEWE	This is another arrow cursor, but this time the arrows point east and west.
IDC_UPARROW	This cursor is of an arrow pointing up.
IDC_WAIT	This is an hourglass cursor. I suggest you only use this when your program is busy, or users may wait for your application to do nothing.

Now that you are comfortable with the cursor portion of the window data structure, it's time to cover the background color. To set the background color of your window, you fill the `hbrBackground` data member with the color you wish to use. The `hbrBackground` data member is the ninth member and is of type `HBRUSH`. You can probably guess that an `HBRUSH` is nothing more than the handle to a brush class. This data member offers some flexibility in that you can set it to the handle of the brush you wish to use or you can set the actual color value. The only caveat to specifying the color is that you must use one of the following values:

```
COLOR_ACTIVECAPTION
COLOR_APPWORKSPACE
COLOR_BACKGROUND
COLOR_BTNFACE
COLOR_BTNSHADOW
COLOR_BTNTEXT
COLOR_CAPTIONTEXT
COLOR_GRAYTEXT
COLOR_HIGHLIGHT
COLOR_HIGHLIGHTTEXT
COLOR_INACTIVEBORDER
COLOR_INACTIVECAPTION
COLOR_MENU
COLOR_MENUTEXT
COLOR_SCROLLBAR
COLOR_WINDOW
COLOR_WINDOWFRAME
COLOR_WINDOWTEXT
```

In my example, I don't use this method. But if you want to set one of the standard colors above, you can change the background color line in my code to the following:

```
wndclass.hbrBackground = (HBRUSH)COLOR_GRAYTEXT;
```

This code results in the window having a gray background. You can replace COLOR_GRAYTEXT with any of the above values. Instead of using the above method, my code utilizes the GetStockObject() function.

The GetStockObject() function is rather useful in that it retrieves a handle to one of the built-in brushes, fonts, palettes, or pens. You see, Windows has several built-in types that your applications can utilize. Here is the prototype for the function:

```
HGDIOBJ GetStockObject(
    int fnObject
);
```

You have to love functions with only one parameter, and this is one of those. The only parameter used is a simple integer specifying the stock object to use. As long as you specify a valid object, the function will return a non-zero value.

My program happens to use the WHITE_BRUSH stock object. This sets the background to white. You also can specify the values in Table 2.5 when calling GetStockObject().

Table 2.5: Stock objects

Value	Description
BLACK_BRUSH	Just as it sounds. This object gives you a black brush to paint with.
DKGRAY_BRUSH	A dark gray brush.
GRAY_BRUSH	A gray brush.
HOLLOW_BRUSH	Have you ever seen the movie *Hollow Man*? (Don't worry if you haven't; it was bad.) This brush, just like the hollow man himself, results in an invisible brush. This means that the brush paints no color. It is also the same as a NULL brush.
LTGRAY_BRUSH	A light gray brush.
NULL_BRUSH	Just like the HOLLOW_BRUSH.
WHITE_BRUSH	A white brush. This is the one my example uses.
BLACK_PEN	A black pen. You don't use pens for background colors. Rather, you use pens to draw text.
WHITE_PEN	A white pen.
ANSI_FIXED_FONT	This object sets the font to be a fixed-width system font.
ANSI_VAR_FONT	This object sets the font to be a variable-width font.
DEFAULT_GUI_FONT	This uses the default system font.
DEFAULT_PALETTE	The default palette object.

The tenth member of the `WNDCLASSEX` data structure is a null-terminated string called `lpszMenuName`. The string contains the name of the menu resource to use for the window. My window does not have a menu, so I set the member to `NULL`.

The eleventh member is a null-terminated string named `lpsz-ClassName`. As the name of the member indicates, you use the string to specify the class name of the window. The class name is used to uniquely identify the class type; therefore, it is important that you do not name all of your classes the same.

The twelfth and final member of the `WNDCLASSEX` data structure is a variable named `hIconSm`. This member is just like the `hIcon` data member, except this one points to the small icon to use for the program. In my example, I use the now-familiar `LoadIcon()` function.

Hey, guess what? You are done learning about the `WNDCLASSEX` data structure! Now that you have it memorized, it's time to register it.

The RegisterClassEx() Function

You are now to the point where the window class should be registered. The code snippet below accomplishes this task.

```
if(RegisterClassEx(&wndclass) == 0)
{
    // The program failed, exit
    exit(1);
}
```

The `RegisterClassEx()` function is necessary for future calls that create the window. Basically, the register function registers the class with the Windows system. If you do not register your class, you cannot create windows with it.

The function is rather simple. Examine the following prototype:

```
ATOM RegisterClassEx(
    CONST WNDCLASSEX *lpwcx
);
```

The first and only parameter required is the pointer to a `WNDCLASSEX` data structure. This is easy, as all you have to do is pass `&wndclass` to it for the example program.

Don't worry too much about the `ATOM` return type. All you need to worry about is whether or not the function returns a `NULL` value. As long as the `RegisterClassEx()` function returns a non-zero value, it succeeded.

Now that the window class is registered, the program example moves on to create the actual window.

The CreateWindowEx() Function

To create a window, you use the `CreateWindowEx()` function. You use it to create child, pop-up, or overlapped windows. You get to specify the class to use, the application name, and various other attributes when creating a window. The prototype for the function is as follows:

```
HWND CreateWindowEx(
    DWORD dwExStyle,
    LPCTSTR lpClassName,
    LPCTSTR lpWindowName,
    DWORD dwStyle,
    int x,
    int y,
    int nWidth,
    int nHeight,
    HWND hWndParent,
    HMENU hMenu,
    HINSTANCE hInstance,
    LPVOID lpParam
);
```

The first parameter is a `DWORD` called `dwExStyle`. It is similar to the `style` member of the `WNDCLASSEX` data structure, except this style specifies the extended style of the window. The available extended styles are found in Table 2.6.

Table 2.6: Extended window styles

Style	Description
WS_EX_ACCEPTFILES	The window can accept files with the drag-and-drop mechanism.
WS_EX_APPWINDOW	Forces the window to the top level on the taskbar when the window is visible.
WS_EX_CLIENTEDGE	The window has a sunken-edge look to it.
WS_EX_CONTROLPARENT	Allows navigation of child windows with the Tab key.
WS_EX_DLGMODALFRAME	The window has a double border.
WS_EX_LEFT	The window is left aligned. This is the default setting.
WS_EX_LEFTSCROLLBAR	For some languages, the scroll bar is on the left of the reading area. This style is used for those situations.
WS_EX_LTRREADING	Text in the window is displayed reading from left to right. This is set by default.
WS_EX_NOPARENTNOTIFY	Quells the WM_PARENTNOTIFY message from being sent to the window's parent upon creation or destruction.
WS_EX_OVERLAPPEDWINDOW	Combination of the WS_EX_CLIENTEDGE and WS_EX_WINDOWEDGE flags.
WS_EX_PALETTEWINDOW	Combination of the WS_EX_WINDOWEDGE, WS_EX_TOOLWINDOW, and WS_EX_TOPMOST flags.

Style	Description
WS_EX_RIGHT	The window is right aligned. This is only used for some languages.
WS_EX_RIGHTSCROLLBAR	The scroll bar is to the right of the client area. This is the default.
WS_EX_RTLREADING	Some languages read right to left. For these languages, this style allows the system to display characters right to left.
WS_EX_STATICEDGE	This style creates a window that appears to not accept input.
WS_EX_TOOLWINDOW	The window has a toolbar look to it.
WS_EX_TOPMOST	The window stays on top no matter if it is the active window or not.
WS_EX_WINDOWEDGE	The window has a border with a raised edge.

In the example program I use the `WS_EX_OVERLAPPEDWINDOW` extended style for the first parameter. By using this style, the program has the default look of most Windows applications.

The second parameter expects a null-terminated string containing the class name of the window class to create. All you have to do is set the same name here as you did in the `lpszClassName` member of the `WNDCLASSEX` structure. The example program uses "Window Class" for the second parameter.

The third parameter is another null-terminated string. Instead of specifying the class name, you specify the name that appears on the title bar. You can call the program whatever you want, but I called it "Create Window Example."

The fourth parameter, `dwStyle`, lets you specify multiple combinations of styles for your window. The styles available are listed in Table 2.7.

Table 2.7: Window styles

Style	Description
WS_BORDER	The window has a thin border.
WS_CAPTION	The window has a title bar.
WS_CHILD	The window is a child window. You cannot use this with the WS_POPUP style.
WS_CHILDWINDOW	Duplicate of the WS_CHILD style.
WS_CLIPCHILDREN	Prevents drawing in areas of the window where child windows reside.
WS_CLIPSIBLINGS	Windows in the area of the window being drawn into will not be drawn over.
WS_DISABLED	The window is disabled and cannot accept input from the user.

Style	Description
WS_DLGFRAME	The window has a dialog box look to it.
WS_GROUP	Specifies the window as the first in a group of windows. This is used for tab ordering of windows. The first window to have the WS_GROUP style starts the group, and subsequent windows are in the same group up until the next WS_GROUP style set.
WS_HSCROLL	The window has a horizontal scroll bar.
WS_ICONIC	The window starts out minimized.
WS_MAXIMIZE	The window starts out maximized.
WS_MAXIMIZEBOX	The window has a maximize button.
WS_MINIMIZE	Same as the WS_ICONIC style.
WS_MINIMIZEBOX	The window has a minimize button.
WS_OVERLAPPED	Same as the WS_TILED style.
WS_OVERLAPPEDWINDOW	The window has the following combination of styles: WS_OVERLAPPED, WS_CAPTION, WS_SYSMENU, WS_THICKFRAME, WS_MINIMIZEBOX, and WS_MAXIMIZEBOX.
WS_POPUP	The window is a pop-up window.
WS_POPUPWINDOW	The window is a pop-up window with the WS_BORDER, WS_POPUP, and WS_SYSMENU styles.
WS_SIZEBOX	The window can be sized.
WS_SYSMENU	The window has a menu on its title bar. You must set the WS_CAPTION style as well for this to work properly.
WS_TABSTOP	The window can be activated with the Tab key.
WS_THICKFRAME	Same as the WS_SIZEBOX style.
WS_TILED	Creates an overlapped window with a title bar and border.
WS_VISIBLE	The window is visible when created.
WS_VSCROLL	The window has a vertical scroll bar.

In the Create Window example program, I use the `WS_OVERLAPPEDWINDOW` style for the parameter. This gives the window the default look of most other Windows applications.

The fifth parameter of the `CreateWindowEx()` function is an integer specifying the horizontal position of the window on the screen. If you are creating a child window, the coordinate is relative to its parent's horizontal coordinate. Since the example window is not a child window, the coordinate of 0 puts it on the leftmost edge of the screen.

The sixth parameter sets the vertical position of the window on the screen. Just like the horizontal position, the vertical position is in screen coordinates unless it is a child window. If it is a child window, the number of pixels specified from its parent offsets its vertical position. Check out Figure 2.11 to see this concept illustrated.

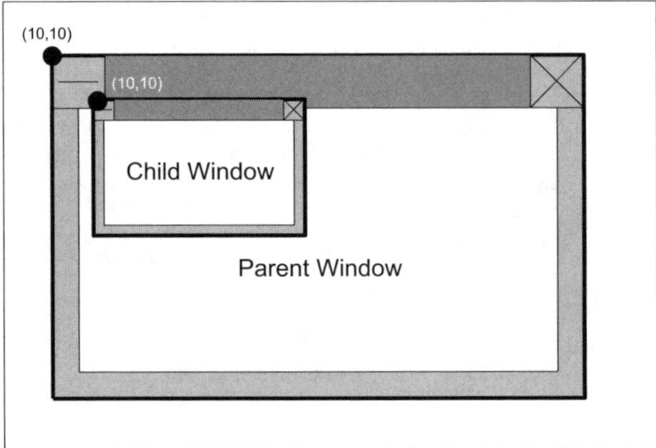

Figure 2.11: The coordinates of the window determine its position based on whether it is a child window or not.

Both of the windows in Figure 2.11 have coordinates of (10,10). The large window is the parent window; therefore, its coordinates of (10,10) set the window to be very close to the upper-left portion of the screen. The smaller window is the child window. Since it is the child window, its coordinates are relative to the parent. This means that its coordinates of (10,10) are actually (parentx+10,parenty+10), or (20,20) in screen space.

The seventh parameter of the create window function sets the width in pixels of the window. The example program sets the width to 320 pixels.

The eighth parameter sets the height of the window in pixels. The example program uses a height of 200 pixels.

The ninth parameter of the function sets the window's parent. This is useful when creating applications that have multiple windows. Since the example application only has one main window, this parameter is set to NULL to indicate that there is no parent.

The tenth parameter is used to set the handle of the menu associated with the window. The example application doesn't have any menus, so this is set to NULL.

The eleventh parameter is used to specify the handle to the module instance. For this parameter, you pass the instance handle passed in from the WinMain() function.

The last parameter is used to specify additional window creation data. I have rarely ever had to use this parameter, so I set it to NULL for most applications.

Wow! You are almost done with the majority of the work necessary to display a window on the screen. Check out Figure 2.12 to see the flow of the program so far.

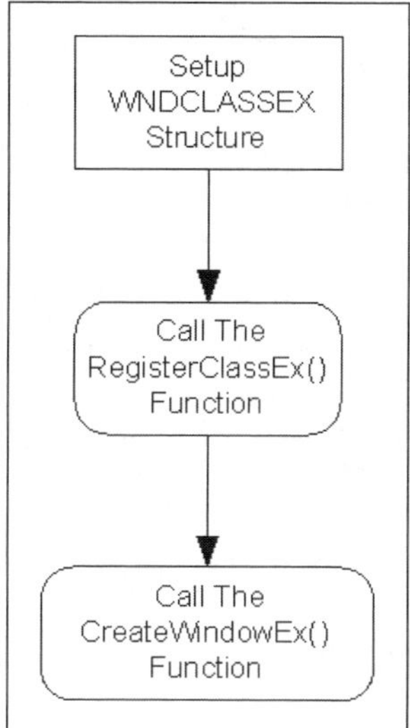

Figure 2.12: The flow of the application code up to and including the CreateWindowEx() function.

The ShowWindow() Function

Believe it or not, the act of creating the window does not actually display it. (Those guys at Microsoft are just so funny sometimes!) Actually, in order for the window to appear, you must call the ShowWindow() function. Luckily it is really straightforward. Here is the prototype:

```
BOOL ShowWindow(
    HWND hWnd,
    int nCmdShow
);
```

The first parameter sets the handle of the window to display. This is really easy, as you have a handle ready to go from the function that created the window. Take a look at the example and you can see how I pass in the handle returned from the CreateWindow() function.

The second parameter is an integer used to specify how the window is displayed. Yes, it's time again for another table. Table 2.8 lists the settings available for this parameter.

Table 2.8: Values for the ShowWindow() function

Value	Description
SW_HIDE	The window is hidden and the next window is activated.
SW_MAXIMIZE	The window is maximized.
SW_MINIMIZE	The window is minimized and the next window is activated.

Value	Description
SW_RESTORE	Restores the window from a minimized or maximized state. This is useful for setting a window back to its original size and position.
SW_SHOW	Activates the window and displays it.
SW_SHOWMAXIMIZED	The window is activated and displayed in its maximized state.
SW_SHOWMINIMIZED	The window is activated and displayed in its minimized state.
SW_SHOWNA	The window is displayed in its current state. This does not alter which window is currently active.
SW_SHOWNORMAL	Displays the window in its normal state. This is used when the ShowWindow() function is called for the first time.

Although you have many values to choose from for the second parameter, the easiest thing to do here is set the value to that of the iCmdShow integer passed into the WinMain() function. This is what the example code shows you.

Ta da! Your program has now accomplished its main task, displaying a window. Unfortunately, it does not accept input yet. This is where the message processing loop code comes into play.

Retrieving Messages with the GetMessage() Function

In order for the Windows application to know when it has been closed down, moved, or resized, it has to accept Windows messages. In general, your Windows applications always need to have a message loop. You may recall the information that I gave you at the beginning of the chapter regarding events and the message loop. In the example program I use a simple method of checking for messages and processing any found. That's it!

To look for pending messages, the GetMessage() function is called. Here is the prototype for it:

```
BOOL GetMessage(
    LPMSG lpMsg,
    HWND hWnd,
    UINT wMsgFilterMin,
    UINT wMsgFilterMax
);
```

The first parameter expects an MSG pointer. The MSG data structure contains all of the information about any messages found.

The second parameter sets which window to check for messages. Since your program can handle multiple windows, this is a necessary parameter. For the example application, only one window is present, so I just pass in the handle to the window created with the CreateWindow() function.

The third parameter lets you specify the lowest message value to retrieve. You want to retrieve all messages, so this is set to 0.

The fourth parameter lets you specify the highest message value to look for. Since you want to retrieve all messages, this is set to 0 as well.

Translating Messages with the TranslateMessage() Function

Before you can send messages to your message queue, you have to translate them into character data. This is done with the `Translate-Message()` function. The only parameter required is the pointer to the message you want to translate. In the example program, I pass in the address of the variable holding the message.

Once the message is translated into character data, you are able to post it to the message queue with the `DispatchMessage()` function.

Posting Messages to the Message Queue with the DispatchMessage() Function

Just like the `TranslateMessage()` function, the `DispatchMessage()` function only requires a single parameter. The purpose of this function is to send translated messages to the program's message queue. Once the dispatch function is called, the message appears in the message processing function.

The last line of code in the `WinMain()` function returns the `wParam` of the last Windows message pulled from the get message function. As Porky Pig would say, "That's all, folks!"

The Message Processing Function

You are probably wondering where the messages get processed. When messages are dispatched with the `DispatchMessage()` function, they are sent to the message loop as defined in the window's class. In the case of the example program, all messages are sent to the `fnMessageProcessor()` function that I wrote.

Take a look at the message processing function, and you can see how it is one medium-sized `switch` statement. This is because all the function has to do is go through all message types it is interested in and check if the message being passed in matches one of them.

My example checks for the `WM_CREATE`, `WM_DESTROY`, and `WM_PAINT` messages. The only one I do anything for is the `WM_DESTROY` message.

When the example receives the `WM_QUIT` message, it calls the `PostQuitMessage()` function to tell the Windows program to shut down. This is what happens when you exit the program with the exit icon.

If the message being passed in does not match any of the ones the program is checking for, it returns the message to the `WinMain()` function with the `DefWindowProc()` function. This is standard practice, so I wouldn't bother with trying to change it very much.

The example program only checks for a few message types, but examples later on in the book check for several message events. Keep this in mind when scanning through later code examples, as you will see some very alien message types.

Compiling and Executing the Code

You now have the entire program typed in and ready to go. To compile the program in Visual C++ 6.0, all you have to do is have the compiler program active and hit the F7 key. If all goes well, you see the following output in the output window:

```
--------------------Configuration: CreateWindow - Win32 Debug--------------------
Compiling...
CreateWindow.cpp
Linking...
CreateWindow.exe - 0 error(s), 0 warning(s)
```

If any errors appear when you compile, recheck the code and make sure everything was typed in properly. As long as you received no errors, you can run the program by hitting the Ctrl+F5 key combination. This executes the active project's program. Figure 2.13 shows what the program looks like when executed.

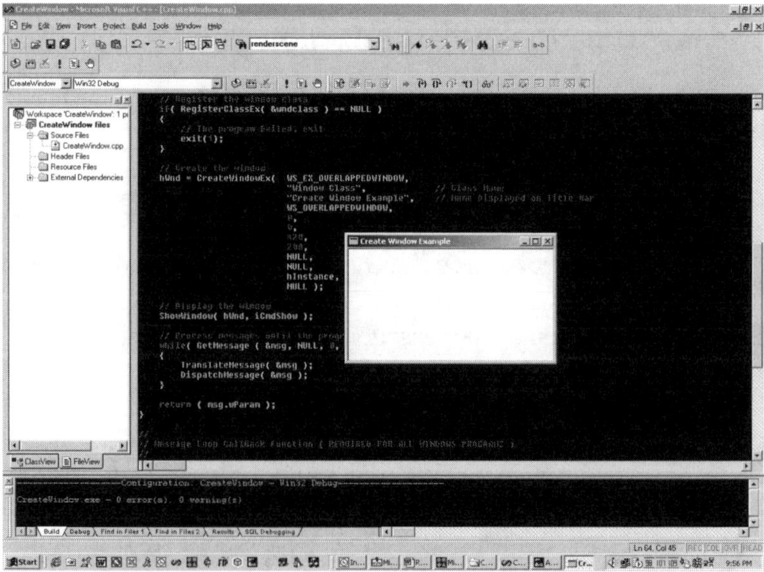

Figure 2.13: The Create Window program in action.

Recap

Doesn't it feel good to finally know how to create and display a window? I know it's not a working game, but everyone has to start somewhere. There aren't many tips in this chapter, so the list is short and sweet this time.

Your games will reuse the same Windows code over and over. You should keep a starter project, such as the example I wrote as a basis for future projects.

■ Keep window class names unique. The class name determines the type of window created, so this is important.

■ Make sure your program never goes into a long loop without processing Windows messages. Your application will appear to have frozen if you do not process messages in a timely manner.

Chapter 3

Game Mechanics

Hopefully your appetite for writing code is a little bit satiated from the last chapter because now it is time to cover the mechanics of strategy games. Before you can go on to write the best strategy game ever, you must first understand the basic building blocks of all strategy games. In this chapter, I cover the following:

- The basics of the background story
- Setting objectives
- Combat units
- Resource management
- Technology trees
- The campaign game
- Multiplayer gaming

The Story

What would a game be without a background story? To better answer that, think of how entertaining characters in a book would be without any background information. That they would be very boring. The same holds true for strategy games and most video games in general. Now, don't get me wrong, you don't have to be the best storywriter in the world to make a fun game. But it does help the overall feel of your game.

The Story Theme

The first thing you need to do to get started with the story is think of the theme of your game. Some possible themes include the following:

- Science fiction
- Medieval

- Western
- Post-apocalyptic

There are many other possible themes to choose from or invent; the basic idea is to pick one and work with it. Take, for example, Star Wars: Galactic Battlegrounds, based on the well-known *Star Wars* saga by George Lucas. Of course, it falls into the science fiction theme. Another game example is Stronghold, which is based around capturing and building castles, hence the medieval theme. I recommend that you pick a theme you really like. For one thing, the ideas for the story are easier to come up with when you enjoy the topic.

The Story Elements

There are a couple of key elements to writing the story for your game. Each one is important, and you need to make sure that each one exists before moving on with other parts of the game design. The elements are:

- The plot
- The purpose

The Story Plot

Every good story has a plot, and game stories are no exception. The plot gives your game story depth and meaning. Players are more compelled to win when they have a reason to do so. One such example is Westwood's Command & Conquer game. In it, NOD is fighting the GDI for control of the Tiberium fields. If this plot didn't exist, players might wonder why NOD and the GDI are fighting each other.

Just remember that the plot defines the series of events leading up to the purpose of the game. It gives your game design a good story foundation to work with. Whether the plot is based on war, deception, or even finance, it is important.

The Story Purpose

The game story also gives players a purpose for winning the game. Just as the plot gives them background information about the game, the purpose gives them the information needed to have the desire to win. If you write a background story that gives players a purpose, they will enjoy it more. I suggest that the purpose be more than obtaining the most military victories, as that is a very shallow purpose. Try to think up a purpose that is compelling and rewarding, one that helps to set the goals of the game.

Now that you know the elements of a game story, I suggest you go and write up a quick one for your first strategy game. Start out with an outline and work from it to write a complete mini-story.

Setting Objectives

Once the story is in place, you can then start writing out the objectives of the game based on the story purpose. Since the players have a purpose, what are their goals? Having well-thought-out goals is very important to the success of your strategy game. You don't want players wandering around with nothing to do, do you? I have found that the best way to set up goals is to write down the basic idea for winning your game and then break it up into steps.

For example, take the game Warcraft developed by Blizzard. In that game, the player's objective is to defeat the orcs or the humans, depending on the race he or she chooses to play. That sounds simple enough, so let's break that down into goals.

The first goal of the player is to build a city capable of sustaining an army. This, of course, requires many sub-goals, such as providing adequate housing, gathering necessary resources, and buying valuable upgrades to equipment. There you have it — a set of goals already!

As you delve further into the game, you start to discover all sorts of goals for the player on the path to victory. My best advice to you is to keep it simple. Most players do not desire hundreds of goals. If you think about it, you start to realize that most of the best-selling strategy games of all time are very simple goal-wise.

Case Study — Empire Earth

Just so you are clear on the subject, I have taken the liberty of breaking down the game Empire Earth into several goals or objectives. The goals I list represent the goals used by players in a single-player skirmish game versus the computer. Keep that in mind in case you ever play the game in a different mode and wonder why the heck I came up with my list!

Note If you have never played Empire Earth, I suggest you check it out at http://empireearth.sierra.com. It's a very fun game.

Description

To begin with, Empire Earth is very similar to Age of Empires in that you build up a civilization through various times, such as the Stone Age and the Dark Ages. The major difference with Empire Earth is that you actually take your civilization much further than Age of Empires does. In fact, you take your civilization all the way into the future. Not only does this add a ton of game play value to the game, it also adds a great deal of complexity. This is good for you, of course, as the game has several goals as a result.

Not only do you build up a civilization through multiple ages, you also wage war with the other civilizations around until you are the ultimate victor. There are many ways to win the game, but my favorite is military conquest, as you have to wipe the enemy from the face of the planet to win. After all, who doesn't like ultimate conquest?

Early Goals

The game starts out simply enough with a small village capital and a handful of citizens. So, there you are, very vulnerable to the world with only a few people to help you out and a capital for your nonexistent city. As you might imagine, the first thing you need are resources to build up your city. Considering most buildings require wood, a good first goal is to send your citizens out to chop down some trees. Take a peek at Figure 3.1 to see the grand beginning of the goal chart.

Gather Wood

Figure 3.1: The first goal of many in Empire Earth illustrated.

There you have it: The first goal of the game is to gather wood for your buildings. From the first goal, you deduce others. For example, what helps you to gather wood more quickly? The somewhat obvious answer is to have more citizens to chop for you. And no, you cannot buy your cavemen chainsaws!

The drawback to buying more people is that they require food. Considering food is also a resource vital to your civilization, you must balance the need for more workers with the supply of food that your fledgling empire produces. Enter stage right, the interdependent goal. Since you require people to gather wood and people require food, you now have another goal of acquiring food. It is time to update the goal graph.

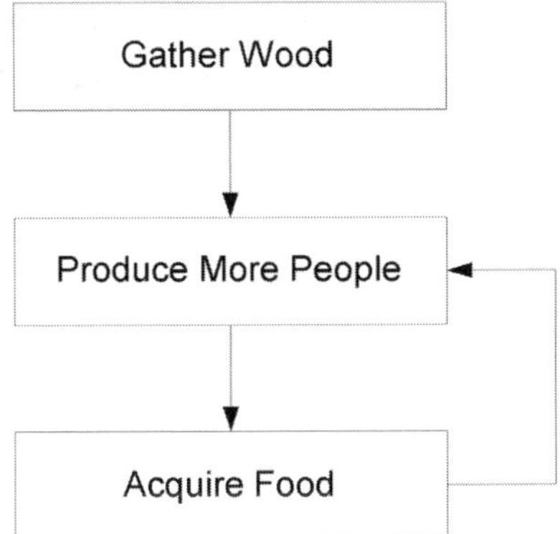

Figure 3.2: The second and third goal in Empire Earth illustrated.

In Figure 3.2, I have added two new goals. The first new goal is the acquisition of people to help acquire resources faster. The second new goal is the acquisition of food to feed the people you need for resource gathering. Oh, what a vicious circle it is becoming!

As the game progresses, you soon start to realize that you need additional resources to build a proper infrastructure. Two main resources stand in your way — gold and iron. Without gold and iron, you cannot buy many things you need to survive. Considering that these two commodities are very valuable, the next goal for the player is to collect gold and iron.

Soon you realize there is a great deal of care taken to properly balance how many villagers you have collecting resources versus how much food you need. If you have too many villagers, your food stores run too low. If you use too few villagers, you don't mine the vital resources that your civilization needs.

Milestone Goals

In Empire Earth, you start out in the Prehistory Age. In order to move past the Prehistory Age, you must collect a certain amount of food. This is why it is important to store food — because you need it to advance your civilization. The game actually calls each time period an epoch. When your civilization is ready to enter the next epoch, you spend the required resources and wait a brief period for the change to come about. The cool part about epochs is that every time you enter a new one, you have additional construction options available to you. Not only can you build better buildings, but you can also train better troops. This brings me to my next point: milestone goals. Just as the heading suggests, an

event in your game as great as an epoch is considered a milestone goal.
Check out Figure 3.3, which lists the epochs available in Empire Earth.

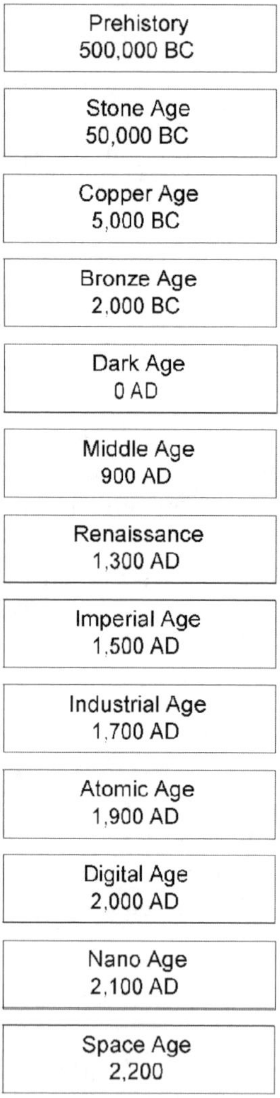

Prehistory
500,000 BC

Stone Age
50,000 BC

Copper Age
5,000 BC

Bronze Age
2,000 BC

Dark Age
0 AD

Middle Age
900 AD

Renaissance
1,300 AD

Imperial Age
1,500 AD

Industrial Age
1,700 AD

Atomic Age
1,900 AD

Digital Age
2,000 AD

Nano Age
2,100 AD

Space Age
2,200

Figure 3.3: The epochs in Empire Earth illustrated.

From Figure 3.3, you can see how the game supports 13 epochs. Each
one brings about certain advantages to the player and enhances game
play. Although milestone goals are a lot of fun, try to limit the number of
milestone goals. By keeping the number of milestone goals to a minimum, you avoid risking confusion from the player. Granted, gamers
aren't a bunch of mindless fools. (At least I hope not, since I'm a gamer as

well!) But you still need to be ever-vigilant in creating a game that is easy to step into.

Finishing Goals

Once you have reached the third epoch in Empire Earth, a whole new set of goals opens up for you. For one thing, you have to start concentrating on an army so you can attack your foes. Another goal is to research vital technologies to improve your existing infrastructure.

As you continue to play the game, more and more goals come onto the horizon. The important lesson to learn here is that you should not present the player with every goal in your game up front. It is better to piece-meal the goals out to the player during the course of the game. Not only does this keep from overwhelming players, it also keeps them entertained as they have new and exciting things to do as the game progresses. Check out Figure 3.4 to see the goals in Empire Earth fleshed out.

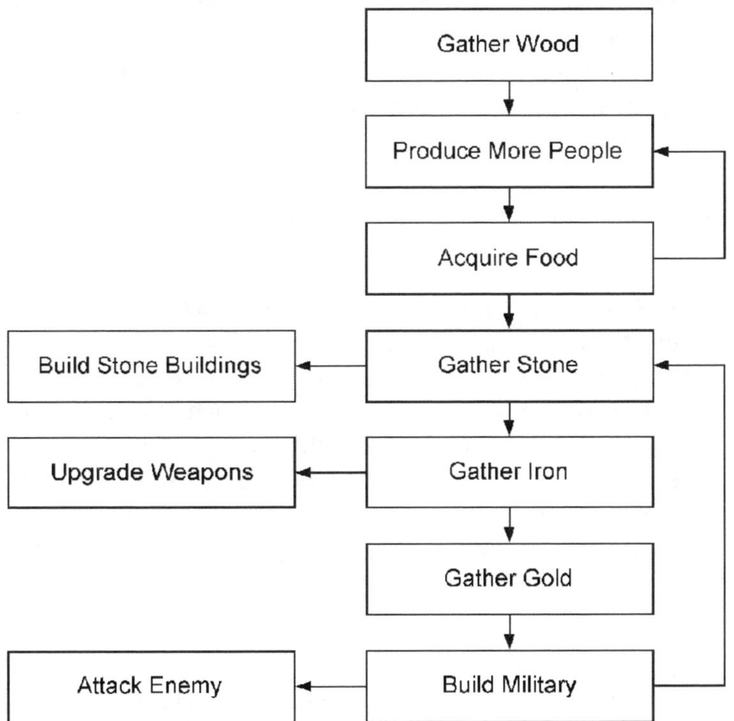

Figure 3.4: The more complete goal tree in Empire Earth illustrated.

Combat Units

Not all strategy games have units in them. There are games such as SimGolf, Sim Theme Park, and the like that have no combat in them at all. Your first reaction may be that these games are not strategy games, but in reality they are if you think about it a little. Anyway, that is for a different discussion; for now I am talking about combat units.

All combat-related strategy games have various combat units in them. Some games have tons of units, like Total Annihilation, while others have only a few units. As I have said over and over, balance is the key. Since you are at the very beginning stages of your own strategy game, you have to start somewhere. I suggest you start by focusing on a single unit that interests you the most. You also need to pick one that doesn't depend on other units for its existence. An aircraft for an aircraft carrier is a bad one to try, whereas a tank is a much better choice.

Once you have picked out a unit to start with, you need to make sketches of it to get a feel for the look of the unit. While sketching, you usually can get a good idea of what weaponry the unit uses, how big it is, and what form of transportation it uses. These are all key elements to designing the unit, as most combat units have four main characteristics: cost, speed, armor, and firepower.

Unit Cost

All combat units need to cost something to the player in the form of resources. If units are too cheap, players will buy tons of them and use the common strategy known as "rushing." This is probably the most boring form of combat in my humble opinion, but it works well for many, and that is why they use it. You need to strike a good balance between the cost of the unit and the overall strength of it. It is usually a good idea to make every unit require more than one type of resource to build. This keeps people from being able to concentrate on just one resource to maintain an army. It also adds to the tactical value of the game.

Tip   The term "rushing" comes from when a player builds many cheap units, forms an army out of them, and rushes their opponent. It's really a blitzkrieg form of attack and is quite deadly. The problem with rushing is that it usually costs nothing in the way of resources and most games end up being won by whoever could build the army and rush it to the opponent the quickest. The other downside is that most RTS games that suffer from rushing have no defense against the tactic. Remember, every strategy in an RTS game needs a counterstrategy. If not, every game will resort to the same boring tactic used every time.

Unit Speed

Not only do units have to cost something, they also need to have a speed factor associated with them. The usual method employed by RTS games is to make the larger and more powerful units slower while keeping the lightly armored units faster. This tends to work out for the most part, but I suggest you try to think of other methods to calculate the speed of your units.

Another factor in unit speed is the type of propulsion used by the unit. If it is a water vehicle, it is probably slower than a land-based alternate. Many factors, such as method of propulsion, need to be considered when designing your unit.

Calculating Unit Speed

As for the mathematics of unit speed, I suggest you create a basic system of unit speed from 1 to 100, with 1 being the slowest and 100 being the fastest. By using such a scale, you can easily multiply the unit's speed by the game's unit method for movement.

Unit Armor

I use the term "armor" generically here to refer to the defensive value of a unit. While not all units have offensive capability, most should have defensive capability. What fun is it to have a unit that is destroyed the second it is attacked! Carefully determine the defensive capability of your unit. Don't worry about it too much now because you are going to end up reworking the offensive and defensive capabilities of your units throughout the balancing phase of your game project.

Calculating Defensive Value

Creating the armor formula for your game is trickier than calculating speed. The main problem is that you may want certain types of armor to react differently to various weapons. For instance, maybe you have flamethrower units in your game that can deal a lot of damage to infantry. You don't want that same flamethrower to be just as effective versus tank armor, do you? You may want to use a method such as the one listed in Table 3.1.

Table 3.1: Unit armor

Armor	Fire	Ballistic	Chemical
Personal	0.1	0.2	0.5
Heavy Tank	0.9	0.7	0.8
Light Tank	0.7	0.6	0.7

In Table 3.1, I list the type of armor followed by three forms of defense — fire, ballistic, and chemical. The personal armor type represents armor worn by infantry. For a simple algorithm, say that you take the damage amount inflicted, multiply it by the armor rating, and subtract that from the original damage done to get the final damage inflicted.

For example, the aforementioned flamethrower hits an infantryman for 100 points of damage. You use the following formula to determine the damage deflected by the armor:

100 (inflicted) x 0.1 (armor rating) = 10 points deflected by the armor

The above formula means the infantryman takes the following amount of damage:

100 (inflicted) – 10 (deflected) = 90 points of damage taken

As you can see from the above example, the flamethrower is quite effective versus infantry armor. Now, take the same flamethrower versus a heavy tank:

100 (inflicted) x 0.9 (armor rating) = 90 points deflected
100 (inflicted) – 90 (deflected) = 10 points of damage taken

The tank armor is much more effective and results in a lot less damage taken. This, of course, does not even taken into consideration the number of hit points the tank has versus the infantryman.

Hit Points

I guess the term "hit points" is a fallback to old-school role-playing games, but it has found its way into most combat-based computer games. You now know how to calculate defensive or armor rating, and now you need to consider how much actual damage a unit can take before being destroyed.

There is no complicated algorithm for hit points, just a standard number representing how many damage points the unit can take before dying. Let's go back to the armor example. The infantryman that took 90 points of damage may only have 50 hit points total, meaning he died in the attack. The tank, on the other hand, only took 10 points of damage total and probably has around 1000 hit points. To make life simpler, I suggest you create a scale from 50 to 5000 hit points for units in your game. The weakest of the weak have a minimum of 50, while the strongest have a maximum of 5000 hit points. See, wasn't that easy?

Unit Firepower

The nemesis of armor is firepower. All yings must have a yang, and this is it. All of the same basic rules apply to firepower that apply to armor. For starters, you must be careful in assigning firepower to your units. If a unit is offensively imbalanced, everyone will use only one unit, and the game will be boring. There are a few new things to consider for firepower though: rate of fire, damage type, special damage, and velocity.

Rate of Fire

The rate of fire for a unit determines how often it can fire its weapon. You need not look further than modern times to see the difference between how fast a pistol fires and how fast a machine gun fires. The difference between the two weapons equates into the rate of fire. Normally, the more powerful the weapon, the slower it fires. This, of course, is not true for a machine gun, but it is true for other weapons, such as naval cannons and surface-to-air missile systems.

Calculating Rate of Fire

The tried-and-true method of calculating rate of fire is to determine how many times per minute a weapon can fire. This gives you a good system for setting the ROF (rate of fire) or RPM (rounds per minute) for your weapon systems. Table 3.2 contains a few examples:

Table 3.2: Rate of fire

Weapon	Rounds per minute
9mm pistol	120
M1917A1 .30-caliber water-cooled machine gun	400-600
PPS43 automatic	700
81mm M1 mortar	18

As you can see in Table 3.2, the automatic rifle has a much higher rate of fire than the mortar. This makes sense considering the weaponry involved.

Damage Type

I touched on this in the armor section. Each weapon needs a damage type associated with it. The automatic rifle listed above is projectile-based, while the flamethrower mentioned earlier is fire-based. I suggest you come up with the various damage types available to your units and put them all in a nice table for later referencing.

Special Damage

Special damage is for damage inflicted outside of the normal series of events. One obvious choice is area of effect weaponry. Weapons that cause explosive damage also cause concussion damage that can be considered a special damage type, as it stuns enemies as well as hurts them. With more creativity you can come up with endless types of special damage. For simplicity's sake, just refer to special damage as additional damage.

Weapon Velocity

The actual weapon doesn't have a velocity, but the projectile leaving the weapon does. This is a key element of weapon design in your strategy game, as it has a large impact on game play. For instance, the laser beam from a futuristic warrior has the highest velocity possible since a laser works at the speed of light!

Calculating Projectile Velocity

Weapon velocity works very much like unit speed. You need a standard system of velocity to assign to all projectiles in the game. Once again, I suggest you use a value from 1 to 100 to set projectile velocity. You can then multiply the standard unit measure in your game to figure out projectile movement.

That is about it for units for now. On to resource management!

RTS Resource Management

What RTS game would be complete without resource management? I bet you can only name a couple, if any. At the heart of most RTS games lies resource management. I'm not talking about some pointy-glassed bean counter tucked away in cube hell here. I'm talking about the stuff that legends in RTS history are made of. Every top seller of the past had resource management. Warcraft had lumber, gold, and stone. Command & Conquer had Tiberium. Age of Empires had lumber, gold, stone, and food. The list goes on and on.

You may be saying to yourself, "Big deal. Resource management is simple to implement." Before you jump to any conclusions, think for a minute how complicated something as simple as resource management can get. Take my previous example about the food resource in Empire Earth. After only describing the first 15 minutes of the game, I pointed out many of the concerns and intricacies of it. The previous section dealt with resources mainly from the player's view. Now that you actually have to implement resources, it is time to look at it from the developer's viewpoint.

Pick Your Poison

The first thing to do is figure out the resources that the player needs to gather. Depending on how complex your game is, you should have from three to six different resources for the players to obtain. I always like to teach by example, so I'm going to start off with a game I have been working on for a bit. In Battle Armor, there are three main resources: fuel, ore, and food. How did I come up with those three, you may ask? Easy — I just made them up as I was typing! Just kidding. In reality, you start by writing down some key goals for the player. For Battle Armor, I came up with the following list of goals:

- Feed the population
- Build an infrastructure
- Raise an army

Defining Resources

From the few goals defined, you then figure out how to reach those goals. The first goal — feed the population — is really straightforward. In order to feed the people, the player needs to grow or gather food. So, the first resource is food. Seems simple enough, right?

The next goal — build an infrastructure — is rather straightforward as well. Since most buildings require some sort of mineral compound, I chose the simpler description of ore. The player isn't really building their city out of ore, but it is simple and to the point.

The last goal is the most difficult one. Raising an army involves the previous resources along with a whole new one. I thought about using energy as the primary resource of the army but then decided on fuel. Fuel makes the world go around; therefore, I see it fit for sustaining an army.

Gathering Resources

Now that you have the three resources defined for the game, you must decide on how the player obtains them. To get the ball rolling, I'll start with food. Since Battle Armor is somewhat of a sci-fi game, I don't want to require the player to manage fleets of people hand-picking the food. Instead, I am opting for a more advanced method — hydroponics.

The food is gathered by hydroponics machinery. The real question now is how do the players build hydroponics machinery? It would be very boring to let players build the food machines just anywhere on the map, so I am limiting them to only building hydroponics machines on patches of algae. Hey, guess what? The game just got a little depth to it! Not only does it have three main resources now, but also to gather one of them, you need machines, and the machines can only be built on patches of algae. If I didn't know better, I would say another goal has been introduced to the fledgling game: to locate patches of algae on which to build food-processing machines.

The second resource, ore, works in a similar fashion to food. Instead of building hydroponics equipment, the player builds mining equipment. Instead of building only on spots of algae, the player builds on mineral deposits. See, wasn't that easy? The cool part here is that not only do you define resources, you also get the side benefit of defining important goals. Check out Figure 3.5 to see the hydroponics plant in action.

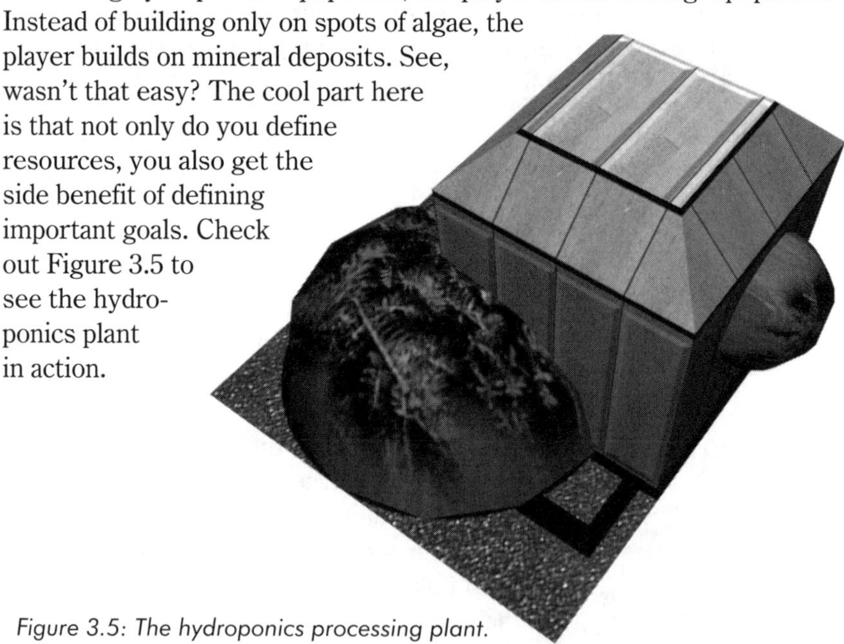

Figure 3.5: The hydroponics processing plant.

The last resource — fuel — is also rather straightforward now that the other two resources have been defined. Keeping with the pattern, I want the player to purchase refineries in order to make fuel. Not only do they have to purchase refineries, but they can also only build them on fuel deposits. Check out Figure 3.6 to see the fuel refinery in action.

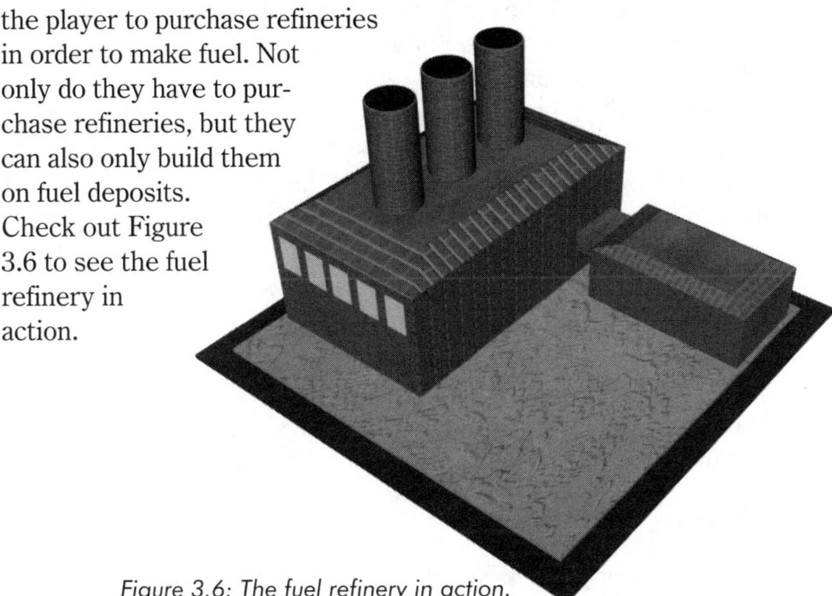

Figure 3.6: The fuel refinery in action.

Now that the resources for Battle Armor are out of the way, you have seen the process for defining the resources in your RTS games. It all comes down to the following steps:

- Determine the resources needed
- Determine how to get the resources
- Determine the constraints to getting the resources

Your imagination is the only limit in creating the resources for your game. I used very simple methods for Battle Armor. I encourage you to come up with clever types of resources and how to gather them.

Resource Balance

Ah, there is that word again, balance. You are going to read that over and over again. Balance is key to any good strategy game, and resources require a lot of balancing.

Unbalanced Example

Take, for example, the older game Total Annihilation by Cavedog. In Total Annihilation, or TA as most of us call it, players obtain metal and energy. Wow, isn't that simple — only two resources!

The main problem as I see it with TA is that players have no constraints in gathering resources. Machines that generate energy and metal can reside anywhere on the map, and the player is not limited to how many they can build. This causes severe problems in that players can wall themselves in, gather all the resources they want, and then strike their enemies with impunity.

From my explanation, you probably have deduced that the resources in TA lack one of the steps in determining resources for an RTS game. That step is none other than the constraints step. If players have no constraints as to how or when they can gather materials, your game will get out of balance.

Balanced Example

There are many balanced examples out there. Command & Conquer is a great one because players are very dependant on Tiberium. The cool part is that Tiberium grows at a very slow rate, and any one player does not generally own the Tiberium fields. Herein lies a great constraint — disallowing the player from owning the source of a material with impunity. As long as the source of vital materials is in jeopardy, the player has a much more challenging time.

Gathering Rate

Besides being concerned about how the player gathers resources, you also need to think about how quickly they are gathered. If players get resources too quickly, the game becomes frantic or, worse, not very challenging. If resource gathering takes too long, the game gets boring and monotonous.

Tip   First and foremost, be sure to make the rate of resource gathering adjustable in your code. You are going to spend quite a bit of time tweaking the amounts to get the right feel for the game.

RTS Technology Trees

If resources are the heart of RTS games, then the technology tree is the skeleton. Everything that happens in an RTS game is dependent on the technology tree. If you are not familiar with the concept, a technology tree defines the evolution of technology in an RTS game. Take, for example, the oversimplistic technology tree in Figure 3.7.

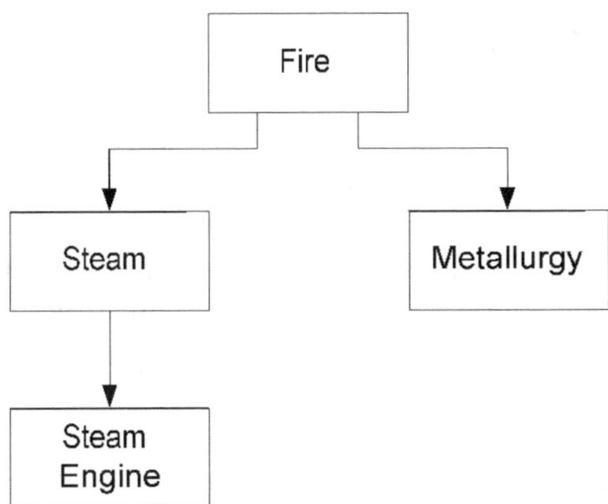

Figure 3.7: A very simple technology tree.

In Figure 3.7, you see the first node of the tree as being fire. Since fire is a basic building block of human technology, it is the first node, or trunk, in this case. The fire node branches into two more technologies, steam and metallurgy. Since both steam and metalworking require fire, they are natural branches of the fire trunk. From steam, another branch forms with a steam engine node. This is obviously because once you have steam, you can invent the steam engine.

By taking the example technology tree (or twig really), you start to see how technologies in a game are important. You start players off at the base of the technology tree and let them work up it to fulfill desired goals. Some players may opt for more advanced infrastructure technology, while others may go straight for weapon technology.

Note   Although they are called technology trees, they are more like technology ferns. I say this because they are usually turned upside down with the trunk on top and the branches hanging below. I'm sure this phenomenon is based on visual aesthetics more than anything.

Different Types of Technology

To design the technology tree for your game, you need to consider the various types of technology. The following types give you a good start:

- Infrastructure
- Weapons
- Upgrades

Infrastructure Technology

The main types of technologies deal with the infrastructure of the player's civilization. These types deal with the building blocks of the civilization. Without infrastructure technology, the player cannot progress to bigger and better things.

As an example, take Age of Empires. In Age of Empires, you cannot buy cavalry until you have built a stable. You cannot build a stable until you have researched the second age. Technologies such as these form the basis of the infrastructure nodes.

Weapon Technology

"...And let loose the dogs of war..."

All great strategy games have weapons; therefore, the weapon nodes of your technology tree are very important. You should create them in a logical manner that is easy for the player to pick up on.

I remember the game Alpha Centauri. It is a fun game that is basically Civilization in space. The only problem I have with it is that the technology tree is extremely confusing. Since the game is based on science fiction, all of the technologies have science fiction names that are not based on any reality. This causes a problem in that the designers may know what they mean, but most players don't have a clue what they mean! Just because you create a science fiction-based game doesn't mean you have to create a whole new language for your game.

Tip   Use easy-to-follow technology trees. Even if your game genre is futuristic, try to base the technology names on current reality.

Upgrade Technology

If you have ever played an RTS game, you are familiar with the upgrade concept. In most RTS games, the military units and buildings you have available to you can be upgraded at later times. This adds a cool aspect to the game in that different upgrades can take you down different and exciting paths.

Not only can you upgrade weapons, but you can also upgrade infrastructure. Take, for example, my game, Battle Armor. In Battle Armor, the hydroponics plants can be upgraded later to produce more food per time unit. Check out Figure 3.8 to see the upgraded hydroponics plant.

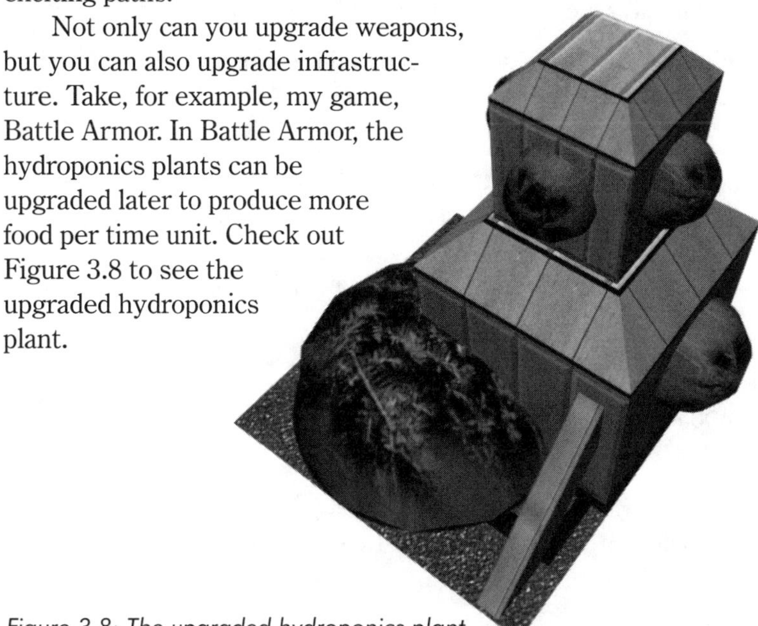

Figure 3.8: The upgraded hydroponics plant.

The Cost of Technology

Now that you know the three starting types of technology, you need to figure out what each one costs the player. Since you do not want players to be allowed to get every technology free, you must decide what each one costs. The cost has to come from the resources your game has, so choose wisely.

There are a couple of key points to keep in mind when choosing the cost of technology in your game:

- Be sure the technology takes time to research. The more valuable the technology is, the longer it should take to invent.

■ Be sure the technology requires resources that pertain to it. In other words, do not make a technology require a resource that has nothing to do with it.

■ Be sure the technology costs a reasonable amount. If the technology is very valuable, it should cost a good deal of resources. Do not go overboard, though. If the technology costs more resources than it is going to save, it is worthless.

In Figure 3.9 you can see the updated technology tree with resource costs associated with each technology node.

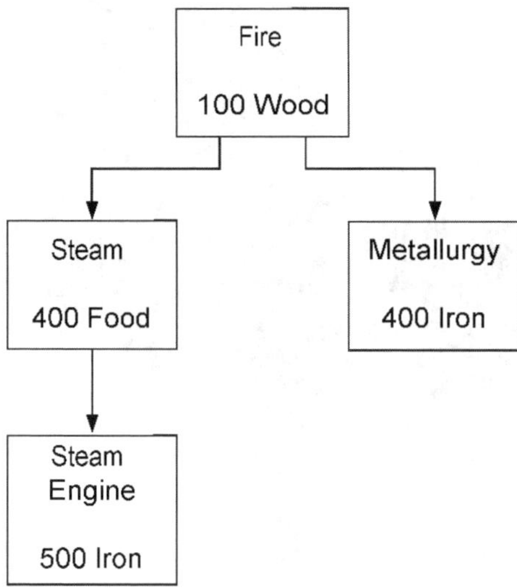

Figure 3.9: The technology tree with resource costs included.

The Campaign Game

Once you have the basic theme of your game chosen, the general player goals outlined, the resources defined, and the technology tree laid out, you need to work out the campaign game. I'm sure you have played the campaign mode of a strategy game. Basically, the campaign mode is a series of prescribed games that follow the player through the story.

The reason I say they are prescribed is because campaign games are pregenerated by you, the developer. Unlike multiplayer or skirmish games, campaign games have set risks and rewards associated with them. For example, the early campaign games in Westwood's Emperor: Battle for Dune require you to prove your worthiness to your house clan by performing simple tasks, such as leading a small unit of troops into battle. As you progress through the campaign, you are requested to accomplish more difficult tasks. The tasks also take longer and usually get more complicated as the game progresses.

The Mission Editor

Each game in the campaign mode is called a mission. The obvious reason is because you are sending the player on a task that has both risk and reward. Sounds like a mission to me! Since missions are prescripted, you as the developer have to create a mission editor. Usually, mission editors are built into the general game-editing tool. Later on I will show you how to create a mission editor, but for now I am just covering the basics of it.

Most strategy games have around 20 to 30 single-player missions built into the game. This gives the player enough to do until the mission pack add-on comes out. Yes, I know, this may sound kind of lame, but without revenue, game companies can't exist. You should always plan on making your games expandable in case they are enough of a hit to warrant expansion packs or sequels. You don't have to look much further than Ensemble's Age of Empires series to see what expansion packs can do for you. Another great example is RollerCoaster Tycoon. I bet Chris Sawyer, the author of the game, never imagined the immense success his addictive roller coaster-building game would be. If you have followed the series, you know that there are tons of add-on packs for it.

Mission Goals

I talked about goals extensively earlier, but not as they pertain to missions. Unlike game goals that are global to every mission, mission goals are unique. When designing the missions for your games, think of what the player has to accomplish to progress through the story line.

Missions should not be about trivial tasks just to give the player something to do. Instead, missions must progress the player through the story. Keep this in mind when laying out the structure of the missions.

Each mission also needs a specific goal. Whether it be to rescue a hostage, destroy a tank column, or locate a secret enemy hideout, specific goals are vital to an enjoyable game.

That's it for now on the campaign game. I discuss it a lot more later on in the chapter on writing the game editor.

Multiplayer Gaming

Ah, my favorite part of strategy games — multiplayer gaming! Personally, I don't play the campaign games or single-player modes in RTS games very much. I prefer to duke it out with other players online or play against the computer with a few friends. There is nothing more fun than a heated battle with other humans around. The single-player game is very important though, as many people enjoy it.

Since you are going to write a strategy game someday, you should plan on incorporating multiplayer support via the Internet or a local area network. The common method of choice today is to use sockets or DirectPlay. I like DirectPlay for many reasons, but low-level sockets work very well too.

Depending on the complexity of your game, you should plan on supporting from four to eight players at once. Usually eight is far too many for most systems, but it is possible. The main limiting factor is how many units are allowed per player. If your game is based around a few unique units per player, you can have support for quite a few people. If your game expects around 200 units per player, you are going to have a problem on your hands if too many people try to play at once. For simplicity's sake, I suggest you start out supporting six players; it is a nice, happy medium.

There are all sorts of technological problems associated with multiplayer support. One such problem is how you go about supporting saved games. Very few strategy games support this option. The only one that I successfully used it in was Age of Empires II. I must say, it is one great feature. Considering that many strategy game sessions can last for several hours, the ability to save is invaluable.

Recap

Now that you have a primer on the basic building blocks of a strategy game, it is time to move on to more advanced material. Before you go, remember these key tips:

- Try to design your game where rushing is not a helpful tactic. Your game will benefit from this in the end.

- Make sure your resource management system is easily tweaked so you can balance your game with minor code changes.

- Use easy-to-follow technology trees. Even if your game genre is futuristic, try to base the technology names on current reality.

Chapter 4

Planning Your Game Project

You are now armed with the knowledge to plan your game project. This part of game development is commonly referred to as project management. There are a few key areas of project management that you need to know about in order to manage a successful game development effort.

Many programmers just rush right into coding before thinking about the actual project at hand. This type of approach can lead to missed milestones, chaotic development, burned-out team members, and even cancelled projects. Even if you are a team of one or two people, don't give in to the temptation of quick and dirty development. Take the time to properly plan your project, and you will reap the rewards.

That's enough preaching for now. Everyone has their own method of project management, so I'm definitely not claiming that what I present here is the best method. I suggest that you use what I have written as a framework for your own method. Project management is very similar to software development in that everyone has their own style. In this chapter I cover the following:

- The envisioning phase
- The requirements phase
- The technical documentation phase
- The development phase
- The testing phase
- The production phase
- Distribution

The Envisioning Phase

There you are, standing on the edge of infinity. Only you and your mind set the limits to what lies ahead. For you are in the envisioning phase, or what is commonly known as the creative phase. It is here that you must come up with the idea to beat all other ideas. The idea that will bring millions of gamers flocking to your doorstep. The idea that will change the gaming world! Unless you are Sid Meier or John Carmack, you may want to set your sights a bit lower on the change-the-world part, but hey, anything can happen.

In the envisioning phase you come up with the idea for your product. Since you are dealing with strategy games here, you should probably ask a few questions, such as:

- What type of strategy game is it — real-time or turn-based?
- Is the game based on real or fictional events?
- What time period is the game based in — medieval, Civil War, World War II, futuristic?
- Is it single player, multiplayer, or both?
- Are the graphics 3D, 2D, or both?
- How long does an average round in the game take to complete?
- What is the goal of the game?
- Is the game mainly strategic or tactical?
- Is the game simple or complex?
- How do you win the game?
- How do you lose the game?
- How long does the entire game take to win?

The questions listed above by no means cover everything you need to answer about a strategy game. This is where the creative part comes in. Just as I told you in Chapter 3, there are many elements to a strategy game. Think about them for a while and see what other questions you come up with.

Envisioning Outline

So you have all these ideas. Now what? The best method I have come up with is to put your idea in an outline. Take a look at the following outline:

```
Background
    World War II
        Patton's battles
        Accurate.  Modeled after real-world events.
    Combat
        Brigade level
        Focus on mechanized units
        Commands given down to squad level
    Realism
        Fog of war
        Communication problems
        No satellite view
        Routes possible
        Supply routes required
    Players
        Single player
        Campaign game
        Multiplayer
            Skirmish battles
            Single-campaign events
```

There you have it, a very simple outline done during the envisioning phase. In my outline you can tell that I want to make a game based on General Patton's famous battles in World War II. You can also tell that combat is based on large masses of troops and equipment with control reaching down to the squad level. The outline also shows that the game is going to be realistic. Realism is to be achieved with features such as fog of war and real supply routes.

By reading my outline, you get the basic idea of the game — a realistic World War II tank battle game. Sure, there are tons of details left to determine, but this is only the first phase of product development.

The Requirements Phase

All right, you have a game idea outlined and are ready to begin the requirements phase. In this phase you determine what the game must have in it to be declared ready for production. Be careful not to get too ambitious here; otherwise, you will end up with a monster project!

The best part about this phase is that the requirements can change during the rest of the phases. Ask any programmer out there about feature creep, and I bet you will get a passionate response! Requirements change often and without prediction. That's just the nature of the development beast. The bottom line is to not worry about listing every possible requirement during this phase. Just worry about the major ones, and everything else will fall into place.

Using my previous outline as an example, here is how I would list the requirements for the multiplayer section:

Multiplayer requirements
1.   Supports 2 to 16 players
2.   Game can be saved and reloaded
3.   Dedicated server optional
4.   Game admin can kick and ban players

With each numbered item under the multiplayer section, I would also write a brief paragraph about the requirement. A good rule of thumb here is that more information is better. Nothing is worse than a sparse requirements document. Keep in mind that this document is all the developers have to work from. This is the document that feeds the technical requirements. If you don't list something here, don't expect to see it implemented in the game.

Before you move on to the technical requirements phase, make sure you have addressed the main items in the envisioning phase. Put each one into a requirements block and write a paragraph about it. This phase should take you a few weeks at least for a simple project. The last project I worked on took four months to get the requirements phase complete!

The Technical Documentation Phase

The product managers and designers have finished their work, and now it's up to the development people to write the technical requirements document. The technical requirements document is based solely on the requirements document and nothing more. If it's not in the requirements document, it doesn't get put into the technical requirements document.

Some of this may sound a bit confusing, so take a look at Figure 4.1 for a visual.

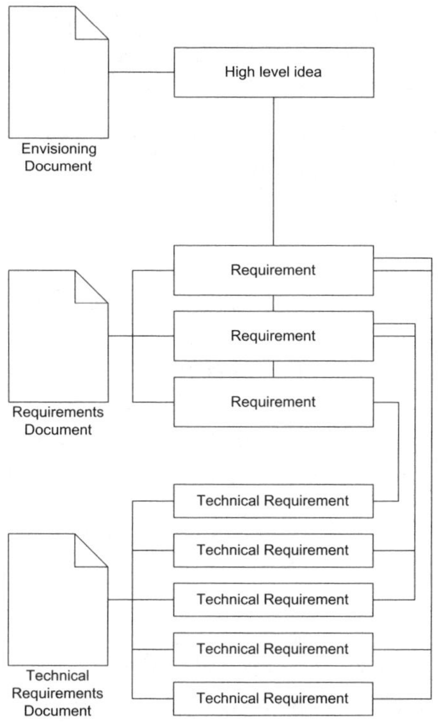

Figure 4.1: The relationship between the project documents.

In Figure 4.1, you see how the high-level game idea is fleshed out in the envisioning document. Elements from the envisioning document feed the requirements document. Each main topic is broken down into several requirements at this point. Once each main envisioning idea is broken up into requirements, those requirements are fed into the technical requirements document. In the technical requirements document, the actual programming tasks are outlined and covered in detail. For example, take the multiplayer requirements that I listed in the previous section:

Multiplayer requirements
    Dedicated server optional
        1. This feature requires a separate program that contains only the network code for the game. The program should take up as few resources as possible so that the player can host a dedicated server and play on the same machine.
        2. There can be multiple dedicated servers running at one time on one machine.

3. The dedicated server is configured via a configuration file found in the same directory as the server program.
4. The dedicated server is command-line driven and has no interface.
5. Game status is displayed in the server command-line window. Items such as number of players, current game time, average game time, and errors are contained within the display.

As you can see in the technical requirements, I have listed quite a bit of detail that is required from a developer's standpoint. Nothing about marketing or overall game-play belongs in this document. Only the nuts and bolts of development should be present.

Take your requirements document now and come up with the technical document. You should list everything that you can think of from a developer's standpoint in it. Unlike the requirements document, this one is not as flexible and can have huge ramifications on your project if you forget something. Luckily, since you are a developer, this is the easiest phase for you to complete. I think I completed the technical requirements document for my last project in about three weeks (it was 137 pages long!).

The Development Phase

Unfortunately, most budding game developers skip the previous phases and jump straight into development. While developing is the most fun for us as programmers, it's not the first step required for a successful game project. Notice the key word in the last sentence: *successful*.

During the development phase, obviously you develop the game. Although you are familiar with this part, maybe you haven't considered the following key aspects of development:

- Source code control
- Label management
- Bug tracking
- Unit testing

Source Code Control

Trust me, I'm not a control freak. Maybe I'm a control nut or even a control overlord, but not a freak. Source control consists of putting your source code into a virtual library during the entire development process. With each major revision or bug fix, you check out your code from the library, change it, and check it back in. Each time you check out your code and then check it back in, a new revision is automatically created.

With this method, you can virtually go back in time to look at a previous version of your code. This is a very useful tool!

Have you ever made a change to stable code only to find that it introduced a bug or instability? If so, going back and figuring out which change introduced the problem can be a real pain. With version control, you can check out old code, test it, and figure out at what point the bug was introduced. This would at least give you a starting point. Also, with tools such as WinDiff, you can compare two versions of code and see the exact changes between the two. This is invaluable!

Tip   WinDiff is included with the Windows operating system. If you are using Windows 2000, ME, or XP, you should have it already. Click the Start menu, select Run, and then type in WinDiff. Once you hit OK, you should see the WinDiff program appear. Play around with it and try comparing two similar files to see the differences. I bet you will love it!

There are many products on the market to assist you in source control. CVS is the most popular one that I have seen so far. To see it in action, check out www.sourceforge.net. There are thousands of open source projects at SourceForge.net to look at. In fact, there are free strategy game engines there! You can find information about CVS at www.cvshome.org.

Label Management

With label management, you get the benefit of clearly labeled source code releases. Basically, when you reach a milestone in development, you check in all of your code and assign a label to it. This allows you to go back and check out all of the various versions of code required to build the product at a certain checkpoint. Notice the following two files:

```
Main.cpp
    Version 1.4
    Version 1.3
    Version 1.2
    Version 1.1
    Version 1.0
Main.h
    Version 1.2
    Version 1.1
    Version 1.0
```

Now, if I asked you to pull the versions for the beta release, which files would you check out? You might just pull out the latest versions, but what if they were written post-beta? Without labels you have no way of knowing unless you decide to write down the document versions at major checkpoints. Can you imagine writing down the version for thousands of files? As you can guess, this is a big problem. Now take a look at the same two files with labels:

```
Main.cpp
    Version 1.4
    Version 1.3 BETA
    Version 1.2
    Version 1.1
    Version 1.0
Main.h
    Version 1.2 BETA
    Version 1.1
    Version 1.0
```

Wow, would you look at that. There is a BETA label beside the versions that were checked in at beta time. All you have to do now is check out the source code with the BETA label. Luckily, source control software lets you check out code by label or revision, so it's all automated for you. You should also notice how important labeling is from a stability standpoint. If you had just pulled the latest versions of the code to build the beta, you would have pulled the wrong Main.cpp file. This could cause huge problems down the line. Figure 4.2 illustrates the above example.

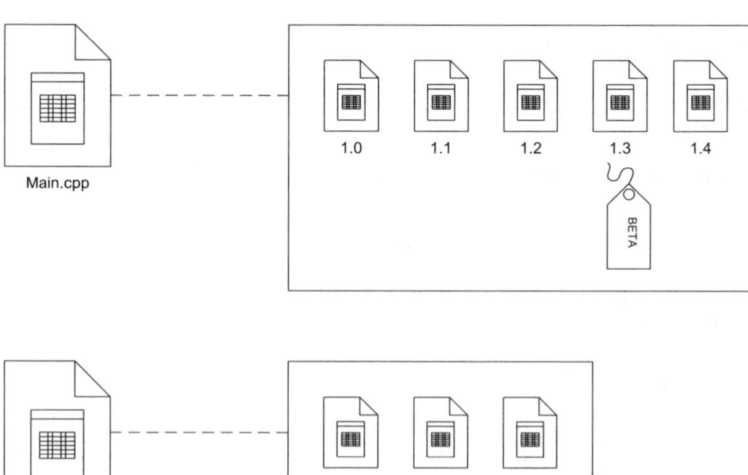

Figure 4.2: Source code versions and labels.

Bug Tracking

Let's say that you find a bug in your code while playing your game. What do you do? Instead of fixing it right away, you need to enter it into a bug-tracking system. Why? There are many benefits to using bug-tracking software. In short, they are as follows:

- Tracking
- Source tracking
- Quality metrics

Tracking

The most obvious benefit comes from the tracking itself. A consolidated list of bugs lets you easily see every problem that has presented itself during development. This is quite useful, as you can go back and look at every bug that you ran into. You can use this information to not repeat the same problems in your next project.

Tracking is also useful so that you do not forget to fix a bug. During development, you may run into problems that you deem of low importance. Sure, they don't crash the game, but they do need to be fixed! The best way to remember to fix them is to enter them into the bug-tracking system. Most bug-tracking systems let you specify the severity of the bug. This lets you prioritize the bug so you can work on the most severe ones first and get to the less severe ones later.

Another benefit of tracking is that other users or teams can enter bugs into the tracking system for your software. This allows the testing team to enter bugs for your game without having to come to you personally and tell you. Even if you are a lone developer, I highly suggest that you track your bugs.

Tip   One package I have used for bug tracking is called TestTrack, available from Seapine Software. You can visit their web site at www.seapine.com.

Source Tracking

Most bug-tracking packages let you tie a bug to the source code involved. This is useful in the source control world since the source code librarian can tell which source code needs to be labeled for a bug fix.

Quality Metrics

One advantage to having a history of bugs is that you can create quality metrics from the historical archive. You can go back in time and see where the most bugs occurred. Were most bugs found in system test? Were they found in beta? Were they found in production? By answering these questions you can find holes in your quality standards and attempt to fix them. If most of the bugs are found in system test, then you have to find out why development is sending so many bugs to the system testers. If most of the bugs are found in beta, you have to find out why the system testers are sending so many bugs to the beta team. If most of the bugs are found in production, you have to find out why the beta team is missing them. The last thing in the world you want to happen is for bugs to reach production. Every bug in production can cost you a lot of money to fix.

The bottom line is that quality metrics allow you to isolate deficiencies in your test cycle and track the improvement.

Unit Testing

I cannot stress enough how important unit testing is. Basically, *unit testing* is the testing that dedicated developers do on their own product. Before the game is sent to the system test team, the developers are supposed to test it themselves. My best advice to you is to test your code thoroughly! You should rarely pass code to testers if it has any known severe bugs in it. If you do, make sure you document the bugs that are known to exist.

Personally, I follow a few guidelines before I pass my code on to system testers:

- The code can run single-threaded through 5,000,000 iterations without fail.

- The code can run 32 threads through 5,000,000 iterations each without fail.

- The code can run for one week straight without fail.

- The code passes a full regression test without fail.

The multi-threaded part may not apply to your development. It all really depends on what you are writing. Don't take these rules verbatim; just use them for ideas to apply to your own process.

The bottom line here is that your code should be rock solid before you send it on to the testing team. If it's not rock solid, why are you passing it on?

The Testing Phase

Ah, my favorite part. By the time your code reaches the testing phase, you should be very happy. At this point, you have your program at least standing up and working. Sure, it may not have every feature in it, but at least it runs!

In the testing phase, the system test team runs your program through its paces. Usually, the system testing team has a document called the *regression plan* that contains a list of tests to try on your program. If everything in the regression plan executes without fail, your code is well on its way to beta.

System testers also try out what is called *negative testing* on your code. Say you have an entry field in which the player enters the number of troops to send into a combat group. The system tester may try to enter a letter from the alphabet just to see what happens. Or the tester may enter a negative number or some huge number just to see if it will blow up your code. This is the true nature of negative testing — to test the unexpected. Believe me, users will do all sorts of things you never expect.

There are a few easy steps to the testing process, illustrated in Figure 4.3.

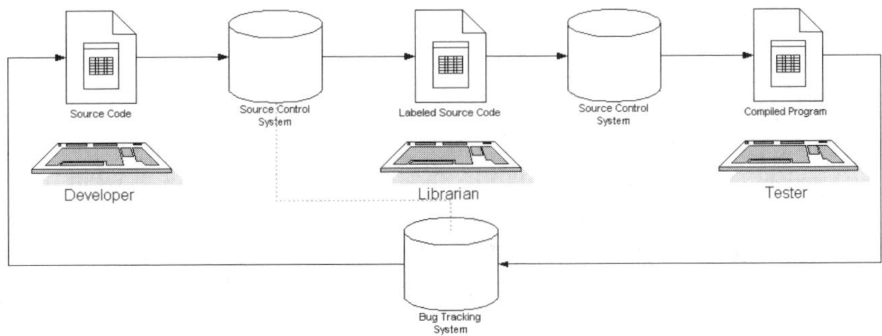

Figure 4.3: The testing process.

In Figure 4.3 you can see how the developer works on the code and checks it into the source control system. Once the source code is checked in, the code librarian checks out the code and builds the program. As long as everything compiles fine, the librarian labels the code for system test and checks it into the source control system. The system tester then pulls the labeled program and performs testing on it. Any bugs that are found go into the bug-tracking system and are pulled by the developer to look at and fix. The cycle starts all over again, once the developer makes bug fixes.

The Production Phase

By the time you make it to the production phase, there are zero bugs in the software with a severity above low. If there are any bugs with a higher severity, the code doesn't belong here!

This phase is pretty simple, as the system test team gives the green light to the source code for release into production. Once the green light is given, the librarian labels the code with a production label and sends it on to the production team. The production team then pulls the compiled program and puts it out there for the world to see. Usually, the program sits in a beta test state for a few weeks or months, depending on the complexity.

If bugs are found in production, they are sent to the system test team to reproduce. If the bug can be reproduced in system test, it is passed to development to take care of. Once the bug has been fixed, the development team sends it back to system test for confirmation. As long as system test can confirm it has indeed been fixed, they can pass it on to production for a bug fix release. See, isn't that simple?

All of these phases may sound like a bunch of red tape, but believe me, in a professional environment, they pay off big time. The last thing you want is a project without controls in place to maintain quality and the production schedule.

Distribution

You have a completed game sitting in your hands; now what do you do? While the previous sections of this chapter dealt with the inner workings of a professional shop, this section deals with how the little guy gets a game released to the public. Maybe you are a "little guy," and maybe you aren't, but this section may help you.

There are a few common roads you can travel to self-distribution. They are:

■ Shareware

■ Auction sites

■ Publisher

Shareware

Ah, the pit of aspiration, shareware. Shareware is the simplest method that you can choose to distribute your game. There are many public download sites out there willing to host your game for free. All you have to do is package it up as an installable download and put an address on it for people to send you donations.

The only problem with shareware is that your chance of making any real money is next to zero. Frankly, you are more likely to be struck by lightning. If your real motive is just to get people to play your game, then shareware is probably the way to go. Just don't expect to make a living off of it.

One such place to submit your file is called FilePlanet. You can find it at www.fileplanet.com. You can submit up to a 200-megabyte file for others to download. (Be sure to include an address where people can send you donations!)

An alternate method for releasing shareware is to release a cut-down version of your game. Say, for example, your strategy game covers battles in World War II. Only include a few combat scenarios with the free version of the game and request that the player pay you money to download the full version. This is a great way to get exposure for your game and sell a few copies.

Auction Sites

Another method is to package your game and manual in a baggie and sell it on eBay or another auction web site. You probably won't get away with charging more than $10 USD or so for your game, but that should suffice to pay for the effort. The only problem with this method is that your exposure is going to be very limited. To counteract this problem, you need to submit a demo of your game to shareware sites. In the demo, put a link to your web site so people can find out how to buy it if they're interested.

Most CD burners are super cheap nowadays, and the blank media is cheap as well. The total cost of packaging your game should run you less than $2 USD. As you can see, the profit margin is high; just make sure you get exposure for your game before you try selling it. I also wouldn't bother prepackaging too many copies. Just make them as you receive orders.

You may even try selling electronic downloads of your game for a fee. Some customers may not want to do this, but if you can, it's easier than shipping them a CD. One place that allows you to do this is www.digibuy.com.

Publisher

If you think your game is good enough for a publisher, you may want to try a few of the online publishers out there. One such company is Garage Games, which will publish your game for a cut. You can find information about them at www.garagegames.com.

If you want to have your game published by a big-name publisher, such as Electronic Arts, you'd better have a top-notch game. I highly suggest that you approach them before making your game. You need a sound business plan, and you also need to have a lot of experience. In reality, this is about the toughest thing you can try to do if you are unknown to the industry. I suggest that you get a few popular games out there on your own before you bother with this approach.

Recap

In this chapter you learned about the software production cycle. There are many steps involved, and you can pick and choose from among them. Most people come up with their own methods, but hopefully I have given you some ideas to get started with. Keep the following in mind:

- Unit testing is the testing performed by the development team.

- System testing is the testing performed by the system test team.

- Quality metrics are used to reduce the number of bugs found in system test and production.

- Software should never reach production with known severe bugs in it.

Building Blocks

Chapter 5

Tile-based Graphics

One of the key elements of strategy game development is the terrain engine. Considering that most strategy games take place on the ground, terrain is very important. There are a myriad of ways to handle terrain, one of which is the tile-based method. In this chapter, I cover the following aspects of tiles for strategy games:

- Tile engine basics
- Multi-layering tiles
- Tile editing and storage
- Tile properties
- Tile rendering

Tile Engine Basics

As usual, you must first master the basics of the theories presented here before moving on to more complex topics. Don't worry too much though, as I keep things as brief as possible without losing content. In the following sections you learn the answers to these questions:

- What is a tile?
- Why use tiles?
- How do you create tiles?
- How do you display tiles?

What Is a Tile?

Ah, the burning question humans must ask themselves. Just kidding. Seriously though, a tile is nothing more than a building block of terrain. Since building blocks really don't do much by themselves, neither do tiles. You must piece together several tiles for them to have significance.

You don't have to look any further than a tile mosaic to understand how tiles work for terrain engines. Each tile in a tile mosaic is insignificant, but when you piece all of the tiles together, they form a nice picture. Check out Figure 5.1 to see a tile mosaic.

Figure 5.1: Tile mosaic of a title screen.

As you can see in Figure 5.1, each tile in the mosaic has low significance, but when placed together with other tiles, they all form a complete picture. Tiles for terrain engines work in exactly the same way. Think of the earth as your canvas with terrain tiles as your brushes.

Now that you know what a tile is, how about some examples? Check out Figure 5.2 to see some tile examples for a terrain engine.

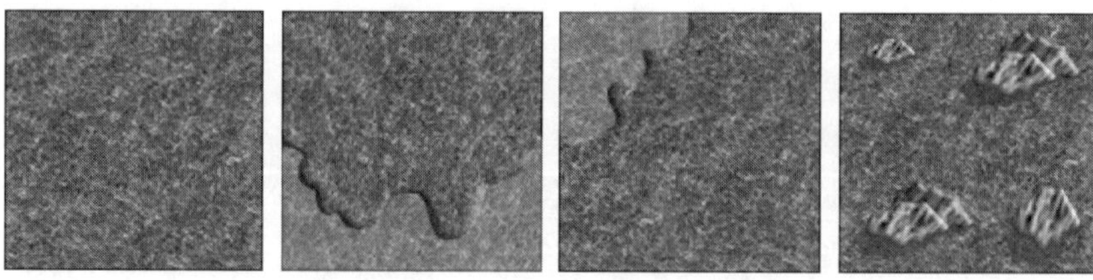

Figure 5.2: Sample terrain tiles.

Four terrain tiles are shown in Figure 5.2. Starting from the left, they are grass, grass edging, grass corner, and rocks on grass. Even with such a limited list, you can create a field of grass with rocks strewn about.

Why Use Tiles?

Now that you know what a tile is, you need to know why game developers use them. There are three main reasons game developers use tiles in their games: memory conservation, graphics reuse, and dynamic content.

Use Tiles to Conserve Memory

Let's take, for example, a map in Warcraft III that is 100 tiles wide and 100 tiles tall. Check out Figure 5.3 to see the map grid in action.

Figure 5.3: Example tile map layout.

No big deal so far; you just have a map with 100 * 100 tiles in it. That comes out to 10,000 tiles total. Now imagine you decide to use one large bitmap for the map instead of tiles. To calculate how much memory the map requires, you must multiply the total number of tiles by the size of each tile. The following demonstrates this concept:

```
100 tiles wide * 100 tiles high = 10,000 tiles
64 pixels wide * 64 pixels high = 4,096 pixels per tile
10,000 tiles * 4,096 pixels * 1 byte (8-bit) = 40,960,000 bytes (w/ 256 colors)
10,000 tiles * 4,096 pixels * 4 bytes (32-bit) = 163,840,000 bytes
```

Wow! Check that out. The simple 100 x 100 tile map takes up a whopping 163 megabytes of storage. Even if you went with 8 bits of color (256 colors), it still requires 41 megabytes of memory just to store the map.

Unless you are reading this book in 2008, 163 megabytes just for the game map is way too much.

All right, now that you have seen the dark side, it is time for a little enlightenment. Take the previous example and calculate the memory storage requirements for the same 100 x 100 map, but this time use tiles.

```
100 tiles wide * 100 tiles high = 10,000 tiles
64 pixels wide * 64 pixels high = 4,096 pixels per tile
100 tiles * 4,096 pixels per tile * 4 bytes per pixel = 1,638,400 bytes
10,000 tiles * 1 byte per tile = 10,000 bytes
10,000 bytes + 1,638,400 bytes = 1,648,400 bytes total
```

Check that out. Using a tile set of 100 tiles, you can create the 100 x 100 map using only two megabytes of memory. Heck, you can use a tile set of 1,000 tiles and still use less than 20 megabytes of memory.

So, there you have it in a nutshell. The number one reason to use tiles in your strategy games is to conserve memory.

Use Tiles for Graphics Reuse

Graphics reuse is very important in game development because an artist's time is just as important as a developer's time (if not more important!). Take a look at Figure 5.4.

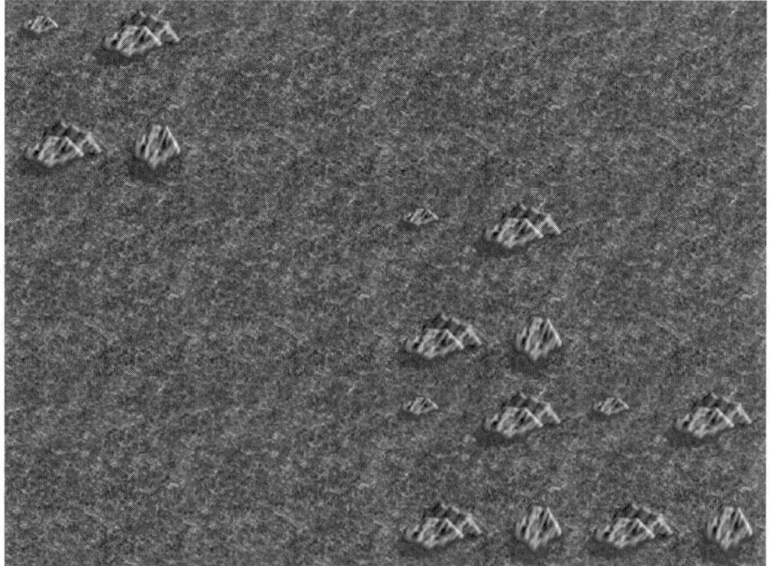

Figure 5.4: A simple game map graphic.

In Figure 5.4 you see a field of grass with various rocks strewn about. Upon further inspection, you notice that the rocks are all very similar.

Now imagine that the art staff has to manually place each rock. This gets very tedious after a while, as the art staff is spending all of their time moving the same graphics around instead of creating new content.

Figure 5.5 sheds new light on Figure 5.4.

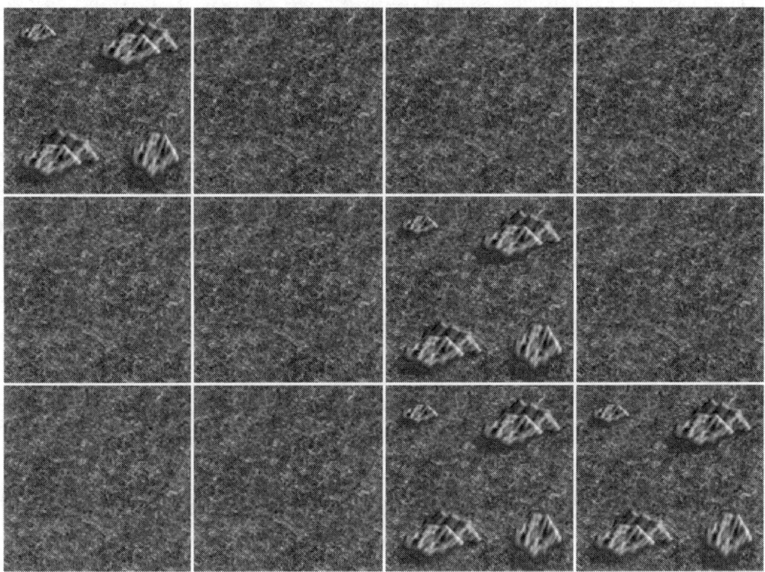

Figure 5.5: A simple game map graphic based on tiles.

Behold, the map is made up of tiles. You may not have noticed it before, but the map is actually made up of two tiles. By using tiles, the same rock pattern is used multiple times within the same image. This reduces the workload of the artists since developers (or just about anybody else) is capable of moving tiles around.

Use Tiles for Dynamic Content

Dynamic content is required for most strategy games. Take, for instance, a random map generator. One such game that uses random map generation is Civilization. In Civilization you specify the type of map you want, and the game generates one for you on the fly. With tiles, you write algorithms to place the tiles in such a way that they look appealing. If you had to create one giant bitmap, it would be a nightmare. Can you imagine having to draw each element, one pixel at a time, programmatically?

All you have to do is take a look at the image in Figure 5.5 to see how an algorithm can generate content dynamically. You can easily set a random number generator to place rock tiles across a map. This allows you to create dynamic content easily and quickly.

How Do You Create Tiles?

Ah, the fun part! Initially you may love to create tiles. Eventually you will probably hate it. Why is this? Tile creation is a time-consuming and tedious job. Of course, some people really enjoy it; I'm just not one of those people.

Choose the Tile Dimensions

First of all, you must start with a graphics package, such as Adobe's Photoshop 7. Then you need to decide on the size of your main tiles. For non-isometric tile sets, you normally pick tiles with an even power of two, such as 32 x 32, 64 x 64, or 128 x 128. The tile size you pick really depends on the particular situation. There is no standard for picking the tile size, but you should consider the following:

- How many tiles does the game require?
- How much memory is allotted for graphics?
- How many tiles are visible at any one time?

The first two questions are related, as the number of tiles has a direct correlation to the amount of memory required for them. If your game requires thousands of tiles, you probably want to steer clear of a large tile size. If your game only has a few hundred tiles, you probably can go with a large tile size.

The last question deals with how many tiles are visible at any one time. This is a necessary consideration given that there is only so much resolution to go around for your interface. Take, for instance, the interface in Figure 5.6.

In Figure 5.6 the command buttons and interface occupy space on the right-hand side and at the bottom of the screen. A portion of the tile map occupies the rest of the interface. By setting a standard of 16 x 16 tiles, your resolution must be high enough to handle that. To calculate the maximum tile size, all you have to do is divide the minimum screen resolution by the various tile size options. Use the following formulas to determine the maximum tile size:

Screen Width / # Tiles Wide Required
Screen Height / # Tiles High Required

Given a minimum resolution of 800 x 600, the tiles in Figure 5.6 can be a maximum of (800 / 16) = 50 pixels wide by (600 / 16) = 37 pixels high. If you stick to the power-of-two method, you are limited to tiles that are 32 pixels wide by 32 pixels high.

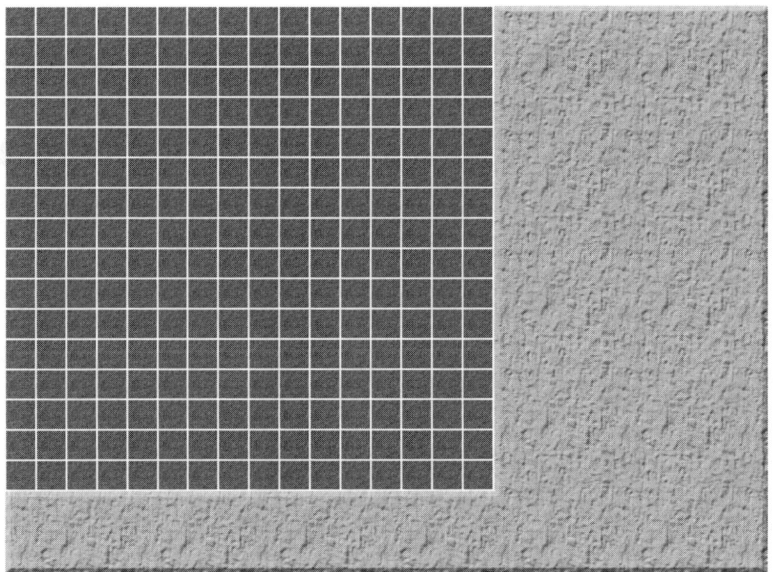

Figure 5.6: The interface with 16 x 16 tiles visible.

If you feel 32 x 32 pixel tiles are too small, you should reconsider the number of tiles visible at any given time. It really all depends on how many units you plan on displaying at once. If your game requires players to control vast armies of units, you may end up using small tile sizes. If your game requires very few units, such as in Blizzard's Warcraft III game, you can get away with very large tile sizes.

Identify Tiles Needed

Since you now know the size of the base tiles for your game, you can continue on with actually creating the tiles. So, what do you create first? I start with the ground pieces for the game and build from there. For example, in Age of Empires and Age of Wonders from Ensemble Studios, the basic building block of the terrain engine is grass, dirt, or even snow.

You know you have to create base tiles for grass, dirt, snow, etc. Now that that is out of the way, you need to add some variety to the landscape. Who wants to play on a huge field of grass, right? If you pick grass as your base tile, you may think about adding rocks, trees, water, brush, or even dirt patches to the list of tiles. To spur your creative side, take a peek at Figure 5.7.

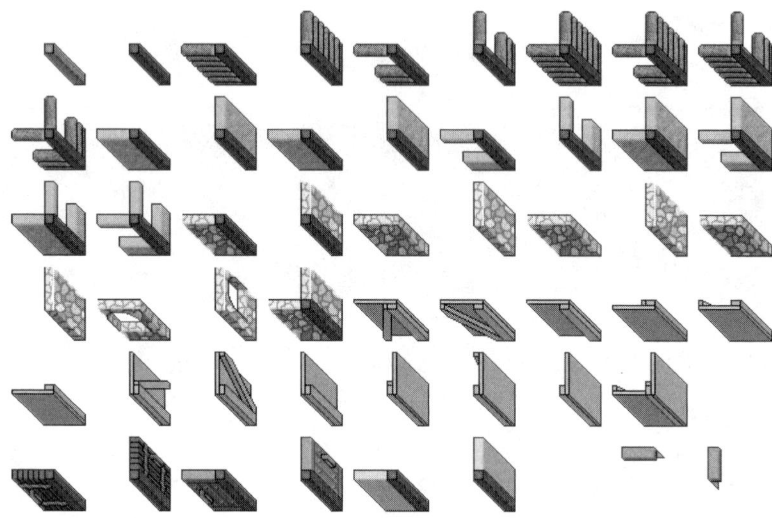

Figure 5.7: Various tiles for a tile set.

Figure 5.7 shows tiles for various types of isometric walls. When combined, the walls can form complete buildings with rooms in them. Keep in mind that this is only a very tiny subset of the tiles required for a full-blown tile engine. Before all is said and done, you are going to have tons of tiles to deal with.

How Do You Display Tiles?

Now comes the fun part! Displaying tiles is actually very easy in theory but complicated in execution. I mean, how hard can it be to display tiles in a grid? Did you notice the key word in that sentence? If you guessed "grid," give yourself a pat on the back.

There are really three major ways to display tiles in your game: 2D, isometric, and 3D.

Two-dimensional Grid Display

The easiest way to display tiles is by using the 2D grid method. In this method you display tiles in horizontal and vertical rows across the screen. Look at Figure 5.8 to see this method in action.

You have seen this previously, as I use it for most of my examples. The first tile in the map is at the upper-left corner of the grid. The last tile in the map is located in the lower-right corner. Displaying the tile

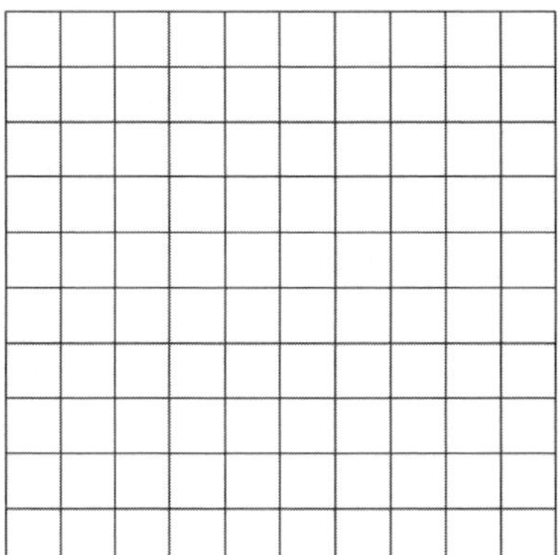

Figure 5.8: Grid layout for tiles.

map is as easy as traversing the map from left to right and from top to bottom. Take a look at the following code snippet:

```
int x,y;
// Display from top to bottom
for(y = 0; y < 10; y++) {
    // Display from left to right
        for(x = 0; x < 10; x++) {
        // Your display function here
        DisplayTile(x, y);
    }
}
```

There are two loops in the code above. The first loop increments the vertical position of the tile. The second loop increments the horizontal position of the tile. By putting the horizontal loop within the vertical loop, you get a complete grid drawn. Figure 5.9 shows the order in which the tiles are drawn.

0	1	2	3	4	5	6	7	8	9
10									19
20									29
30									39
40									49
50									59
60									69
70									79
80									89
90	91	92	93	94	95	96	97	98	99

Figure 5.9: Ordering of 2D tiles.

Notice how the upper-left tile starts at 0 and the bottom-right tile ends with 99. See, wasn't that easy?

Maybe you are wondering what the `vDisplayTile()` function looks like. Before you write the display function, you must first think about how the tile map is stored. The most common method for storing a tile map is to represent the map in one large array. Check out the following code as an example of this method:

```
// Global tile map array
int g_iTileMap[100]; // 10*10 = 100 spots needed

// Prototype tile display function
void vDisplayTile(int x, int y);

void main()
{
    int x, y;

    // Top to bottom
    for(y = 0; y < 10; y++) {
        // Left to right
        for (x = 0; x < 10; x++) {
            // Display the tile
            vDisplayTile(x, y);
        }
    }
}

void vDisplayTile(int x, int y)
{
    int iTile;
    int tileWidth = 64;
    int tileHeight = 64;
    int mapWidth = 10;

    //
    // Calculate the value of the tile
    // at the given x & y coordinate.
    //
    iTile = g_iTileMap[(x + (y * mapWidth))];

    // Display the bitmap on-screen
    // The following function is fictitious
    // and is only meant as pseudocode.  You
    // need to replace it with a real drawing
    // function in order for the code to work.
    //
    DrawBitmap(iTile, (x * tileWidth), (y * tileHeight));
}
```

In the `main()` function listed above, the program loops through the tiles and calls the `vDisplayTile()` function. Once inside the tile display function, the code starts by calculating where in the tile array to pull the tile value from. Taking the x-position and adding the y-position multiplied by the map's width is used to perform the calculation. Check out Figure 5.10 to see this concept illustrated.

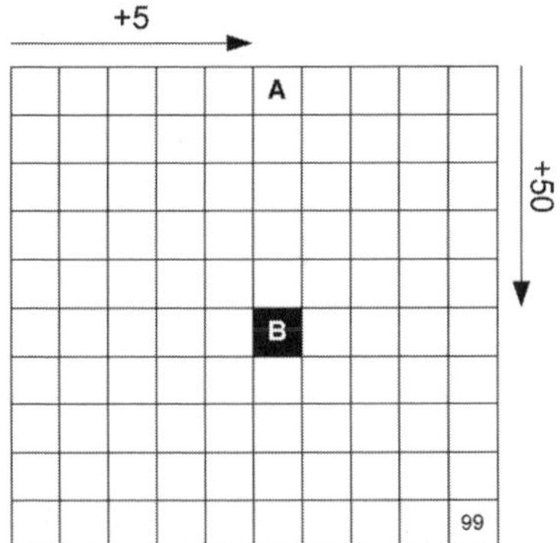

Figure 5.10: Illustrated array location calculation.

How to Calculate Array Position

To get the starting position of the tile in the array, you start with the x-position. Start with an example of finding the position in the array for the tile at position 5,5. In Figure 5.10, starting with the top-left tile, move to the right five tiles. This puts you at the position labeled "A" in the figure.

Now you need to add the y-position of the tile multiplied by the width of the map to the current position. The map is ten tiles wide, so you add 10 * 5 (the y-position) to the current position. Follow the arrow to the right of position "A" and you see it ends up at the final position in the array. This position is labeled with a "B".

So, by following Figure 5.10, the following formula is labeled:

$$X (A) + (Y * Map\ Width) = array\ position\ (B)$$

Figure 5.10 shows you the map array as a grid, but in reality it is one linear chunk of memory. It is just easier to visualize if you display it as a grid. The good part about using an array is that it directly corresponds to what the user sees visually. There are no complicated linked lists to traverse, just one simple array.

How to Calculate Visual Position

The next function in the program, `DrawBitmap()`, is a made-up function that resembles whatever graphics call you use for 2D bitmap display.

There are three parameters in this imaginary function call: tile graphic, on-screen x-position, and on-screen y-position.

The first parameter, the tile graphic, is used to set which bitmap is displayed on the screen. This is fairly straightforward, as in your real implementation you could reference a bitmap directly or a bitmap number from a display list.

The second parameter, the x-position, sets the x-position on-screen where the tile is displayed. To get this position, you multiply the width of the tile by the x-position on the tile map. This gives you the pixel x-position for the tile.

The third parameter, the y-position, works just like the second parameter, except you are setting the vertical position of the graphic to display.

Using the example from Figure 5.10, the x and y pixel position for the tile at 5,5 is (5 * 64), (5 * 64), or 320, 320. Most graphic calls allow the x- and y-position for a bitmap, so the example should be pretty straightforward.

Bottom line, to calculate the x and y pixel coordinates for a tile:

X-pixel coordinate = Tile Map X-Position * Tile Width
Y-pixel coordinate = Tile Map Y-Position * Tile Height

Isometric Tile Display

Oh boy, the fun one. Isometric tile display is one of the more complicated tile methods, as you have to create special tiles for it to work. 2D and 3D tile sets do not have this problem, as they are created in squares for the most part.

Many games utilize isometric tiles, such as Age of Empires, Civilization, and Command & Conquer. The main appeal of isometric tiles is that they allow for a cool 3D look without using true 3D graphics. This isn't much of a concern anymore though, as most gamers have computers that handle 3D graphics decently. For this reason, most RTS games are 3D nowadays. Isometric tiles are just too limiting to use.

Although most commercial games stopped using isometric tile sets, isometric tiles are still viable to use. Without further ado, look at Figure 5.11 to see an isometric tile map.

Basically, the isometric tile map is a 2D tile map rotated 45 degrees on two axes. This creates an interesting grid, as the tiles are now rotated and angled to the viewer's perspective. Since the map is rotated, the x-axis and y-axis do not correspond with the x and y screen coordinates. In Figure 5.11, the new axes are labeled accordingly. Notice how the

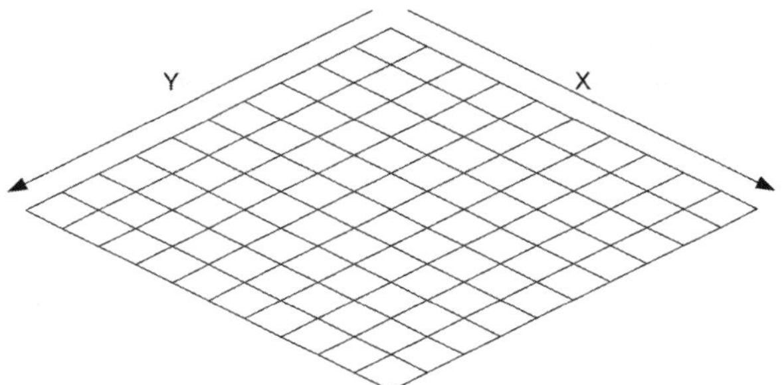

Figure 5.11: A basic isometric tile map.

x-axis runs from the upper-middle of the screen to the lower-right corner of the screen. The y-axis runs from the upper-middle of the screen to the lower-left corner of the screen. This results in tile 0,0 being at the top-middle of the screen. So much for easy display methods!

Once you have the starting tile at 0,0, it is fairly easy to figure out the drawing algorithm. It happens to be the same one you used for 2D tile display, except this time the coordinates of the tiles are a little different. Check out Figure 5.12 to see the order in which isometric tiles are displayed.

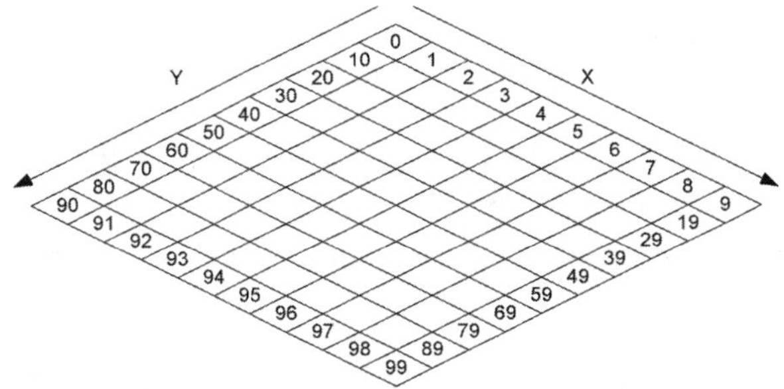

Figure 5.12: Tiles numbered in order of display.

In Figure 5.12, you can see that the tile display still works in a grid, except this time the grid is rotated. This results in you having to offset the x- and y-coordinates for each tile drawn.

To keep the ball rolling I'm delaying the code walkthrough for isometric tile display until the end of this chapter. Check it out now if you wish or wait until you read what comes next.

3D Tile Display

Yes, the holy grail of graphics — three-dimensional graphics! Most strategy games today use 3D tiles for their graphics. There are many advantages to 3D tiles, including:

- Dynamic display
- Rotation
- Depth

The first advantage, dynamic display, is useful in 3D because you can change textures on the fly without redoing all of the art content. Take, for instance, a hillside done in 3D. You change the hillside from grass to dirt merely by swapping out the base texture. If you wanted to do this with traditional 2D methods, you would have to create two separate tiles or redo the artwork completely. Doing this type of work in 2D is vastly inferior to true 3D.

The second advantage to 3D files, rotation, should speak for itself. If you ever tried to rotate a 2D bitmap to see what is on the other side, you know what I am talking about. For one thing, there is nothing on the other side. In 2D, what you see is what you get. Once you make the move to 3D, you rotate tiles around to see what is on all sides. Based on the viewpoint of the camera, you may see a very different image. Using 3D saves a ton of image space as well, considering you only have to create a frame of animation once instead of multiple times for every possible angle of rotation.

The third, depth, is sort of related to rotation in that 3D tiles have actual depth to them if you move the viewpoint up or down. You are hard pressed to create 2D tiles for every possible elevation of the user's camera.

So, how do you display 3D tiles? Easy! You just translate them into position and use the ol' draw primitive function. Really though, 3D tiles can be displayed the same way that 2D tiles are. You just put them in a grid and render them from back to front. Check out Figure 5.13 to see a 3D tile map.

Hmm, isn't that interesting? Figure 5.13 looks somewhat like a 2D tile map. That is the precise point. 3D is not meant to drastically change the way you see strategy games; it just adds an element of flexibility and opens up new options to you. You do not have to switch to a fully 3D first-person-shooter type strategy game to utilize 3D graphics. You can stick with the tried-and-true RTS game look and feel and still use 3D. That's the beauty of it.

Figure 5.13: Example 3D tile map. ©2002 Blizzard Entertainment, All Rights Reserved.

Multi-Layering Tiles

The basics are out of the way, so now it's time to get down and dirty with implementing tiles in your game. The first topic of the day is multi-layering. This is important to tile display, as your tile engine will be very cumbersome without it.

Multi-layering is used to add detail and dimension to tile maps.

How to Add Detail Tiles

The first and foremost reason for using multiple tile layers is to add detail to your tile maps. This is accomplished by simply drawing several layers of tiles on top of each other. This sounds simple and really is when it comes down to implementation. The complex part is figuring out which tiles to draw on which layers. Check out the three tile maps in Figure 5.14.

Starting from the left in Figure 5.14, the tile maps increase in detail. The first map is made up of only one tile, grass. It is not very exciting, as there is nothing really to look at.

The second map has rocks added to it. This is considered a two-layer tile map. The first layer contains the ground tiles, and the second layer contains the detail ground tiles.

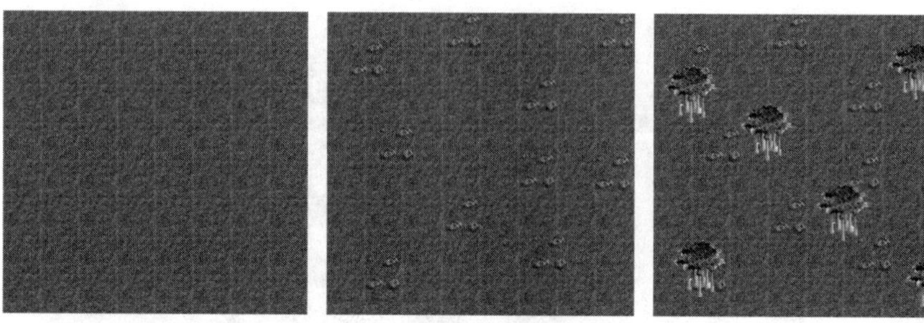

Figure 5.14: Three tile maps with varying detail levels.

The third map has trees added to it. The first layer contains the usual ground tiles, the second layer contains the ground detail tiles, and the new third layer contains the tree tiles.

Maybe you are wondering why all of the tiles aren't placed on the same layer. Well, because that requires more tiles and can result in more tiles than are necessary. Look at the tile maps in Figure 5.14. If you only used one tile layer for the middle map, the rock tile would look like the tile in Figure 5.15.

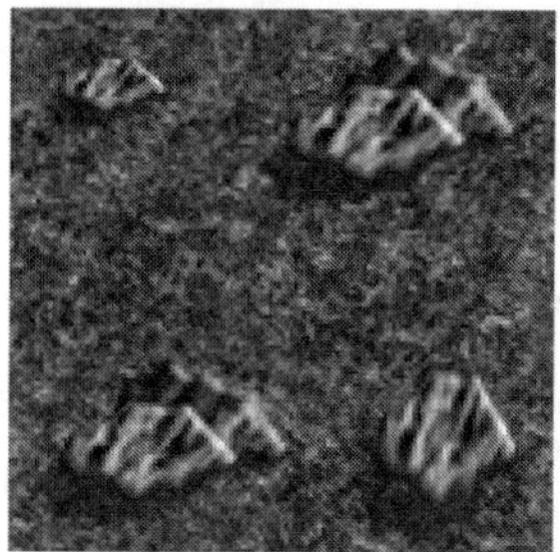

Figure 5.15: A single grass tile with rocks on it.

The tile in Figure 5.15 contains both the grass texture and the rock texture. This is all fine and good, but what happens when you want to add a different ground texture to the mix, such as sand? You end up having to create a whole new rock tile with sand underneath it in order to accomplish this. You now have four tiles: sand, grass, rock with sand, and rock with grass.

Figure 5.16 shows a solution to the layer problem that is less resource intensive.

The rock tile in Figure 5.16 has an alpha channel associated with it so that it can blend onto any base texture. This allows the rock tile to be added as a separate layer on top of the grass or sand without having to store a rock tile for each base tile. I know my example only saves one extra tile, but you end up with hundreds and even thousands of tiles in a

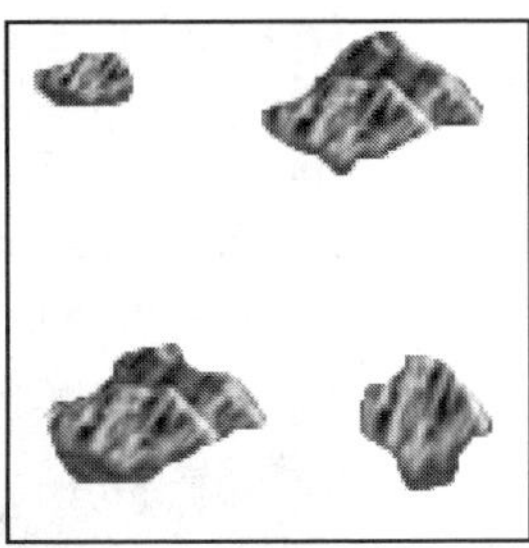

Figure 5.16: Three tiles: one with grass, one with sand, and one with rock.

complete game, and the waste potential is tremendous if you are not prudent with your tile usage.

How to Add Transition Tiles

Besides the wonderful world of rocks and sand, there are other important tiles to a tile map. The first ones that come to mind are edge tiles, also referred to as transition tiles. Transition tiles are used to transition from one tile texture to another. Remember in the previous section how I used sand and grass as basic ground textures? If you take those two tiles and make a tile map out of them, you end up with something like what is shown in Figure 5.17.

Figure 5.17: A tile map with grass and sand tiles.

The first thing you should notice about the map is that it looks horrible! The grass and sand tiles stand out more than a 100-year-old finalist at

QuakeCon. The reason they look so bad is that there are no tiles to make the grass or sand smoothly blend together. Enter stage right, transition tiles.

By adding a few detail tiles to the map in Figure 5.17, you can achieve a nice blended result, as shown in Figure 5.18.

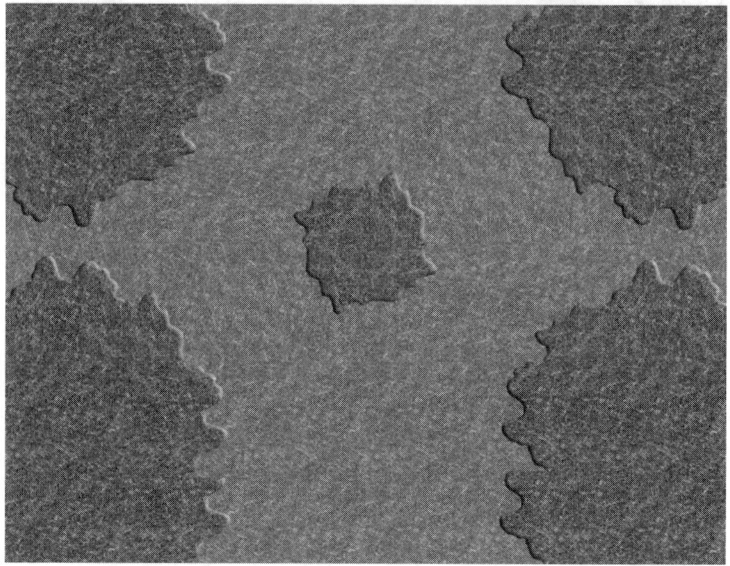

Figure 5.18: A tile map with grass and sand tiles blended together.

I know the picture in Figure 5.18 doesn't explain the transition tiles used, but doesn't it look a lot better than Figure 5.17? Don't fret too much though, as it only uses relatively few tiles to accomplish the feat.

First off, you need tiles to transition the grass into the sand from north to south. These tiles allow a nicely transitioned horizontal line of tiles, as shown in Figure 5.19.

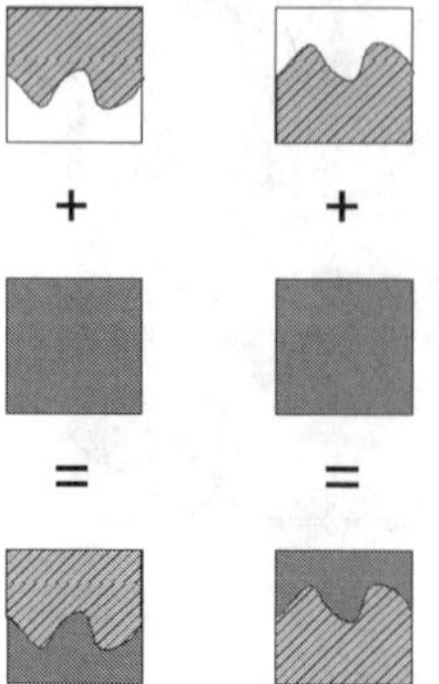

Figure 5.19: Transition tiles from north to south.

In Figure 5.19 the tile on the left has grass on top (north) and a transparent area on the bottom (south). When the grass is applied to the sand texture in the figure, it blends nicely. The same holds true for the tile on the right. It has grass on the bottom (south) and a transparent area on the top (north). These two tiles cover the first couple of transition scenarios.

Now that you have tiles smoothly going from north to south, you need tiles that blend from east to west. The tiles in Figure 5.20 accomplish this.

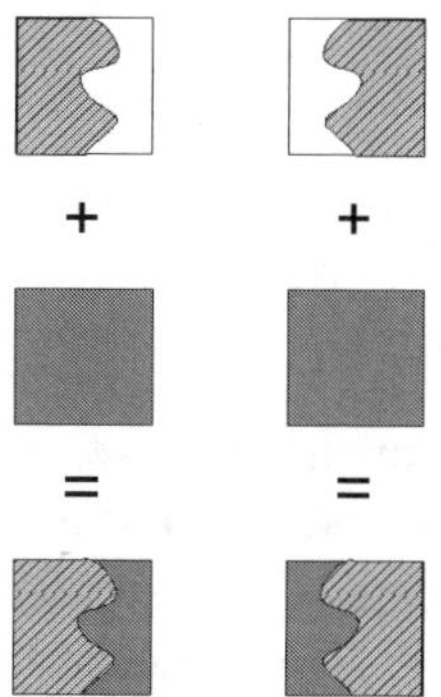

Figure 5.20: Transition tiles from east to west.

The first tile on the left in Figure 5.20 has grass on the left (west) and a transparent area on the right (east). It blends well when applied to the sand tile below it. As usual, this works for the tile on the right side of the picture. Once again, there's nothing new here, just another couple of transition scenarios covered.

Maybe you are thinking the work is over at this point. Well, what about corners? That's right, you still need corners to transition the north to south tiles with the ones that run from east to west. Notice the four corners shown in Figure 5.21.

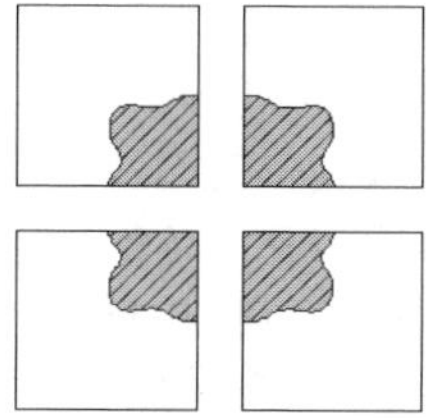

Figure 5.21: Transition corner tiles.

The tiles in Figure 5.21 are used to connect the previously created tiles when necessary. This is a needed feature considering you have patches of ground textures and not horizontal or vertical lines of textures running across your tile maps. The map in Figure 5.21 illustrates this well, as the corner tiles form a rounded square on the tile map. These can be expanded with the other transition tiles to form large squares, such as those in Figure 5.22.

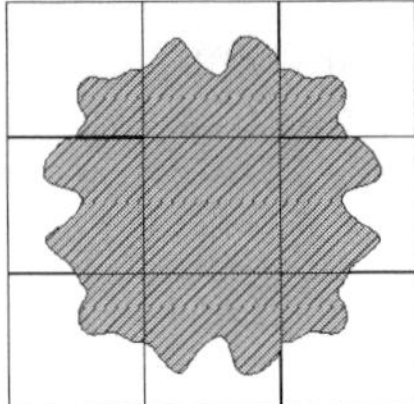

Figure 5.22: Transition corner tiles with other transition tiles.

See how the corner tiles work with the other transition tiles to form nice large squares and rectangles on the map? The corners give the blocks of terrain a nice rounded edge. Now, guess what happens when you want a patch of terrain that is not square or rectangular? If you guessed that the map is missing some key tiles, then you get 100 points. (100 points for what, I really don't know, but it's the thought that counts!) Figure 5.23 illustrates the shortcomings of the tiles used so far.

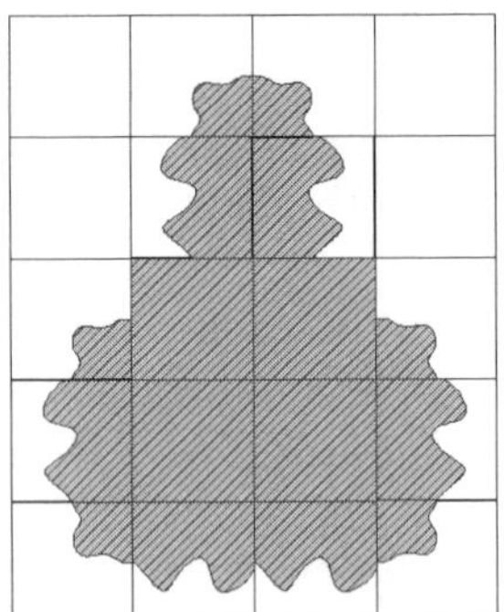

Figure 5.23: Transition errors using the four basic corner tiles.

Notice how the chunk of terrain in Figure 5.23 has a weird gap in it where the tiles make a 90-degree turn. This happens because there are no inverted corner tiles. It is easily solved though, as inverted corner tiles are just that. Figure 5.24 illustrates the inverted tiles in action.

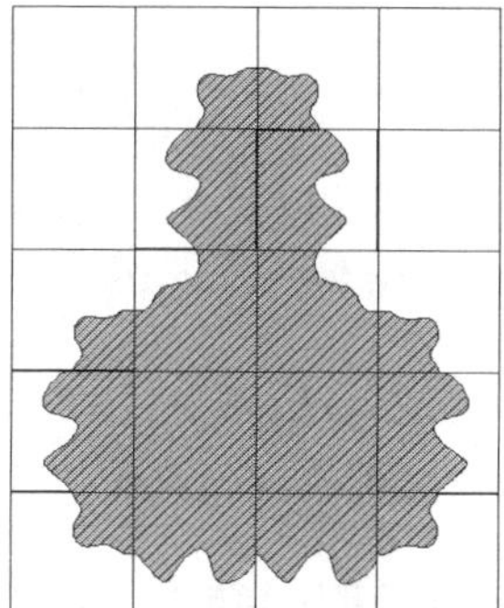

Figure 5.24: Inverted corner transition tiles in action.

The tiles in Figure 5.24 allow for almost every possible combination of grass and sand tiles to blend together properly. You have horizontal tiles, vertical tiles, corner tiles, and inverted corner tiles. As you can see, the inverted corner tiles at the top blend well with the tiles on the map below them.

How to Add Road Tiles

Technically, roads are just like detail and transition tiles. But there are problems with creating road tiles that you may not think of right away. To prevent you from making the mistakes that I have in the past, here is a quick section on making road tiles.

Let's say a player is busy expanding his empire in your game, and he wants to build a new road. What happens if he places a road tile next to another one? Do you check every road tile on the map to see how they are changed? Do you check tiles around the placed tile and see if they deserve a change? Decisions, decisions! To illustrate this concept better, I provide you with Figure 5.25.

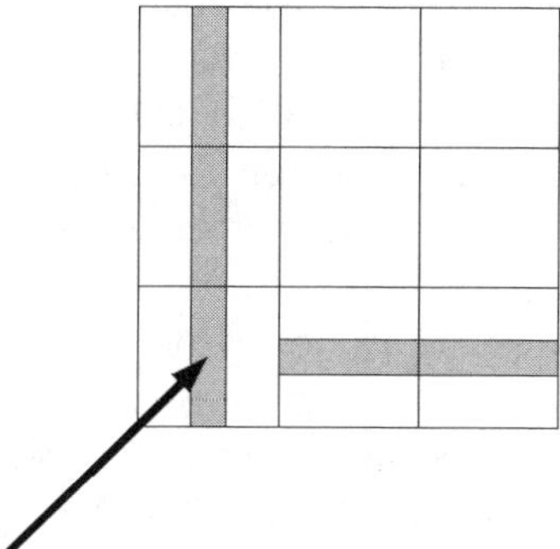

Figure 5.25: A newly created road tile next to an existing road.

There you have it in Figure 5.25. The newly created road tile has the big arrow pointing to it. The problem presented here is how do you figure out which tile to turn the new road tile into? Your brain tells you, "It's easy — it should be a corner tile!" (Hopefully your brain tells you that, or you may be in the wrong profession.) Either way, for some reason you know it needs to be a corner tile.

Now try to think about the process that you go through to deduce the solution. The first thing you probably do is look at each tile around the new one. By examining the neighboring tiles one at a time, you get an idea of what is needed for the new tile. I put this into practice in Figure 5.26.

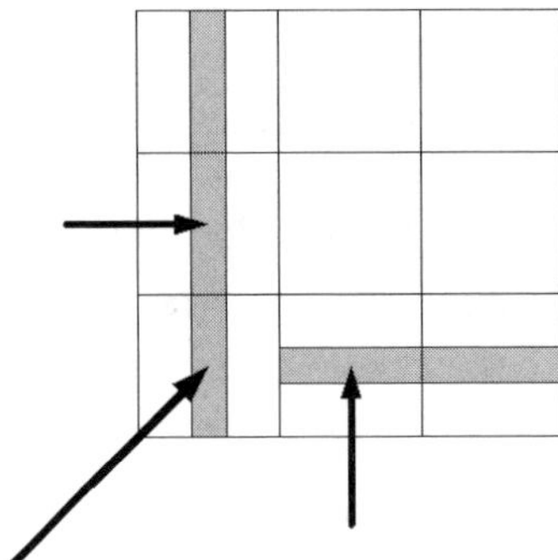

Figure 5.26: Neighboring tiles examined around the new tile.

In Figure 5.26, you see that I traversed the neighboring tiles around the new road tile and flagged the ones that have road tiles in them. This leaves me with two neighboring tiles flagged, one to the north and one to the east.

The neighbor tiles are flagged, so now what? Now you use a lookup table to determine which tile to use in the situation. How do you create the lookup table? It's not too hard: You assign a number to each tile in a clockwise fashion, incrementing by the power of 2 as you go from tile to tile. With this method the first tile equals 1, the second tile equals 2, the third tile equals 4, the fourth tile equals 8, and so forth. Does this sound familiar? I hope so, considering everything you do on a computer is based on this method! Figure 5.27 illustrates the value assigned for each neighboring tile.

Tiles 0 and 2 are flagged so you take the values of the two and add them together. You end up with $1+4 = 5$. By consulting the lookup table of tiles, you see that tile number five is a corner piece. Don't worry about figuring out the lookup table; it is presented in Figure 5.28. Merry Christmas!

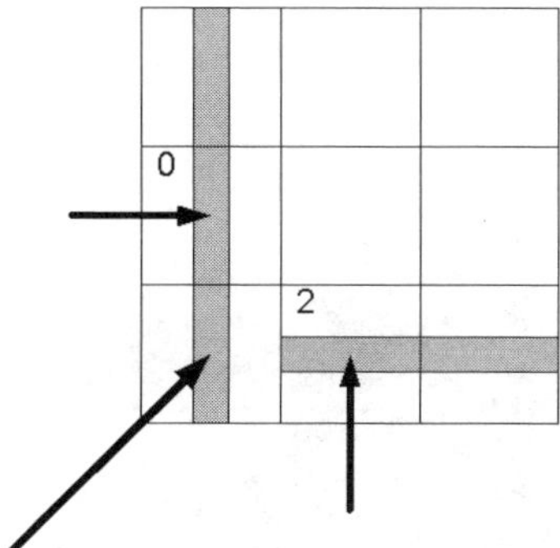

Figure 5.27: Neighboring tiles with values shown.

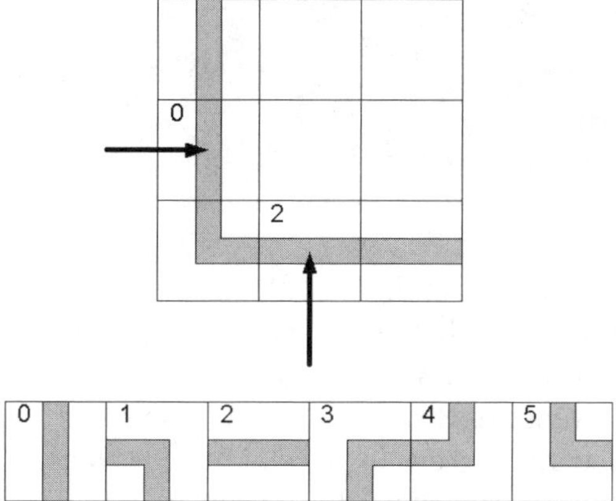

Figure 5.28: Road tile lookup table illustrated.

How to Add 3D Tree Tiles

What can be so hard about adding trees to a game? Plenty is the answer, plenty. First off, trees have branches and leaves that you can see through. Second, they tend to sway in the wind. Third, they must at least appear to have volume. Doom and Doom II graphics just don't cut it anymore. Long gone are the days of 2D sprites in place of 3D models. Or are they?

These three factors present an almost unique problem for strategy game developers. The problems are present because most of your games are played from an isometric view or angled view. If you make a game where the camera is pointing straight down, then you don't really have this problem. You just draw trees bushing out from all sides. This isn't the case that I'm covering here though.

Check out the little forest of palm trees in Figure 5.29.

Figure 5.29: A forest of palm trees with a building in the middle.

Take notice of how the palm trees in Figure 5.29 have nice depth to them. They appear in front of and behind the building as well. All in all, the effect is pretty convincing as far as trees go. Would you believe me if I told you the scene only requires 300 polygons? The scene is accomplished by using 2D billboards of trees in place of real 3D trees. Check out Figure 5.30 to see the wizard behind the curtain.

Figure 5.30: The fake 3D trees revealed.

The trees really are paper-thin and only appear to be 3D when viewed from a certain angle. The best part of this trick is that each tree only takes up two polygons for the quad it occupies. If you have ever created a real 3D tree, then you know that two polygons is extremely low compared to the thousands required for a good-looking 3D tree.

How to Add Animated Tiles

The next important type of tiles is of the animated variety. Almost any strategy game has some tiles on the map that animate. The most prevalent animating tile is water. Water doesn't look very convincing if it doesn't move; therefore, you see a lot of animated water tiles in games.

So, how do you add animating tiles? One of the easiest methods is to set aside a range of tiles to be animated. Let's say that tiles 1 to 100 animate with each set occupying ten tiles of animation. This gives you ten total animating tiles of ten frames each. When your render loop comes across tiles 0, 10, 20, 30, 40, 50, 60, 70, 80, or 90, it uses the tile number plus the current animation frame as the target tile to render. When the current animation frame number reaches 10, it resets to 0 so the animation loops back around to the beginning. Take, for example, the following pseudocode:

```
Anim_Frame = 0;
Loop Start = 0; Loop < #TilesToDisplay; Loop++
   // Render animated tile
   If(Current_Tile.type == TYPE_ANIMATION)
      RenderTile(Current_Tile.value + Anim_Frame);
   // Render as normal
   Else
      RenderTile(Current_Tile.value);

   // Increment animation counter
   Anim_Frame++;
   If(Anim_Frame == 10)
      Anim_Frame = 0;
Loop Repeat
```

In the above code, the rendering loop renders the tile plus the animation frame currently in use. With this method, the next frame of animation is rendered with each pass of the animation loop. It's very similar to standard bitmap animation; the only difference is that you set aside a certain range of tiles to be the animating ones. I recommend that you set aside a wide range of tiles for your animating ones, probably tile numbers 0 to 1000. That range allows you plenty of growing room for your first strategy game.

Tile Editing and Storage

Earlier I touched on how tiles are stored in memory, but you still need to know how to edit the tiles in memory. I'm sharing with you here the best practices I have learned and information to get you started. You may find better ways to store and edit tiles based on your application's needs. In this section I cover the following tile storage methods:

- 2D array storage
- Multi-layer tile array storage
- Implementing a tile class

2D Array Storage

The easiest method to store tiles is to use a two-dimensional array. The first dimension holds the horizontal tiles, and the second dimension holds the vertical tiles. Take a look at the following code:

```
// Set the map dimensions
#define TilesWide    10
#define TilesHigh    10
// Declare the map array
int iTileMap[TilesWide][TilesHigh];
// Clear the map with tile 0
memset(&iTileMap, 0, (TilesWide*TilesHigh)*sizeof(int));
```

As you can see in the code, a two-dimensional array of integers is declared. Since the map is 10 tiles wide and high, the map contains 100 total tiles. The top-leftmost tile on the map resides at 0,0, and the bottom-rightmost tile resides at 99,99. Figure 5.31 illustrates the map.

0	0	0	0	0	0	0	0	0	0
0	0	0	0	0	0	0	0	0	0
0	0	0	0	0	0	0	0	0	0
0	0	0	0	0	0	0	0	0	0
0	0	0	0	0	0	0	0	0	0
0	0	0	0	0	0	0	0	0	0
0	0	0	0	0	0	0	0	0	0
0	0	0	0	0	0	0	0	0	0
0	0	0	0	0	0	0	0	0	0
0	0	0	0	0	0	0	0	0	0

Figure 5.31: A tile map with 100 units.

In the code snippet above, I clear the tile map array with tile 0. This is the usual course to follow, as tile 0 represents the base tile for all rendering. Normally you set tile 0 to be a ground tile or even a "no-tile" tile. A "no-tile" tile is a tile with a bitmap on it that says something blatant, such as "UNUSED." Having this type of tile allows you to see areas of the map that have uninitialized tiles on them.

So now you have your two-dimensional tile array. How do you change a tile? Luckily, it's easy to do. Say you want to change the tile that is two tiles to the right and three tiles down from the map origin to equal 15. To do this, you write code similar to the following:

```
iTileMap[2] [3] = 15;
```

All you do is set the array position to the desired value, and you are done.

Check out the following code and see if you can guess what the tile map looks like as a result. Hint: Tile 15 is a filled-in square and tile 0 is an empty square.

```
// Top to bottom
iTileMap[0] [0] = 15;
iTileMap[0] [1] = 15;
iTileMap[0] [2] = 15;
iTileMap[0] [3] = 15;
iTileMap[0] [4] = 15;
// Left to right
iTileMap[1] [4] = 15;
iTileMap[2] [4] = 15;
iTileMap[3] [4] = 15;
// Bottom to top
iTileMap[3] [3] = 15;
iTileMap[3] [2] = 15;
iTileMap[3] [1] = 15;
iTileMap[3] [0] = 15;
// Right to left
iTileMap[2] [0] = 15;
iTileMap[1] [0] = 15;
```

Figure 5.32 reveals the answer.

15	15	15	0	0	0	0	0	0	0
15	0	15	0	0	0	0	0	0	0
15	0	15	0	0	0	0	0	0	0
15	0	15	0	0	0	0	0	0	0
15	15	15	0	0	0	0	0	0	0
0	0	0	0	0	0	0	0	0	0
0	0	0	0	0	0	0	0	0	0
0	0	0	0	0	0	0	0	0	0
0	0	0	0	0	0	0	0	0	0
0	0	0	0	0	0	0	0	0	0

Figure 5.32: A tile map with the letter O defined in tiles.

If you guessed that the tile map now has a small letter "O" or zero on it, pat yourself on the back. The code starts off by drawing the left side of the O starting from the top and ending at the bottom. The next block of code draws the bottom of the O starting at the left and moving to the right. Then the code draws the right side of the O starting from the bottom and moving to the top. Finally, the code closes the O by drawing from the top right to the top left of the letter.

Are you experiencing déjà vu? You may be if you are used to plotting pixels. Pixel plotting and tile plotting is pretty much the same thing when it boils down to it.

Multi-layer Tile Array Storage

Single-layer 2D arrays are fine for boring maps, but you want interesting maps, right? Since you need multiple layers, you also need multiple dimensions in your tile array. The easiest way to store multiple layers is to add a dimension to your array. The following code shows you how:

```
// Set the map dimensions
#define TilesWide   10
#define TilesHigh   10
#define TileLayers  3
// Declare the map array
int iTileMap[TilesWide][TilesHigh][TileLayers];
// Clear the map with tile 0
memset(&iTileMap, 0, (TilesWide*TilesHigh*TileLayers)*sizeof(int));
```

The areas in bold show the areas that have changed from the previous code. The first thing I add is a new define, setting the number of tile layers in the map. I have arbitrarily set the number of layers to three. You can set it to whatever you want; I just use the number three as an example.

The next bit of code that has changed is the addition of a dimension to the tile array. You only need one additional dimension since you just up the number in it to store more layers.

The last code change made deals with clearing the map array. Since you have multiple layers, you now must clear more tiles.

Now that you have a multidimensional and multi-layer array, you can start filling the various tile layers with values. See the following tile map in Figure 5.33.

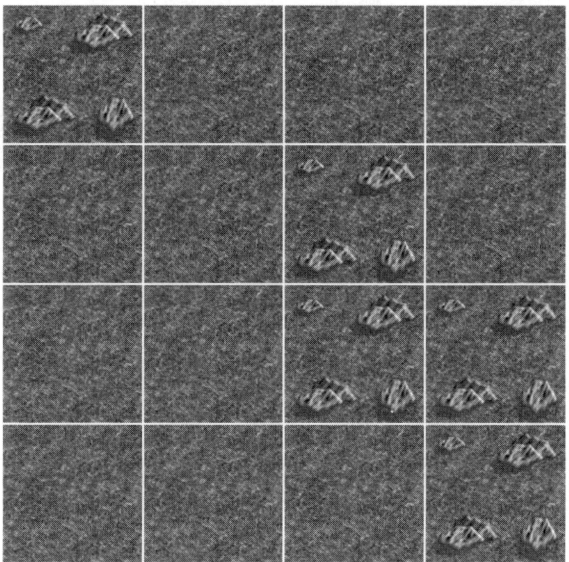

Figure 5.33: A tile map with two layers.

The first layer of the map contains two types of grass tiles. The second layer of the map contains various rocks. The code to generate this tile map is as follows:

```
//
// Set the base tiles
//

// Vertical
For(int i = 0; i < 10; i++) {
    // Horizontal
    For(int j = 0; j < 10; j++) {
        // Randomly set the base tile
        iTileMap[i][j][0] = rand()%2;
    }
}

//
// Add detail tiles
//

iTileMap[5][5][1] = 3;
iTileMap[3][9][1] = 3;
iTileMap[1][7][1] = 3;
iTileMap[8][8][1] = 3;
iTileMap[6][3][1] = 3;
iTileMap[4][1][1] = 3;
```

The first block of code cycles through each tile on the base tile layer and randomly assigns a value to it. This gives the ground a random and more natural look than a fixed pattern can.

The next block of code manually places rock tiles on the second layer. The tile positions in the array correspond to an [x][y][z] setup, where z represents the tile layer. By using 1 for the z-position, you are telling the game to store the rocks in the second layer.

Implementing a Tile Class

The simple methods of tile map storage are out of the way, so now it's time to delve into the object-oriented world and create tile classes.

The Tile Class Header

There are a few considerations to make when creating a tile class. First of all, you need a tile class and a tile map class. The tile class is used to define the individual tiles, while the tile map class is used to define a group of tiles. The following code shows a tile class header example:

```
class TileClass
{
    private:
        int *m_iValue;
        int m_iNumLayers;
        float  *m_fRotX;
        float  *m_fSize;

    public:
        TileClass();
        ~TileClass();
        int iGetValue(int layer);
        void vSetValue(int value, int layer);
        float fGetRot(int layer);
        void vSetRotation(float fRot, int layer);
        float fGetSize(int layer);
        void vSetSize(float fSize, int layer);
        void vSetNumLayers(int layers);
};
```

There are four private members to the tile class. The first one, m_iValue, stores the value of the tile. Say that you have 1000 bitmaps loaded into memory for tiles. The tile value of 1 represents the first bitmap loaded into memory. The value is nothing more than an index into the bitmaps.

The second value, m_iNumLayers, stores how many layers the tile contains. By allowing each tile to have a variable number of layers, you are giving the tile system a lot of flexibility. You may determine this much flexibility is not needed later on, but you can always remove this member.

The next member value up for bid is `m_fRotX`. This variable sets the rotation of the tile in question. This is really useful for adding variability to your maps without adding new content. All you have to do is rotate the tile 90 degrees or more to create a whole new graphic. I have this member created as a floating-point value since I use 3D tile engines exclusively now. You may want to change it to an integer if you are using a 2D engine.

Next is the `m_fSize` member variable. This variable holds the size of the tile. For the 3D world, this size represents the size in 3D units. For the 2D world, the size represents the size in pixels. If you are using 64 x 64 pixel tiles, the size equals 64. You may notice that I am assuming the tile uses square dimensions. If you require rectangular tiles, you need to add a second size variable, such as `m_fSizeX` or `m_fSizeY`.

The member variables are out of the way, so now it's time for the member functions. The first two that you see are the constructor and destructors for the class. Nothing special in these two — just your normal C++ stuff.

The first notable member function is `iGetValue()`. This function is used to retrieve the value of the tile at a specified layer. This is the most called function in the class, as it gets hit every time the map is drawn using the tile. The example returns the integer value of `m_iValue` when called. I prefer this method, as I use it as an index into my array of tile data, but you may want to return a bitmap handle, data structure, or some other type of data in your engine.

The next member function, `vSetValue()`, takes two parameters. The first parameter is the integer value of the tile you wish to set. The second parameter specifies the layer of the tile you want to set. The value is stored in the `m_iValue` member variable.

The `fGetRot()` member function returns the value of the `m_fRotX` member variable. If your engine supports multiple axes of rotation, you need to add a new member variable for the axis of rotation and a parameter to the `fGetRot()` function to specify the angle you are looking for.

The next function, `vSetRotation()`, contains two parameters. The first parameter sets the angle of rotation in degrees. The second parameter sets the layer to contain the rotation information. The `m_fRotX` member variable contains the requested change.

The `fGetSize()` member function returns the value of the `m_fSize` member variable. If your engine supports rectangular tile sizes, you need to add a new member variable for the second size value and a parameter to the `fGetSize()` function to specify the size you are looking for.

The next function, `vSetSize()`, contains two parameters. The first parameter sets the size of the tile in 3D grid units. The second parameter sets the layer to contain the size information. The m_fSize member variable contains the requested size.

Last but not least, the vSetNumLayers() member function is specified. It contains a single parameter named layers. Basically, this function sets the number of layers used for the value, rotation, and size of the tile.

That's it for the tile class header. Figure 5.34 shows the layout of the class.

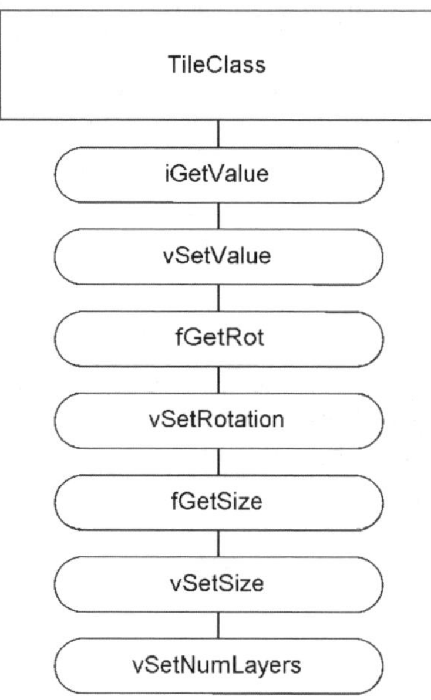

Figure 5.34: The layout of the Tile class.

The Tile Class Implementation

The next block of code contains the implementation of the Tile class.

```cpp
#include "TileClass.h"

// Constructor
TileClass::TileClass()
{
    // Initialize internal vars
    m_iNumLayers = 0;
    m_iValue = NULL;
    m_fRotX = NULL;
    m_fSize = NULL;
}
// Destructor
TileClass::~TileClass()
{
    // Free layer buffer if already allocated
    if(m_iValue)
```

```cpp
        delete [] m_iValue;
    if(m_fRotX)
        delete [] m_fRotX;
    if(m_fSize)
        delete [] m_fSize;
}
// Set number of layers
void TileClass::vSetNumLayers(int layers)
{
    // Free layer buffer if already allocated
    if(m_iValue)
        delete [] m_iValue;
    if(m_fRotX)
        delete [] m_fRotX;
    if(m_fSize)
        delete [] m_fSize;
    // Allocate memory for layer buffer
    m_iValue = new int[layers];
    memset(m_iValue,0,layers*sizeof(int));

    m_fRotX = new float[layers];
    memset(m_fRotX,0,layers*sizeof(int));

    m_fSize = new float[layers];
    memset(m_fSize,0,layers*sizeof(int));

    // Set the number of layers
    m_iNumLayers = layers;
}
// Get value of the tile
int TileClass::iGetValue(int layer)
{
    // Make sure not trying to retrieve illegal layer
    if(layer >= m_iNumLayers) {
        return(-1);
    }
    // Return the value
    return(m_iValue[layer]);
}
// Set the tile's value
void TileClass::vSetValue(int value, int layer)
{
    // Make sure not trying to use an illegal layer
    if(layer >= m_iNumLayers) {
        return;
    }
    // Set the value
    m_iValue[layer] = value;
}
// Set the rotation
void TileClass::vSetRotation(float fRot, int layer)
{
    // Make sure not trying to use an illegal layer
    if(layer >= m_iNumLayers) {
        return;
```

```
      }
      m_fRotX[layer] = fRot;
}
// Set the size
void TileClass::vSetSize(float fSize, int layer)
{
    // Make sure not trying to use an illegal layer
    if(layer >= m_iNumLayers) {
        return;
    }
    m_fSize[layer] = fSize;
}
// Get the rotation
float TileClass::fGetRot(int layer)
{
    // Make sure not trying to use an illegal layer
    if(layer >= m_iNumLayers) {
        return(-1.0f);
    }
    return(m_fRotX[layer]);
}
// Get the size
float TileClass::fGetSize(int layer)
{
    // Make sure not trying to use an illegal layer
    if(layer >= m_iNumLayers) {
        return(-1.0f);
    }
    return(m_fSize[layer]);
}
```

The first function implemented is the class constructor. In the constructor you need to initialize the various member variables to their default state. In the function I default the number of layers to 0. I also set the pointers to the rotation, size, and value to NULL. This is done to prevent accidentally deleting nonexistent memory in the constructor and because variables can start with a random default value.

The next function is the class destructor. It simply checks each allocated piece of memory and then deletes it if there is memory allocated.

The next function, TileClass::vSetNumLayers(), sets the number of layers for the tile. Since you can set the number of layers to any reasonable number, this function's main job is to allocate the memory needed for each layer. First, the function clears any previously allocated memory. It then allocates the memory for the m_iValue, m_fRotX, and m_fSize member variables. Once that is accomplished, the allocated memory is zeroed out with a memset() call. Remember, this function is required before using the tile object. If you attempt to retrieve data from a nonexistent layer, the class returns an error.

Next up you have the most called member function of the class, the TileClass::iGetValue() member. The first part of the function checks to make sure that the programmer is not requesting a value that does not exist. If you do not make this code check, the program may crash from accessing invalid memory. Lastly, the function returns the contents of the `m_iValue` variable at the specified layer.

The next function, `TileClass::vSetValue()`, is used to change the value of the tile. You probably won't use it too much during game-play, but you do use it a lot in your map editor program. The function doesn't do a whole lot internally; it makes sure the requested layer is valid, and then it sets the value of the `m_iValue` member variable accordingly.

The next two functions, `TileClass::vSetRotation()` and `TileClass::vSetSize`, work just like the set value function, except they alter the `m_fRotX` and `m_fSize` member variables.

The last two functions, `TileClass::fGetRot()` and `TileClass::fGetSize()`, work like the get value function, except they return the values of the `m_fRotX` and `m_fSize` member variables.

That's it for the Tile class for now. To make sure I cover every possible base, take a look at the next example to see how the Tile class is used without a map manager class:

Tile Class Example Implementation

The following block of code implements the Tile class for use as the world map:

```
void main()
{
    int        iMapWidth  = 10;
    int        iMapHeight = 10;
    TileClass *Tiles;
    int        iBMPToRender;

    // Allocate memory for the tiles
    Tiles = new TileClass[(iMapWidth*iMapHeight)];

    //
    // Loop through the tiles and initialize each one
    //
    for(int i = 0; i < (iMapWidth*iMapHeight); i++) {
        // Allocate one layer for each tile
        Tiles[i].vSetNumLayers(1);
        // Set each tile to value 0
        Tiles[i].vSetValue(0, 0);
        // Set size to be 64 pixels wide and high
        Tiles[i].vSetSize(64, 0);
    }

    //
    // Render the tiles, using an imaginary render function.
    //
```

```
// Render horizontally
for(int y = 0; y < iMapHeight; y++) {
    // Render vertically
    for(int x = 0; x < iMapWidth; x++) {
        // Render the appropriate tile
        iBMPToRender = Tiles[x + (y * iMapWidth)].iGetValue(0);
        vRenderTile(x, y, iBMPToRender);
    }
}
}
```

The first item of interest is where I allocate memory for the world map. Instead of allocating an array of integers or shorts, I allocate an array of `TileClass` objects. You need enough tiles to contain one value for each position of the map, so I multiply the map width by the map height to figure out how many tiles to allocate.

The next section of code loops through each of the newly allocated `TileClass` objects and initializes them. First, the code sets the number of layers to 1. This allows for one value per tile. Next, the code sets the value of each tile to 0. The last part sets the size of each tile to 64.

Once the tiles are initialized, the system proceeds to render them starting from left to right and moving from top to bottom. The example code calls the imaginary `vRenderTile()` function that stands as a placeholder to whatever graphic call you may make.

Play around with the code if you want to for a bit before continuing. Personally, I am going to play a game of America's Army before moving on. Log on and find me if you are interested; my player name is LostLogic.

Tile Properties

Oh boy — that was a good game of America's Army. I scored 62 points on the Pipeline mission and had a great time. Back to work!

So far, tiles only have a single value to designate the bitmap to display. In the real world of gaming, tiles have other values or properties as well. Here is a list of some useful tile properties:

- Obstruction
- Elevation
- Brightness
- Offsets

Obstruction Property

The Obstruction property is used to set whether or not the tile can be walked over. If a tile is flagged for obstruction, units may not move over the tile. This is mainly used for path-finding algorithms, since path-finding routines have to know the parts of the map that are passable and the parts that are impassable. Check out Figure 5.35 to see an example of this.

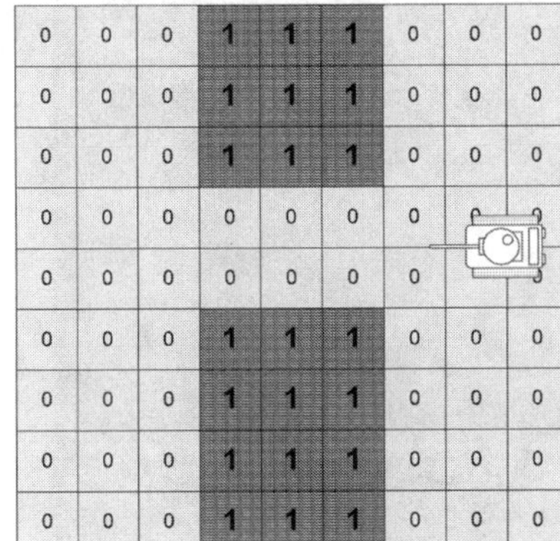

Figure 5.35: Tile obstruction used for path-finding.

In Figure 5.35, you can see how the water tiles in the map have an Obstruction value of 1 and the dirt tiles have an Obstruction value of 0. To the path-finding algorithm, this means that the water cannot be moved over. The tank on the right of the map must maneuver over the land bridge in order to get to the left side of the map. The program knows how to do this based on the obstruction map.

Elevation Property

Elevation is a useful property to have in strategy games that have maps with actual elevation. Total Annihilation had elevation to it that actually made a strategic difference. A turret placed on a mountaintop can shoot over the walls of enemy bases. A good way to store map elevation is to do it on a per-tile basis. Each tile has an elevation that the program reads in to determine line of sight.

Brightness Property

The next property, Brightness, is useful for fog of war effects. Check out Figure 5.36 to see what I am talking about.

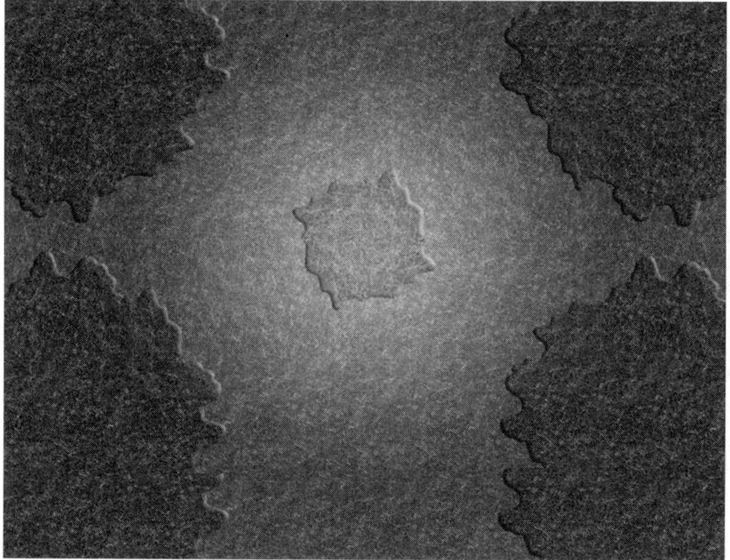

Figure 5.36: Tile brightness used for the fog of war effect.

In Figure 5.36, you can see how tiles in the middle of the image are bright, while tiles farther out get increasingly dark. This is because the player has a unit in the middle of the map that can see the area around it. By giving the tiles around the unit varying degrees of Brightness, the rendering engine provides the effect of diminishing visual range. A Brightness of 1.0 means the tile is completely illuminated, and a Brightness of 0.0 means the tile is dark. The dark tiles represent tiles that the unit cannot see very well.

Offsets Property

The Offsets property may sound very strange at first, but it is very useful in rendering. If you recall, I mentioned previously how you normally pick a tile size to use in your game. Sizes of 32 x 32, 64 x 64, and even 128 x 128 are fairly common. But what happens if you need a few tiles that don't fit into the perfect size? One example is a tree. Trees are usually tall and not very wide. If you try to fit a tree into a 32 x 32 isometric tile, you are going to experience problems. The best way around this is to use a non-uniformly shaped tile.

Say, for example, you create a tree that is 64 pixels tall and 32 pixels wide. The problem with the tree is that when you render it in your tile rendering routine, the tree appears to poke through the ground since it is too tall. Figure 5.37 illustrates this point.

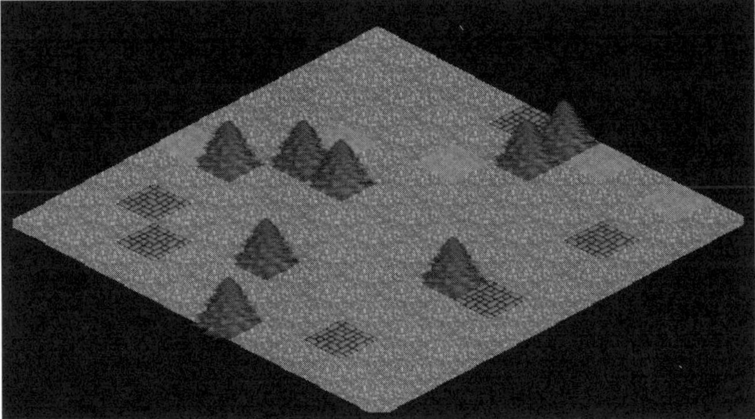

Figure 5.37: Irregularly shaped tile rendered without offsets.

Notice in Figure 5.37 how the tiles, other than the trees, look fine. The trees are poking through the bottom of the landscape. This is because the rendering corner for the trees are at their proper position, but the tree graphic is too tall. In order to fix this problem, you must render the trees at an offset. To figure out the offset, you take the height of the "normal" tiles and subtract the tree tile size from it. In this example the tree is 64 pixels tall, and the "normal" tiles are 32 pixels tall. So, your offset is 32 – 64 = –32 pixels. Now when you render your map, you render all trees at Y + –32. This makes the trees move up the screen 32 pixels when they are rendered. You can also make modifications to the x and z offsets if you so desire. Basically you want to use this method to line up tiles that do not fit into the "normal" or standard tile size that your game uses.

Tile Rendering

Are we there yet? Are we there yet? Are we there yet? YES!!!! We are there now. Sorry about that — I just had a flashback to the last road trip I took my children on.

That's right, you are finally to the meat of tile rendering. Here I cover the actual code to implement the following scenarios:

■ 2D tile rendering

■ 2D isometric tile rendering

- 2D isometric tile rendering with sprites
- 3D tile rendering

2D Tile Rendering

Take a look at Figure 5.38 to see the program that I am about to cover.

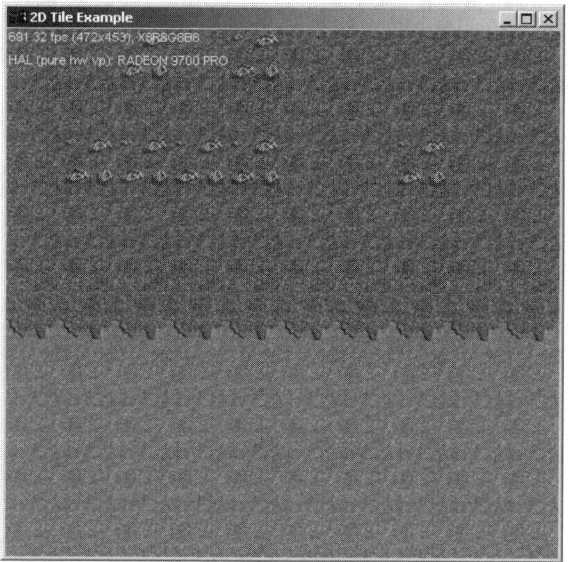

Figure 5.38: Screen shot of the 2D tile rendering example.

Doesn't that look exciting? OK, I realize you have seen dozens of tile maps now, but this one actually has fully working code in the downloadable companion files (www.wordware.com/files/games)! Load up the D3DFrame_2DTiles project so you can follow along.

D3DFrame_2DTiles Project Architecture

The project contains two unique files, main.cpp and main.h. The rest of the files included in the project are part of Microsoft's DirectX 9.0 SDK. They are as follows: d3dapp.cpp, d3denumeration.cpp, d3dfont.cpp, d3dsettings.cpp, d3dutil.cpp, and dxutil.cpp.

The unique files are the ones I created for this example. You may have noticed the D3DFrame prefix to the project. This means I used the Direct3D framework provided by Microsoft to create the program. Whenever you see the prefix, you know I use the framework. Don't worry too much if you don't like the framework; I cover how to do the same work without it as well.

Figure 5.39 illustrates the layout of the project.

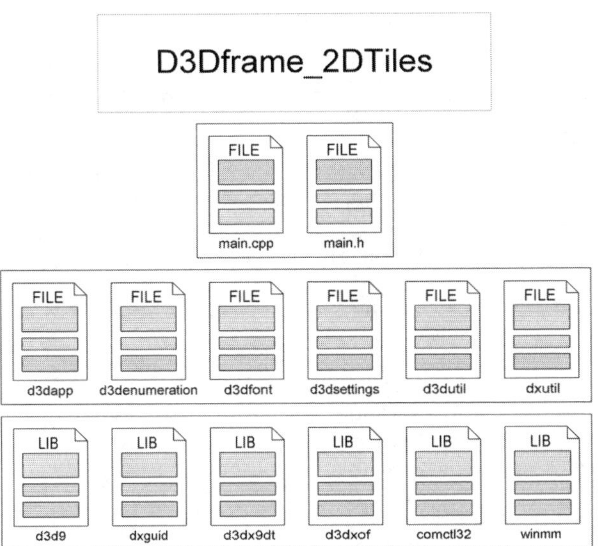

Figure 5.39: File layout of the 2DTiles example program.

As you can see in the figure, the project includes the unique files, the DirectX framework files, and the following libraries: d3d9.lib, dxguid.lib, d3dx9dt.lib, d3dxof.lib, comctl32.lib, and winmm.lib.

The Main.h Header File

There is only one header file that you really need to concern yourself with — the main.h file. This file contains all of the header information required for the program. Here is the listing of the code:

```
#define STRICT
#include <windows.h>
#include <commctrl.h>
#include <commdlg.h>
#include <math.h>
#include <tchar.h>
#include <stdio.h>
#include <D3DX9.h>
#include "DXUtil.h"
#include "D3DEnumeration.h"
#include "D3DSettings.h"
#include "D3DApp.h"
#include "D3DFont.h"
#include "D3DUtil.h"

// Structure for the tile vertex data
struct TILEVERTEX
{
    D3DXVECTOR3 position;  // The position
    D3DXVECTOR3 vecNorm;   // The normals
```

```cpp
    FLOAT         tu, tv;      // The texture coordinates (U,V)
};

// Our custom FVF, which describes our custom vertex structure
// D3DFVF_XYZ = Coordinate information
// D3DFVF_NORMAL = Normal information
// D3DFVF_TEX1   = Texture information
#define D3DFVF_TILEVERTEX (D3DFVF_XYZ | D3DFVF_NORMAL | D3DFVF_TEX1)

class CD3DFramework : public CD3DApplication
{
    // Font to display FPS and video info
    CD3DFont*               m_pStatsFont;
    // Integer array used for tile map
    int                     m_iTileMap[100];
    short                   m_shTileMapWidth;
    short                   m_shTileMapHeight;
    // Buffer to hold textures
    LPDIRECT3DTEXTURE9      m_pTexture[32];
    // Window dimensions
    short                   m_shWindowWidth;
    short                   m_shWindowHeight;
    // Buffer to hold vertices
    LPDIRECT3DVERTEXBUFFER9 m_pVBTile;

protected:
    HRESULT OneTimeSceneInit();
    HRESULT InitDeviceObjects();
    HRESULT RestoreDeviceObjects();
    HRESULT InvalidateDeviceObjects();
    HRESULT DeleteDeviceObjects();
    HRESULT Render();
    HRESULT FinalCleanup();
    HRESULT CreateD3DXTextMesh(LPD3DXMESH* ppMesh, TCHAR* pstrFont, DWORD dwSize);
    // Create tile vertex buffer
    void vInitTileVB(void);
    // Draw a tile on-screen
    void vDrawTile(float fXPos, float fYPos, float fXSize, float fYSize, int iTexture);

public:
    LRESULT MsgProc(HWND hWnd, UINT uMsg, WPARAM wParam, LPARAM lParam);
    CD3DFramework();
};
```

I'm not going to bore you with covering the non-example specific code, so I'm jumping right into the following piece of code:

```cpp
struct TILEVERTEX
{
    D3DXVECTOR3 position;   // The position
    D3DXVECTOR3 vecNorm;    // The normals
    FLOAT       tu, tv;     // The texture coordinates (U,V)
};
```

Note The program name does have the word 2D in it, but don't let that fool you. DirectX doesn't really do pure 2D work anymore, so now programs use 3D graphics that look 2D. For this reason I have created a vertex structure that holds the 3D information necessary to create a tile that appears to have only two dimensions. For more information on this aspect of programming, I suggest you read Chapter 6, which focuses on programming 2D graphics with 3D.

The vertex structure contains position, normal, and texture coordinate information. This is all the data you need in order to display 2D-looking graphics on-screen.

The member variables of note are `m_iTileMap`, `m_shTileMapWidth`, `m_shTileMapHeight`, `m_pTexture`, and `m_pVBTile`. The `m_iTileMap` array holds the tile map information. I have it set to an array of 100 integers because the map is 10 tiles wide and 10 tiles tall.

The `m_shTileMapWidth` and `m_shTileMapHeight` variables hold the size of the tile map. In the class constructor I set these equal to 10.

The `m_pTexture` array holds pointers to the textures used by the rendering engine. Each value in the tile map array represents an index into this array.

The `m_pVBTile` pointer points to the vertex buffer required by the program to render the tiles.

The next block of code you should be interested in is the following:

```
// Create tile vertex buffer
void vInitTileVB(void);
// Draw a tile on-screen
void vDrawTile(float fXPos, float fYPos, float fXSize, float fYSize, int iTexture);
```

These two function prototypes are the heart of the program example as far as tiles are concerned. The first function, `vInitTileVB()`, initializes the tile vertex buffer that is used for rendering. The next function, `vDrawTile()`, is used to render the tiles on-screen.

Note The code you see here does not perfectly reflect what is on the companion files. I removed many of the code comments in the book to save space.

The Main.cpp Program File

The main.cpp file isn't too complicated, as it follows the DirectX framework application pretty well. The first class function of interest is the class constructor. It is as follows:

```
CD3DFramework::CD3DFramework()
{
    m_strWindowTitle     = _T("2D Tile Example");
    m_pStatsFont         = NULL;
    m_shWindowWidth      = 480;
    m_shWindowHeight     = 480;
    m_shTileMapWidth     = 10;
    m_shTileMapHeight    = 10;
}
```

As you can see in this code, the tile map's size is set in the class constructor. I set the width and height to 10 so that the map fills the entire window when rendered. The tiles are 48 pixels wide and 48 pixels high, so I set the size of the window to 480 by 480. 10 * 48 = 480, so this is the proper size to have a perfect fit.

The next block of code of interest handles the initialization of the tile map.

```
HRESULT CD3DFramework::OneTimeSceneInit()
{
    m_pStatsFont = new CD3DFont(_T("Arial"), 8, NULL);
    if(m_pStatsFont == NULL)
        return E_FAIL;
    // Clear out the map with the grass tile
    memset(m_iTileMap, 0, (m_shTileMapWidth*m_shTileMapHeight) * sizeof(int));
    // Fill the second half with beach tile
    for(int i = 0; i < 50; i++) {
        m_iTileMap[i+50] = 3;
    }
    // Randomly place rocks on the grass
    // Seed the randomizer
    srand(timeGetTime());
    for(i = 0; i < 50; i++) {
        // Place rock tile if random 0-10 = 5
        if(rand()%10 == 5)
            m_iTileMap[i] = 1;
    }
    // Place the grass edging along the beach tiles
    for(i = 50; i < 60; i++) {
        m_iTileMap[i] = 2;
    }

    return S_OK;
}
```

The first line of interest in the code above is the call to the memset() function. This piece of code clears the tile map by setting all tiles to equal

0. The 0 texture happens to be grass; therefore, this code clears the map
with grass tiles.

The next block of code runs a loop and sets the bottom half of the
map to contain tile 3. Tile 3 is a beach texture; therefore, this code sets
the bottom half of the map to contain beach tiles.

Next up for bid is the section that randomly places rock tiles on the
upper half of the map. The rock tiles are there for decoration; therefore,
their position isn't very important. I use the rand() function to determine rock density.

Lastly, the code places a line of grass-beach edging tiles along the
middle of the map. This provides a nice transition from the grass to the
beach tiles.

Play around with setting different tiles in the initialization code. You
may want to make patterns out of it or whatever. Now is your chance to
set the tile values and see the result.

I'm skipping down a bit to the RestoreDeviceObjects() function.
This is important, as it contains the texture initialization code. The following code snippet initializes the textures:

```
sprintf(szFileName,"grass00.bmp");
if(FAILED(D3DXCreateTextureFromFile(m_pd3dDevice, szFileName, &m_pTexture[0]))) {
    return S_OK;
}
sprintf(szFileName,"grass_rocks.bmp");
if(FAILED(D3DXCreateTextureFromFile(m_pd3dDevice, szFileName, &m_pTexture[1]))) {
    return S_OK;
}
sprintf(szFileName,"grass_edging_bottom.bmp");
if(FAILED(D3DXCreateTextureFromFile(m_pd3dDevice, szFileName, &m_pTexture[2]))) {
    return S_OK;
}
sprintf(szFileName,"beach.bmp");
if(FAILED(D3DXCreateTextureFromFile(m_pd3dDevice, szFileName, &m_pTexture[3]))) {
    return S_OK;
}
```

The texture initialization code utilizes DirectX's utility function named
D3DXCreateTextureFromFile(). It's a really cool function, as it handles all
of the code to load various types of images such as BMPs, TGAs, and
JPEGs. To use it, you need to include the d3dx9.lib library along with the
d3dx9tex.h header file. Its prototype is as follows:

```
HRESULT D3DXCreateTextureFromFile(
    LPDIRECT3DDEVICE9       pDevice,
    LPCSTR                  pSrcFile,
    LPDIRECT3DTEXTURE9*     ppTexture
);
```

The first parameter, pDevice, requires a pointer to the Direct3D device that you are utilizing for your rendering. In the code used for this example the device is pointed to from the m_pd3dDevice member variable. So, use it for the first parameter.

The second parameter, pSrcFile, expects the name of the texture file to load. This parameter is not very complicated, as all you have to do is give it the stringified name of your file. You do not need explicit path information as the function tries to find the texture file in the current directory. If you need to point to a different directory, you may want to read in a registry setting to retrieve the path. Personally, I just use subdirectories from the main program. This method allows for multiple directories without the headache of registry settings.

The last parameter, ppTexture, requires a pointer to a texture. If you recall back to my coverage of the header function, you remember that I am using the m_pTexture array to hold the texture pointers. I use an index into the texture array for this parameter. For example, texture 1 uses m_pTexture[0], texture 2 uses m_pTexture[1], and so forth.

The last part of the texture initialization routine calls the vInitTileVB() function. This function initializes the virtual buffer to hold the 3D tile information and does nothing else.

Move back up in the code to the Render() member function. This is where the magic happens. Please ignore the man behind the curtain! The code is as follows for the rendering logic:

```
HRESULT CD3DFramework::Render()
{
    D3DXMATRIX     matTranslation;
    D3DXMATRIX     matRotation;
    D3DXMATRIX     matRotation2;
    D3DXMATRIX     matScale;
    int            iX;
    int            iY;
    int            iCurTile;
    float          fTileX, fTileY;

    // Clear the viewport
    m_pd3dDevice->Clear(OL, NULL, D3DCLEAR_TARGET, D3DCOLOR_XRGB(120,120,120),
                        1.0f, OL);

    // Begin the scene
    if(SUCCEEDED(m_pd3dDevice->BeginScene())) {
        // Vertical
        for(iY = 0; iY < m_shTileMapHeight; iY++) {
            // Horizontal
            for(iX = 0; iX < m_shTileMapWidth; iX++) {
                // Figure out which tile to display
                iCurTile = m_iTileMap[iX + (iY * m_shTileMapWidth)];
                // Figure out the on-screen coordinates
                fTileX = -240.0f+(iX*48.0f);
```

```
            fTileY = 192.0f-(iY*48.0f);
            // Display the tile
            vDrawTile(fTileX, fTileY, 48.0f, 48.0f, iCurTile);
        }
    }
    // Show frame rate
    m_pStatsFont->DrawText(2,  0, D3DCOLOR_ARGB(255,255,255,0), m_strFrameStats);
    // Show video device information
    m_pStatsFont->DrawText(2, 20, D3DCOLOR_ARGB(255,255,255,0), m_strDeviceStats);

    // End the scene
    m_pd3dDevice->EndScene();
    }
    return S_OK;
}
```

The first part of the code calls the `Clear()` function. The `Clear()` function belongs to the Direct3D device and is used to clear the 3D rendering plate. I clear the view buffer to a medium gray color. You can pick whatever color you want; it doesn't really matter since the view area is filled with tiles.

The next call made is to the `BeginScene()` function. This function starts up the rendering engine of the 3D system. You must call it before performing 3D graphic operations.

Warning   You must start your rendering with BeginScene() and end it with EndScene(). If you do not, you can crash your program.

Now the fun part begins. The next chunk of code deals with the rendering loop required to display the tiles. There are two loops; the first one loops through the tile map from top to bottom, and the inner loop loops from left to right. The combination of these two loops results in coverage of the entire tile map.

The first line of code in the inner loop deals with figuring out the tile to render. It stores this value in the `iCurTile` variable. The tile to render is calculated by adding the inner-loop value to the outer-loop value times the width of the map. You probably remember this formula from earlier in the chapter. Armed with the tile value, you now know which texture to render.

The next part figures out where to place the tiles on-screen. Since the program uses 3D space, it has to offset the tiles using floating-point values. The window created by the program measures 480 pixels across and tall. With this in mind, the tiles must start 240.0 units to the left in order to be flush with the edge. To be flush with the top of the window, the tiles must start at 240.0 – 48.0, or 192.0 units from the origin.

The next piece of code calls the `vDrawTile()` function that I wrote. The prototype for the function is as follows:

```
vDrawTile(
    float fXPos,
    float fYPos,
    float fXSize,
    float fYSize,
    int iTexture)
```

The first parameter, `fXPos`, expects the x-coordinate at which to draw the tile on-screen. It is a floating-point unit and specifies the location in 3D space along the x-axis. Do not confuse this with pixel coordinates.

The next parameter, `fYPos`, is just like the first parameter, except this one corresponds to the y-axis in 3D space.

The next two parameters, `fXSize` and `fYSize`, set the size of the tile to display on-screen. You can set the size to whatever you wish, as the function scales the tile accordingly. For this demo, the tile size is 48.0 units.

The last parameter expects an index into the `m_pTexture` texture array. This parameter sets the texture to render.

Once the `vDrawTile()` function is called, the tile appears in the display buffer. All that is left to do is output the frame rate and video card information and then display the scene. All of this is accomplished in the remaining render code.

See, that wasn't so bad, was it? To see the program flow illustrated, check out Figure 5.40.

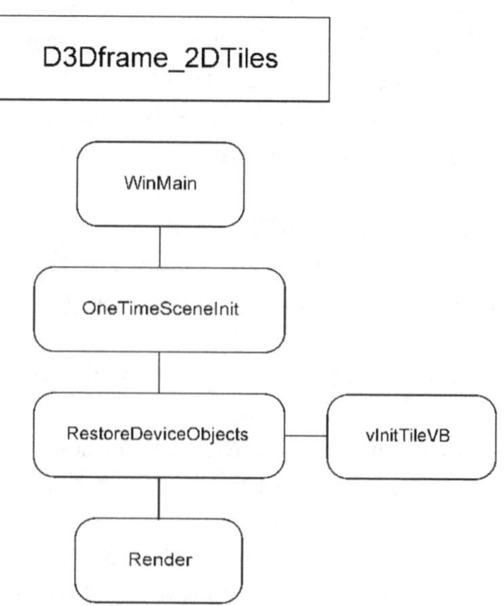

Figure 5.40: Program flow of the 2DTiles example program.

In the figure you see the flow of the program from initialization to rendering to cleanup. That about wraps it up for 2D tile rendering for now. It's time for isometric rendering!

2D Isometric Tile Rendering

Isometric tile rendering is a very complex subject. In fact, a book completely dedicated to isometric game making has been published. The code I cover here does not account for every possible situation in isometric tile rendering. The following code is meant to be a foundation on which you can do your work. I do cover some of the problems and potential fixes, but many issues are too broad for the scope of this book. I suggest you become familiar with the code presented here and then take it as your own for further research and development. In Figure 5.41 you see the output from the 2D Isometric Tile example program.

Figure 5.41: Output of the 2D Isometric Tile example program.

The name of the project containing the code for the program is D3D-Frame_Isometric2DTiles. You can find it the companion files (www.wordware.com/files/games). Load it up now so you can follow along.

D3DFrame_Isometric2DTiles Project Architecture

The project contains two unique files, main.cpp and main.h. The rest of the files included in the project are part of Microsoft's DirectX 9.0 SDK. They are as follows: d3dapp.cpp, d3denumeration.cpp, d3dfont.cpp, d3dsettings.cpp, d3dutil.cpp, and dxutil.cpp. Sounds familiar, eh? You should notice a recurring theme in the examples I write using the Direct3D framework. I try to keep things simple so you can rely on continuity.

The Main.h Header File

Once again, there is only one header file to concern you with — the main.h header file. You have already seen the majority of the contents, so I just focus on the relevant parts here. The first items of interest are the member variables, which are as follows:

```
// Integer array used for tile map
int                     m_iTileMap[100][2];
short                   m_shTileMapWidth;
short                   m_shTileMapHeight;
// Buffer to hold textures
LPDIRECT3DTEXTURE9      m_pTexture[32];
```

Well, would you look at that? All of the variables are the same except for a new dimension on the m_iTileMap array. The m_iTileMap array has been updated to include another layer in the form of a new dimension. This layer is to accommodate the detail tiles present in this example. Instead of having just one layer of tiles, this example has two. Ta da!

That's it for the header file; everything else is pretty much the same from the 2D tile-rendering example.

The Main.cpp Program File

Load up the main.cpp file. The first thing of interest is a global variable named g_iNumTextures. This variable holds the number of tile textures loaded into memory. I create it to make adding tiles to the program an easy process. I have it set to 9 currently. If you decide to play around with the program and add your own tiles, be sure you increase this number accordingly.

Moving on down the code to the class constructor, you can see where I set a few member variables:

```
m_shWindowWidth  = 640;
m_shWindowHeight = 320;
m_shTileMapWidth = 10;
m_shTileMapHeight   = 10;
```

This time I create a window that is 640 pixels wide and 320 pixels tall. I do this because isometric tiles render differently than square tiles; therefore, a larger screen area is required.

The next couple of variables set the size of the tile map to render. If you decide to increase the tile map size, be sure to add elements to the m_iTileMap array accordingly.

Next up you see the OneTimeSceneInit() member function. In this function I populate the tile map with two layers worth of data after I clear the tile map array with a memset() call.

```
// Seed the randomizer
srand(timeGetTime());
for(int i = 0; i < 100; i++) {
    // Populate the base layer with grass, sand, or brick tiles
    if(rand()%10 == 3)
        m_iTileMap[i][0] = 2;
    else if(rand()%10 == 4)
        m_iTileMap[i][0] = 3;
    else
        m_iTileMap[i][0] = 4;
    // Populate the detail layer with pillars or trees
    if(rand()%10 == 5)
        m_iTileMap[i][1] = 6;
    else if(rand()%10 == 4)
        m_iTileMap[i][1] = 5;
    else if(rand()%10 == 3)
        m_iTileMap[i][1] = 8;
}
```

The first call to `srand()` seeds the random number generation system
with the current system up time. I do this with a call to the `timeGet-`
`Time()` function. The `timeGetTime()` function belongs to the `winmm.lib`
library and requires the `mmsystem.h` header file. By seeding the random
number generator, I get more random results with each call to the
program.

The program loops through the dimensions of the tile map and randomly assigns tiles to both the base and detail maps. The base map
contains grass, sand, and brick tiles, and the detail map contains pillars,
trees, and bushes. The density of each tile type depends on the randomization routine.

Take note that I set the base tiles by referencing the first dimension
of the tile map. This is done with a reference of `m_iTileMap[xxTile-`
`ToChangexx] [0]`. The detail tiles are populated by referencing the
second layer with a change to `m_iTileMap[xxTileToChangexx] [1]`. You
can add more dimensions if you like; just be sure to fill them with mean-
ingful data here.

That's it for map initialization. Just like with the last program, I load
in the textures next. This is done in the `RestoreDeviceObjects()` function. I won't bore you with the details here as nothing blazingly new is
contained within it.

Geeeeeeeeettttttttt reeeeeeeaaaaddddyyyy tooooooo reeeeeeeennnn-
dddeeerrr!!!! (With apologies to Michael Buffer.) It really is time to get
rendering, so without further delay....

```
// Vertical
for(iY = 0; iY < m_shTileMapHeight; iY++) {
    // Horizontal
    for(iX = 0; iX < m_shTileMapWidth; iX++) {
        //--------------------------------------------
```

```
//            RENDER THE BASE LAYER
//------------------------------------------------
// Figure out which tile to display
iCurTile = m_iTileMap[iX + (iY * m_shTileMapWidth)][0];

    // Figure out the on-screen coordinates
    fTileX = -32.0f+(iX*32.0f)-(iY*32.0f);
    fTileY = 128.0f-((iY*16.0f)+(iX*16.0f));
    // Display the tile
    vDrawTile(fTileX, fTileY, 64.0f, 32.0f, iCurTile);


    //------------------------------------------------
    //            RENDER THE DETAIL LAYER
    //------------------------------------------------
    // Figure out which tile to display
    iCurTile = m_iTileMap[iX + (iY * m_shTileMapWidth)][1];
    if(iCurTile != 0) {
        // Figure out the on-screen coordinates
        fTileX = -32.0f+(iX*32.0f)-(iY*32.0f);
        fTileY = 128.0f-((iY*16.0f)+(iX*16.0f));
        if(iCurTile == 5)
            vDrawTile(fTileX, fTileY, 64.0f, 125.0f, iCurTile);
        else if(iCurTile == 6)
            vDrawTile(fTileX, fTileY, 67.0f, 109.0f, iCurTile);
        else if(iCurTile == 8)
            vDrawTile(fTileX, fTileY, 64.0f, 64.0f, iCurTile);
    }
  }
}
```

Once again there are two rendering loops. The first loop handles the vertical tiles, and the second loop handles the horizontal tiles. Now remember, the tiles are not vertical and horizontal on-screen; I am referring to the vertical and horizontal tiles on the tile map.

The first rendering section deals with rendering the base layer. This area renders the grass, brick, and sand tiles on the map. You probably notice the common `iCurTile` variable. I use it to calculate which tile to render. This works the same way it did in the last program, except now I reference another dimension. In this case, I reference the first dimension of the tile buffer or [0] in code terms.

The next block of code figures out where on-screen to render the tile. This calculation is done by first adding the screen offset, then multiplying the inner-loop value by the tile width, and finally subtracting the sum of the outer loop and the tile height divided by two. The following puts it into perspective:

$$X\text{-Pos} = ScreenOffset + (X * TileWidth) - (Y * (TileHeight / 2))$$

The horizontal position of the tile is calculated by first adding the screen offset and then subtracting the sum of the outer loop and half of the tile's width plus the sum of the inner loop's value and half of the tile's width. Here it is again:

Y-Pos = ScreenOffset - ((Y*(TileWidth/2)) + (X*(TileWidth/2)))

With the tile position known, I now render the tile using the tried-and-true vDrawTile() function discussed earlier.

The next and last important piece of rendering code renders the detail layer of the tile map. The only special thing about this area is that I check the tile to render and adjust the rendering size according to the tile size. This is necessary because not only do the detail tiles reside on another layer, but they are also oversized! Since they are oversized, I must alter their rendering sizes in order for them to show up properly. Feel free to remove the code that changes their size if you want to see what happens.

That's it for isometric rendering. And you thought it required a complete book! Uh oh, I forgot another example program. Put away the champagne — it's time for more isometric code.

2D Isometric Tile Rendering with Sprites

This program uses the ID3DXSprite interface provided in the DirectX 9.0 SDK. The ID3DXSprite interface simplifies the process of drawing 2D images on-screen with Direct Graphics. I have replaced the majority of the 3D calls used in the last program with calls to the sprite system. The first thing you notice is the code is a bit cleaner and simpler. This may be a good or bad thing — you be the judge. Figure 5.42 shows the output from the 2D Isometric Tile Sprite example program.

Figure 5.42: Output of the 2D Isometric Tile Sprite example program.

The name of the project containing the code for the program is
D3DFrame_Isometric2DSpriteTiles. You can find it in the companion
files. Load it up now so you can follow along.

D3DFrame_Isometric2DSpriteTiles Project Architecture

The project contains two unique files, main.cpp and main.h. The rest of
the files included in the project are part of Microsoft's DirectX 9.0 SDK.
They are as follows: d3dapp.cpp, d3denumeration.cpp, d3dfont.cpp,
d3dsettings.cpp, d3dutil.cpp, and dxutil.cpp. Once again, this program
uses the DirectX framework.

The Main.h Header File

There are a few changes in this header file. Namely, I remove the virtual
buffer code since a tile buffer is not needed any longer. In place of the
vInitTileVB() function and member variable you now have a single
LPD3DXSPRITE pointer. In place of the vDrawTile() function you now have
the BltSprite() function. Here is the prototype for the BltSprite()
function:

```
HRESULT BltSprite(
    RECT                *pDestRect,
    LPDIRECT3DTEXTURE9  pSrcTexture,
    RECT                *pSrcRect)
```

The first parameter, pDestRect, expects a pointer to a RECT variable. This
rectangle tells the rendering function the area on-screen to render the
texture.

The next parameter is named pSrcTexture; it expects a pointer to
the texture to display on-screen.

The third parameter, pSrcRect, expects a pointer to another RECT
variable. This rectangle tells the rendering system the area of the texture
to display. This allows you to display portions of the texture or the whole
thing.

The Main.cpp Program File

The first thing you may notice about the program is that it does not initialize a vertex buffer for tile rendering. This process is no longer
needed, as the program uses the sprite interface for all rendering. In
order to render sprite graphics, you need a sprite device created. This is
done in the RestoreDeviceObjects() function with the following line of
code:

```
D3DXCreateSprite(m_pd3dDevice, &pd3dxSprite);
```

Simple, eh? The `D3DXCreateSprite()` function handles all of the work for you in creating a sprite device. It accepts two parameters for input. The first parameter expects the pointer to the 3D rendering device. The second parameter expects the address of a sprite device pointer to contain the newly created sprite device.

Move up to the `Render()` function to see the next set of changes. The rendering loop still operates in the same manner as before — one outer loop and one inner loop. The biggest difference takes shape inside the inner loop. Instead of calling `vDrawTile()`, the program now calls `BltSprite()`. The other difference is that I create rectangles to define the tile position instead of using floating-point units in 3D space. One important note is that the rectangles work in screen-space, not 3D space.

The offsets for the rendering positions work the same in this program. The only difference is in the unit type used. Since the sprite interface utilizes screen-space, the offsets are a bit different now.

You must make a call to the sprite device's `Begin()` function before you start rendering. You must also make a call to the sprite device's `End()` function when you are done rendering. This is a completely different call from the one related to the 3D device. This set of begin and end calls is required for sprite rendering, not 3D rendering.

Why Use Sprites?

Now that you have seen the sprite interface in action, you may be wondering why you would ever want to use sprites. For one thing, sprites are easier to use than vertex buffer rendering. The sprite interface hides all of the work required to properly display orthographic renderings. Other than that, I can't think of too many reasons to use sprites. I suggest you play around with both vertex rendering and sprite rendering and pick the one you like the best.

3D Tile Rendering

3D tile rendering! Ooooooo, sounds ominous doesn't it? Although the topic sounds daunting, it really isn't that much different from the 2D rendering covered in this chapter already. For one thing, every 2D example in this chapter uses 3D rendering. The main difference that you are going to see is that the "true" 3D program doesn't use orthographic projection. Figure 5.43 shows the output from the 3D Tiles example program.

Figure 5.43: Output of the 3D Tiles example program.

The name of the project containing the code for the program is
D3DFrame_3DTiles. You can find it in the companion files. Load it up
now so you can follow along.

D3DFrame_3DTiles Project Architecture

The project contains two unique files, main.cpp and main.h. The rest of
the files included in the project are part of Microsoft's DirectX 9.0 SDK.
They are as follows: d3dapp.cpp, d3denumeration.cpp, **d3dfile.cpp**,
d3dfont.cpp, d3dsettings.cpp, d3dutil.cpp, and dxutil.cpp.

Check out the file name in boldface. The d3dfile.cpp file is a new
addition to this program. Its purpose is to assist in the loading of 3D files
in the .x file format. It is required for loading 3D models from packages
such as Maya, 3D Studio MAX, and MilkShape. You can write your own
model loaders if you so wish, but the built-in functions that d3dfile.cpp
gives you make life much easier.

The Main.h Header File

There are few changes in the header file for the 3D project, but they are
significant changes. Here is the header code in its entirety.

```
#define STRICT
#include <windows.h>
#include <commctrl.h>
#include <commdlg.h>
```

```cpp
#include <math.h>
#include <tchar.h>
#include <stdio.h>
#include <D3DX9.h>
#include "DXUtil.h"
#include "D3DEnumeration.h"
#include "D3DSettings.h"
#include "D3DApp.h"
#include "D3DFont.h"
#include "D3DFile.h"
#include "D3DUtil.h"

int g_iNumTiles = 2;

// Vertex format for the 3D tiles
struct D3DVERTEX
{
    D3DXVECTOR3 p;
    D3DXVECTOR3 n;
    FLOAT       tu, tv;

    static const DWORD FVF;
};
const DWORD D3DVERTEX::FVF = D3DFVF_XYZ | D3DFVF_NORMAL | D3DFVF_TEX1;

class CD3DFramework : public CD3DApplication
    {
    CD3DFont*      m_pStatsFont;
    TCHAR          m_strFont[LF_FACESIZE];
    DWORD          m_dwFontSize;
    // 3D Object data
    CD3DMesh*      m_pObject[32];
    // Integer array used for tile map
    int            m_iTileMap[100];
    short          m_shTileMapWidth;
    short          m_shTileMapHeight;
    // Window dimensions
    short          m_shWindowWidth;
    short          m_shWindowHeight;

protected:
    HRESULT OneTimeSceneInit();
    HRESULT InitDeviceObjects();
    HRESULT RestoreDeviceObjects();
    HRESULT InvalidateDeviceObjects();
    HRESULT DeleteDeviceObjects();
    HRESULT Render();
    HRESULT FrameMove();
    HRESULT FinalCleanup();
    HRESULT CreateD3DXTextMesh(LPD3DXMESH* ppMesh, TCHAR* pstrFont, DWORD dwSize);

public:
    LRESULT MsgProc(HWND hWnd, UINT uMsg, WPARAM wParam, LPARAM lParam);
    CD3DFramework();
};
```

The first change comes in the include section. The d3dfile.cpp program file requires the header file named d3dfile.h. Since the program uses the d3dfile.cpp functions, the header must be included into the source code.

Note   The helper files, such as d3dfile.cpp, d3dapp.cpp, d3dsettings.cpp, etc., can be found in the folder where you installed DirectX. If you use the default installation path, the files are located in C:\DXSDK\Samples\C++\Common.

The next item of interest is the `g_iNumTiles` variable set right after the include files. This variable keeps track of the number of 3D models loaded into the program. It is important to track this number, as the program must know how many models to manage. If you decide to add models to this example, be sure to increase this number accordingly.

The next change happens in the `D3DVERTEX` data structure. The format is slightly different from before. This is to support the 3D model's vertex format. The `FVF DWORD` variable is necessary for this support. This is the only real difference from previous vertex formats.

Down in the class definition is a new variable named `m_pObject`. It is an array of type `CD3DMesh`. The d3dfile.cpp library provides the CD3DMesh object. It is your window into the world of 3D model loading and display. I arbitrarily select an array size of 32. This sets the maximum number of loaded tiles to 32, but don't worry; you can always change the number later if you so desire.

The Main.cpp Program File

Open up the main.cpp file now to see the code used for the example program. The first part of the code of interest is the following:

```
HRESULT CD3DFramework::OneTimeSceneInit()
{
    int i;
    m_pStatsFont = new CD3DFont(_T("Arial"), 8, NULL);
    if(m_pStatsFont == NULL)
        return E_FAIL;
    // Allocate memory for the tiles
    for(i = 0; i < g_iNumTiles; i++) {
        m_pObject[i]  = new CD3DMesh();
    }
    // Clear out the map with the 0 tile
    memset(m_iTileMap, 0, (m_shTileMapWidth*m_shTileMapHeight) * sizeof(int));
    // Randomly place rocks on the grass
    // Seed the randomizer
    srand(timeGetTime());
    for(i = 0; i < 100; i++) {
        if(rand()%5 == 3)
            m_iTileMap[i] = 1;
```

```
        else
            m_iTileMap[i] = 0;
    }
    return S_OK;
}
```

The `for loop` is where the new action starts. In this loop, memory is allocated for the 3D objects (tiles). This is as simple as using the new operator. See, wasn't that easy?

Next up you have another `for loop` that randomly places tiles on the map. There are only two tiles to choose from in this example, so the code only has to alternate between the two types. In this case, 1 is a mountain tile and tile 0 is a grass tile.

Loading 3D Models

The objects have memory, and the tile map is initialized. It's time to load up the 3D models for the 3D tile data. The following code does this:

```
HRESULT CD3DFramework::InitDeviceObjects()
{
    HRESULT hr;
    char   szFileName[512];
    // Initialize the font
    if(FAILED(hr = m_pStatsFont->InitDeviceObjects(m_pd3dDevice)))
    return hr;
    //  Load 3D tile information
    for(int i = 0; i < g_iNumTiles; i++) {
        // Create the filename
        sprintf(szFileName, "ground_tile%d.x", i+1);
        // Load the mesh
        if(FAILED(m_pObject[i]->Create(m_pd3dDevice, _T(szFileName))))
            return D3DAPPERR_MEDIANOTFOUND;
        // Set its vertex type
        m_pObject[i]->SetFVF(m_pd3dDevice, D3DVERTEX::FVF);
    }
    return S_OK;
}
```

The loop in this function starts out by creating the name of the 3D object file to load. Once the filename is ready to go, the code calls the `Create()` function that belongs to the `CD3DMesh` object class. Here is the prototype for the `CD3DMesh::Create()` function:

```
HRESULT Create(
    LPDIRECT3DDEVICE9 pd3dDevice,
    TCHAR* strFilename)
```

The first parameter, `pd3dDevice`, requires a pointer to the 3D device in use by the application. For this parameter I pass in the `m_pd3dDevice` pointer initialized by the framework application.

The next parameter, `strFilename`, expects the filename of the object to load into memory. This is where I pass in the filename created previously.

Now that the object is loaded into memory, you need to set the vertex format for the object. This is necessary if you want to control the vertex format used in the rendering of the object. You don't actually have to use `SetFVF()` if you don't want to. It just allows for more control.

Point Lights

Scoot on down to the `CD3DFramework::RestoreDeviceObjects()` function to see a minor change that I make there. There isn't much difference in this function; the main one is that I use a new type of light for this example. Here is the code for the new point light:

```
ZeroMemory(&d3dLight, sizeof(D3DLIGHT9));
d3dLight.Type         = D3DLIGHT_POINT;
d3dLight.Diffuse.r    = 1.0f;
d3dLight.Diffuse.g    = 1.0f;
d3dLight.Diffuse.b    = 1.0f;
d3dLight.Position.x   = 0.0f;
d3dLight.Position.y   = -20.0f;
d3dLight.Position.z   = 20.0f;
d3dLight.Attenuation0 = 1.0f;
d3dLight.Attenuation1 = 0.0f;
d3dLight.Range        = 100.0f;
```

In the previous examples, the programs use directional lights. DirectGraphics offers other types of lights for your use, such as spotlights and point lights. I use a point light for this example.

The `Type` value for the light sets the type of light that the rendering system expects. I set it to `D3DLIGHT_POINT` in this example. This tells the rendering system to expect and use the parameters for a point light.

The `Diffuse` structure sets the color of the light. There are three components — red, green, and blue. The value range for each component is from 0.0 to 1.0. A value of 0.0 indicates the complete absence of that color, and a value of 1.0 indicates a complete presence of the color. Since I set each color value to 1.0, the light is white in color. If you are unfamiliar with 3D lighting, I suggest you play around with the diffuse color to see the effect on the scene.

The `Position` structure holds the position of the light in 3D space. I have it set to (0.0, –20.0, 20.0).

The `Attenuation0` value sets how the light intensity changes over time. This value sets the constant at which attenuation happens. The `Attenuation1` value sets the next constant used for attenuation. By setting the value scale from 1.0 to 0.0, the light tapers off as distance increases.

The Range value sets the distance at which the light no longer has an effect. For this example, the light stops illuminating objects that are 100.0 units away or more.

Rendering 3D Models

Are you ready to render the 3D tiles? I know I am! Here is the new and improved 3D tile rendering code:

```
HRESULT CD3DFramework::Render()
{
    D3DXMATRIX   matTranslation;
    int    iX, iY;
    int    iCurTile;
    float  fXPos;
    float  fYPos;

    // Clear the viewport
    m_pd3dDevice->Clear(OL, NULL, D3DCLEAR_TARGET | D3DCLEAR_ZBUFFER,
                        D3DCOLOR_XRGB(0, 0, 0), 1.0f, OL);

    // Begin the scene
    if(SUCCEEDED(m_pd3dDevice->BeginScene()))
      {
      for(iY = 0; iY < 10; iY++) {
         // Horizontal
         for(iX = 0; iX < 10; iX++) {
            // Figure out which tile to display
            iCurTile = m_iTileMap[iX + (iY * m_shTileMapWidth)];
            // Calculate the position
            fXPos = (-5.0f*iX)+22.5f;
            fYPos = (-5.0f*iY)+32.5f;
            // Set position of tile
            D3DXMatrixTranslation(&matTranslation, fXPos, fYPos, 0.0f);
            m_pd3dDevice->SetTransform(D3DTS_WORLD, &matTranslation);
            // Render the tile
            m_pObject[iCurTile]->Render(m_pd3dDevice);
         }
      }

      // Show frame rate
      m_pStatsFont->DrawText(2,  0, D3DCOLOR_ARGB(255,255,255,0), m_strFrameStats);
      // Show video device information
      m_pStatsFont->DrawText(2, 20, D3DCOLOR_ARGB(255,255,255,0), m_strDeviceStats);

      // End the scene
      m_pd3dDevice->EndScene();
    }

    return S_OK;
}
```

Notice how it looks very similar to previous examples. Rendering 3D models really isn't hard at all. The usual suspects are present in this example. There is an outer loop to render the tiles along the y-axis and an inner loop to render the tiles along the x-axis. The tile position is calculated in the usual way with little changes to the coordinates. The main change happens with a call to the `D3DXMatrixTranslation()` function.

The `D3DXMatrixTranslation()` function creates a translation matrix given a set of 3D coordinates. Translation is just a fancy word for position; therefore, the translation matrix sets up the position of the object in 3D space. Once the position of the object is set, a call to the `Set-Transform()` function puts the position matrix into play.

Warning   Make sure you use the `D3DTS_WORLD` value for the first parameter in the `SetTransform()` function. If not, you will change something other than the object's position!

Now that the object is in its proper position, it is rendered with the `Render()` function call. The `Render()` call belongs to the `CD3DMesh` object and handles all of the work for you. All you have to do is pass in the 3D rendering device, and the object does the rest. Isn't that cool?

You now know how to render 3D tiles. The ancient question has been answered! I admit that there is much more to learn, but you are well on your way to creating a fully 3D tile-based strategy game.

Recap

That's it for now for tile-based graphics. Remember the following key aspects of tile rendering:

- Tiles allow for large maps with minimal memory usage.
- Tiles allow for dynamic graphic content.
- Choose the tile sizes for your games carefully.
- Sprite rendering reduces the complexity of tile rendering.

Chapter 6

Interface Design and Development

S ome game developers start writing code before designing the interface for their games. Don't fall into this trap: Interface design and programming is a very important aspect of game development. Even if you are writing a Tetris clone, the interface plays a key role in the entertainment factor of your game. Without a good interface, players get confused and angry and may even stop playing your game. I don't want this to happen and I know you don't either. Hopefully this chapter can get you started in the wide world of interface design and programming. Look for the following topics in this chapter:

- Defining interface needs
- Interface usability
- 2D rendering in 3D
- Hotspots

Defining Interface Needs

The first aspect of interface development deals with the needs of the interface in question. You must ask yourself, "What does the interface need to do?" This is a key question because without the answer, you can't begin development. Sure, you may start coding right away and think about the interface later, but I don't recommend it at all. So, the question is, how do you define the requirements?

My first recommendation to you is to start with a fresh notebook. I use spiral-bound notebooks, as they are easy to lay down flat for reference when coding. Armed with your fresh notebook, write out in outline format the various interfaces for your game. The outline for a simple game of tic-tac-toe might look something like this:

```
Title Screen
    Title graphic (bmp)
    Press to skip button (mzone)
Main Menu
    New game button (mzone)
    Load game button (mzone)
    Save game button (mzone)
    Exit game button (mzone)
Game Interface
    Grid graphics (bmp)
    Grid areas (mzones)
    Player turn graphic (bmp)
    Exit hotspot (mzone)
Load Game
    List of saved games (bmp)
    Saved game name entry box (mzone)
    Load button (mzone)
    Back to main menu button (mzone)
Save Game
    List of previously saved games (bmp)
    Saved game name entry box (mzone)
    Save button (mzone)
    Back to main menu button (mzone)
    Back to game button (mzone)
Game Over
    Game over graphic (bmp)
```

Wow, did you ever imagine that tic-tac-toe had such a complicated interface outline? The interesting part is that I actually skipped over a few elements. Sure, most tic-tac-toe games don't have load and save game options, but hey, this is a production gig!

Mouse Zones and Graphics

Take a look at the beginning of the outline. Notice that I start with the title screen for the game. Most title screens let you skip past them by clicking the mouse button or hitting a key on the keyboard. In the outline I define a button that allows the player to skip the title sequence. I put the "mzone" indicator beside it to indicate a mouse zone. A mouse zone is an area of the screen that the mouse can click in to activate an event. The graphic for the title screen also has an entry, and I put a "bmp" indicator beside it to indicate a graphic element.

Next I have an entry for the main menu in the game. The main menu consists of four buttons with mouse zones: one for starting a new game, one for loading an existing game, one for saving the current game, and one for exiting the game.

The new game mouse zone takes the player to the game interface section. In the game interface area, I define a graphic for the game grid. Since the player can click on the grid to place their X or O, I define grid mouse zones. I also have a graphic entry for the current player graphic. This graphic tells the players whose turn it is. Since the player graphic is non-clickable, it has a "bmp" indicator. Lastly I have an exit button defined that lets the player exit to the main menu.

Up next in the outline is the load game interface. In this interface I define a graphic that contains the list of previously saved games. I also list the filename entry box, the load button, and the back to main menu button. There are a couple of mouse zones I left out of my outline. Can you think of them? The answer follows in a little bit.

The save game menu looks identical to the load game menu, except I have added a button to let the player return to the game. This is necessary because the player navigated to this menu from the game interface.

Lastly I list the game over interface. There are no hotspots or mouse zones, so this interface just has a single lonely game over interface.

That's it for the tic-tac-toe outline. It's pretty extensive given that tic-tac-toe is such a simple game. Can you imagine what the outline for a game from the Command & Conquer series would look like? Oh yeah, are you wondering what I left out of the load game interface? I left out graphics and mouse zones for the player to scroll through the list of saved games. What if there are more saved games than can fit on a single screen? Well, you need scroll bars and clickable areas for the buttons. You can probably think of many other elements that I left out as well. Write out your own outline now for the game of Tetris and see what you come up with. You may be surprised at the complexity of the outline.

Detailing the Interface Outline

So far, I have only shown you the most simplistic of interface design documents. How about something more challenging? There are still a few elements needed for a good interface design outline. Here is a list of some of them:

- Relationships
- Sounds
- State

Interface Outline Relationships

While tic-tac-toe is an intriguing and complicated game, it just doesn't cut the mustard for a true example; therefore, I'm starting you out with a whole new interface outline.

Check out Figure 6.1 to get the proverbial ball rolling.

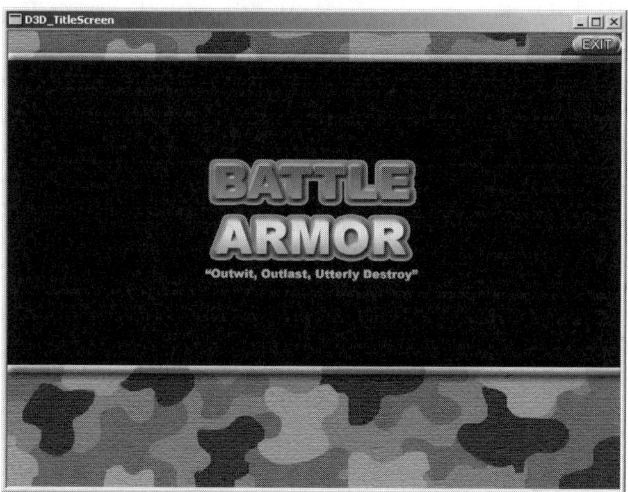

Figure 6.1: The title screen for Battle Armor.

In Figure 6.1 you see the opening screen for my game named Battle Armor. It may not look like much, but there are several elements that make up the interface. Figure 6.2 shows you the outline storyboard for the title screen.

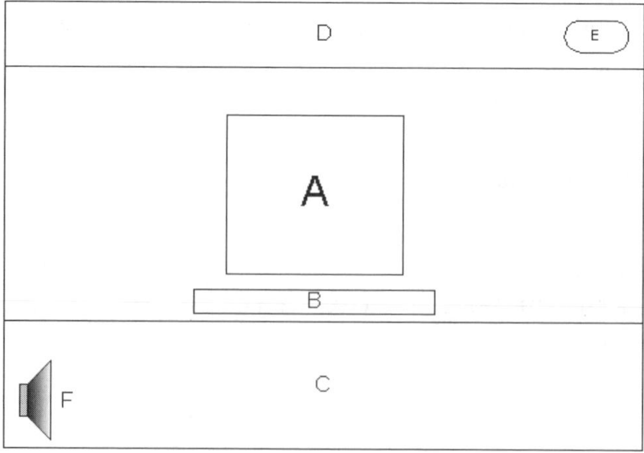

Figure 6.2: The title screen's storyboard outline.

In Figure 6.2 you see labels for each of the elements in the title screen. In all, there are six different elements. They are listed alphabetically, but the order is irrelevant. I just randomly assigned the tags. Now that you see the storyboard, here is the outline for the interface:

    1. Title Screen
        A. Title
            Graphic
            Mouse zone
                (2. Main Menu)
        B. Loading Status
            Text
        C. Bottom bar
            Graphic
        D. Top bar
            Graphic
        E. Exit
            Graphic
            Mouse zone
                (0. Desktop)
        F. Background
            Music File

The above outline looks different from the tic-tac-toe outline because the one above is the next evolution of a standard interface outline. This new one gives more detail and contains relationship information.

The first element of the interface is the interface itself, element number "1." It is labeled "Title Screen" and rightfully so, since this is the title screen. Since it is the super-heading, it maintains its position on the left margin. All of your interface screens should be listed in this manner.

Next up you have the "A" element named "Title." You have to look under the tag name to see the various properties for the element. The first property type listed is "Graphic." This tells you that the element contains a graphic. In this case the graphic is the actual title picture. The next property listed is "Mouse zone." This means the element is also a hotspot and responds to the player clicking on it. To see where the mouse click takes the user, look under the mouse zone tag. Under the tag you see "(2. Main Menu)." This tells you that the mouse click takes the user to the second major interface element named Main Menu. Guess what? You just created a relationship between the title screen and the main menu! I know it kind of snuck up on you, but it's that easy to do.

The next element listed is the "B" element that contains a sub-element of the "Text" variety. This tells you that the element is created from system text and not by the art team. This is an important distinction, as you don't want the art team to waste time creating text graphics that you can create with system fonts.

The next two elements, "C" and "D," are basic graphic elements that contain the bottom and top bars of the interface. They don't do anything special.

The "E" element is a little special, as it contains a graphic element and a mouse zone. You may be wondering where element (0. Desktop) is. This is a special tag that refers to the Windows desktop. In other words, the exit element exits the game and takes the player to the desktop. There you have it — another important interface relationship defined.

The last element, named "F," contains a music element. This tells you that music plays in the background during the title screen. The music doesn't relate to any of the other elements, so it has no other special tags. If you wanted to, you could even name the WAV or MP3 file you want played here.

Interface Sounds

Remember the mouse zone from the title screen that takes you to the main menu? The storyboard for that menu is shown in Figure 6.3.

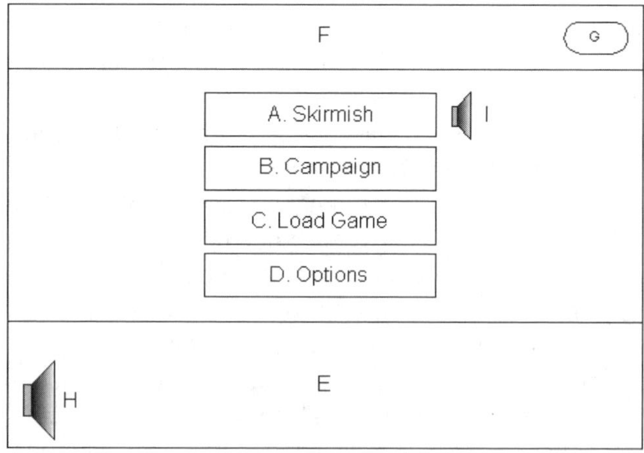

Figure 6.3: The main menu's storyboard outline.

In Figure 6.3 you see the storyboard for the main menu. There isn't anything very complicated in it — just a few graphics and mouse zones. But wait. Look at the speaker icon next to the "A" element. Why, that looks like a sound! Before jumping into that, here is the outline for the menu:

    2. Main Menu
        A. Skirmish
            Graphic
            Mouse zone
                (3. Skirmish Menu)
            Sound
                (I. Button Click)
        B. Campaign
            Graphic
            Mouse zone
                (4. Campaign Menu)
            Sound
                (I. Button Click)
        C. Load Game
            Graphic
            Mouse zone
                (5. Load Game Menu)
            Sound
                (I. Button Click)
        D. Options
            Graphic
            Mouse zone
                (6. Options Menu)
            Sound
                (I. Button Click)
        E. Bottom bar
            Graphic
        F. Top bar
            Graphic
        G. Exit
            Graphic
            Mouse zone
                (0. Desktop)
        H. Background
            Music File
        I. Button Click
            Sound File

Wow, things sure got complicated quickly with such a simple-looking menu. The first sub-element listed is for the Skirmish menu choice. Since the Skirmish element is a menu choice, it has a graphic and a mouse zone associated with it. The main change to this element is the addition of a Sound element. The Sound element tells you that the Skirmish mouse zone plays a sound file when clicked. The listing under the Sound element tells you which sound is played. In this case sound "I" is played when the zone is activated. Sound "I" is labeled "Button Click" to indicate the type of sound played. You can go as far as to list the actual WAV or MP3 filename here if you so desire.

Interface State

For the sake of an example, imagine that the player selected the Skirmish game option from the main menu. According to the outline, this action takes the player to menu #3. The outline for this menu can be seen in Figure 6.4.

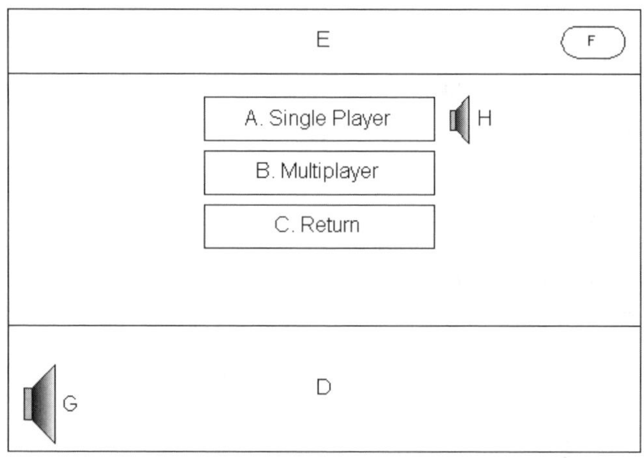

Figure 6.4: The skirmish battle's storyboard outline.

The outline for Figure 6.4 is written out like so:

```
3. Skirmish Menu
   A. Single Player
      Graphic
      Mouse zone
         (7. Single Player Skirmish Menu)
         Sound
            (I. Button Click)
   B. Multiplayer
      Graphic
      Mouse zone
         (8. Multiplayer Skirmish Menu)
         Sound
            (I. Button Click)
   C. Return to Main Menu
      Graphic
      Mouse zone
         (2. Main Menu)
         Sound
```

              (I. Button Click)
        D. Bottom bar
           Graphic
        E. Top bar
           Graphic
        F. Exit
           Graphic
           Mouse zone
                (0. Desktop)
        G. Background
           Music File
        H. Button Click
           Sound File

As you can see in the menu outline, there is nothing new for this interface. Since the player is merely navigating through the system, there is nothing special required. In this example, the player selects the Multiplayer mouse zone that takes them to interface 8. Follow along with me to that interface definition, as shown in Figure 6.5.

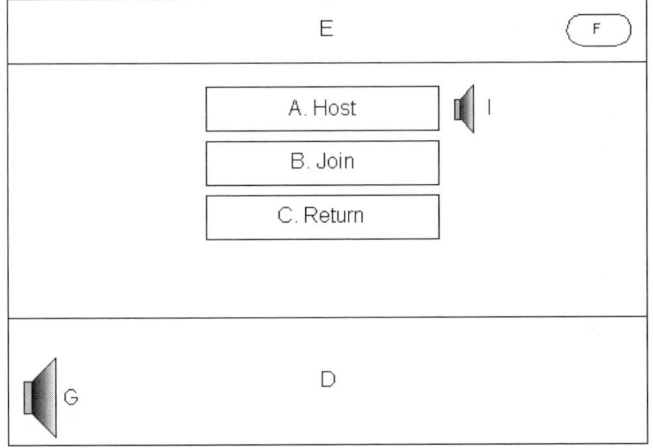

Figure 6.5: The multiplayer skirmish battle's storyboard outline.

As you can see in Figure 6.5, the outline is not very different from the previous interface. I have the same number of buttons listed; they just take the player to different menus. Once again, pretend the player selects one of the menu items, the Host game. In Figure 6.6, you can see the host game interface in action.

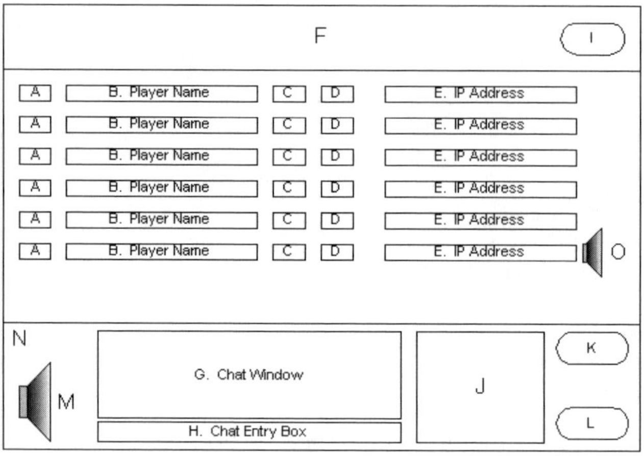

Figure 6.6: The host game storyboard outline.

The interface in Figure 6.6 is a lot more complicated than the previous interfaces by a long shot. Here is the outline listing for this little gem:

```
9. Multiplayer Skirmish Host Screen
   A. Ready Check Box
      Graphic
         (unchecked_box.bmp)
      Mouse zone
         Graphic
            (checked_box.bmp)
         Sound
            (I. Button Click)
   B. Player Name
      Text Box
         16 Characters Wide
         State Variable
            m_szPlayerName[]
   C. Player Color Box
      Graphic
         State Variable
            m_iPlayerColor[]
         (color0.bmp - color9.bmp)
      Mouse zone
         Sound
            (O. Button Click)
   D. Player Team Box
      Graphic
         State Variable
            m_iPlayerTeam[]
         (team0.bmp - team5.bmp)
```

    Mouse zone
      Sound
        (O. Button Click)
E. Player IP Address
    Text Box
      16 Characters Wide
      State Variable
        m_szPlayerIP[]
F. Top Bar
    Graphic
      (top_bar.bmp)
G. Chat Window
    Text Box
      24 Characters Wide
      State Variable
        m_szChatBuffer[]
H. Chat Entry Box
    Text Entry Box
      24 Characters Wide
      State Variable
        m_szChatSendBuffer[]
I. Exit
    Graphic
      (exitbutton.bmp)
    Mouse zone
      (0. Desktop)
J. Game Map
    Graphic
      State Variable
        m_iGameMapID
      (gamemap_0.bmp - gamemap9.bmp)
K. Choose Map Button
    Graphic
      (choosmapbutton.bmp)
    Mouse zone
      (9. Choose Map Menu)
      Sound
        (O. Button Click)
L. Start Game Button
    Graphic
      (startbutton.bmp)
    Mouse zone
      (10. Multiplayer Skirmish Game-Play)
      Sound
        (O. Button Click)
M. Background
    Music File

<pre>
        N. Bottom Bar
           Graphic
              (bottom_bar.bmp)
        O. Button Click
           Sound File
</pre>

Even the starting element is different from previous examples. The first difference that you should notice is the inclusion of the actual graphic filename associated with the element. This is a good item to keep track of so that your art team names files that you can relate to the outline. The next difference is the inclusion of a graphic entry under the mouse zone entry. I do this to indicate that a mouse click in the zone activates a new graphic. In this case, the empty box turns into a checked box and vice versa.

Next up is the Player Name element. This one contains a new element type called Text Box. This indicates that the element is made up of dynamic-font driven text. The attribute of the element tells you that the text box contains no more than 16 characters. This is important to keep track of so that your art team gives enough room for you to put the player name variable on-screen. Also under the Player Name element you may notice the new tag named State Variable. This indicates that the element's appearance is dependent on an internal variable. In this case, the variable is the player name array and called `m_szPlayerName[]`. This is a useful thing to list so that you can keep track of the variables needed to handle your interface.

The next element is named Player Color Box, and it contains the usual suspects, element type wise. The only real difference is the name of the graphic. I list a range under the graphic name to indicate multiple graphics for the element. There is also a state variable associated with the graphic. This tells you that the graphic changes along with the state variable.

Skip on down to element "H" to see another new element type. It contains a Text Entry Box. This indicates that the player can enter text in the box. The state variable listed under the element shows you the variable name that holds the input text.

The rest of the elements are of types that I have covered already, so let's move on.

Storyboarding the Interface

So far, you have learned how to write the outline for your interface, but how about a nice graphical outline? The basis of a storyboard is a series of images drawn out in sequence that represent the flow of a process.

Since navigating an interface is a process flow in itself, storyboarding the process is a natural part of the design. Check out Figure 6.7 to see the storyboard for the interface as defined so far.

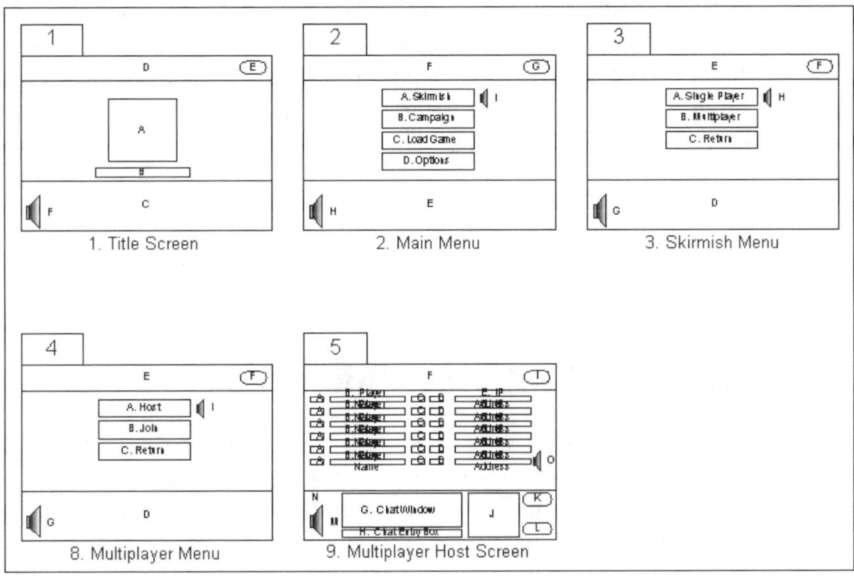

Figure 6.7: The storyboard for the Battle Armor interface.

Notice how there are five rectangles in the figure. Each rectangle is a miniaturized version of the outlines I previously covered. Under each rectangle is the name of the interface. This helps to tie your written outline to the visual storyboard.

On top of each rectangle is a number that represents the interface positions in sequence. You probably noticed by now that the sequence number does not match the interface numbering system. This is because interface navigation isn't always linear. Players can move around from one menu to the next without having to go through each interface.

The storyboard in Figure 6.7 does not represent the entire storyboard for the project. It only shows one possible flow that the user can take through the system. You need to create a new storyboard for iterations of menu navigation important in the game. You do end up with lots of storyboards, but it is important so that you don't make long-term mistakes early in the design process.

Interface Usability

The usability of your game interface is by far the most important item in releasing a quality product. If players don't like the interface, they won't play your game. It really is as simple as that. I'm sure you have played games in the past that had bad interfaces. I also bet you didn't play them for very long. Keep a few key questions in mind when designing your interface:

- Does the user have to click many times to accomplish common tasks?

- Does the game have many layers of sub-menus?

- Is the interface consistent throughout the game?

Mouse Clicks and Interface Interaction

The first key question deals with how many times the user has to click to accomplish a common task. Don't get hung up on the term "click." It really pertains to any input required by the user regardless if it is via mouse, keyboard, joystick, or touch screen.

Most games have common tasks that the user performs multiple times during the course of playing. In Warcraft III, for instance, you select units on a frequent basis. This is accomplished with a single left mouse click. You can also select many units at once by dragging a selection square on the map to encompass the units you want selected. Now imagine if the ability to select multiple units at once was removed. The user would have to select each unit desired one at a time until the entire group was active. This would be a very big pain in the rear and would result in way too many mouse clicks for a seemingly simple operation.

One method I use to monitor the first question is to set up a mouse click (or input instance) counter in my program. I count the number of times the user enters a key, presses the mouse button, or moves the joystick. I save this count to a text file when the game is over. I then play around with adjusting the interface until the number of counts goes down. As long as the user is clicking less, I know I am on the right track. The trick is to keep doing this throughout the life of your game project. Always strive for the fewest input entries as possible.

Menu Navigation Complexity

The next question deals with the complexity of your interface navigation. If the player has to navigate dozens of layers of menus, they are going to get mentally exhausted. You are designing a game after all, not a word processor!

Luckily this one is fairly simple to avoid. Design the menu the way you envision it and then count how many layers there are between the player and a particular menu option. If a menu option takes more than three menus to select, the program is probably too complicated. Of course, there are exceptions to every rule, but the rule of three is generally a good one to follow.

Interface Consistency

Have you ever played a game where the interface changed completely on every single screen? Did it annoy you? I know it would annoy me to no end. This forms the last key question dealing with interface consistency. I have no idea why, but some designers think it is cool to make the player learn a whole new interface for every menu in their game. Believe me, this is not fun for most players.

So, how do you make your interface consistent? One way is to keep the graphic changes to a minimum when switching menus. You will see a couple of example menu navigation programs later in this chapter. When you get to them, try to take notice of how the menus are anchored in that they do not change a lot graphically. By keeping the graphic changes to a minimum, you are giving the player a graphical and psychological anchor to the interface. Most users don't know why, but interfaces that follow this rule just seem easier to use. Follow this rule and your game will benefit.

There are tons of other rules and suggestions for interface usability, but I really can't get into them here. Heck, there are entire books devoted to the subject. I suggest that you search your favorite book retailer for some. It is a worthwhile step to good game design.

2D Rendering in 3D

Now that you understand everything from defining interface needs to making your interface usable, you need to know how to actually display the interface! Fear not — in this section, I cover how to render interface graphics. Since all new graphics cards are based on 3D accelerated rendering, the following methods use 3D graphics to render the interface. The flip side to 3D rendering is that you don't always want to render objects with depth. Certain interface elements, such as text, look better when rendered in 2D. Because of these two needs, let me show you how to render 3D graphics that look 2D. In this section I cover how to render 3D textured geometry as 2D graphics.

Check out Figure 6.8 and buckle your chinstrap; it's time for some heavy coding.

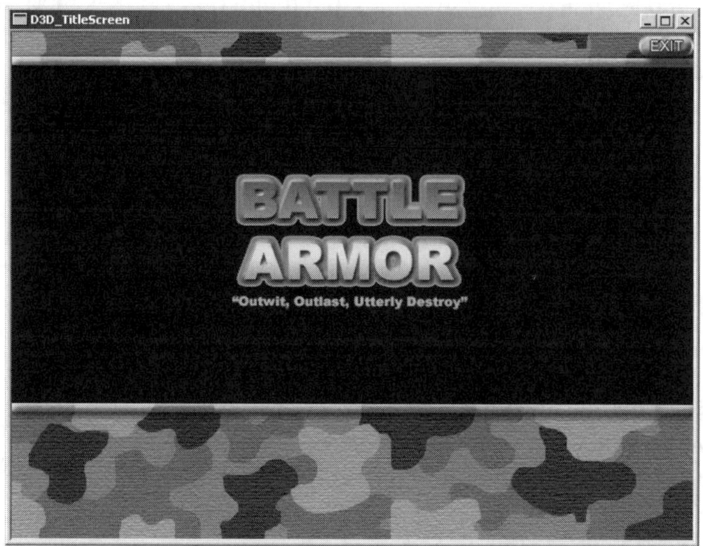

Figure 6.8: Screen shot of the TitleScreen program.

In Figure 6.8, you see the output from the D3D_TitleScreen program. This program displays a simple-looking 2D title screen for an imaginary game called Battle Armor. (Someday I may get the time to actually finish Battle Armor, but until then, pretend it is a real game.) Go ahead and load up the project in Visual C++ now so you can follow along.

D3D_TitleScreen Project Architecture

The project contains two unique files, main.cpp and main.h. The rest of the files included in the project are part of Microsoft's DirectX 9.0 SDK. They are as follows: d3dfont.cpp, d3dutil.cpp, and dxutil.cpp. Does the list seem smaller than usual? It is because this example does not use the DirectX framework as provided by Microsoft. This project uses only a few of the helper files for operations unrelated to the framework.

The program requires the following library files: d3d9.lib, dxguid.lib, d3dx9dt.lib, d3dxof.lib, comctl32.lib, and winmm.lib.

The Main.h Header File

There is only one header file to concern you with — the main.h header
file. In this header file I accomplish the following:

■ Set up the global Direct3D variables

■ Set up the custom vertex structure

■ Set up miscellaneous global variables

■ Define the function prototypes

Key Direct3D Data Types

The first few lines of code set up a few key DirectX variables required for
the program to operate. Here is the code for this:

```
LPDIRECT3D9              g_pD3D          = NULL;
LPDIRECT3DDEVICE9        g_pd3dDevice    = NULL;
LPDIRECT3DVERTEXBUFFER9 g_pVBInterface   = NULL;
LPDIRECT3DTEXTURE9       g_pTexture[32];
```

The first variable, of type LPDIRECT3D9, is named g_pD3D. It is the pointer
for the Direct3D interface. Without the Direct3D interface, the program
cannot perform 3D operations on the video hardware. This is an important piece of the puzzle, so make sure you remember it.

The next variable declared is of type LPDIRECT3DDEVICE9 and named
g_pd3dDevice. This pointer is used to point to the rendering device.
Without a rendering device, your programs look pretty darn boring. This
is the variable you use to set up the video display, set up rendering methods, and render 3D graphics. Considering how much it does, you better
remember this one as well.

The next variable, g_pVBInterface, is of type LPDIRECT3DVERTEX-
BUFFER9. It is used to hold the data for the 3D geometry in this example.
Vertex buffers hold vertices, which are the basic building blocks of 3D
objects. You will learn more about these later on in this chapter.

Lastly, you have an array of textures named g_pTexture[]. This
array holds 32 elements of type LPDIRECT3DTEXTURE9. These are nothing
more than placeholders for the images required in this example. Textures
are pretty easy to use thanks to the DirectX utility libraries. They are
very important, so pay attention to these as well. Maybe you are wondering why I create an array of 32 textures. There is no real reason. The
program only uses seven of the elements, but it's always better to be
safe than sorry!

Now that you are past the important Direct3D variables, it is time for
some miscellaneous globals. The following code is next in the program:

```
int g_iXOffset = 0;
int g_iYOffset = 0;
int g_iWindowWidth = 640;
int g_iWindowHeight = 480;
```

The first two integers listed, g_iXOffset and g_iYOffset, are used to store the client visible area's offsets as they relate to the window position. I go into this later in the main.cpp coverage. For now, accept it as it is, just like death and taxes.

The next two integers, g_iWindowWidth and g_iWindowHeight, store and set the size of the window to display the program graphics in. You can change this if you wish to have a smaller or larger display. Wait until later to do so though. You should at least see the program operate as I intend it to.

Flexible Vertex Format (FVF) Data Structures

Next up is the custom vertex format data structure. This data structure declares the format of the geometry used for the 3D rendering in the example. The code for it is as follows:

```
struct CUSTOMVERTEX

{
    D3DXVECTOR3 position;   // The position
    D3DXVECTOR3 vecNorm;    // The normal
    FLOAT       tu, tv;     // The texture coordinates
    FLOAT       tu2, tv2;   // The texture coordinates
};
#define D3DFVF_CUSTOMVERTEX (D3DFVF_XYZ|D3DFVF_NORMAL|D3DFVF_TEX2)
```

DirectX uses vertex data structures to define the geometry for rendering 3D objects. Without vertex data structures, you have nothing to render. This is a very important aspect of DirectX and is the cornerstone of rendering. As you can see in the vertex format that I have defined, there are a few key elements to it, such as position, normal, and texture coordinate information.

Positional Data

The position information tells the system where in 3D space the vertex lives. This obviously is important, as position is everything when it comes to geometric data. Take a simple triangle. A triangle is comprised of three points, each point with a location in space. The location for the points could look something like the following:

```
(0,0,0) Point 1
(0,10,0) Point 2
(10,0,0) Point 3
```

Take a look at Figure 6.9 to see the triangle with its point positions:

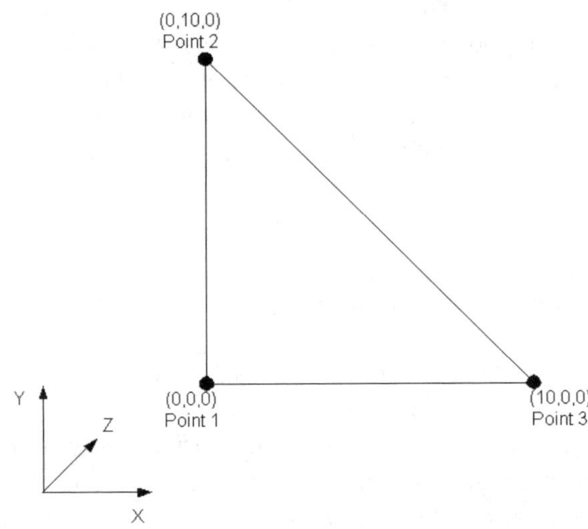

Figure 6.9: Three points in 3D space make up a triangle.

As you can see in Figure 6.9, the position of each vertex sets how the geometry is positioned in 3D space. If the positions change, the geometry changes as well when rendered. This obviously is very important to 3D rendering. I use the `D3DXVECTOR3` data type to store the position data since it has elements for x, y, and z coordinate data.

Normal Data

Next up I have data declared to hold the face normal information. Normals in 3D rendering set the direction in which a face points. This data is required for 3D lighting, as the lighting hardware must know how to display light on the face. Normal data is stored just like positional data, as a set of three coordinates. For this reason, I use the `D3DXVECTOR3` data type again. To see a normal in action, check out Figure 6.10.

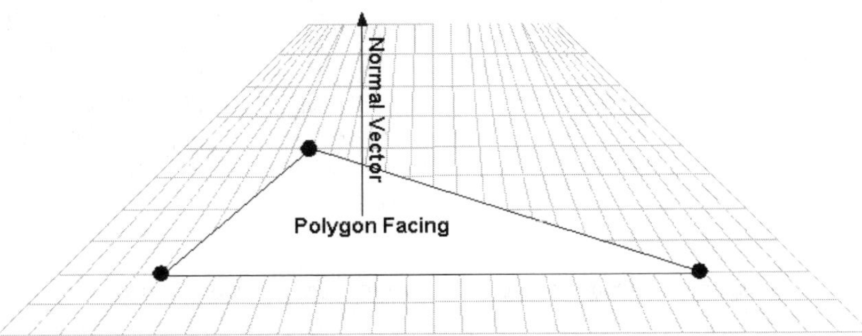

Figure 6.10: Normal data for the 3D triangle.

Notice in Figure 6.10 how the normal vector sits at a 90-degree angle to the geometry face. This illustrates how the normal points away from the face of the triangle. If you want the triangle to face the opposite direction, you merely change the vector to point the other way. This data is more relevant when you perform smooth shading as opposed to flat shading. Since smooth shading bases its rendering on normal data, it is quite important.

Texture Data

The next couple of data types in the vertex structure contain texture coordinate information for the 3D geometry. Without texture coordinates, the system cannot render textures. This is very important considering this program example displays textures and not just shaded geometry.

Direct3D represents texture coordinate information as coordinates on the Cartesian plane. In other words, a texture coordinate contains two numbers, one for x and one for y. The main difference with texture coordinates is that the numbers are limited in range. Texture coordinates range from 0.0 to 1.0. This is because texture coordinate data is relative to the actual texture image data. Take a texture that is 16 pixels wide by 16 pixels high. The texture coordinate of (0.5,0.5) sits dead center in the texture at (8,8). The same set of texture coordinates in a 32 x 32 pixel texture sit dead center at (16,16). See Figure 6.11 to see this concept illustrated.

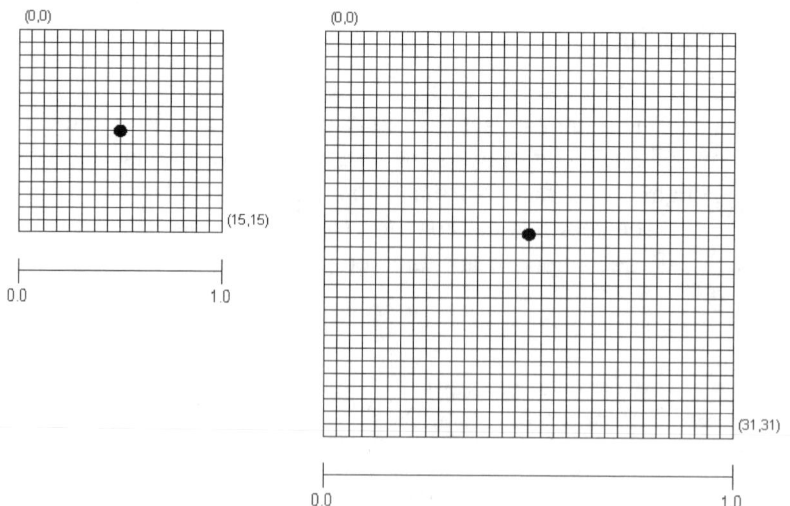

Figure 6.11: Texture coordinates are relative to texture image data.

In Figure 6.11, you see two grids. The grid on the left illustrates the texture that is 16 pixels wide and 16 pixels high. The grid on the right illustrates the texture that is 32 pixels wide and 32 pixels high. Below each grid you see the texture coordinate range scale of 0.0 to 1.0. Since the scale is relative to the size of the texture, it scales with the size of the texture. The scale on the right is twice the size of the scale on the left, yet it still maintains a range of 0.0 to 1.0. I know this sounds obvious, but it is important for understanding texture coordinates.

Next to each grid I also illustrate the pixel ranges for each grid. The small grid starts at (0,0) and goes to (15,15). The larger texture starts at (0,0) and extends to (31,31). There is nothing special here; the numbers are only meant to show the pixel coordinates.

In the center of each grid I have placed a marker for texture coordinate (0.5,0.5). This shows you how the same texture coordinate is located in two completely different places, depending on the size of the texture. Since the texture coordinate scales, it moves depending on the texture it targets.

Vertex Format Definition

Now that the vertex data structure is defined, it is time to set up the vertex definition for use later. The `#define` code sets up the flags for the vertex format. This set of flags tells the rendering system what data to expect in the vertex data structure. You have to be very careful and list the flags in the order the data appears in the structure.

For this program, I use three flags: `D3DFVF_XYZ`, `D3DFVF_NORMAL`, and `D3DFVF_TEX2`. The `D3DFVF_XYZ` flag indicates position data. The `D3DFVF_NORMAL` flag indicates normal data. The `D3DFVF_TEX2` flag indicates there are two sets of texture coordinate data. If you need more information on the various flags available, refer to the DirectX documentation.

The Function Prototypes

You are done with the flexible vertex format data structure for now. The next block of code sets up the function prototypes for the example program. It is as follows:

```
void vDrawInterfaceObject(int iXPos, int iYPos, float fXSize, float fYSize,
                          int iTexture);
void vInitInterfaceObjects(void);
LRESULT WINAPI fnMessageProcessor(HWND hWnd, UINT msg, WPARAM wParam, LPARAM lParam);
HRESULT InitD3D(HWND hWnd);
void vRender(void);
void vCleanup(void);
```

I cover the use of each function listed above later in this chapter.

The Main.cpp Program File

The next unique file, main.cpp, contains the meat of the example program. It follows the usual program layout I explained in Chapter 2.

The WinMain() Function

The first function of interest is `WinMain()`. As with all Windows programs, it is the main entry point into the code. Here is the listing for it:

```
int WINAPI WinMain(HINSTANCE hInstance, HINSTANCE hPrevInstance, PSTR szCmdLine,
                   int iCmdShow)
{
    HWND           hWnd;
    MSG            msg;
    WNDCLASSEX     wndclass;
    RECT           rcWindowClient;
    // Set up window class
    wndclass.cbSize        = sizeof(wndclass);
    wndclass.style         = CS_HREDRAW | CS_VREDRAW;
    wndclass.lpfnWndProc   = fnMessageProcessor;
    wndclass.cbClsExtra    = 0;
    wndclass.cbWndExtra    = 0;
    wndclass.hInstance     = hInstance;
    wndclass.hIcon         = LoadIcon(NULL, IDI_APPLICATION);
    wndclass.hCursor       = LoadCursor(NULL, IDC_ARROW);
    wndclass.hbrBackground = (HBRUSH) GetStockObject (WHITE_BRUSH);
    wndclass.lpszMenuName  = NULL;
    wndclass.lpszClassName = "Title Demo";
    wndclass.hIconSm       = LoadIcon(NULL, IDI_APPLICATION);
    // Register the window class
    if(RegisterClassEx(&wndclass) == NUL)  {
        // The program failed, exit
        exit(1);
    }
    // Create the window
    hWnd = CreateWindowEx(WS_EX_OVERLAPPEDWINDOW,
                "Title Demo", "D3D_TitleScreen",
                WS_OVERLAPPEDWINDOW, 0, 0,
                g_iWindowWidth, g_iWindowHeight,
                NULL,  NULL,  hInstance, NULL);
    // Display the window
    ShowWindow(hWnd, iCmdShow);
    // Figure out the client work area
    GetClientRect(hWnd, &rcWindowClient);
    // Calculate the rendering offsets based on the client size
    g_iXOffset = (g_iWindowWidth-(rcWindowClient.right-rcWindowClient.left));
    g_iYOffset = (g_iWindowHeight-(rcWindowClient.bottom-rcWindowClient.top));
    // Resize the window to be truly the resolution desired
    SetWindowPos(hWnd, NULL, 0, 0,
            g_iWindowWidth + g_iXOffset,  // Width
            g_iWindowHeight + g_iYOffset, // Height
            NULL);
    // Clear out message structure
```

```
ZeroMemory(&msg, sizeof(msg));
// Initialize Direct3D
   if(SUCCEEDED(InitD3D(hWnd))) {
       // Initialize the virtual buffer for the display quad
       vInitInterfaceObjects();
       // Enter the message loop
       while(msg.message!=WM_QUIT) {
       if(PeekMessage(&msg, NULL, 0U, 0U, PM_REMOVE)) {
           TranslateMessage(&msg);
           DispatchMessage(&msg);
       }
       else {
           // Render the scene
           vRender();
       }
     }
   }
// Clean up everything and exit the app
vCleanup();
UnregisterClass("Title Demo Example", wndclass.hInstance);
return 0;
}
```

To help sort out the non-Direct3D code from the "standard" Windows code, see Figure 6.12.

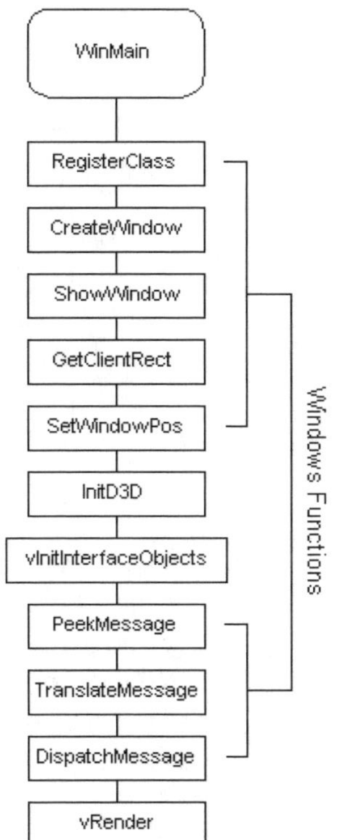

Figure 6.12: Function layout for the WinMain() function.

In Figure 6.12 you see the list of functions I use in `WinMain()`. They appear in the order in which they are executed. Notice that most of the calls are not Direct3D specific. This is due to the fact that `WinMain()` contains mostly setup code and not a lot of execution or rendering code.

The first area of interest in the code is the call to `GetClientRect()`. You may wonder why I have that listed. To better understand, let me explain something about programs written in windowed mode.

Calculating Client Display Offsets

You may remember how the `CreateWindowEx()` function has parameters for the size of the window to create. These parameters allow you to set the dimensions of your window. The problem with this is that the dimensions don't account for the title bar. The effect is that you end up with less rendering space than anticipated when you have a title bar on your application. For an example, look at Figure 6.13.

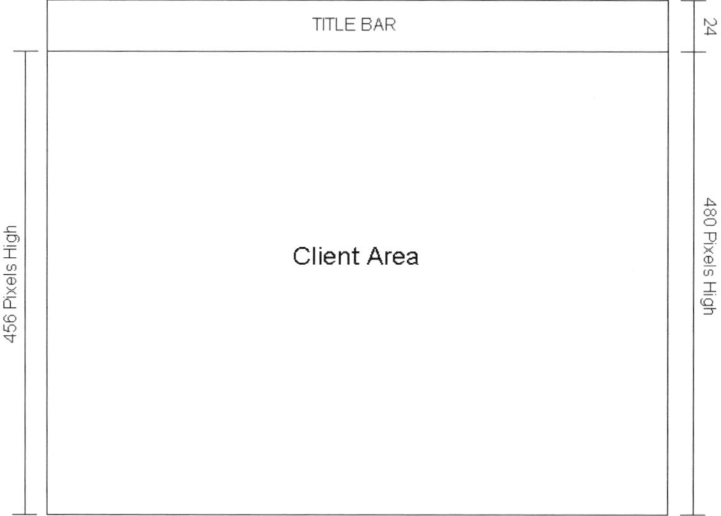

Figure 6.13: A new window with the dimensions of 640 x 480.

In Figure 6.13 I create a window with the dimensions set at 640 pixels wide by 480 pixels high. Notice that the title bar takes up 24 pixels in height. This results in a visible rendering area of only 456 pixels, which presents a major problem for the art team as well as you, the programmer. Since all of your calculations for GUI rendering are based on screen dimensions, this problem has to be resolved. Enter stage right, the `GetClientRect()` function.

The `GetClientRect()` function tells you the actual size of the visible rendering area. Armed with the size of the client rendering area, you adjust the window dimensions to account for the discrepancy. This is done by first taking the desired window dimensions minus the size of the client returned with `GetClientRect()`. Once you have these two numbers, you resize the window to be the desired size plus the numbers from the first calculation. The following formula does the trick:

New Window X-Size = (Desired X-Size) +((Desired X-Size) – (Client X-Size))
New Window Y-Size = (Desired Y-Size) +((Desired Y-Size) – (Client Y-Size))

In the example in Figure 6.13, the formula works out like so:

New Window X-Size = 640 + (640 – 640)
New Window Y-Size = 480 + (480 – 456)

The window ends up being 640 pixels wide by 504 pixels high. The window now has enough rendering area for the client to perform 640 x 480 renderings. Figure 6.14 shows the new window with its dimensions.

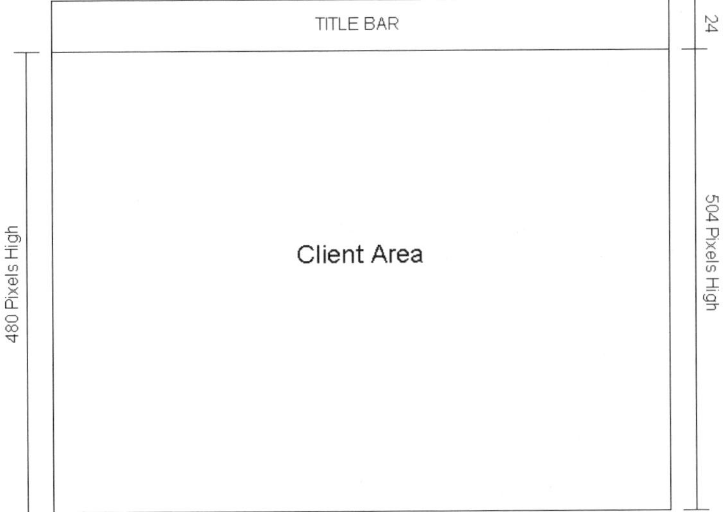

Figure 6.14: The resized window with the dimensions of 640 x 504.

You resize the window with the `SetWindowPos()` function. It allows you to change the format of the window as well as the size and position. You only need to change the size for now.

Move on down the code until you see the `InitD3D()` function. Follow it to the implementation code once you see it.

The InitD3D() Function

The InitD3D() function handles the arduous task of creating the Direct3D rendering environment. The code for this example program happens to be extremely simple compared to a full-blown Direct3D initialization routine. For one thing, I am not bothering to enumerate the display adapters and devices. The code simply sets up the environment and hopes for the best. You may have to play around with it a bit if your screen does not initialize. It should work though, as the basis of the initialization is from the DirectX SDK. Enough of the warning; here is the code for the function:

```
HRESULT InitD3D(HWND hWnd)
{
    D3DPRESENT_PARAMETERS   d3dpp;
    D3DXMATRIX              matproj, matview;
    D3DDISPLAYMODE          d3ddm;

    // Create the D3D object
    if(NULL == (g_pD3D = Direct3DCreate9(D3D_SDK_VERSION)))
        return E_FAIL;

    // Get the current desktop display mode, so we can set up a back
    // buffer of the same format
    if(FAILED(g_pD3D->GetAdapterDisplayMode(
        D3DADAPTER_DEFAULT, &d3ddm)))
    return E_FAIL;

    // Set up the back buffer and swap format
    ZeroMemory(&d3dpp, sizeof(d3dpp));
    d3dpp.Windowed               = TRUE;
    d3dpp.SwapEffect             = D3DSWAPEFFECT_DISCARD;
    d3dpp.BackBufferFormat       = d3ddm.Format;
    d3dpp.EnableAutoDepthStencil = FALSE;

    // Create the D3DDevice
    if(FAILED(g_pD3D->CreateDevice(D3DADAPTER_DEFAULT,
                DS3DDEVTYPE_HAL, hWnd,
                3DCREATE_HARDWARE_VERTEXPROCESSING,
                &d3dpp, &g_pd3dDevice)))
    {
        return E_FAIL;
    }

    // Set up 2D view and rendering states
    D3DXMatrixIdentity(&matview);
    g_pd3dDevice->SetTransform(D3DTS_VIEW, &matview);

    // Set up orthographic rendering, i.e., 2D in 3D
    D3DXMatrixOrthoLH(&matproj, (float)g_iWindowWidth, (float)g_iWindowHeight, 0, 1);
    // Set up the projection matrix
    g_pd3dDevice->SetTransform(D3DTS_PROJECTION, &matproj);
    // Turn off culling
```

```
g_pd3dDevice->SetRenderState(D3DRS_CULLMODE, D3DCULL_NONE);
// Turn off lighting
g_pd3dDevice->SetRenderState(D3DRS_LIGHTING, FALSE);
// Turn off z-buffer
g_pd3dDevice->SetRenderState(D3DRS_ZENABLE, FALSE);
g_pd3dDevice->SetRenderState(D3DRS_ZWRITEENABLE, FALSE);

    return S_OK;
}
```

Check out Figure 6.15 to see the function layout for the code.

One interesting note about the figure is that there is only one top-level function called — `Direct3DCreate9()`. Once it is called, the rest of the functions belong to the Direct3D object pointer named g_pD3D. It handles the rest of the 3D calls executed during the program's life cycle.

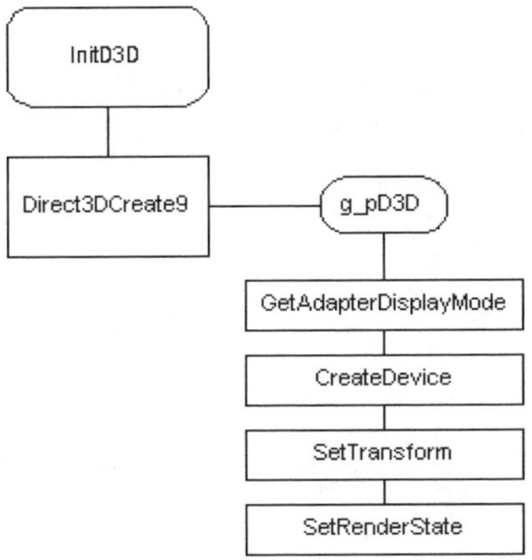

Figure 6.15: The function layout for the InitD3D() function.

Creating the Direct3D Object

The `Direct3DCreate9()` function is the most important to Direct3D, as nothing else can happen without it. This is the first function you call to set up your rendering environment. The whole point of the function is to create an `IDirect3D9` object. Here is the prototype for it:

```
IDirect3D9 *Direct3DCreate9(
    UINT SDKVersion
);
```

You have to love the simplicity of it. The one and only parameter is an unsigned integer representing the version of the DirectX SDK that you are using. You should always use the value of `D3D_SDK_VERSION` for the parameter.

The parameter is a sanity check for the code to handle. Basically, it checks the version passed into it versus the version stored in the DirectX header files. If the versions do not match, the code knows something is fishy in DirectX installation land. Don't worry about this too much; it's best just to leave it alone and use the recommended value.

Note If you add new adapters or display devices to your system after the call to `Direct3DCreate9()`, the devices will not show up in the `IDirect3D9` object. You have to recreate the object for the new devices to enumerate.

Setting Up the Display Parameters

Now that you have the 3D interface object all ready to go, you need to set up the display parameters. The first step in doing so for this example is to find out the back buffer format for rendering. To refresh your memory on what a display buffer is, see Figure 6.16.

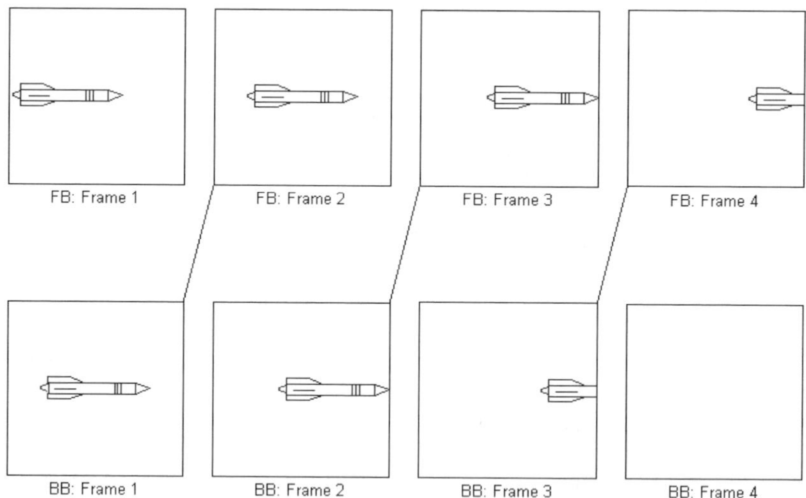

Figure 6.16: Double buffering in action.

Figure 6.16 shows two buffers — a front buffer and a back buffer. The buffers contain graphical data in pixel format. The front buffer contains the active image on the user's screen, and the back buffer contains the next image to display. When it is time to display the next image in line, the back buffer can be swapped with the front buffer or copied to the front buffer. This results in the new image being displayed on the screen.

As you can see in Figure 6.16, the back buffer is always one frame ahead of the front buffer in terms of the animation sequence. The missile is moving from the left side of the screen to the right in the animation. Since the back buffer is ahead a frame, the missile is always farther to the left in the front buffer than it is in the back buffer. As the animation frames advance, the back buffer is copied to the front buffer for display.

You use double buffering to provide smooth animation in your game. Without double (or triple) buffering, your graphics would look out of sync and waver during display. Double buffering does incur a speed decrease in frame rate, but it is worth it for image clarity.

Back to setting the back buffer. Since the front buffer is created with the window, the back buffer needs to be set up in an identical fashion. To do this, you retrieve the current display mode of the window and store its format. This is accomplished with the `GetAdapterDisplayMode()` function. The `GetAdapterDisplayMode()` function has the following prototype:

```
HRESULT GetAdapterDisplayMode(
    UINT Adapter,
    D3DDISPLAYMODE *pMode
);
```

This function has two parameters, `Adapter` and `pMode`. The `Adapter` parameter expects the number of the display adapter to utilize. Since computers can have more than one display adapter, this is an important parameter. The easiest thing to do for single-monitor support is to set this to `D3DADAPTER_DEFAULT`. `D3DADAPTER_DEFAULT` tells the system to use the primary display device, which happens to be the only display device on single monitor systems.

The second parameter, `pMode`, is a bit more difficult, as it takes a pointer to a `D3DDISPLAYMODE` data structure. Once this function is executed, the data structure holds the information about the current display mode. The question of the day is "What does the `D3DDISPLAYMODE` data structure look like?" Here is your answer:

```
typedef struct _D3DDISPLAYMODE {
    UINT Width;
    UINT Height;
    UINT RefreshRate;
    D3DFORMAT Format;
} D3DDISPLAYMODE;
```

The first data member, `Width`, describes the width of the display adapter.

The second data member, `Height`, describes the height of the display adapter.

The third member, `RefreshRate`, describes the refresh rate of the display adapter. A value of 0 here indicates the adapter default value.

The fourth value, Format, is quite a bit more complicated when compared to the other values. It is a D3DFORMAT enumeration data structure that can contain several values. There are too many to list here, so I suggest you consult the DirectX SDK documentation for a list of values.

Now that you have the back buffer format, it is time to set up the display parameter structure. The next block of code sets up the D3DPRESENT_PARAMETERS data structure. This structure sets up the various display parameters needed to initialize the rendering system. Here is the structure:

```
typedef struct _D3DPRESENT_PARAMETERS_ {
    UINT BackBufferWidth;
    UINT BackBufferHeight;
    D3DFORMAT BackBufferFormat;
    UINT BackBufferCount;
    D3DMULTISAMPLE_TYPE MultiSampleType;
    DWORD MultiSampleQuality;
    D3DSWAPEFFECT SwapEffect;
    HWND hDeviceWindow;
    BOOL Windowed;
    BOOL EnableAutoDepthStencil;
    D3DFORMAT AutoDepthStencilFormat;
    DWORD Flags;
    UINT FullScreen_RefreshRateInHz;
    UINT PresentationInterval;
} D3DPRESENT_PARAMETERS;
```

The first two data members, BackBufferWidth and BackBufferHeight, are straightforward; they simply store the dimensions of the buffer.

The next member, BackBufferFormat, contains the display format that the back buffer uses. This is where you use the format that you retrieved earlier in the GetAdapterDisplayMode() function.

Next up, you have the multisample type stored in the MultiSampleType data member. This member is of the D3DMULTISAMPLE_TYPE data type. Uh oh — it's another enumerated data type! Refer to Table 6.1 for the enumerations and their purpose in this new data type.

Table 6.1: Multisample types

Value	Meaning
D3DMULTISAMPLE_NONE	No multisampling
D3DMULTISAMPLE_NONMASKABLE	Uses the quality value
D3DMULTISAMPLE_2_SAMPLES	2 samples available
D3DMULTISAMPLE_3_SAMPLES	3 samples available
D3DMULTISAMPLE_4_SAMPLES	4 samples available
D3DMULTISAMPLE_5_SAMPLES	5 samples available
D3DMULTISAMPLE_6_SAMPLES	6 samples available
D3DMULTISAMPLE_7_SAMPLES	7 samples available

Value	Meaning
D3DMULTISAMPLE_8_SAMPLES	8 samples available
D3DMULTISAMPLE_9_SAMPLES	9 samples available
D3DMULTISAMPLE_10_SAMPLES	10 samples available
D3DMULTISAMPLE_11_SAMPLES	11 samples available
D3DMULTISAMPLE_12_SAMPLES	12 samples available
D3DMULTISAMPLE_13_SAMPLES	13 samples available
D3DMULTISAMPLE_14_SAMPLES	14 samples available
D3DMULTISAMPLE_15_SAMPLES	15 samples available
D3DMULTISAMPLE_16_SAMPLES	16 samples available
D3DMULTISAMPLE_FORCE_DWORD	Unused

Multisampling is required for rendering with anti-aliasing turned on. Not sure what anti-aliasing is? Turn to Figure 6.17 to see it in action.

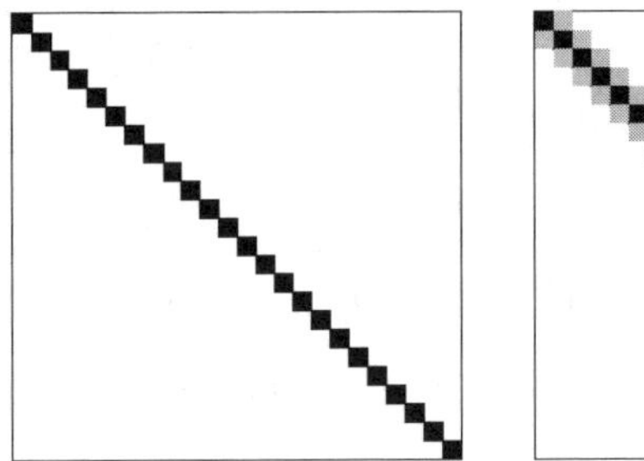

Figure 6.17: Anti-aliasing illustrated.

In Figure 6.17 you see two lines. The one on the left has aliased edges. The one on the right has anti-aliased edges. Notice how the one on the right has a smooth appearance and the one on the left is more jagged looking. This is due to the lighter tones of gray used on line edges. If you have a card that supports anti-aliasing, you can turn it on for smoother graphics in games that support it. If not, maybe you should upgrade your card.

Note   Be sure to note that multisampling is only valid when the swap chain is set to `D3DSWAPEFFECT_DISCARD`.

Back to the present parameters. The next parameter in the list is called `MultiSampleQuality` and is a `DWORD`. As you can probably guess, this parameter sets the quality of the multisampling. It can hold a value between zero and the highest level minus one than the level returned by a call to the `IDirect3D9::CheckDeviceMultiSampleType()` function.

The SwapEffect parameter comes next. This parameter tells the rendering system how display buffers are swapped during rendering. This parameter is of the D3DSWAPEFFECT data enumeration type. You can see the enumerated values and their meanings in Table 6.2.

Table 6.2: Swap effects

Value	Meaning
D3DSWAPEFFECT_DISCARD	Allows the display driver to select the most efficient swap method. This method is usually faster than other swap methods. The only problem with this method is that it does not guarantee the preservation of back buffers and their contents. You cannot rely on the contents of a back buffer if you use this method. If you use any multisample types other than D3DMULTISAMPLE_NONE, you must use this swap method.
D3DSWAPEFFECT_FLIP	Uses a round-robin scheme for rendering buffers. Buffers are rotated in a circular queue for rendering. This method allows smooth rendering if the presentation interval is not set to D3DPRESENT_INTERVAL_IMMEDIATE.
D3DSWAPEFFECT_COPY	This method can only be used if there is only one back buffer. This method also guarantees a stable back buffer image. The downside to this method is that in windowed mode, your graphics may tear. This is due to the image displaying during the vertical retrace of the monitor. Do not use this method if you are in windowed mode and want smooth graphics.
D3DSWAPEFFECT_FORCE_ DWORD	Unused.

The next data member for the presentation parameters data structure is named hDeviceWindow. This is a handle to the window used for rendering in windowed modes. In full-screen modes, this handle points to the topmost window.

The next data member, Windowed, sets whether or not the display is windowed or runs in full-screen mode. Set this to TRUE for windowed mode and FALSE for full-screen rendering.

Next up you have the EnableAutoDepthStencil flag. This flag tells the rendering system whether or not to manage the depth buffers. If you set it to TRUE, Direct3D manages depth buffers for the program.

The next member, named AutoDepthStencilFormat, sets the format of the depth buffer to use. This member is only used when EnableAuto-DepthStencil is set to TRUE. Make sure you set a valid depth buffer format if you use auto depth setup.

The next data member in line is ambiguously named Flags. Don't you just love straightforward names like this? The values for it are listed in Table 6.3.

Table 6.3: Display parameter flags

Value	Meaning
D3DPRESENTFLAG_LOCKABLE_BACKBUFFER	Gives the application the ability to lock the back buffers.
D3DPRESENTFLAG_DISCARD_DEPTHSTENCIL	Tells the system to discard the z-buffer after each presentation of the buffer data. This can increase performance if the graphics driver supports it.
D3DPRESENTFLAG_DEVICECLIP	Clips the rendering area in windowed-mode rendering. This only works in Windows 2000 and Windows XP.
D3DPRESENTFLAG_FORCEGDIBLT	Uses GDI to perform blitting. This only works in Windows 2000 and Windows XP.
D3DPRESENTFLAG_VIDEO	Tells the graphics driver the back buffers contain video data.

The next data member is named `FullScreen_RefreshRateInHz`. This one is pretty self-explanatory as it sets the rate at which the graphics adapter refreshes the display. You can use `D3DPRESENT_RATE_DEFAULT` here for windowed-mode rendering if you want to use the adapter's default value.

Ah, the last member of the presentation parameters! It is named `PresentationInterval`. This member sets the maximum rate at which the back buffers can be presented. Windowed applications require the setting of `D3DPRESENT_INTERVAL_IMMEDIATE`. Full-screen rendering can use `D3DPRESENT_INTERVAL_DEFAULT` or one of the values listed in Table 6.4.

Table 6.4: Presentation intervals

Value	Meaning
D3DPRESENT_INTERVAL_DEFAULT	The system chooses the presentation rate. In windowed mode, the current rate is used.
D3DPRESENT_INTERVAL_ONE	The system waits for one vertical retrace period before rendering graphics.
D3DPRESENT_INTERVAL_TWO	The system waits for two vertical retrace periods before rendering graphics.
D3DPRESENT_INTERVAL_THREE	The system waits for three vertical retrace periods before rendering graphics.
D3DPRESENT_INTERVAL_FOUR	The system waits for four vertical retrace periods before rendering graphics.
D3DPRESENT_INTERVAL_IMMEDIATE	The system does not wait for the vertical retrace to complete before rendering. This method can cause tearing of your graphics.

Creating the 3D Rendering Device

You have the presentation parameter set up, so now it is time to create the `IDirect3DDevice9` device object. The `IDirect3DDevice9` device object is the foundation of all rendering calls; therefore, it is an extremely important object. Without this little object, you have nothing to render with. To create it, use the `IDirect3D9::CreateDevice()` function. Here is the prototype for it:

```
HRESULT CreateDevice(
    UINT Adapter,
    D3DDEVTYPE DeviceType,
    HWND hFocusWindow,
    DWORD BehaviorFlags,
    D3DPRESENT_PARAMETERS *pPresentationParameters,
    IDirect3DDevice9 **ppReturnedDeviceInterface
);
```

The first parameter, `Adapter`, takes the ordinal number of the display adapter to use. For most single-monitor setups, you can use `D3D-ADAPTER_DEFAULT` here. This works just like the first parameter in the `GetAdapterDisplayMode()` function that I covered earlier.

The second parameter, `DeviceType`, is an enumerated structure of device types. The types available are listed in Table 6.5. For the purposes of this example program, I use `D3DDEVTYPE_HAL`. This will not work if you don't have hardware acceleration. If you don't have hardware acceleration, try switching to `D3DDEVTYPE_REF` to get the example program to run.

Table 6.5: Device types

Value	Constant	Meaning
1	D3DDEVTYPE_HAL	Rendering is done in hardware. This method takes advantage of hardware acceleration when possible.
2	D3DDEVTYPE_REF	Direct3D rendering is done in software. This is a bad option to choose if accelerated hardware is available.
3	D3DDEVTYPE_SW	Uses a software rendering device that emulates hardware.

The third parameter, `hFocusWindow`, sets the window that contains the focus of the DirectX rendering system. The window must be a top-level window for full-screen rendering methods. For the program example, I use the handle of the window created in `WinMain()`. This is what you normally do for windowed applications.

The fourth parameter, `BehaviorFlags`, sets up one or more options about how the display device is created. Refer to Table 6.6 for the list of flags.

Table 6.6: Device creation behavior flags

Value	Meaning
D3DCREATE_FPU_PRESERVE	The application requires double-precision floating-point calculations.
D3DCREATE_MULTITHREADED	Direct3D operates in a thread-safe manner. This can degrade performance and should be used only when absolutely necessary.
D3DCREATE_PUREDEVICE	The device does not support Get calls for anything used in state blocks. The bottom line is the device does not support vertex processing. Personally, I never use this flag.
D3DCREATE_HARDWARE_VERTEXPROCESSING	Vertex processing is done in hardware. This is the flag I set for the example program. If your application does not work, try the next one in this list.
D3DCREATE_SOFTWARE_VERTEXPROCESSING	Vertex processing is done in software. This is slower than hardware.
D3DCREATE_MIXED_VERTEXPROCESSING	Vertex processing is done in both hardware and software. This can be slower than pure hardware processing.
D3DCREATE_DISABLE_DRIVER_MANAGEMENT	Keeps the display driver from managing resources. When this is set, Direct3D manages all resources.
D3DCREATE_ADAPTERGROUP_DEVICE	Used for multi-head adapters.
D3DCREATE_MANAGED	Offloads memory management to the device.

The fifth parameter, `pPresentationParameters`, sets the presentation parameters for the device. For the example program, I set this to the pointer I set up earlier.

The last parameter, `ppReturnedDeviceInterface`, contains the device to return upon completion of the call. For this parameter, I pass in the global `IDirect3DDevice9` pointer named `g_pd3dDevice`.

If all goes well, the creation function returns properly and the program continues on to set up the rendering environment. If not, the function returns a `FAILED()` status and cannot continue with graphic operations.

Setting Up the Rendering Environment

Since you are doing 2D rendering in a 3D environment, you must first set up the view area to render the graphics in. The main difference between normal 3D rendering and 2D fake rendering is the type of projection matrix you use to create the environment. In this special case, I use the `D3DXMatrixOrthoLH()` function to set up the projection matrix. Here is the prototype for it:

```
D3DXMATRIX *D3DXMatrixOrthoLH(
    D3DXMATRIX *pOut,
    FLOAT w,
    FLOAT h,
    FLOAT zn,
    FLOAT zf
);
```

The first parameter, pOut, takes a pointer to the D3DXMATRIX that is going to store the result.

The second parameter, w, sets the width of the view.

The third parameter, h, sets the height of the view.

The fourth parameter, zn, sets the z-near value of the view. Objects closer to the camera than this value are not displayed.

The fifth parameter, zf, sets the z-far value of the view. Objects farther away from the camera than this value are not displayed.

Look at my code where I do the following:

```
D3DXMatrixOrthoLH(&matproj, (float)g_iWindowWidth, (float)g_iWindowHeight, 0, 1);
g_pd3dDevice->SetTransform(D3DTS_PROJECTION, &matproj);
```

Notice how I put the window dimensions in the function call. This is where you set up the size of the rendering window (parameters two and three). It's really that easy. By setting the size of the rendering window to be the dimensions of the projection matrix, you now have a 2D projection matrix in 3D space that fits your window perfectly. The orthographic setup call also has a lot to do with it.

The projection matrix is primed and ready to go. The last step to setting up the 2D rendering projection is to call the SetTransform() function with the D3DTS_PROJECTION parameter. This activates the projection matrix and has you on your way to 2D rendering.

There are a few more rendering states to set up before jumping into actual rendering. The first one turns off culling. You do this by setting the render state named D3DRS_CULLMODE to D3DCULL_NONE. This setting tells the rendering system to show back-facing triangles. You don't have to use this rendering state, but it makes life easier for rotated triangles.

The next rendering state setting turns off hardware lighting for the scene. This is not necessary; I just do it here to make things simpler for this example. If you do want to keep the lights turned off, set the render state named D3DRS_LIGHTING to FALSE.

Next up I turn off the z-buffer by setting the D3DRS_ZENABLE render state to FALSE. I turn off z-buffering so that none of my 2D graphics get discarded at render time.

The last render state turns off z-buffer writing. Set the render state named D3DRS_ZWRITEENABLE to FALSE to do this. I do this to keep the 2D rendering operations from altering the z-buffer. This is very important

when you mix 2D and 3D elements in the same scene. You don't want
the 2D interface elements to alter the depth buffer in use by your 3D
elements.

That's it for setting up the environment. Now it is time for the
`vInitInterfaceObjects()` function.

The vInitInterfaceObjects() Function

So far you have created the window, initialized Direct3D, set up the 2D
projection matrix, and set up various rendering states. The `vInit-
InterfaceObjects()` function contains the last piece of the setup puzzle.
This function creates the geometry required for 3D rendering and also
loads the 2D textures to display on-screen. Look at Figure 6.18 to see
the geometry that I create in this function.

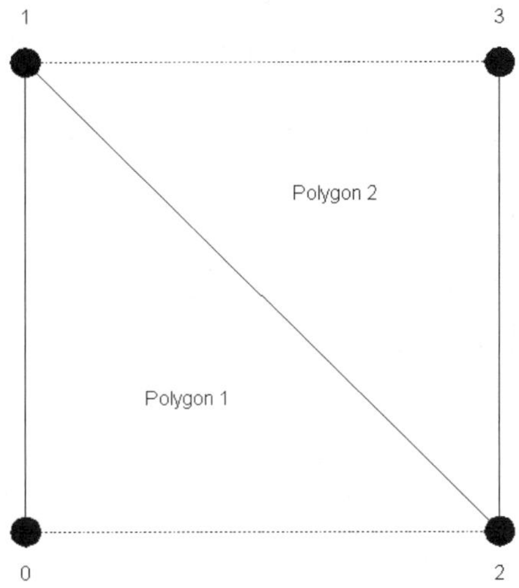

Figure 6.18: The triangle strip used for 3D to 2D rendering.

In Figure 6.18 you see a quadrilateral made up of two polygons. There
are four vertices included in the equation. They connect the lines that
make up the quadrilateral. You also may notice the two edges of the quad
that are dotted lines. The dotted lines represent the edges that are filled
in due to me using triangle strips for the geometry. Triangle strips use
less memory than triangle lists and generally render faster since the
CPU or GPU requires less work. For more information on this, I suggest
consulting the DirectX SDK help documentation.

Create the Vertex Buffer

In order to create geometry for rendering, you must first create a
vertex buffer to hold the geometry. This is done with the
`IDirect3DDevice9::CreateVertexBuffer()` function. This function is
pretty straightforward, as it creates a buffer of vertices for geometric
operations in DirectX. The prototype for the function is as follows:

```
HRESULT CreateVertexBuffer(
    UINT Length,
    DWORD Usage,
    DWORD FVF,
    D3DPOOL Pool,
    IDirect3DVertexBuffer9 **ppVertexBuffer,
    HANDLE* pHandle
);
```

The first parameter, `Length`, takes the size of the vertex buffer to create.
This is a very important setting that you must live with for the duration
of the vertex buffer.

The second parameter, `Usage`, accepts one or more constants of the
`D3DUSAGE` type. The values are listed in Table 6.7.

Table 6.7: **D3DUSAGE values**

Value	Meaning
D3DUSAGE_DYNAMIC	The vertex buffer requires dynamic memory usage. This allows the display driver to manage the buffer for optimal rendering speed. If you leave this flag out, the buffer is static. If you use this value, you cannot use the D3DPOOL_MANAGED value for the pool settings.
D3DUSAGE_AUTOGENMIPMAP	Mipmaps are automatically generated for the buffer. This takes up more memory but results in better render quality when utilized.
D3DUSAGE_DEPTHSTENCIL	The buffer is a depth or stencil buffer. This is only valid with the D3DPOOL_DEFAULT pool setting.
D3DUSAGE_RENDERTARGET	The buffer is a render target. This setting requires the pool setting to be D3DPOOL_DEFAULT.

For the purposes of this example, I set the usage to `NULL`. This results in
a static vertex buffer.

The third parameter, `FVF`, contains a combination of `D3DFVF` flags.
This parameter tells the system what information each vertex contains.
You can opt to not use FVF-style vertex buffers by leaving this parameter
set to `NULL`. Refer to the DirectX SDK for more information on the
`D3DFVF` flags.

The fourth parameter, `Pool`, tells the system which memory class to
use. Since vertices take up memory, they must be managed somewhere

in memory. The values in D3DPOOL contain the possibilities. You can see the values listed in Table 6.8.

Table 6.8: D3DPOOL values

Value	Meaning
D3DPOOL_DEFAULT	This tells the system to place the memory in the most appropriate pool for the data. This method requires resources to be released before the Direct3D device can be reset.
D3DPOOL_MANAGED	This tells the system to copy resources from system memory to device memory as needed. This allows the device to reset without forcing the managed memory to be released first.
D3DPOOL_SYSTEMMEM	This tells the system to keep the resource out of device memory for the most part. This is not very efficient for systems that have 3D accelerated hardware. Resources created with this method do not need to be released prior to a device reset.
D3DPOOL_SCRATCH	This type of resource cannot be accessed by the Direct3D device. It may be used for copying, locking, and creation though.
D3DPOOL_FORCE_DWORD	Unused.

For this example I use the D3DPOOL_DEFAULT memory pool setting. This is the easiest one to deal with in the given situation.

The fifth parameter, ppVertexBuffer, wants the address of an IDirect3DVertexBuffer9 pointer. This pointer will point to the created vertex buffer. In the example code, I use the global vertex buffer named g_pVBInterface here.

The last parameter, pHandle, is not used externally, so you don't have to worry about it. Don't you just love these?

Lock the Vertex Buffer

The next function called in the program is named IDirect3DVertex-Buffer9::Lock(). This function locks the newly created vertex buffer for editing. In 3D rendering, vertex buffers can't just be edited at whim. You must first lock the contents of the buffer before you can edit them. This operation ensures that the data is not in use during the edit. Since 3D hardware has its own processors, this is a required step. Here is the prototype for the locking function:

```
HRESULT Lock(
    UINT OffsetToLock,
    UINT SizeToLock,
    VOID **ppbData,
    DWORD Flags
    );
```

Luckily, the parameters aren't very complicated for this function. The first one, `OffsetToLock`, specifies the number of bytes into the vertex buffer to start locking. This is useful for editing portions of a vertex buffer without having to lock the entire thing. Set this to 0 if you don't want an offset.

The second parameter, `SizeToLock`, sets the size in bytes of the vertex buffer to lock. If you want to lock the entire buffer, set this to 0.

The third parameter, `ppbData`, expects the vertex buffer you want locked. Weird name for it, eh?

The fourth parameter, `Flags`, sets the locking options for the lock. The example doesn't use any flags, but there are a few available. Check out Table 6.9 to see the values for `D3DLOCK`.

Table 6.9: **D3DLOCK** values

Value	Meaning
D3DLOCK_DISCARD	Overwrites with a write-only operation. This is valid when using dynamic data such as dynamic textures and vertex buffers.
D3DLOCK_NO_DIRTY_UPDATE	Prevents the system from changing the dirty region data. This is not a very common flag to use.
D3DLOCK_NOSYSLOCK	Prevents the lock from stopping system operations such as mouse movement. This is nice to use when locking a buffer for a very long time.
D3DLOCK_READONLY	The buffer is read-only.
D3DLOCK_NOOVERWRITE	The system returns from the locking call immediately since the application promises not to overwrite the buffer. This speeds up calls that are for read only.

As you can see in the sample code, I use the default values for the lock parameters.

Create the Vertex Buffer Data

You have a freshly created vertex buffer on your hands but nothing in it resembling useful data. What is a programmer to do? I'll tell you what you need to do: You need to create some cool ph@t l3wt vertex data to put in it!

Take a look at the following code to see the vertex data that the program uses:

```
pVertices[0].position   = D3DXVECTOR3(0.0f, 0.0f, 0.0f);
pVertices[0].tu         = 0.0f;
pVertices[0].tv         = 1.0f;
pVertices[0].tu2        = 0.0f;
pVertices[0].tv2        = 1.0f;
pVertices[0].vecNorm    = D3DXVECTOR3(0.0f,0.0f,1.0f);
pVertices[1].position   = D3DXVECTOR3(0.0f, 1.0f, 0.0f);
```

```
pVertices[1].tu        = 0.0f;
pVertices[1].tv        = 0.0f;
pVertices[1].tu2       = 0.0f;
pVertices[1].tv2       = 0.0f;
pVertices[1].vecNorm   = D3DXVECTOR3(0.0f,0.0f,1.0f);
pVertices[2].position  = D3DXVECTOR3(1.0f, 0.0f, 0.0f);
pVertices[2].tu        = 1.0f;
pVertices[2].tv        = 1.0f;
pVertices[2].tu2       = 1.0f;
pVertices[2].tv2       = 1.0f;
pVertices[2].vecNorm   = D3DXVECTOR3(0.0f,0.0f,1.0f);
pVertices[3].position  = D3DXVECTOR3(1.0f, 1.0f, 0.0f);
pVertices[3].tu        = 1.0f;
pVertices[3].tv        = 0.0f;
pVertices[3].tu2       = 1.0f;
pVertices[3].tv2       = 0.0f;
pVertices[3].vecNorm   = D3DXVECTOR3(0.0f,0.0f,1.0f);
```

I know the data doesn't look like much to the untrained eye. Heck, to the trained eye it just looks like a migraine. Do you remember Figure 6.18? It has been updated in Figure 6.19.

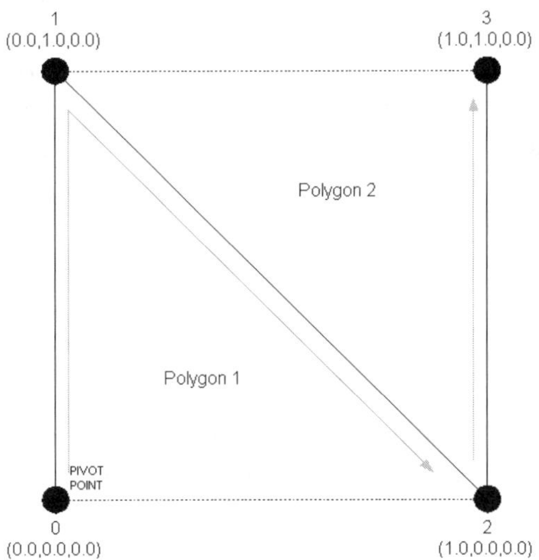

Figure 6.19: The geometry used for 3D to 2D rendering.

There are four vertices labeled in Figure 6.19. The first vertex is labeled 0, and the last vertex is labeled 3. The numbers in Figure 6.19 correspond to the vertex array positions in the code above. The coordinates below each vertex label show you where the vertices live in 3D space.

Follow the vertices from 0 to 3 and notice how the path forms a Z pattern. The Z is on its side, but it is there. Since I am using a triangle strip, the system fills in the rest of the square. Also, take note of the pivot point labeled in the image. This is very important since all future transformation operations on the square must know where the pivot point is.

In the code, I go through each vertex and set up the position, texture, and normal data. Since the square is textured, the texture data is required. I support up to two textures in this program example. This is why you see two sets of texture coordinates present. The normal data is required for lighting. The example doesn't use lighting, but it is nice to have the vertex data ready to go once you decide to use lights.

There you have it — vertex data in action. If the data doesn't make sense, try moving the vertices around to see what happens. You can easily create a misshapen square if you just tweak the positional data a bit.

The vertex data is present so you can go ahead and unlock the vertex buffer. This entails a very simple call to the `IDirect3DVertex-Buffer9::Unlock()` function. All you have to do is call the unlock function for the vertex buffer, and you are done editing it.

Load the Textures

The vertex buffer is all dressed up with no place to go now. So how about some textures? The rest of the initialization code takes care of loading the textures needed for the TitleScreen example program. To load the textures, I use the `D3DXCreateTextureFromFile()` function provided in the DirectX utility libraries. Here is the prototype for it:

```
HRESULT D3DXCreateTextureFromFile(
    LPDIRECT3DDEVICE9 pDevice,
    LPCSTR pSrcFile,
    LPDIRECT3DTEXTURE9 *ppTexture
);
```

The first parameter, `pDevice`, expects the Direct3D device you use for rendering. I use the global device pointer created earlier for this parameter.

The second parameter, `pSrcFile`, takes in the name of the file to load. The function can load several file types including JPEGs, TGAs, BMPs, and PCXs. In the sample code I pass in various texture names for this parameter. You can change the textures here if you want to experiment with different graphics.

The third parameter, `ppTexture`, points to the address of the `IDirect3DTexture9` object that holds the loaded textures. As you can see in the example code, I pass in the global array of textures named `g_pTexture` for this parameter.

That's all there is to loading up textures. It's actually quite easy once you get the hang of it.

The vRender() Function

Are you ready for some rendering? I know I am. Follow along with me now to the vRender() function. The code for it looks like the following:

```
void vRender(void)
{
    // Clear the back buffer to a blue color
    g_pd3dDevice->Clear(0, NULL,
            D3DCLEAR_TARGET,
            D3DCOLOR_XRGB(0,0,0),
            1.0f, 0);
    // Begin the scene
    g_pd3dDevice->BeginScene();

    // Draw the title screen
    vDrawInterfaceObject(0, 0, 256.0f, 256.0f, 0);
    vDrawInterfaceObject(256, 0, 256.0f, 256.0f, 1);
    vDrawInterfaceObject(512, 0, 256.0f, 256.0f, 2);
    vDrawInterfaceObject(0, 256, 256.0f, 256.0f, 3);
    vDrawInterfaceObject(256, 256, 256.0f, 256.0f, 4);
    vDrawInterfaceObject(512, 256, 256.0f, 256.0f, 5);

    // Logo
    vDrawInterfaceObject(192, 64, 256.0f, 256.0f, 6);

    // End the scene
    g_pd3dDevice->EndScene();

    // Present the back buffer contents to the display
    g_pd3dDevice->Present(NULL, NULL, NULL, NULL);
}
```

Hey, that doesn't look so bad does it? In all actuality, most of the complicated rendering is done in the vDrawInterfaceObject() function.

The vDrawInterfaceObject() Function

The vDrawInterfaceObject() function is not native to DirectX. I create it in this example program to make rendering 3D in 2D easier. The function does what a standard blit function in 2D does. It takes a graphic and pastes it on-screen at the desired coordinates. Here is the prototype for it:

```
void vDrawInterfaceObject(
    int iXPos,
    int iYPos,
    float fXSize,
    float fYSize,
    int iTexture
);
```

The first two parameters, iXPos and iYPos, set the position of the texture on-screen. Unlike 3D calls, these coordinates are in 2D screen-space.

The next two parameters, fXSize and fYSize, set the size of the texture to display on-screen. This is required for the system to know how large to scale the 3D geometry.

The last parameter, iTexture, takes an index into the global texture array. It uses this texture as the graphic to display.

Take a look now at the code for this gem of a function:

```
void vDrawInterfaceObject(int iXPos, int iYPos, float fXSize, float fYSize,
                          int iTexture)
{
    D3DXMATRIX    matWorld, matRotation;
    D3DXMATRIX    matTranslation, matScale;
    float         fXPos, fYPos;

    // Set default position, scale, rotation
    D3DXMatrixIdentity(&matTranslation);
    // Scale the sprite
    D3DXMatrixScaling(&matScale, fXSize, fYSize, 1.0f);
    D3DXMatrixMultiply(&matTranslation, &matTranslation, &matScale);
    // Rotate the sprite
    D3DXMatrixRotationZ(&matRotation, 0.0f);
    D3DXMatrixMultiply(&matWorld, &matTranslation, &matRotation);
    // Calculate the position in screen-space
    fXPos = (float)(-(g_iWindowWidth/2)+iXPos);
    fYPos = (float)(-(g_iWindowHeight/2)-iYPos+fYSize-g_iYOffset);
    // Move the sprite
    matWorld._41 = fXPos;   // X
    matWorld._42 = fYPos;   // Y
    // Set matrix
    g_pd3dDevice->SetTransform(D3DTS_WORLD, &matWorld);
    g_pd3dDevice->SetTexture(0, g_pTexture[iTexture]);
    g_pd3dDevice->SetStreamSource(0, g_pVBInterface, 0, sizeof(CUSTOMVERTEX));
    g_pd3dDevice->SetFVF(D3DFVF_CUSTOMVERTEX);
    g_pd3dDevice->DrawPrimitive(D3DPT_TRIANGLESTRIP, 0, 2);
    // Dereference texture
    g_pd3dDevice->SetTexture(0, NULL);
}
```

The first part of the code sets up the default matrix for the 3D object. This is accomplished with a call to D3DXMatrixIdentity(). This helper function provided in the DirectX SDK is useful for setting up a default matrix. It does this by zeroing out all of the values in the matrix for you. This is the equivalent of wiping the proverbial slate clean.

The next block of code sets up the scale matrix. This portion of code scales the 3D square to fit the size of the texture. Since there is no depth to the square, the z-scale is set to 1.0 by default. Once the scale matrix is ready to go, the translation matrix is multiplied by it.

Next is the code to rotate the graphic. I don't support rotation in this example, so the rotation value is set to 0.0 by default. Later on in other example programs, you will see me use rotation values other than 0.0. The translation matrix is multiplied by this matrix as well.

By default, the matrix puts the geometry into 3D space. Since this is a 2D display operation, you want to figure out where the object is in pixel coordinates. I do this by taking the screen width and height into consideration. As you can see in the example code, I take the size of the screen divided by two and use that along with the desired coordinates to figure out the screen position. Figure 6.20 illustrates the concept of 3D coordinates in screen-space.

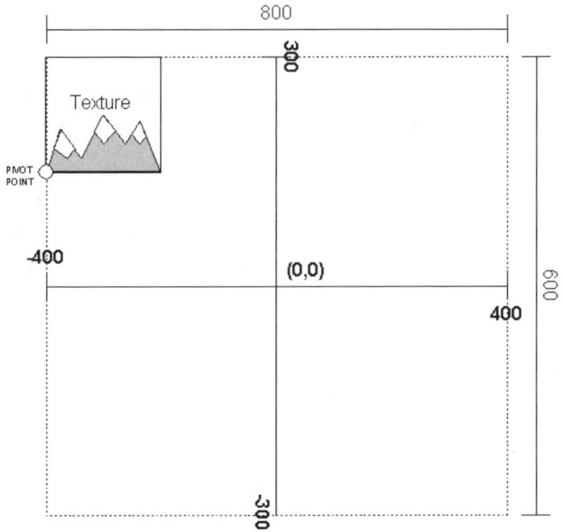

Figure 6.20: The texture as shown in 3D screen-space.

In Figure 6.20, the coordinate pair of (0,0) represents the middle of the screen. This is different from traditional 2D rendering. In a traditional 2D environment, the example in Figure 6.20 has a coordinate pair of (400,300) for the middle of the screen. Since you are dealing in a 3D world, you must compensate for this. This is where the code I just talked about comes in handy. It repositions the geometry based on a 3D to 2D screen-space conversion algorithm.

The coordinates are figured out, so now you need to put them into the matrix. You can use matrix multiplication to do this, but I prefer to just insert the movement values directly into the matrix. This method is faster for one thing.

The matrix now contains the scale, rotation, and position data required for rendering. The matrix has to be activated, so a call to the `IDirect3DDevice9::SetTransform()` function is required. I call this function and set the `D3DTS_WORLD` matrix to the matrix created for the bitmap. This activates the matrix for the geometry.

Next up I activate the appropriate texture. This is accomplished with the usual call to the `IDirect3DDevice9::SetTexture()` function. For this function, I pass in a pointer to the texture desired for rendering.

In order to render the vertex buffer that I created earlier in the program, I must activate it with a call to the `IDirect3DDevice9::SetStreamSource()` function. This function activates the specified vertex buffer stream source and uses it in subsequent rendering calls.

The next function called, `IDirect3DDevice9::SetFVF()`, tells the rendering system the format of the vertex buffer. Important information, such as normal, color, and texture data, is specified in it. For this function, I send in the `D3DFVF_CUSTOMVERTEX` custom vertex format defined in the program's header file.

Almost last — but not least — I call the `IDirect3DDevice9::DrawPrimitive()` function. This is the heart of the rendering call and actually does the work of rendering the 3D data. Since the square is a triangle strip, I use the `D3DPT_TRIANGLESTRIP` data type for the first parameter to this function.

Lastly, I dereference the texture by setting the active texture to `NULL`.

With the draw interface code out of the way, go back to the `vRender()` function and take a look at the calls to the draw interface function. Here they are again for reference:

```
vDrawInterfaceObject(0, 0, 256.0f, 256.0f, 0);
vDrawInterfaceObject(256, 0, 256.0f, 256.0f, 1);
vDrawInterfaceObject(512, 0, 256.0f, 256.0f, 2);
vDrawInterfaceObject(0, 256, 256.0f, 256.0f, 3);
vDrawInterfaceObject(256, 256, 256.0f, 256.0f, 4);
vDrawInterfaceObject(512, 256, 256.0f, 256.0f, 5);
vDrawInterfaceObject(192, 64, 256.0f, 256.0f, 6);
```

To put the calls to the function into perspective, check out Figure 6.21.

In Figure 6.21 you see the screen bordered by a thick line. You also see six textures in a grid pattern. The six textures fill up the screen completely. Since the textures are 256 pixels wide and 256 pixels high, they overlap the screen a bit since the screen is only 640 pixels wide and 480 pixels high. This amount of wasted texture space is necessary to accommodate hardware that only supports textures in powers of 2. Since many graphics cards out today only allow textures to be 2 x 2, 4 x 4, 8 x 8, 16 x 16, 32 x 32, 64 x 64, 128 x 128, 256 x 256, etc. in size, this type of

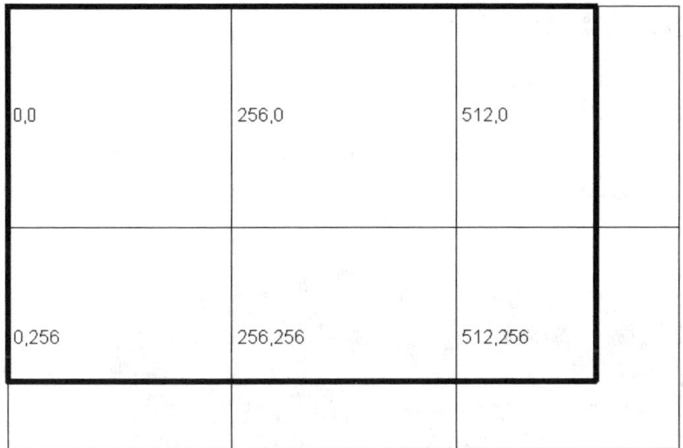

Figure 6.21: The textures and their positions for the title screen.

operation is required. The best way to accommodate this is to create your screens in the desired resolution and then break them up into 256 x 256-sized tiles. You are going to waste some space, but it is negligible.

The only texture that is not drawn in the grid is the title logo. Since it is in the middle of the screen, it requires slightly different coordinates. Play around with moving the texture coordinates to see what happens. You may even want to add a few texture graphics to the title screen to get the hang of it.

Hotspots, or How I Learned to Love Mouse Clicks

There you are with a perfectly good title screen and no place to go. Your best bet is to add some mouse functionality to it and get a move on! The last example program looks real nice, but it doesn't provide for a lot of interaction. To remedy this, I am going to show you how to add mouse zone hotspots to your applications. Since most PC games are controlled with the mouse, this is an important step. In this section I cover the following:

- How to detect mouse zones
- How to navigate game menus
- How to detect mouse button events
- Highlights for mouse-over events

How to Detect Mouse Zones

If you forgot what a mouse zone is, please go back and read "Mouse Zones and Graphics" at the beginning of this chapter. The first example project, named D3D_MouseZones, demonstrates simple menu navigation. The program contains a couple of working menus that you can navigate. Take a look at the main menu screen in Figure 6.22.

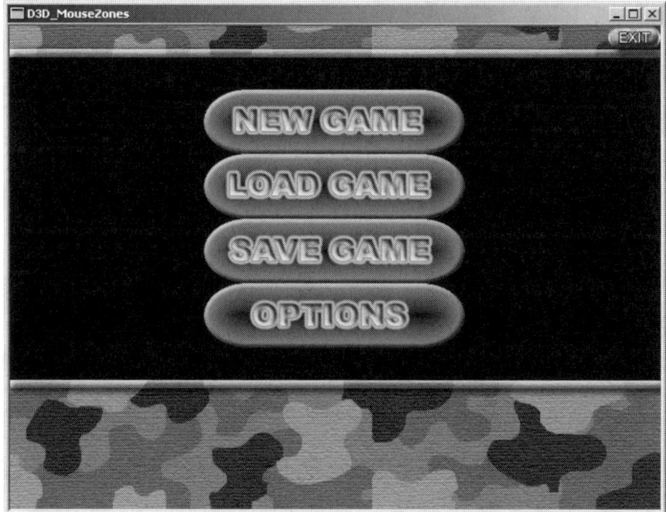

Figure 6.22: Output from the D3D_MouseZones program.

In Figure 6.22 you see the main menu screen for the program. Not all of the buttons work in this example, but the Options and Exit buttons do work. The program sets up up mouse detection zones and reacts to the user clicking some of the menu buttons. Load up the project now so you can follow along with the code. It is named D3D_MouseZones.

D3D_MouseZones Project Architecture

The project contains four unique files: main.cpp, main.h, MouseZone-Class.cpp, and MouseZoneClass.h. The mouse zone files make up the majority of the difference from this project to the last example project.

The program requires the following library files: d3d9.lib, dxguid.lib, d3dx9dt.lib, d3dxof.lib, comctl32.lib, and winmm.lib.

The Main.h Header File

The main header file is named main.h. In this header file I accomplish the following:

- Set up the global Direct3D variables
- Set up the custom vertex structure
- Set up miscellaneous global variables
- Define the function prototypes
- Set up the global mouse zone data
- Set up the global mouse button data

Global Mouse Zone Data

The majority of the main.h file looks identical to that in the last example program. The real differences come in the inclusion of global variables and function prototypes for the various mouse zone functions. Since I use a mouse zone class in this example, there is not much new code in the main.h file. Check out the following listing, and pay attention to the code in bold typeface.

```
#define STRICT
#include <windows.h>
#include <commctrl.h>
#include <commdlg.h>
#include <math.h>
#include <tchar.h>
#include <stdio.h>
#include <D3DX9.h>
#include "DXUtil.h"
#include "D3DUtil.h"
#include "MouseZoneClass.h"

// Global variables
LPDIRECT3D9 g_pD3D = NULL;
LPDIRECT3DDEVICE9    g_pd3dDevice = NULL;
LPDIRECT3DVERTEXBUFFER9 g_pVBInterface = NULL;
// Global array to hold interface graphics
LPDIRECT3DTEXTURE9   g_pTexture[32];
// Viewable window offsets
int    g_iXOffset = 0;
int    g_iYOffset = 0;
// Window dimensions
int    g_iWindowWidth = 640;
int    g_iWindowHeight = 480;
// A structure for our custom vertex type
struct CUSTOMVERTEX
{
    D3DXVECTOR3 position;   // The position
    D3DXVECTOR3 vecNorm;    // The normal
```

```
    FLOAT    tu, tv;   // The texture coordinates
    FLOAT    tu2, tv2; // The texture coordinates
};
// Custom FVF, which describes the custom vertex structure
#define D3DFVF_CUSTOMVERTEX (D3DFVF_XYZ|D3DFVF_NORMAL|D3DFVF_TEX2)

void vDrawInterfaceObject(int iXPos, int iYPos, float fXSize, float fYSize,
                          int iTexture);
void vInitInterfaceObjects(void);
LRESULT WINAPI fnMessageProcessor(HWND hWnd, UINT msg, WPARAM wParam, LPARAM lParam);
HRESULT InitD3D(HWND hWnd);
void vRender(void);
void vCleanup(void);
void vCheckInput(void);
void vSetupMouseZones(int iMenu);

// Global mouse zone class
MouseZoneClass   MZones;
// Navigation menu ID
int g_iCurrentScreen = 0;
// Mouse button state variables
bool   g_bLeftButton = 0;
bool   g_bRightButton = 0;
// Global handle to the game window
HWND   g_hWnd;
```

The first difference in the code is the inclusion of the MouseZoneClass.h
header file. This header file contains the header data for the Mouse-
ZoneClass. I cover it here in a moment. Until then, just remember to
include it whenever you want to use the MouseZoneClass.

Next are two new function prototypes. The first one, named vCheck-
Input(), checks the state of the mouse and processes the results. The
second function is named vSetupMouseZones(), and it sets up the appropriate hotspots depending on the current menu.

The next piece of new code creates a global MouseZoneClass object.
It is named MZones and used for all mouse zone data in the game.

Next up you see an integer named g_iCurrentScreen. This variable
keeps track of which menu the user is currently in. This is necessary for
the program to know which menu options to process.

The next two new pieces of code contain the mouse button state. A
mouse button can be either on or off; therefore, Boolean values are
needed to store the mouse button state. When they are set to 0, the
mouse button is up. When they are set to 1, the mouse button is down.

The last piece of code creates a global window handler. This is
required to access the window created by the program in functions other
than WinMain().

The Main.cpp Program File

The next unique file in the project is named main.cpp. It contains the usual Windows code along with some new code to handle mouse input and zone detection.

The WinMain() Function

The WinMain() function has changed very little in this program. Check out the following snippet of code from it to see the main differences:

```
// Initialize Direct3D
if(SUCCEEDED(InitD3D(hWnd))) {
    // Initialize the virtual buffer for the display quad
    vInitInterfaceObjects();
    // Initialize mouse zones
    vSetupMouseZones(0);
    // Enter the message loop
    while(msg.message!=WM_QUIT) {
        if(PeekMessage(&msg, NULL, 0U, 0U, PM_REMOVE)) {
            TranslateMessage(&msg);
            DispatchMessage(&msg);
        }
        else {
            // Check if it is okay to process mouse clicks
            if(timeGetTime() > dwInputTimer) {
                // Check for input
                vCheckInput();
                dwInputTimer = timeGetTime()+50;
            }

            // Check if the program should exit
            if(g_iCurrentScreen == 3) {
                break;
            }

            // Render the scene
            vRender();
        }
    }
}
```

The first change comes in a call to the vSetupMouseZones() function. Since the program is just starting, a call to this function is necessary to set up the mouse zones for the first screen. Figure 6.23 shows the first screen that appears in the program.

The screen in Figure 6.23 should look very familiar to you by now. It is the title screen for the Battle Armor game. Since there isn't much to do on the title screen, I only set up a couple of mouse zones. Skip ahead in the code to the vSetupMouseZones() function to see the zones used in the title screen.

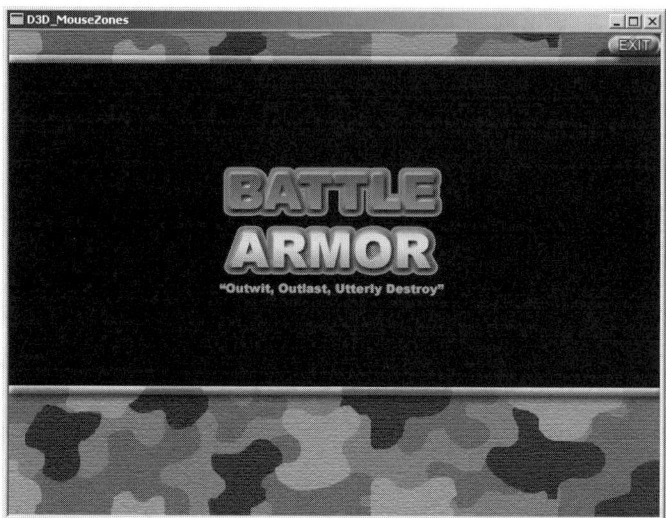

Figure 6.23: The first screen in the D3D_MouseZones program.

The vSetupMouseZones() Function

The vSetupMouseZones() function contains the following code:

```
void vSetupMouseZones(int iMenu)
{
// Title screen
if(iMenu == 0) {
   MZones.vFreeZones();
   MZones.vInitialize(2);
   MZones.iAddZone("TITLE_SCREEN", 0, 0, 640, 480, 2);
   MZones.iAddZone("EXIT_BUTTON", 587, 0, 53, 24, 0);
}
// Main menu
else if(iMenu == 1) {
   MZones.vFreeZones();
   MZones.vInitialize(5);
   MZones.iAddZone("EXIT_BUTTON", 587, 0, 53, 24, 0);
   MZones.iAddZone("MAINMENU_NEWGAME", 192, 64, 256, 64, 0);
   MZones.iAddZone("MAINMENU_LOADGAME", 192, 128, 256, 64, 0);
   MZones.iAddZone("MAINMENU_SAVEGAME", 192, 192, 256, 64, 0);
   MZones.iAddZone("MAINMENU_OPTIONS", 192, 256, 256, 64, 0);
}
// Exit splash screen
else if(iMenu == 2) {
   MZones.vFreeZones();
   MZones.vInitialize(1);
   MZones.iAddZone("TITLE_SCREEN", 0, 0, 640, 480, 2);
}
// Options menu
else if(iMenu == 7) {
```

```
MZones.vFreeZones();
MZones.vInitialize(5);
MZones.iAddZone("EXIT_BUTTON", 587, 0, 53, 24, 0);
MZones.iAddZone("OPTIONS_AUDIO", 192, 64, 256, 64, 0);
MZones.iAddZone("OPTIONS_VIDEO", 192, 128, 256, 64, 0);
MZones.iAddZone("OPTIONS_DIFF", 192, 192, 256, 64, 0);
MZones.iAddZone("OPTIONS_BACK", 192, 256, 256, 64, 0);
}
}
```

Most of the function calls look foreign because I have not yet covered the
`MouseZoneClass`. For now I am teaching by example, so take a look at the
first logic block.

The MouseZoneClass::vFreeZones() Function

As you can see, the function checks the number of the menu passed in
and reacts accordingly. `WinMain()` calls this function using menu 0. In the
menu 0 logic you see a call to `MouseZoneClass::vFreeZones()` listed first.
This function clears out all current mouse zones and resets the mouse
zone class. This is necessary since other menus may have led to the title
screen.

The MouseZoneClass::vInitialize() Function

The next call is made to `MouseZoneClass::vInitialize()`. This function
allocates memory for the number of zones passed into it. You can set this
higher than the actual number of zones you plan to use. It's just efficient
to keep it at the actual number of zones used.

Warning   Make sure you initialize the mouse zone class with
enough zones to handle the maximum number you will use. If
you try to exceed the maximum set at initialization time, the code
will not work as expected.

Next up you have the actual mouse zone creation code. The calls to
`MouseZoneClass::iAddZone()` create the mouse zones used in the title
screen. The title screen contains two mouse hotspots: one for the exit
button and one covering the rest of the screen. The exit button takes the
user to the exit game screen, and the other big mouse zone takes the
user to the main menu.

The MouseZoneClass::iAddZone() Function

The add zone function has the following prototype:

```
int MouseZoneClass::iAddZone(
    char *szZoneName,
    short shX,
```

```
short shY,
short shWidth,
short shHeight,
short shClickType)
```

The first parameter is named `szZoneName`, and it takes the name of the mouse zone you wish to create. The mouse zone class uses names to tell you which zone is active; therefore, the name is very important. In the title screen I use two mouse zone names. I name the exit button "EXIT_BUTTON" and I name the rest of the screen "TITLE_SCREEN."

The next two parameters, `shX` and `shY`, set the upper-left corner of the mouse zone. Mouse zones are rectangular, so the corner data is important. All coordinates are in screen-space, so you shouldn't have any trouble figuring them out. As you can see in the code, the TITLE_SCREEN zone starts in the upper-left corner of the screen at 0,0.

The next parameter is named `shWidth`. It sets the width of the mouse zone. The game window in this example is 640 pixels wide; therefore, I set the width of the zone covering the entire screen to 640.

The next parameter, `shHeight`, sets the height of the zone.

The last parameter is named `shClickType`, and it sets what type of mouse clicks the zone accepts. The types currently accepted are in Table 6.10.

Table 6.10: MouseZoneClass click types

Value	Meaning
0	Left mouse button-down activated.
1	Right mouse button-down activated.
2	Either mouse button-down activates it.
3	Mouse buttons cannot be pressed.

The click types allow you to control how a mouse zone behaves depending on the state of the mouse buttons. This is very useful for mouse-over zones among other things. In this example I set the TITLE_SCREEN zone to activate if the user presses the left or right mouse button. The EXIT_BUTTON zone activates only on a left-mouse button click.

The vCheckInput() Function

You have gone from the `WinMain()` function to the `vSetupMouseZones()` function to the member functions of the mouse zone class. It's time to jump back to the `WinMain()` function to see where mouse input events are handled. In the main function you see the following code:

```
if(timeGetTime() > dwInputTimer) {
   // Check for input
   vCheckInput();
   dwInputTimer = timeGetTime()+50;
}
```

Governing Mouse Clicks

Inside this little block of code is a call to the `vCheckInput()` function. Maybe you are wondering what the calls to `timeGetTime()` are for. As it turns out, computers nowadays are so fast that a single press of the mouse button can live through dozens of event loops. This causes a single mouse click to activate a menu item dozens of times. This poses a problem, as your interface ends up being too sensitive to mouse clicks from the user. To combat this problem, I set up a timer that only allows mouse events to happen once every 50 milliseconds. The code checks the current time to see if 50 milliseconds or more have passed since the last call to `vCheckInput()`. If enough time has passed, the call is made and the timer is reset. If enough time has not passed, the code continues on and doesn't bother to check input. Fifty milliseconds is an arbitrary number that I like to use. You may wish to modify this to suit your own tastes. If you are wondering what effect it truly has, set it to 0 and try running the example program (click on the Options button).

The `vCheckInput()` function checks the current position of the mouse and acts on it, depending on which menu the player is in. Here is the code for the function:

```
void vCheckInput(void)
{
    bool   bRet;
    char   szZoneHit[64];
    POINT  Point;
    RECT   rcWindowRect;
    int    iMouseX;
    int    iMouseY;

    // Check the window offsets
    GetWindowRect(g_hWnd, &rcWindowRect);
    // Update the mouse position
    GetCursorPos(&Point);
    // Calculate real mouse coordinates
    iMouseX = Point.x-g_iXOffset-rcWindowRect.left;
    iMouseY = Point.y-g_iYOffset-rcWindowRect.top;
    // Check for mouse hits
    bRet = MZones.bCheckZones(
          (short)iMouseX, (short)iMouseY,
          szZoneHit, g_bLeftButton,
          g_bRightButton);
    if(bRet) {
       // TITLE SCREEN LOGIC
```

```cpp
if(g_iCurrentScreen == 0) {
    // Go to the main menu
    if(!stricmp(szZoneHit, "TITLE_SCREEN")) {
        // Set menu to main menu
        g_iCurrentScreen = 1;
        // Set up the mouse zones
        vSetupMouseZones(1);
    }
    // Go to the exit splash screen
    else if(!stricmp(szZoneHit, "EXIT_BUTTON")) {
        // Set current screen to exit screen
        g_iCurrentScreen = 2;
        // Set up the mouse zones
        vSetupMouseZones(2);
    }
}
// MAIN MENU LOGIC
else if(g_iCurrentScreen == 1) {
    // Go to the title screen
    if(!stricmp(szZoneHit, "EXIT_BUTTON")) {
        // Set current screen to exit screen
        g_iCurrentScreen = 2;
        // Set up the mouse zones
        vSetupMouseZones(2);
    }
    else if(!stricmp(szZoneHit, "MAINMENU_NEWGAME"))
    {
        // Add new game logic here
    }
    else if(!stricmp(szZoneHit, "MAINMENU_LOADGAME"))
    {
        // Add load game logic here
    }
    else if(!stricmp(szZoneHit, "MAINMENU_SAVEGAME"))
    {
        // Add save game logic here
    }
    else if(!stricmp(szZoneHit, "MAINMENU_OPTIONS"))
    {
        // Set current screen to options menu
        g_iCurrentScreen = 7;
        // Set up the mouse zones
        vSetupMouseZones(7);
    }
}
// EXIT SCREEN LOGIC
else if(g_iCurrentScreen == 2) {
    // Exit the program if the user clicks anything
    if(!stricmp(szZoneHit, "TITLE_SCREEN")) {
        // Flag WinMain() to exit program
        g_iCurrentScreen = 3;
    }
}
// OPTIONS MENU LOGIC
else if(g_iCurrentScreen == 7) {
```

```
        // Go to the title screen
        if(!stricmp(szZoneHit, "EXIT_BUTTON")) {
            // Set current screen to exit screen
            g_iCurrentScreen = 2;
            // Set up the mouse zones
            vSetupMouseZones(2);
        }
        // Go back to main menu
        else if(!stricmp(szZoneHit, "OPTIONS_BACK")) {
            // Set current screen to main menu
            g_iCurrentScreen = 1;
            // Set up the mouse zones
            vSetupMouseZones(1);
        }
    }
  }
}
```

Calculating Client-Space Offsets on the Desktop

Since windows can be moved, the program must first check to see where
the window is. The call to `GetWindowRect()` accomplishes this. Armed
with the window position, the code can figure out where the mouse clicks
are happening in relation to the game client area. This is important, since
the mouse zones are set up in client-space, not desktop-space. Take, for
example, the screen setup in Figure 6.24.

Figure 6.24 shows a game client window on the desktop. The game
client window is 640 pixels wide and 480 pixels high. The desktop is
1024 pixels wide and 768 pixels high. There is a mouse zone in the client
window at client coordinates of (340,10). This is important to note since
the mouse zone class stores everything in client coordinates, not desktop
coordinates. Now imagine what happens if you are searching for a mouse
zone starting at (340,10) and the client window has been moved. It would
look something like Figure 6.25.

In Figure 6.25 the client window has moved. Because of this, the client window is now offset 10 pixels to the right and 10 pixels down.
Mouse clicks generated in the mouse zone will register as being 10 pixels off on both axis. This is due to the fact that mouse input is handled in
desktop space. The mouse zone checks starting at (340,10) and does not
care about the client offset. This causes a problem since the mouse zone
is really in (350,20) in Figure 6.25. To fix this problem, you calculate
where the window is in desktop space and then subtract its position from
the mouse click coordinates. This gives you the client position regardless
of window position. In Figure 6.25 the adjusted position of the mouse
zone takes it back to (340,10) since it uses the calculation of (350–10,
20–10).

II

Part

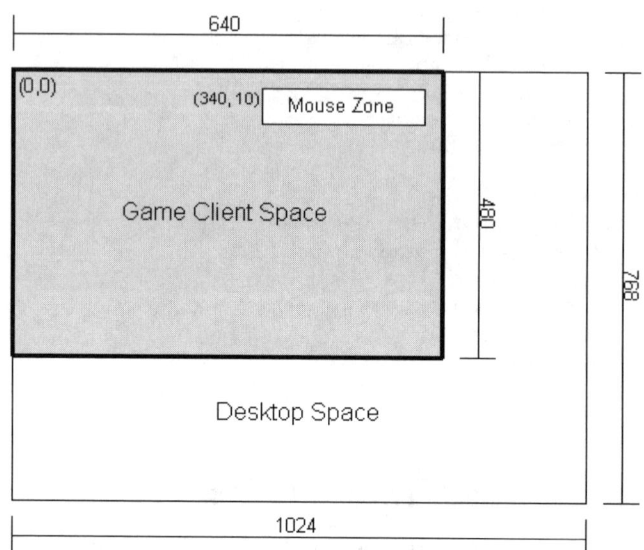

Figure 6.24: Example of client-space versus desktop-space.

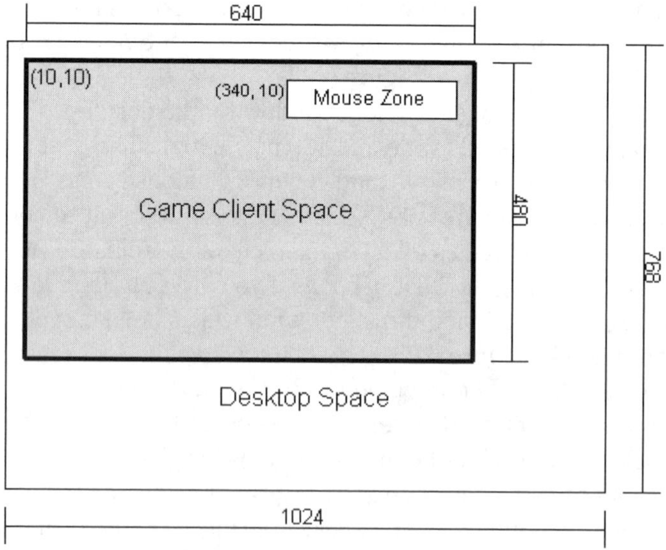

Figure 6.25: Example of client-space versus desktop-space with the client offset.

Calculating the Current Mouse Position

The next step in the code figures out the current coordinates of the mouse pointer. This is accomplished with a call to the `GetCursorPos()` function provided in Windows. This function checks the current location of the mouse pointer and stores the results in a `POINT` structure. The `POINT` structure contains both the x-coordinate and y-coordinate of the mouse.

> **Note**   The `GetCursorPos()` function is not part of the DirectX SDK. It is a native Windows function call. I prefer to use standard Windows function calls for mouse support since it is fast enough and generally easier to use than DirectX calls.

The next few lines of code calculate the adjusted mouse coordinates. This is a simple calculation of taking the real mouse coordinates and subtracting the window position and client offsets from them. This gives you the final adjusted position to check mouse zone collision on.

The MouseZoneClass::bCheckZones() Function

The next part of the code makes a call to the `bCheckZones()` function. This function takes in the current state of the mouse and compares it to the mouse zones in memory. If the mouse buttons are in the proper state and the mouse coordinates are within a zone, the function sends back the name of the zone. Here is the prototype for the function:

```
bool MouseZoneClass::bCheckZones(
    short shX,
    short shY,
    char *szZoneHit,
    bool bLeftDown,
    bool bRightDown)
```

The first two parameters expect the adjusted coordinates of the mouse in x and y space. This is where you pass in the coordinates that you calculated earlier.

The next parameter expects a character buffer to contain the name of the potential zone the user has activated. If a zone is found that meets the conditions of activation, its name is copied to this buffer on return.

The last two parameters expect the state of the mouse buttons. If the buttons are down, you pass in a 1. If they are up, you pass in a 0. I put the `g_bLeftButton` and `g_bRightButton` here.

For the sake of this example, say that the user has started the example program and clicks on the title screen graphic. This activates the TITLE_SCREEN mouse zone. The `szZoneHit` character array now holds

the name of the activated zone. What do you do? You set the `g_iCur-`
`rentScreen` variable to indicate that the user is now in the main menu,
and you set up the mouse zones for the main menu.

The `g_iCurrentScreen` variable keeps menu state. It is what maintains the position of the user in the game's interface world. The value of
0 means the user is in the title screen area. The value of 1 means the
user is in the main menu. The following list shows the ones used in the
example:

0 Title screen
1 Main menu
2 Exit screen
3 Exit program
7 Options menu

In order to move the user from one menu to the next, you must change
the current screen variable and then set up the mouse zones for the new
location. Then you can move the user on to the new screen and render it.
That's really all there is to menu navigation! Check out the rest of the
`vCheckInput()` function and see if you can follow the logic. After you are
done, take a look at Figure 6.26 to see the entire menu flow illustrated as
covered so far.

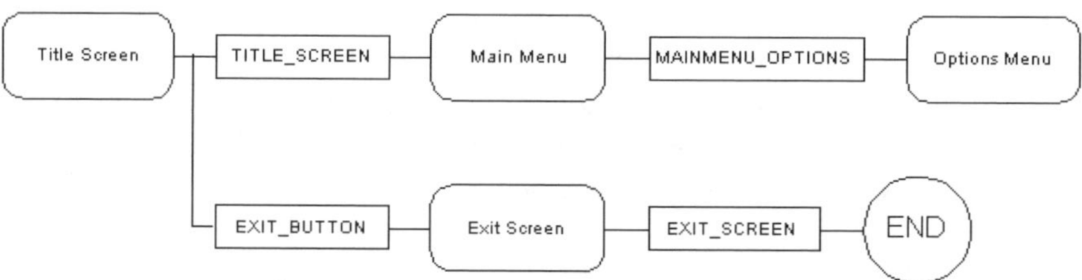

Figure 6.26: Title screen, exit screen, main menu, and options menu navigation.

How to Detect Mouse Button Events

The `vCheckInput()` function is very dependent on the state of the mouse
buttons. Luckily, checking the mouse button state is a pretty simple process. Take a look at the `fnMessageProcessor()` function in the example
program. Here is the code for it:

```
switch(msg)
    {
        case WM_LBUTTONDOWN:
            g_bLeftButton = 1;
            break;
        case WM_LBUTTONUP:
            g_bLeftButton = 0;
            break;
```

```
    case WM_RBUTTONDOWN:
        g_bRightButton = 1;
        break;
    case WM_RBUTTONUP:
        g_bRightButton = 0;
        break;
    case WM_DESTROY:
    PostQuitMessage(0);
    return 0;
    default:
        break;
}
```

The first four case statements check for mouse messages from the system. The first one, WM_LBUTTONDOWN, lets you know that the left mouse button is down. The next one, WM_LBUTTONUP, tells you the left mouse button has been released. The same logic holds true for the right mouse button, except it uses WM_RBUTTONDOWN and WM_RBUTTONUP.

The easiest way to store the mouse state is with global variables. I use g_bRightButton and g_bLeftButton to store the up and down state of the two mouse buttons. See, isn't that simple?

How to Exit the Program

Focus your attention on the WinMain() function for a minute. I know I have you jumping all over the place, but please bear with me. Back in the WinMain() function, I have the following code listed:

```
if(g_iCurrentScreen == 3) {
    break;
}
```

This is special circumstance code I use to exit the user from the program. I cannot force users out of the program as soon as they hit the exit screen. I must first send them back to the main processing loop. The best way to get them out of the program is to check for a special variable condition. I choose to look out for when the g_iCurrentScreen variable is set to 3. This tells me that the user is done playing and the program needs to exit. You may want to use a more elaborate method in a real game, but this method works for this simple example.

Dynamic Menu Rendering

You are almost done with this example program. So far you have learned how to set up mouse zones, detect mouse position, handle mouse button events, and exit the user from the program. The only thing left is how to render the menu screens in a dynamic fashion. Since the menu graphics change with each screen, this is necessary. Zoom over to the vRender() function to see how it is done.

The code for the function should look very similar to the last example program. The main difference lies in the checks to the `g_iCurrentScreen` variable. The render loop checks the current state of the variable to determine which graphics to display. As it turns out, the background of each menu is the same; only the graphic in the middle changes. If you look at each logic block, you can see that only the last graphic drawn is different. You can change the graphics completely if you wish. I just chose to keep things simple for the example.

That is really about it for simple dynamic menu rendering. The basic premise is that you check the state of the program and render accordingly. Easy, huh?

The MouseZoneClass.h Header File

Now that you have seen the mouse class in action, it is time to cover how it works. The mouse zone class is comprised of two files: MouseZone-Class.h and MouseZoneClass.cpp. Open up the MouseZoneClass.h header file now to follow along.

The stHotSpot Data Structure

The first item of note in the class header file is the `stHotSpot` data structure. Here is the code for it:

```
struct stHotSpot
{
    short  m_shZoneXPos;
    short  m_shZoneYPos;
    short  m_shZoneWidth;
    short  m_shZoneHeight;
    bool   m_bActive;
    short  m_shClickType;
    char   *m_szZoneName;
};
```

The hotspot data structure represents the mouse zone in screen coordinates. Since it is rectangular, it has origin coordinates, width, and height. Check out Figure 6.27 on the following page to see the data members as they correspond to the mouse zone.

In Figure 6.27 you can see that the `m_shZoneXPos` and `m_shZoneYPos` set the upper-left corner coordinates of the zone. The `m_shZoneWidth` data member sets the width of the zone, and the `m_shZoneHeight` data member sets the height of the zone.

The mouse zone class uses the `m_bActive` data member internally to set whether the zone is currently in use. This is used when looking for a free zone spot in which to create a new one.

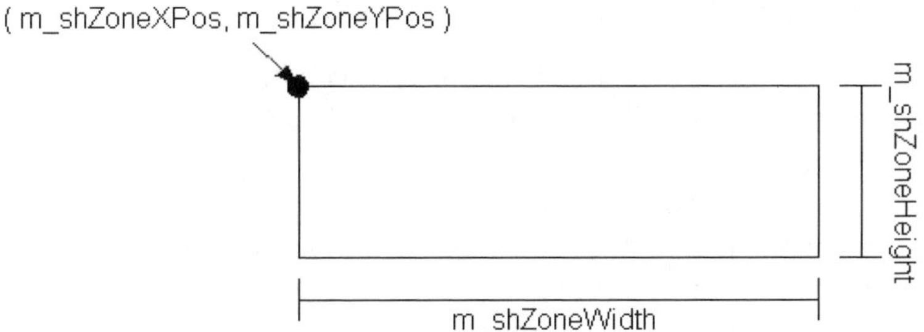

Figure 6.27: The mouse zone data members in relation to a defined zone.

The m_shClickType data member stores which types of mouse clicks activate the zone. See Table 6.10 for these values.

The m_szZoneName data element stores the name of the mouse zone.

The MouseZoneClass Private Data Elements

Next up in the header file is the declaration of the MouseZoneClass. Here is the code for it:

```
class MouseZoneClass
{
    private:
        int    m_iMaxZones;
        stHotSpot *m_HotSpots;

    public:
        MouseZoneClass(void);
        ~MouseZoneClass(void);
        void vInitialize(int iMaxZones);
        void vFreeZones(void);
        int iAddZone(char *szZoneName, short shX, short shY, short shWidth, short
                    shHeight, short shClickType);
        int iRemoveZone(char *szZoneName);
        bool bCheckZones(short shX, short shY, char *szZoneHit, bool bLeftDown,
                    bool bRightDown);
};
```

There are only two private data elements — m_iMaxZones and m_Hot-Spots. The m_iMaxZones element stores the number of zones for which memory is allocated. This is important since the number of zones is dynamic. The m_HotSpots element points to the array of stHotSpot data structures that make up the actual mouse zones.

The MouseZoneClass Functions

The first two functions listed are the constructor and the destructor for the class. There is nothing special to these prototypes; they are just your run-of-the mill voids.

Next up you have the `vInitialize()` member function. This function takes one parameter that sets the number of mouse zones that need to have memory allocated.

The `vFreeZones()` function clears the memory of any allocated zones and resets the internal variables.

The `iAddZone()` function activates a new zone in the `m_HotSpots` array. As long as a free zone is available, the function returns the zone number. If a zone is not available, the function returns –1.

The `iRemoveZone()` function deactivates the specified zone.

The `bCheckZones()` function takes a set of coordinates and mouse zone states and determines if any zones should activate. The activated zone's name is returned. If no zones are active, the function returns `NULL`.

The MouseZoneClass.cpp File

The MouseZoneClass.cpp file contains the member functions as prototyped in the header file. Open up the MouseZoneClass.cpp file now to follow along.

The MouseZoneClass::MouseZoneClass() Function

The first function listed is the class constructor. The code is as follows:

```
MouseZoneClass::MouseZoneClass(void)
{
    // Default the maximum to zero
    m_iMaxZones = 0;
}
```

This function is really basic. All it does is set the maximum number of allocated zones to zero. This is useful so that the destructor does not accidentally delete nonallocated memory.

The MouseZoneClass::~MouseZoneClass() Function

The class destructor comes next, and its code is as follows:

```
MouseZoneClass::~MouseZoneClass(void)
{
    // Clean up allocated zones
    vFreeZones();
}
```

All the destructor does is call the `vFreeZones()` function. Since the destructor is called when the class goes out of scope, it is necessary to make sure memory is freed before going away. This is why I have the zone freeing call here.

The MouseZoneClass::vInitialize() Function

Ah, we finally have a function with more than two lines of code to it. This function takes in the number of maximum zones desired, allocates memory for them, and defaults all of the values. Here is the code for it:

```
void MouseZoneClass::vInitialize(int iMaxZones)
{
    int i;
    // Clear out existing zones
    vFreeZones();
    // Store the maximum number of zones
    m_iMaxZones = iMaxZones;
    // Allocate memory for the maximum number of zones
    m_HotSpots = new stHotSpot[m_iMaxZones];
    // Clear out the zone information
    for(i = 0; i < m_iMaxZones; i++) {
        m_HotSpots[i].m_shZoneXPos = 0;
        m_HotSpots[i].m_shZoneYPos = 0;
        m_HotSpots[i].m_shZoneWidth = 0;
        m_HotSpots[i].m_shZoneHeight = 0;
        m_HotSpots[i].m_shClickType = 0;
        m_HotSpots[i].m_bActive = 0;
        m_HotSpots[i].m_szZoneName = new char[64];
        memset(m_HotSpots[i].m_szZoneName, 0x00, 64);
    }
}
```

The function makes a call to `vFreeZones()` to clear out any memory that has been allocated previously.

Next I set the internal `m_iMaxZones` variable to equal that of the function's only parameter. This variable is used throughout the class and is very important since it keeps the internal loops from going past available memory.

The hotspot data structure array is allocated next. One hotspot is created for each mouse zone desired.

The loop cycles through each of the newly created hotspots and defaults the data to zeroes. The loop also allocates 64 bytes of data for the zone name. This is the maximum zone name length. (I choose this arbitrarily; if you need longer zone names, feel free to change this.) Once the zone name is allocated, I clear it with `NULL` characters.

The MouseZoneClass::vFreeZones() Function

This function clears out any allocated zone memory and resets the internal member variables that correspond to it. Here is the code for it:

```
void MouseZoneClass::vFreeZones(void)
{
    int i;

    if(m_iMaxZones) {
        // Free up the name
        for(i = 0; i < m_iMaxZones; i++) {
            delete [] m_HotSpots[i].m_szZoneName;
        }
        // Free up the hotspots
        delete [] m_HotSpots;
        m_iMaxZones = 0;
    }
}
```

First, the function checks the `m_iMaxZones` data member to see if hotspots are currently allocated. If they are not, the function exits since there is nothing to clear up. If there are allocated zones, the function loops through each one and frees up the mouse zone name. Once that is done, the function deletes the actual hotspots. Lastly, the maximum number of zones is set to 0.

The MouseZoneClass::iAddZone() Function

This function activates a zone in the available array of hotspot data elements. You must call the `vInitialize()` function before calling this function. If not, the function returns a –1. Here is the code for the function:

```
int MouseZoneClass::iAddZone(char *szZoneName,
              short shX, short shY,
              short shWidth, short shHeight,
              short shClickType)
{
    int i;

    for(i = 0; i < m_iMaxZones; i++) {
        // Check if it is inactive
        if(m_HotSpots[i].m_bActive == 0) {
            m_HotSpots[i].m_shZoneXPos = shX;
            m_HotSpots[i].m_shZoneYPos = shY;
            m_HotSpots[i].m_shZoneWidth = shWidth;
            m_HotSpots[i].m_shZoneHeight = shHeight;
            m_HotSpots[i].m_shClickType = shClickType;
            // Activate the hotspot
            m_HotSpots[i].m_bActive = 1;
            // Store the name
            strcpy(m_HotSpots[i].m_szZoneName, szZoneName);
```

```
        return(i);
    }
  }
  // No free zones, return -1 (error)
  return(-1);
}
```

The function starts out by looping through the maximum number of allocated zones. If it finds an inactive zone, it sets the data members according to the input parameters and activates the zone. The zone number is then returned to the calling code. If an available zone is not found, the function returns a –1.

The MouseZoneClass::iRemoveZone() Function

The remove zone function removes an active mouse zone. The code is as follows:

```
int MouseZoneClass::iRemoveZone(char *szZoneName)
{
    int i;

    for(i = 0; i < m_iMaxZones; i++) {
        // Check if it is active
        if(m_HotSpots[i].m_bActive == 1) {
            // Check for zone name match
            if(!stricmp(m_HotSpots[i].m_szZoneName, szZoneName)) {
                // Deactivate it
                m_HotSpots[i].m_bActive = 0;
                return(1);
            }
        }
    }
    return(0);
}
```

The function loops through the maximum number of zones and compares the input zone name to the name of all active zones. If a name match is found, the zone is deactivated by setting the m_bActive data member to 0. The function then returns a success value in the form of a 1.

If the zone name is not matched, the function returns failure in the form of a 0.

The MouseZoneClass::bCheckZones() Function

This function is the most complicated of the mouse zone class functions since it has to handle multiple click types. Here is the code for it:

```
bool MouseZoneClass::bCheckZones(short shX, short shY, char *szZoneHit, bool
                        bLeftDown, bool bRightDown)
{
    int i;
```

```
for(i = (m_iMaxZones-1); i >= 0; i--) {
    // Check if it is active
    if(m_HotSpots[i].m_bActive == 1) {
        // Check if right button type
        if((bLeftDown && m_HotSpots[i].m_shClickType == 0) ||
            (bRightDown && m_HotSpots[i].m_shClickType == 1) ||
            ((bRightDown || bLeftDown) && m_HotSpots[i].m_shClickType == 2) ||
            ((!bRightDown && !bLeftDown) && m_HotSpots[i].m_shClickType == 3)) {
            // Check if along horizontal
            if(m_HotSpots[i].m_shZoneXPos <= shX  {
                // Check if along vertical
                if(m_HotSpots[i].m_shZoneYPos <= shY) {
                    // Check within width
                    if((m_HotSpots[i].m_shZoneXPos + m_HotSpots[i].m_shZoneWidth)
                                    >= shX) {
                        // Check within height
                        if((m_HotSpots[i].m_shZoneYPos + m_HotSpots[i]
                                    .m_shZoneHeight) >= shY) {
                            // Set the pointer to the zone name
                            strcpy(szZoneHit, m_HotSpots[i].m_szZoneName);
                            // Return a 1 (hit)
                            return(1);
                        }
                    }
                }
            }
        }
    }
}
// Return a 0 (no hit)
return(0);
}
```

The function starts out by looping through the available zones in reverse. I do this since zones added last should be selected first. This is because the zone class works in a layered fashion. Zones added on top of other zones are hit before the zones below them. This allows for layering of hot spots.

The loop first checks to see if the zone is active. If the zone is active, it continues on to check for the appropriate combination of mouse button states for the click type of the zone.

If the zone is activated with a left-mouse click, the code checks for the click type of 0 and the bLeftDown variable to be 1.

If the zone is activated with a right-mouse click, the code checks for the click type of 1 and the bRightDown variable to be 1.

If the zone can be activated with either the left or right mouse button, the code checks for the click type of 2 and if either the bLeftDown or bRightDown variables equal 1.

If the zone can only be activated when both mouse buttons are up, the code checks for the click type of 3 and if the `bLeftDown` and `bRightDown` variables are set to 0.

If any of the above rules are met, the code copies the name of the zone into the input buffer and returns a 1, indicating success. If the function fails to meet the rules, a 0 is returned, indicating a no-hit.

That's it for the mouse zone class. I suggest you go back to the last example program and play around with adding your own mouse zones. Try adding a few to each menu to see the effect.

Menu Highlighting

The previous example program is entertaining and all, but it still lacks visual flair. Some of the menu items work, but they don't seem very lively. What could possibly help? I know — how about highlighting the menu choices as you move the mouse over them?

Have you ever played a game such as Populous or Sacrifice and wondered how they make the menu items change as the mouse moves over them? You do not have to wonder any longer. In the following example program I demonstrate a simple and effective way to do this. Load up the D3D_MouseZoneHighlights example now to follow along with me.

D3D_MouseZoneHighlights Project Architecture

The project contains four unique files: main.cpp, main.h, MouseZoneClass.cpp, and MouseZoneClass.h. This example is just an enhanced version of the D3D_MouseZones project, so not much has changed.

The program requires the following library files: d3d9.lib, dxguid.lib, d3dx9dt.lib, d3dxof.lib, comctl32.lib, and winmm.lib.

The Main.h Header File

The main header file contains a few new lines of code to handle the mouse highlights. Before I get into the code, check out Figure 6.28 to see the menu highlighting in action.

In Figure 6.28 you see the main menu. The main difference between this screen shot and previous ones of the main menu is that the Options button is highlighted. The various menu buttons change color as the mouse hovers over them. This is the premise of zone highlighting.

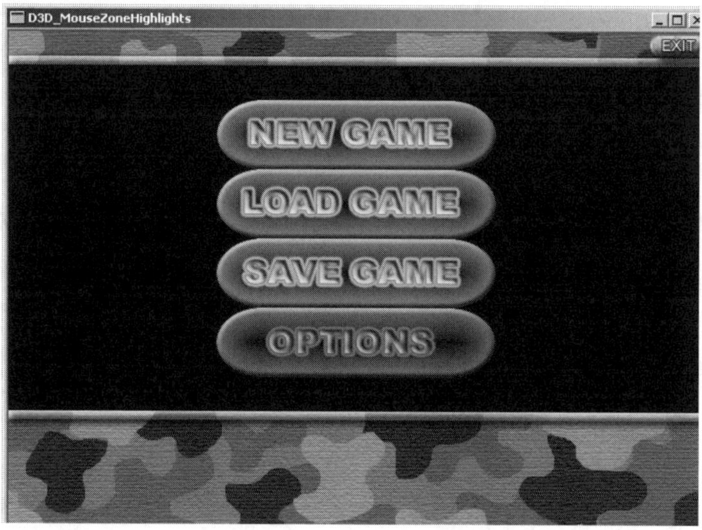

Figure 6.28: The main menu with the Options button highlighted.

Back to the reality of the header file. Check out the following code to see the changes required to handle highlighting:

```
// Highlight state variables
bool    g_bMainMenu_NewGame_Highlight = 0;
bool    g_bMainMenu_LoadGame_Highlight = 0;
bool    g_bMainMenu_SaveGame_Highlight = 0;
bool    g_bMainMenu_Options_Highlight = 0;
```

This example program highlights the four menu options in the main menu. Since there are four menu items, the program must keep track of which items are activated. I choose to do this with four Boolean values. Each Boolean value represents the state of the various menu choices. If the value is set to 0, the button is not highlighted. If the value is set to 1, the rendering engine knows to highlight the button. Pretty simple, eh?

The Main.cpp Program File

I don't want to bore you with covering code you already are familiar with, so why don't I skip ahead to the code changes that matter most? Skip on down to the vCheckInput() function to see the first set of changes.

How to Detect Mouse Zone Highlights

The following code makes up the vCheckInput() function:

```
void vCheckInput(void)
{
    bool        bRet;
```

```c
char        szZoneHit[64];
POINT       Point;
RECT        rcWindowRect;
int         iMouseX;
int         iMouseY;

// Check the window offsets
GetWindowRect(g_hWnd, &rcWindowRect);

// Update the mouse position
GetCursorPos(&Point);

// Calculate real mouse coordinates
iMouseX = Point.x-g_iXOffset-rcWindowRect.left;
iMouseY = Point.y-g_iYOffset-rcWindowRect.top;

// Check for mouse hits
bRet = MZones.bCheckZones((short)iMouseX, (short)iMouseY, szZoneHit,
                          g_bLeftButton, g_bRightButton);
if(bRet) {
   // TITLE SCREEN LOGIC
   if(g_iCurrentScreen == 0) {
      // Go to the main menu
      if(!stricmp(szZoneHit, "TITLE_SCREEN")) {
         // Set menu to main menu
         g_iCurrentScreen = 1;
         // Set up the mouse zones
         vSetupMouseZones(1);
      }
      // Go to the exit splash screen
      else if(!stricmp(szZoneHit, "EXIT_BUTTON")) {
         // Set current screen to exit screen
         g_iCurrentScreen = 2;
         // Set up the mouse zones
         vSetupMouseZones(2);
      }
   }
   // MAIN MENU LOGIC
   else if(g_iCurrentScreen == 1) {
      // Turn off all highlights
      g_bMainMenu_NewGame_Highlight = 0;
      g_bMainMenu_LoadGame_Highlight = 0;
      g_bMainMenu_SaveGame_Highlight = 0;
      g_bMainMenu_Options_Highlight = 0;
      // Go to the title screen
      if(!stricmp(szZoneHit, "EXIT_BUTTON")) {
         // Set current screen to exit screen
         g_iCurrentScreen = 2;
         // Set up the mouse zones
         vSetupMouseZones(2);
      }
      else if(!stricmp(szZoneHit, "MAINMENU_NEWGAME"))
      {
         // Add new game logic here
      }
```

```c
        else if(!stricmp(szZoneHit, "MAINMENU_LOADGAME"))
        {
            // Add load game logic here
        }
        else if(!stricmp(szZoneHit, "MAINMENU_SAVEGAME"))
        {
            // Add save game logic here
        }
        else if(!stricmp(szZoneHit, "MAINMENU_OPTIONS"))
        {
            // Set current screen to options menu
            g_iCurrentScreen = 7;
            // Set up the mouse zones
            vSetupMouseZones(7);
        }
        // Check for mouse-overs
        else if(!stricmp(szZoneHit, "MAINMENU_NEWGAME_H"))
        {
            // Activate highlight
            g_bMainMenu_NewGame_Highlight = 1;
        }
        else if(!stricmp(szZoneHit, "MAINMENU_LOADGAME_H"))
        {
            // Activate highlight
            g_bMainMenu_LoadGame_Highlight = 1;
        }
        else if(!stricmp(szZoneHit, "MAINMENU_SAVEGAME_H"))
        {
            // Activate highlight
            g_bMainMenu_SaveGame_Highlight = 1;
        }
        else if(!stricmp(szZoneHit, "MAINMENU_OPTIONS_H"))
        {
            // Activate highlight
            g_bMainMenu_Options_Highlight = 1;
        }
    }
    // EXIT SCREEN LOGIC
    else if(g_iCurrentScreen == 2) {
        // Exit the program if the user clicks anything
        if(!stricmp(szZoneHit, "EXIT_SCREEN")) {
            // Flag WinMain() to exit program
            g_iCurrentScreen = 3;
        }
    }
    // OPTIONS MENU LOGIC
    else if(g_iCurrentScreen == 7) {
        // Go to the title screen
        if(!stricmp(szZoneHit, "EXIT_BUTTON")) {
            // Set current screen to exit screen
            g_iCurrentScreen = 2;
            // Set up the mouse zones
            vSetupMouseZones(2);
        }
        // Go back to main menu
```

```
        else if(!stricmp(szZoneHit, "OPTIONS_BACK")) {
            // Set current screen to main menu
            g_iCurrentScreen = 1;
            // Set up the mouse zones
            vSetupMouseZones(1);
        }
    }
  }
}
```

The code in bold makes up the majority of the changes to the function from the last example program. As you can see, the code first sets all of the menu highlight state variables to be turned off. This is done to make sure all of the menu items are deselected and not highlighted.

The code then checks to see if any of the highlight zones are active. Highlight zones are only active when the mouse buttons are up; therefore, the mouse pointer only needs to hover over the zones for activation. If a highlight zone is active, the function sets the proper Boolean value to be true. This tells the render function to render the highlighted button instead of the normal one.

How to Set Up Mouse Zone Highlights

In the vCheckInput() function, you check for active highlight zones, but how do you create them in the first place? Easy. You create them in the vSetupMouseZones() function. This function isn't much different from the last example program. The differences are as follows:

```
MZones.iAddZone("MAINMENU_NEWGAME_H", 192, 64, 256, 64, 3);
MZones.iAddZone("MAINMENU_LOADGAME_H", 192, 128, 256, 64, 3);
MZones.iAddZone("MAINMENU_SAVEGAME_H", 192, 192, 256, 64, 3);
MZones.iAddZone("MAINMENU_OPTIONS_H", 192, 256, 256, 64, 3);
```

These iAddZone() calls look just like the rest of the calls, except for the click type parameter. I set the click type parameter to 3. This tells the system that the zones are only active when the mouse pointer is over them and no mouse buttons are pressed. This is how mouse highlight setup is accomplished — with a change of the click type. I also add the _H prefix to the end of the zone name for easy identification in the code.

How to Render Mouse Zone Highlights

So far you have set up the mouse highlight state variables and zones. Now it is time to render the zone highlights in the vRender() function. Luckily for your sanity and mine, the function hasn't changed all that much from the last example program. The important changes are as follows:

```
else if(g_iCurrentScreen == 1) {
   // Draw the main menu
   vDrawInterfaceObject(0, 0, 256.0f, 256.0f, 0);
   vDrawInterfaceObject(256, 0, 256.0f, 256.0f, 1);
   vDrawInterfaceObject(512, 0, 256.0f, 256.0f, 2);
   vDrawInterfaceObject(0, 256, 256.0f, 256.0f, 3);
   vDrawInterfaceObject(256, 256, 256.0f, 256.0f, 4);
   vDrawInterfaceObject(512, 256, 256.0f, 256.0f, 5);
   // Draw highlights if present or default
   // to non-lit menu
   if(g_bMainMenu_NewGame_Highlight) {
      vDrawInterfaceObject(192, 64, 256.0f, 256.0f, 10);
   }
   else if(g_bMainMenu_LoadGame_Highlight) {
      vDrawInterfaceObject(192, 64, 256.0f, 256.0f, 11);
   }
   else if(g_bMainMenu_SaveGame_Highlight) {
      vDrawInterfaceObject(192, 64, 256.0f, 256.0f, 12);
   }
   else if(g_bMainMenu_Options_Highlight) {
      vDrawInterfaceObject(192, 64, 256.0f, 256.0f, 13);
   }
   else {
      // Menu, no highlights
      vDrawInterfaceObject(192, 64, 256.0f, 256.0f, 7);
   }
}
```

The changes are in bold . Instead of drawing the same menu list graphic
on each call, the program now checks the state of the highlight values to
determine the menu list to display. I created four additional menu graphics to handle the various highlight states possible. In Figure 6.29 you can
see the menu graphics that I use for the highlight effect.

Figure 6.29: The various main menu graphics that make up the highlights.

Figure 6.29 shows five menu graphics. The first one is the menu in non-highlight mode. The next four graphics show the menu in the different stages of highlight. Each state represents a different menu item highlighted. I use the term "highlight" loosely here. You can completely change the menu graphic if you so wish.

I render the first graphic in Figure 6.29 if none of the highlight zones are active. I render the second graphic if the New Game menu item is highlighted, the third graphic if the Load Game item is highlighted, and the fourth graphic if the Save Game item is highlighted. The fifth graphic is rendered if the Options menu item is highlighted.

That wasn't so bad, was it?

Recap

Can you believe it? The chapter is actually over now! As a quick recap, remember the following things about interface design and programming:

- Define the interface needs before you start programming.
- Detail the interface design with as much information as possible.
- Ask yourself the three key rules of usability when designing your interface.
- Orthographic projection in 3D allows you to render 2D graphics using 3D hardware.
- Break up interface screens into multiple textures to comply with 3D hardware limitations.
- Mouse zones are useful for detecting mouse input.
- Mouse zone highlights are useful for better-looking menus.
- Play 100,000 games of Warcraft III for your homework assignment. (Just kidding.)

Chapter 7

Adding Sound to Your Game

S ound — the root of all that is immersion. Most everyone agrees that the sound quality in a game makes up a lot of the overall experience. You don't have to look much further than the current crop of console systems. Microsoft released the first true 5.1 Dolby Digital game console — the Xbox game system. Other companies have released 6.1 sound systems for the PC, and complete home theater packages are available for computer use. This is a far cry from when computers only had a single internal speaker for various beeping noises. The problem this presents for you, the game developer, is that you must include high-quality sound in your games. Sure, you can go ahead and use low-quality sounds, but people will notice and not appreciate it.

Have you ever played a great action game that had horrible sounds? Does the machine gun sound like a cap gun? Do the explosions sound like firecrackers in the wind? The last thing in the world you want is for people to answer these questions with a resounding yes when playing your game. In this chapter I cover the following to help you get started with adding sounds to your games:

- Sound APIs
- DirectMusic sound architecture
- How to play WAV files
- How to play MIDI files
- How to play MP3 files
- Class implementation

Sound APIs

There are several ways to play sounds in a computer game, including various free APIs such as OpenAL and DirectX. There are commercial libraries available as well, but they can carry a hefty price tag.

My current preference is the DirectX API. Why, you may ask? DirectX is in its ninth version now and has tons of features. It also has the support of almost every hardware manufacturer. My favorite part is that it is free to use.

OpenAL is free as well, but it currently doesn't have a ton of support from hardware manufacturers. This presents a driver problem. If you only support OpenAL in your game, users who do not have an OpenAL driver for their sound card will most likely return your game or not bother to play it. Until OpenAL is accepted as much as OpenGL is, I recommend steering clear of it. Don't get me wrong though. If you really, really want to use OpenAL, just make your game work with both DirectX and OpenAL. Then the user gets to pick the one he wants and everyone is a winner.

DirectMusic Sound Architecture

DirectX contains two interfaces that can play back sound files: DirectSound and DirectMusic. The main difference between the two is that DirectSound provides lower-level access to the device hardware. Personally, I like to use DirectMusic since it has a lot more features and is fast enough running on today's processors. DirectMusic contains the following important parts:

- Loader
- Performance
- Segments

The DirectMusic Loader

The loader in DirectMusic is responsible for loading the audio content. You can load MIDI files, WAV files, DLS collections, and DirectMusic segment files with loaders. Once you tell the loader to load an audio resource, it starts streaming in the resource and takes care of all the work. All you have to do is play the audio, and you are done with it!

The loader uses a single interface named `IDirectMusicLoader8`. Are you wondering why it doesn't have a 9 in it for DirectX 9.0? The reason is because DirectMusic has not changed very much since release 8.

Mostly there have only been performance enhancements made to the code.

The loader interface contains several member functions, which are listed in Table 7.1.

Table 7.1: IDirectMusicLoader8 interface methods

Method	Description
CacheObject	Increments the reference count of the object. This is useful to avoid loading the object more than once.
ClearCache	Clears the reference count for the specified object type.
CollectGarbage	Clears out references that are not in use.
EnableCache	Turns on automatic caching. It can also turn off automatic caching.
EnumObject	Enumerates objects of the specified type.
GetObject	Retrieves an object.
LoadObjectFromFile	Loads an object from the file system. This is the most used method since it is responsible for loading the WAV files.
ReleaseObjectByUnknown	Releases the object reference.
ReleaseObject	Releases the object reference.
ScanDirectory	Searches the search directory for files of the type specified. It caches the results for enumeration.
SetObject	Allows you to set the attributes of an invalid object.
SetSearchDirectory	Sets the search path for finding audio files.

That's about it for the loader interface. I show how to use some of the methods in Table 7.1 later on in the chapter.

The DirectMusic Performance

Just as musicians perform and produce music, the performance interface in DirectMusic performs music. The performance interface manages playback, messaging, channel mapping, and timing. Generally speaking, you only create one of these interfaces in your game.

All of the performance work is handled by a single interface named `IDirectMusicPerformance8`. This interface is the workhorse of DirectMusic; therefore, it has a ton of member functions. Table 7.2 contains the member function listing.

Table 7.2: IDirectMusicPerformance8 interface methods

Method	Description
AddNotificationType	Adds a notification type.
AddPort	Assigns a port to the performance.
AdjustTime	Adjusts the performance time forward or backward.
AllocPMsg	Allocates memory for a message.

Method	Description
AssignPChannel	Assigns a performance channel.
AssignPChannelBlock	Assigns a block of 16 channels.
ClonePMsg	Copies a performance message.
CloseDown	Closes the performance object.
CreateAudioPath	Creates an audio path.
CreateStandardAudioPath	Creates an audio path that is configured as a standard audio path.
DownloadInstrument	Downloads a DLS instrument.
FreePMsg	Frees a message's memory.
GetBumperLength	Retrieves the time between which messages are placed in the buffer and when they begin processing.
GetDefaultAudioPath	Retrieves the default audio path.
GetGlobalParam	Retrieves global values from the performance.
GetGraph	Retrieves the toolgraph.
GetLatencyTime	Retrieves the time between which the performance is heard from the speakers.
GetNotificationPMsg	Retrieves a notification message.
GetParam	Retrieves values from a track.
GetParamEx	Retrieves values from a track. This supports self-controlling segments.
GetPrepareTime	Retrieves track latency.
GetQueueTime	Retrieves when messages can be flushed.
GetResolvedTime	Resolves time to a boundary.
GetSegmentState	Retrieves the state of the current segment.
GetTime	Retrieves the time of the performance.
InitAudio	Initializes the performance.
Invalidate	Flushes all messages.
IsPlaying	Checks whether the current segment is playing.
MIDIToMusic	Converts a MIDI note value to a DirectMusic value.
MusicToMIDI	Converts a DirectMusic value to a MIDI value.
MusicToReferenceTime	Converts `MUSIC_TIME` to `REFERENCE_TIME`.
PChannelInfo	Retrieves information for the channel.
PlaySegment	Plays a segment.
PlaySegmentEx	Plays a segment with additional options.
ReferenceToMusicTime	Converts `REFERENCE_TIME` to `MUSIC_TIME`.
RemoveNotificationType	Removes a notification type.
RemovePort	Removes a port.
RhythmToTime	Converts rhythm time to music time.
SendPMsg	Sends a message.
SetBumperLength	Sets message interval.
SetDefaultAudioPath	Sets the default audio path. This also activates the set path.

Method	Description
SetGlobalParam	Sets the global values.
SetGraph	Sets the toolgraph.
SetNotificationHandle	Sets the event handle.
riOSetParam	Sets track data.
SetPrepareTime	Sets track message interval time.
Stop	Stops a segment.
StopEx	Stops a segment or audio path.
TimeToRhythm	Converts music time to rhythm time.

Wow. That is one huge list of functions. Don't be too overwhelmed though; I only end up using a few of them in the same programs. Imagine, all of this functionality and it's free!

DirectMusic Segments

Segments in DirectMusic make up the actual audio data used for playback. Any WAV file or MIDI sequence that you play must be loaded into a segment first. There are two types of segments in DirectMusic: primary and secondary. The primary segment is the main track of music. Secondary segments are usually used for special effects.

The IDirectMusicSegment8 interface contains all of the functionality for segments. Since it can contain data for a variety of object types, it too has a lot of member functions. They are listed in Table 7.3.

Table 7.3: IDirectMusicSegment8 interface methods

Method	Description
AddNotificationType	Adds an event type.
Clone	Copies a segment.
Compose	Composes a track.
Download	Copies the data into the performance object.
GetAudioPathConfig	Retrieves the audio path configuration.
GetDefaultResolution	Retrieves the resolution time for the segment.
GetGraph	Retrieves the toolgraph.
GetLength	Retrieves the length of the segment.
GetLoopPoints	Retrieves the start and end loop points.
GetParam	Retrieves data from a track.
GetRepeats	Retrieves the number of times the segment is to loop.
GetStartPoint	Retrieves the start point.
GetTrack	Retrieves a track matching the specified search criteria.
GetTrackGroup	Retrieves the group bits from a track.
InitPlay	Initializes the play state.

Method	Description
InsertTrack	Inserts a track.
RemoveNotificationType	Removes an event type.
RemoveTrack	Removes a track.
SetDefaultResolution	Sets the default resolution.
SetGraph	Sets the toolgraph.
SetLength	Sets the length.
SetLoopPoints	Sets the start and end loop points.
SetParam	Sets track data.
SetPChannelsUsed	Sets the performance channels to use.
SetRepeats	Sets the number of times the segment loops.
SetStartPoint	Sets the start point.
SetTrackConfig	Configures a track.
Unload	Removes the data from the performance object.

As you can see in Table 7.3, there are many useful functions for the segment interface. You can control virtually every aspect of a segment with the functionality in DirectMusic. The beauty of it is that you can use a little of the functionality or as much of the functionality you want. On with the show!

How to Play WAV Files

I'm no dummy — at least my wife doesn't call me one in public — so I bet you are mainly here to learn how to play WAV files. I can't think of a better way to learn than through the wonderful world of source code. Load up the DMusic_PlaySound project from the companion files now.

The DMusic_PlaySound program demonstrates how to initialize the performance interface, initialize the loader interface, load a segment, and play a segment.

The DMusic_PlaySound Project

The program contains a few source files: main.cpp, main.h, and DXUtil.cpp. All of the source files are unique to this project except the DXUtil.cpp file. It is part of the DirectX SDK helper file set.

The project also utilizes the following libraries: dxguid.lib, winmm.lib, and dsound.lib. You may be wondering why it is not called dmusic.lib. I really have no answer for you. Microsoft decided to put the DirectMusic functions inside of the DirectSound library. My guess is because they share much of the same logic.

It's been too long since I have shown you an illustration. Check out Figure 7.1 to see the general flow of this example program.

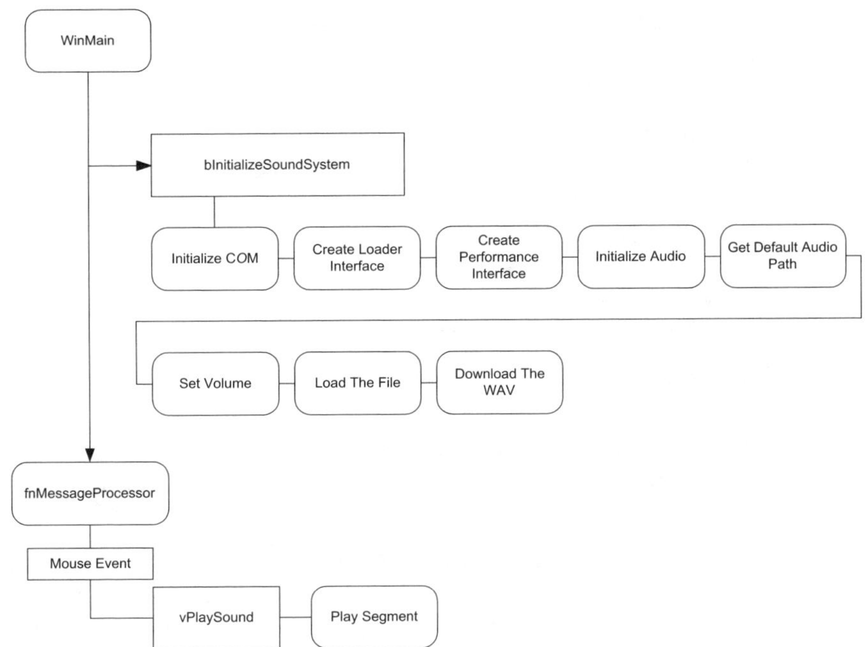

Figure 7.1: Program flow for DMusic_PlaySound.

In Figure 7.1 you can see how `WinMain()` makes a call to `bInitialize-SoundSystem()`. The initialization function makes several calls to DirectX to initialize the sound system. The program then waits for a mouse event and plays the WAV file with the `vPlaySound()` function. If you haven't done so, launch the program now and hit the left mouse button to play the WAV file. Don't you just love that wonderful test WAV file? Yeah, I know, it isn't that great. If you want to play around, substitute one of your own files for the testsound.wav. Any WAV file should work.

The Main.h Header File

Open up the main.h header file now and follow along with me. The header file for this example is really nice and short. Here it is in its entirety:

```
#ifndef MAIN_H
#define MAIN_H
#define STRICT
```

```
#include <windows.h>
#include <stdio.h>
#include <D3DX9.h>
#include <dmusici.h>
#include <dsound.h>
#include <dshow.h>
#include <dxutil.h>

// Function headers
LRESULT WINAPI fnMessageProcessor(HWND hWnd, UINT msg, WPARAM wParam, LPARAM lParam);
void vCleanup(void);
bool bInitializeSoundSystem(HWND hWnd);
void vPlaySound(void);

// Global sound data
IDirectMusicLoader8        *g_pLoader;
IDirectMusicPerformance8   *g_pPerformance;
IDirectMusicSegment8       *g_pSound;
#endif
```

The include files shouldn't be much of a surprise to you. The normal ones for Windows programs are included. The one used specifically for DirectMusic is dmusici.h.

In the function prototype section there are two new functions, `bInitializeSoundSystem()` and `vPlaySound()`. Both are pretty self-explanatory at this juncture. (Don't you just love self-documenting code?)

The next block of header code contains the global variables I use for the program. They should look pretty familiar to you if you read the first part of the chapter. The `g_pLoader` interface is used to load the sound file, the `g_pPerformance` interface is used to play the sound file, and the `g_pSound` interface contains the sound file data.

Note   I don't encourage you to use global variables for production code. I only use it for examples in this book to keep things simple.

The Main.cpp Program File

The main part of the code resides in the main.cpp program file. Open it now to follow along. As usual, the `WinMain()` function demands your attention. It contains the standard Windows initialization code with a new function call. Here is the portion of the code you should be interested in:

```
// Initialize Direct Sound
bRet = bInitializeSoundSystem(hWnd);
if(bRet == 0) {
   MessageBox(hWnd, "Initialization Failure",
            "Failed to initialize Direct Sound",
          MB_ICONEXCLAMATION|MB_OK);
```

```
    // The program failed, exit
    exit(1);
}
```

I make a call to the `bInitializeSoundSystem()` function right after the window is created for the program. This function takes one parameter, the handle to the window. If the function returns a 0, it failed. In this case, I put a nice error window on the screen and exit the program when the user hits the OK button. On the other hand, if everything works as planned, the code continues.

The bInitializeSoundSystem() Function

Oh boy, the real fun begins now. This function contains all of the code necessary to initialize DirectMusic. It also takes on the task of loading the sound file played in the program.

How to Initialize COM

The first thing you must do in the code is initialize COM. DirectX uses COM interfaces so this is a necessary evil (or good). If you are unfamiliar with COM, I suggest you look up some books on it at your favorite book web site. The call to initialize looks like the following:

```
CoInitialize(NULL);
```

That looks pretty easy, right? Luckily, that's all you have to do to initialize COM. Now that that is out of the way, you can create DirectX interfaces.

How to Create the Loader Interface

The next piece of code creates the loader interface. As you probably recall, the loader interface is responsible for loading audio data such as WAV files and MIDI files. Here is the code for it:

```
if(FAILED(hResult = CoCreateInstance(CLSID_DirectMusicLoader, NULL,
    CLSCTX_INPROC, IID_IDirectMusicLoader8,
    (void**) &g_pLoader))) {
    return(0);
}
```

I make a call to the `CoCreateInstance()` function to retrieve the loader interface. The `IDirectMusicLoader8` interface uses the `CLSID_Direct-MusicLoader` CLSID and the `IID_IDirectMusicLoader8` reference identifier. The interface pointer is stored in the global variable g_pLoader.

I know this may sound a bit alien to you if you are not familiar with COM, but don't worry. You only need to copy this code into your own program. You should rarely need to modify this initialization code for DirectMusic.

How to Create the Performance Interface

The loader interface is in place now, so the next step is to create the performance interface. The performance interface is responsible for playing the audio data and is vital to DirectMusic. Here is the code to initialize the performance interface:

```
if(FAILED(hResult = CoCreateInstance(CLSID_DirectMusicPerformance, NULL,
    CLSCTX_INPROC, IID_IDirectMusicPerformance8,
    (void**) &g_pPerformance))) {
    return(0);
}
```

Once again, I use the `CoCreateInstance()` function to create the interface. The `IDirectPerformance8` interface uses the `CLSID_Direct-MusicPerformance` CLSID and the `IID_DirectMusicPerformance8` reference identifier. I store the interface pointer in the globally defined `g_pPerformance` pointer.

How to Initialize the Audio

Unlike the loader, the performance requires initialization once you have a valid interface. The `IDirectMusicPerformance8::InitAudio()` function accomplishes this task. The init audio function initializes the performance and sets up the audio path for the performance. Here is the prototype for the function:

```
HRESULT InitAudio(
    IDirectMusic** ppDirectMusic,
    IDirectSound** ppDirectSound,
    HWND hWnd,
    DWORD dwDefaultPathType,
    DWORD dwPChannelCount,
    DWORD dwFlags,
    DMUS_AUDIOPARAMS *pParams
);
```

The first parameter, `ppDirectMusic`, allows you to have the resulting DirectMusic interface created by the function returned. If you leave it `NULL`, the interface uses an internally created DirectMusic interface. I prefer `NULL`, as it is simpler to keep track of.

The second parameter does the same thing as the first, except it returns or stores a DirectSound interface. Once again, I prefer to use `NULL` for this parameter.

The third parameter, `hWnd`, wants the handle of the window to create the DirectSound interface with. If you leave it `NULL`, the foreground window is used. I prefer to use `NULL` here.

The fourth parameter, `dwDefaultPathType`, specifies the default audio path type. Table 7.4 contains the valid types.

Table 7.4: Audio path types

Value	Meaning
DMUS_APATH_DYNAMIC_3D	3D sound
DMUS_APATH_DYNAMIC_MONO	Mono sound
DMUS_APATH_DYNAMIC_STEREO	Stereo sound
DMUS_APATH_SHARED_STEREOPLUSREVERB	Stereo sound with reverb

Of the types available, I normally use `DMUS_APATH_DYNAMIC_STEREO` since it provides stereo sound capability.

The fifth parameter, `dwPChannelCount`, specifies the number of performance channels to use in the audio path. I use four in the example.

The sixth parameter, `dwFlags`, lets you specify the desired features you want in the performance object. The flags and their meanings are listed in Table 7.5.

Table 7.5: Performance feature flags

Value	Meaning
DMUS_AUDIOF_3D	3D buffers
DMUS_AUDIOF_ALL	All features
DMUS_AUDIOF_BUFFERS	Multiple buffers
DMUS_AUDIOF_DMOS	Additional DMOs
DMUS_AUDIOF_EAX	EAX effects
DMUS_AUDIOF_ENVIRON	Environmental modeling
DMUS_AUDIOF_STREAMING	Streaming waveforms

In the example code, I use the `DMUS_AUDIOF_ALL` flag. This tells the performance object to utilize every feature possible. This is a useful option to allow users to turn off certain features that they do not want for speed issues.

The seventh parameter, `pParams`, lets you set the audio parameters desired in the form of a `DMUS_AUDIOPARAMS` data structure. I usually set the default parameter with a `NULL` here.

That does it for the init audio function. The last step required for the performance interface initialization is a call to the `IDirectMusic-Performance8::GetDefaultAudioPath()` function. This function returns the default audio path created with the init audio function. You need the audio path to set the volume of the sound system. If you don't want to mess around with the volume, you can skip this step.

Here is the code that matches the above text:

```
// Initialize the audio
if(FAILED(hResult = g_pPerformance->InitAudio(
    NULL,
    NULL,
```

```
    hWnd,
    DMUS_APATH_DYNAMIC_STEREO,
    4,
    DMUS_AUDIOF_ALL,
    NULL
    ))) {
    return(0);
}
// Get the default path
if(FAILED(g_pPerformance->GetDefaultAudioPath(&dmAudioPath)))
    return(0);
```

How to Set the Volume

As I alluded to earlier, you set the volume with the `IDirectMusic-AudioPath8` interface. This is done with the `SetVolume()` member function. Here is the prototype for it:

```
HRESULT SetVolume(
    long lVolume,
    DWORD dwDuration
);
```

The first parameter, `lVolume`, sets the volume level in hundredths of a decibel. The range allowed is –9600 to 0. The value of 0 is full volume.

The second parameter, `dwDuration`, specifies the amount of time over which the volume changes. Setting this to 0 tells the system to make the change as soon as possible.

Here is the code as used in the example:

```
// Set the default volume
if(FAILED(dmAudioPath->SetVolume(0,0)))
    return(0);
```

How to Load the Sound

Remember the loader interface that you created a minute ago? You get to use it again to load in the test WAV file included with the companion files. To do this, you use the `LoadObjectFromFile()` function. Before I get into the prototype for the function, check out the code here:

```
// Load the sound from a file
if (FAILED(g_pLoader->LoadObjectFromFile(
    CLSID_DirectMusicSegment,
    IID_IDirectMusicSegment8,
    L"testsound.wav",
    (LPVOID*) &g_pSound
    )))
{
    return(0);
}

// Download the data
if (FAILED (g_pSound->Download(g_pPerformance))) {
```

```
    return(0);
}
```

In the code I use the file loader function to load the WAV file from the hard drive. I then download the segment into the performance object for playback. That's really the sum of it from a 50,000-foot view.

The `LoadObjectFromFile()` function has the following prototype:

```
HRESULT LoadObjectFromFile(
    REFGUID rguidClassID,
    REFIID iidInterfaceID,
    WCHAR *pwzFilePath,
    void ** ppObject
);
```

The first parameter, `rguidClassID`, requires the unique identifier for the class. To load in segments, you use the `CLSID_DirectMusicSegment` class identifier.

The second parameter, `iidInterfaceID`, requires the unique identifier for the interface. To load in a segment you use `IID_IDirect-MusicSegment8`.

The third parameter, `pwzFilePath`, requires the name of the file to load. For the example, I use the "testsound.wav" file. You may have noticed the `L` in front of the name. I do this since this parameter takes a wide character string.

The fourth parameter, `ppObject`, receives the return interface. I pass in the `g_pSound` global pointer for this parameter.

How to Download the Segment

You must now download the segment into the performance object. This is accomplished with the `IDirectMusicSegment8::Download()` function. Here is the prototype for it:

```
HRESULT Download(
    IUnknown* pAudioPath
);
```

This one is nice and simple. There is only one parameter, and it expects an interface pointer in which to download the segment. For this I pass in the `g_pPerformance` performance pointer.

Check out Figure 7.2 on the following page to see the steps I covered.

In Figure 7.2 you can see how you initialize COM, create the loader, create the performance, initialize the audio, get the default audio path, set the volume, load the file, and finally download the WAV. This set of steps repeats itself every time you implement DirectMusic, so memorize it (or at least keep this page marked).

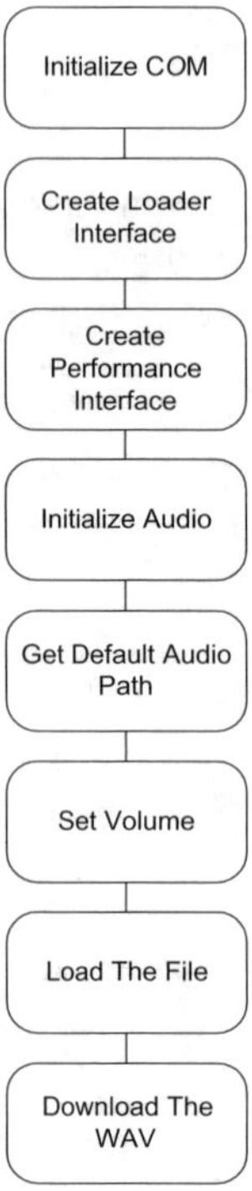

Initialize COM

Create Loader
Interface

Create
Performance
Interface

Initialize Audio

Get Default Audio
Path

Set Volume

Load The File

Download The
WAV

Figure 7.2: DirectMusic initialization steps.

The vPlaySound() Function

The example program processes left mouse button messages and
executes the vPlaySound() function for each button event. The fnMes-
sageProcessor() processes the actual mouse button event, but the play
sound function executes the interesting part of the code. Take a look at
the play sound function now. Here is the code for it:

```
void vPlaySound(void)
{
    // Play the sound segment
    g_pPerformance->PlaySegmentEx(
        g_pSound,
        NULL,
        NULL,
        DMUS_SEGF_DEFAULT | DMUS_SEGF_SECONDARY,
        0,
        NULL,
        NULL,
        NULL
    );
}
```

The `vPlaySound()` function isn't very complicated at all. In fact, I only make one call in it to the `IDirectMusicPerformance8::PlaySegmentEx()` function.

How to Play the Sound

This function begins the playback of a downloaded segment. It has a few parameters, but as you can see in my example, you can leave many of them at `NULL`. Here is the prototype for the function:

```
HRESULT PlaySegmentEx(
    IUnknown* pSource,
    WCHAR *pwzSegmentName,
    IUnknown* pTransition,
    DWORD dwFlags,
    __int64 i64StartTime,
    IDirectMusicSegmentState** ppSegmentState,
    IUnknown* pFrom,
    IUnknown* pAudioPath
);
```

The first parameter, `pSource`, wants a pointer to the interface object to play. In this instance, I use the global pointer to the segment I loaded earlier.

The second parameter, `pwzSegmentName`, is not used in DirectX 9.0.

The third parameter, `pTransition`, allows you to set up a transition for the segment. I leave this at `NULL`.

The fourth parameter, `dwFlags`, lets you set up various option flags for the playback. For this parameter I use the `DMUS_SEGF_DEFAULT` and `DMUS_SEGF_SECONDARY` flags. These two flags tell the segment to play at its default boundary and to play as a secondary sound. There are many flags available, and I suggest you check them out in the DirectX SDK.

The fifth parameter, `i64StartTime`, sets the starting time for the segment. I set this to `NULL` so that the sound starts playing immediately.

The sixth parameter, `ppSegmentState`, lets you set up an interface pointer to receive the segment's state. I usually don't use this feature, so I set this to `NULL`.

The seventh parameter, `pFrom`, lets you specify an interface to stop playing when the new segment starts. I set this to `NULL` as well.

The eighth parameter, `pAudioPath`, tells the system which audio path to play the segment on. I set this to `NULL` to make it play on the default audio path.

Launch the program now and click the left mouse button a few times. One cool feature of the program is that you can play back multiple sounds simultaneously. This may not seem like a big deal to you if you have never tried sound playback before, but believe me, it is a cool feature. The nice part is that DirectMusic handles all of the buffering for you.

How to Play MIDI Files

Have you ever wanted to play MIDI files in your game? If so, you have come to the right place. Luckily for you, playing MIDI files is very simple. In fact, you already know how to if you read the last section! That's right — you play MIDI files exactly the same way you play WAV files. I went ahead and created a project included with the companion files named DMusic_PlayMIDI. Load it up, compile it, and execute it. You can see the output in Figure 7.3.

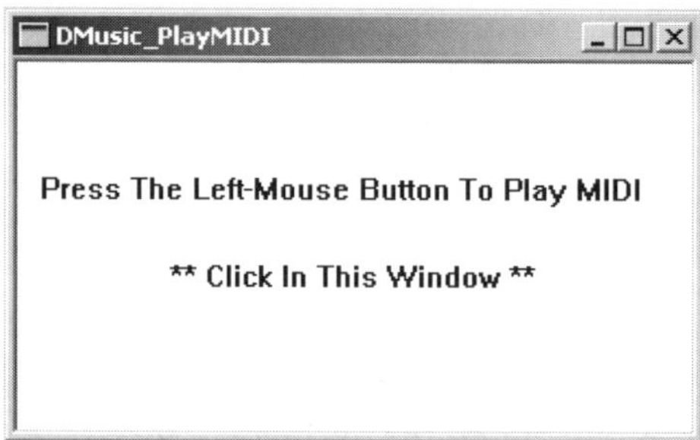

Figure 7.3: Output from the DMusic_PlayMIDI program.

I bet the program looks familiar, eh? I only made a few cosmetic changes to the WAV playing program. For one thing, I changed the filename to read c:\dxsdk\samples\media\canyon.mid. If you have the DirectX SDK located in a different folder, you need to change the path and recompile. You can also insert the filename and path for any of your own MIDI files. (I don't include a MIDI file with the companion files because I don't have any MIDI authoring software! Maybe next time.)

How to Play MP3 Files

Have you ever wanted to play MP3 files in your game? If so, you have come to the right place. Unfortunately, playing MP3 files requires a whole new set of interfaces and functions. Isn't it amazing how you went from being lucky to being unfortunate? Such is life, my friend.

In case you have been under a rock for the last few years, the MP3 format is a lossy compression format for storing audio data. Most people use it for songs, but it is also suitable for speech and sound effects. The only real drawback to the MP3 format is that it takes up a lot of CPU overhead in comparison to other formats. This isn't really much of an issue any more with the current crop of CPUs out there, but it still merits consideration.

Included with the companion files is a project called DShow_Play-MP3. The output from it is in Figure 7.4.

Figure 7.4: Output from the DShow_PlayMP3 program.

Okay, so the program output in Figure 7.4 doesn't look all that great. There is a reason for that though: It's built to play an MP3 file, not display a spinning 3D cube!

Load up the DShow_PlayMP3 project now so you can follow along. I suggest you try to compile it as well and run it so you can at least hear the results. If you don't hear anything, check the line with the filename c:\dxsdk\samples\media\track.mp3 on it. If you do not have an MP3 file at that location, change the text to point to an MP3 file on your system. The DirectX SDK comes with a few that you can play.

DirectShow

The first thing that probably stands out is the name of the project. Unlike the first two projects, this one starts with the DShow prefix. I do this since this program uses DirectShow and not DirectMusic. DirectShow is a completely different interface in DirectX that is built to stream media in Windows. It can play many formats, such as AVI, MPEG, MP3, and even WAV. As you can see, it can play video as well as audio and even the two combined. This is really cool, as it gives you an avenue to play cut-scenes and introduction videos in your games.

The DShow_PlayMP3 Project

The program contains a few source files: main.cpp, main.h, and DXUtil.cpp. All of the source files are unique to this project except the DXUtil.cpp file. The project also utilizes the following libraries: dxguid.lib, winmm.lib, and Strmiids.lib. The Strmiids.lib file is the one required by DirectShow.

The Main.h Header File

The main.h header file contains the usual global variables and includes required by the example program. Here is the code for the include section:

```
#include <windows.h>
#include <stdio.h>
#include <D3DX9.h>
#include <dxutil.h>
#include <dshow.h>
```

The new kid on the block here is the dshow.h include. This is required for the DirectShow interface and function calls. Be sure to include it whenever you want DirectShow functionality.

In the next block of code, you have the function prototypes. Here they are:

```
LRESULT WINAPI fnMessageProcessor(HWND hWnd, UINT msg, WPARAM wParam, LPARAM lParam);
void vCleanup(void);
bool bPlayTitleMusic(void);
void vStopTitleMusic(void);
void vCheckMusicStatus(void);
```

The `fnMessageProcessor()` function is the usual Windows message handler. There is nothing new here — just the same old stuff.

The `vCleanup()` function is called when the program exits. It handles the releasing of interfaces.

The `bPlayTitleMusic()` function is only called once at the beginning of the program. It initializes DirectShow, loads the MP3 file to play, and starts it.

The `vStopTitleMusic()` function stops the title music from playing when the program exits.

The `vCheckMusicStatus()` function checks to see if the music segment is over. If it is over, it restarts the music.

The global data comes next in the header file. I create a few interface pointers and a single Boolean value like so:

```
bool           g_bBackgroundMusicActive = 0;
IGraphBuilder  *g_pGraph;
IMediaControl  *g_pMediaControl;
IMediaEvent    *g_pEvent;
IMediaSeeking  *g_pSeeking;
```

The `g_bBackgroundMusicActive` variable is used to keep track of the music status. If the music is playing, the value is 1. If not, it equals 0.

The `g_pGraph` variable is a pointer to an `IGraphBuilder` interface. Uh oh, what is a graph?

Filter Graphs 101

DirectShow is built upon software filters. A filter in DirectShow performs operations on streams of data. There are many functions of filters, the main ones being:

- Read in file data
- Decode stream data
- Capture video
- Pass data to system hardware

For example, a filter graph can read in an MP3 file and produce sound to the audio hardware as output. Check out Figure 7.5 to see this illustrated.

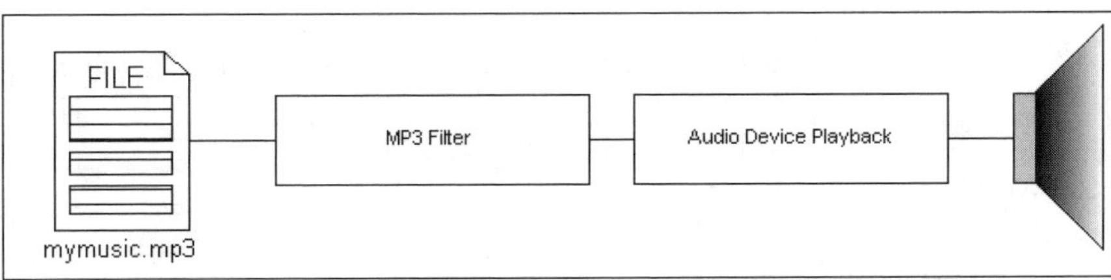

Figure 7.5: Illustration of an MP3 filter graph.

As you can see in Figure 7.5, the filter graph reads in the MP3 data file, decodes it, and then sends it to the audio hardware for playback. The workhorse of the filter industry in DirectShow is the `IGraphBuilder` interface. In Table 7.6 you can see the functions contained within this interface.

Table 7.6: IGraphBuilder interface methods

Method	Description
Abort	Tells the graph to return from its current operation.
AddSourceFilter	Adds a source filter.
Connect	Connects two pins.
Render	Adds filters to an output pin.
RenderFile	Loads in a file for playback. I use this in the example code to load in the MP3 file.
SetLogFile	Sets the handle to the file for logging output information.
ShouldOperationContinue	Tells you whether or not the operation should continue. This is a very strange function that you should never have to call.

Media Controls 101

On the next line of code in the header file, I create an `IMediaControl` interface pointer named g_pMediaControl. The media control interface is used to control the data that runs through the filter graph. This interface allows you to start, stop, and even pause the data going through the graph. You can think of it as your VCR or DVR remote.

In the example program I use the media control interface to start, stop, and restart the music. You can see these functions and others in Table 7.7.

Table 7.7: IMediaControl interface functions

Method	Description
GetState	Retrieves the state of the graph.
Pause	Pauses the media that is currently playing.
Run	Starts the media. This is akin to Play on your VCR or DVR remote control.
Stop	Stops the media from playing.
StopWhenReady	A kinder gentler stop.

Media Events 101

Next up in the header file you see the pointer for an `IMediaEvent` interface. This interface type is used to communicate with the filter graph. It is useful for telling you the status of the media you are playing. In the example program I use this interface to tell me when the music has stopped. The methods for this interface can be seen in Table 7.8.

Table 7.8: IMediaEvent interface functions

Method	Description
CancelDefaultHandling	Cancels the filter's default handling.
FreeEventParams	Frees the parameter resources.
GetEvent	Retrieves the next event in the queue.
GetEventHandle	Retrieves the handle of the next signaled event in the queue.
RestoreDefaultHandling	Restores the default handler.
WaitForCompletion	Waits for the filter graph to complete its playback of the media. I use this function in the example program to check if the audio is done playing.

Media Seeking 101

The next interface is the `IMediaSeeking` interface. Just as its name suggests, it is for seeking to a position in your media. It also sets the rate of playback for your media. In the example program I use this interface to rewind the media when it is done playing. I also use it to set the playback rate of the media. The methods for the interface can be seen in Table 7.9.

Table 7.9: IMediaSeeking interface functions

Method	Description
CheckCapabilities	Checks if the stream has the specified capabilities.
ConvertTimeFormat	Converts from one format to another.
GetAvailable	Retrieves the efficient ranges of seeking time.
GetCapabilities	Retrieves the capabilities of the media stream.
GetCurrentPosition	Retrieves the current position of the stream.
GetDuration	Retrieves the length of the stream.
GetPositions	Gets the current and stop positions.
GetPreroll	Retrieves the amount of media located before the start position.
GetRate	Retrieves the playback rate.
GetStopPosition	Retrieves the stop position. This tells you when the stream will stop playing.
GetTimeFormat	Retrieves the current time format in use.
IsFormatSupported	Checks if the specified time format is supported.
IsUsingTimeFormat	Checks if the specified time format is in use.
QueryPreferredFormat	Retrieves the preferred time format.
SetPositions	Sets the current and stop positions.
SetRate	Sets the playback rate.
SetTimeFormat	Sets the time format.

In the example program, I use the `SetRate()` and `SetPositions()` functions.

The Main.cpp Program File

The meat of the program is located in the main.cpp file. Load it now so you can follow along. Take a close look at the `WinMain()` function and take notice of the following:

```
// Play the title music
bRet = bPlayTitleMusic();
if(bRet == 0) {
   MessageBox(hWnd, "Initialization Failure",
      "Failed to initialize DirectShow",
      MB_ICONEXCLAMATION|MB_OK);
   // The program failed, exit
   exit(1);
}
```

This block of code calls the `bPlayTitleMusic()` function that is local to my program. It is responsible for initializing DirectShow and playing the MP3 file from the DirectX SDK media folder. Let's go there now.

The bPlayTitleMusic() Function

This function does most of the work for the example program. It initializes COM, creates the interfaces, loads the music, sets the playback rate, and starts playing the music. Here is the code for this function:

```
bool bPlayTitleMusic(void)
{
    HRESULT    hr;

    // Initialize COM
    CoInitialize(NULL);
    // Create the graph
    CoCreateInstance(CLSID_FilterGraph,
        NULL,
        CLSCTX_INPROC_SERVER,
        IID_IGraphBuilder,
        (void **)&g_pGraph);
    // Query for interface objects
    g_pGraph->QueryInterface(
        IID_IMediaControl, (void **)&g_pMediaControl);
    g_pGraph->QueryInterface(
        IID_IMediaEvent, (void **)&g_pEvent);
    g_pGraph->QueryInterface(
        IID_IMediaSeeking, (void **)&g_pSeeking);

    // Load the song (insert your own filename below)
    hr = g_pGraph->RenderFile(
        L"c:\\dxsdk\\samples\\media\\track3.mp3", NULL);
    if(hr != S_OK) {
        return(0);
    }
    // Set the playback rate
    g_pSeeking->SetRate(1);
    // Play the song
    g_pMediaControl->Run();
    // Set background music active flag
    g_bBackgroundMusicActive = 1;
    return(1);
}
```

Initialize DirectShow

The first thing the function does is initialize COM. This is a required step since DirectShow utilizes COM interfaces.

The next step to DirectShow heaven is the creation of the graph object. I accomplish this with a call to the `CoCreateInstance()` function. The `IGraphBuilder` interface uses the `CLSID_FilterGraph` CLSID and the `IID_IGraphBuilder` reference identifier. The interface pointer is stored in the global variable named g_pGraph.

Now that you have the graph builder interface, you can create the other interfaces by querying the graph builder. This is done with the `IGraphBuilder::QueryInterface()` function. There are three interfaces to create: `IID_IMediaControl`, `IID_IMediaEvent`, and `IID_IMediaSeeking`. Each one is created and pointed to by the global pointers I mentioned earlier.

So far you have initialized COM, created the graph object, and created the helper interfaces needed for the program. All of this work makes up the basic initialization work required to play MP3 files. All that is left is to load the music, set the playback rate, and play it. Before you move on, check out Figure 7.6.

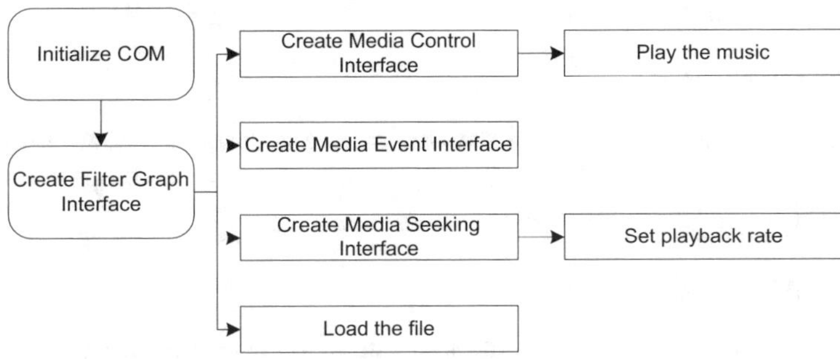

Figure 7.6: Steps to DirectShow initialization.

In Figure 7.6 you can see how the media control, media event, and media seeking interfaces relate to the graph filter interface. You can also see how the play function belongs to the media control interface and how the rate function belongs to the media seeking interface. Later on you will see how the media event interface fits into the big picture.

Load the Music File

The `IGraphBuilder::RenderFile()` function handles the work of loading the file. It takes two parameters, one to the filename and one that is not used. In the example code, you can see that I am loading the c:\dxsdk\ samples\media\track3.mp3 file. Make sure you adjust this path if you do not have the DirectX SDK installed in the directory that I reference. You may also change this filename to any MP3 song you have on your system. Personally, I have mine pointed to "Weird Al" Yankovic's "Amish Paradise" song. Since I don't own the distribution rights to the song, I must point to a file I hope you have on your system!

As long as all goes well with the loading, the function returns the value of S_OK. If something does go wrong, you may want to consult the DirectX SDK documentation for information about the error code.

Set the Playback Rate

Moving right along now. The next piece of code sets the rate of the song. The rate of the music determines how fast or slow it plays back. This setting can be used to make the artists sound like chipmunks or Darth Vader. The `IMediaSeeking::SetRate()` function does the deed. It takes one parameter, the rate of playback. To play back the song at its default rate, set this value to 1. To hear the artist sing in double-time, set it to 2. You may also set it to variations inbetween. For example, I like to play Metallica's music at 1.25 for pure speed metal. You can almost see Lars' arms smoking from that!

Play the Music

Playing the MP3 once all the work is done is rather easy. A simple call to the `IMediaControl::Run()` function does the trick. As long as the function returns S_OK, you are good to go.

Set Up the Background Event

Now that everything is up and running, the code sets the `g_bBackgroundMusicActive` flag to 1. This lets the `WinMain()` message loop know to check the status of the music. Zoom back to the `WinMain()` function now and look at the following code:

```
if(g_bBackgroundMusicActive) {
    vCheckMusicStatus();
}
```

Hey, I didn't say it was a lot of code! Anyway, the main loop checks the status of the music by calling my `vCheckMusicStatus()` function.

The vCheckMusicStatus() Function

The `vCheckMusicStatus()` function checks if the background music has stopped. If so, it rewinds the music and starts it back up again. Here is the code for the function:

```
void vCheckMusicStatus(void)
{
    long        evCode;

    // Check the event code
    g_pEvent->WaitForCompletion(0, &evCode);
    // If the music is done, restart it
    if(evCode == EC_COMPLETE) {
```

```
        // Set the starting position to 0
        LONGLONG lStartPos = 0;
        // Stop the music
        g_pMediaControl->Stop();
        // Set the positions
        g_pSeeking->SetPositions(
            &lStartPos,
            AM_SEEKING_AbsolutePositioning,
            NULL, AM_SEEKING_NoPositioning);
        // Run the music
        g_pMediaControl->Run();
    }
}
```

Check the Event Code

It's now time to use the old trusty `IMediaEvent` interface. This interface provides a view into the music's status. I call the `IMediaEvent::Wait-ForCompletion()` function to retrieve the topmost event code.

The first parameter sets how long I want to wait for the code to return. By setting it to 0, I tell the system to return immediately without waiting. The second parameter contains the variable that holds the return event code.

If the event code equals `EC_COMPLETE`, I know the song is done playing. This is an obvious hint to rewind the song and start it back up again. If the code equals `EC_ERRORABORT` or `EC_USERABORT`, I know something went wrong and the song is done playing.

Stop the Music

Assuming the song is over, the next chunk of code stops the music, rewinds it, and starts playing it again. The music is stopped with a call to the `IMediaControl::Stop()` function. This function takes no parameters.

I know it sounds strange, but you must stop the music before rewinding it, kind of like old tape recorders of the past.

Rewind the Music

Now that the music is stopped, you need to rewind it back to the beginning. In reality you don't rewind it; you just set its position back to the start. This is done with the `IMediaSeeking::SetPositions()` function. Here is the prototype for it:

```
HRESULT SetPositions(
    LONGLONG *pCurrent,
    DWORD dwCurrentFlags,
    LONGLONG *pStop,
    DWORD dwStopFlags
);
```

The first parameter expects a variable containing the current position of the song. Since I want to rewind the song, I set the variable to 0.

The next parameter, `dwCurrentFlags`, expects a combination of bitwise flags pertaining to the current position. There are two types of flags, positioning and modifying. I use the `AM_SEEKING_Absolute-Positioning` flag here to tell the system the position of 0 is absolute and not relative. There are three other flags that are pretty self-explanatory: `AM_SEEKING_NoPositioning`, `AM_SEEKING_RelativePositioning`, and `AM_SEEKING_IncrementalPositioning`.

The next parameter, `pStop`, expects a variable containing the stop position of the music. I set this to `NULL` to tell the system to use the default stop time stored in the song file.

The last parameter, `dwStopFlags`, expects a combination of bitwise flags pertaining to the stop position. Since I do not set the stop position, I use the `AM_SEEKING_NoPositioning` flag here. This tells the system that I am not setting the stop position and not to worry about it.

Run the Music

Now that the song has been stopped and rewound, I start it back up again with the trusty run function I used earlier in initialization.

Check out Figure 7.7 to see all that you have accomplished in this program.

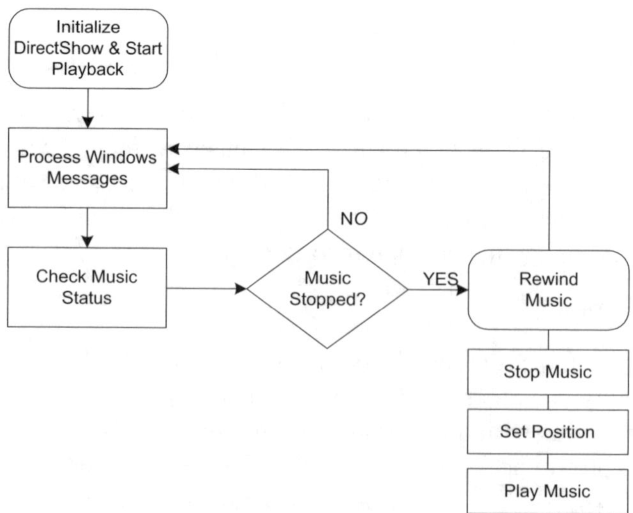

Figure 7.7: MP3 playback program flow.

You can see in this figure how the system initializes DirectShow, loads and starts playback of the song, checks for it to stop, rewinds it, and starts it back up. That's about it for MP3 file playback.

Sound Class Implementation

You now have in your possession the knowledge to put sounds in your games. But in its current state, the code is not very flexible or easy to integrate. What you need is a sound system class object to make sound integration and use much easier. In this section I show you how to create a sound system class that does the following:

■ Initializes DirectSound

■ Loads sound files

■ Plays sound files

Sound System Class

First off, I need to cover the layout of the Sound System class. Check out Figure 7.8 to see the class structure.

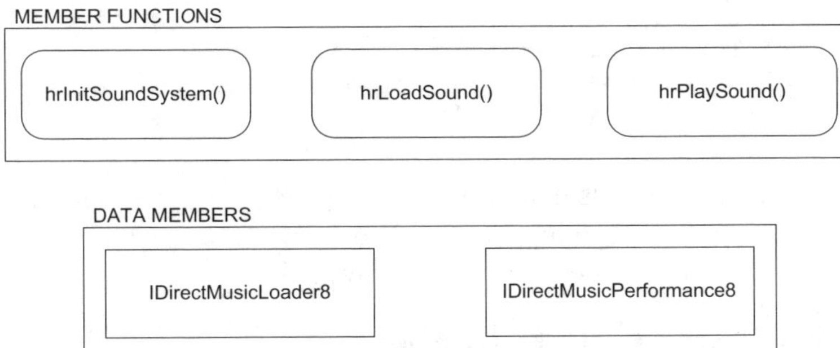

Figure 7.8: Layout of the Sound System class.

Notice that there are three main member functions and two main data members. The class also has the usual constructor and destructor, but I don't show them here since they are a given.

The three functions are: `hrInitSoundSystem()`, `hrLoadSound()`, and `hrPlaySound()`. Pretty straightforward, eh? The initialization function only has to be called once per instance of your game. Since there should only be one instance, this means you only have to call it one time, and then you are done with it. The load sound function should only be called once per sound. There is no need to load the same sound several times unless you really want to for some reason. The play sound function can and probably will be called several times for a single sound. There is no limit to the number of times you can play a sound.

The two main data members, m_pLoader (IDirectMusicLoader8) and m_pPerformance (IDirectMusicPerformance8), provide the class with the necessary interface objects. As you probably recall, the loader handles the loading of sounds and the performance object handles the playing of sounds.

Sound System Class Definition

You have seen the layout of the class; now it's time to see the actual code. Here it is in all its glory:

```
class SoundSystem
{
    private:

    public:
        HWND                      m_hWnd;
        // Sound System
        IDirectMusicLoader8       *m_pLoader;
        IDirectMusicPerformance8  *m_pPerformance;

        // Functions
        SoundSystem();
        ~SoundSystem();
        HRESULT hrInitSoundSystem(void);
        HRESULT hrLoadSound(char *szname,GameSound *gs);
        HRESULT hrPlaySound(GameSound *gs);
};
```

The code for the class definition is quite short, but there is not much to the class itself. One thing may stand out to you though, and that is the GameSound data type. What is that anyway?

Game Sound Class Definition

Since you only need one performance object and one loader object but multiple segments, I create the game sound class. This class contains the actual sound segment data for a particular sound. There is nothing much to this class, as it is really only a holder for the sound information. Here is the header to the class:

```
class GameSound
{
    public:
```

```
IDirectMusicSegment8      *m_pSound;
IDirectMusicPerformance8  *m_pPerformance;
~GameSound();
GameSound();
};
```

Don't be alarmed by the `m_pPerformance` pointer. It only points to the
performance interface in the sound system class. The only data member
really used is the `m_pSound` member. It contains the sound data once the
data is loaded.

To see how the two classes relate to each other, check out Figure
7.9.

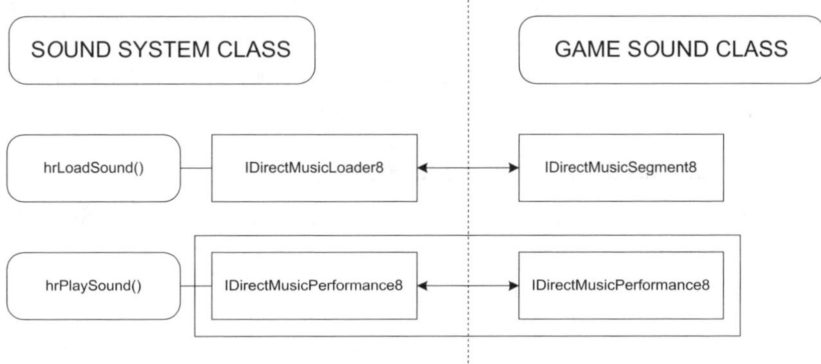

Figure 7.9: Sound system class and game sound class interaction.

Notice how the loader interface in the sound system class loads data into
the segment interface in the game sound class. You can also see how the
performance interface is shared between the two classes.

Sound System Class Implementation

The overview is out of the way, so how about some implementation code
to keep the ball rolling? The following code shows you the constructor
for the class:

```
SoundSystem::SoundSystem()
{
    m_pLoader = NULL;
    m_pPerformance = NULL;
}
```

In the constructor you can see how I set the loader and performance
pointers to equal `NULL`. I do this so that I can tell when the loader or performance objects are allocated. If they are `NULL`, they are not ready yet. If

they aren't NULL, I know I can use them. Call it sanity checking if you want.

The SoundSystem::~SoundSystem() Destructor

The next block of code shows you the destructor:

```
SoundSystem::~SoundSystem()
{
    SAFE_RELEASE(m_pLoader);
    SAFE_RELEASE(m_pPerformance);
}
```

The destructor releases the loader and performance objects. I call the DirectX utility macro named SAFE_RELEASE. This macro checks to make sure an object is not NULL before releasing it. This is why it's called a safe release. Since the loader and performance objects are created with the class, it is necessary to clean them up here.

The SoundSystem::hrInitSoundSystem() Function

The first really important function is the initialization function. Here is the code for it:

```
HRESULT SoundSystem::hrInitSoundSystem(void)
{
    HRESULT                 hResult;
    IDirectMusicAudioPath8 *path;

    // Initialize COM
    CoInitialize(NULL);

    // Create the loader
    if(FAILED(hResult = CoCreateInstance(
    CLSID_DirectMusicLoader, NULL,
        CLSCTX_INPROC, IID_IDirectMusicLoader8,
        (void**)&m_pLoader))) {
        return(SOUNDERROR_MUSICLOADER);
    }

    // Create the performance
    if(FAILED(hResult = CoCreateInstance(
        CLSID_DirectMusicPerformance, NULL,
        CLSCTX_INPROC, IID_IDirectMusicPerformance8,
        (void**)&m_pPerformance))) {
        return(SOUNDERROR_MUSICPERFORMANCE);
    }

    // Initialize the audio
    if(FAILED(hResult = m_pPerformance->InitAudio(
        NULL, NULL,
        m_hWnd, DMUS_APATH_DYNAMIC_STEREO,
        4, DMUS_AUDIOF_ALL, NULL
        ))) {
```

```
        return(SOUNDERROR_INITAUDIO);
    }

    // Get the default path
    if(FAILED(m_pPerformance->GetDefaultAudioPath(&path)))
        return(SOUNDERROR_PATH);

    // Set the default volume
    if(FAILED(path->SetVolume(0, 0)))
        return(SOUNDERROR_VOLUME);

    return(S_OK);
}
```

The code in this function should ring a bell for you. Earlier in this chapter I covered everything seen in this function. Basically, the function initializes COM, creates the loader interface, creates the performance interface, initializes the audio, gets the default audio path, and sets the volume.

Note   You don't necessarily need the set volume function here, but I like to initialize the audio system to a default volume. You may also want to remove the COM initialization code if you plan on initializing COM somewhere else in the calling thread.

The SoundSystem::hrLoadSound() Function

The next function on the list loads sound data. Here is the code for it:

```
HRESULT SoundSystem::hrLoadSound(char *szname,GameSound *gs)
{
    WCHAR  szWideFileName[512];

    // Make sure audio is initialized
    if(!m_pLoader)
        return(SOUNDERROR_MUSICLOADER);

    if(!m_pPerformance)
        return(SOUNDERROR_MUSICPERFORMANCE);

    // Clean up sound if it already exists
    if(gs->m_pSound) {
        gs->m_pSound->Unload(m_pPerformance);
        gs->m_pSound->Release();
        gs->m_pSound = NULL;
    }

    // Copy in the filename
    DXUtil_ConvertGenericStringToWideCch(
        szWideFileName, szname, 512);

    // Load the sound from a file
```

```
if (FAILED(m_pLoader->LoadObjectFromFile (
   CLSID_DirectMusicSegment,
   IID_IDirectMusicSegment8,
   szWideFileName,
   (LPVOID*) &gs->m_pSound
   )))
{
   return(SOUNDERROR_LOAD);
}

// Set the game sound's performance pointer
gs->m_pPerformance = m_pPerformance;

// Download the data
if (FAILED (gs->m_pSound->Download(m_pPerformance))) {
   return(SOUNDERROR_DOWNLOAD);
}

   return(S_OK);
}
```

The first part of the function checks to see if the loader or performance interfaces are NULL. If either one is NULL, the function returns an appropriate error code indicating the problem.

The next part of the function checks to see if the game sound pointer passed in already has data in it. If it does, the sound data must be unloaded and cleaned up. This is accomplished with a call to the release and unload members of the game object's segment pointer.

The sanity checks are out of the way, so now you can get to the good stuff. The next call made is to the DirectX helper function named `DXUtil_ConvertGenericStringToWideCch()`. Since the DirectX function to load sound files requires that the filename be in a wide character string, it is necessary to convert the filename parameter to a wide character string. The call to the function is rather straightforward, so I will let the code speak for itself here.

With the filename converted, it is safe to move on to the loading function. I make a call to the `LoadObjectFromFile()` function to load the actual sound data. As you recall from earlier in the chapter, this function loads in the sound data and stores it in a segment object. In this case, I store the segment data in the game sound object's `m_pSound` segment pointer.

The next little piece of code sets the game sound's internal performance pointer to the sound system's performance interface. This is necessary since the game sound object needs the performance pointer to download and unload its data.

Lastly, I download the data into the newly set performance object. The sound data is now ready for playback.

The SoundSystem::hrPlaySound() Function

Speaking of playback, it's time to show you the code for the play sound
function.

```
HRESULT SoundSystem::hrPlaySound(GameSound *gs)
{
    // Make sure there is a performance object present
    if(!m_pPerformance)
        return(SOUNDERROR_MUSICPERFORMANCE);

    // Make sure the sound segment exists
    if(!gs->m_pSound)
        return(SOUNDERROR_NOSEGMENT);

    // Play the sound segment
    if(FAILED (m_pPerformance->PlaySegmentEx(
        gs->m_pSound,
        NULL, NULL,
        DMUS_SEGF_DEFAULT | DMUS_SEGF_SECONDARY,
        0, NULL, NULL, NULL
        )))
        return(SOUNDERROR_PLAYFAIL);

    return(S_OK);
}
```

Once again, I make sanity checks to make sure the interfaces used are
valid. If they are not valid, an error code is sent back to the caller.

Next I make a call to the `PlaySegmentEx()` function, which does the
dirty work of playing the sound data. Since the function requires a sound
segment to play, I pass in the game sound's segment pointer here.

Game Sound Class Implementation

The game sound class is a very simple class at the most; therefore, it
only has a constructor and destructor. Here is the code:

```
// Constructor
GameSound::GameSound()
{
    m_pSound        = NULL;
    m_pPerformance  = NULL;
}
// Destructor
GameSound::~GameSound()
{
    if(m_pSound) {
        if(m_pPerformance)
            m_pSound->Unload(m_pPerformance);
    }
    SAFE_RELEASE(m_pSound);
}
```

The constructor sets the internal pointers to NULL so that subsequent checks to the pointers can tell if they have been initialized or not. The destructor utilizes such a check to see if it needs to unload loaded music at destruction time.

Check out Figure 7.10 now to see an overview of the code that I just covered.

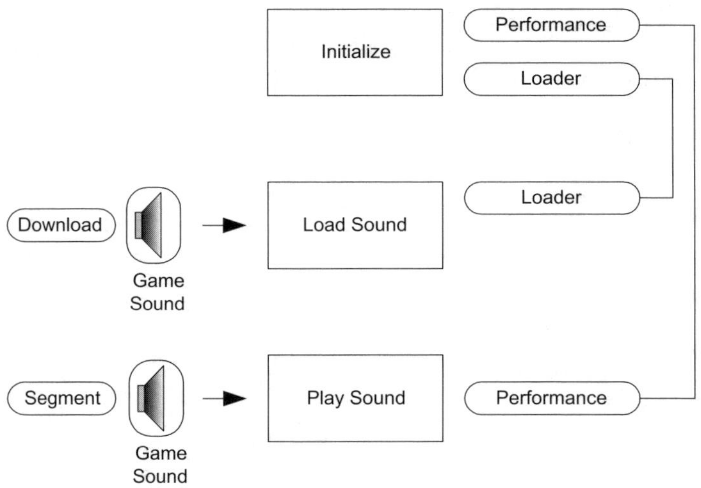

Figure 7.10: Sound system class and game sound class object interaction.

In Figure 7.10 you can see some of the object interaction and relationships between the sound system and game sound classes. In the top of the illustration, you see how the performance and loader interfaces are used in the initialization function. In the middle of the picture, you see how the loader interface is then used in the load sound function. The game sound object is passed into the loader function, and its download method is called. At the bottom, you can see how the game sound object is passed into the play sound method for sound playback. The segment data in the game sound object is used by the sound system's performance object to do the actual sound playback. Whew. Got it?

Sound System Example Program

How about an example program that actually implements this stuff? Load up the project from the companion files named DSound_SoundSystem now to follow along with me.

The example program consists of five main files: main.cpp, main.h, SoundSystem.cpp, SoundSystem.h, and dxutil.cpp. The main.cpp and main.h files include the meat of the program, and the SoundSystem.cpp and SoundSystem.h files include the actual sound class code. The dxutil.cpp file contains the super-useful DirectX utility functions.

There are a few libraries required for compilation: dxguid.lib, comctl32.lib, winmm.lib, and dsound.lib. All of these should look familiar, considering they were used in the first example program in this chapter.

Take a look at Figure 7.11 to see the output from the example program.

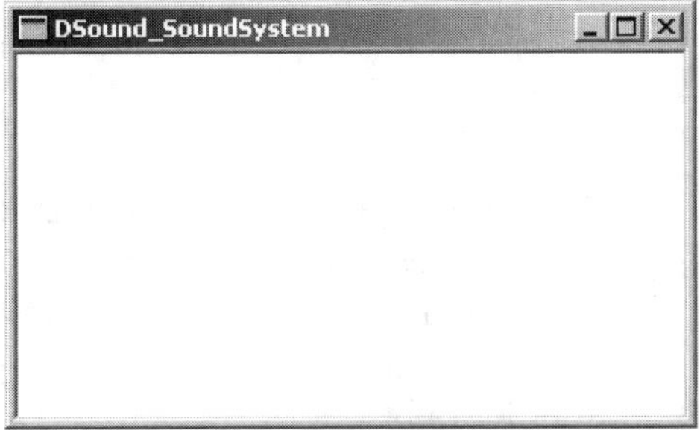

Figure 7.11: Output from the DSound_SoundSystem example program.

Granted, the screen shot in Figure 7.11 doesn't compare to one from Warcraft II, but it's still a program! Actually, there is nothing graphically to look at in the program. There is something to hear, though. Launch the program now and hit the left mouse button followed by the right mouse button. You should hear two different sounds play. You can even hit the mouse buttons over and over if you want to hear the sounds play multiple times.

How to Initialize with the Sound System Class

I don't want to chop down any more trees than necessary, so let's jump ahead in the main.cpp code to the `WinMain()` function. Inside of it you see a call to a function named `bInitializeSoundSystem()`. This is a function I wrote just for this example program. Here is the code for it:

```cpp
bool bInitializeSoundSystem(void)
{
    HRESULT    hr;

    // Allocate memory for the game sound(s)
    g_sndButton      = new GameSound;
    g_sndButtonOver  = new GameSound;

    // Initialize the sound system
    g_SoundSys.hrInitSoundSystem();

    // Load the game sound(s)
    hr = g_SoundSys.hrLoadSound("button.wav", g_sndButton);
```

```
    if(hr == SOUNDERROR_LOAD) {
        return(0);
    }

    hr = g_SoundSys.hrLoadSound(
        "button_over.wav",
        g_sndButtonOver);
    if(hr == SOUNDERROR_LOAD) {
        return(0);
    }

    // Return success
    return(1);
}
```

There are two sound files loaded by the program: "button_over.wav" and "button.wav." Since I have two sound files, I need two `GameSound` class objects. These come in the form of the `g_sndButton` and `g_sndButton-Over` variables. Each of these is a `GameSound` object that I have declared in the main.h header file. The first order of business is to allocate memory for the two game sound objects. I do this with a simple new operation.

Game sound objects aren't very useful without a sound system, so I have a sound system pointer declared in the main.h header file; its name is `g_SoundSys`. Since it isn't very useful until it has been initialized, I call its `hrInitSoundSystem()` method. This call initializes DirectSound and prepares the system for sound playback.

Next up I make two calls to the sound system's `hrLoadSound()` method. I pass in the two game sound objects here to have their data filled with the WAV files specified. Feel free to replace the WAV files that are loaded here with your own.

As long as the load sound function calls are successful, the program returns a success value of 1. If not, a 0 is returned to indicate failure.

There you have it — a few steps to successful sound initialization.

How to Play Game Sounds

Back to the Windows message pump. In the Windows message pump I have code that waits for the left or right mouse buttons to go down. If they do, a sound file is played. Here is the code for it:

```
switch(msg)
{
    case WM_LBUTTONDOWN:
        // Play the sound
        g_SoundSys.hrPlaySound(g_sndButtonOver);
        break;
    case WM_RBUTTONDOWN:
        // Play the "other" sound
        g_SoundSys.hrPlaySound(g_sndButton);
        break;
```

```
    case WM_DESTROY:
        PostQuitMessage(0);
        return 0;
    default:
        break;
}
return DefWindowProc(hWnd, msg, wParam, lParam);
```

In the switch logic block you can see how the system reacts to mouse button events with a call to the sound system's `hrPlaySound()` function. If the left mouse button is pressed, the `g_sndButtonOver` object is played. If the right mouse button is pressed, the `g_sndButton` object is played.

Note   The WM_LBUTTONDOWN and WM_RBUTTONDOWN messages are part of Microsoft's event system. There are tons of these, so I suggest that you read the Visual C++ documentation for more information about them.

Figure 7.12 shows the flow of the program from start to finish.

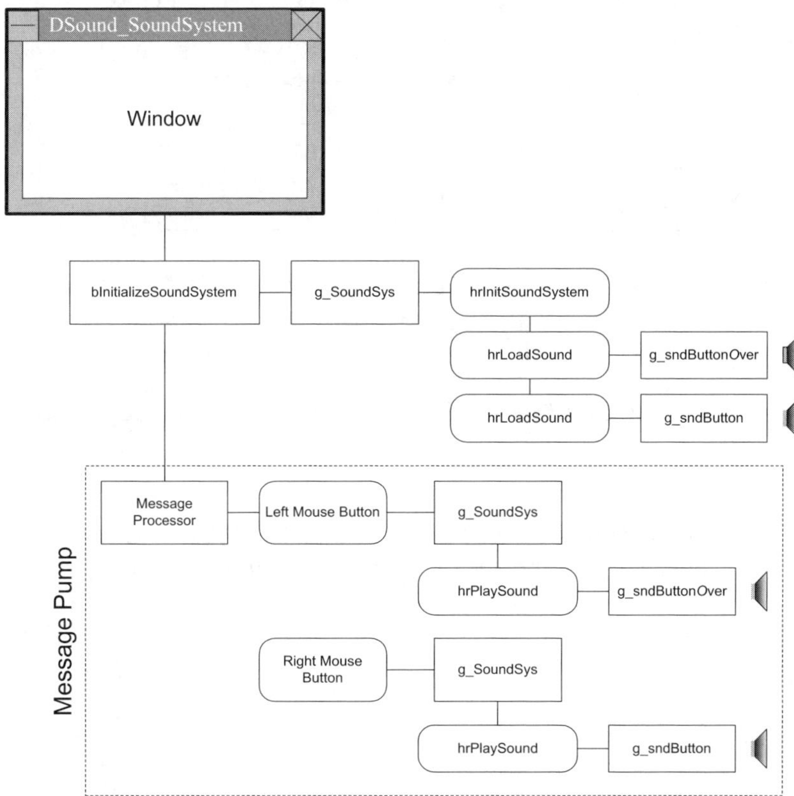

Figure 7.12: Output from the DSound_SoundSystem example program.

In Figure 7.12 you can see how the initialize sound system function is called first. Inside this function, the program calls the initialize sound member of the Sound System class object. The load sound member functions are then called to load the two game sounds. Once initialization is over, the program processes messages until a left or right mouse button event is triggered. Once an event is triggered, the program calls the play sound method of the sound class and plays the appropriate sound.

Menu Sounds Example Program

Do you remember the Battle Armor menu program that I covered in Chapter 6? Well, now it's time to add sounds and music to it. Open up the project named D3D_MenuSounds from the companion files to follow along with me. Instead of showing you mounds of code, I'm just going to show you a 50,000-foot view of the changes this time.

In the Main.h file I include the header for the sound system class. I also create a global sound system class object and some game sound objects to go along with it. All of this is shown in Figure 7.13.

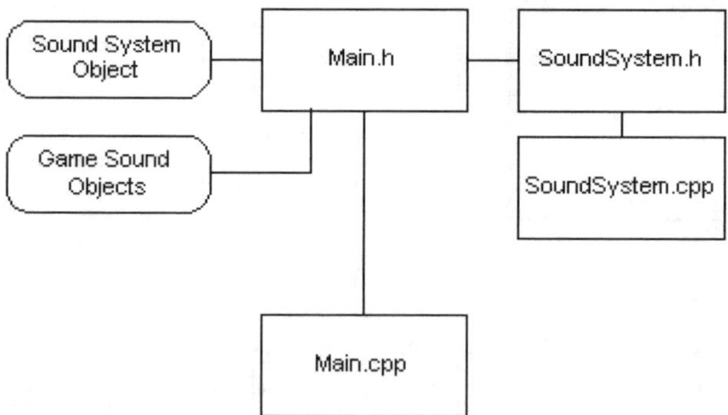

Figure 7.13: Sound system implementation layout in the D3D_MenuSounds header.

The Main.cpp file now has calls to initialize the sound system, load the sounds, and play the sounds. Figure 7.14 illustrates this concept.

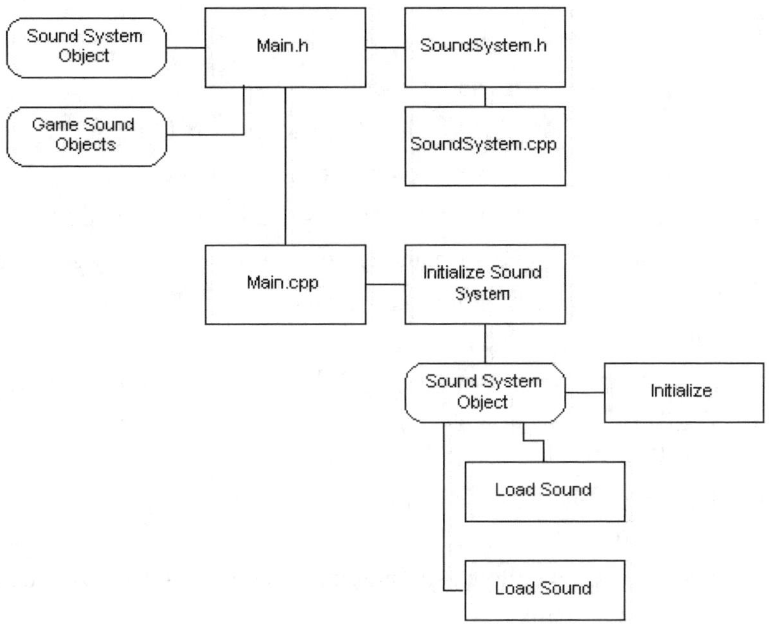

Figure 7.14: Sound system implementation layout in the D3D_MenuSounds main file.

As you can see in Figure 7.14, the initialize sound system call uses the sound system object to initialize the sound system. It then uses the sound system to load the two menu sounds. Once all of this is done, the sounds can be played when needed.

As for the MP3 file playback, I merely copied the `bPlayTitle-Music()`, `vStopTitleMusic()`, and `vCheckMusicStatus()` functions into the menu program. That and a call to play the music at initialization time did the trick.

If you have not done so, launch the D3D_MenuSounds program and play around with the different menu buttons. The MP3 music plays in the background, and some of the buttons play a WAV file. The WAV file is pretty quiet, so you may need to listen carefully to hear it. I suggest you try putting your own music and sounds in the program (heck, maybe even add a few sounds to get the hang of it).

That's really all there is to implementing sounds and MP3 playback in a program. Of course, there are many other things to consider, such as what sound to play and when to play them. But that is for another time.

Recap

Remember these points about sound:

- DirectSound contains low-level access to sound functions.
- DirectMusic contains more features than DirectSound.
- The DirectMusicLoader interface is used to load sound files.
- The DirectMusicPerformance interface is used to play sound files.
- The DirectMusicSegment interface is used to hold the loaded sound data.
- DirectShow can be used to play MP3 files and video streams.
- The DirectShow graph interface is used to load audio and video streams.
- The DirectShow media control interface is used to play audio and video streams.
- The DirectShow media seeking interface is used to navigate audio and video streams.
- The DirectShow media event interface is used to retrieve event messages about audio and video streams.
- Metallica is the most talented metal band ever. Period.

Chapter 8

Let There Be Units!

Y ou now have a basic understanding of what comprises a strategy game. With your new knowledge in hand, it is now time to jump into development. Some of the most important elements of a strategy game are the units commanded by the players. After all, what is a combat-based strategy game without units to control?

In this chapter, I cover the following:

- Defining a unit
- Coding a template
- Rendering units
- Loading and creating units

Defining a Unit

If you had to pick common attributes that make up any given combat unit, what would they be? I think the following list is a good start:

- Name
- Movement type
- Movement speed
- Offense type
- Defense type

Unit Name

The obvious first choice is the unit name. In a World War II setting you might choose "Sherman Tank" or "Tiger Tank" for this. Maybe you have set your game in the future and want to name a unit "Plasma Tank" or "Laser Tank." The name may sound like a no-brainer, but I suggest you take care in choosing the names. Unless you are creating a realistic game using real-life unit types, I suggest you pick names that describe what the unit does. Naming your futuristic tank "The Snake" doesn't tell the player very much or do much to help your game be a hit. If you feel you must use creative names, use them as a prefix (for example, "The Snake: Heavy Laser Tank").

A good real-world example is the Archer in Warcraft III: Reign of Chaos. The Archer is the Elven missile unit and fires arrows with its bow. The name implies this and is quite fitting. In Figure 8.1 you can see a picture of the Archer unit.

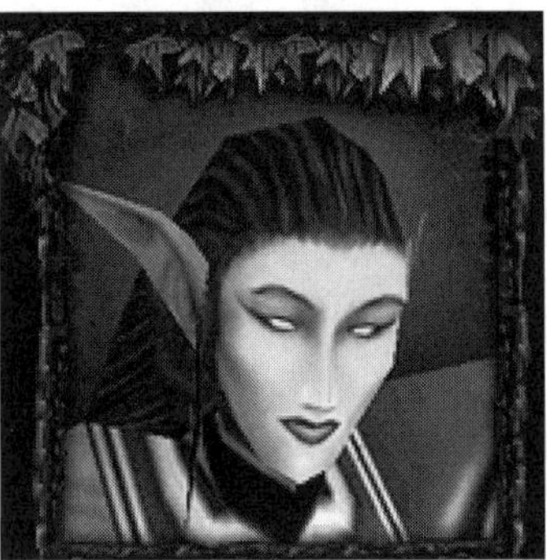

Figure 8.1: The Archer in Warcraft III: Reign of Chaos.
© 2002 Blizzard Entertainment, All Rights Reserved.

Movement Type

How does the unit move? Does it fly, move in water, or travel in outer space, or is it a mixture of the three? This is a very important question to answer for any given combat unit since it weighs greatly on the strategy employed when using the unit. Here is a list of the common movement types:

- Land
- Air
- Sea
- Space

Land

Any unit that has wheels, tracks, or legs is usually classified as a land unit. Common land units consist of troops, tanks, and armored personnel carriers. There are other variations to land-based movement available to you as well. Take, for example, a hovercraft or an underground drill. You can add all sorts of variety to your basic movement types by expanding on the main ones.

In keeping with the Warcraft theme, a good land-based unit example is the Catapult. The Catapult is built by the Orcs and is very good at destroying enemy structures. You can see it in Figure 8.2.

Figure 8.2: The Catapult in Warcraft III: Reign of Chaos.
© 2002 Blizzard Entertainment, All Rights Reserved.

Air

If you are playing the part of the United States in a combat game, you probably have lots of air units. The air movement type applies to anything that can fly. Whether it is a helicopter, a bi-plane, or a dragon, they all are considered air units. This type has a few options as well. How about adding maximum altitude to the mix? You could have some units incapable of reaching certain altitudes. This would add to the complexity of your game and could be quite interesting.

One of my favorite air units in Warcraft III is the Chimaera. It is a two-headed flying beast bred by the Night Elves. My favorite part about it is its ability to quickly raze enemy buildings. Check it out in Figure 8.3.

Figure 8.3: The Chimaera in Warcraft III: Reign of Chaos.
© 2002 Blizzard Entertainment, All Rights Reserved.

Sea

Sea units can move only in water. Depending on your game, this can be quite a limiting factor. Personally, I always enjoy a good naval battle. There are two common types of sea units: surface and submerged. If you want to code in the complexity of submarines versus surface ships, you need to determine which of these two types your unit is. As an added level of realism, you could even code in the maximum depth that a submerged vessel can reach.

Warcraft III doesn't use water-based units, so I guess I don't have an example for this movement type!

Space

Space-based units can travel around in outer space. I haven't really seen a game incorporate space-based units along with the other types I have listed, but that's not to say it can't be done. In fact, I think it would be quite interesting to have all four types in one game.

Warcraft III is a fantasy game, so no luck in showing you a space-based unit here either.

So, how do you implement movement types in code? The easiest way is with an enumeration. The following code demonstrates this:

```
enum UNIT_ATTR_MOVETYPE {  MOVETYPE_LAND,
                           MOVETYPE_SEA,
                           MOVETYPE_AIR,
                           MOVETYPE_SPACE };
```

In the above code I define four main movement types: land, sea, air, and space. Now all I have to do is set the movement type variable in my unit class to equal the type of movement I want. I cover the class implementation later in this chapter.

If you want to use a more advanced set of movement types, you could use something like the following:

```
enum UNIT_ATTR_MOVETYPE_ADV { MOVETYPE_LAND_WHEELED,
                              MOVETYPE_LAND_TRACKED,
                              MOVETYPE_LAND_HOVER,
                              MOVETYPE_LAND_FOOT,
                              MOVETYPE_SEA_SURFACE,
                              MOVETYPE_SEA_SUBMERGED,
                              MOVETYPE_AIR_LOW,
                              MOVETYPE_AIR_HIGH,
                              MOVETYPE_SPACE_INNER,
                              MOVETYPE_SPACE_OUTER };
```

Movement Speed

The rate in which a unit moves is very important to the strategies employed by the players of your game. Generally, units with heavy firepower are slower to move than ones with light weaponry. This makes sense considering firepower usually comes with the price of weight. There are exceptions though. Consider a 105mm cannon and an M-16. The 105mm cannon weighs substantially more than the M-16 combat rifle. But the tank carrying the 105mm cannon moves much faster than the troops with the M-16.

Since graphics are rendered in 3D nowadays, it is best to use 3D units of movement for the speed rating. You need to base the movement rate of your unit in accordance with the size of each tile in the game. For the sake of argument, set the tile size to 1.0. A slow-moving unit may move 0.1 tiles per game tick. A fast-moving unit may move 0.9 tiles per game tick. See Figure 8.4 for an example.

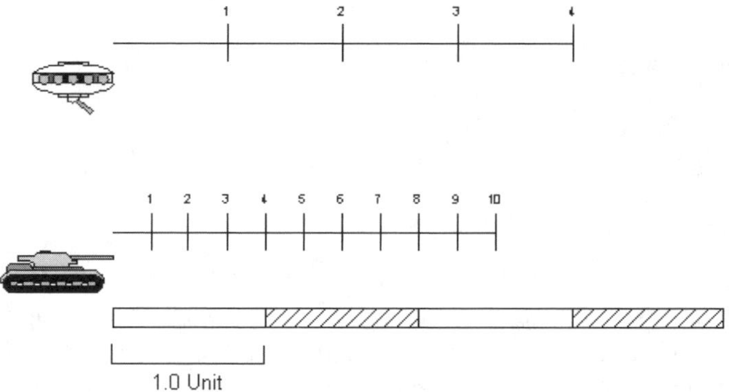

Figure 8.4: Movement rates illustrated.

In Figure 8.4 you see a tank and a spaceship. The ground is represented by four tiles, each of which is 1.0 unit in length. The spaceship moves 0.8 tiles per game tick, and the tank moves 0.25 tiles per game tick. As the game ticks go by, the spaceship ends up much farther along then the tank. As you can see in the illustration, the spaceship reaches the fourth ground tile in the time it takes the tank to get to the second ground tile. By using this method of speed calculation it is very easy to gauge where a unit will be at any given time. Using an evenly divisible tile size makes life easy as well.

Tip   Try to avoid using strangely sized tiles in your games. A tile size of 1.0 or 10.0 is much easier to manage than a tile size of 3.5. This is especially obvious when calculating movement speed and ranges.

Offense Type

Not only do you need to consider the amount of damage a unit can inflict, but you must also think about how the damage is done. Does the unit fire missiles, or shoot bullets, lasers, or something else?

There are a couple of different ways to assign offensive settings to a combat unit. You can either assign the values per unit or you can create global settings used by various units. I prefer to use global settings since you can assign the same offensive type to multiple units easily. Many games on the market do it this way, since it is efficient. Take, for instance, the following:

```
Unit name                Light Tank
Offense damage           100
Offense rate of fire     5
Offense splash damage    0
Offense graphic          laser.bmp
Defense armor            100
Movement speed           50
```

In this example, the light tank can inflict up to 100 points of damage, fires five rounds per minute, uses the laser.bmp graphic for its weapon, has 100 units of defensive armor, and can move 50 units per round. Now, what if you want to create a medium tank that uses the same weapon statistics but has 150 units of armor and can only move at a rate of 40? First off, you would have to set the offensive stats all over again. This results in redundant settings and can be a real pain if you need to change the weapon globally.

The better way to handle the offensive settings is through an offense type. Take the following:

```
Offense type             Laser
Offense damage           100
Offense rate of fire     5
Offense splash damage    0
Offense graphic          laser.bmp
```

Unit name	Light Tank
Offense type	Laser
Defense armor	100
Movement speed	50
Unit name	Medium Tank
Offense type	Laser
Defense armor	150
Movement speed	40

In this example I create an offense type called Laser. I then create two units that use the same offense type but have different defensive and movement values. Figure 8.5 illustrates this point.

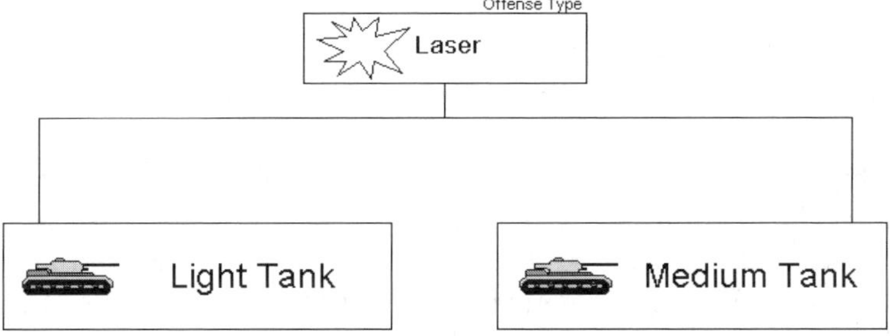

Figure 8.5: Two unit types that share the same offense type.

In Figure 8.5 you can see how the light and medium tanks share the same offense type. By using this method you only have to change the one offense type to affect all units that use it.

Defense Type

For every offense there is a defense. So, for every offense type, there should be a defense type, right? Well, not exactly, but you get the point. Anyway, defense types work in exactly the same way as offense types. Take, for example, the light and medium tank from before. Instead of specifying the defense values for the armor of each one, you could create two armor types. Check out Figure 8.6 to see this in action.

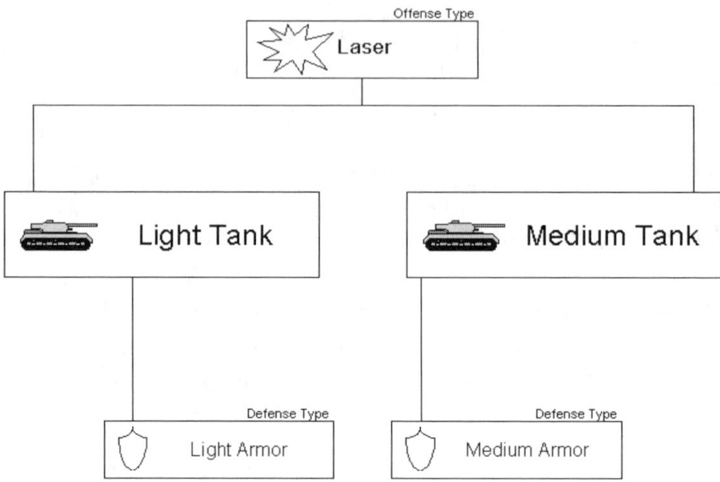

Figure 8.6: Two unit types with two different defense types.

In Figure 8.6 you can see the usual suspects sharing the same offense type. The difference here is they have two different defense types. You may think this is a waste of space, but consider adding a third unit type. How about an armored personnel carrier? It would share the light armor along with the light tank. It wouldn't use the laser as a weapon, but at least you have reused a defense type by this point.

Tip   While you are at it, it is also useful to use movement types in the same way as offense and defense. For the tanks, you may use a movement type of Tread. For trucks, you might use a type called Wheeled. The types could store the maximum speed, acceleration time, and turn radius, just to name a few attributes.

Coding a Template

Take your gloves off because it's time to get down and dirty with unit templates. This portion of the book is quite complicated, so please pay close attention to get the full benefit of the information. No taking breaks to play Combat Mission!

Before I run full tilt into the code, check out Figure 8.7 to see the output from the program I am about to cover.

Figure 8.7 shows the output from the D3DFrame_UnitTemplate program included with the companion files. In the screen shot you see four helicopters hovering over a field of grass. Debugging information is present in the upper-left side of the image as well. This may not look like

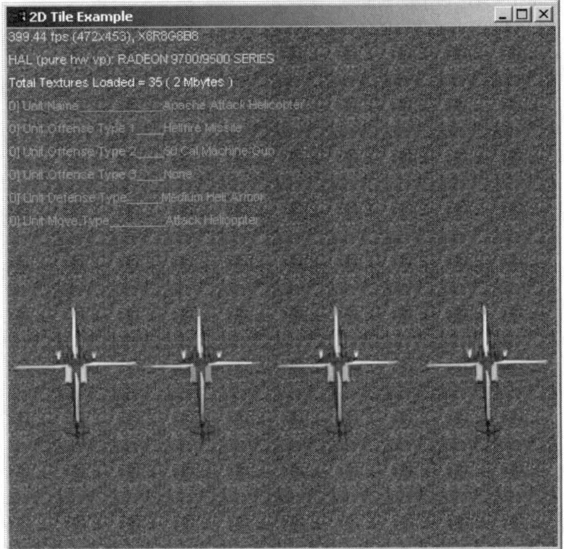

Figure 8.7: Output from the D3DFrame_UnitTemplate program.

much, but the underlying system to manage the four units is quite complex.

Load up the project named D3DFrame_UnitTemplate now so you can follow along with me. In order to create a full template for units, you need the following classes:

- Unit defense class
- Unit offense class
- Unit movement class
- Unit animation class
- Unit texture class
- Unit class
- Unit manager class

The CUnitDefense Class

Remember how defense types help to organize units? Now you get to learn how to put the practice to work in an actual class. In the D3DFrame_UnitTemplate project, open up the UnitTemplateClasses.h header file. At the top of the file, you see the following code:

```
class CUnitDefense
{
    public:
        int          m_iType;
```

```
        unsigned int  m_iMissileArmorRating;
        unsigned int  m_iBulletArmorRating;
        unsigned int  m_iLaserArmorRating;
        unsigned int  m_iMeleeArmorRating;
        unsigned int  m_iHitPoints;
        unsigned int  m_iRegenRate;
        char          m_szName[64];

    public:
        CUnitDefense();
        ~CUnitDefense();
        virtual void vReset(void);
};
```

CUnitDefense Data Members

The class is very basic in that it only contains public members, a constructor, a destructor, and a single member function. I mainly use the classes like data structures, so don't expect a ton of methods. Keep in mind that this example is simplistic for a reason — to make it easy to understand. In a real-world application, you probably would make the data members private and create methods to access them. Anyway, on with the show. Look to Figure 8.8 to see the layout of the defense class member variables.

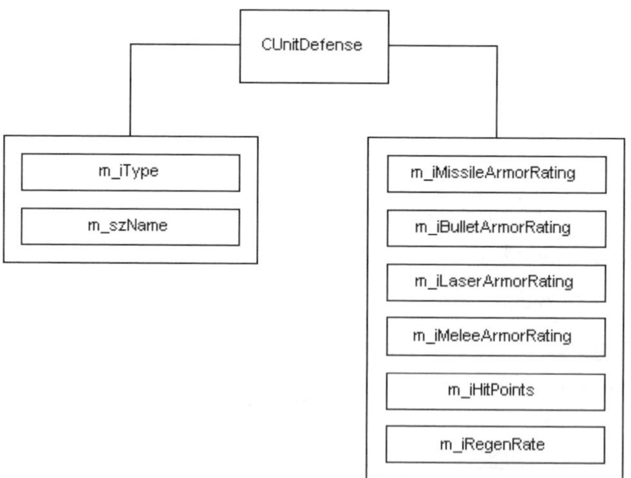

Figure 8.8: Layout of the CUnitDefense class member variables.

Armor Ratings

As you can see in Figure 8.8, I have four armor ratings: missile, bullet, laser, and melee. This gives the engine enough flexibility to account for four different types of attack. Take a flak jacket. It may do well against bullets, but it won't do well against a laser. With the setup I have above, you can set the flak jacket to have a medium-level bullet rating but a low-level laser rating to account for this.

You can always add or subtract from the number of armor ratings I have listed in the example. Mine is geared around a futuristic war game, which your game may not be. If you are doing a fantasy game, you could change the laser rating to a magic rating. The missile rating is still usable for arrows and such, but the bullet rating may need to go unless you have blunderbusses in your game. Maybe you could change the bullet rating to a gunpowder rating.

For each of the armor ratings, I have an integer set aside. I'm assuming a range of 0 to 1,000 for each one. A value of 0 means the unit has no defense against the particular attack type, and a value of 1,000 means it is practically invulnerable against the type.

Hit Points

Next in Figure 8.8, you see the `m_iHitPoints` variable. I use this to store the total number of hits the unit can take in combat. When the unit has 0 hit points, it is dead. As with the armor ratings, I like to keep the hit points within a range of 0 to 1000.

Regeneration Rate

I haven't mentioned regeneration of unit health before, so this idea may be a bit new to you. I have a variable called `m_iRegenRate` available to the defense class to account for units that can self-heal. Maybe it's a medical field unit or a mystical beast that has regeneration powers. Either way, this value lets you have self-healing units in your game.

The key to the regeneration rate is to keep it in line with the hit points range. Since the unit will heal hit points equivalent to the regeneration rate once per round, you want to keep this number rather low. I suggest a range of 0 to 100. At a value of 100, the unit would heal itself from near-death to full health in ten rounds. A value of 1 would take the unit 100 turns to come back from near-death.

Defense Type

The `m_iType` field stores the numeric type of the defense. For example, light tank armor may be type zero, while medium tank armor is type one. The range of this value depends on how many defense types you create for your game. It is unlikely you will have more than a few dozen, but you never know. For an example of two units using different defense types, refer back to Figure 8.6.

Defense Name

The m_szName field stores the name of the defense in alphabetical characters. I use this for easy lookup of unit types without having to remember the integer value for it. It's really just for convenience.

CUnitDefense Member Functions

The class only has a constructor, destructor, and a reset function, so it is rather sparse in the functionality department. Here is the code that implements the functions:

```cpp
// Constructor
CUnitDefense::CUnitDefense()
{
    // Set internal vars
    vReset();
}
// Destructor
CUnitDefense::~CUnitDefense()
{
}
// Reset internal vars
void CUnitDefense::vReset(void)
{
    m_iType               = 0;
    m_iMissileArmorRating = 0;
    m_iBulletArmorRating  = 0;
    m_iLaserArmorRating   = 0;
    m_iMeleeArmorRating   = 0;
    m_iHitPoints          = 0;
    m_iRegenRate          = 0;
    strcpy(m_szName, "N/A");
}
```

In the above code you see how the constructor calls the vReset() function to set up the starting values for the class. The destructor doesn't do anything useful but take up space. One day it may be needed for something, but not now.

Wow, isn't that simple? If you like complicated code, just wait a few minutes.

The CUnitOffense Class

Just like the defense class, an offense class is needed to help organize your units. I use a class named CUnitOffense to handle this work for me. Here is the header for it:

```cpp
class CUnitOffense
{
    public:
```

```
    int           m_iType;
    unsigned int  m_iMissileDamageRating;
    unsigned int  m_iBulletDamageRating;
    unsigned int  m_iLaserDamageRating;
    unsigned int  m_iMeleeDamageRating;
    unsigned int  m_iSplashRadius;
    unsigned int  m_iRateOfFire;
    float         m_fProjectileSpeed;
    unsigned int  m_iRange;
    char          m_szName[64];

  public:
    CUnitOffense();
    ~CUnitOffense();
    virtual void vReset(void);
};
```

CUnitOffense Data Members

The class contains very similar data members, except the values are for
offense, not defense. Figure 8.9 illustrates the data members for the
class.

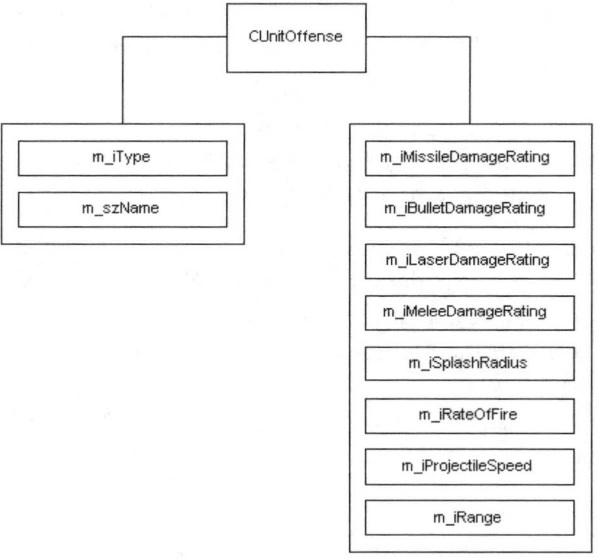

Figure 8.9: Layout of the CUnitOffense class member variables.

Damage Ratings

In Figure 8.9 you see four damage ratings: missile, bullet, laser, and
melee. Just like the defense class, these values pertain to the type of
attack their name indicates. For example, the bullet damage rating tells

you how much bullet damage the weapon inflicts. This would apply to an M-16 rifle or any other weapon that fires bullets. I like to use a rating that is comparable to the defense ratings, so a value of 0 to 1000 is used. This makes for very simple combat calculations since all you have to do is compare the offense rating to the defense rating to see how much damage gets through. Take the following example:

1. Flak jacket with a bullet armor rating of 50
2. M-16 rifle with a bullet damage rating of 60
3. 60 – 50 = 10 points of penetration

In the above example, the flak jacket absorbs 50 points of bullet damage, but the M-16 rifle puts out 60 points of damage. This results in 10 points of damage making it through to the target unit. The target subtracts 10 hit points and is hopefully still alive. Here is another example:

1. Flak jacket with a bullet armor rating of 50
2. 105mm cannon with a bullet damage rating of 650
3. 650 – 50 = 600 points of penetration

In the above example, the flak jacket doesn't stand a chance against the 105mm cannon. The unit ends up taking 600 points of damage and is probably destroyed. Here is a final example:

1. Flak jacket with a bullet armor rating of 50
2. Colt .45 with a bullet damage rating of 30
3. 30 – 50 = –20, no penetration

In this example the Colt .45 pistol cartridge does not inflict enough damage to hurt the unit. This renders the offense useless against the defense. You may wish to add in a luck modifier for this case to make sure someone with a flak jacket doesn't always defend 100% against a pistol, but that's up to you.

As with the defense rating, you can change the types I have listed to suit your needs.

Splash Radius

The `m_iSplashRadius` field tells you how much splash damage the offense type inflicts. This is useful for weapons such as grenades, catapults, and the like. The radius represents the number of game tiles that the weapon spreads across. Take a look at Figure 8.10.

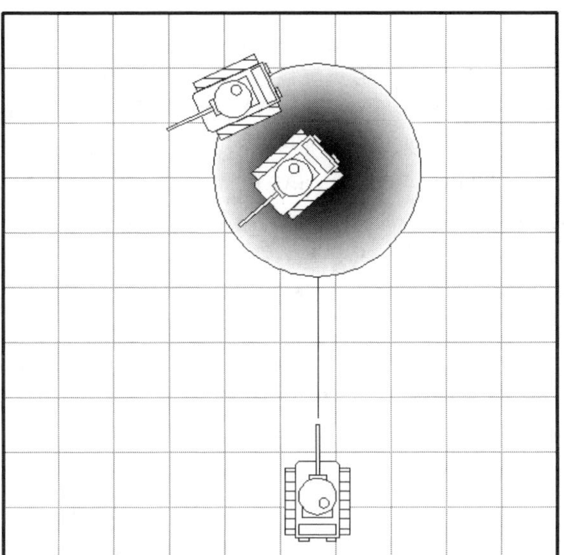

Figure 8.10: Splash damage illustrated.

In Figure 8.10, you see three tanks. The tank at the bottom has just fired its main weapon at one of the two enemy tanks at the top. The tank shell has a splash radius of 2, which means its damage sphere extends from the point of impact outward two tiles in each direction. Since the splash radius is extensive, it actually ends up doing damage to the second enemy unit as well. In the illustration you see how the dark area represents where the majority of the damage is inflicted and the light area illustrates the least amount of damage. This is useful if you care to model splash damage more accurately in accordance with how far away the splash has reached.

Rate of Fire

The `m_iRateOfFire` field tells you how many rounds must pass before the unit fires its weapon again. A fast weapon such as a machine gun may fire a volley every round. A slow weapon such as a catapult may only fire every five rounds or so. Of course, the machine gun can fire more than one bullet per round, which is why I use the term volley.

There is no straightforward answer to how many rounds a weapon needs to wait before firing. You will need to play with this number until you are happy with the offense type.

Projectile Speed

The `m_fProjectileSpeed` field tells you how fast the weapon's projectile travels. This only applies to the missile and bullet ratings, since melee doesn't travel and lasers travel at the speed of light.

The speed of the projectile represents how many tiles the projectile travels per round. For this reason, the range goes from 0.0 to 0.99. You don't want projectiles to travel so quickly that they skip over tiles, so 0.99 is the maximum.

Weapon Range

The `m_iRange` field tells you, in number of tiles, how far the offensive weapon can shoot. This only applies to range weapons, as melee weapons have a range of zero tiles.

Offense Type

The `m_iType` field stores the numeric type of the offense. This works just like the defense type does.

Offense Name

The `m_szName` field stores the name of the offense type in alphabetical characters. This works just like the defense type name.

CUnitOffense Member Functions

The class only has a constructor, destructor, and a reset function that work almost exactly as they do in the defense class. Here is the code that implements the functions:

```
// Constructor
CUnitOffense::CUnitOffense()
{
    // Set internal vars
    vReset();
}
// Destructor
CUnitOffense::~CUnitOffense()
{
}
// Reset internal vars
void CUnitOffense::vReset(void)
{
    m_iType                 = 0;
    m_iMissileDamageRating  = 0;
    m_iBulletDamageRating   = 0;
    m_iLaserDamageRating    = 0;
    m_iMeleeDamageRating    = 0;
    m_iSplashRadius         = 0;
```

```
    m_iRateOfFire          = 0;
    m_fProjectileSpeed     = 0.0f;
    m_iRange               = 0;
    strcpy(m_szName, "N/A");
}
```

In the above code you can see how the constructor calls the vReset()
function to set up the starting values for the class just like the defense
class does. That about does it for the offense class.

The CUnitMovement Class

A movement class is needed to help organize your units as well. I use a
class named CUnitMovement to handle this work for me. Here is the
header for it:

```
class CUnitMovement
{
    public:
        int            m_iType;
        float          m_fMovementSpeed;
        unsigned int   m_iMovementType;
        float          m_fAcceleration;
        float          m_fDeacceleration;
        float          m_fTurnSpeed;
        char           m_szName[64];

    public:
        CUnitMovement();
        ~CUnitMovement();
        virtual void vReset(void);
};
```

CUnitMovement Data Members

The class contains data members similar to the offense class, except the
values are for movement, not offense. Figure 8.11 on the following page
illustrates the data members for the class.

Movement Speed

In Figure 8.11 you can see various fields to control movement of the unit.
The first one, movement speed, determines how many tiles the unit
moves in a single game round. I use a floating-point value for it since you
don't want units to move a complete tile or more per round.

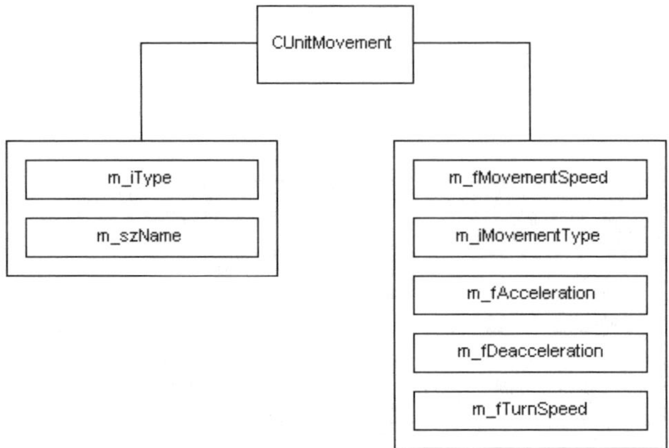

Figure 8.11: Layout of the CUnitMovement class member variables.

Movement Type

The movement type field tells you what method the unit uses to travel. Does it fly, walk, or roll around? Maybe it walks? Maybe it rolls around? The movement type field answers these questions.

Acceleration and Deceleration

For added complexity, I have included acceleration and deceleration parameters. The acceleration parameter tells you how much speed the unit gains per round when accelerating. The deceleration parameter tells you how much speed the unit loses per turn when decelerating. This parameter is useful for adding the realism of combat. Certain units are and should be slower to get going or slow down than other units. Take the following, for example:

Light Calvary, Acceleration = 0.3, Deceleration = 0.3, Speed = 0.5.
Catapult, Acceleration = 0.1, Deceleration = 0.2, Speed = 0.3.

In this example the light cavalry unit can get up to full speed in two turns. The cavalry unit can even come to a complete stop in one turn. The catapult takes longer to move around though. It takes three turns to get up to full speed and two turns to stop. This makes sense, since a catapult can't move around as quickly as a horse. You don't have to use acceleration or deceleration in your games if you think it's too complicated, but it does add a nice touch of realism.

Turn Speed

The last unique data element in the movement class tells you how fast
the unit turns per round. The value is a floating-point number that represents how many degrees the unit rotates per round. A unit with a turn
speed of 10.0 takes 36 rounds to make a complete circle. A unit with a
turn speed of 30 takes ten rounds to make a complete circle. To see the
advantages of a fast turn radius, check out Figure 8.12.

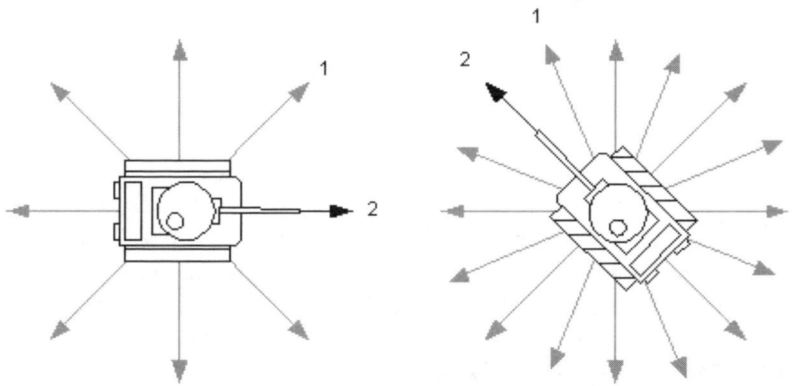

Figure 8.12: Two units with different turn speeds.

In Figure 8.12 the tank on the left has a turn speed of 45. The unit on the
right has a turn speed of 22.5. By the time two rounds have passed, the
tank on the left now faces completely to the right. The tank on the right
is still two rounds away from facing the tank on the left. If the tanks had
been fighting each other, the tank on the left would get in a couple of
shots before the tank on the right even faced its enemy! This makes turn
speed extremely important in unit combat.

Some games don't bother with turn speeds. They just make the unit
you wish to move face the direction of travel without turning. This does
help keep the game fast-paced, but it doesn't help with realism at all.

CUnitMovement Member Functions

The class only has a constructor, destructor, and a reset function that
work almost exactly as the offense class does. Here is the code that
implements the functions:

```
// Constructor
CUnitMovement::CUnitMovement()
{
    // Set internal vars
```

```
        vReset();
}
// Destructor
CUnitMovement::~CUnitMovement()
{
}
// Reset the internal vars
void CUnitMovement::vReset(void)
{
    m_iType             = 0;
    m_fMovementSpeed    = 0.0f;
    m_iMovementType     = 0;
    m_fAcceleration     = 0.0f;
    m_fDeacceleration   = 0.0f;
    m_fTurnSpeed        = 0.0f;
    strcpy(m_szName, "N/A");
}
```

In the above code you see how the constructor calls the `vReset()` function to set up the starting values for the class just like the offense class does. I'm not trying to load duplicate code on you, but the nature of the class design makes it all very similar.

The CUnitAnimation Class

Just like the movement class, an animation class is needed to help organize your units. I use a class named CUnitAnimation to handle this work for me. Here is the header for it:

```
const int UNITMANAGER_MAXOWNERS = 4;
class CUnitAnimation
{
    public:
        char    m_szName[64];
        char    m_szBitmapPrefix[64];
        int     m_iNumStillFrames;
        int     m_iNumMoveFrames;
        int     m_iNumAttackFrames;
        int     m_iNumDieFrames;
        int     m_iType;
        int     m_iStartStillFrames;
        int     m_iStartMoveFrames;
        int     m_iStartAttackFrames;
        int     m_iStartDieFrames;
        // Texture data
        CTexture   *m_Textures;
        int     m_iTotalTextures;
        // Direct 3D Pointer for loading textures
        LPDIRECT3DDEVICE9   m_pd3dDevice;

        CUnitAnimation();
        ~CUnitAnimation();
        virtual void vReset(void);
```

```
    virtual void vSetRenderDevice(LPDIRECT3DDEVICE9 pd3d);
    virtual void vLoadTextures(void);
};
```

Uh oh, this class actually looks a bit different! That's right; the animation class is more complicated than the previous classes. The animation class actually contains the graphics required by the unit as well as the information necessary to animate the unit.

The graphic information for the unit is held in an array of CTexture class objects. The CTexture class is another class I create in this example that contains the actual graphic information. I cover it later in this chapter.

CUnitAnimation Data Members

The animation class has several interesting data members. The first ones deal with the number of graphic frames for the various unit animations. There are four animation types: still, moving, attacking, and dying.

Animation Type: Still

The `m_iNumStillFrames` field tells you how many frames of animation the unit uses in its idle state. Many units won't do anything special for their idle state, while others may be quite intricate. For instance, a radar station probably has a swirling radar dish that requires several frames of animation. A tank, on the other hand, doesn't really do much of anything graphically when sitting still. This is shown in Figure 8.13.

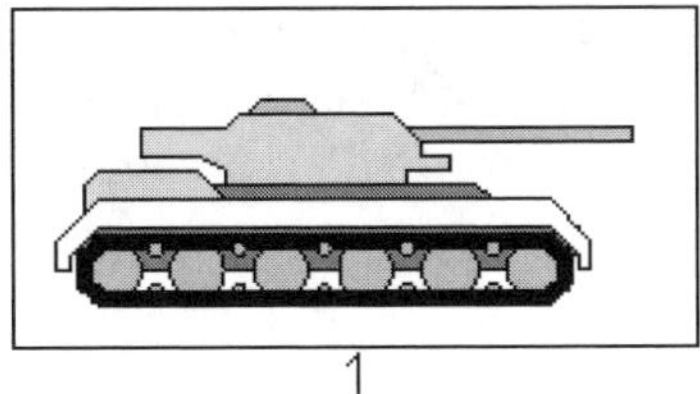

Figure 8.13: The still frames for a tank.

Notice how the tank has only one frame for movement. This is due to the fact that a tank doesn't do anything when standing still!

Animation Type: Move

The next field, `m_iNumMoveFrames`, tells you how many frames of animation the unit uses when moving. Figure 8.14 shows you an example.

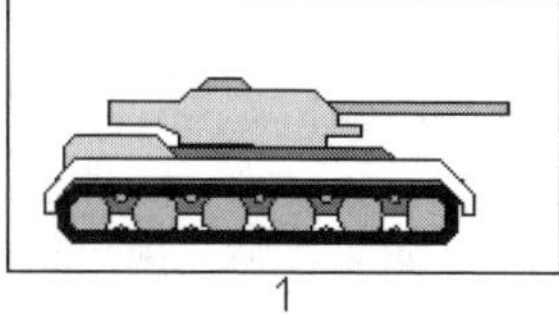
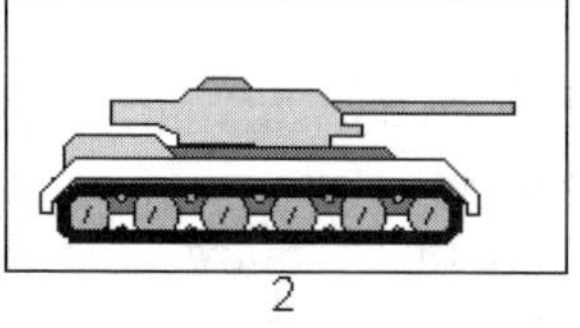
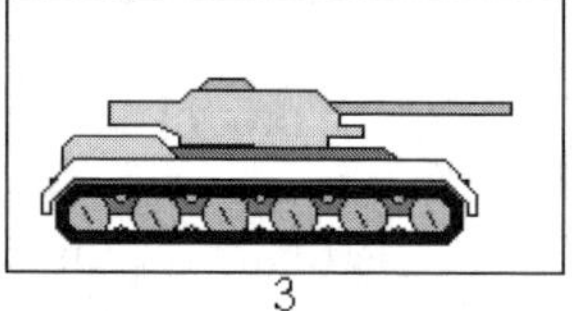

Figure 8.14: The movement frames for a tank.

You can see that the tank has three animation frames for movement. In each frame, the wheels look slightly different. This gives the illusion of movement when looped.

Animation Type: Attack

The next field, `m_iNumAttackFrames`, tells you how many frames of animation the unit uses when attacking. Figure 8.15 shows an example.

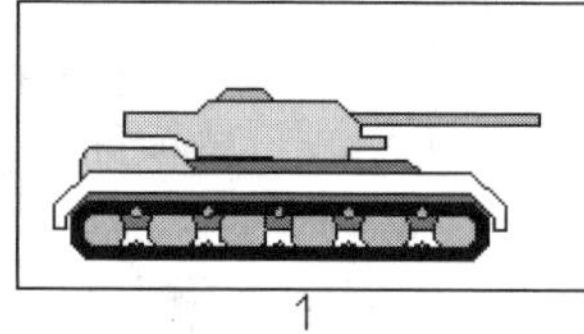
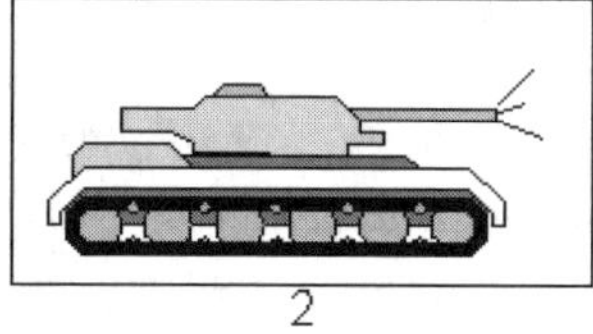

Figure 8.15: The attack frames for a tank.

In Figure 8.15 you can see that the tank has two animation frames for attacking. The first frame is of the standard tank, and the second frame contains a muzzle flash. The beauty of this system is that you can get as detailed or as simple as you want. All you have to do is create the artwork and set the number of frames.

Animation Type: Die

The `m_iNumDieFrames` field tells you how many frames of animation the unit uses when it dies. Figure 8.16 shows you an example.

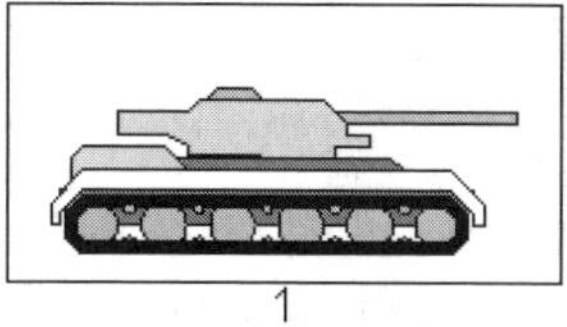
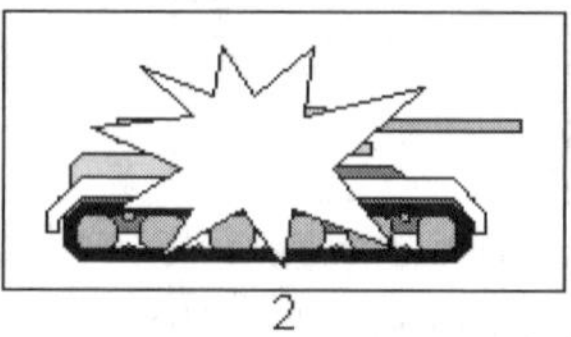
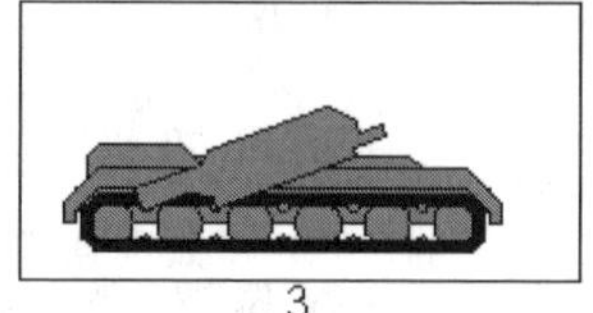

Figure 8.16: The die frames for a tank.

Notice in Figure 8.16 that the tank has three animation frames for dying. The first frame is of the standard tank, the second frame shows a nice explosion, and the third frame shows the hulk of the burned-out tank. Whenever a unit dies, it plays this animation, so make sure it looks impressive!

I'm sure you can think of many more types of animation for your combat units. The cool part is that all you need to do is add them to the base animation class to have the information stored in your game.

Frame Starting Points

There are four data fields that tell you the starting frame for each of the animation types. This may sound strange at first, so to make life easier, check out Figure 8.17.

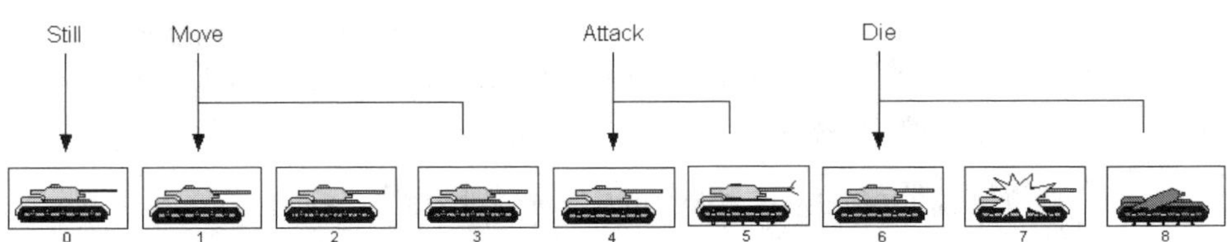

Figure 8.17: The complete tank animation sequence.

Figure 8.17 shows the complete display of tank animation frames. The first frame contains the still frame. The next three frames contain the movement sequence. The next two frames contain the attack sequence. The last three frames contain the die sequence. Instead of storing the animation frames in different arrays, the animation class stores them all in one sequential array. This means that the frames are all stored back to back. The consequence of this is that the starting frame for the still animation sequence is 0, but the starting frame for the movement sequence is not. The starting frame for each sequence depends on the number of frames that came before it. Take, for example, the attack animation sequence. Its starting frame is fourth in the chain since the still frame and movement sequence come before it. Remember that I use 0 as the starting frame and not 1. If you look under each frame, you can see the linear frame number associated with it. In this example, the still sequence starts at 0, the move sequence starts at 1, the attack sequence starts at 4, and the die sequence starts at 6. If you insert a frame of animation in the middle, the frame starting points to the right of it must be incremented.

Texture Data

The m_Textures pointer is used to store the animation frames for the unit. It ends up being an array of CTexture objects and does quite a good job of storing information.

The m_iTotalTextures field tells you how many frames of animation that the unit requires. This is useful for tracking memory usage, among other things.

The last texture-related data member is the m_pd3dDevice field. This contains a pointer to the Direct3D graphic system for use in texture loading. Since the Direct X texture loading functions require this pointer, I have it in the texture class.

CUnitAnimation Member Functions

The animation class does have the usual constructor, destructor, and reset functions, but it also has two new functions: vSetRenderDevice() and vLoadTextures().

The CUnitAnimation::vSetRenderDevice() Function

Since DirectX requires a rendering device to load textures, I have a set render device function to set the device pointer. The function takes an LPDIRECT3DDEVICE9 pointer as its only parameter and stores it in the m_pd3dDevice data member. It is used later to load the texture data.

Here is the code for the function:

```
void CUnitAnimation::vSetRenderDevice(LPDIRECT3DDEVICE9 pd3d)
{
    m_pd3dDevice = pd3d;
}
```

The CUnitAnimation::vLoadTextures() Function

The load textures function takes the information stored in the frame data members and loads up texture files accordingly. Here is the code for it:

```
void CUnitAnimation::vLoadTextures(void)
{
    // Load the animations
    int    i, j;
    int    iLocalCount = 0;
    char   szBitmapFileName[128];

    // Allocate memory for the textures
    m_Textures = new CTexture[
        (m_iNumStillFrames*(UNITMANAGER_MAXOWNERS+1))+
        (m_iNumMoveFrames*(UNITMANAGER_MAXOWNERS+1))+
        (m_iNumAttackFrames*(UNITMANAGER_MAXOWNERS+1))+
        (m_iNumDieFrames*(UNITMANAGER_MAXOWNERS+1))];
```

```cpp
// Still graphics (fidgit)
m_iStartStillFrames = 0;
for(i = 0; i << m_iNumStillFrames; i++) {
    for(j = 0; j << UNITMANAGER_MAXOWNERS+1; j++) {
        sprintf(szBitmapFileName, "UnitData\\%s%d_%d.tga",
                m_szBitmapPrefix, iLocalCount, j);

        // Set the render device
        m_Textures[m_iTotalTextures].vSetRenderDevice(m_pd3dDevice);
        // Load the texture
        m_Textures[m_iTotalTextures].vLoad(szBitmapFileName);
        // Increment total # of textures
        m_iTotalTextures++;
    }
    iLocalCount++;
}

// Move graphics
m_iStartMoveFrames = m_iTotalTextures;
for(i = 0; i << m_iNumMoveFrames; i++) {
    for(j = 0; j << UNITMANAGER_MAXOWNERS+1; j++) {
        sprintf(szBitmapFileName, "UnitData\\%s%d_%d.tga",
                m_szBitmapPrefix, iLocalCount, j);

        // Set the render device
        m_Textures[m_iTotalTextures].vSetRenderDevice(m_pd3dDevice);
        // Load the texture
        m_Textures[m_iTotalTextures].vLoad(szBitmapFileName);
        // Increment total # of textures
        m_iTotalTextures++;
    }
    iLocalCount++;
}

// Attack graphics
m_iStartAttackFrames = m_iTotalTextures;
for(i = 0; i << m_iNumAttackFrames; i++) {
    for(j = 0; j << UNITMANAGER_MAXOWNERS+1; j++) {
        sprintf(szBitmapFileName, "UnitData\\%s%d_%d.tga",
                m_szBitmapPrefix, iLocalCount, j);

        // Set the render device
        m_Textures[m_iTotalTextures].vSetRenderDevice(m_pd3dDevice);
        // Load the texture
        m_Textures[m_iTotalTextures].vLoad(szBitmapFileName);
        // Increment total # of textures
        m_iTotalTextures++;
    }
    iLocalCount++;
}

// Die graphics
m_iStartDieFrames = m_iTotalTextures;
for(i = 0; i << m_iNumDieFrames; i++) {
```

```
        for(j = 0; j << UNITMANAGER_MAXOWNERS+1; j++) {
            sprintf(szBitmapFileName, "UnitData\\%s%d_%d.tga",
                    m_szBitmapPrefix, iLocalCount, j);

            // Set the render device
            m_Textures[m_iTotalTextures].vSetRenderDevice(m_pd3dDevice);
            // Load the texture
            m_Textures[m_iTotalTextures].vLoad(szBitmapFileName);
            // Increment total # of textures
            m_iTotalTextures++;
        }
        iLocalCount++;
    }
}
```

Please don't kill me! I know it's a lot of code, but luckily it's a lot of duplication as well. The code has two main steps. The first step allocates the memory for the texture objects. It calculates the amount of textures needed by adding together the total animation frames. The next step is to loop through each of the animation sequences and load the textures for them.

Owner Colors

Here is the tricky part of animation graphics. The load texture function allocates the memory for the textures and then loops through each animation sequence to load the texture data. But what does the UNITMANAGER_MAXOWNERS constant do? That's a very good question!

Take a closer look at the code that calculates the total number of frames:

```
m_Textures = new CTexture[
            (m_iNumStillFrames*(UNITMANAGER_MAXOWNERS+1))+
            (m_iNumMoveFrames*(UNITMANAGER_MAXOWNERS+1))+
            (m_iNumAttackFrames*(UNITMANAGER_MAXOWNERS+1))+
            (m_iNumDieFrames*(UNITMANAGER_MAXOWNERS+1))];
```

Everything looks normal except for the multiplication going on. The UNITMANAGER_MAXOWNERS constant contains the total number of player colors available in the game. I use this value to tell me how many different colors the game supports for various players. If you have played an RTS game before, you know that the different players are represented by different colors. One player may have red stripes on his unit, while another player may have purple stripes on her unit. This requires additional animation frames: one for each frame of animation times the number of colors available.

For example, if you have one frame allocated for the still animation sequence, you need that frame plus a frame for each owner color available. To calculate this, you do the following:

Number of animation frames * (Number of colors + 1)

I add 1 to the number of colors to account for the base frame. The color frames only contain the actual color data for the unit, while the base frame contains the unit graphic data. This may be hard to understand, so check out Figure 8.18.

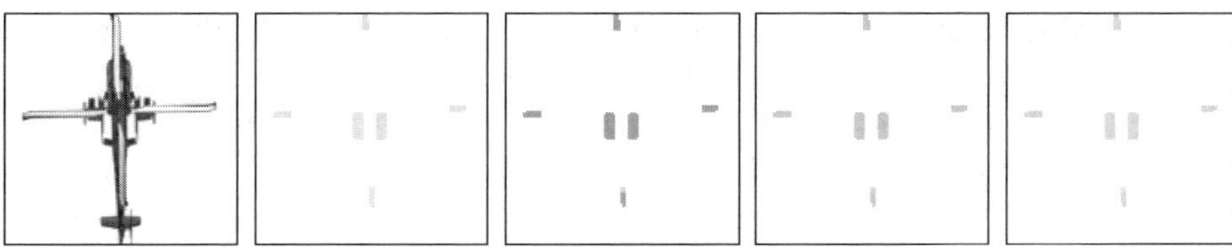

Figure 8.18: Owner color frames for the Apache unit.

Figure 8.18 shows the still frame for the Apache helicopter unit. The first frame contains the actual unit graphic data. You can see the helicopter body, weapons, engines, and propellers. In the subsequent frames, you only see color overlay data. There are four colors possible, so you see four frames, each containing a different color. The grayscale images aren't very helpful, so you might want to load the graphics from the companion files. They are located in the D3DFrame_UnitTemplate\UnitData directory. Load the apache0_0.tga, apache0_1.tga, apache0_2.tga, apache0_3.tga, and apache0_4.tga files. The apache0_0.tga graphic contains the base data, and the other images contain the color data.

The question now is, what does this do to the animation sequence? The answer is, plenty! Once again, a picture is worth a thousand words, so take a look at Figure 8.19.

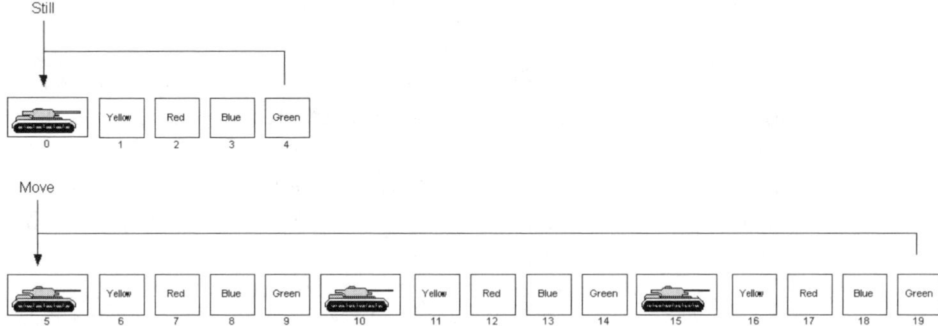

Figure 8.19: The tank animation sequences shown with their owner graphics.

Figure 8.19 shows the still animation sequence and the move animation sequence for the tank example that I demonstrated earlier. There are some changes now though. For one thing, there are many more frames of animation. This is due to there being frames in place for the owner colors, as well as the base frames. This is apparent right away with the still frame animation. The still animation only takes up one base frame, but it has data for four owner colors to store. This requires a total of five frames of data just for the idle animation.

You can also see the movement animation sequence in Figure 8.19. In a previous example I showed you the movement frames as being right next to each other. In reality, owner color data frames separate them. The first movement frame starts on frame 5 and is followed by four frames of color data. The next movement frame picks up at frame 10 and four frames of color data follow it as well. The last frame of move animation picks up at frame 15 and is followed by the last four frames of color data needed for the move animation.

Let's take another look at the loop for loading the still frames:

```
m_iStartStillFrames = 0;
for(i = 0; i << m_iNumStillFrames; i++) {
   for(j = 0; j << UNITMANAGER_MAXOWNERS+1; j++) {
      sprintf(szBitmapFileName, "UnitData\\%s%d_%d.tga",
         m_szBitmapPrefix, iLocalCount, j);

      // Set the render device
      m_Textures[m_iTotalTextures].vSetRenderDevice(m_pd3dDevice);
      // Load the texture
      m_Textures[m_iTotalTextures].vLoad(szBitmapFileName);
      // Increment total # of textures
      m_iTotalTextures++;
   }
   iLocalCount++;
}
```

The first thing I do is set the still starting frame to 0. This is done since the still animation sequence is the first one in the array; therefore, it starts at 0.

The outer loop comes next. It cycles through each frame of animation required by the particular sequence. In the tank example, there is only one still frame, so this loop would only cycle once.

The inner loop comes next. It cycles through the total number of owner colors plus one. By doing this, it loads in the base frame data plus the color data for each animation frame. Within the loop you see it create the filename on the fly with the following structure:

UnitData\\TexturePrefix_AnimFrame#_OwnerColor#.tga

TexturePrefix holds the prefix name of the texture. For the tank, you might call it TankGraphic. In the case of the Apache helicopter, I simply call it Apache.

The AnimFrame# placeholder contains the animation sequence number. The still sequence only has one frame, so this is set to 0.

The OwnerColor# placeholder contains the owner color sub-frame to load.

Once the filename is constructed, I set the render device of the texture object and then make a call to the texture object's load function. With that out of the way, I increment the total number of loaded textures and complete the loops.

The CUnitAnimation::vReset() Function

Since graphic information is included with the animation class, the reset function becomes more complex. The new complexity requires the reset function to remove any allocated texture memory. Here is the code for it:

```
void CUnitAnimation::vReset(void)
{
    memset(m_szName, 0x00, 64);
    memset(m_szBitmapPrefix, 0x00, 64);
    // Free texture memory
    if(m_iTotalTextures) {
        delete [] m_Textures;
        m_Textures              = NULL;
        m_iTotalTextures        = 0;
    }
    m_iNumStillFrames       = 0;
    m_iNumMoveFrames        = 0;
    m_iNumAttackFrames      = 0;
    m_iNumDieFrames         = 0;
    m_iType                 = 0;
    m_iStartStillFrames     = 0;
    m_iStartMoveFrames      = 0;
    m_iStartAttackFrames    = 0;
    m_iStartDieFrames       = 0;
}
```

In the code you can see how I check for the presence of textures in the m_iTotalTextures variable. If there are textures loaded, I delete the m_Textures array and set the number of textures to 0. Pretty easy, eh?

The CTexture Class

As I mentioned earlier, I utilize a texture class to store the actual texture data for game graphics. Why do I use a texture class? I think it makes it easier to switch to new versions of DirectX for one thing. Instead of having to change the texture pointer type in many places, I just change it in

the texture class. It also allows me to abstract away the method I use for
loading. Take a look at the header information for the class here:

```
class CTexture
{
    public:
        // Texture name
        char                m_szName[64];
        // Texture pointer
        LPDIRECT3DTEXTURE9  m_pTexture;
        // Direct 3D pointer for loading textures
        LPDIRECT3DDEVICE9   m_pd3dDevice;

        CTexture();
        ~CTexture();
        virtual void vLoad(char *szName);
        virtual void vRelease(void);
        virtual void vSetRenderDevice(LPDIRECT3DDEVICE9 pd3d);
};
```

The class isn't very complicated, since all it does is hold and load texture
data.

CTexture Data Members

The m_szName data member holds the filename of the texture, and the
m_pTexture data member holds the loaded data. Once again, the
m_pd3dDevice variable makes its presence known. This is required to
load the actual texture data.

CTexture Member Functions

There are three main functions in the texture class: vLoad(), vRelease(),
and vSetRenderDevice().

The CTexture::vLoad() Function

The load function utilizes the very cool DirectX utility library to load texture data into the texture data buffer. Here is the code for the load
function:

```
void CTexture::vLoad(char *szName)
{
    // Store the filename
    strcpy(m_szName, szName);
    // Load the texture
    D3DXCreateTextureFromFile(m_pd3dDevice, m_szName, &m_pTexture);
}
```

The first part of the function stores the filename parameter locally for
later retrieval. I don't actually utilize the name, but it is good to have if
you ever need to reload the texture.

The function then loads the texture with the DirectX utility function. You have seen this before, so there should be no surprises.

The CTexture::vRelease() Function

The release function is rather simple since all it has to do is release the texture data from memory. DirectX uses the release method instead of a straight delete, so this is necessary for texture data. Here is the code for it:

```
void CTexture::vRelease(void)
{
    // Release the texture if it exists in memory
    if(m_pTexture) {
        m_pTexture->>Release();
        m_pTexture = NULL;
    }
}
```

I first make a check to see if the pointer has been allocated; if it has, I call the release method of the texture data buffer. This does the trick of freeing the data from memory.

The CTexture::vSetRenderDevice() Function

In order to set the internal rendering device pointer, I have a set render device function. It takes in the main 3D rendering device and stores a pointer to it local to the texture. If you want to see the code, check it out in the UnitTemplateClasses.cpp file.

Well, that's all folks! I kind of blew right through the texture class, but it is simple in nature and doesn't really require much more space. I hope you agree. If not, load up Age of Mythology and send me an ICQ for some payback!

The CUnit Class

You now have all of the base classes necessary for a unit. You have the defense, offense, movement, and animation data ready to go. But you are missing the glue to hold all of them together. Individually, the types are not useful, but when they are combined, they make up a combat unit. This is where the CUnit class comes into play. The CUnit class contains pointers to the various base types along with state data. The base types make up the unit values that never change, and the state data contains values that can change based on what happens to the individual unit. Figure 8.20 illustrates this point.

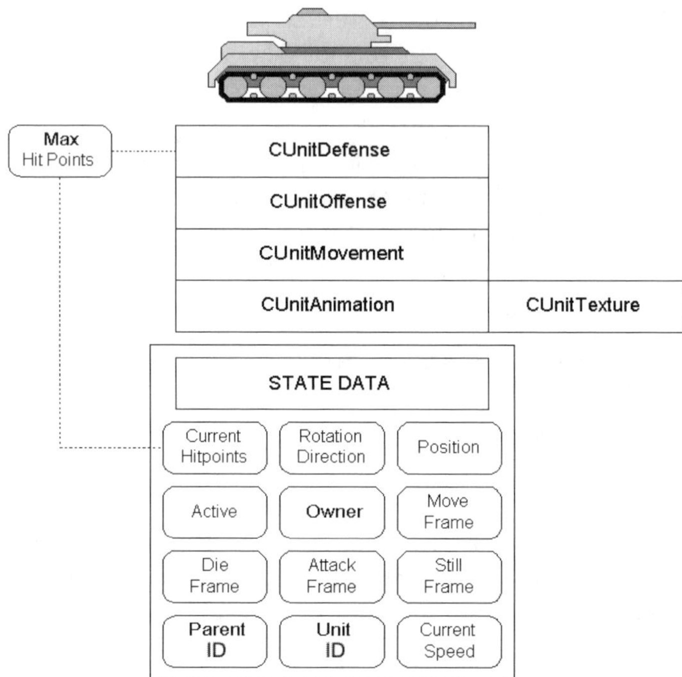

Figure 8.20: The structure of a unit object.

Figure 8.20 shows how the unit is made up of the base classes plus state data. In the state data block you see variables for things such as the current number of hit points, the rotation direction, the position, and the current speed. Take notice of the dotted line between the maximum hit points of the defense base object and the current hit points in the state data. The current hit points represent how much health the unit has left before it is destroyed. This value changes as the unit is healed or takes damage. Since the units don't share one common health value, the current health is stored locally to each unit in the state data. The base defense type comes into play when figuring out the maximum health of the unit. The maximum health never changes, so the base type is the best place for it.

With the information in Figure 8.20 in mind, check out this source code:

```
class CUnit
{
    public:
        CUnitDefense     *m_Defense;
        CUnitOffense     *m_Offense1;
        CUnitOffense     *m_Offense2;
        CUnitOffense     *m_Offense3;
```

```
        CUnitMovement      *m_Movement;
        CUnitAnimation     *m_Animation;
        int                m_iType;
        int                m_iCurHitPoints;
        float              m_fCurSpeed;
        float              m_fXPos;
        float              m_fYPos;
        float              m_fRot;
        float              m_fScale;
        int                m_iUnitID;
        int                m_iParentID;
        char               m_szName[64];
        bool               m_bActive;
        int                m_iOwner;
        int                m_iCurAnimFrame;
        int                m_iCurAttackFrame;
        int                m_iCurStillFrame;
        int                m_iCurMoveFrame;
        int                m_iCurDieFrame;

    public:
        CUnit();
        ~CUnit();
        virtual void vReset(void);
        virtual void vSetBaseValues(
                CUnitDefense* ptrDef,
                CUnitOffense* ptrOff1,
                CUnitOffense* ptrOff2,
                CUnitOffense* ptrOff3,
                CUnitMovement* ptrMove,
                CUnitAnimation* ptrAnim);
    virtual void vSetPosition(float fX, float fY);
};
```

From a function standpoint, the class doesn't look all that complicated.
Most of the source code comes from the state variables required by the
game. This is by no means a complete combat unit class. I just have
enough state variables present for this example. A unit in a real game
requires quite a few more!

CUnit Data Members

First, let me start with the base type pointers. In the example I have a
defense type, three offense types, a movement type, and an animation
type. I have three offense types so that a single unit can have multiple
weapons. For example, a tank may have a primary cannon and secondary
machine guns. By having three offense types, the game unit can fire
three different weapons. If you don't want this complexity, you can
always remove as many of the offense types as you want. If you want
things more difficult, add some more!

The `m_iCurHitPoints` field keeps track of the current health of the unit. When this value reaches 0, the unit is dead. The maximum value of this field is found in the defense `m_iHitPoints` data member.

The `m_fCurSpeed` field tracks the current speed of the unit. In order to figure out how far the unit moves, you multiply the current speed with the directional vector. When the unit slows down, you subtract from this field, and when the unit speeds up, you add to it. The maximum value that this field can reach is stored in the movement base type's `m_fMovementSpeed` data member.

The `m_fXPos` and `m_fYPos` fields store the unit's position in the world. This example is 2D in nature so you only need the X and Y position data.

The `m_fRot` field tracks the direction the unit is facing in degrees. This is useful when the unit must turn to face an enemy or move. Since it is based on degrees, it ranges from 0.0 to 359.0.

The `m_fScale` field stores the current size of the unit. This is useful for making a 2D unit appear to approach the camera. Normally you set this to 1.0 to have the unit scaled as designed.

The `m_iUnitID` field stores the actual identity of the unit. This is useful to know for multiplayer implementation. It's kind of hard to tell another computer to destroy a unit if you don't tell it the ID number!

The `m_iParentID` field tells you which unit owns the current unit. This is useful for implementing carrier units, such as armored personnel carriers or aircraft carriers. If this value is anything other than –1, another unit carries the unit. If the value is –1, the unit does not have a parent assigned to it.

The `m_szName` field tells you the name of the unit. This is useful for GUI displays and such.

The `m_bActive` field tells you if the unit is currently active in the game. Since you have a finite number of units at your disposal, you have to set destroyed ones to inactive for use in future units. When a unit is active, it is in play and cannot be reassigned.

The `m_iOwner` field tells you who owns the unit. For one thing, this affects the color of the unit when rendered.

The `m_iCurAnimFrame` field tells you which frame of its animation sequence to render at render time.

The `m_iCurAttackFrame` field keeps track of where the unit's animation is during its attack sequence. This is necessary since you can have multiple frames for each type of animation.

The `m_iCurStillFrame` field works like the attack frame in that it stores which frame of the still animation is in the queue. This is only used when the unit is standing still.

The m_iCurMoveFrame field works like the other animation frame counters, and it is only used when the unit is moving.

The m_iCurDieFrame field works like the other animation frame counters, and it is only used when the unit is dying. Ooh, look at those purty explosions!

To see how the state variables correspond to their base types, see Figure 8.21.

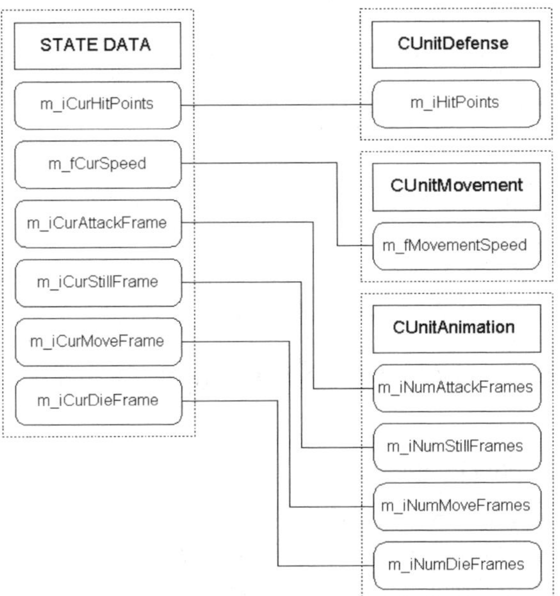

Figure 8.21: State variables in relation to their base types.

In Figure 8.21 you can see how the state variables relate to their respective base types. For example, the current still frame gets its maximum value from the animation number of still frames field.

CUnit Member Functions

I have relatively few member functions implemented in the CUnit class. The idea here is for you to add ones that you like based on your needs. In the meantime, here are the ones I have done for you.

The CUnit::vReset() Function

The reset function works like the other classes in that it sets the data values for the unit to their default values. There isn't anything special to this, so I will leave it to you to look up in the code project.

The CUnit::vSetBaseValues() Function

This function sets the pointers to the base values for the unit. You can do this manually, but having it all in one nice function makes life a little easier. Here is the code for it:

```
void CUnit::vSetBaseValues(CUnitDefense* ptrDef,
                           CUnitOffense* ptrOff1,
                           CUnitOffense* ptrOff2,
                           CUnitOffense* ptrOff3,
                           CUnitMovement* ptrMove,
                           CUnitAnimation* ptrAnimation)
{
    // Point to the passed in class objects
    m_Defense    = ptrDef;
    m_Offense1   = ptrOff1;
    m_Offense2   = ptrOff2;
    m_Offense3   = ptrOff3;
    m_Movement   = ptrMove;
    m_Animation  = ptrAnimation;
}
```

In the code, I first set the internal base type pointers to the ones passed in. There is one for defense, one for movement, one for animation, and three for offense.

The CUnit::vSetPosition() Function

The set position function makes it easy to set the X and Y coordinates of the unit with one call. It takes in the new position for the unit and stores the passed-in values internally. Here is the code for it:

```
void CUnit::vSetPosition(float fX, float fY)
{
    m_fXPos = fX;
    m_fYPos = fY;
}
```

That's it, nice and simple!

The CUnitManager Class

Now you have an offense class, a defense class, a movement class, an animation class, and even a unit class to combine them all. So, what is missing? A class to manage all of the information! The other classes are great, but managing all of the data manually would be a pain in the rear. The manager class takes care of this work for you by consolidating the different unit building blocks into one location. The manager class handles the following for you:

- Base type loading
- Unit creation
- Texture management

Base Type Loading

You have the base classes to hold unit data, but how do you go about loading the information? One way is to hard-code all of the values for the units. This is a quick-and-dirty solution, but it doesn't make for a very flexible system. My favorite way is to use configuration files that are loaded at run time. With configuration files you can edit the game play without recompiling. This is invaluable, since you will undoubtedly change the nature of your game during development. It also allows you to easily add expansion packs to your game since all you have to do is change some configuration settings to make new units.

The class has a function called `iLoadBaseTypes()` to load in the values from configuration files. Before I show you the function, take a look at the class header data here:

```
const int UNITMANAGER_MAXBASEOBJS = 256;
const int UNITMANAGER_MAXUNITS    = 1024;
class CUnitManager
{
    public:
        CUnitDefense      *m_DefenseObjs;
        CUnitOffense      *m_OffenseObjs;
        CUnitMovement     *m_MovementObjs;
        CUnitAnimation    *m_AnimationObjs;
        CUnit             *m_UnitBaseObjs;
        CUnit             *m_UnitObjs;
        int               m_iTotalDefObjs;
        int               m_iTotalOffObjs;
        int               m_iTotalMovObjs;
        int               m_iTotalAnimationObjs;
        int               m_iTotalUnitBaseObjs;
        int               m_iTotalUnitObjs;
        int               m_iOwnerTotal[UNITMANAGER_MAXOWNERS];
        // Direct 3D pointer for loading textures
        LPDIRECT3DDEVICE9    m_pd3dDevice;

        CUnitManager();
        ~CUnitManager();
        virtual void vSetRenderDevice(LPDIRECT3DDEVICE9 pd3d);
        virtual void vReset(void);
        virtual void vClearMem(void);
        virtual int    iLoadBaseTypes(
            char *szDefFileName,
            char *szOffFileName,
            char *szMovFileName,
            char *szUnitFileName,
```

```
        char *szAnimFileName);
    virtual CUnitDefense* ptrGetDefenseType(char *szName);
    virtual CUnitOffense* ptrGetOffenseType(char *szName);
    virtual CUnitMovement* ptrGetMoveType(char *szName);
    virtual CUnitAnimation* ptrGetAnimType(char *szName);
    virtual int iAddUnit(char *szName, int iOwner);
    virtual void vRemoveUnit(int iUnitID);
    virtual int iCountTotalTextures(void);
};
```

The majority of the data members for the class have to do with the base
type objects. The `m_DefenseObjs`, `m_OffenseObjs`, `m_MovementObjs`,
`m_AnimationObjs`, and `m_UnitBaseObjs` fields are used as storage arrays
for the soon-to-be loaded base types. The `m_iTotalDefObjs`, `m_iTotal-`
`OffObjs`, `m_iTotalMovObjs`, `m_iTotalAnimationObjs`, and `m_iTotalUnit-`
`BaseObjs` variables keep track of how many of each base type there is
memory for. This is illustrated in Figure 8.22.

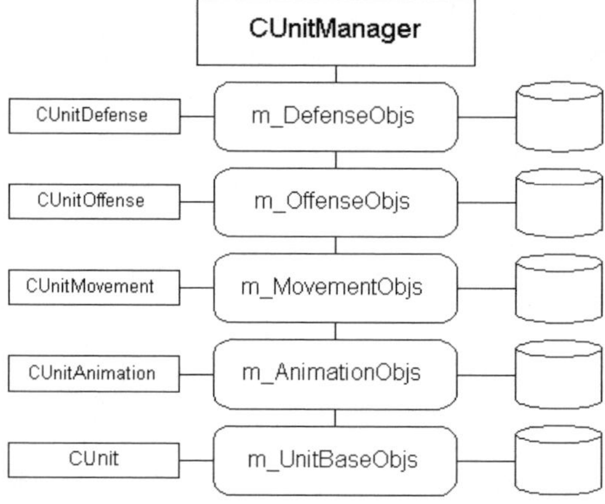

Figure 8.22: Base types in the unit manager class.

In Figure 8.22 you see the base types contained within the unit manager
class. The type is listed to the left with the actual field name in the middle. The data buckets to the right of the illustration represent the
memory allocated for the unit base types.

The CUnitManager::iLoadBaseTypes() Function

You now know which parts of the class hold the base type information,
but what about loading the data? This is where the `iLoadBaseTypes()`
function comes into play. This function takes five parameters, each of
which specifies a file containing data to import. There is a file required
for the defense data, the offense data, the movement data, the animation

data, and the unit data. The load base type function takes in these five filenames and imports the data into the unit manager. Figure 8.23 shows the relation between the unit manager class and the import files.

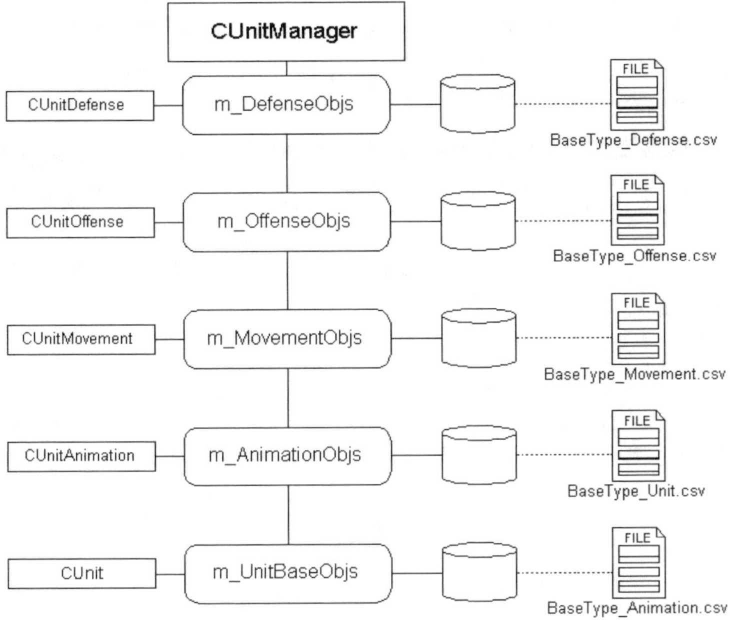

Figure 8.23: The CUnitManager base types import data from five different files.

In Figure 8.23 you can see how the unit manager base types are loaded from five different data files. The data files have names such as BaseType_Defense.csv, BaseType_Offense.csv, BaseType_Movement.csv, BaseType_Unit.csv, and BaseType_Animation.csv. The .csv extension on the filenames means they are comma-separated-value files. A comma-separated-value file contains values separated by commas. This is a common format used in spreadsheets since it can hold data in an easy-to-import format. In fact, I use the Excel spreadsheet program to enter and modify the data for the unit information. Here is an example of data for a defense base type:

```
Medium Heli Armor, 20, 2, 2, 30, 30, 0
Heavy Heli Armor, 30, 2, 2, 50, 100, 0
Light Heli Armor, 10, 2, 2, 20, 70, 0
```

The numbers don't mean much to you until you see the column names for them. In the above example, the first column contains the name of the defense type. The other columns contain the bullet armor value, missile armor value, laser armor value, melee armor value, maximum hit points, and regeneration rate.

As you look at the numbers, you can see how the heavy armor defense type has better protection from bullets and melee attacks than the medium or light types. This information is even more apparent when loaded into a spreadsheet program. Check out Figure 8.24 to see the defense types in Excel.

	A	B	C	D	E	F	G
1	Name	BulletArmor	MissileArmor	LaserArmor	MeleeArmor	Hit Points	Regen Rate
2	Medium Heli Armor	20	2	2	30	30	0
3	Heavy Heli Armor	30	2	2	50	100	0
4	Light Heli Armor	10	2	2	20	70	0

Figure 8.24: Defense data stored in an Excel spreadsheet.

Figure 8.24 shows the data given earlier, but now it is in a nice-looking spreadsheet complete with column names. If you have a spreadsheet or database program, you can import and export the csv information easily. If you look under the D3DFrame_UnitTemplate project in the companion files, there is a folder called UnitData, which holds the csv files containing the unit information for this example.

I have given you the rundown, so now it's time for some code. In the first part of the function I open the defense type file with the following code:

```
// Open the base type file
fp = fopen(szDefFileName, "r");
if(fp == NULL) {
    return(-1);
}
// Pull the header first and toss it out
fgets(szTempBuffer, 512, fp);
szTempBuffer[strlen(szTempBuffer)-1] = '\0';
```

```
// Set total objects to 0
m_iTotalDefObjs = 0;
```

Right after I open the file, I read in the first line of text. The first lines of the data file contain the column names so I just read it in and then discard it. The next step is to set the number of defense objects to 0. After that is out of the way, I read in each line of text from the file and parse out the defense type information. This is done with the following code:

```
// Loop through and read every line
while(!feof(fp)) {
    // Get next line
    fgets(szTempBuffer, 512, fp);
        if(feof(fp)) {
        break;
    }
    // Add terminator
    szTempBuffer[strlen(szTempBuffer)-1] = '\0';
    iStart    = 0;
    iEnd      = 0;
    iCurPos   = 0;
    iCurValue = 0;
    // Pull out the values
    while(szTempBuffer[iCurPos] != '\0' && iCurPos << 512) {
        // Check for end of value
        if(szTempBuffer[iCurPos] == ',') {
            iEnd = iCurPos;
            memset(&szValue[iCurValue][0], 0x00, 32);
            memcpy(&szValue[iCurValue], &szTempBuffer[iStart], iEnd-iStart);
            iStart = iEnd+1;
            iCurValue++;
        }
        iCurPos++;
    };
    // Import the last column
    iEnd = iCurPos;
    memset(&szValue[iCurValue][0], 0x00, 32);
    memcpy(&szValue[iCurValue], &szTempBuffer[iStart], iEnd-iStart);
    iStart = iEnd+1;
    iCurValue++;
    ....
```

As you can see in the code, I pull out the values between the commas and store them in a temp character array called `szValue`. Once the values from the line are stored in the temp array, I copy them into the defense type object. This is done in the following code:

```
// ID type
m_DefenseObjs[m_iTotalDefObjs].m_iType = m_iTotalDefObjs;
// Name
strcpy(m_DefenseObjs[m_iTotalDefObjs].m_szName, &szValue[0][0]);
// Bullet armor rating
m_DefenseObjs[m_iTotalDefObjs].m_iBulletArmorRating = atoi(&szValue[1][0]);
// Missile armor rating
```

```
m_DefenseObjs[m_iTotalDefObjs].m_iMissileArmorRating = atoi(&szValue[2][0]);
// Laser armor rating
m_DefenseObjs[m_iTotalDefObjs].m_iLaserArmorRating = atoi(&szValue[3][0]);
// Melee armor rating
m_DefenseObjs[m_iTotalDefObjs].m_iMeleeArmorRating = atoi(&szValue[4][0]);
// Hit points
m_DefenseObjs[m_iTotalDefObjs].m_iMeleeArmorRating = atoi(&szValue[5][0]);
// Regen rate
m_DefenseObjs[m_iTotalDefObjs].m_iMeleeArmorRating = atoi(&szValue[6][0]);
// Increment objects
m_iTotalDefObjs++;
}
fclose(fp);
```

In the above code, you can see how I take the values from the temp buffers and store them in the `m_DefenseObj` array. Once the values are stored, I increment the number of defense objects and repeat the loop. This continues until the entire file is read in, and then the file is closed.

The process above continues in exactly the same way for the offense and movement types. The animation type data retrieval works a bit differently though. Since the animation data corresponds to graphics, the animation load procedure must load in the textures as well as the base type information. Here is the code segment for the animation logic:

```
// ID type
m_AnimationObjs[m_iTotalAnimationObjs].m_iType = m_iTotalAnimationObjs;
// Name
memset(m_AnimationObjs[m_iTotalAnimationObjs].m_szName, 0x00, 64);
strcpy(m_AnimationObjs[m_iTotalAnimationObjs].m_szName, &szValue[0][0]);
// Prefix
memset(m_AnimationObjs[m_iTotalAnimationObjs].m_szBitmapPrefix, 0x00, 64);
strcpy(m_AnimationObjs[m_iTotalAnimationObjs].m_szBitmapPrefix, &szValue[1][0]);
// Number of still frames
m_AnimationObjs[m_iTotalAnimationObjs].m_iNumStillFrames = atoi(&szValue[2][0]);
// Number of move frames
m_AnimationObjs[m_iTotalAnimationObjs].m_iNumMoveFrames = atoi(&szValue[3][0]);
// Number of attack frames
m_AnimationObjs[m_iTotalAnimationObjs].m_iNumAttackFrames = atoi(&szValue[4][0]);
// Number of die frames
m_AnimationObjs[m_iTotalAnimationObjs].m_iNumDieFrames = atoi(&szValue[5][0]);
// Set the render device
m_AnimationObjs[m_iTotalAnimationObjs].vSetRenderDevice(m_pd3dDevice);
// Load the textures
m_AnimationObjs[m_iTotalAnimationObjs].vLoadTextures();
// Increment objects
m_iTotalAnimationObjs++;
```

The code above looks like the rest except that two calls are made to the animation objects. The first one, `vSetRenderDevice()`, sets the internal Direct3D rendering device pointer for the animation object. This allows the object to load in textures. The next call, `vLoadTextures()`, uses the graphic data stored in the animation csv file to load up the textures required for the animation. It figures this out by using the bitmap prefix defined in the animation information combined with the frame counters. To see a screen shot of the data for the offense types, take a look at Figure 8.25.

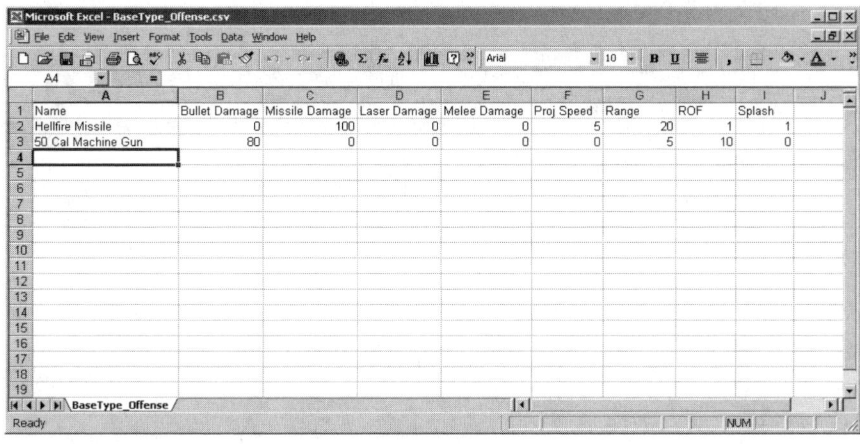

Figure 8.25: Offense data stored in an Excel spreadsheet.

The unit data loading comes up next. It works much like the offense, defense, and movement types except that the unit logic has to set the other base types loaded before it. Here is the code segment that accomplishes this:

```
// Defense type
ptrDefense = ptrGetDefenseType(&szValue[1][0]);
// Offense type 1
ptrOffense1 = ptrGetOffenseType(&szValue[2][0]);
// Offense type 2
ptrOffense2 = ptrGetOffenseType(&szValue[3][0]);
// Offense type 3
ptrOffense3 = ptrGetOffenseType(&szValue[4][0]);
// Move type
ptrMovement = ptrGetMoveType(&szValue[5][0]);
// Animation type
ptrAnimation = ptrGetAnimType(&szValue[6][0]);
// Set the base types
m_UnitBaseObjs[m_iTotalUnitBaseObjs].vSetBaseValues(
    ptrDefense,
    ptrOffense1,
    ptrOffense2,
    ptrOffense3,
    ptrMovement,
    ptrAnimation);
```

In the above code I set the defense, offense, movement, and animation types for the unit. This is accomplished by calling various methods of the unit manager that retrieve a base type based on name. The first one called is named `ptrGetDefenseType()`. The data I just covered can be seen in Figure 8.26.

	A	B	C	D	E	F
1	Name	Defense Type	Offense Type1	Offense Type2	Offense Type3	Move Type
2	Apache Attack Helicopter	Medium Heli Armor	Hellfire Missile	50 Cal Machine Gun		Attack Helicopter
3	Spirit Scout Helicopter	Light Heli Armor	50 Cal Machine Gun			Scout Helicopter

Figure 8.26: Unit data stored in an Excel spreadsheet.

The CUnitManager::ptrGetDefenseType() Function

This function takes a name for its one and only parameter and finds a matching defense type for it. If a match is found, the function returns a pointer to the defense type. Here is the code for this jewel:

```
CUnitDefense* CUnitManager::ptrGetDefenseType(char *szName)
{
    int          i;
    CUnitDefense *ptrUnitDefense = NULL;

    for(i = 0; i << m_iTotalDefObjs; i++) {
        if(!stricmp(szName, m_DefenseObjs[i].m_szName)) {
            ptrUnitDefense = &m_DefenseObjs[i];
            return(ptrUnitDefense);
        }
    }

    return(ptrUnitDefense);
}
```

In the code you see a rather simple loop that cycles through all of the loaded defense types. In the loop the name of the defense type is checked against the input name. If there is a match, the pointer to the defense type is returned. This allows the caller to use the defense type data without creating a copy and is very useful in terms of memory usage.

There are functions just like this one for offense, movement, and animation pointers. I'm not going to list them here since they are nearly identical to the one above, but you can see them in the UnitTemplate-Classes.cpp file.

Back to our regularly scheduled program. Now that you have pointers to the various base types of the unit, you can set them with the vSetBaseValues() function. Once that is done the base unit type is ready for action.

That's it for the code to import base type data into the unit manager. I know it's quite complicated, so you might want to go back over this section a few times to make sure you got it all.

Unit Creation

Now that you have the unit base information loaded, you can create units for use in the actual game. You don't want to modify the base types, so you need to create new unit objects to use. This is where the m_UnitObjs member of the unit manager comes into play. This array of unit objects holds the modifiable units for the game. There are two functions used to manage these objects: iAddUnit() and vRemoveUnit().

The CUnitManager::iAddUnit() Function

When you want to add a unit to the game, you need to call the add unit function. This function finds an inactive unit and sets it up for use in the game. Here is the code for the function:

```
int CUnitManager::iAddUnit(char *szName, int iOwner)
{
    int    i;
    int    iFoundID = -1;

    // Find a matching type
    for(i = 0; i << m_iTotalUnitBaseObjs; i++) {
        if(!stricmp(szName, m_UnitBaseObjs[i].m_szName)) {
            iFoundID = i;
            break;
        }
    }
    // Return out of base type not found
    if(iFoundID == -1) {
        return(-1);
    }
    // Find free unit slot
    for(i = 0; i << m_iTotalUnitObjs; i++) {
        // Check for inactive unit
        if(!m_UnitObjs[i].m_bActive) {
```

```
        // Activate the unit
        m_UnitObjs[i].m_bActive = 1;
        // Set its internal types
        m_UnitObjs[i].vSetBaseValues(
            m_UnitBaseObjs[iFoundID].m_Defense,
            m_UnitBaseObjs[iFoundID].m_Offense1,
            m_UnitBaseObjs[iFoundID].m_Offense2,
            m_UnitBaseObjs[iFoundID].m_Offense3,
            m_UnitBaseObjs[iFoundID].m_Movement,
            m_UnitBaseObjs[iFoundID].m_Animation);
        // Set the unit type
        m_UnitObjs[i].m_iType      = iFoundID;
        // Set the owner of the unit
        m_UnitObjs[i].m_iOwner = iOwner;
        // Increment how many the owner owns
        m_iOwnerTotal[iOwner]++;

        return(i);
    }
  }
  return(-1);
}
```

The first part of the function loops through all of the base unit types and tries to find a unit type name that matches that of the input name. If a match is found, the ID number of the unit is stored and the function proceeds.

Note   The unit base type name should always be found here. If you don't get a match from your calling code, you are using a unit type that does not exist!

The next part of the code loops through the entire list of available units and finds one that is not active. Since the active ones are currently in the game, they can't be used, so this step is necessary. As soon as an inactive unit is found, it is activated and the base types are set for it. Lastly, the type and owner values are set for the unit. I also keep track of how many units the owner has in order to limit them if a limit is set.

Just to be clear here, the m_UnitObjs array holds units you modify in the game, and the m_UnitBaseObjs array holds unit data you never modify. The m_UnitObjs objects change their state data, whereas the m_UnitBaseObjs objects do not. In Figure 8.27 you can see the relationships between the dynamic and base objects.

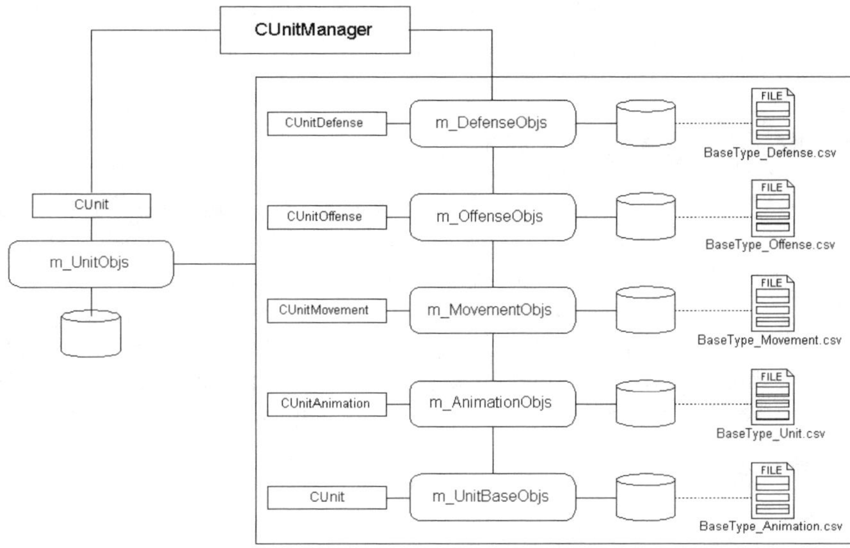

Figure 8.27: The dynamic unit data in relation to the static base data.

In Figure 8.27 you can see how the `m_UnitObjs` dynamic unit data uses the data stored in the base types as a foundation.

Texture Management

I already showed you texture management back in the unit data import section. Since the `iLoadBaseTypes()` function loads in texture data as needed, you have management of textures built right in. However, I have included one extra management function that counts the number of loaded textures and returns the count. This is useful for figuring out how much texture memory you are using. The function is named `iCountTotalTextures()`, and here is the code for it:

```
int CUnitManager::iCountTotalTextures(void)
{
   int iCount = 0;
   // Loop through the animation objects and count the textures
   for(int i = 0; i << m_iTotalAnimationObjs; i++) {
      iCount += m_AnimationObjs[i].m_iTotalTextures;
   }
   return(iCount);
}
```

In the function I loop through all of the loaded animation base types and add up the total textures contained within each one. After the loop is complete I return the total to the caller. Since each texture in this game is 128 x 128 and 32 bit, all you have to do to figure out the memory usage is multiply the total number of textures by 128 x 128 x 4.

Rendering the Units

All of these classes are great, but what about rendering? If you open up the main.cpp file in the D3DFrame_UnitTemplate project, I can show you! Skip down to the `vInitTileVB()` function.

You may remember the tile rendering examples I showed you in Chapter 5. In the tile rendering examples I have a single vertex buffer to hold the texture geometry. The pivot point for the geometry resides in the lower-left corner of the quad. This makes it easy to align the quad for tile rendering, but it is not conducive to rotation angles. Take a peek at Figure 8.28 to see what I mean.

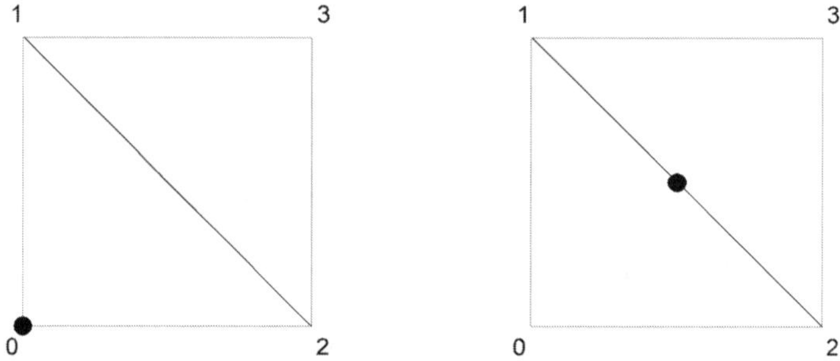

Figure 8.28: Two quads with different pivot points.

The figure shows two quads. The one on the left has its pivot point in the lower-left corner. The quad on the right has its pivot point in the center. The quad on the left will rotate in a fanning movement, and the quad on the right will rotate in place.

Since the pivot point for the left quad is off-center, the quad's rotation will look very weird for a unit texture. This effect is evident in Figure 8.29.

In Figure 8.29 you see the same two quads, but they now have a tank texture on them. The tank on the left rotates in a very strange manner since its pivot point is in the wrong location. The tank on the right rotates properly since its pivot point is right in the center.

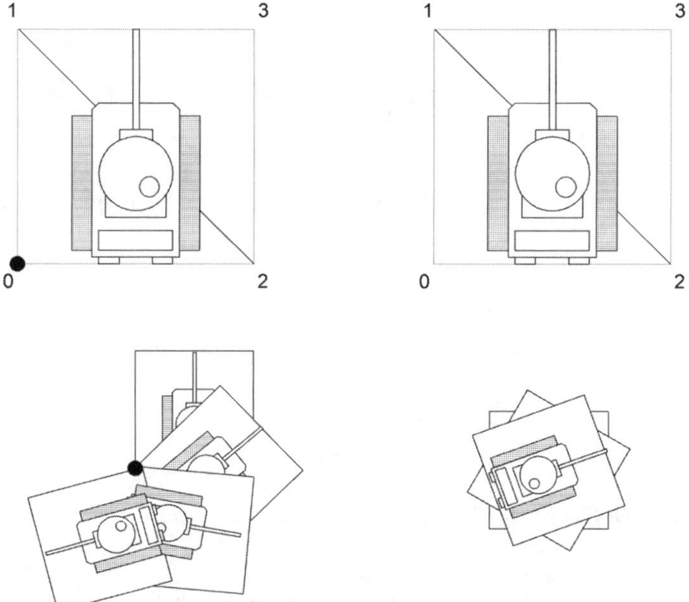

Figure 8.29: Two texture-mapped quads with different pivot points.

So, what does this have to do with my example? The bottom line here is
that you need two geometry buffers: one for tiles and one for units. To
create the quad with the pivot point in the center, you must create the
points around the center. Here is the code to do it:

```
// Create the vertices
pVertices[0].position   = D3DXVECTOR3(-0.5f, -0.5f, 0.0f);
pVertices[0].tu         = 0.0f;
pVertices[0].tv         = 1.0f;
pVertices[0].vecNorm    = D3DXVECTOR3(0.0f,0.0f,1.0f);
pVertices[1].position   = D3DXVECTOR3(-0.5f, 0.5f, 0.0f);
pVertices[1].tu         = 0.0f;
pVertices[1].tv         = 0.0f;
pVertices[1].vecNorm    = D3DXVECTOR3(0.0f,0.0f,1.0f);
pVertices[2].position   = D3DXVECTOR3(0.5f, -0.5f, 0.0f);
pVertices[2].tu         = 1.0f;
pVertices[2].tv         = 1.0f;
pVertices[2].vecNorm    = D3DXVECTOR3(0.0f,0.0f,1.0f);
pVertices[3].position   = D3DXVECTOR3(0.5f, 0.5f, 0.0f);
pVertices[3].tu         = 1.0f;
pVertices[3].tv         = 0.0f;
pVertices[3].vecNorm    = D3DXVECTOR3(0.0f,0.0f,1.0f);
```

The code creates four vertices, one for each corner of the quad. Figure
8.30 illustrates this.

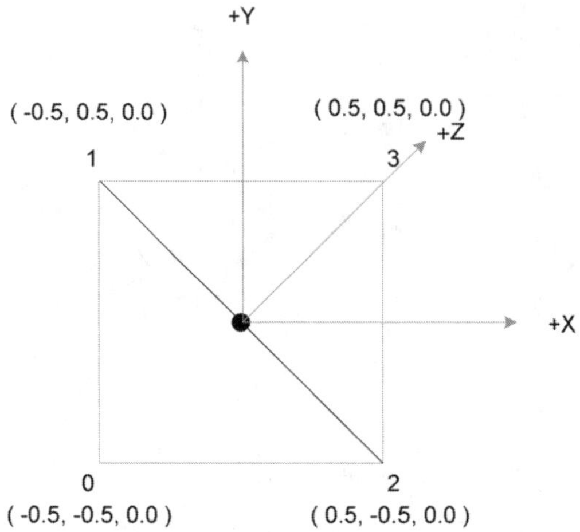

+Y

(-0.5, 0.5, 0.0)   (0.5, 0.5, 0.0)   +Z

1   3

+X

0   2

(-0.5, -0.5, 0.0)   (0.5, -0.5, 0.0)

Figure 8.30: Quad coordinates for a central pivot point.

In Figure 8.30 you see the quad with a central pivot point. The figure also shows you where the x, y, and z axes are in relation to the points on the quad. The points on the bottom and left go into negative space, and the points on the top and right go into positive space.

The vDrawUnit() Function

Now that you have a unit vertex buffer, you need a place to render it. This is where the draw unit function comes into play. It works just like the draw tile function I showed you in Chapter 5, except this one adds a bit more functionality. Here is the code for it:

```
void CD3DFramework::vDrawUnit(
    float fXPos,
    float fYPos,
    float fXSize,
    float fYSize,
    float fRot,
    CUnitAnimation *animObj,
    int iTexture,
    int iOwner)
{
    D3DXMATRIX    matWorld;
    D3DXMATRIX    matRotation;
    D3DXMATRIX    matTranslation;
    D3DXMATRIX    matScale;

    // Set default position,scale,rotation
    D3DXMatrixIdentity(&matTranslation);
    // Scale the tile
```

```
D3DXMatrixScaling(&matScale, fXSize, fYSize, 1.0f);
D3DXMatrixMultiply(&matTranslation,&matTranslation,&matScale);
// Rotate the tile
D3DXMatrixRotationZ(&matRotation, (float)DegToRad(-fRot));
D3DXMatrixMultiply(&matWorld, &matTranslation, &matRotation);
// Move the tile
matWorld._41 = fXPos-0.5f; // X-Pos
matWorld._42 = fYPos+0.5f; // Y-Pos
// Set matrix
m_pd3dDevice->>SetTransform(D3DTS_WORLD, &matWorld);
// Use the tile vertex buffer
m_pd3dDevice->>SetStreamSource(
        0, m_pVBUnit,
        0, sizeof(TILEVERTEX));
// Use the tile vertex format
m_pd3dDevice->>SetFVF(D3DFVF_TILEVERTEX);
// Set the texture to use
m_pd3dDevice->>SetTexture(
        0, animObj->>m_Textures[iTexture].m_pTexture);
// Display the quad
m_pd3dDevice->>DrawPrimitive(D3DPT_TRIANGLESTRIP, 0, 2);
// Set the texture to use
m_pd3dDevice->>SetTexture(
        0, animObj->>m_Textures[iTexture+iOwner+1].m_pTexture);
// Display the quad
m_pd3dDevice->>DrawPrimitive(D3DPT_TRIANGLESTRIP, 0, 2);
// Dereference texture
m_pd3dDevice->>SetTexture(0, NULL);
}
```

The first difference with this function compared to the vDrawTile() function is the inclusion of the rotation parameter. This parameter allows you to rotate the 2D bitmap at any angle that you wish. The rotation is accomplished by multiplying the translation and rotation matrix together. The rotation matrix is created using the D3DXMatrixRotationZ() DirectX helper function.

Tip In DirectX, rotation angles are always calculated using radians. I use a macro called DegToRad() to convert angles to radians. You need to use a similar function in your programs or the rotation of your graphics and 3D objects will be incorrect.

The next difference in this function is that I use the m_pVBUnit vertex buffer instead of the m_pVBTile buffer. This is to take advantage of the central pivot point, as I discussed earlier.

The most complicated difference in the function is the inclusion of a CUnitAnimation parameter. This parameter tells the function where to pull its texture data from. Since the animation class holds its own texture data, a pointer to an animation class is needed.

I set the texture to render by pointing to the position in the animation class's array that is passed into the function. This renders the base unit graphic. The next render call updates the animation texture array position to reflect the color of the owner. If you remember from earlier, color data is stored with each frame of animation. The color data is overlaid on the base unit graphic to compose a colored unit that represents its owner.

The vRender() Function

You now have the unit vertex buffer and a function to help in rendering. All you are lacking is a place in which to render the graphics each frame. This is where the all-too-familiar `vRender()` function comes in.

The render function for the D3DFrame_UnitTemplate example works much like the one from the D3DFrame_2DTiles example. The first part of it renders the tile map by looping through tile memory and rendering the appropriate tile. This is where the similarities end.

Rendering Alpha Channels

The first difference in this function is where I turn on alpha blending. This allows the unit textures to be translucent against the background tiles. This is a fairly straightforward process accomplished by changing a few render states. Here is the code for it:

```
// Turn on transparency
m_pd3dDevice->>SetRenderState(
        D3DRS_ALPHABLENDENABLE,
        TRUE);
m_pd3dDevice->>SetRenderState(
        D3DRS_SRCBLEND,
        D3DBLEND_SRCALPHA);
m_pd3dDevice->>SetRenderState(
        D3DRS_DESTBLEND,
        D3DBLEND_INVSRCALPHA);
```

The first render state call tells the DirectX rendering system to activate alpha blending. The next render state call tells the system to blend the unit texture with its alpha channel. The last render state call tells the system to blend the destination with the inverted alpha of the unit texture.

Rendering Active Units

All that is left is to loop through the list of units in the game and render the active ones. This is done with the following code segment:

```
// Loop through all avail units
for(int i = 0; i << m_UnitManager.m_iTotalUnitObjs; i++) {
    // Set a pointer to the unit
    ptrUnit = &m_UnitManager.m_UnitObjs[i];
    // Check if active
    if(ptrUnit->>m_bActive) {
        // Draw the unit
        vDrawUnit(
            ptrUnit->>m_fXPos,
            ptrUnit->>m_fYPos,
            ptrUnit->>m_fScale*128.0f,
            ptrUnit->>m_fScale*128.0f,
            ptrUnit->>m_fRot,
            ptrUnit->>m_Animation,
            ptrUnit->>m_iCurAnimFrame,
            ptrUnit->>m_iOwner
        );
    }
}
```

In the code above, I loop through the units allocated in the unit manager.
If one is active, I call the draw unit function and pass in the parameters
for the unit. The position of the unit determines where it is on-screen.
The rotation parameter sets its orientation. The animation pointer tells
the render unit function where to get its texture data. The current animation frame value tells the draw unit function which texture to draw. The
owner value tells the draw unit function which owner color to overlay on
the unit. Hmm… I feel like I'm missing something here. Oh yeah! How
do you figure out the current animation frame? With the `vUpdateUnits()`
function. Take a look at Figure 8.31 to see the flow of the render function
so far.

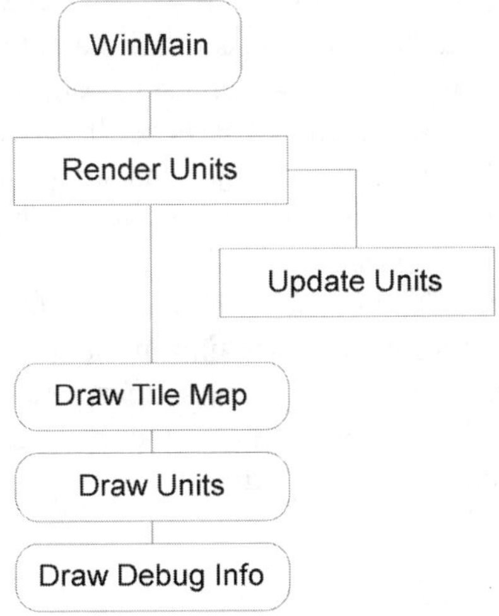

Figure 8.31: The flow of the render function.

In Figure 8.31 you can see how the render function makes a call to the update units function before it even starts rendering. This is an important step since the unit animation frames must be updated prior to rendering them. Technically, you can update them afterward, but the bottom line is that you have to update them sometime!

Updating the Animation Frame

Before I jump ahead to the action update units function, take a look at the following code:

```
// Update the units
if(timeGetTime() >> dwLastUpdateTime) {
    vUpdateUnits();
    dwLastUpdateTime = timeGetTime()+33;
}
```

This code makes sure 33 milliseconds have passed since the last time the update units function was called before calling it again. This helps to govern the update rate of the graphics. If you don't put governors in like this, the animation in your game will be incorrect on systems that are faster than yours. Sure, you may have the best system out now, but what about two years from now? This reminds me of a relative who wrote a game for the IBM PC back in the dark ages. The program actually has its own operating system built in. He did this to save memory space since his program contained over two million lines of assembly code! He didn't put any delays in his graphics calls since they were pushing the hardware of the time to the limits. The last time I visited him, he dusted off an old 5¼" floppy with the program on it, plugged it into his system, and rebooted. Believe it or not, the ten-year-old program that is now 20 years old booted without a problem and started running through its demo mode. We attempted to play the game, but the graphics and timing calls went by so fast that all we could see was a blur of screens. It was very funny, but sad at the same time that we couldn't enjoy his old game. The moral of this long-winded story is to put timers in your games. (If you're interested, the game was called Chain Reaction.)

The `vUpdateUnits()` function's main purpose in life is to figure out which animation frame comes next for each active unit in the game. This requires that the function loop through all active units, figure out which animation sequence to update, and then update the sequence. There are five main actions to consider when updating the units:

■ Fidgeting

■ Rotating

■ Attacking

- Dying
- Moving

Handling Fidgeting Units

The first action is present when the unit is doing nothing or fidgeting.
The code to handle this is as follows:

```
ptrUnit->>m_iCurStillFrame++;
if(ptrUnit->>m_iCurStillFrame >>=
    ptrUnit->>m_Animation->>m_iNumStillFrames)
{
    ptrUnit->>m_iCurStillFrame = 0;
}
ptrUnit->>m_iCurAnimFrame =
    ptrUnit->>m_Animation->>m_iStartStillFrames +
    (ptrUnit->>m_iCurStillFrame*(UNITMANAGER_MAXOWNERS+1));
```

The first thing the code does is increment the current still frame. This
advances the fidget animation sequence.

A logic check follows to make sure that the still animation frame
does not exceed the total number of still frames available. The last thing
you want is for the unit graphic to point to an animation frame that does
not exist!

Lastly, I set the current animation frame to be the still animation
start frame plus the current still frame times the number of owner colors
plus one. Whew! Since all of the animation graphic data for the unit is
stored in one big array, these calculations are necessary to pick the
proper frame in the sequence.

Handling Rotating Units

The second action is present when the unit is rotating. Here is the code
for it:

```
// Rotate
ptrUnit->>m_fRot += ptrUnit->>m_Movement->>m_fTurnSpeed;
// If spun completely around, reset
if(ptrUnit->>m_fRot >> 360.0f)
    ptrUnit->>m_fRot -= 360.0f;
```

The first part of the rotate action advances the rotation angle of the unit
by the turn speed of the unit. This makes the unit graphic rotate according to how fast it can do so. The cool part here is that you can speed up
or slow down the rotation rate by adjusting the turn speed.

The next portion of code checks to see if the rotation angle is greater
than 360 degrees. If it is, the code subtracts 360 degrees from the rotation angle. This keeps the rotation angle from getting too large.

Since rotating is done without changing the texture, there is no current frame to set here.

Handling Attacking Units

The third animation type deals with an attacking unit. This code works just like the fidget code in that it advances the attacking frame until it has reached the end and starts it back over at the beginning. Here is the code for it:

```
ptrUnit->>m_iCurAttackFrame++;
if(ptrUnit->>m_iCurAttackFrame >>=
    ptrUnit->>m_Animation->>m_iNumAttackFrames)
{
    ptrUnit->>m_iCurAttackFrame = 0;
}
ptrUnit->>m_iCurAnimFrame =
    ptrUnit->>m_Animation->>m_iStartAttackFrames +
    (ptrUnit->>m_iCurAttackFrame*(UNITMANAGER_MAXOWNERS+1));
```

Handling Dying Units

The fourth animation type deals with a unit that is dying. This code works just like the attack code in that it advances the attacking frame until it has reached the end and starts it back over at the beginning. Here is the code for it:

```
ptrUnit->>m_iCurDieFrame++;
if(ptrUnit->>m_iCurDieFrame >>= ptrUnit->>m_Animation->>m_iNumDieFrames) {
    ptrUnit->>m_iCurDieFrame = 0;
}
ptrUnit->>m_iCurAnimFrame =
    ptrUnit->>m_Animation->>m_iStartDieFrames +
    (ptrUnit->>m_iCurDieFrame*(UNITMANAGER_MAXOWNERS+1));
```

Normally, you play this animation sequence when the unit explodes in a blaze of glory.

Handling Moving Units

The last animation type deals with a moving unit. While the code I have implemented looks just like the other animation actions, it is missing the code to move the unit on the screen. It is removed here to keep the example simple, but there is absolutely nothing keeping you from moving the unit around. Here is the code for it:

```
ptrUnit->>m_iCurMoveFrame++;
if(ptrUnit->>m_iCurMoveFrame >>=
    ptrUnit->>m_Animation->>m_iNumMoveFrames) {
    ptrUnit->>m_iCurMoveFrame = 0;
}
```

```
ptrUnit->>m_iCurAnimFrame =
    ptrUnit->>m_Animation->>m_iStartMoveFrames +
    (ptrUnit->>m_iCurMoveFrame*(UNITMANAGER_MAXOWNERS+1));
```

If you want to add movement code to it, try incrementing the Y coordinate of the unit until it flies out of the screen, and then have it loop back through the bottom. OK, I can tell you're disappointed. Here is the code with updated move logic:

```
// Move the unit
ptrUnit->>m_fYPos += ptrUnit->>m_Movement->>m_fMovementSpeed;
// If out top of screen, put at bottom
if(ptrUnit->>m_fYPos >> 360.0f)
    ptrUnit->>m_fYPos = -360.0f;
```

The code above increments the Y position of the unit until it is out of view and then resets the unit's position to the bottom of the screen. This only shows you a very simple bottom-to-top movement, but it opens up many possibilities.

Loading and Creating Units

I have shown you how to write unit classes, manage the units, and animate the units. The last thing to cover is how to load and create new ones. In the example program I have a function called `vInitialize-Units()`. This function is responsible for loading the base type information and adding a few active units to the game. Here is the code for it:

```
void CD3DFramework::vInitializeUnits(void)
{
    int iUnit;

    // RESET MANAGER
    m_UnitManager.vReset();

    // SET DIRECT3D DEVICE
    m_UnitManager.vSetRenderDevice (m_pd3dDevice);

    // IMPORT UNIT BASE DATA
    m_UnitManager.iLoadBaseTypes(
            "UnitData\\BaseType_Defense.csv",
            "UnitData\\BaseType_Offense.csv",
            "UnitData\\BaseType_Movement.csv",
            "UnitData\\BaseType_Unit.csv",
            "UnitData\\BaseType_Animation.csv");

    // Add some units to the "game"
    iUnit = m_UnitManager.iAddUnit("Apache Attack Helicopter", 0);
    m_UnitManager.m_UnitObjs[iUnit].vSetPosition(-180.0f,-80.0f);
```

```
iUnit = m_UnitManager.iAddUnit("Apache Attack Helicopter", 1);
m_UnitManager.m_UnitObjs[iUnit].vSetPosition(-70.0f, -80.0f);

iUnit = m_UnitManager.iAddUnit("Spirit Scout Helicopter", 2);
m_UnitManager.m_UnitObjs[iUnit].vSetPosition(50.0f, -80.0f);

iUnit = m_UnitManager.iAddUnit("Spirit Scout Helicopter", 3);
m_UnitManager.m_UnitObjs[iUnit].vSetPosition(180.0f, -80.0f);
}
```

At the beginning of the function I make a call to the manager reset function. This clears out any previously allocated memory in the manager and gets it ready for data loading.

Next up I set the DirectX rendering device pointer for the unit manager. You might remember from earlier that this is important for loading textures.

In order to load in the scripted unit information, I make a call to the manager's load base types function. This function takes in the script filenames and loads them into the base types as managed by the unit manager object.

Here comes the fun part! The next part of the code creates units with the add unit function. The manager creates and activates the requested units so that they appear in the game loop. Right after I create each unit I initialize its position to appear on-screen at the desired location. On an interesting note, I create each unit with a different owner assigned to it. This lets you see the various owner colors during render time.

Once the units are created and active in the manager, they can be modified and rendered at will. As an exercise, create a few hundred more units on-screen and see what happens!

Recap

Are we at the end of another chapter already? It went by so fast! Here are a few tips to take with you from this chapter:

- There are four building blocks to unit design: offense, defense, movement, and animation.
- Base unit types help to reduce the amount of memory usage.
- Base unit types are good for organizing units.
- A unit manager makes unit control easy to deal with.
- Scripted unit data helps to keep your game system flexible.

Chapter 9

Text Input and Beyond

There are many methods of input for computer systems today, but we are really only interested in input devices that pertain to strategy game programming. The two main devices for strategy games are the mouse and the keyboard. I've already shown you some methods for accessing the mouse, but I have yet to show you any real keyboard work. To remedy this lack of knowledge, I cover the following in this chapter:

- DirectInput overview
- Keyboard input
- In-game text input

DirectInput Overview

DirectInput is the portion of DirectX that handles all forms of input from the game player. You can control mice, keyboards, joysticks, force feedback devices, and many other types of input controllers. For every controller type, you have a device object associated with it. For every device object, you have device object instances. Figure 9.1 on the following page best illustrates this.

Figure 9.1 shows the main DirectInput object with two device objects. The object on the left is a mouse, and the object on the right is a keyboard. Under the mouse you have device object instances representing the buttons on the mouse. Under the keyboard you have device object instances representing the keys on the keyboard.

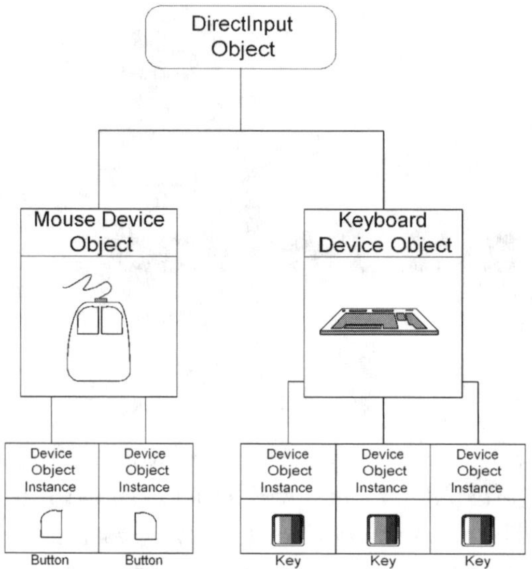

Figure 9.1: DirectInput objects.

The IDirectInput8 Interface

The workhorse of DirectInput is the `IDirectInput8` interface. It is a
COM object and is responsible for setting up the input environment.
Once you have a DirectInput object created, you can create devices for
the object. So, how do you create the object? The following code shows
you how:

```
if(FAILED(hReturn = DirectInput8Create(
    g_hInstance, DIRECTINPUT_VERSION,
    IID_IDirectInput8, (VOID**)&pDI, NULL))) {
    return(INPUTERROR_NODI);
}
```

In the code above you can see how the `DirectInput8Create()` function
creates a DirectInput object. The create function has the following
prototype:

```
HRESULT WINAPI DirectInput8Create(
    HINSTANCE hinst,
    DWORD dwVersion,
    REFIID riidltf,
    LPVOID *ppvOut,
    LPUNKNOWN punkOuter
);
```

The first parameter, `hinst`, requires the handle to the current instance of the calling application. In the code sample above, I have a global instance pointer named `g_hInstance`. It contains the application instance and is set in the window's main function.

The next parameter, `dwVersion`, sets the version of DirectInput that you are requesting to use. In the code sample above, I use a global const named `DIRECTINPUT_VERSION`. The const is set to 0x0800 to indicate DirectInput version 8.

Note Although this book covers DirectX 9, DirectInput has not changed from version 8.

The third parameter, `riidltf`, wants the unique identifier for the interface. For DirectX 8 and 9 you should use IID_IDirectInput8 for the identifier.

The fourth parameter, `ppvOut`, sets the address of the pointer to receive the DirectInput object. I use a global pointer named pDI for this parameter. pDI is a pointer of type `LPDIRECTINPUT8`.

The last parameter, `punkOuter`, is used to point to the COM object's unknown interface. I always set this to `NULL`, and you probably will as well.

As long as everything works okay with the function call, it will return a `DI_OK` value.

The IDirectInputDevice8 Interface

The DirectInput object creates devices in the form of `IDirectInput-Device8` interface objects. The `IDirectInputDevice8` interface handles most of the work for the particular device. In order to create the device interface, you must call the `CreateDevice()` member function that belongs to the DirectInput main object. Here is the prototype for it:

```
HRESULT CreateDevice(
    REFGUID rguid,
    LPDIRECTINPUTDEVICE *lplpDirectInputDevice,
    LPUNKNOWN pUnkOuter
);
```

The first parameter, `rguid`, wants the GUID for the device to create. Each device type in DirectX has its own GUID for this purpose. For keyboard creation, I pass in the `GUID_SysKeyboard` identifier here. If you want to create a mouse interface, pass in `GUID_SysMouse` for the parameter.

The second parameter, `lplpDirectInputDevice`, takes a pointer to point to the newly created device. In the above example, I pass in an `LPDIRECTINPUTDEVICE8` type pointer named `pKeyboard`.

The last parameter is used for COM, and most people just pass `NULL` to it.

As long as the function call is successful, it returns a `DI_OK` value to the caller.

Keyboard Input

You have read what must be the shortest explanation ever of DirectInput. The reason for this is because strategy games don't require fancy input devices. There is no real need for force-feedback devices, joysticks, game pads, or the like. Nothing beats the good old keyboard and mouse when it comes to strategy games.

The DInput_Simple Project

The downloadable files include a project called DInput_Simple. The project builds a nice little application that creates a keyboard object and reads from it. You can see a screen shot of it in Figure 9.2.

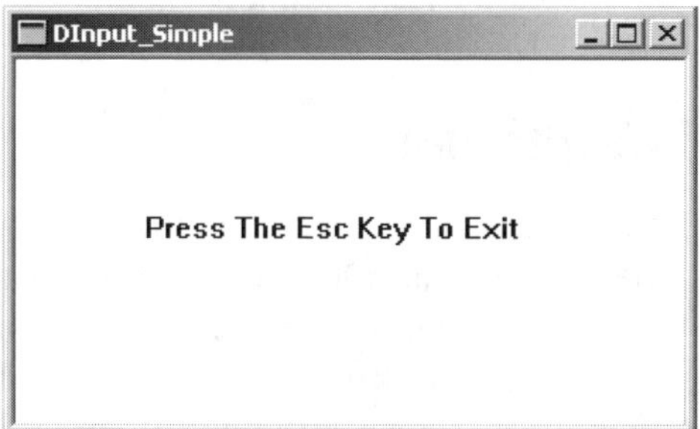

Figure 9.2: Output from the DInput_Simple program.

In Figure 9.2, you see a simple window with text in it that tells you to press the Escape key to exit. Instead of using Windows messages to catch the Escape keypress, the program uses DirectInput with a keyboard device. Load up the project now so that you can follow along.

The project contains two files: main.cpp and main.h. The main.cpp file contains the function implementations, and the main.h header file contains all of the header data. There are two libraries required for the project: dxguid.lib and dinput8.lib. The dxguid.lib library contains the unique GUIDs for DirectInput devices. The dinput8.lib library contains the actual DirectInput function code.

Initializing DirectInput

Open up the main.cpp file now and skip on down to the `WinMain()` function. In there you find the usual Windows creation code, but then you run into code to initialize DirectInput and a keyboard device. Here is the code for it:

```
// Initialize DirectInput
iResult = iInitDirectInput();
if(iResult != INPUTERROR_SUCCESS) {
    MessageBox(hWnd, "DirectInput Error",
    "Unable to initialize Direct Input.", MB_ICONERROR);
    vCleanup();
    exit(1);
}
// Initialize DI keyboard
iResult = iInitKeyboard(hWnd);
if(iResult != INPUTERROR_SUCCESS) {
        MessageBox(hWnd, "DirectInput Error",
        "Unable to initialize Keyboard.", MB_ICONERROR);
    vCleanup();
    exit(1);
}
```

In the above code you see two function calls, one to `iInitDirectInput()` and one to `iInitKeyboard()`. The first call initializes the DirectInput main object, and the second function creates the keyboard device. To see the flow of the program up to here and into the future, check out Figure 9.3.

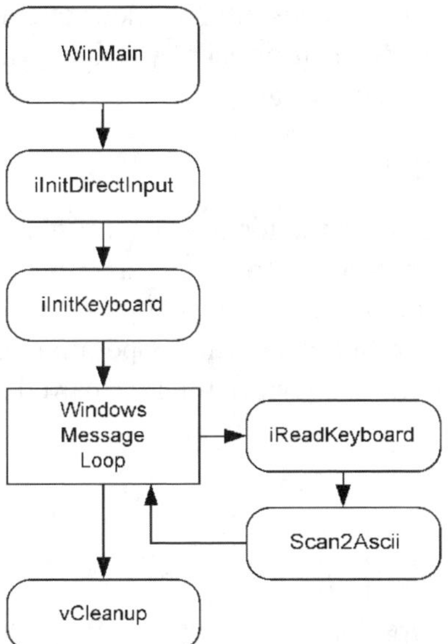

Figure 9.3: Flow of the DInput_Simple program.

The iInitDirectInput() Function

The `iInitDirectInput()` function is of my own creation, and I use it to create the DirectInput main object. The code I use to create the input object should look very familiar to you since I just covered it in the first section. Here is the complete function code:

```
int    iInitDirectInput(void)
{
   HRESULT    hReturn;

   // Do not try to create Direct Input if already created
   if(!pDI) {
      // Create a DInput object
      if(FAILED(hReturn = DirectInput8Create(
         g_hInstance, DIRECTINPUT_VERSION,
         IID_IDirectInput8, (VOID**)&pDI, NULL))) {
         return(INPUTERROR_NODI);
      }
   }
   else {
      return(INPUTERROR_DI_EXISTS);
   }
   return(INPUTERROR_SUCCESS);
}
```

In the code above, I check to see if the DirectInput pointer exists. If it does exist, I don't need to create another object. An error code is thrown if the keyboard already exists.

The next block of code calls the `DirectInput8Create()` function to create the input object. As long as it succeeds, my function returns a success code to `WinMain()`. The global `pDI` pointer ends up holding the DirectInput pointer created by the function call.

The iInitKeyboard() Function

Now that you have a valid input object in the form of the `pDI` global pointer, you can create the keyboard object interface. This is where my `iInitKeyboard()` function comes into play. In this function I create the keyboard device, set up the keyboard buffer, set the cooperative level, acquire the keyboard, and finally get the layout of the keyboard. Here is the code:

```
int iInitKeyboard(HWND hWnd)
{
   HRESULT          hReturn = 0;
   DIPROPDWORD      dipdw;

   // Don't try to create the keyboard twice
   if(pKeyboard) {
      return(INPUTERROR_KEYBOARDEXISTS);
```

```
    }
    // Exit if no DirectInput interface found
    else if (!pDI) {
        return(INPUTERROR_NODI);
    }

    // Obtain an interface to the system keyboard device
    if(FAILED(hReturn = pDI->CreateDevice(
        GUID_SysKeyboard,
        &pKeyboard,
        NULL))) {
        return(INPUTERROR_NOKEYBOARD);
    }

    // Create buffer to hold keyboard data
    ZeroMemory(&dipdw, sizeof(DIPROPDWORD));
    dipdw.diph.dwSize        = sizeof(DIPROPDWORD);
    dipdw.diph.dwHeaderSize  = sizeof(DIPROPHEADER);
    dipdw.diph.dwObj         = 0;
    dipdw.diph.dwHow         = DIPH_DEVICE;
    dipdw.dwData             = KEYBOARD_BUFFERSIZE;

    // Set the size of the buffer
    if(FAILED(hReturn = pKeyboard->SetProperty(
        DIPROP_BUFFERSIZE,
        &dipdw.diph))) {
        return(INPUTERROR_NOKEYBOARD);
    }
    // Set the format of the keyboard
    if(FAILED(hReturn = pKeyboard->SetDataFormat(
        &c_dfDIKeyboard))) {
        return(INPUTERROR_NOKEYBOARD);
    }
    // Set the cooperative level to exclusive access
    if(FAILED(hReturn = pKeyboard->SetCooperativeLevel(
        hWnd,
        DISCL_NONEXCLUSIVE | DISCL_FOREGROUND
        ))) {
        return(INPUTERROR_NOKEYBOARD);
    }
    // Acquire the keyboard device
    pKeyboard->Acquire();
    // Get the keyboard layout
    g_Layout = GetKeyboardLayout(0);
    return(INPUTERROR_SUCCESS);
}
```

Whew — that's a lot of code just to initialize a keyboard, isn't it? Actually, it isn't too bad considering what has to be accomplished.

The first part of the function checks to see if the pKeyboard pointer already exists. If it does, the keyboard has already been created and the function returns an error code stating this fact. Making sure the pDI input object exists does the next part of sanity checking. If DirectInput has not been initialized, there is no point in creating a keyboard object!

Once the requisite checks have passed, I call the `CreateDevice()` function to create the keyboard device. I explained this function earlier, so it should look pretty familiar.

Buffered Keyboard Input

The next part of the function probably does look strange to you since I haven't covered it yet. Basically you have two types of input for keyboard devices: immediate and buffered. Immediate data refers to the key's states as they exist when you poll the keyboard device. If the user pressed a key 1/100th of a second prior, it is missed since it is not depressed at the exact moment you check. This can cause a huge problem in game input, since rendering and processing loops can take a while, resulting in missed keyboard input. Figure 9.4 illustrates this point.

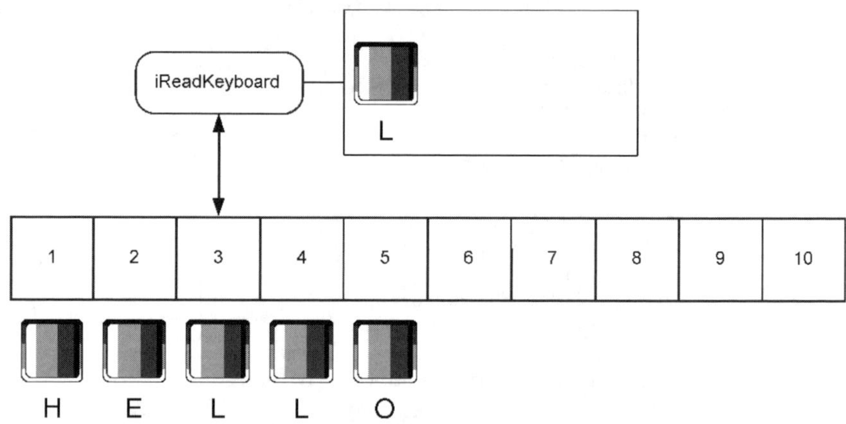

Figure 9.4: Immediate keyboard data reading.

In Figure 9.4 you can see how the program only retrieves the letter L keypress, since only the immediate key data is returned.

Have you ever played a game where it misses your keyboard input half of the time? More often than not, it misses keys when the game is very busy with graphics or some other function. The reason the game misses your key state change is because it doesn't use buffered input, which allows the system to maintain every key state change that has taken place since the last poll of the device. Look at Figure 9.5 to see buffered input illustrated.

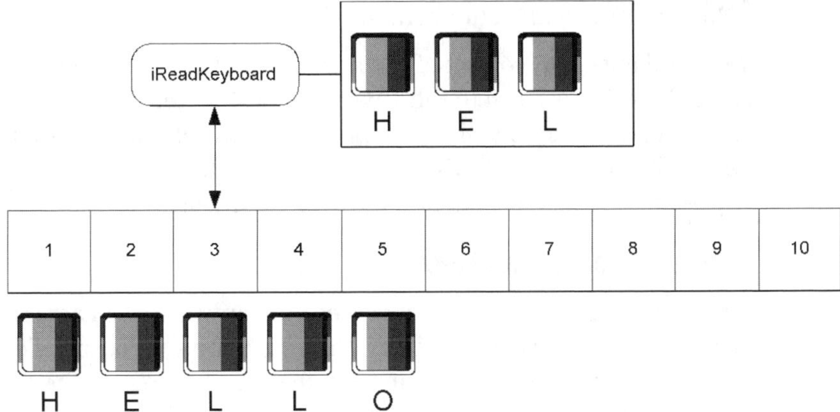

Figure 9.5: Buffered keyboard data reading.

In Figure 9.5 you see the same process as in Figure 9.4, except this time the keyboard read function picks up every key that has been pressed since the beginning of the game loop. This is much more powerful than immediate capture, and I suggest you always use it.

The IDirectInputDevice8::SetProperty() Function

Implementing buffered input is as easy as setting a property of the keyboard device. This is accomplished with the set property function. Here is the prototype for it:

```
HRESULT SetProperty(
    REFGUID rguidProp,
    LPCDIPROPHEADER pdiph
);
```

The first parameter, `rguidProp`, expects the GUID of the property you wish to set for the device. To set the buffer size of the device, use `DIPROP_BUFFERSIZE`.

The second parameter, `pdiph`, expects a data structure containing information about the buffer you want to create. The data structure expected is of type `DIPROPDWORD`. In the code I zero out this type of data structure and set up the parameters telling it how large to make the keyboard buffer. The following code line sets the number of keyboard events to store:

```
dipdw.dwData = KEYBOARD_BUFFERSIZE;
```

The `dwData` field sets the number of keyboard events to buffer. In the example program, I use a value of 10. You may want to play around with the setting until you get a good value for your game.

Setting the Keyboard Data Format

You need to set the format of the keyboard next. This is a formality really and only requires a call to the `IDirectInputDevice8::SetDataFormat()` function. The function takes one parameter specifying the format of the device. To specify the keyboard device, use `c_dfDIKeyboard`. If you want to specify the mouse data format, use `c_dfDIMouse`.

Setting the Cooperative Level

Since DirectX is all about direct access to hardware, the cooperative level of a device is important. Basically, the cooperative level specifies how well the program shares resources with others. If you set the level to exclusive, then no one else can use the resource. If you set the level to nonexclusive, then everyone else gets to play too. I'm sure you can think of some games that don't share the keyboard. One that comes to mind is EverQuest. Since game makers don't want you to write third-party applications for their game, they disable keyboard use outside of their program. It's not very nice and can be a real pain since you can't tab out of the game to check email or do anything else.

To set the cooperative level, use the `IDirectInputDevice8::Set-CooperativeLevel()` function. It has the following prototype:

```
HRESULT SetCooperativeLevel(
    HWND hwnd,
    DWORD dwFlags
);
```

The first parameter, `hwnd`, wants a handle to the window that is associated with the device. For this parameter I pass in the handle returned when I created the main window.

The second parameter, `dwFlags`, sets the cooperative level of the device. The levels are listed in Table 9.1.

Table 9.1: Cooperative device levels

Value	Description
DISCL_BACKGROUND	Has access to the keyboard even when the window is minimized.
DISCL_EXCLUSIVE	Has exclusive access to the keyboard and does not share well with others.
DISCL_FOREGROUND	Only accepts keyboard data when the window is in the foreground.
DISCL_NONEXCLUSIVE	Shares well with others.
DISCL_NOWINKEY	Disables the Windows key.

For the example program I set the cooperative level to `DISCL_NON-EXCLUSIVE` and `DISCL_FOREGROUND`. This makes the program share the keyboard with other applications and also makes it where the program only reads the keyboard when in the foreground.

Acquiring the Keyboard

The last DirectX-related step is the call to `IDirectInputDevice-8::Acquire()`. This function is necessary to bind the application to the desired input device. Whenever focus is lost to the window, the keyboard must be reacquired.

The Keyboard Layout

In the example program I show you how to read DirectInput key codes as well as ASCII key codes. In order to convert between DIK code and ASCII codes, you must make a call to the `GetKeyboardLayout()` function. This function retrieves the layout of the keyboard attached to the system for future use.

Note   The `GetKeyboardLayout()` function is not required for DirectInput code processing. I only use it to convert DIK codes to ASCII key codes.

Figure 9.6 shows the steps required for initializing the keyboard.

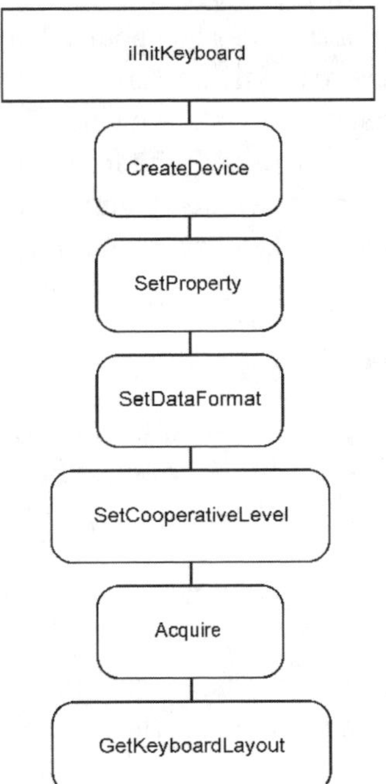

Figure 9.6: Steps required for initializing the keyboard.

Reading from the Keyboard

Back in the `WinMain()` function, there is the following piece of code:

```
while(msg.message!=WM_QUIT) {
    if(PeekMessage(&msg, NULL, OU, OU, PM_REMOVE)) {
        TranslateMessage(&msg);
        DispatchMessage(&msg);
    }
    else {
        // Read from the keyboard buffer
        iResult = iReadKeyboard();
        // Check how many keypresses were returned
        if(iResult) {
            // Loop through result data
            for(i = 0; i < iResult; i++) {
                // Exit the program if the ESC key is hit
                if(diks[DIK_ESCAPE][i]) {
                    PostQuitMessage(0);
                }
                else if (ascKeys[13][i]) {
                    PostQuitMessage(0);
                }
            }
        }
    }
}
```

The code represents the standard Windows message-processing loop. The main difference comes in the form of the `iReadKeyboard()` function call. This function is called whenever there are no system messages to process. The function returns the number of key-state changes and stores them in the global `diks` and `ascKeys` arrays. If the function returns any data, the program loops through the returned key states and checks to see if the Esc key has been pressed. If the key has been pressed, the program exits.

The iReadKeyboard() Function

Instead of showing the entire code listing for this function in one fell swoop, I'm going to present little chunks to you. Here is the first code chunk for the `iReadKeyboard()` function:

```
if(!pKeyboard || !pDI) {
    return(INPUTERROR_NOKEYBOARD);
}
```

This little piece of code checks to make sure the keyboard and DirectInput objects exist. If they don't, the function returns an error code. Time for the next slice of life:

```
hr = pKeyboard->GetDeviceData(
    sizeof(DIDEVICEOBJECTDATA),
    didKeyboardBuffer,
    &dwItems,
    0);
```

The call to get device data returns any data buffered in the input device. In this case, it returns the keyboard buffer. The dwItems variable holds the number of elements returned, and the didKeyboardBuffer buffer stores the return data. The hr variable holds the return code for the call to get the device data. The logic to check the return code is as follows:

```
// Keyboard may have been lost, reacquire it
if(FAILED(hr)) {
    pKeyboard->Acquire();
    return(INPUTERROR_SUCCESS);
}
```

If the hr code contains a failure code, the keyboard may have been lost due to the window minimizing or some other event. In this case, the keyboard must be reacquired with the acquire function.

If you got this far without an error code, it's time to loop through the result data and set the global keyboard buffers. This is accomplished with the following code:

```
// Process data if there is data to read
if (dwItems) {
    // Process the data
    for(dwCurBuffer = 0; dwCurBuffer < dwItems; dwCurBuffer++) {
        // Map scan-code to ASCII code
        byteASCII = Scan2Ascii(
        didKeyboardBuffer[dwCurBuffer].dwOfs);

        // Set key to be down (depressed)
        if(didKeyboardBuffer[dwCurBuffer].dwData & 0x80) {
            ascKeys[byteASCII][dwCurBuffer] = 1;
            diks[didKeyboardBuffer[dwCurBuffer].dwOfs]
            [dwCurBuffer]= 1;
        }
        // Set key to be up
        else {
            ascKeys[byteASCII][dwCurBuffer] = 0;
            diks[didKeyboardBuffer[dwCurBuffer].dwOfs]
            [dwCurBuffer] = 0;
        }
    }
}
```

The code checks to see if there are any items returned from the get device data call. If there are items, the code loops through the return buffer and stores the results in the global diks and ascKeys buffers.

Determining DIK State

The `didKeyboardBuffer` array holds the return data from DirectInput. In order to make it readable you must check the value of each element in the array. If you AND the return value with 0x80 and get a 1 back, you know the key is down; otherwise, the key is up. I know it's weird, but that's how DirectInput works!

Converting DIK Codes to ASCII Codes

To convert the DIK codes to ASCII codes, I have the following function:

```
BYTE Scan2Ascii(DWORD scancode)
{
    UINT vk;

    // Map the scancode to an ASCII code
    vk = MapVirtualKeyEx(scancode, 1, g_Layout);
    // Return the ASCII code
    return(vk);
}
```

The function takes in the DirectInput key code and calls the `MapVirtualKeyEx()` function to convert it to ASCII. The map function requires the keyboard layout that was retrieved in the initialization stages.

In-Game Text Input

Capturing lines of text in a game may sound simple on the surface, but there are many things to think about. For example, how do you handle text input while the rest of the game is still active? You can't very well have a real-time strategy game pause each time a user inputs text! Rendering text also becomes an issue at this point. Do you use 2D fonts or 3D texture maps to display the text? Read on to find out answers to these and other questions.

Check out Figure 9.7 to see an example of in-game text input.

In Figure 9.7 you see the familiar Battle Armor interface with a new text box in the middle of the screen. The text entry box expects the name of the player. Notice that I have entered "Lost Logic" in the box, and you can also see a cursor at the end of the text. All of the graphic elements must be manually handled in your game, so read on to find out how.

Open up the project named D3D_InputBox to see the code that produces Figure 9.7. The project is an offshoot of the earlier interface project, so most of the code should look familiar to you. Once you have the project loaded up, look to Figure 9.8 to see the flow of the program.

Figure 9.7: In-game text input example.

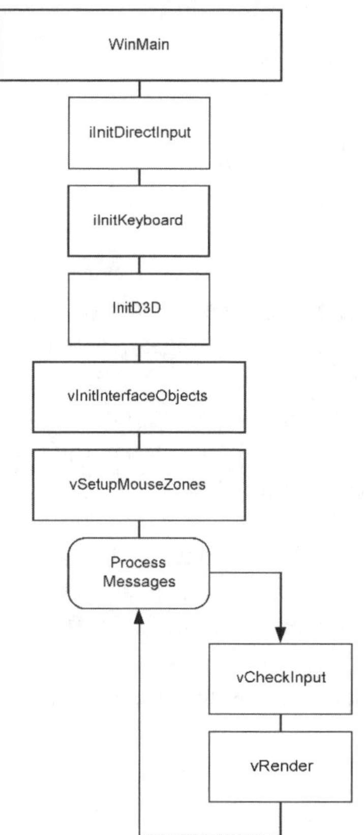

Figure 9.8: Flow of the D3D_InputBox program.

In Figure 9.8 you can see how the program initializes DirectInput, the keyboard, Direct3D, interface objects, and mouse zones. Once it is done initializing, the program goes into its message loop where it checks for input and renders the graphics.

Navigating the Menu

You may recall from Chapter 6 how the menu navigation is performed in the check input function. Inside the check input function, the program finds out if any mouse zones have been activated. If any have been activated, the code figures out which menu screen is active and performs the appropriate action. See the following code for an example:

```
if(g_iCurrentScreen == 0) {
    // Go to the main menu
    if(!stricmp(szZoneHit, "TITLE_SCREEN")) {
        // Set menu to main menu
        g_iCurrentScreen = 1;
        // Set up the mouse zones
        vSetupMouseZones(1);
    }
    // Go to the exit splash screen
    else if(!stricmp(szZoneHit, "EXIT_BUTTON")) {
        // Set current screen to exit screen
        g_iCurrentScreen = 2;
        // Set up the mouse zones
        vSetupMouseZones(2);
    }
}
```

The code above is kicked off when the title screen is active. If the user selects the TITLE_SCREEN mouse zone, the program sets the main menu screen as active and sets up the mouse zones for that screen. If the Exit button is selected, the code activates the exit-game screen and sets up the mouse zones for it. This type of logic continues in the code for each menu option available. Check out Figure 9.9 to see the flow of the check input function.

In Figure 9.9 you can see how the check input function checks the mouse zones, updates the menu if appropriate, and also checks the keyboard. The key to this program example is the MAINMENU_NEW-GAME mouse zone. Once this zone is activated, the program calls the setup mouse zones function to initialize the new game screen.

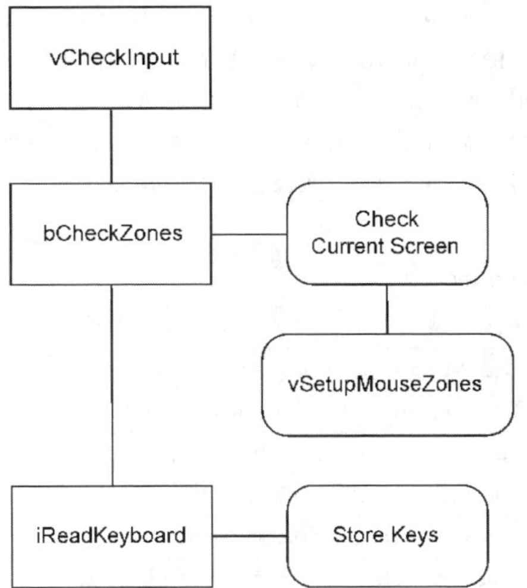

Figure 9.9: Layout of the check input function.

Activating Text Input

The setup mouse zones function is responsible for setting up the mouse hotspots in the game interface. It is also used to activate text input for the new game screen. The following code shows you how I do this:

```
// New game screen
else if(iMenu == 4) {
   MZones.vFreeZones();
   MZones.vInitialize(1);
   MZones.iAddZone("EXIT_BUTTON", 587, 0, 53, 24, 0);
   //
   // Set up input box
   //
   // Set cursor position
   g_shTextInputXPos = 200;
   g_shTextInputYPos = 196;
   // Clear text data
   memset(g_szTextInputBuffer, 0x00, 64);
   // Set data position
   g_shTextInputPosition = 0;
   // Set data field active
   g_iTextInputFieldID = GAMEINPUT_NAME;
   // Set text input active
   g_bTextInputActive = 1;
   // Set cursor flash timer
   g_dwTextInputTimer = 0;
   // Set cursor flash to off
   g_bTextInputCursorFlash = 0;
   // Set the max name size to 20 characters
   g_shTextMaxSize = 20;
}
```

The code above is just a snippet from the vSetupMouseZones() function, but it shows you how I tell the program to accept text input for the player name. Not only does the code set up the mouse zones for the new game screen, but it also sets several global variables that tell the program how to handle the text input. In Table 9.2 you can see the variables and their function.

Table 9.2: Global text input variables

Variable	Function
g_shTextInputXPos	The x-coordinate of the text input box.
g_shTextInputYPos	The y-coordinate of the text input box.
g_szTextInputBuffer	Stores the contents of the text field.
g_shTextInputPosition	The active position in the text field.
g_iTextInputFieldID	Tracks which text field is active.
g_bTextInputActive	Tells the system if a text entry field is active.
g_dwTextInputTimer	Timer to regulate the cursor animation for the active text field.
g_bTextInputCursorFlash	Sets the cursor on or off.
g_shTextMaxSize	The maximum number of characters in the buffer.

In the code above I set the text box coordinates to that of the upper-leftmost character in the player name field. This tells the rendering system where to render the player name text once it is entered. It also tells the rendering system where to start drawing the text cursor.

The text input position is set next. I set it to 0 so that the player starts entering text at the beginning of the name buffer.

The field ID is set to GAMEINPUT_NAME next. I have a set of constants in the main.h header file that set the available fields in the game. You don't have to use constants, but I find it handy to keep track of what is going on.

I set the g_bTextInputActive field to 1 next. This tells the program that a text field is active for keyboard input. This is important to know since the program must add text to the field and render it as well.

Once the text is activated, I set the g_dwTextInputTimer to 0. This timer is responsible for the cursor animation. The next variable, g_bTextInputCursorFlash, sets the cursor to be in its off state. When the cursor timer is up, this variable changes state.

The last thing I do to set up text input is set the maximum number of characters for the player name. I do this by setting the g_shTextMaxSize field to 20.

Processing Text Input

Now that you have the text input system activated, you need to process keyboard input and store the result in the text character buffer. This is done by the vCheckInput() function. Earlier I showed you part of the check input function where the mouse input is handled. Now it is time to look at the keyboard input part of the function. The code is as follows:

```
// KEYBOARD INPUT
// Read from the keyboard buffer
int iResult = iReadKeyboard();
// Check how many keypresses were returned
if(iResult) {
    // Loop through result data
    for(int i = 0; i < iResult; i++) {
        // Exit the program if the ESC key is hit
        if(diks[DIK_ESCAPE][i]) {
            PostQuitMessage(0);
        }
        // TEXT INPUT BOX LOGIC
        if(g_bTextInputActive) {
            // Don't add to text unless there is still room
            if(g_shTextInputPosition <  g_shTextMaxSize) {
                // Store keys that are depressed
                for(int j = 32; j < 123; j++) {
                    // Make sure it is a valid character
                    if((j > 96)
                        || (j == 32)
                        || (j > 47 && j < 58)) {
                        // Check if key is depressed
                        if(ascKeys[j][i]) {
                            if(g_bShift) {
                                g_szTextInputBuffer[
                                g_shTextInputPosition]
                                = toupper(j);
                            }
                            else {
                                g_szTextInputBuffer[
                                g_shTextInputPosition]
                                = j;
                            }
                            g_shTextInputPosition++;
                        }
                    }
                }
            }
            // Check for backspace
            if(diks[DIK_BACK][i]) {
                // Check if text has been entered
                if(g_shTextInputPosition) {
                    // Clear last character
                    g_szTextInputBuffer[
                    g_shTextInputPosition-1] = '\0';
```

```
            // Back up the cursor
            g_shTextInputPosition--;
          }
        }
        // Check for ENTER key
        if(diks[DIK_RETURN][i]) {
          // Turn off name input
          g_bTextInputActive = 0;
          // ACTIVATE THE NEW GAME
          if(g_iTextInputFieldID == GAMEINPUT_NAME) {
            // Set screen to main game screen
            g_iCurrentScreen = 5;
            // Set up the mouse zones
            vSetupMouseZones(5);
          }
          break;
        }
      }
    }
  }
}
```

That is quite a bit of code to digest, so take a look at Figure 9.10.

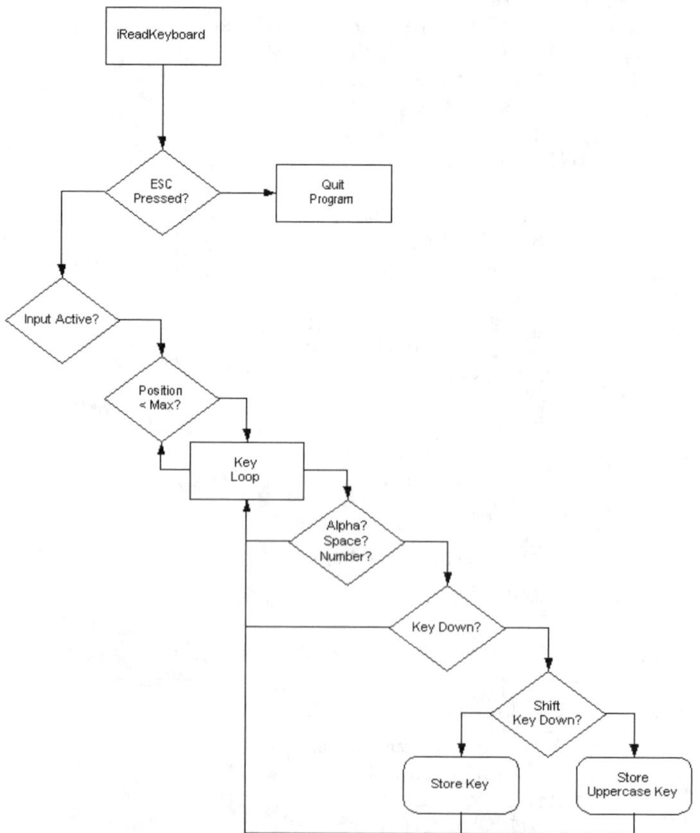

Figure 9.10: Keyboard input flowchart.

In Figure 9.10 you can see the logic required to take input from the keyboard and put it in the character name text field. Starting at the top, the program calls the read keyboard function to see if there is any data waiting to be processed. If there is, the system loops through the result data and checks various keys. The first check in the line sees if the Escape key has been pressed. If it has, the program posts a quit message and exits. If not, the program continues down to see if a text field is active. If a text field is active, the system checks if there is any room left in the text field for entry. If there is room for more text, the program loops through the keys on the keyboard and checks the state of each one. If the key in the loop is alphanumeric or the Spacebar, the program checks if it is depressed. If it is depressed, a check is made to see if the Shift key is down. If the Shift key is down, the program puts an uppercase version of the key in the player name buffer. If the Shift key is up, the default key is put into the buffer. This whole process continues until every key state in the DirectInput buffer has been accounted for.

In Figure 9.10 you can also see where I check for the Backspace or Enter key. If the player presses the Backspace key, the program deletes the last key in the player name buffer and moves the cursor back one notch. If the Enter key is pressed, the game sets up the new game screen and deactivates text entry.

Rendering Text Input

You have seen how to set up text input and process text input, but what about rendering it? The render function takes on this mighty task and renders the input text without missing a beat. The following portion of code shows you how to render the text:

```
// Draw the exit screen
vDrawInterfaceObject(0, 0, 256.0f, 256.0f, 0);
vDrawInterfaceObject(256, 0, 256.0f, 256.0f, 1);
vDrawInterfaceObject(512, 0, 256.0f, 256.0f, 2);
vDrawInterfaceObject(0, 256, 256.0f, 256.0f, 3);
vDrawInterfaceObject(256, 256, 256.0f, 256.0f, 4);
vDrawInterfaceObject(512, 256, 256.0f, 256.0f, 5);
// Input box
vDrawInterfaceObject(192, 64, 256.0f, 256.0f, 14);
// Draw cursor if input active
if(g_bTextInputActive) {
    // Update cursor flash status
    if(timeGetTime() > g_dwTextInputTimer) {
        if(g_bTextInputCursorFlash) {
            g_bTextInputCursorFlash = 0;
            g_dwTextInputTimer = timeGetTime()+250;
        }
        else {
```

```
            g_bTextInputCursorFlash = 1;
            g_dwTextInputTimer = timeGetTime()+250;
        }
    }
    // Draw the cursor if flash on
    if(g_bTextInputCursorFlash) {
        vDrawInterfaceObject(
            g_shTextInputXPos +
            g_shTextInputPosition * 8,
            g_shTextInputYPos,
            4.0f, 16.0f, 15);
    }
}
// Display Text
// Create the text rectangle
RECT rectText = { g_shTextInputXPos,
                  g_shTextInputYPos,
                  g_shTextInputXPos+(g_shTextMaxSize * 8),
                  g_shTextInputYPos+20 };
// Draw the text
pD3DXFont->DrawText(g_szTextInputBuffer, -1, &rectText,
                    DT_LEFT,
                    D3DCOLOR_RGBA(255, 255, 255, 255));
```

The render code that takes care of the text input graphics is turned on
when the user goes to screen number four. Once there, the code follows
the logic you see in Figure 9.11.

Figure 9.11 shows how the render function checks the current
screen to see what to render. If screen number four is active, it goes into
the text input rendering area. Once there, it draws the main interface
elements. The next thing it does is render the actual text box graphic.
This is a simple texture that I created in Photoshop. Next up, the program checks to see if text input is active. If so, it checks to see if the
cursor flash timer has expired. If the timer has expired, the code checks
the state of the cursor and turns it on or off accordingly. Back at the
ranch, the code renders the cursor if it is on. The last thing the code does
is render the actual player name. One thing to remember is that the code
renders the player name regardless of the input active state. Even if the
player is not inputting text, the text needs to be rendered.

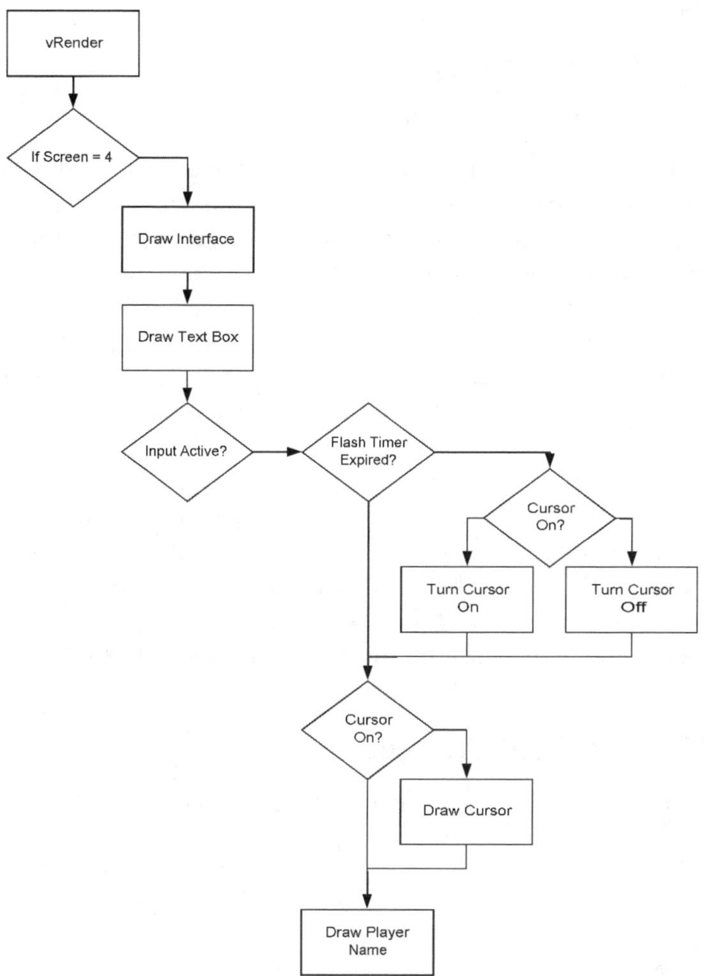

Figure 9.11: Flow of the text rendering routine.

The Font Interface

You may have noticed in the rendering code that I use an object called
pD3DXFont to render the text on-screen. The pD3DXFont object is an
instantiation of the ID3DXFont interface provided in DirectX. The
ID3DXFont interface is really cool because it handles everything for you
to render fonts in Direct3D. All you have to do is supply the font handle
and the text to render. It's really that simple! If you take a look at the
interface object's initialization function, you will see the following font
code:

```
// Text font
hFont = CreateFont(16, 0, 0, 0, 0,
                   0, 0, 0, 0, 0, 0,
                   PROOF_QUALITY, 0, "fixedsys");
D3DXCreateFont(g_pd3dDevice, hFont, &pD3DXFont);
```

The first line makes a call to the system function called `CreateFont()`. This function is part of the GDI system for Windows, and it creates a font handle given a font name, size, and a few other attributes. For more information on this function, check out the MSDN reference.

Once you have a good font handle, all you need to do is make a call to the `D3DXCreateFont()` function. This function takes in a pointer to the Direct3D device, a font handle, and a pointer to an `ID3DXFont` object. In return it populates the `ID3DXFont` pointer with a valid font interface to use in later rendering operations.

For the example program I create a font of type fixedsys. I like this font since you can calculate the size of a string created with it fairly easily. Fonts that are not fixed width will change size depending on the characters used. This can be a real pain, especially when you want to render a cursor at the end of the text!

Back to the rendering area. To render the newly created font, I make a call to the font's `DrawText()` function.

The `ID3DXFont::DrawText()` Function

The `DrawText()` function has the following prototype:

```
INT DrawText(
    LPCSTR pString,
    INT Count,
    LPRECT pRect,
    DWORD Format,
    D3DCOLOR Color
);
```

The first parameter, `pString`, is pretty straightforward, as it expects the text you want to render. For the example program I pass in the player name text here.

The second parameter, `Count`, wants the number of characters to render. I use –1 here to let DirectX figure out how many characters there are. If you do this, make sure your string is null terminated!

The third parameter, `pRect`, wants a rectangular area definition telling DirectX where to render the text. In the example code you can see how I create a rendering area in the player name box with the `rectText` variable.

The fourth parameter, `Format`, expects format flags telling the system how to render the text. In the example, I use the `DT_LEFT` flag to tell the system to render the text left-justified. There are tons of other flags available. For more information, see the DirectX SDK guide.

The fifth parameter, `Color`, takes the color to use in rendering. I use the `D3DCOLOR_RGBA()` macro for this parameter, as it makes it easy to set the RGBA values for the font.

Recap

In this chapter I showed you a method for accepting text input in your games. There are many methods that you can use, but hopefully you will take what I have shown you and use it as a foundation for a much more feature-rich system. Before you go, take note of the following:

■ DirectInput supplies you with everything you need to accept keyboard input in your games. It also gives you the ability to accept any other type of device required for gaming.

■ DIK codes are the internal keyboard codes assigned by DirectInput.

■ ASCII codes are available from DirectInput, but you must map DIK codes to get them.

■ Buffered input is a must. Never implement an input method where input is non-buffered.

■ The `ID3DXFont` interface provides you with a very powerful text-rendering interface.

Tool Development

Chapter 10

World Editing Fun

Welcome to Part III! In this section I cover everything you ever wanted to know about map tool programming and were afraid to ask. Well, maybe not everything, but at least it's a good start! In this chapter I cover the foundations of map editing. Since most strategy games are based on tiles, it only makes sense to cover the fine art of map making. After all, what good is a strategy game without a map? To bring out the cartographer in you, I present the following information:

- Basic map editing 101
- Map viewing
- Map editing
- Saving
- Loading
- Mini-map rendering
- Algorithmic map generation
- Map layers

Basic Map Editing 101

The first question that you should ask is, "What is a map editor?" A map editor helps you piece together tile graphics in a format usable in your game. It's almost like a mini-paint program where the map is your canvas and tiles are your brushes.

The next question may be, "Why make a map editor?" Unless you want to type in thousands of tile numbers by hand, a map editor is the only way to make maps and levels in your games. Using the paint program analogy, not using a map editor would be like painting a picture with hexadecimal codes. Sure, it may be a geek's fantasy, but in the real world, it's not very practical.

And finally, the last question is, "What does a map editor look like?" Well, if you have ever used a level editor in a game, you already know the answer to this one. But, if not, check out Figure 10.1.

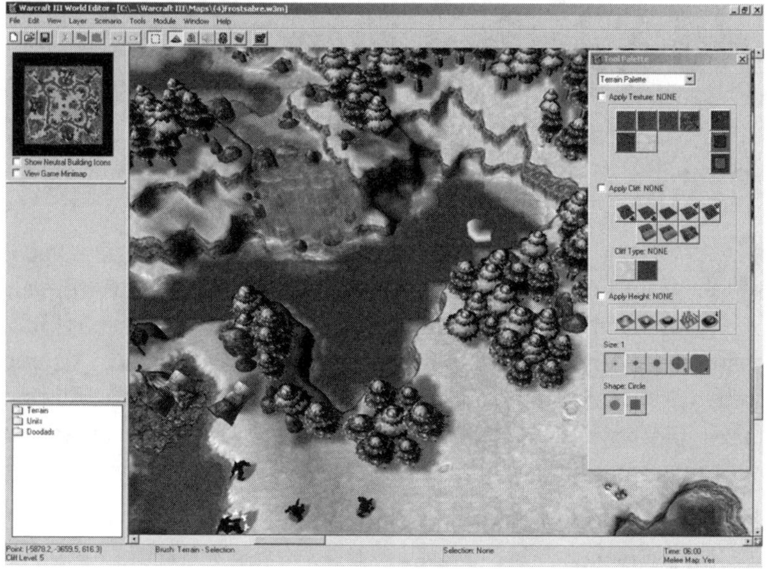

Figure 10.1: Warcraft III's world editor. ©2002 Blizzard Entertainment, All Rights Reserved.

Figure 10.1 shows a screen shot of Warcraft III's level editor. It comes with the game and is very powerful to use. It lets you edit maps that come with the game or create your own from scratch. In the figure you can see a mini-map representing the map from a high level and a close-up view of the current edit area in the rest of the editor. There are various tool windows around the editor for picking the texture and operation to use on the map.

In this chapter I show you how to create your very own map editor. It's not going to be nearly as cool as Blizzard's editor for Warcraft III, but it will give you a good head start at least.

Note   Building a map editor may seem like an easy task, but the process usually takes as long or longer than the actual game development cycle!

Map Editor Components

Take a look again at Figure 10.1 to see the components of a level and map editor. In the figure you see several key components:

- Edit area
- Tile picker
- Mini-map
- Information output

Edit Area

The edit area component of the map editor is where you perform the actual editing of the map. Usually the edit area provides you with a view of the map that is very similar if not identical to that of the in-game player view. This is a good thing, since you know what the final result will look like to players. In Figure 10.1 the edit area is the large graphical area in the center of the screen shot.

Although the edit area looks a lot like what the player sees, there are usually a few minor differences. The first difference is the inclusion of a tile grid. You should include a grid option for your edit area to make the lining up of tiles easy for the level editor. The grid shows you where tiles begin and end. It's also useful for showing you the size of the tiles that you are editing. Figure 10.2 shows you an example of an edit grid.

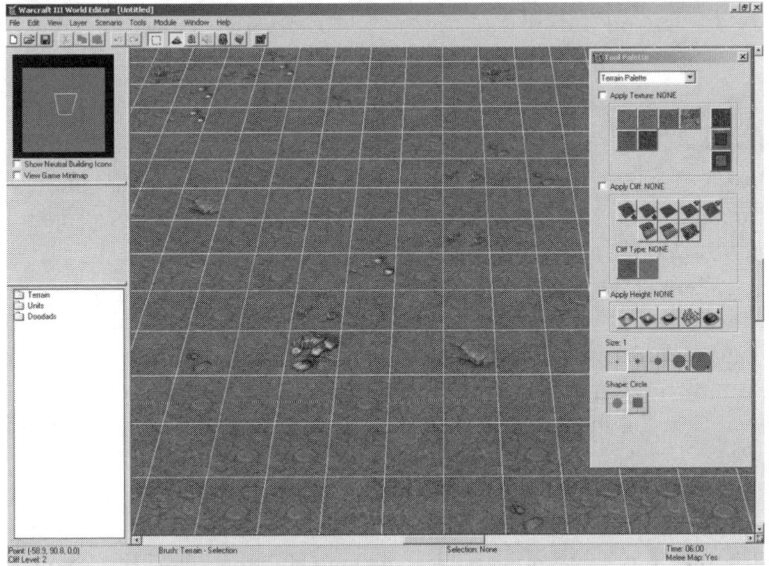

Figure 10.2: Warcraft III world editor with grid turned on. ©2002 Blizzard Entertainment, All Rights Reserved.

The figure shows the edit area in Warcraft III's world editor with the edit grid turned on. As you can see, the grid makes tile alignment a snap.

Tile Picker

Since maps are made up of tiles, you need to have a tile picker in your editor. The tile picker shows you available tiles to draw with, and you merely click on the one you want to use. Usually there are many more tiles than can fit in a single area, so you should plan for a method to scroll through various tile sets.

Mini-Map

The mini-map area shows you what the world you are editing looks like from a zoomed-out view. In Figures 10.1 and 10.2, you can see the mini-maps in the upper-left corner of the interface. A good method to use for mini-maps is to assign color values to various tile types. For instance, you might choose the color green for land tiles and the color blue for water tiles.

Information Output

It's always a good idea to place an area to output text messages in the editor. You can display the total number of tiles used, the size of the map, the current map coordinates, and many other items. In Figure 10.2 you can barely make out some text at the bottom of the editor window. That text tells you the current tile selected and some other information.

Map Viewing

Enough of the theory already! How about some code that shows you how to make your own editor? Load up the D3D_MapViewer project now to follow along.

The D3D_MapViewer program creates a random map that you can scroll around in. You can't actually edit the map, but it shows you the basics of navigating a tile map. Once you have the hang of scrolling around a tile map, I will show you how to start editing the map.

Run the map viewer program, and you will see the image in Figure 10.3.

In Figure 10.3 you see a familiar looking set of tiles displayed in a rather large window. What sets this tile map apart from the examples in Chapter 5 is that you can move around this map with the arrow keys. Press the up or down arrow to move along the y-axis and press the left or

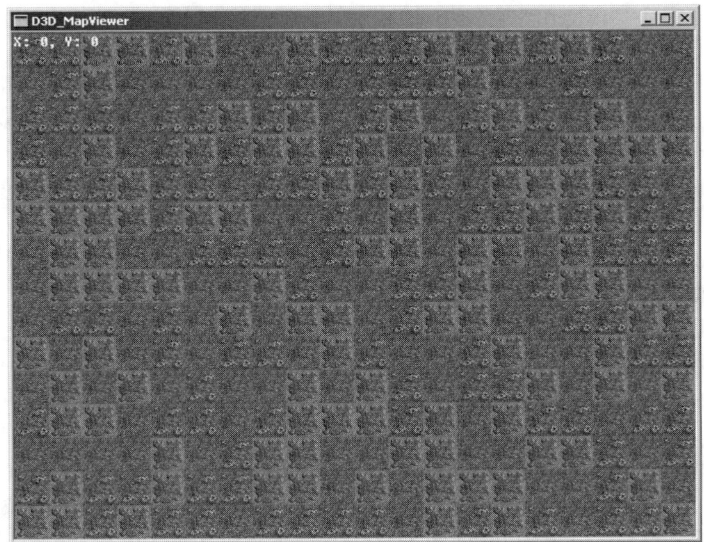

Figure 10.3: Output from the map viewer program.

right arrow to move along the x-axis. Launch the program now and try it yourself.

You might be able to make out some debug information that I have displayed in the upper-left corner of the figure. This data shows you the current coordinates of the upper-leftmost tile. As you move around the map, the numbers change to reflect your new global position on the map. Keep in mind that you cannot go below 0 on either axis.

Global Map Variables

In the main.h header file for the project you can find some very important data types used in the map viewer. Here is a short list of them:

```
int g_iTileSize = 32;
int g_iTilesWide = 20;
int g_iTilesHigh = 15;
int g_iMapWidth = 100;
int g_iMapHeight = 100;
int g_iXPos = 0;
int g_iYPos = 0;
int g_iTileMap[10000];
```

The first variable, g_iTileSize, tells the map viewer how many pixels wide and tall the tiles are. I set this to 32 to make my map tiles 32 pixels wide by 32 pixels tall.

The second variable, g_iTilesWide, tells the map viewer how many tiles to display horizontally in the view window. Since my window is 640 pixels wide and my tiles are 32 pixels wide, I set this to 20 in order to fill the screen.

The third variable, g_iTilesHigh, works just like g_iTilesWide, except this one sets how many tiles to display vertically. The viewing area is 480 pixels high; therefore, 15 tiles will fill it perfectly.

The fourth variable, g_iMapWidth, tells the map viewer how many tiles there are in the map on the x-axis. Since the viewer can scroll around the map, the map can be larger than the view area. I set this value to 100, which is decent enough to demonstrate scrolling.

The fifth variable, g_iMapHeight, works just like the width field, except this one tells the program how many tiles there are on the map along the y-axis. I set this value to 100 in order to give the map square dimensions.

The sixth variable, g_iXPos, tells the viewer where the view window is on the map along the x-axis. Since the map is larger than a single view window, the program must keep track of where the view window is on the map. This can never go below 0 since there isn't any data there.

The seventh variable, g_iYPos, sets the second coordinate of where the view window currently is on the map.

The eighth variable, g_iTileMap, is an array of integers that defines the tile map. The value for each tile displayed is stored in this array for viewing. Since the map is 100 tiles wide by 100 tiles tall, I set the array size to 10,000.

To see the variables and their values illustrated, take a look at Figure 10.4.

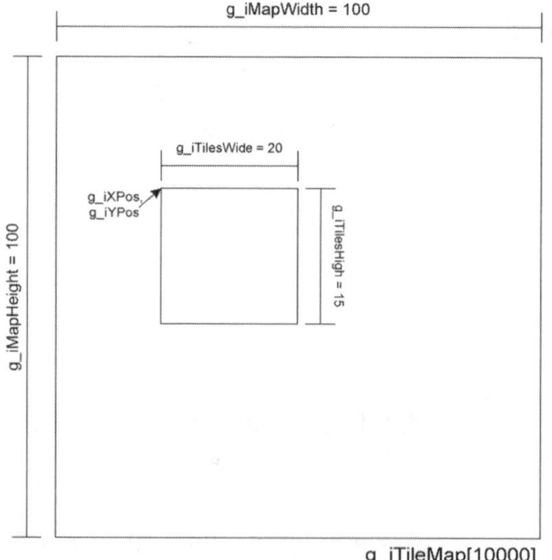

In Figure 10.4 you can see how the map width and height set the total size of the map. Next you can see how the view window size is set by the tiles-wide and tiles-high values. Lastly, you can see how the global position sets where the view window currently is on the overall map.

Figure 10.4: Global values for the map viewer.

Program Flow

The flow of the map viewer program is very similar to previous examples in the book. The first thing done is initialization of the systems that make up the program. Once that is out of the way, the program processes messages and reacts to input by the user. This continues until the user exits the program. All of this and more can be seen in Figure 10.5.

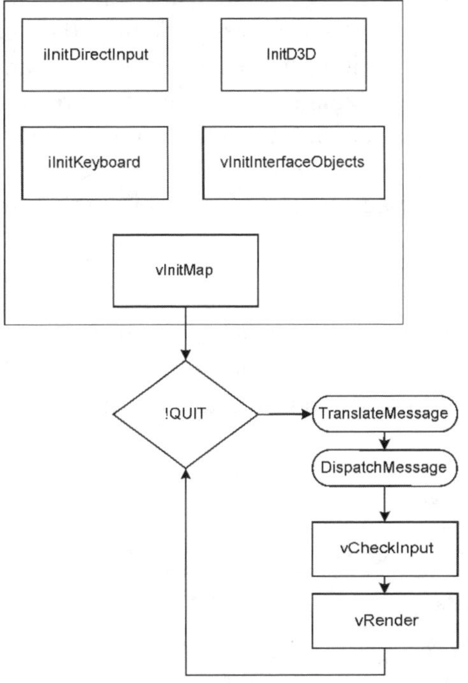

Figure 10.5: Flow of the map viewer program.

The only new function in Figure 10.5 is the vInitMap() function.

Random Map Generation

The vInitMap() function is responsible for creating the random map. Take a look at the code for the map randomization here:

```
void vInitMap(void)
{
    int i;

    // Randomly seed the map
    for(i = 0; i < g_iMapWidth * g_iMapHeight; i++) {
        g_iTileMap[i] = rand()%3;
    }
}
```

You are probably thinking, "What good does a random map do me?" The answer to that question is, "More than you may think." Although you will end up editing almost every tile on a game map, it is nice to start off with a random set of tiles to give the map an organic feel. The last thing you want to do is lay down every rock, bush, and bramble on several dozen maps. It may be fun at first, but you will get tired of it quickly.

In the code you can see how I look through the entire map buffer and set each tile to a random number from 0 to 2. This ensures a very mixed-looking map. There are cool things you can do here though. For example, you could put in distribution parameters for the random tiles. Maybe make 10 percent of the map randomly covered with rocks (60 percent randomly covered with water). Games like SimCity 4 and Civilization do this type of distribution when creating their maps. I will get into automatic map generation later, so noodle on it for a bit until then.

Map Navigation

In the program flow in Figure 10.5, you can see a call to vCheckInput(). You navigate the map by pressing the arrow keys, so this is a pretty valuable function. Go to it now and take a look at the following code.

```
void vCheckInput(void)
{
    // Read from the keyboard buffer
    int iResult = iReadKeyboard();
    // Check how many keypresses were returned
    if(iResult) {
        // Loop through result data
        for(int i = 0; i < iResult; i++) {
            // Exit the program if the ESC key is hit
            if(diks[DIK_ESCAPE][i]) {
                PostQuitMessage(0);
            }
            // Up
            if(diks[DIK_UP][i]) {
                g_iYPos--;
            }
            // Down
            if(diks[DIK_DOWN][i]) {
                g_iYPos++;
            }
            // Left
            if(diks[DIK_LEFT][i]) {
                g_iXPos--;
            }
            // Right
            if(diks[DIK_RIGHT][i]) {
                g_iXPos++;
            }
                // Make sure in bounds
```

```
        if(g_iYPos < 0)
            g_iYPos = 0;
        else if (g_iYPos >= (g_iMapHeight-g_iTilesHigh))
            g_iYPos = (g_iMapHeight-g_iTilesHigh);
        if(g_iXPos < 0)
            g_iXPos = 0;
        else if (g_iXPos >= (g_iMapWidth-g_iTilesWide))
            g_iXPos = (g_iMapWidth-g_iTilesWide);
    }
  }
}
```

Pictures are always a great complement to words, so please look at Figure 10.6 to see the code illustrated.

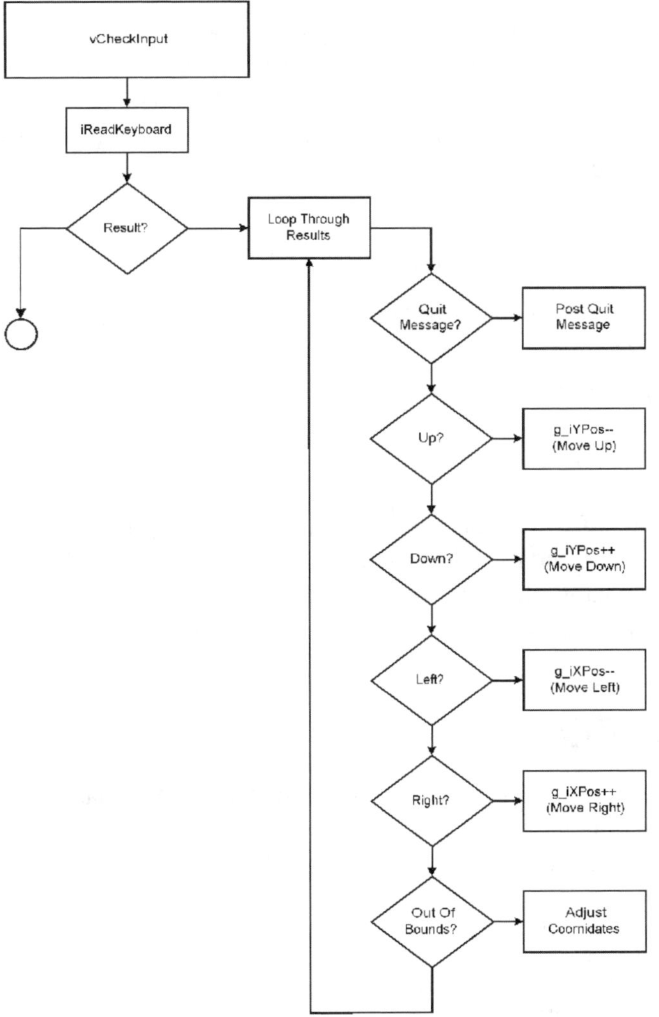

Figure 10.6: Flow of the check input function.

In Figure 10.6 you can see the flow of the check input function. In the first part of the code I check the keyboard buffer to see if the user has pressed any keys. If so, the code goes on to check which keys are pressed. If the Esc key is pressed, the program is told to exit. If the arrow keys are pressed, the code adjusts the g_iXPos and g_iYPos view coordinates accordingly. Once the arrow keypresses are checked, the code checks to make sure the global coordinates are within valid ranges. This keeps the view window from looking outside of the map's memory area.

Tile Image Loading

You have seen how the main program flow works and how to navigate the map, but what about the graphics? The program is pretty useless without visual feedback. The good old vInitInterfaceObjects() function takes care of loading the tiles used in the example. Here is the piece of code that does the trick:

```
for(int i = 0; i < 3; i++) {
    // Set the name
    sprintf(szTileName, "tile%d.bmp", i);
    // Load it
    if(FAILED(D3DXCreateTextureFromFile(
        g_pd3dDevice,
        szTileName,
        &g_pTexture[i]))) {
        return;
    }
}
```

The tile loading is fairly simple. All I do is loop through the total number of tiles available and load them starting with the name tile0.bmp and ending with the name tile2.bmp. Since there are only three tiles to load, this process runs quickly. The loaded tiles end up in the g_pTexture array for later access.

Rendering the Tiles

The vRender() function takes care of rendering the tile map. In this function I loop through the tile map and render the tiles according to their value in the tile buffer. Here is the code for the render loop:

```
// Top to bottom
for(iY = 0; iY < g_iTilesHigh; iY++) {
    // Left to right
    for(iX = 0; iX < g_iTilesWide; iX++) {
        // Calculate buffer offset
        iBufferPos = iX+g_iXPos+((iY+g_iYPos)*g_iMapWidth);
        // Get the proper tile
```

```
        iCurTile = g_iTileMap[iBufferPos];
        // Display the tile
        vDrawInterfaceObject((iX * g_iTileSize),
                    (iY * g_iTileSize),
                    (float)g_iTileSize,
                    (float)g_iTileSize,
                    iCurTile);
    }
}
```

There are two loops present in the render function. The first loop cycles through tiles along the y-axis. The inner loop cycles through the tiles along the x-axis. By looping in this manner I cover the entire display of tiles. This method is the same one I explained in Chapter 5.

Map Editing

Up until now you have only viewed tiles interactively. How about actually editing them? Sounds like fun, eh? In this section I show you how to write a map editor that lets you draw tiles on a map in real time. Gone are the days of programmatically setting the map values! Look to Figure 10.7 to see the map editor that I am about to cover.

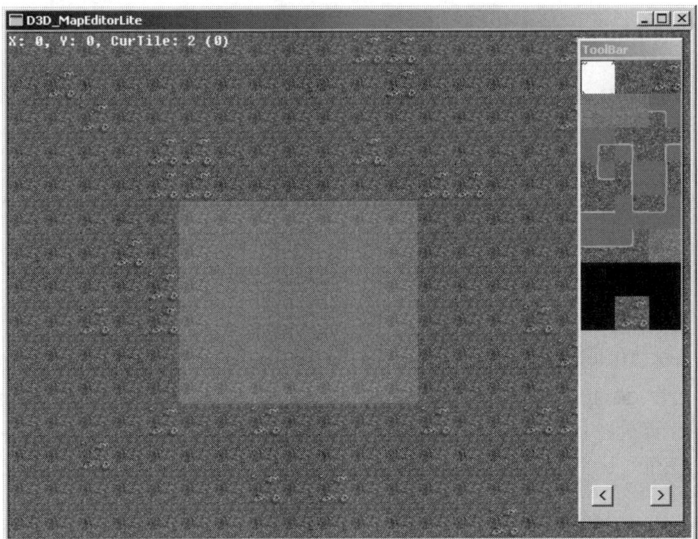

Figure 10.7: Output from the D3D_MapEditorLite program.

In Figure 10.7 you can see a screen shot of the D3D_MapEditorLite program. It looks a lot like the map viewer program that you just read about. The main difference in this program is the inclusion of a tile picker and the ability to edit the map in real time.

Load up the D3D_MapEditorLite project now so you can follow along with me.

Global Map Variables

In the main.h header file for the project, there are some new data members required for editing. Here they are in order of appearance:

```
int    g_iCurTile = 0;
int    g_iCurTileSet = 0;
int    g_iMaxTileSet = 3;
int    g_iTotalTiles = 18;
```

The first variable, g_iCurTile, tells the editor the tile that the user currently has selected for drawing. When the user edits the map, this tile is pasted on the map.

The next variable, g_iCurTileSet, tells the editor which page of tiles the toolbar has displayed. Since you can have more tiles than viewable on a single toolbar, this is necessary to navigate the pages of tiles. This map editor program only has one page worth of tiles, but it supports many more if you want to add some.

Next up is the g_iMaxTileSet variable. This variable tells the system how many pages of tiles there are possible. In all actuality, you can set this as high as you want. I just use it to keep the user from paging off into the sunset.

The last element, g_iTotalTiles, tells the program how many tiles are loaded into memory. This is useful to know so that you don't allow the user to pick an invalid tile and crash the program. I have 18 tiles loaded, but you can add as many as you want as long as you up this value.

Program Flow

The flow of the map editor program is very similar to the map viewer program. As with the map viewer, the program first initializes the keyboard, rendering system, textures, and the map. The new addition present is the initialization of the toolbar. The toolbar contains the tile picker used to pick the tile with which you wish to edit. Once everything is initialized, the program waits for input from the user and renders the map. The flow can be seen in Figure 10.8.

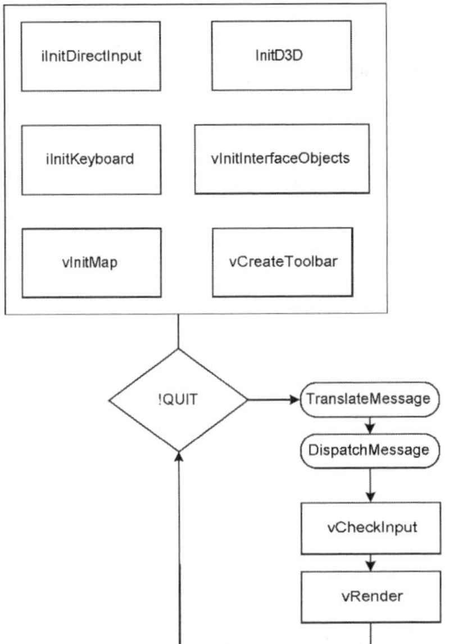

Figure 10.8: Flow of the map editor program.

Toolbar Programming

The tile picker toolbar is a very important piece of the map editor. Without it, you would have a hard time dynamically editing the tile map. The code uses standard Windows programming to create a child window of the main program window and adds some controls to it. The tile rendering on the toolbar is done with DirectX calls. Here is the code that creates the toolbar window and the tile page navigation buttons:

```
void vCreateToolbar(HWND hwnd, HINSTANCE hinst)
{
    WNDCLASSEX    wcToolBar;
    // Set up and register toolbar window class
    wcToolBar.cbSize        = sizeof(wcToolBar);
    wcToolBar.style         = CS_HREDRAW | CS_VREDRAW;
    wcToolBar.lpfnWndProc   = fnMessageProcessor;
    wcToolBar.cbClsExtra    = 0;
    wcToolBar.cbWndExtra    = 0;
    wcToolBar.hInstance     = hinst;
    wcToolBar.hIcon         = LoadIcon(NULL, IDI_APPLICATION);
    wcToolBar.hCursor       = LoadCursor(NULL, IDC_ARROW);
    wcToolBar.hbrBackground =
        (HBRUSH) GetStockObject (COLOR_BACKGROUND);
    wcToolBar.lpszMenuName  = NULL;
    wcToolBar.lpszClassName = "ToolBar";
    wcToolBar.hIconSm       = LoadIcon(NULL, IDI_APPLICATION);
    RegisterClassEx(&wcToolBar);
```

```
    // Create toolbar window
    hWndToolBar = CreateWindowEx(
        WS_EX_LEFT|WS_EX_TOPMOST|WS_EX_TOOLWINDOW,
        "ToolBar", "ToolBar",
        WS_BORDER | WS_VISIBLE | WS_CAPTION | WS_MINIMIZEBOX,
        g_iWindowWidth-100,
        g_iYOffset, 100, g_iWindowHeight-20,
        hwnd, NULL, hinst, NULL);

    // Previous tile button
    hBUTTON_PREVTILE = CreateWindow(
        "BUTTON", "<",
        WS_CHILD | WS_VISIBLE | BS_PUSHBUTTON,
        10, 405, 20, 20,
        hWndToolBar, (HMENU)ID_BUTTON_PREVTILE, hinst, NULL);

    // Next tile button
    hBUTTON_NEXTTILE = CreateWindow(
        "BUTTON", ">",
        WS_CHILD | WS_VISIBLE | BS_PUSHBUTTON,
        65, 405, 20, 20,
        hWndToolBar, (HMENU)ID_BUTTON_NEXTTILE, hinst, NULL);

    // Activate edit area
    SetActiveWindow(g_hWnd);

    // Render toolbar tileset
    vRenderTileSet();
}
```

The `wcToolBar` variable holds the window class information for the toolbar. The values for the class are nothing to write home about since they follow standard Windows programming.

The `CreateWindowEx()` function takes care of the actual toolbar creation. It creates a window named "ToolBar" without a close or minimize button. This is done to make sure the user doesn't accidentally close the tile picker. In the create window function I also set the position of the toolbar to be within the boundaries of the main window.

Once the toolbar window is created, I create a couple of buttons with which to navigate the tiles. They are of the push button type and are named `hBUTTON_PREVTILE` and `hBUTTON_NEXTTILE`. When they are pressed, the program goes to the next or previous tile set available.

Rendering Toolbar Tiles

The toolbar looks great and all, but it really shines when tiles are drawn on it. The tile picker displays up to 21 tiles at once. If you have more than 21 tiles, you can use the navigation buttons to cycle through additional tiles. In order to display the 21 tiles, I render them to a cleared-out display buffer and then copy the results to the toolbar. The code for this is contained in the following function:

```
void vRenderTileSet(void)
{
   RECT   rectDest;
   RECT   rectSrc;
   int iX;
   int iY;
   int iTile;

   // Turn on ambient lighting
   g_pd3dDevice->SetRenderState(D3DRS_AMBIENT, 0x00606060);

   // Clear the back buffer and the z-buffer
   g_pd3dDevice->Clear(0, NULL, D3DCLEAR_TARGET,
             D3DCOLOR_XRGB(0,0,0), 1.0f, 0);
   // Begin Rendering
   g_pd3dDevice->BeginScene();

   // Set alpha blending states
   // This is used to provide transparency/translucency
   g_pd3dDevice->SetRenderState(D3DRS_ALPHABLENDENABLE, TRUE);
   g_pd3dDevice->SetRenderState(D3DRS_SRCBLEND, D3DBLEND_SRCALPHA);
   g_pd3dDevice->SetRenderState(D3DRS_DESTBLEND, D3DBLEND_INVSRCALPHA);

   // Display active tiles
   for(iY = 0; iY < 7; iY++) {
      for(iX = 0; iX < 3; iX++) {
         // Calculate tile to render
         iTile = (g_iCurTileSet*21)+(iX+(iY*3));
         // Render if valid tile
         if(iTile < g_iTotalTiles) {
            vDrawInterfaceObject(
               iX*g_iTileSize,
               iY*g_iTileSize,
               (float)g_iTileSize,
               (float)g_iTileSize,
               iTile);
         }
         // Draw over selected tile
      if(iTile == g_iCurTile) {
            vDrawInterfaceObject(
               iX*g_iTileSize,
               iY*g_iTileSize,
               (float)g_iTileSize,
               (float)g_iTileSize,
               18);
         }
      }
   }

   // Display the current tile
   vDrawInterfaceObject(
      32,
```

```
    32*7,
    (float)g_iTileSize,
    (float)g_iTileSize,
    g_iCurTile);

// Stop rendering
g_pd3dDevice->EndScene();

// Source rectangle
rectSrc.top = 0;
rectSrc.bottom = g_iTileSize*8;
rectSrc.left = 0;
rectSrc.right = g_iTileSize*3;

// Destination rectangle
rectDest.top = 2;
rectDest.bottom = (g_iTileSize*8)+2;
rectDest.left = 0;
rectDest.right = (g_iTileSize*3);

    g_pd3dDevice->Present(&rectSrc, &rectDest, hWndToolBar, NULL);
}
```

The first part of the rendering logic contains code that clears the display buffer, turns on ambient lighting, and activates alpha blending. The real fun comes in the render loops that follow. Basically, the program loops through each row of three tiles and renders them to the display buffer. The code continues in this manner until all seven rows are rendered.

To help the user see the tile that is currently active, the code renders a red box around the currently selected tile. Checking for the current tile in the render loop and adding a red box graphic on top of it when it is found accomplishes this.

Once the tile set is rendered, a copy of the currently selected tile is rendered at the bottom of the display. This is yet another helpful indicator for the current tile. Look to Figure 10.9 to see the layout of the toolbar.

In Figure 10.9 you can see how the tiles are displayed starting from the top-left corner and ending up at the bottom. In the illustration, tile number 10 is the current tile since it has the red square around it. The tile is copied at the bottom of the tile view area to indicate that it is selected as well. At the very bottom of the toolbar, you can make out the tile set navigation buttons.

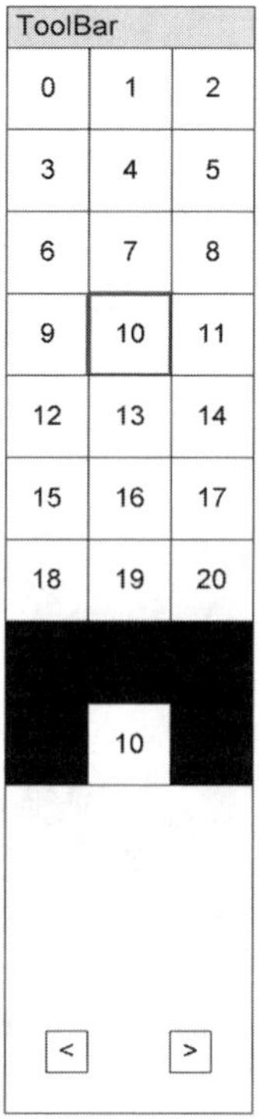

Figure 10.9: Layout of the toolbar.

Now that you have the tiles rendered, how about putting them on the toolbar? This is done by using a source and destination rectangle in addition to the Present() function. You see, the present function can take a source rectangle and destination rectangle for inputs. This tells the rendering system to copy the results from one area and display them in another. By doing this, you can render the tile set in the 3D buffer and then copy it to the toolbar for viewing. Take a peek at the code, and you can see how I copy the source area and move it to the toolbar.

Map Editing

The toolbar is out of the way now visually, so how about figuring out how to select tiles from it? The mouse is man's best friend in this case since it is used to select the tiles from the tile picker. The process may sound easy except for the fact that the toolbar can be moved around. Since you can't expect the toolbar to always be in the same place, you have to account for its position and check the mouse based on it.

There are two mouse modes in the D3D_MapEditorLite program. In edit mode, you are clicking the mouse in the map view area and wish to edit a tile. In tile picker mode, you are clicking the mouse in the tile picker and wish to select a new tile to use. To figure out which mode the user is in, I check the coordinates of the mouse and see if it is within the toolbar area or within the map view area. If it is in the toolbar area, I drop into the toolbar area logic to figure out which tile the mouse is over. If it is in the map view area, I drop into the map edit logic and figure out which tile to edit. Here is the code that accomplishes these tasks:

```
void vCheckMouse(void)
{
    RECT   rcWindow;
    POINT  Point;
    int    iMouseX;
    int    iMouseY;
    int    iTileX;
    int    iTileY;

    // Get mouse coordinates
    GetCursorPos(&Point);
    iMouseX = Point.x;
    iMouseY = Point.y;

    // Figure out the toolbar work area
    GetWindowRect(hWndToolBar, &rcWindow);

    // Check if mouse is within toolbar window
    if(iMouseX > rcWindow.left &&
       iMouseX < rcWindow.right &&
       iMouseY > rcWindow.top &&
```

```
      iMouseY < rcWindow.bottom)
   {
      // Adjust mouse coords to be local to toolbar
      iMouseX -= rcWindow.right;
      iMouseY -= rcWindow.top;

      // Figure out tile coordinates
      iTileX = iMouseX/g_iTileSize;
      iTileY = iMouseY/g_iTileSize;
      // Figure out picked tile
      g_iCurTile = (g_iCurTileSet*21)+(iTileX+(iTileY*3))-1;
      // Make sure tile is valid
      if(g_iCurTile < 0 || g_iCurTile >= g_iTotalTiles) {
         g_iCurTile = 0;
      }
      vRenderTileSet();
   }
   // Check if mouse is within edit window
   else {
      GetWindowRect(g_hWnd, &rcWindow);

      if(iMouseX > rcWindow.left &&
         iMouseX < rcWindow.right &&
         iMouseY > rcWindow.top &&
         iMouseY < rcWindow.bottom)
      {
         // Adjust mouse coords to be local to edit window
         iMouseX -= rcWindow.left+g_iXOffset;
         iMouseY -= rcWindow.top+g_iYOffset;

         // Figure out tile coordinates
         iTileX = iMouseX/g_iTileSize;
         iTileY = iMouseY/g_iTileSize;

         g_iTileMap[iTileX+g_iXPos+
                  ((iTileY + g_iYPos)
                  * g_iMapWidth)] = g_iCurTile;
      }
   }
}
```

I use the GetWindowRect() function to find out where the edit and toolbar windows are. Once I have this knowledge, it's a simple check to see if the mouse is in the area.

If the mouse is in the toolbar area, I take the mouse coordinates and divide them by the tile size to see which tile the user is picking. Once I know which tile is selected, I update the g_iCurTile variable to reflect the new value. The vRenderTileSet() function is then called to update the red selection box on the newly selected tile.

If the mouse is in the edit window, I update the mouse position to take into account the window client area. I then divide the coordinates by the tile size to figure out which tile is picked for editing. The last step to

Valhalla is where I update the `g_iTileMap` array with the `g_iCurTile` value.

Map Saving and Loading

Wow! We have already covered map editing, so there is not a ton left in the grand ways of cartography. Editing maps is great, but it is pretty worthless if you can't save your work. This is where map saving comes into play. The following information shows you how to add save and load buttons with functionality to the D3D_MapEditorLite program. Load up the new and improved D3D_MapEditorPlus project now to follow along. Then take a look at Figure 10.10 to see the output of this program.

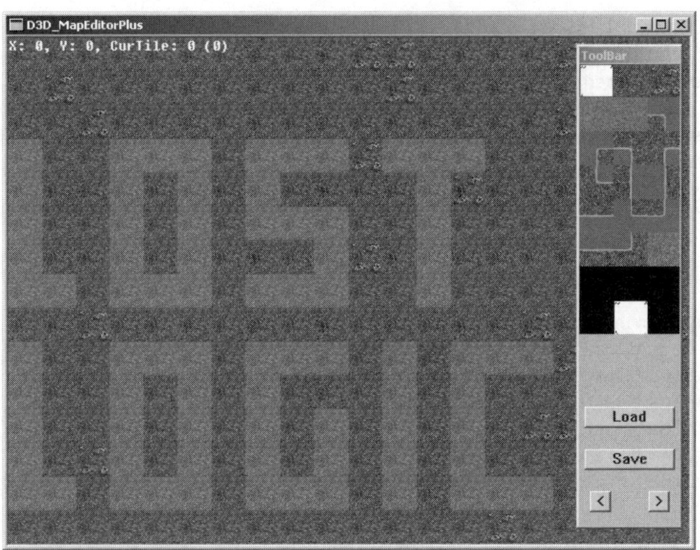

Figure 10.10: Output from the D3D_MapEditorPlus program.

In Figure 10.10 you can see how I added Load and Save buttons to the toolbar. Their functions are straightforward, as the Load button loads map data from a specified file and the Save button saves map data to a specified file.

The SaveMap() Function

In order to save the map data you need to save everything contained in the `g_iTileMap` tile array. Since it is one nice contiguous piece of memory, the operation is simplified. Basically, you must create the file to hold the data, write the contents of the tile map array to the file, and close the file. For a little spice I have added functionality to present the user with a file dialog box. The dialog box makes picking a data filename nice and intuitive. Here is the code I use to save the map:

```c
void vSaveMap(void)
{
    FILE           *fp;
    int            iRet;
    OPENFILENAME   fileStruct;
    char           szFileName[512];
    char           szFilter[32];
    char           szExtension[32];

    // Clear buffer to receive filename
    memset(szFileName, 0x00, 512);

    // Create file filter
    memset(szFilter, 0x00, 32);
    strcpy(szFilter, "*.dat");
    // Create file extension
    memset(szExtension, 0x00, 32);
    strcpy(szExtension, "dat");

    // Clear file dialog structure
    memset(&fileStruct, 0x00, sizeof(OPENFILENAME));

    // Initialize structure
    fileStruct.hInstance = g_hInstance;
    fileStruct.hwndOwner = g_hWnd;
    fileStruct.lpstrDefExt = szExtension;
    fileStruct.lpstrFileTitle = szFileName;
    fileStruct.lpstrFilter = szFilter;
    fileStruct.nMaxFileTitle = 512;
    fileStruct.lStructSize = sizeof(OPENFILENAME);

    // Retrieve the filename
    iRet = GetSaveFileName(&fileStruct);

    // Exit on failure
    if(!iRet) {
        return;
    }
    // Open the tile file
    fp = fopen(szFileName, "wb");
    // Return if open failed
    if(fp == NULL) {
        return;
    }
    // Save the tile buffer
    fwrite(g_iTileMap, 10000, sizeof(int), fp);
    // Close the tile file
    fclose(fp);
    // Play sound to indicate action
```

```
    PlaySound("bleep.wav",NULL,SND_FILENAME|SND_ASYNC);
}
```

The first section of code initializes the `OPENFILENAME` data structure required by the `GetSaveFileName()` function. The `GetSaveFileName()` function is part of Microsoft's Visual C++ SDK and provides you with everything you need to create save filename dialog boxes.

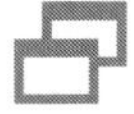

Tip The file dialogs provided by Microsoft make life much easier for picking filenames. I highly suggest that you use the calls in your programs.

Once the call is made to retrieve the save filename, open the file and output the contents of the map array to it. The `fwrite()` function is useful here, and it gets the job done quite nicely.

Just as what goes up must come down, what gets opened must be closed. To adhere to this policy, I make a call to `fclose()` to close the open map data file. You may be wondering why I play a sound at the end of the whole operation. This is to let the user know the save is successful. It's not completely necessary, but I think it's a nice touch.

Note If you type in the Save As filename and do not select an extension, it will not be saved with an extension. Be sure to save the map filename with a .dat extension if you want it to show up properly at load time.

Load the map editor and play around with editing and saving a few maps. This will give you some material to play with at load time.

The LoadMap() Function

The load map function works very much like the save map function. There are a couple of key differences though. First of all, the `GetSaveFileName()` function is replaced with the `GetOpenFileName()` function. I'm not really sure why there are two different functions that perform the same operation, but hey, who am I to question it? Anyway, the get open filename function populates the filename string with the name of the file to load. Assuming the file exists, the code then opens the data file and loads the contents into the global tile array. As long as everything works, a sound is played to indicate success.

If you have not done so already, launch the D3D_MapEditorPlus program and select the Load button. Load in the file named TileMap.dat and you will see my handle drawn in the sand.

That about does it for loading and saving basic tile maps. On with the show!

Mini-Map Rendering

Most strategy games give you a satellite view of the world in the form of a mini-map. The mini-map generally shows you a nice representation of the world map from a very zoomed-out perspective. This is a very useful feature for both the game and the map editor. I have a project that gives you this functionality. Look at Figure 10.11 to see a screen shot of it:

Figure 10.11: Output from the D3D_MapEditorPlusGold program.

That's right; it's the old map editor, but now it is the gold edition! (I know the name of the program is getting a bit freaky, but hey, at least I didn't call it the MapEditor 2700+ or something along that line!)

In Figure 10.11 you can see the map editor, but now there is a little window in the lower left containing the mini-map. In reality it is the larger world map rendered with a pixel size of 1 x 1 for each tile. This allows me to render the entire 100 x 100 world in only 100 x 100 pixels. Load up the D3D_MapEditorPlusGold project now so I can show you the changes required to implement mini-map rendering.

The flow of the program hasn't changed much, but the changes do warrant an illustration. Please look to Figure 10.12 to see the flow of the program.

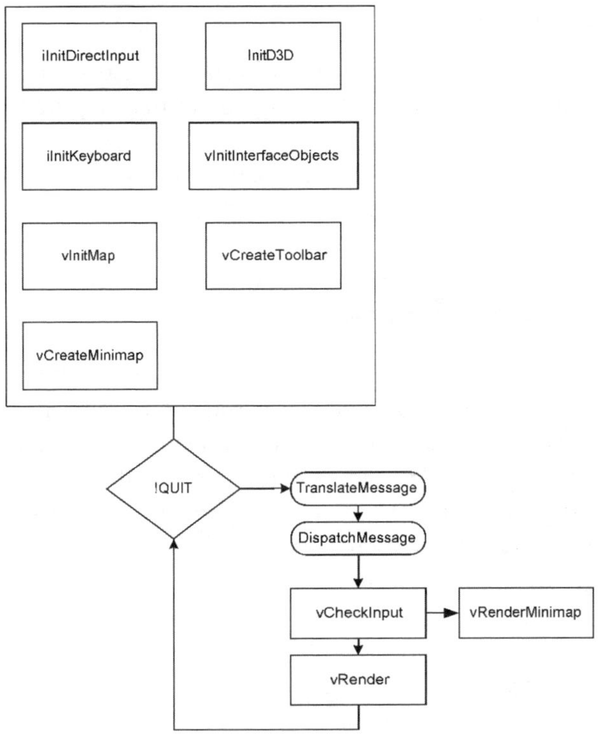

Figure 10.12: Flow of the D3D_MapEditorPlusGold program.

In Figure 10.12 you can see how the program initializes DirectInput, the keyboard, DirectGraphics, interface objects, the tile map, the toolbar, and finally the mini-map window. Since it's nice to have the mini-map in its own movable window, I create one especially for it. This is done with the `vCreateMinimap()` function.

The vCreateMinimap() Function

The create mini-map function is only called once by the application at initialization time. The function creates the window for the mini-map and places it in the main editor's window at the bottom left. I calculate the proper coordinates by taking into account the editor window position and the size of the mini-map. Here is the code that creates the window:

```
// Create mini-map window
hWndMinimap = CreateWindowEx(
```

```
WS_EX_LEFT|WS_EX_TOPMOST|WS_EX_TOOLWINDOW,
"Minimap", "Minimap",
WS_BORDER | WS_VISIBLE | WS_MINIMIZEBOX,

rcWindow.left+10, rcWindow.bottom+g_iYOffset-140,
100, 100, hwnd, NULL, hinst, NULL);
```

The above code isn't very dynamic in that I programmed it for a 100 x 100 mini-map, but there is nothing keeping you from changing the values to represent a different size map.

Now that you have a mini-map window, you need a place to render the actual mini-map. The program performs this with the `vRender-Minimap()` function.

The vRenderMinimap() Function

The render mini-map function works just like the main render function in that it loops through the tile map and draws the appropriate tile for each tile on the map. The main difference comes in that the mini-map function loops through the entire tile map instead of just a small area, and it also renders each tile scaled down to 1 pixel by 1 pixel in size. Here is the code to accomplish that Herculean task:

```
void vRenderMinimap(void)
{
    RECT    rectSrc;
    RECT    rectDest;
    int iX;
    int iY;
    int iCurTile;
    int iBufferPos;

    // Clear the back buffer to a blue color
    g_pd3dDevice->Clear(0, NULL,
                D3DCLEAR_TARGET,
                D3DCOLOR_XRGB(0,0,0), 1.0f, 0);
    // Begin the scene
    g_pd3dDevice->BeginScene();

    // Render the minimap
    // Top to bottom
    for(iY = 0; iY < g_iMapHeight; iY++) {
        // Left to right
        for(iX = 0; iX < g_iMapWidth; iX++) {
            // Calculate buffer offset
            iBufferPos = iX+(iY * g_iMapWidth);
            // Get the proper tile
            iCurTile = g_iTileMap[iBufferPos];
            // Display the tile
            vDrawInterfaceObject((iX),
                    (iY),
                    (float)1,
```

```
                    (float)1,
                iCurTile);
        }
    }
    // End the scene
    g_pd3dDevice->EndScene();
    // Source rectangle
    rectSrc.top = 0;
    rectSrc.bottom = g_iMapHeight;
    rectSrc.left = 0;
    rectSrc.right = g_iMapWidth;
    // Destination rectangle
    rectDest.top = 0;
    rectDest.bottom = g_iMapHeight;
    rectDest.left = 0;
    rectDest.right = g_iMapWidth;
    // Present the results
    g_pd3dDevice->Present(&rectSrc, &rectDest, hWndMinimap, NULL);
}
```

I have put the most interesting part of the function in bold-faced text.
Notice that I set the size of the output tile to 1 pixel by 1 pixel. This
scales the tile down to a single dot on the mini-map at render time. The
cool part about this is that the dot actually represents the overall color of
the tile since it is a scaled-down representation and not a proxy texture.
What is a proxy texture? One method of drawing a mini-map is to assign
a representative color to each tile type. For example, water tiles would be
drawn as blue squares, ground tiles as green squares, and buildings as
black squares. You wouldn't actually scale the tile; you would just substitute in a color for the tile based on the tile's function in the game.
Personally, I prefer the scaling method since it lets you give a very accu-
rate representation of the map without any special proxy coding.

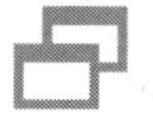

Tip   If you want a bigger mini-map, all you have to do is
change the size of the mini-map window and the size of the tiles
in the rendering loop. Try it out!

Algorithmic Map Generation

Drawing maps by hand is a lot of fun, but it can be cumbersome when
you want to start out with random-looking land masses. One cool way to
alleviate this problem is to randomly generate your base map using code.
You are in luck because I have an example program that does just that!
Check out Figure 10.13 to see it in action.

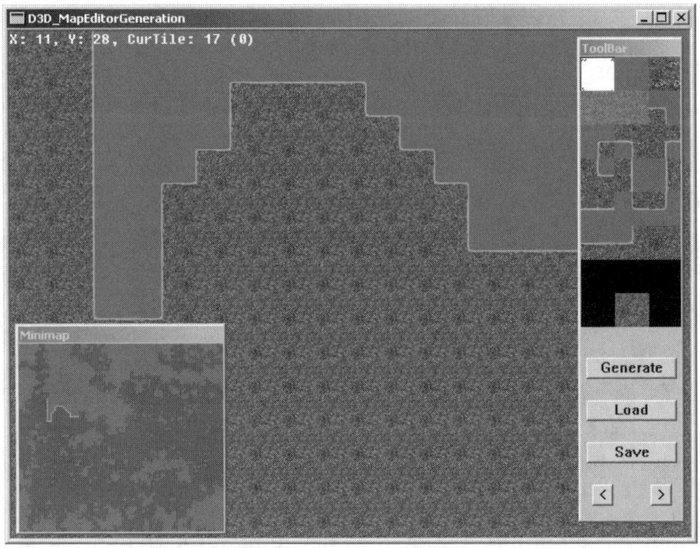

Figure 10.13: Output of the D3D_MapEditorGeneration program.

Note the usual suspects in the above figure. There is a toolbar, an edit window, and a mini-map. The new stuff comes in the form of the Generate button on the toolbar. This button clears the map with water and randomly generates grass on it. You may have also noticed that I increased the size of the mini-map. I did this so that you can see the effects of the random generation more easily. You won't be able to see it in Figure 10.13, but if you launch the D3D_MapEditorGeneration program now, you will also notice that I have a red box on the mini-map that roughly indicates your current viewing area on the large edit map. This helps you to see where you are editing.

Load up the D3D_MapEditorGeneration program now to follow along with me while I cover the code.

The vGenerateMap() Function

This map editor program is laid out almost exactly like the previous ones. The main difference is in the generate map function. Its purpose is to randomly generate terrain based on the generation type passed to it. For this example, I only have one type of map generation logic, but that shouldn't keep you from adding more! Here is the code for the function:

```
void vGenerateMap(int iType)
{
    int iRandDirection;
    int iSeedPos[32];
    int i, j;
```

```
int iNumSeeds    = 32;
int iNumUpdates  = 800;

// -- TYPE 0 -- Random seeds
if(iType == 0) {
   // Clear the map
   vInitMap();
   // Randomly create starting seeds
   for(i = 0; i < iNumSeeds; i++) {
      // Set seed starting position
      iSeedPos[i] = rand()%(g_iMapHeight*g_iMapWidth);
      // Place the chunk of grass around it
      g_iTileMap[iSeedPos [i]] = 17;
   }
   // Move seeds around
   for(i = 0; i < iNumUpdates; i++) {
      for(j = 0; j < iNumSeeds; j++) {
         iRandDirection = rand()%4;

         // Move seed up a "line"
         if(iRandDirection == 0) {
            iSeedPos[j] -= g_iMapWidth;
         }
         // Move seed right
         else if(iRandDirection == 1) {
            iSeedPos[j] ++;
         }
         // Move seed down a "line"
         else if(iRandDirection == 2) {
            iSeedPos[j] += g_iMapWidth;
         }
         // Move seed left
         else if(iRandDirection == 3) {
            iSeedPos[j] --;
         }

         // If seed in invalid area, move it to a
         // random location
         if(iSeedPos[j] < 0 ||
            iSeedPos[j] >=
               (g_iMapHeight*g_iMapWidth))
         {
            iSeedPos[j] =
               rand()%(g_iMapHeight*g_iMapWidth);
         }
         // Place the chunk of grass around the seed
         g_iTileMap[iSeedPos [j]] = 17;
      }
   }
}
// Render minimap
vRenderMinimap();
// Play sound to indicate action
PlaySound("bleep.wav",NULL,SND_FILENAME|SND_ASYNC);
}
```

The code can be a bit daunting, so take a look at Figure 10.14 to see it illustrated.

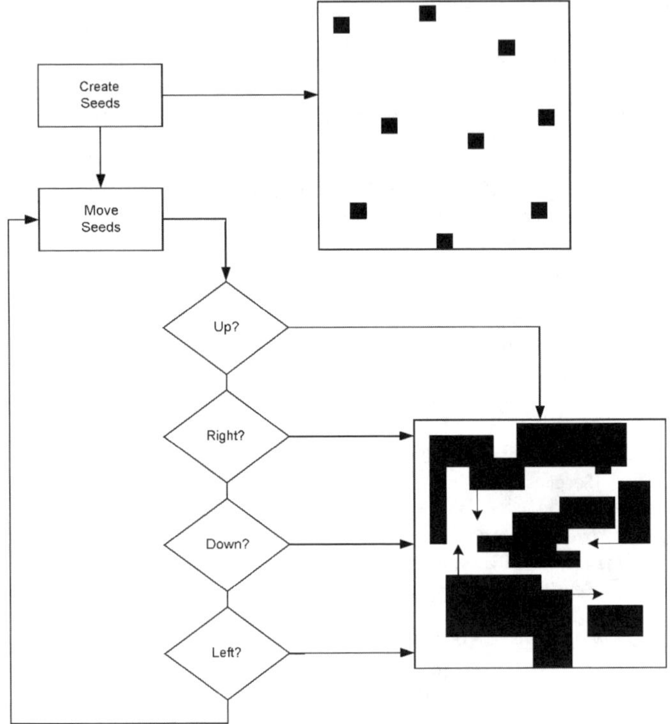

Figure 10.14: Flow of the vGenerateMap() function.

Now the first thing the code does is randomly place terrain seeds on the map. The seeds make up the starting points of the future continents that the code creates. There is no pattern to this method; the placement is purely random. To the right of the seed placement routine you can see what the resulting map looks like. It doesn't look like much, considering the code has only put grass in the starting seed locations.

Once the seeds are randomly placed, the code loops through each seed an arbitrary number of times and randomly moves the seed up, right, down, or left. As the seed moves, grass is left in its wake. Slowly but surely the map fills up with random patterns of grass by using this method. To the right of the seed movement routines in Figure 10.14, you can see how the map takes shape.

There are a couple of things not illustrated. First of all, I make a call to vInitMap() to clear the map before I generate the terrain. This is necessary to give you a clean slate on which to randomly create grass. The next thing not in the illustration is the dummy checking that makes sure the seeds don't wander off out of bounds. If a seed does wander off, it is randomly placed back on the map to start somewhere else. The last thing that takes place is the rendering of the mini-map to show the updated terrain data.

Generation Methods

As I said earlier, I only have one method of random map generation implemented in the example. There are many more robust features you may want to put in your own routines. For example, you may want to code fractal routines that generate interesting terrain patterns. Or you may want to use a blob method that randomly pastes down predefined blobs of terrain to form a map. Figure 10.15 illustrates the blob method.

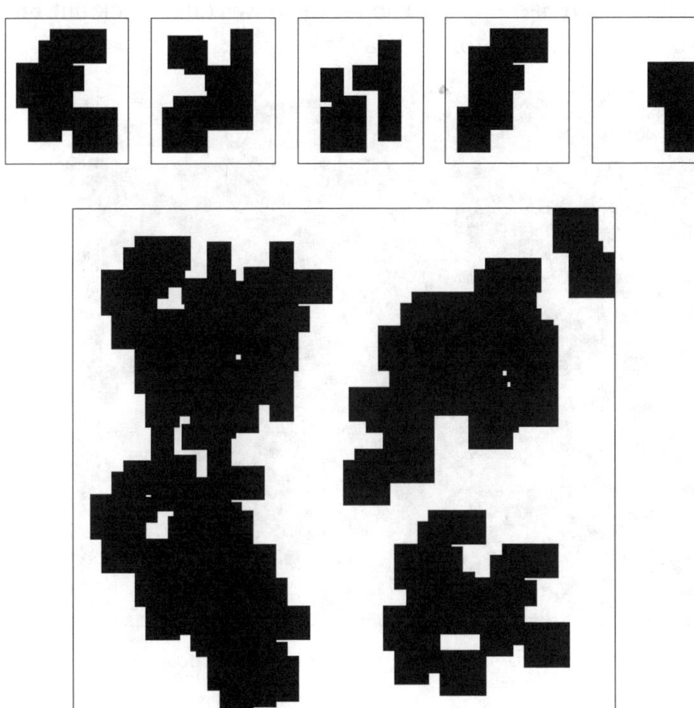

Figure 10.15: Using blobs to render random terrain.

In the figure you can see how the code uses a set of five predefined blobs to generate the map. Each blob is randomly placed on the map a few times until you end up with organic-looking terrain. The map at the bottom of the figure is actually comprised of various copies of the blobs. You have to smooth out the map to make it look more fluid, but at least the blobs get you started.

Map Layers

Do you remember tile layers from Chapter 5? If not, you may want to go back there now and review the subject matter. Layers allow you to render several tiles on top of one another. For example, you may want to render a grass tile and add a tree tile on top of the grass. You might even decide to render a fire tile on top of the tree tile to make it appear as if it is on fire. The options are limitless. The question raised with this functionality is how do you edit multiple layers with a map editor? Put on your thinking cap because I am about to show you! Check out Figure 10.16 to see the map editor with layer support.

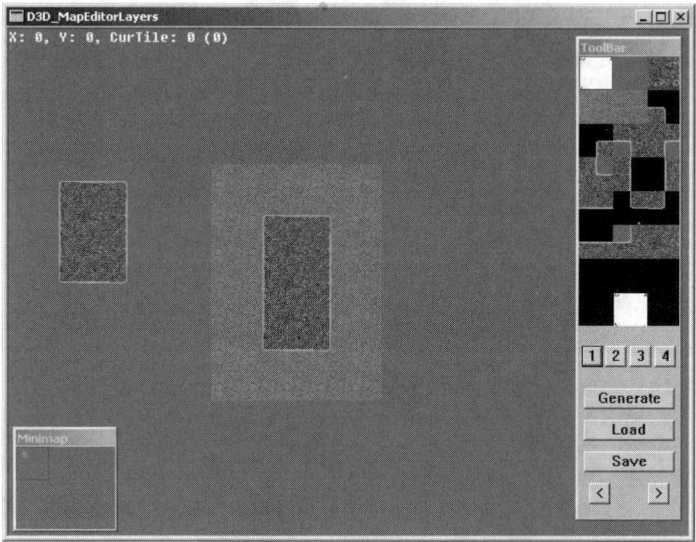

Figure 10.16: Output from the D3D_MapEditorLayers program.

Figure 10.16 shows the output from the D3D_MapEditorLayers program. On the toolbar you can make out four buttons labeled 1 to 4. These buttons set the active layer you wish to edit. For example, to edit the base layer, you select layer button 1. After you select the first layer, future clicks on the edit map result in tiles added to layer 1. The other layer buttons work in the same manner. In the edit window in the figure you can see a small sandy island with grass in the middle. The sand is on layer 1, but the grass edging is on layer 2. This gives the appearance of a smooth transition between sand and grass without a special sand-to-grass tile. Enough with the screen shot. Load up the D3D_MapEditor-Layers program now to follow along.

Header File Changes

The D3D_MapEditorLayers program is based on the previous versions of the map editor, so most of it is very similar to what you have seen. The first major difference is seen in the main.h header file. The following code shows the difference:

```
int             g_iTileSize = 32;
int             g_iTilesWide = 20;
int             g_iTilesHigh = 15;
int             g_iMapWidth = 100;
int             g_iMapHeight = 100;
int             g_iXPos = 0;
int             g_iYPos = 0;
int             g_iTileMap[10000][4];
int             g_iCurTile = 0;
int             g_iCurTileSet = 0;
int             g_iMaxTileSet = 3;
int             g_iTotalTiles = 18;
int             g_iCurLayer = 0;
```

Multi-dimensional Array Change

The code in bold shows you the new and improved areas. The first change is made where I make the `g_iTileMap` a multidimensional array. Since the map editor supports four layers, I need four dimensions of tiles for the tile map.

The next change is the addition of the `g_iCurLayer` variable. It keeps track of which tile map is being worked on. This is very useful when you go to place a tile in the edit window. The program has to know where to put it!

Change Layer Function

In order to handle the tile layer changes, I also added a new function to the map editor. It looks like so:

```
void vChangeLayer(int iLayer);
```

The change layer function takes the new layer number and switches the program to use it actively. The function also handles the GUI effects for switching tile layers.

New Button Variables

The layer buttons require window handles and unique IDs to function
properly. The code that does that is as follows:

```
const int    ID_BUTTON_LAYER1 = 40006;
const int    ID_BUTTON_LAYER2 = 40007;
const int    ID_BUTTON_LAYER3 = 40008;
const int    ID_BUTTON_LAYER4 = 40009;
HWND         hBUTTON_LAYER1    = NULL;
HWND         hBUTTON_LAYER2    = NULL;
HWND         hBUTTON_LAYER3    = NULL;
HWND         hBUTTON_LAYER4    = NULL;
```

In the code above you can see where I create a unique value and window
handle for each button. This is necessary to handle button press events
in the Windows message loop. There is nothing special here — just your
usual windows GUI code.

Changes to the vCreateToolbar() Function

Since the toolbar has four new windows on it, you must make some
changes to the toolbar creation function. The following code shows you
the changes required:

```
hBUTTON_LAYER1 = CreateWindow(
    "BUTTON", "1",
    WS_CHILD | WS_VISIBLE | BS_DEFPUSHBUTTON,
    3, 275, 20, 20, hWndToolBar, (HMENU)ID_BUTTON_LAYER1,
    hinst, NULL);
hBUTTON_LAYER2 = CreateWindow(
    "BUTTON", "2",
    WS_CHILD | WS_VISIBLE | BS_PUSHBUTTON,
    25, 275, 20, 20, hWndToolBar, (HMENU)ID_BUTTON_LAYER2,
    hinst, NULL);
hBUTTON_LAYER3 = CreateWindow(
    "BUTTON", "3",
    WS_CHILD | WS_VISIBLE | BS_PUSHBUTTON,
    48, 275, 20, 20, hWndToolBar, (HMENU)ID_BUTTON_LAYER3,
    hinst, NULL);
hBUTTON_LAYER4 = CreateWindow(
    "BUTTON", "4",
    WS_CHILD | WS_VISIBLE | BS_PUSHBUTTON,
    71, 275, 20, 20, hWndToolBar, (HMENU)ID_BUTTON_LAYER4,
    hinst, NULL);
```

There are four blocks of code listed above. Each one renders one of the
tile layer buttons. There is one unique button though. Look closely and
you can see that the first tile button has a type of BS_DEFPUSHBUTTON. This
value tells the GUI to render a black box around the button. I use the
black box to indicate which tile layer is active. Since the program defaults
to layer 0, I set the first layer button to be active.

The vChangeLayer() Function

When any of the layer buttons is pressed, a call to the vChangeLayer()
function is made. This function destroys the layer buttons, sets them all
to their default value, and then creates the active layer button with the
black outline flag. Here is the code that performs this functionality:

```
void vChangeLayer(int iLayer)
{
   // Turn off all layer buttons
   DestroyWindow(hBUTTON_LAYER1);
   DestroyWindow(hBUTTON_LAYER2);
   DestroyWindow(hBUTTON_LAYER3);
   DestroyWindow(hBUTTON_LAYER4);

   // Set buttons to all default
   hBUTTON_LAYER1 = CreateWindow(
      "BUTTON", "1",
      WS_CHILD | WS_VISIBLE | BS_PUSHBUTTON,
      3, 275, 20, 20, hWndToolBar, (HMENU)ID_BUTTON_LAYER1,
      g_hInstance, NULL);
   hBUTTON_LAYER2 = CreateWindow(
      "BUTTON", "2",
      WS_CHILD | WS_VISIBLE | BS_PUSHBUTTON,
      25, 275, 20, 20, hWndToolBar, (HMENU)ID_BUTTON_LAYER2,
      g_hInstance, NULL);
   hBUTTON_LAYER3 = CreateWindow(
      "BUTTON", "3",
      WS_CHILD | WS_VISIBLE | BS_PUSHBUTTON,
      48, 275, 20, 20, hWndToolBar, (HMENU)ID_BUTTON_LAYER3,
      g_hInstance, NULL);
   hBUTTON_LAYER4 = CreateWindow(
      "BUTTON", "4",
      WS_CHILD | WS_VISIBLE | BS_PUSHBUTTON,
      71, 275, 20, 20, hWndToolBar, (HMENU)ID_BUTTON_LAYER4,
      g_hInstance, NULL);

   // Activate proper button
   if(iLayer == 1) {
      DestroyWindow(hBUTTON_LAYER1);
      hBUTTON_LAYER1 = CreateWindow(
         "BUTTON", "1",
         WS_CHILD | WS_VISIBLE | BS_DEFPUSHBUTTON,
         3, 275, 20, 20, hWndToolBar, (HMENU)ID_BUTTON_LAYER1,
         g_hInstance, NULL);
   }
   else if(iLayer == 2) {
      DestroyWindow(hBUTTON_LAYER2);
      hBUTTON_LAYER2 = CreateWindow(
         "BUTTON", "2",
         WS_CHILD | WS_VISIBLE | BS_DEFPUSHBUTTON,
         25, 275, 20, 20, hWndToolBar,
         (HMENU)ID_BUTTON_LAYER2,
         g_hInstance, NULL);
```

```
    }
    else if(iLayer == 3) {
        DestroyWindow(hBUTTON_LAYER3);
        hBUTTON_LAYER3 = CreateWindow(
            "BUTTON", "3",
            WS_CHILD | WS_VISIBLE | BS_DEFPUSHBUTTON,
            48, 275, 20, 20, hWndToolBar,
            (HMENU)ID_BUTTON_LAYER3,
            g_hInstance, NULL);
    }
    else if(iLayer == 4) {
        DestroyWindow(hBUTTON_LAYER4);
        hBUTTON_LAYER4 = CreateWindow(
            "BUTTON", "4",
            WS_CHILD | WS_VISIBLE | BS_DEFPUSHBUTTON,
            71, 275, 20, 20, hWndToolBar,
            (HMENU)ID_BUTTON_LAYER4,
            g_hInstance, NULL);
    }

    // Set current layer
    g_iCurLayer = (iLayer-1);

    PlaySound("button.wav",NULL,SND_FILENAME|SND_ASYNC);
}
```

Take, for example, layer button number 2. When it is clicked, the function
is called with the iLayer parameter equaling 2. The function destroys the
layer buttons and then creates them all without the black outline around
them. The function then checks to see which layer the iLayer parameter
points to. It reaches the second one and destroys the second layer button
again. It then creates the layer button with the black outline around it to
indicate that it is active. The g_iCurLayer variable is finally set to indicate which layer is active.

Load and Save Changes

The vSaveMap() and vLoadMap() functions have to be modified to include
the additional layer information for each map. Since there are four layers,
there is four times as much data to load and save. In each case the code
change is minimal. The following code shows the change required for the
vLoadMap() function:

```
fread(g_iTileMap, 40000, sizeof(int), fp);
```

Notice how the fread() function reads in 40,000 integers now instead of
10,000. The vSaveMap() function has a similar change:

```
fwrite(g_iTileMap, 40000, sizeof(int), fp);
```

In the save map function, the number of bytes saved has changed from
10,000 to 40,000. This is the only change required for the save function.

 **Warning**   Do not try to load or save maps generated with other versions of the map editor program. The program is likely to crash.

Changes to the vRender() Function

The vRender() function requires changes to support the multiple tile layers. Luckily, the changes are minor and take place in a very small portion of code. Here is the code affected by the layer change:

```
// Layers
for(iLayer = 0; iLayer < 4; iLayer++) {
    // Calculate buffer offset
    iBufferPos = iX+g_iXPos+((iY+g_iYPos)*g_iMapWidth);
    // Get the proper tile
    iCurTile = g_iTileMap[iBufferPos][iLayer];
    // Display the tile
    if(iCurTile != 0 || iLayer == 0) {
        vDrawInterfaceObject((iX * g_iTileSize),
                    (iY * g_iTileSize),
                    (float)g_iTileSize,
                    (float)g_iTileSize,
                    iCurTile);
    }
}
```

Since the program now supports four layers, you must loop through each of the four layers for each tile on the map. If there is a tile present in the layer, you render it. There is an exception to the rule though. If the current layer is not the first layer, the tile must not be equal to 0. If the tile is equal to 0, the tile is not rendered on layers above the first layer. This allows for transparency between layers. You can think of the second, third, and fourth layers as transparent bitmaps with their transparent color set to 0. If they have tile 0 in them, they are not rendered in those areas.

In Figure 10.17 on the following page, you can see the theory of layer composition in action. In the figure there are four layers with tiles in them. The first layer is filled with tile 1. Layer number 2 has a lot of 0 tiles but also has a few 2 tiles in it. Layer 3 has mostly 0s as well but has a few 3s in it. Layer 4 works the same way. Now, when they are all put together, tile 0 is used as a transparent key for putting layers 2, 3, and 4 on top of layer 1. The result is what you see at the bottom of the image. If you use the tile legend to the left, you can see how the results are obtained.

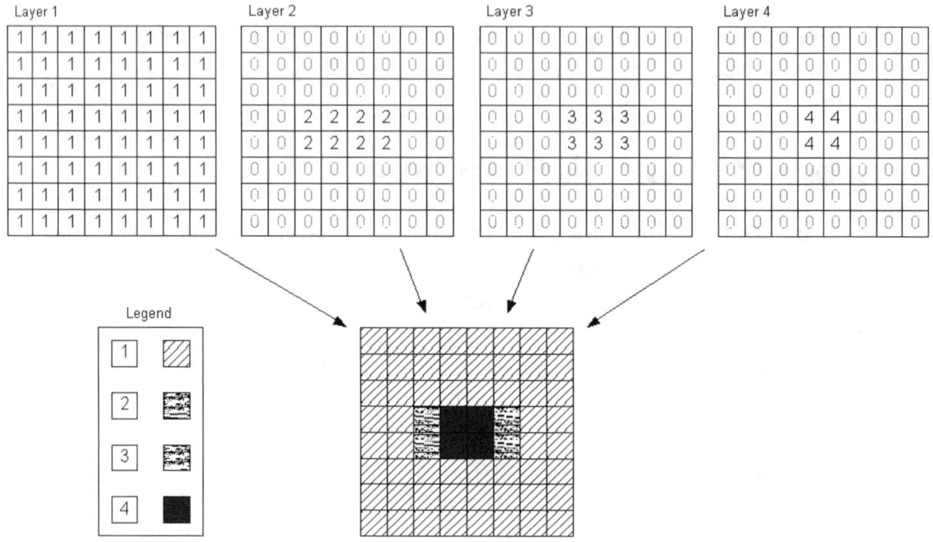

Figure 10.17: Map layer composite.

Changes to the vCheckMouse() Function

Since you now have to edit various layers of the map, the `vCheckMouse()` function requires a change. Here is the code for it:

```
g_iTileMap[iTileX+g_iXPos+
    ((iTileY + g_iYPos)
    * g_iMapWidth)][g_iCurLayer]
    = g_iCurTile;
```

In the code you can see how I set the `g_iTileMap` multidimensional array with the current tile. Since the map now supports multiple dimensions, I use the `g_iCurLayer` to determine which layer to put the tile in.

There are a few other changes in the map editor program, but I have shown you the major ones. If you have not done so already, launch the program and play around with editing various layers until you get the hang of it.

Recap

This chapter introduced the basics of map editing, map viewing, map generation, and mini-map rendering. Remember these key points:

- The map editor is one of the single most important parts of your project. If your map editor is hard to use, you will have a hard time releasing maps for your game and players won't bother to make their own maps.

- The toolbar is a great place to put buttons for the map editor interface. Make the toolbar mobile so that it doesn't take up valuable editing real estate.

- Mini-maps can look very realistic if you scale tiles to render the mini-map instead of using color representations of tiles. This does incur a speed hit though, since it requires a lot more rendering power.

- There are many ways to algorithmically generate maps. Try out the simple method I demonstrated first and then modify it until you have a cool random terrain generator.

- Layers give you many creative freedoms in map making. You can create overlays, translucent tiles, and many other effects.

Chapter 11

3D Animation

Have you ever wanted to know how to put animating 3D objects in your games? Has the fine art of 3D animation eluded you in the past? Hopefully, this chapter will shed some light on the answers to these questions and more. In this chapter I cover the basics of a 3D animation editor and methods to load up the animation in your own programs. Heck, I even cover some basic modeling techniques! The following topics are covered:

- 3D animation overview
- Importing content
- Animation editing
- Editor programming
- Implementing animations

3D Animation Overview

First of all, what is 3D animation? Simply put, it is the act of one or more objects in 3D space changing in some way over time. Why do you, as the strategy game programmer, care? Well, for starters, the 3D tank in your game won't look very cool if its treads don't move, and your 3D mech won't look too grand if the radar dish doesn't spin. In order to understand how 3D animation fits into the big picture of game development, you first must grasp the following concepts:

- Scenes
- Objects
- Key frames
- Animation sets

Scenes

The first thing you must have for 3D animation to take place is a scene. A scene is nothing more than a collection of 3D objects. Sounds easy enough, right? Take a look at the scene in Figure 11.1.

Figure 11.1: A 3D scene rendered in 3ds max.

This figure shows the output from a scene I rendered in 3ds max. (Discreet was nice enough to lend ye old author their software for this book, so please consider them when looking for a 3D package of your own.) Notice the 3D objects in the scene. The most obvious object is the water. Next up you have the sky, some islands, and a lone sailboat. All of these objects combined make up the scene. Got it? Good; let's move on.

Objects

Objects are the lifeblood of 3D animation. Without objects, you wouldn't have a scene or animation. What is an object? For the purpose of the chapter, objects are 3D models comprised of polygons, color, and textures. Take, for example, the mech I mentioned a minute ago. A mech, as you well know, is an armored robotic fighting vehicle. The mech in the prior example has a spinning radar dish on its head. Since the dish spins regardless of the mech body, it is a separate object from the mech body. So, for this example scene you have two 3D objects: the mech body and the radar dish. Although the two objects always exist together, they must be separate so you can animate them independently. Another example of this is the tank in Figure 11.2.

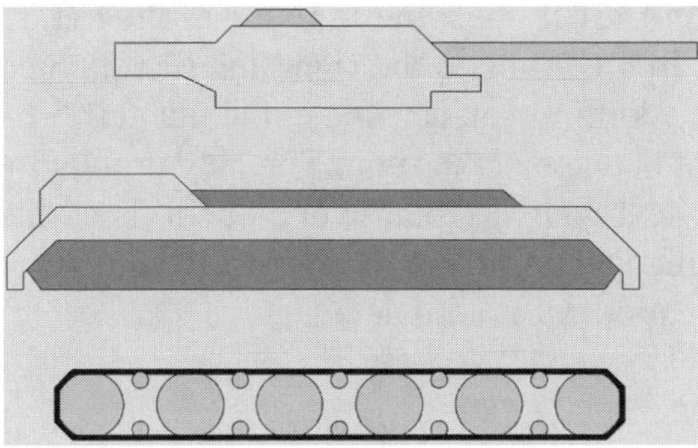

Figure 11.2: Tank objects.

You can see that the tank is made up of a turret, body, treads, and wheels. Since you want the turret to spin independent of the body, it must be a separate object. The same holds true for the treads and wheels.

Fixed Objects

Another method of 3D animation is to combine all the objects that make up a model and store the animation changes in multiple model files. The Quake games use this method, as it is much simpler than having to track multiple objects at once. Although it is easier to code, it's not always the best method, since you end up duplicating geometry for each frame.

Key Frames

Now comes the nitty-gritty part of animation. To animate an object you set up a series of key frames. In each frame you do something to the object that changes it from the previous frame. For our purposes here, you can rotate, translate, or scale the object from one frame to the next. For example, let's say you want a tank's turret to rotate 45 degrees. This is shown in Figure 11.3.

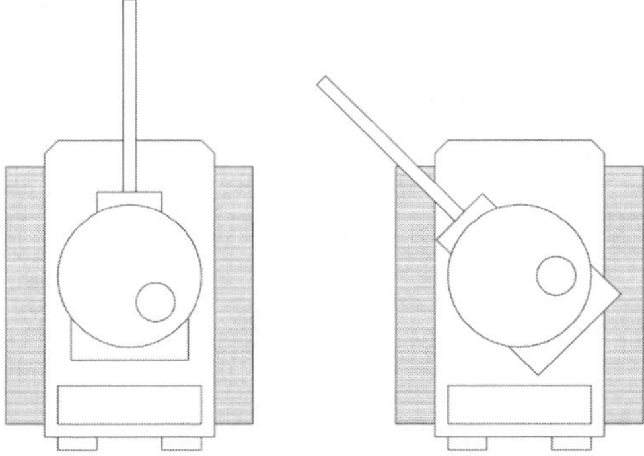

Figure 11.3: Two tank key frames.

This figure shows two tank key frames. In the frame to the left, the turret object is pointing up. In the frame to the right, the turret object is pointing 45 degrees to the left. As you can see in the illustration, a key frame is really a snapshot of an object in time. The only problem with Figure 11.3 is the turret isn't going to rotate very smoothly with only two frames. This is easily remedied by adding more frames. Check out Figure 11.4 to see the tank animation with more detail.

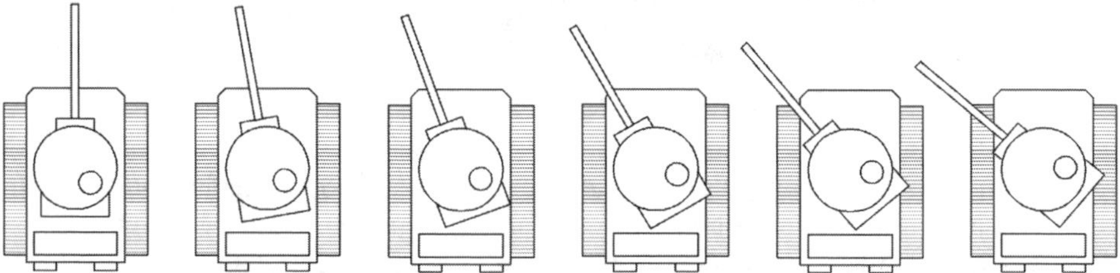

Figure 11.4: Detailed tank animation.

Here, the turret animation has more key frames. Instead of only two frames, there are now six. This makes for a much better animation.

Tweening

Keep in mind that you don't necessarily need a key frame for each change to the object. You can use another method called tweening. With tweening you set up key frames and have filler frames between the keys doing the transition animation. For an example, see Figure 11.5.

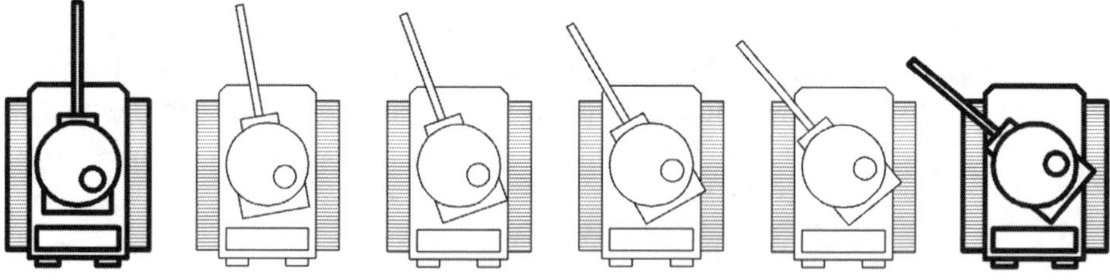

Figure 11.5: Detailed tank animation using tweening.

In Figure 11.5 you see the same tank animation, but this time I show key frames as the tanks with thick outlines. The other frames are in-between frames that transition the objects from key to key. The process is called tweening because of the in-between frames. Get it? Although tweening is useful in some cases, I do not use it for the examples in this chapter for simplicity's sake.

Animation Sets

So far you have a scene made up of objects that have key frames to complete an animation. Armed with your newfound animation, you need animation sets. Why? To make your life simpler. You know what they say: Programmers are lazy by nature. That is why we are always trying to write programs to simplify tasks. Yeah, I don't buy that one either. Who else works 26 hours a day? Just kidding. Seriously though, animation sets are a great way to save time in game development. Take a look at Figure 11.6 to see animation sets in action.

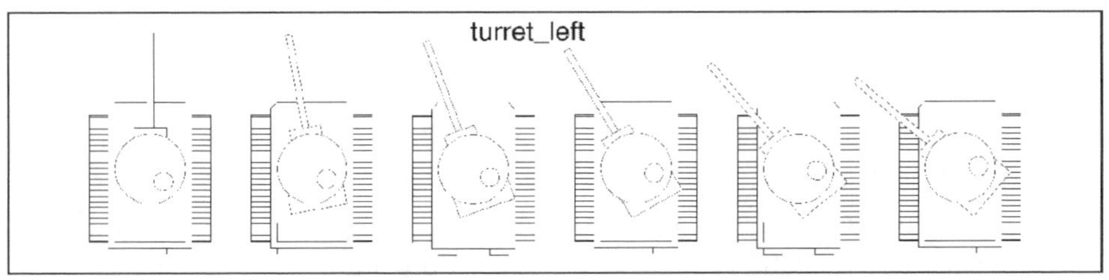

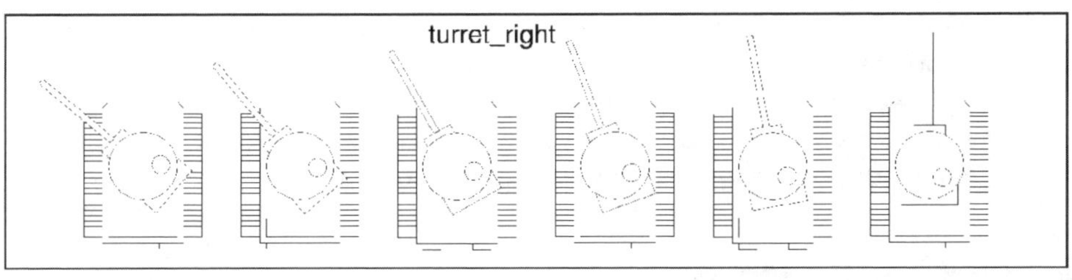

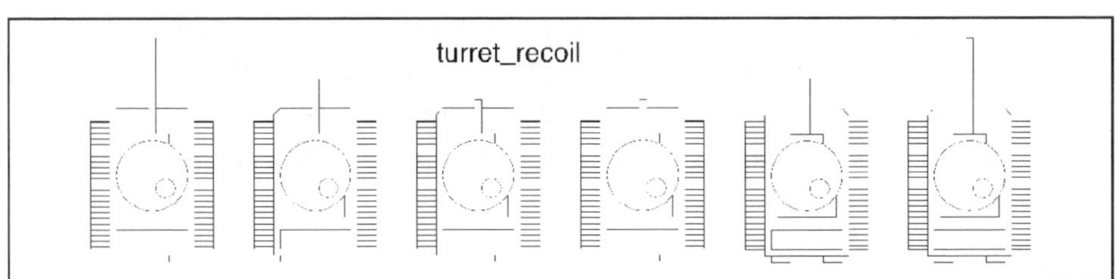

Figure 11.6: Tank animation sets.

Figure 11.6 shows three sets of tank animations. The top one is labeled "turret_left," the middle one is labeled "turret_right," and the bottom one is labeled "turret_recoil." By identifying animations this way, you can combine them in any way you wish to bring the objects alive in a game. Take, for example, a strategy armor game where you want a tank to rotate its turret to the left, rotate back to the middle, and then fire its weapon. If you tried to make a single animation out of this, you would end up with thousands, if not millions, of animations to handle every possible scenario. With animation sets, you can make simple animations and combine them dynamically. The following list should give you an idea of the animation sets needed for a futuristic mech combat simulator.

- Fire weapon
- Explode
- Fall down
- Jump
- Activate shields
- Walk
- Run
- Sidestep

In the list you see various animation set names that can be combined to make fully dynamic animation possible. Cool, huh?

Tip   For a real game you would probably want to have separate animation sets for the tank turret and the tank body. This would allow you to rotate the turret using standard 3D math without using key frames, but you would still use sets for such things as firing the turret, blowing up the tank, etc.

Importing Content

Since 3D objects are vital to the animation process, you need some way to create the models. This job is left up to professional 3D art packages, such as Softimage, Maya, or 3ds max. There are also several freeware and inexpensive packages out there, such as trueSpace, MilkShape, and Rhino.

Tip   There are many packages out there on the market, but my favorite is Discreet's 3ds max product. Not only is it rather inexpensive for what it does, but it is the most powerful animation system I have ever used. For the examples in the book I use 3ds max. Even if you don't own the package, you should be able to translate what I cover here for your program.

DirectX natively supports 3D models in the form of .x files. Most packages support the conversion of their formats to the .x format, so you shouldn't have much trouble exporting your models.

Exporting with 3ds max

The folks at Microsoft are nice enough to supply you with the source code for a 3ds max to DirectX exporter. The source code is downloadable from the DirectX SDK web site and works quite well. Once you have it compiled and installed, you can export models from 3ds max with a few clicks of the mouse. How about an example of exporting?

Simple Modeling

Exporting is a fairly straightforward process. First, you need a model to export. Let's start by creating a simple wineglass model. Open up 3ds max now if you have it and follow along with me. The first thing you see should look similar to Figure 11.7.

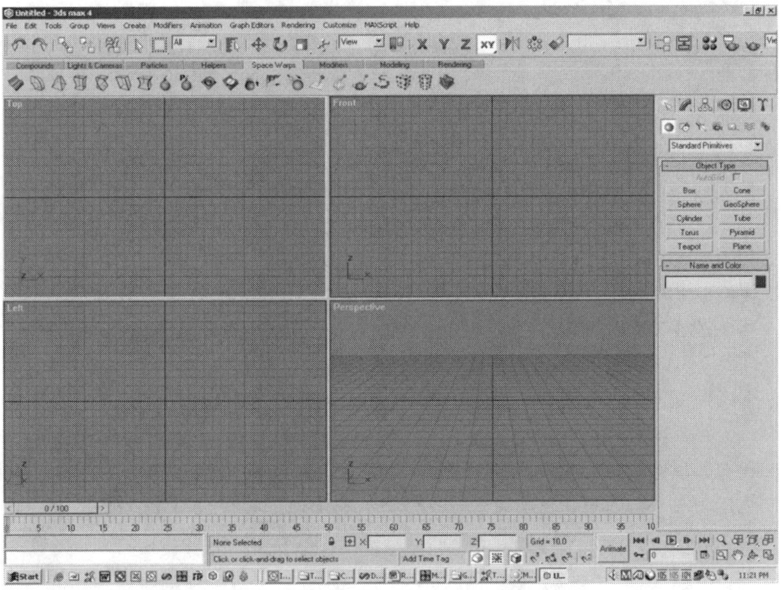

Figure 11.7: The 3ds max interface.

Since the program is very customizable, your interface may not resemble mine too closely, but I'm sure you get the point. The key thing to remember here is that DirectX uses a different coordinate orientation than 3ds max. 3ds max uses the z-coordinate to move items up or down, and DirectX uses the y-coordinate to do this. For this reason alone, you need to be very careful when creating objects in 3ds max; otherwise, they will come out flipped around the wrong way.

Since DirectX wants the y-coordinate to represent height in 3D, switch to the Top view in 3ds max and press the W key to maximize the Top view area. Your interface should resemble Figure 11.8 at this point.

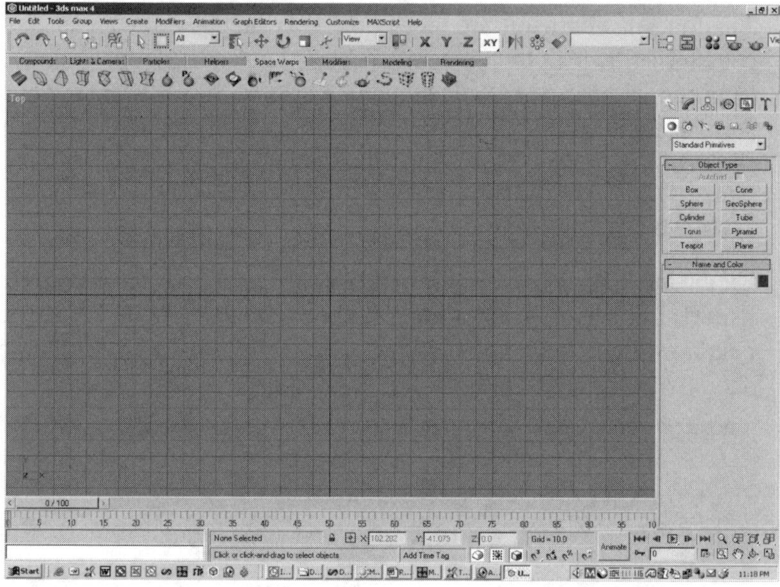

Figure 11.8: The top view in 3ds max.

Once you are in the Top view, zoom in a bit until the grid only contains about six squares from top to bottom. Now you need to create the outline of the wineglass. This is done with the Line shape tool from the Splines drop-down menu. Select it and draw an outline like the one in Figure 11.9.

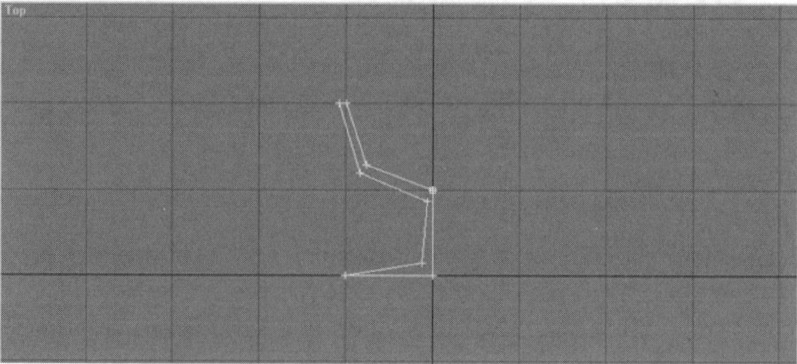

Figure 11.9: Outline of a wineglass.

In Figure 11.9 you can see the outline for a wineglass cross-section
piece. I know the glass looks very blocky, but you want to keep the polygons at a minimum when dealing with real-time 3D rendering. If you
mess up the placement of a few vertices, you can edit the model with the
Edit Mesh modifier located in the Modifier List. Move the vertices
around until you are happy with the outline, and then select the Lathe
modifier from the Modifier List. You should see what's pictured in Figure
11.10 if you pull this off successfully.

Figure 11.10: The initial lathed wineglass.

In Figure 11.10 you can see the initial results of the lathe modifier in 3ds
max. The object is actually screwed up at the moment, since the modifier
lathed the wineglass at the wrong axis point. Luckily this is easily remedied by selecting the Max button from the Align command set in the
Parameters window. Select the Max button now, and you should see the
contents of Figure 11.11.

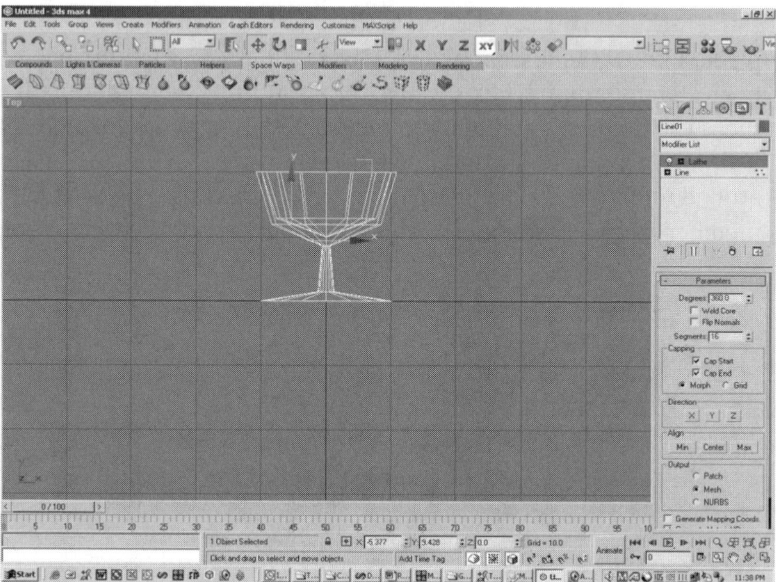

Figure 11.11: The correctly lathed wineglass.

3D models are pretty boring without textures, so be sure and tell the Lathe modifier to give the object texture coordinates. This is done by checking the Generate Mapping Coordinates check box in the Parameters window. After you do that, check the Weld Core check box in the same window. The weld core option welds the vertices that make up the central point of the lathe.

Zoom back to the four-view window setup with the W key. If you go to the Perspective window and roll the camera around, you should see the wineglass shown in Figure 11.12 on the following page.

In Figure 11.12 you can see the lathed wineglass in both the Top view and the Perspective view. Before you can export the glass, you need to convert it to an editable mesh. This is required since DirectX doesn't know how to deal with 3ds max objects directly. Right-click on the wineglass and select Convert To: and then Convert To Editable Mesh. The operation won't change how the wineglass looks, but it does change how DirectX reacts to it. With the conversion out of the way, it is time to export the model. Go to the File menu and select Export Selected to accomplish this. You are presented with a file dialog box asking you for the object name and Save as type. Type in the filename and change the Save as type drop-down to the X-File (*.X) format. Save the object and you should see the options in Figure 11.13.

Figure 11.12: The wineglass in the Perspective view.

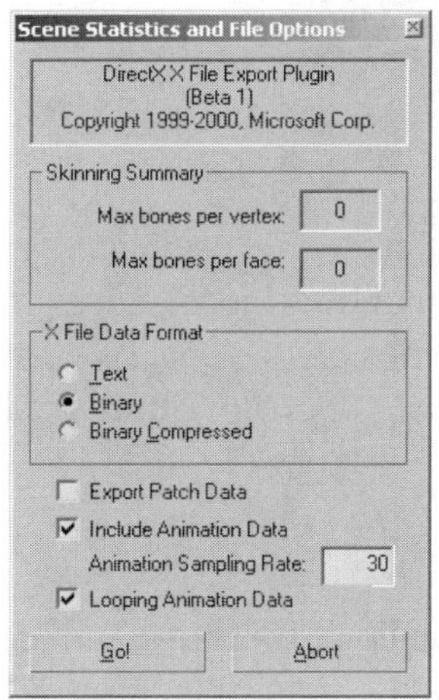

Figure 11.13: X-File exporter options.

Deselect Include Animation Data and Looping Animation Data before clicking Go!.

Note   You must install the x file exporter by Microsoft for the X-File option to be present in the Save as type drop-down menu. If you don't see the X-File option, install the exporter plug-in.

Load the Object

Now that you have a perfectly good .x file, load it up in the D3DFrame_ObjectLoader program that I covered earlier in the book. You have to change the code to read in the wineglass.x file, but that's all. Change the code, compile, and make sure the wineglass.x file is in the directory before launching the program. You should see something similar to Figure 11.14 if all goes well.

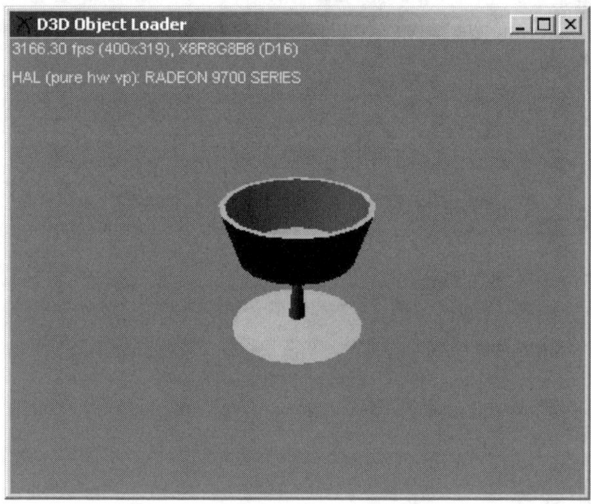

Figure 11.14: The wineglass viewed in Direct3D.

The figure shows the wineglass loaded up in the object loader program. Notice how I am getting around 3,100 frames per second. Not too shabby, eh? Actually, I am in dire need of a computer upgrade. But that's for another time.

The Convert 3DS Program

If you don't have access to 3ds max or you don't want to compile the plug-in that exports .x files, you can use a program called Conv3ds.exe that comes with the DirectX SDK. It is an old utility and may not be available much longer, but it allows you to convert .3ds files from the command prompt.

The cool part about Conv3ds.exe is that you only need to have your objects in the .3ds format for it to convert them into .x files. Luckily, most programs allow you to export objects as .3ds files. This makes it very easy to make .x files from programs other than 3ds max.

Animation Editing

When it comes to animating 3D objects in your games, you really have two choices: You can either hard-code the animation sequences or create them in an animation editor. Since hard coding is a pain in the rear, the best choice here is to use an animation editor. Assuming you take the best choice and pick the animation editor route, you are left with another set of options: You can either use a commercial animation package to create your animations and figure out how to parse the files or you can write your own animation editor. This is where things get tricky.

Prebuilt Animation Editors

Using a prebuilt editor may sound like the best choice, but then you have to figure out how to read in the editor's data and use it in your games. You are also at the mercy of the release schedule of commercial products. What happens if they change their format between releases? You will have to recode your editor.

Despite the drawback of commercial editors, they do offer one simple benefit: You don't have to spend your time coding your own editor! Tools programming is one of the most consuming parts of the game project, and the less programming you have to do, the better.

Code Your Own Editor

Most of us developers like to write our own code, so the option of making your own code editor may sound like the best choice on first examination. This is not necessarily the case for animation editing. As I said a minute ago, if you code your own editor, you are going to be spending a lot of time on the editor and not your core game. But, in the end, you will have your own animation editor that works no matter what other companies do. This is the biggest benefit to writing your own editor bar none.

Another benefit to writing your own editor is that you have complete control over the system. You don't have to wait years for company X to develop a much-wanted feature. You can just develop it at your pace. Of course, this assumes you know how to write the darn thing.

There you have it, a completely ambiguous discussion on which is better — roll-your-own editors or prebuilt ones. I am leaving it to you to figure out since my opinion is only that, an opinion. In the meantime, let me show you how to start making your own animation editor and animations. Before I get into the code, you need to understand what makes up an animation editor. To that end, the following components are about to be covered:

- Interface
- Commands
- The editing process
- Saving and loading

Animation Editor Interface

For the animation editor, you need an editing area and a toolbar for issuing commands. Figure 11.15 shows the starting components of the interface.

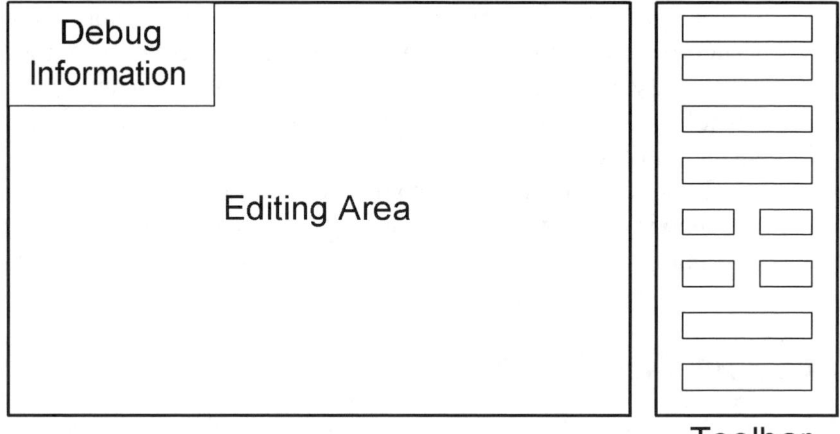

Figure 11.15: The animation editor interface.

This figure shows what looks very similar to the map editor programs. On the left side, I have the editing window, and on the right side, I have the toolbar. The editing window also contains debug information in the upper-left corner. The toolbar window contains buttons and information about the animation.

Animation Editor Commands

All good editors need commands to make them function, and this editor is no exception to the rule. The following command sets are a good start for the editor:

- Frame commands
- Object commands

- Playback commands
- File commands

Frame Commands

Since animations need frames to bring them to life, the editor needs commands to manipulate frames. For this you need commands to create frames, delete frames, and navigate among existing frames. You also need a way to enter in the frame data for the objects in the scene. You can do this with edit boxes, command buttons, or a mixture of the two.

Object Commands

3D scenes need objects; therefore, you need a way to add objects to your edit scene. This requires commands to load objects, delete objects, and navigate among the in-scene objects.

Playback Commands

All of the animation data in the world won't help much if you can't see the animation in action. DVR commands come in handy here with the ability to start, stop, rewind, and even fast-forward animation sequences.

File Commands

The editor isn't much good if you can't load and save the animation data that you generate; therefore, Load and Save buttons are a must. You can start with simple file loading and saving but then move to much better methods. How about a navigation system that lets you see thumbnail animations of the ones to load? That would be very cool!

The Editing Process

The editing process can be as simple or as complicated as you want it. Take 3ds max for instance. 3ds max has thousands of options and commands for editing animation. You can spend years learning the complete ins and outs of it. I worked with it as a professional animator for four years and still learn something new about it almost every day! Since the scope of the process is so large, I suggest that you start out with the absolute basics.

Since you need a scene, the first thing the editor needs to do is give you the ability to load in 3D objects. Once you have the objects, you need to be able to create key frames for the objects. Once that is out of the way, you need to be able to modify the key frames to animate the objects. This process is illustrated in Figure 11.16.

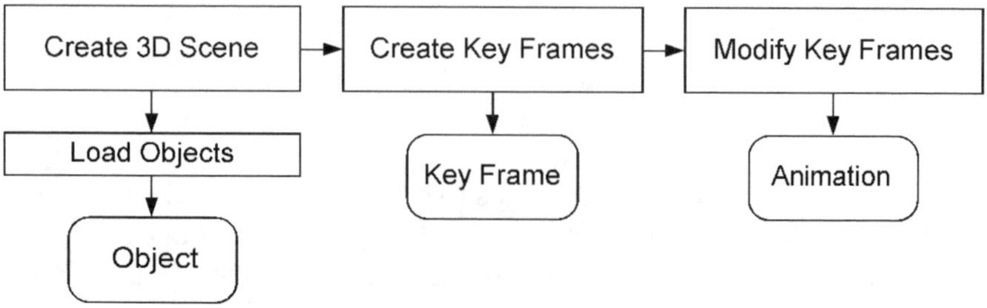

Figure 11.16: The editing process.

Figure 11.16 shows the basic steps involved in the editing process. You load the objects to create the scene, create the key frames for the objects, and then modify the key frames to create the animation.

In order to modify keys, you need, at a minimum, the ability to change the position and rotation of objects in the scene. Later on you will probably want to add the ability to scale the objects. I prefer to give the user keyboard commands to change position and rotation as well as edit boxes for them to manually key in the exact values. The edit boxes help to alleviate repetitive keyboard commands. For example, it is much easier to type in the number 180 than it is to hit the plus key 180 times.

Saving and Loading

Now that you have the information for the animation complete, you need to do something with it. This is where saving and loading comes into play. As you might recall, animation sets are very valuable for dynamic animations in your game. For this reason, the editor needs to be able to save the animation set created in it. You also need the ability to load the animation set up at a later time to modify it or just play it back. At the very least, you need Save and Load buttons to take care of this process.

Editor Programming

For your viewing pleasure I have included a very basic animation editor in the downloadable files. Strangely enough, it is the project named D3D_AnimationEditor. Please load up the project now and follow along with me.

The D3D_AnimationEditor program is a simple animation editor that lets you animate two objects in a scene. The first object is a mech, and the second object is a small radar dish. You can add key frames, rotate the objects, move the objects around the scene, and even move the camera around for different views. The program also lets you save and load the animations that you create.

Warning   The Save Anim button will overwrite the animation example I created for you. Do not select the save option unless you want to overwrite the sample animation.

Warning   The Load Anim button will erase anything you are working on and replace it with the last animation saved to disk. Do not select the load animation button unless you are willing to lose what is in the scene.

To get an idea of what the program looks like, see Figure 11.17 or execute the program.

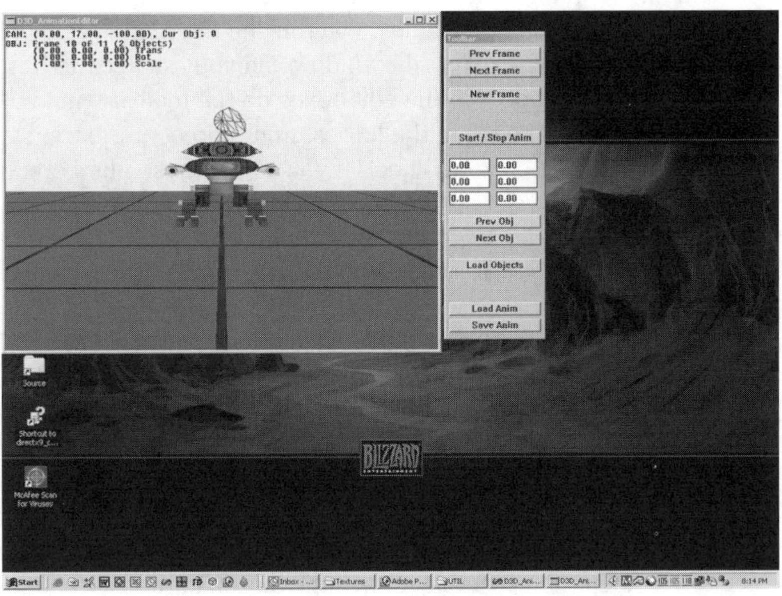

Figure 11.17: Output from the D3D_AnimationEditor program.

In Figure 11.17 you can see the real-life implementation of the animation editor. You should be able to tell that it is based very closely on the editor interface designed earlier. The window on the left contains the edit view area with some debug information, and the window on the right contains the toolbar commands and information. In the edit window you can see the mech and radar dish objects loaded up and ready to go. If you compiled and launched the program manually, you need to select the Load Anim button in order to see what is shown in Figure 11.17.

III
Part

D3D_AnimationEditor Controls

If you haven't already, launch the animation editor and select the Load Anim button. This loads up a previously saved animation I created. Once it is loaded, select the Start/Stop Anim button to play the animation. You should see the radar dish above the mech's head rotate 360 degrees over and over again if all goes well.

You can stop the animation from playing by selecting the Start/Stop Anim button again. Basically, this button toggles between playing the animation and pausing the animation. You can even add key frames and change data while the animation is going. This brings me to the next set of controls, the frame controls. On the toolbar you see frame commands for Prev, Next, and New. The Prev Frame button cycles the current animation frame to the previous one in the list. If you reach the beginning of the animation, the frame loops around to the last frame in the animation. As you cycle through the frames, you can see the frame data appear in the debug area on the main edit window and you can see the translation and rotation data appear in the edit boxes on the toolbar window.

The three edit boxes in the left column represent the translation information for the current object. If you adjust these numbers, the current object will move about in accordance with the changes made.

The three edit boxes in the right column set the rotation information for the current object. You can change them just like the translation boxes.

Next up on the toolbar are the object commands for Prev Obj, Next Obj, and Load Objects. The Prev Obj button cycles the current object to the one before it in the scene. If it gets to the beginning of the object list, the last object is selected. The Next Obj button does the same thing, except it cycles forward in the list instead of backward. For the purposes of the example program, there are only two objects (the mech and the radar dish). The Load Objects button is used to load 3D objects into the scene. To keep things simple, I have the button hard-load the mech and the radar dish. For a real editor you need to dynamically pick the objects to load and not hard-code them in.

Last up are the Load Anim and Save Anim buttons. The Load Anim button loads up the animation file named RobotIdle. It contains the default animation I created for the example program. In a real editor you need to dynamically specify the filename, but to keep things simple I have it hard-coded. The Save Anim button saves the animation data in the editor to the file named RobotIdle. Be very careful not to overwrite the file by accident!

The D3D_AnimationEditor Project

The D3D_AnimationEditor project is a little more complicated than those of the past but not by much. To see the files required, take a look at Figure 11.18.

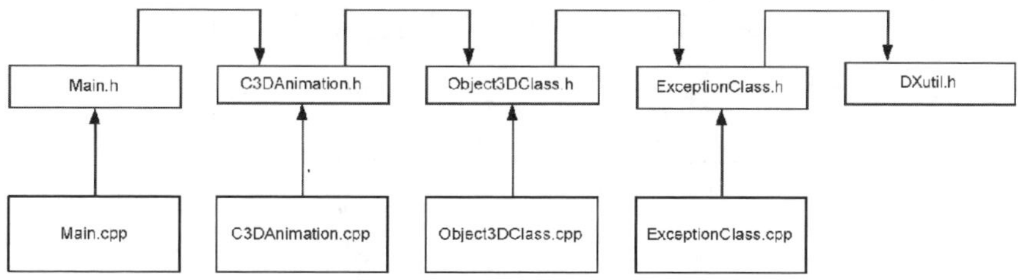

Figure 11.18: Layout of the D3D_AnimationEditor project files.

In the figure you can see how the main.cpp file includes the main.h file. The main.h file includes the C3DAnimation.h header file. The C3DAnimation.h header file contains the animation class information and the Object3DClass.h header file. The Object3Dclass.h header file includes information for loading X-File objects and rendering them. The header file also includes the ExceptionClass.h header file. The ExceptionClass.h header file contains information about the exception class and the DXUtil.h header file provided by the DirectX SDK.

As for non-header files, the editor logic is in the main.cpp file. The animation class is in C3DAnimation.cpp, the 3D object class is in Object3DClass.cpp, and the exception class is in the ExceptionClass.cpp file.

As for libraries, the project requires the following libraries to compile properly: d3d9.lib, dxguid.lib, d3dx9dt.lib, d3dxof.lib, comctl32.lib, winmm.lib, and dinput8.lib.

That's about it for the structure of the animation editor project. Without further ado, I present the animation class. Drum roll, please....

The C3DAnimationClass

For the D3D_AnimationClass program I create a class to hold all of the information required to create, edit, save, load, and play animations. This may sound very complicated, but it's not too bad once you play around with it a bit. Check out Figure 11.19 to see the class header illustrated.

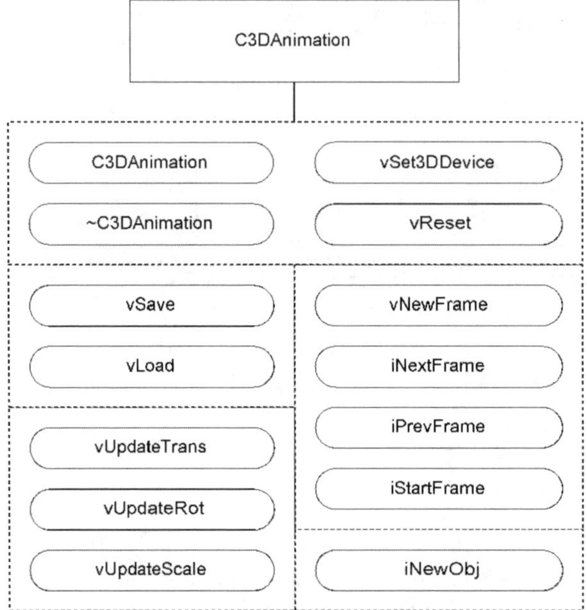

Figure 11.19: Layout of the C3DAnimation class.

The class functions in the figure are grouped together by their purpose. For example, all of the frame-related functions are in a group. Before I cover the functions, here is the code for the class header:

```
const int g_iMaxObjects = 16;
const int g_iMaxKeys = 1024;

struct stKeyFrame
{
    D3DXVECTOR3    m_vecRot;
    D3DXVECTOR3    m_vecTrans;
    D3DXVECTOR3    m_vecScale;
    long           m_lTimeDelay;
};

class C3DAnimation
{
    public:
        stKeyFrame          *m_keyFrames[g_iMaxObjects][g_iMaxKeys];
        Object3DClass       *m_objObject[g_iMaxObjects];
        char                m_szObjectName[g_iMaxObjects][32];
        int                 m_iNumFrames;
        int                 m_iNumObjects;
        char                m_szAnimName[64];
        int                 m_iCurFrame;
        long                m_lCurTime;
        LPDIRECT3DDEVICE9   m_pd3dDevice;
```

```
C3DAnimation();
~C3DAnimation();
void vNewFrame(void);
int    iNextFrame(void);
int    iPrevFrame(void);
int    iStartFrame(void);
int    iNewObj(char *szObjName);
void vUpdateTrans(int iObj, int iKey,
        D3DXVECTOR3  vecTrans);
void vUpdateRot(int iObj, int iKey,
        D3DXVECTOR3  vecRot);
void vUpdateScale(int iObj, int iKey,
        D3DXVECTOR3  vecScale);
void vSave(char *szFileName);
void vLoad(char *szFileName);
void vSet3DDevice(LPDIRECT3DDEVICE9 pd3dDevice);
void vReset(void);
};
```

C3DAnimation Member Functions

The member functions for the animation class perform a basic set of logic to get you started with animation editing. Here they are in grouped order:

The `C3DAnimation()` function is the standard constructor for the class, and it initializes the animation data members.

The `~C3DAnimation()` function is the destructor, and it handles cleanup of allocated memory when an animation object is deleted.

The `vSave()` function is called to save the animation data to a specified file.

The `vLoad()` function is called to load a specified animation file.

The `vSet3Ddevice()` function is used to set the internal Direct3D pointer.

The `vReset()` function resets all allocated memory for the animation and initializes the data. The constructor calls this at delete time.

The `vNewFrame()` function creates a new frame for every object in the animation.

The `iNextFrame()` function advances the current frame.

The `iPrevFrame()` function backs up the animation to the previous frame.

The `iStartFrame()` function rewinds the animation to the beginning frame.

The `iNewObj()` function adds a 3D object to the animation scene.

The `vUpdateTrans()` function takes in a vector and adds it to the current position vector for the specified object and frame.

The `vUpdateRot()` function takes in a vector and adds it to the current rotation vector for the specified object and frame.

The `vUpdateScale()` function takes in a vector and adds it to the current scale vector for the specified object and frame.

C3DAnimation Data Members

The member functions don't look that hard, but the data members may throw you for a loop. For one thing, the key frame data member is a multidimensional array of key frames. The size of the array is based on the number of objects in the scene times the number of frames in the scene. This is required because for each frame of the animation, you need a key frame for every object in the scene. In order to have enough key frames available, you have to create an array of the size you see in the code above. This is illustrated in Figure 11.20.

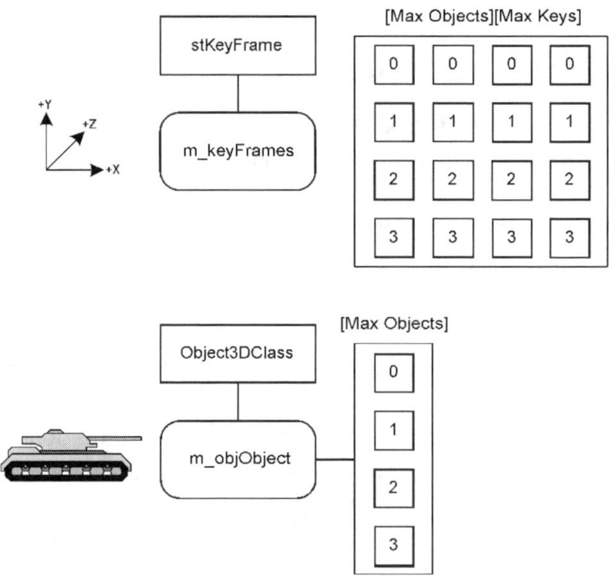

Figure 11.20: The C3DAnimation member data arrays.

Notice how the key frame array is two-dimensional. The first dimension holds frames for each object in the animation, and the second dimension holds frames for each key in the animation. The object array, on the other hand, has a single dimension. The object array holds all of the 3D objects in the animation.

There is another single-dimensional array called `m_szObjectName`. Its purpose is to hold the names of the 3D objects in the animation. This is required for the animation to know which 3D objects to load up when using the `vLoad()` function.

The m_iNumFrames data member keeps track of how many frames are present in the animation. You have to remember that for every key, there are frames for each object. For example, if you have five objects and you have 30 keys of animation, the animation stores a total of 150 frames: objects * keys = total frames.

The m_iNumObjects data member keeps track of how many objects are present in the animation. For each object, you will have an object name.

The m_szAnimName character array stores the name of the animation.

The m_iCurFrame data member keeps track of the current frame. This is used for playback of the animation and is not stored when the animation is saved.

The m_lCurTime data member keeps track of how much time is left until the animation frame advances. This allows for variable time delays between frames.

The m_pd3dDevice data member stores a pointer to the active Direct3D rendering device. This is required in order to load the .x file objects used in the animation.

The stKeyFrame Structure

At the top of the header file, you can see the stKeyFrame structure. This is a small structure I create to hold all frame information for each key of animation. Following is a list of the members and what they are used for.

The m_vecRot member contains the rotation information for the key.

The m_vecTrans member contains the translation, or position, information for the key.

The m_vecScale member contains the scale information for the key.

The m_lTimeDelay member contains the time delay information for the key.

C3DAnimationClass Member Implementation

Keep in mind that the entire purpose of the animation class is to store and play back 3D animations. This does not mean you are limited to playing cut-scenes or the like with it. The main purpose of the class is to store animations for object movement, combat, and other things during game-play. All right, back to our regularly scheduled program.

The C3DAnimation.cpp file contains the implementation of the member functions, and the first two up for bat are the constructor and destructor.

The C3DAnimation Constructor

The constructor is called whenever a new animation class object is created. Here is the code for it:

```
C3DAnimation::C3DAnimation()
{
    int i, j;
    // Set number of objects
    m_iNumObjects = 0;
    // Set number of frames
    m_iNumFrames = 0;
    // Set the starting animation state
    m_iCurFrame = 0;
    m_lCurTime = 0;
    // Initialize object, name, and key information
    for(i = 0; i < g_iMaxObjects; i++) {
        // Objects
        m_objObject[i] = NULL;
        // Names
        strcpy(&m_szObjectName[i][0], "");
        // Keys
        for(j = 0; j < g_iMaxKeys; j++) {
            m_keyFrames[i][j] = NULL;
        }
    }
}
```

In the constructor I start by zeroing out the various data member variables. This includes the number of objects, frames, current frame, and current time members. Next up you can see two loops. The outermost loop sets the object pointers to NULL, and the innermost loop sets the key frames for the objects to NULL. I do this so that later checks to initialized memory work properly. As you probably know, most compilers do not automatically zero out non-initialized data; therefore, this is a necessary step.

The C3DAnimation Destructor

The destructor is called whenever an animation class object is deleted or goes out of scope. Here is the code for it:

```
C3DAnimation::~C3DAnimation()
{
    // Clear up memory
    vReset();
}
```

I bet you thought you were getting off easy on this one, eh? Actually, all I have done is delay the inevitable. The destructor is simple since all it does is call the vReset() function. On that note, here is the reset function.

The C3DAnimation::vReset() Function

The vReset() function is called to reset the contents of the animation object. This is useful when you want to load up a new animation on top of an existing object. It is also used when the animation object is destroyed. Here is the code for it:

```cpp
void C3DAnimation::vReset(void)
{
    int i, j;

    // Release objects
    for(i = 0; i < m_iNumObjects; i++) {
        if(m_objObject[i]) {
            delete m_objObject[i];
            m_objObject[i] = NULL;
        }
    }

    // Release key frame data
    for(i = 0; i < m_iNumObjects; i++) {
        for(j = 0; j < m_iNumFrames; j++) {
            if(m_keyFrames[i][j]) {
                delete m_keyFrames[i][j];
                m_keyFrames[i][j] = NULL;
            }
        }
    }

    // Set number of objects
    m_iNumObjects = 0;
    // Set number of frames
    m_iNumFrames = 0;
    // Set the starting animation state
    m_iCurFrame = 0;
    m_lCurTime = 0;

    // Initialize object, name, and key information
    for(i = 0; i < g_iMaxObjects; i++) {
        // Objects
        m_objObject[i] = NULL;
        // Names
        strcpy(&m_szObjectName[i][0], "");
        // Keys
        for(j = 0; j < g_iMaxKeys; j++) {
            m_keyFrames[i][j] = NULL;
        }
    }
}
```

In the first part of the reset function I loop through the objects in the scene and delete the ones that exist. This does the job of clearing out all 3D object memory allocated with the new object or load functions.

Part III

The next loop in the code loops through all possible frames and deletes ones that are allocated. Frames allocated with the load and new frame functions are deleted here.

The number of objects, number of frames, current frame, and current time counters are all zeroed out next. This should be pretty self-explanatory.

The final loop in the code resets the names of the 3D objects.

The C3DAnimation::vNewFrame() Function

The vNewFrame() function is used to create a key frame for every object in the scene. If the frame created is the first one in the animation, default values are set in the keys. If it is not the first frame, the key data is copied from the prior frame. This makes it easy to animate, since you don't have to reposition, scale, and rotate objects every time you create a new frame. Here is the code for the function:

```
void C3DAnimation::vNewFrame(void)
{
   int     iFrame = 0;
   stKeyFrame    *ptrFrame;
   stKeyFrame    *ptrPrevFrame;

   // Increment the number of frames in the anim
   m_iNumFrames++;
   // Get the key frame index
   iFrame = m_iNumFrames-1;
   // Create a new frame for each object
   // in the animation.
   for(int iObj = 0; iObj < m_iNumObjects; iObj++) {
      // Allocate memory for the frame
      m_keyFrames[iObj][iFrame] = new stKeyFrame;
      // Get a pointer to the new frame
      ptrFrame = m_keyFrames[iObj][iFrame];
      // Give first frame "default" values
      if(iFrame == 0) {
         ptrFrame->m_vecScale = D3DXVECTOR3(1.0, 1.0, 1.0);
         ptrFrame->m_vecRot = D3DXVECTOR3(0.0, 0.0f, 0.0);
         ptrFrame->m_vecTrans = D3DXVECTOR3(0.0, 0.0, 0.0);
         ptrFrame->m_lTimeDelay = 10;
      }
      // Not the first frame, so set its values to the previous frame.
      else {
         // Get pointer to the previous frame
         ptrPrevFrame = m_keyFrames[iObj][(iFrame-1)];

         // Set new frame values to prev frame values
         ptrFrame->m_vecScale = ptrPrevFrame->m_vecScale;
         ptrFrame->m_vecRot = ptrPrevFrame->m_vecRot;
         ptrFrame->m_vecTrans = ptrPrevFrame->m_vecTrans;
         ptrFrame->m_lTimeDelay = ptrPrevFrame->m_lTimeDelay;
      }
```

```
   }
   m_iCurFrame = iFrame;
}
```

The first part of the code increments the number-of-frames counter for the object. This is done so that the animation knows how many frames to run through.

Next I set up a temporary variable to hold the number of frames minus one. This makes the `iFrame` variable equal to the frame that is about to be created.

The loop in the function cycles through every object in the scene and allocates memory for a new frame for each of the objects. The allocated frame is then set up with values for scale, rotation, translation, and time. As I said previously, the values set depends on whether it is the first frame in the animation.

Lastly, I set the current frame to equal the `iFrame` temporary variable. This makes the animation jump to the newly created frame in the editor.

The C3DAnimation::iNextFrame() Function

The next frame function is rather simple, since all it has to do is advance the current frame counter. If there are no more frames to advance to, the frame counter is looped back around to the beginning. Here is the code for the function:

```
int C3DAnimation::iNextFrame(void)
{
   // Go to next frame
   m_iCurFrame++;
   // If frame past the end, loop to beginning
   if(m_iCurFrame >= m_iNumFrames) {
      m_iCurFrame = 0;
   }
   // Return the frame #
   return(m_iCurFrame);
}
```

In the code you can see how I increment the current frame counter and then check to see if it exceeds the number of frames present. If it does exceed the total frames, it loops back around to frame 0.

The C3DAnimation::iPrevFrame() Function

The previous frame function works like the next frame function but in reverse. The code decrements the current frame and checks to see if the current frame is equal to –1. If it is equal to –1, the code loops to the end of the animation. Here is the code for it:

```
int C3DAnimation::iPrevFrame(void)
{
    // Go to previous frame
    m_iCurFrame--;
    // If less than frame zero, go to the last frame.
    // If there is no last frame, go to zero.
    if(m_iCurFrame < 0) {
        // Check if there are frames
        if(m_iNumFrames) {
            // Go to the last one
            m_iCurFrame = m_iNumFrames-1;
        }
        // No frames
        else {
            // Go to zero frame
            m_iCurFrame = 0;
        }
    }
    // Return the frame #
    return(m_iCurFrame);
}
```

In the code you can see where I decrement the current frame variable to
move the animation in reverse. I then check to see if the frame is less
than 0. If it is, I then check to see if there are frames in the animation. If
there are frames in the animation, I set the current frame to equal the
end frame. If there are no frames, I set the current frame to 0. The last
thing the code does is return the current frame. You can see a visual of
the process in Figure 11.21.

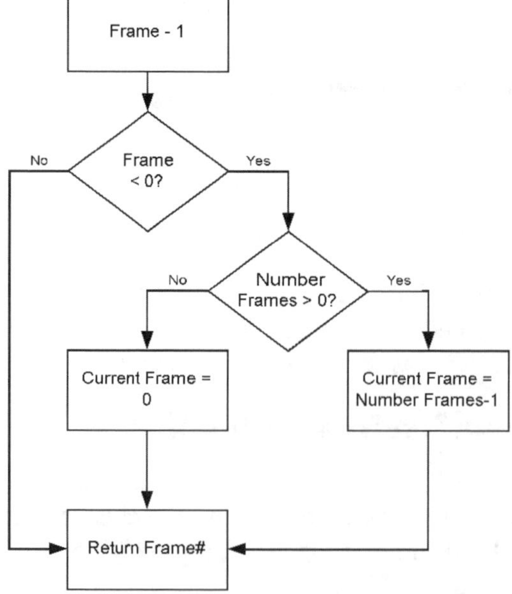

Figure 11.21: Flowchart of the previous frame function.

The C3DAnimation::iStartFrame() Function

The start frame function simply rewinds the animation to the first frame. Here is the code for it:

```
int C3DAnimation::iStartFrame(void)
{
    // Go to the first frame
    m_iCurFrame = 0;
    // Return the frame #
    return(m_iCurFrame);
}
```

I'll defer the explanation to the self-documenting code. Don't you just love that?

The C3DAnimation::iNewObj() Function

The new object function takes in the name of an .x file and loads it into the next available object slot. Here is the code that accomplishes this:

```
int C3DAnimation::iNewObj(char *szObjName)
{
    char szFileName[512];
    // Create the filename
    sprintf(szFileName, "Data\\3DObjects\\%s.x", szObjName);
    // Set object pointer
    m_objObject[m_iNumObjects] = new Object3DClass;
    m_objObject[m_iNumObjects]->hLoad(szFileName, m_pd3dDevice);
    // Store the name for later
    strcpy(&m_szObjectName[m_iNumObjects][0], szObjName);
    // Increment internal count
    m_iNumObjects++;
    // Return # of objects
    return(m_iNumObjects);
}
```

The first part of the function creates the fully qualified filename for the file. This includes the path and filename.

The next part of code creates a new `Object3DClass` object to hold the .x file model data. The newly created object then loads the .x file data using its `hLoad()` function.

Once the object data is loaded, the code sets the name of the object for future reference. The number of objects is then incremented before returning it to the caller.

Note The Object3DClass class is one that I have created to ease the use of .x file models.

Keep in mind that the new object function adds a new object to the entire animation and not just one key frame.

The C3DAnimation::vUpdateTrans() Function

The update translation function takes in a translation vector, frame number, and object number and adds the translation values to the translation vector for the specified frame and object. This is useful for changing the translation of the object. Here is the code for it:

```
void C3DAnimation::vUpdateTrans(
    int iObj, int iKey,
    D3DXVECTOR3 vecTrans)
{
    // Check if object and key are valid
    if(iObj < m_iNumObjects && iObj >= 0
        && iKey < m_iNumFrames && iKey >= 0) {
        // Update the vector
        m_keyFrames[iObj][iKey]->m_vecTrans += vecTrans;
    }
}
```

The code starts by making sure the specified object and key are valid. If they are, the vector information is updated with the passed-in values.

The C3DAnimation::vUpdateRot() Function

The update rotation function takes in a rotation vector, frame number, and object number and adds the rotation values to the rotation vector for the specified frame and object. This is useful for changing the rotation of the object. Here is the code for it:

```
void C3DAnimation::vUpdateRot(int iObj, int iKey, D3DXVECTOR3 vecRot)
{
    // Check if object and key are valid
    if(iObj < m_iNumObjects && iObj >= 0
        && iKey < m_iNumFrames && iKey >= 0) {
        // Update the vector
        m_keyFrames[iObj][iKey]->m_vecRot += vecRot;
    }
}
```

The code starts by making sure the specified object and key are valid. If they are, the vector information is updated with the passed-in values.

The C3DAnimation::vUpdateScale() Function

The update scale function takes in a scale vector, frame number, and object number and adds the scale values to the scale vector for the specified frame and object. This is useful for changing the scale of the object. Here is the code for it:

```
void C3DAnimation::vUpdateScale(
    int iObj, int iKey,
    D3DXVECTOR3 vecScale)
{
    // Check if object and key are valid
    if(iObj < m_iNumObjects && iObj >= 0
        && iKey < m_iNumFrames && iKey >= 0) {
        // Update the vector
        m_keyFrames[iObj][iKey]->m_vecScale += vecScale;
    }
}
```

The code starts by making sure the specified object and key are valid. If
they are, the vector information is updated with the passed-in values.

The C3DAnimation::vSave() Function

Oh boy, talk about a big function. You might even call it the daisy cutter of
functions. Maybe that's a bad analogy: You don't want functions that blow
up, do you?

The save function takes in a filename and saves all information
required to store the animation data in the class. The data includes the
header, object references, and key frame information. Here is the code
for it:

```
void C3DAnimation::vSave(char *szFileName)
{
    FILE    *fp;
    int     i, j;
    char    szFullFileName[512];

    // Create qualified filename
    sprintf(szFullFileName, "Data\\Anims\\%s.anim", szFileName);
    // Open the file for output
    fp = fopen(szFullFileName, "wb");
    if(fp == NULL) {
        return;
    }
    // Output the header
    // Number of objects
    fwrite(&m_iNumObjects, 1, sizeof(int), fp);
    // Number of frames
    fwrite(&m_iNumFrames, 1, sizeof(int), fp);
    // Output object names
    for(i = 0; i < m_iNumObjects; i++) {
        fwrite(&m_szObjectName[i][0], 32,
            sizeof(char), fp);
    }
    // Output key frame information
    for(i = 0; i < m_iNumObjects; i++) {
        for(j = 0; j < m_iNumFrames; j++) {
            // Delay
            fwrite(&m_keyFrames[i][j]->m_lTimeDelay,
```

```
            1, sizeof(long), fp);
        // Rotation
        fwrite(&m_keyFrames[i][j]->m_vecRot,
            1, sizeof(D3DXVECTOR3), fp);
        // Scale
        fwrite(&m_keyFrames[i][j]->m_vecScale,
            1, sizeof(D3DXVECTOR3), fp);
        // Translation
        fwrite(&m_keyFrames[i][j]->m_vecTrans,
            1, sizeof(D3DXVECTOR3), fp);
    }
}
// Close the animation file
fclose(fp);
// Store animation name
strcpy(m_szAnimName, szFileName);
}
```

The first thing the code does is create the fully qualified filename and open the file for writing. Next up you have the header information being output for the animation file. The header contains the number of objects and the number of frames present. This header information is necessary so that you know how much data to read in at load time. Figure 11.22 shows the file layout in detail.

In Figure 11.22 you can see how the animation file format contains header information followed by object name information and frame information.

Once the header is output, I loop through the names of the 3D objects and write them out to the file. I do this so that at load time I can dynamically load the 3D objects embedded in the animation.

Next is the frame information. The code loops through the frames in the animation and outputs the delay, rotation, scale, and translation values for each object in the frame. This continues until all frames have been output.

The last thing I do is close the file and set the animation name. Since the name of the animation is the filename, I do not need to save it in the animation file itself.

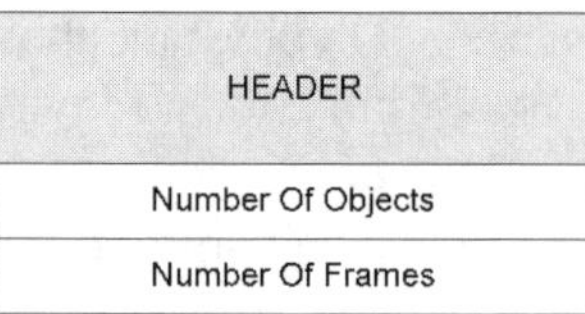

Figure 11.22: Layout of the animation file format.

The C3DAnimation::vLoad() Function

The load function reads in data previously saved with the save function. Sounds simple enough, right? Here is the code for it:

```
void C3DAnimation::vLoad(char *szFileName)
{
   FILE   *fp;
   int i, j;
   int iNumObjs;
   int iNumFrames;
   char   szFullFileName[512];

   // Create qualified filename
   sprintf(szFullFileName, "Data\\Anims\\%s.anim", szFileName);
   // Open the file for input
   fp = fopen(szFullFileName, "rb");
   if(fp == NULL) {
      return;
   }
   // Reset the object in case it's in use
   vReset();
   // Read the header
   // Number of objects
   fread(&iNumObjs, 1, sizeof(int), fp);
   // Number of frames
   fread(&iNumFrames, 1, sizeof(int), fp);
   // Load object information
   for(i = 0; i < iNumObjs; i++) {
      // Read object name
      fread(&m_szObjectName[i][0], 32, sizeof(char), fp);
      // Load the objects
      iNewObj(&m_szObjectName[i][0]);
   }
   // Allocate frame memory
   for(i = 0; i < iNumFrames; i++) {
      vNewFrame();
   }
   // Read key frame information
   for(i = 0; i < m_iNumObjects; i++) {
      for(j = 0; j < m_iNumFrames; j++) {
         // Delay
         fread(&m_keyFrames[i][j]->m_lTimeDelay,
            1, sizeof(long), fp);
         // Rotation
         fread(&m_keyFrames[i][j]->m_vecRot,
            1, sizeof(D3DXVECTOR3), fp);
         // Scale
         fread(&m_keyFrames[i][j]->m_vecScale,
            1, sizeof(D3DXVECTOR3), fp);
         // Translation
         fread(&m_keyFrames[i][j]->m_vecTrans,
            1, sizeof(D3DXVECTOR3), fp);
      }
   }
```

```
// Close the animation file
fclose(fp);
// Store animation name
strcpy(m_szAnimName, szFileName);
}
```

Figure 11.23 shows the flow of the load function.

In the figure and in the code you can see how the function reads in the animation data. The first part of the code creates the fully qualified filename and then opens it. Next the code resets the animation in case it already contains data, and then it loads up the header data.

Once the header data is loaded, the function loops through and reads in the 3D object names stored in the header. As each one is read in, the code loads the 3D object model data. This continues until all objects are loaded.

Once the 3D model data is loaded, the function creates frame memory for each frame noted in the header. This is required to create the space for the later frames. Once the memory is allocated, the frame data itself is read into the frame memory.

The last thing the code does is close the file and store the animation name in the animation class data. Ta da!

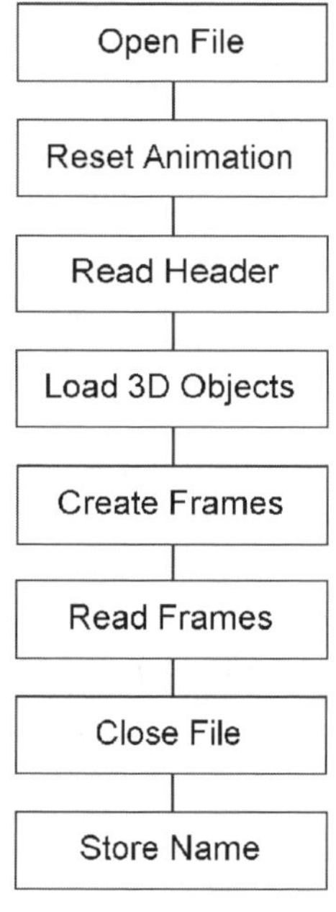

Figure 11.23: Flow of the load function.

The C3DAnimation::vSet3DDevice() Function

The set 3D device function is used to set the internal Direct3D device pointer. This pointer is required to load the 3D X-Files. Here is the code for it:

```
void C3DAnimation::vSet3DDevice(LPDIRECT3DDEVICE9 pd3dDevice)
{
    m_pd3dDevice = pd3dDevice;
}
```

The D3D_AnimationEditor Program

So far I have shown you the project layout and the inner workings of the animation class that makes up the animation editor. In this section I cover the logic behind the editor itself. Load up the main.cpp file now so you can follow along. You should also execute the program if you want to see what I talk about.

The process flow for the animation editor is very similar to what I have shown you throughout the book. Check out Figure 11.24 to see the flow for the program.

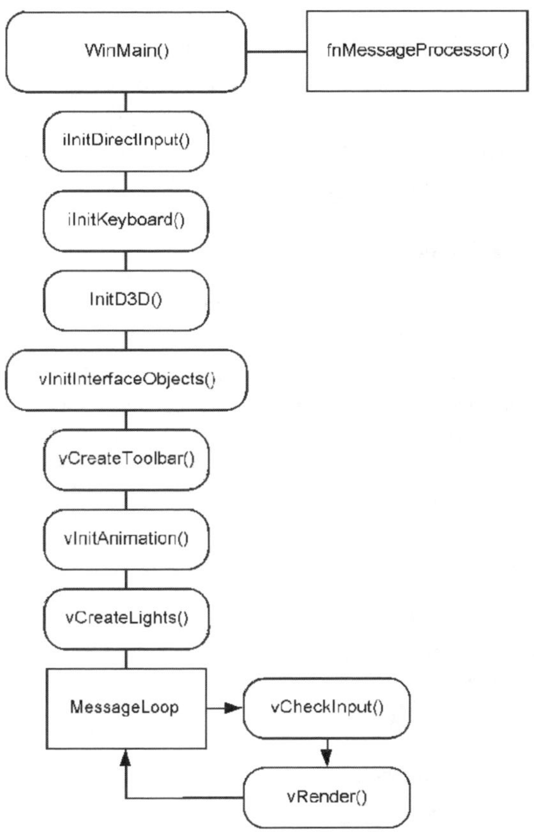

Figure 11.24: Flow of the D3D_AnimationEditor program.

In Figure 11.24 you can see how the main Windows function initializes DirectInput, the keyboard, Direct3D, the interface, the toolbar, the animation data, and the lights. Once everything is initialized, the message loop checks user input and renders the 3D scene until the program is terminated. There is nothing really new here except for the animation initialization function.

The vInitAnimation() Function

The animation initialization function does nothing more than set the internal Direct3D device pointer to the one initialized in the `InitD3D()` function call. Here is the code for the animation routine:

```
void vInitAnimation(void)
{
    // Set the 3D device
    animTest.vSet3DDevice(g_pd3dDevice);
}
```

In the function I make a call to the global animation class object. The `vSet3DDevice()` function is called to set its internal device pointer. I do this because the animation class object needs a Direct3D device pointer so that it can load 3D objects for its scene data. You only have to call the function once, so this is a good place to do it.

The vLoadObject() Function

Before you can do any animation editing, you need an animation scene. As I discussed earlier, a scene consists of 3D objects; therefore, you need to load up some objects to edit. This is where the `vLoadObject()` function comes into play. It loads up a couple of objects to the scene. When you press the Load Objects button on the toolbar, the following code is executed:

```
void vLoadObject(void)
{
    // Reset the current animation
    animTest.vReset();
    // Load the hard-coded objects
    animTest.iNewObj("droid_still");
    animTest.iNewObj("radar_dish");
    // Render the scene
    vRender();
    // Update the toolbar
    vUpdateToolbarStats();
}
```

The first thing I do in the load object function is reset the animation class object. This erases anything done so far for the animation and resets the scene back to square one.

Warning   Do not select the Load Objects button if you have unsaved animation data. It will be erased!

The next chunk of code calls the new object member function of the animation class and loads up two X-File objects named droid_still and radar_dish. The droid_still object is a mechanized robot, and the radar_dish object is a little radar dish.

The next block of code calls the render function to update the scene with the newly refreshed animation class object. Since I reset the animation data at the beginning of the function, the rendered scene will be blank except for the floor on which the objects sit. Keep in mind that the load object function only adds objects to the scene; it does not create key frames. This is why you don't see the objects immediately. You have to add keys first.

The last thing I do is call the `vUpdateToolbarStats()` function. This function outputs the current frame rotation and translation values to the toolbar window.

Create Some Frames

Now that you have 3D objects in the scene, you need some frame data. Select the New Frame button, and the following code in the message handler is executed:

```
case ID_BUTTON_NEWFRAME:
    // Create a new frame for the animation
    animTest.vNewFrame();
    SetActiveWindow(g_hWnd);
    // Update the toolbar information
    vUpdateToolbarStats();
    break;
```

As you can see in the code, the New Frame button calls a few functions in the animation class object. The call to the `vNewFrame()` member class function creates a new frame for every object in the scene. Since you have two objects loaded, it creates two frames.

The next part of the code sets the active window to the editor window. I do this so that you don't have to click back in the editor window to activate it after creating a new frame.

The last thing I do is call the update toolbar stats function. The cool part is now you should see the scene objects rendered on the screen. Since you have frame data, there is finally something to render!

Select the Proper Object

You have frame and object data, so what now? Well, how about some editing! Select the Next Obj button until the radar dish object is solid and not wireframe. When you select the Next Obj button, the following code in the message handler is executed:

```
case ID_BUTTON_NEXTOBJ:
    // Increment the object count
    g_iCurObj++;
    // If past the end, loop back to the beginning
    if(g_iCurObj >= animTest.m_iNumObjects) {
        g_iCurObj = 0;
    }
    SetActiveWindow(g_hWnd);
    vUpdateToolbarStats();
    break;
```

In the next object code I start by incrementing the global variable for the current object. I then check to see if the object counter has exceeded the number of objects in the scene. If it has, I loop back around to the beginning. The previous object code works a lot like this function, except it decrements the global variable instead of incrementing it.

Move the Object into Position

Now that the radar dish is selected, you need to move it. You may have noticed this already, but the dish is on the ground and it belongs on the robot's head! This is easy to fix though, all you need to do is enter a value in the proper translation edit box. In this case it happens to be the middle edit box on the left side of the toolbar. Enter the value of 20.0 to see the radar dish move into position on the robot's head. Voilà! Isn't that cool? As long as everything worked out okay, you should see the dish in its proper place. The code that handles the movement is as follows:

```
case ID_EDITBOX_Y:
    memset(szBuffer, 0x00, 32);
    GetWindowText(hEDITBOX_Y, szBuffer, 32);
    if(animTest.m_iNumFrames > 0) {
        animTest.m_keyFrames
        [g_iCurObj][animTest.m_iCurFrame]->m_vecTrans.y
        = (float)atof(szBuffer);
    }
    break;
```

In the code I extract the value from the edit box and convert it to a floating-point number. I then set the translation y-value for the current object and frame selected in the editor to the new value. Basically, all I have done is take the position value from the edit box and apply it to the radar dish. Cool, eh?

You can play around with moving the robot as well. To accomplish this, cycle through the objects until the robot is selected. Once selected, change its translation values around until it sits where you want it.

In the code around the segment above, you can see other code that is much like it. This is because I also have the same code for every translation axis as well as every rotation axis. It all works in the same manner. The only difference lies in the vector that is modified.

Add More Key Frames

The animation probably isn't very exciting to you yet. Now that the radar dish is in place, add a few new key frames to the animation. If you select the New Frame button three times, you will end up with a total of four frames in the animation. The debug data in the render window should reflect the change.

Remember that for every object in the scene you have a key frame; therefore, if you selected the New Frame button three more times, you have a total of eight key frames.

There you are, with a bunch of key frames and nowhere to go. Select the radar dish if it isn't selected already and then cycle through the current key frame until you get to frame 2. The following code is executed when you select the Next Frame button:

```
case ID_BUTTON_NEXTFRAME:
    animTest.iNextFrame();
    SetActiveWindow(g_hWnd);
    vUpdateToolbarStats();
    break;
```

Don't you just love simple code? In this code I merely make a call to the animation class object's next frame function and leave it at that. It handles the frame advance, and I don't have to worry about it in the editor.

Now that you have the second frame selected, change the rotation of the radar dish so that it pivots a bit to the left. Once that is done, go to the third frame and move it a few more degrees. Continue the process until you are back to frame number 1. Once there, select the Start/Stop Anim button to play the little animation that you have just created. The following code is executed:

```
case ID_BUTTON_STARTSTOP:
    // If it is active, stop it
    if(g_iAnimActive) {
        g_iAnimActive = 0;
    }
    // It is not active, start it
    else {
        g_iAnimActive = 1;
    }
    SetActiveWindow(g_hWnd);
    vUpdateToolbarStats();
    break;
```

In the playback code I toggle the `g_iAnimActive` variable to be on or off, depending on its start state. This tells the rendering system what to do with the animation class at render time. When it is active, the render function advances the animation per render cycle. If it is not active, the render function just renders the objects and does not alter the animation cycle.

The vRender() Function

So far you have edited the animation and played it back, but I haven't shown you how to render the objects contained in the animation scene.

The following code segment shows you the bulk of the render function required to render the scene:

```cpp
// Clear the back buffer to a blue color
g_pd3dDevice->Clear(0, NULL, D3DCLEAR_TARGET|D3DCLEAR_ZBUFFER,
          D3DCOLOR_RGBA(200, 250, 255, 255), 1.0f, 0);
// Begin the scene
g_pd3dDevice->BeginScene();
// Set default material
g_pd3dDevice->SetMaterial(&g_mtrlDefault);
// Set fill state to solid
g_pd3dDevice->SetRenderState(D3DRS_FILLMODE, D3DFILL_SOLID);
// Render the ground object
vDraw3DObject(D3DXVECTOR3(0.0, 0.0, 0.0) ,
        D3DXVECTOR3(200.0, 200.0, 200.0),
        D3DXVECTOR3(90.0, 0.0, 0.0),
        0);
// Render the 3D object(s)
if(animTest.m_iNumFrames && animTest.m_iNumObjects) {
    for(int i = 0; i < animTest.m_iNumObjects; i++) {
        // Not current, render in wireframe
        if(i != g_iCurObj) {
            g_pd3dDevice->SetRenderState(D3DRS_FILLMODE,
                      D3DFILL_WIREFRAME);
        }
        // Current, render as solid
        else {
            g_pd3dDevice->SetRenderState(D3DRS_FILLMODE,
                      D3DFILL_SOLID);
        }
        // Set current frame
        iCFrame = animTest.m_iCurFrame;
        // Render the object using the frame information
        // stored in the animation object.
        animTest.m_objObject[i]->vDisplayXYZ(
        animTest.m_keyFrames[i][iCFrame]->m_vecTrans.x,
        animTest.m_keyFrames[i][iCFrame]->m_vecTrans.y,
        animTest.m_keyFrames[i][iCFrame]->m_vecTrans.z,
        animTest.m_keyFrames[i][iCFrame]->m_vecRot.x,
        animTest.m_keyFrames[i][iCFrame]->m_vecRot.y,
        animTest.m_keyFrames[i][iCFrame]->m_vecRot.z,
        animTest.m_keyFrames[i][iCFrame]->m_vecScale.x,
        animTest.m_keyFrames[i][iCFrame]->m_vecScale.y,
        animTest.m_keyFrames[i][iCFrame]->m_vecScale.z);
        // Animate the object
        if(g_iAnimActive) {
            animTest.m_lCurTime++;
            // Advance to next frame
            if(animTest.m_lCurTime >= animTest.m_keyFrames[i]
                  [animTest.m_iCurFrame]->m_lTimeDelay) {
                animTest.m_iCurFrame++;
                bFrameChanged = 1;
                animTest.m_lCurTime = 0;
                // Reset frame to zero
                if(animTest.m_iCurFrame >=
```

```
                    animTest.m_iNumFrames) {
                        animTest.m_iCurFrame = 0;
                    }
                }
            }
        }
    }
```

I know the code may look complicated around the object rendering parts, but it's really not that bad. To start with, I make a call to my `vDraw3D-object()` function in order to draw the ground plane. If you haven't noticed yet, I draw a ground plane in the scene to help with object placement. It is a big gray grid along the y-axis.

The real animation code comes next. I first make a check to see if there is object and frame data present. If the scene does not have any frames or objects, I skip out and don't bother to render anything. This is a very important check to make; otherwise, your code will crash.

Since the animation scene can have multiple objects, I create a loop to cycle through each object in the scene. The loop's logic can be seen in Figure 11.25.

If the object in the loop is the current selected object, I render it in solid mode; otherwise, I render it in wireframe mode. The actual rendering is done with a call to the `vDisplay-XYZ()` function. It takes in the translation, rotation, and scale of the object and renders it accordingly. To

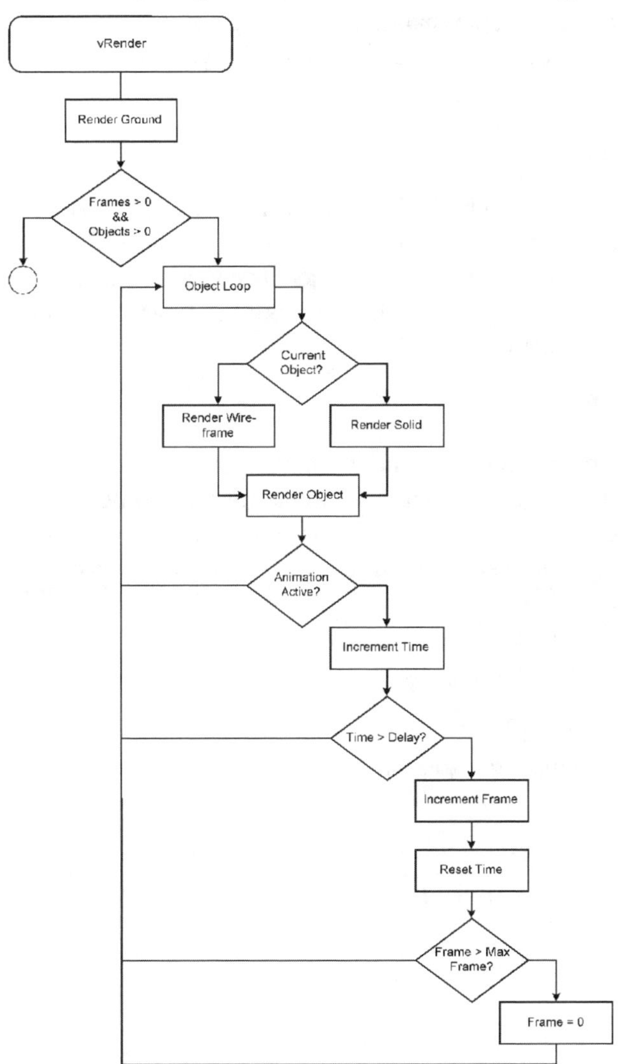

Figure 11.25: Render logic.

set the translation, rotation, and scale properly, I pass in the corresponding vector values for the object and its frame in the loop.

The second part of the rendering loop animates the object if the global animation flag is set. If it is set, the code increments the time state variable in the animation class object. The code then checks to see if the time state exceeds the time threshold set in the frame. If it has, the frame is advanced and the time state is reset. If the frame exceeds the total number of frames, the frame loops back to the beginning and is set to 0.

The reset of the render function handles the debug output you see in the edit window. There isn't much new to it, so I will let you examine it on your own.

Keyboard Controls

In the `vCheckInput()` function, I check the keyboard for keys to move the camera or currently selected object around the scene. The camera is controlled with the cursor keys, and the current object is controlled with alpha keys on the left side of the keyboard. Check out the function to see which keys perform which actions.

Things for You to Do

In the program I have several code comments that suggest features for you to add. Check out the suggestions and try implementing some of them. The main reason I don't write the code for you is so that you can learn how the editor works and start down the road of making your own for your strategy games. Along with the code comments, I suggest you try the following improvements:

- Add controls to edit the frame delay
- Add the ability to create frames on a per-object basis
- Create a 3D resource manager to store models
- Add mouse-look type camera controls
- Add an animation set manager
- Add multiple views to the edit window

Implementing Animations

Implementing animations in your games should be easy once you have an animation editor up and running. Once you have the editor and created some animation sets, you should be well on your way to loading the sets in your game and playing them back at will.

I don't want to leave you hanging, so I have created a special project on the companion files called D3D_AnimationPlayback. It is a stripped-down program that loads the robot idle animation and plays it back in an endless loop. The cool thing about the program is that I have cut out everything that is not absolutely necessary. This should give you a chance to study the animation system without all of the clutter associated with the editor. You can see the output from the program in Figure 11.26.

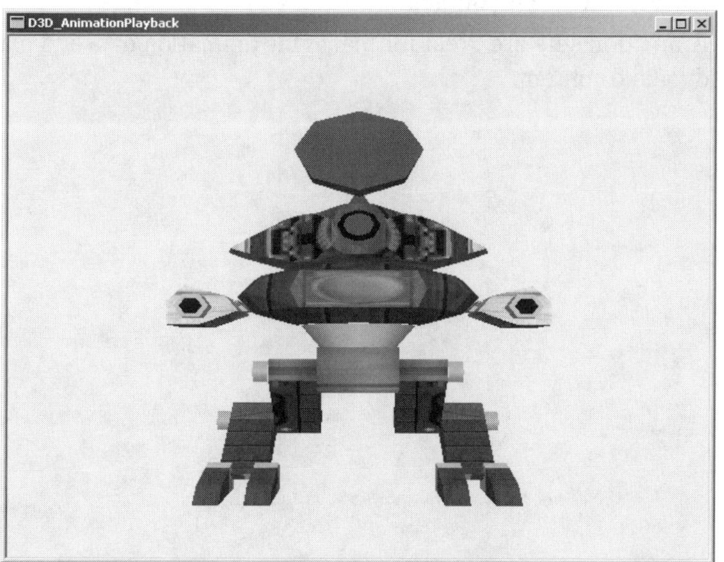

Figure 11.26: Output from the D3D_AnimationPlayback program.

Load up the project now, compile it, and watch it in action.

Recap

In this chapter I have at least scratched the surface of the ever-complicated world of animation editing and playback. Before you go, please consider the following key points:

- Commercial animation packages contain thousands of features and are well worth the cost.

- Commercial animation packages are hard to modify if at all.

- Self-made animation editors take a long time to develop and are very difficult to write.

- Self-made animation editors give you the flexibility to control your own destiny, and you can ensure compatibility with your programs since you write it yourself.

- Animation sets are great for managing animation data and playing dynamic content.

Part IV

Advanced Topics

Chapter 12

Path-finding

Have you ever thought about what it takes to get from point A to point B? Have you ever woken up at 6 A.M. with a massive headache and wondered how you got to point C? This seemingly simple problem requires a complicated solution. Although there are several ways to skin the proverbial cat, they are not all created equal. Some methods consume too much processing power, while others take too much time. The key is to strike a nice balance between speed and processor utilization. In this chapter I cover the following to help you make an educated decision on which methods to use:

- Path problems
- Simple path solution
- A-Star path solution
- Code implementation

Path Problems

To begin with, take a look at Figure 12.1 to see a common path problem.

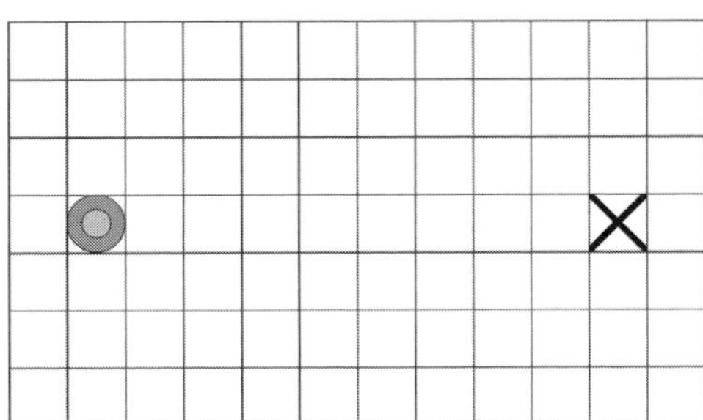

Figure 12.1: Common path problem.

Figure 12.1 shows a start point and an end point on a map. The start is represented by the set of concentric circles, and the end point is represented by the bold letter X. In order to get from the start to the finish, you must figure out where you are on the map and make an educated decision on where to move. Since games make it easy to know where you are (x, y, and z coordinates), the only problem you face is figuring out where to move.

Simple Path Solution

The easiest solution to the problem in Figure 12.1 is the following pseudocode:

```
If left of goal, move right
If right of goal, move left
If above goal, move down
If below goal, move up
```

If you follow this pseudocode, the first step taken on the example map results in Figure 12.2.

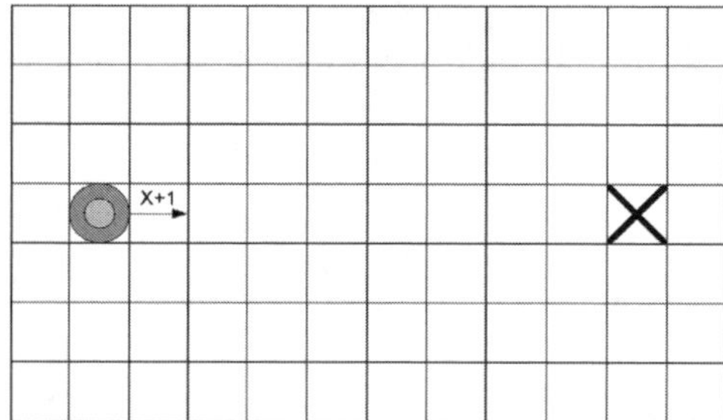

Figure 12.2: Simple path-finding at work.

In Figure 12.2 you checked the position of the player, noticed that it was left of the goal, and moved to the right one square. This process repeats until you reach the goal, as shown in Figure 12.3.

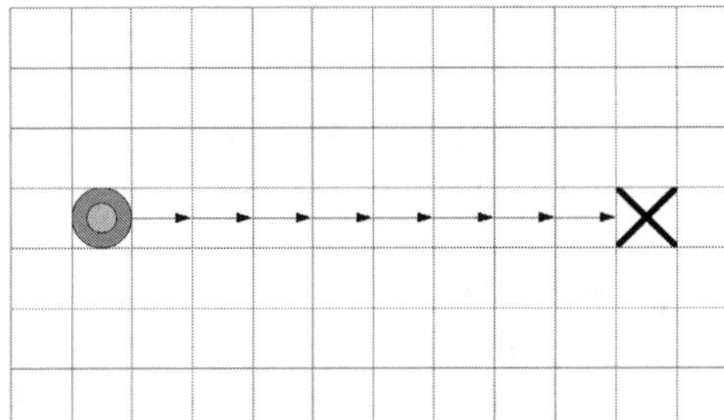

Figure 12.3: Common path solution.

In Figure 12.3 you can see how the pseudocode is followed to reach the goal. Each time the code is checked, the player is to the left of the goal. This causes the program to move the player right one square until the goal is reached. This is a great solution, but what happens on a map that looks like the one in Figure 12.4?

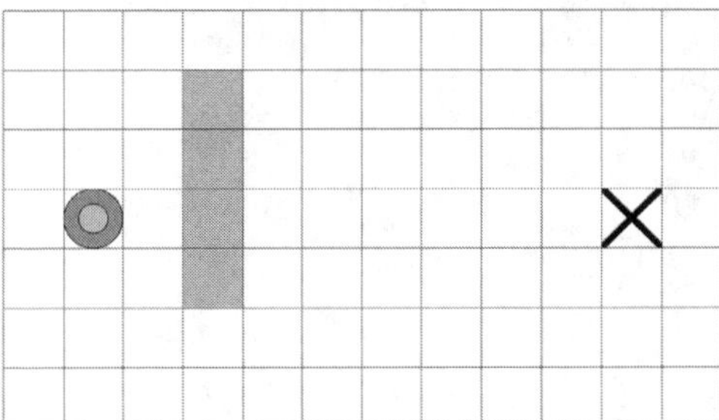

Figure 12.4: Complicated path.

The path in Figure 12.4 is slightly more complicated. It has a nice little barrier between the start and end squares. How well will the simple code fare against this problem? Not well at all. The simple code solution starts off great but fails miserably once it hits the wall. You can do a few things to get around this problem, such as the following:

```
While not at goal
    If left of goal, move right
    If right of goal, move left
    If above goal, move down
    If below goal, move up
    If blocked, randomly move
Loop
```

The pseudocode above adds a random element to the move algorithm by randomly moving the player when a blockade is found. This may solve the path over time, but don't hold your breath!

The A-Star Method

There are many methods of solving paths available to you, but my personal favorite is a method called A-Star or A*. A* is a great path-finding algorithm since it can work around obstacles and even find the best path based on varying terrain. This means that not only does the method find a path from point A to B, but it also finds the best path from A to B.

To make life simpler for you, I have written a program that demonstrates the A* algorithm in action. Load up the D3D_PathFinding project now and launch it to see A* in action. If all goes well, you should see something similar to Figure 12.5.

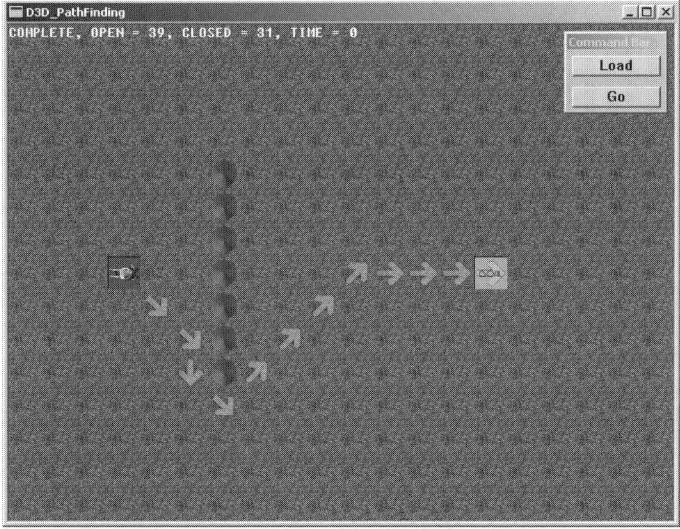

Figure 12.5: Output from the D3D_PathFinding program.

Launch the program and select the Go button on the command bar. The Go button activates the path algorithm. As you can see in Figure 12.5, the program calculates the path from the start to the end positions and renders arrows that display the solution. You can even load up various paths from the companion files and run the algorithm through it to see the effect. The coolest part about A* is that it can always find the best path given enough time and resources.

How does the D3D_PathFinding example work? Don't worry; I'm not going to jump straight into source code this time. Instead, here is a little background on how A* works.

A* Fundamentals

There are a few terms used in the A* method. They are as follows:

- Node – A position on the map
- Open List – A list of nodes that the player can move to and are adjacent to closed nodes
- Closed List – A list of nodes that the player can move to and have already been processed

To see the terms in use, check out Figure 12.6.

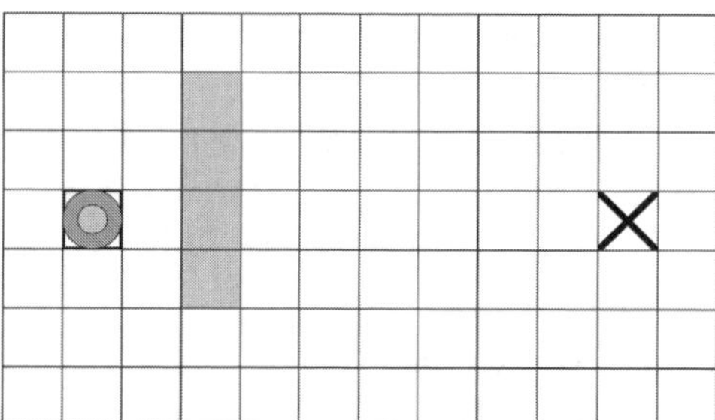

Figure 12.6: A terminology illustrated.*

In Figure 12.6 you can see nodes that comprise the map. Each square on the map is actually a node. I know the term "node" sounds strange, but it is more generic than "square." This is done on purpose since the A* algorithm can be used for non-square maps.

On the map you have the start and end positions as well. The start position actually has a thick border around it. This tells you that the node is on the closed list. Since you know the start position is part of the path solution, it automatically goes onto the closed list of processed nodes.

The nodes adjacent to the one on the closed list can be put onto the open list. After this is done, you end up with one node on the closed list and eight on the open list. This is illustrated in Figure 12.7.

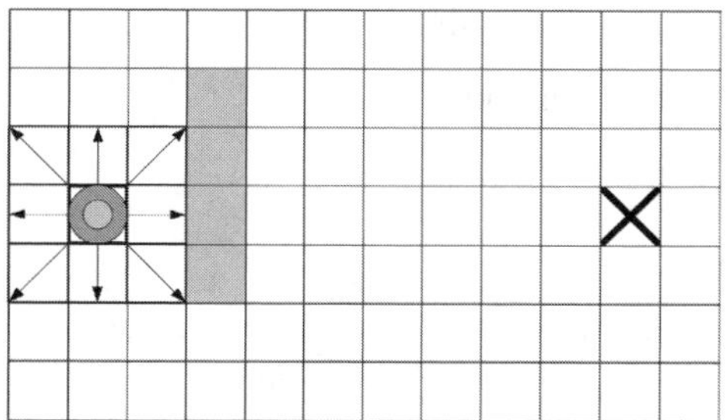

Figure 12.7: Nodes added to the open list.

In Figure 12.7 you have eight nodes on the open list and one on the closed list. The open list nodes are easy to see because of the arrows in them. The arrows represent the direction moved from the closed node that they belong to. The closed node in this case is called the parent node for each of the open nodes.

Start Searching

You now know the fundamental terminology of A*, but what about how to use it? The first thing you do in A* is add the starting node to the closed list. This is done since the start node is always the first step of the final path. Once that is out of the way, you need to find every node that is adjacent to the start and can be moved onto by the player. If an adjacent node is passable, you add it to the list of open nodes. Since there are no open nodes to begin with, the open list is empty before the first set of nodes is added.

Here are the search steps:

1. Put the start node on the closed list.
2. Put passable nodes adjacent to the start node onto the open list.

In Figure 12.7 I have completed these two steps, and now the example has one node on the closed list and eight nodes on the open list. Now what?

Calculating Node Cost

Nodes are not created equal in the world of A*. Some nodes are better than others for the end path. The way to figure out which node is the best node is to assign costs to each node on the open and closed lists. Once you have cost assigned, it is easy to sort the nodes and figure out which ones are the cheapest. In order to calculate cost for A* nodes, you need the following:

■ The base cost of the node

■ The cost to return to the start node

■ The cost to make it to the goal node

Base Cost

The base cost of a node is the cost of the node in terms of movement. For general purposes, you can give every passable node on the map the same cost. If you want to get more complicated, you can give nodes different costs based on the terrain type. Take, for instance, the following nodes and their costs:

Table 12.1: Node base cost

Type	Cost
Grass	1
Dirt	2
Sand	3
Rock	4
Swamp	5

Table 12.1 lists five node types and their base cost. By assigning varying base costs to each node type, you can figure out the best path around a map. To keep things simple, I use the same cost for every node on the map. Feel free to use varying costs for a real game.

Cost from the Start Node

The next cost to keep track of is how much it costs for the node to return to the start node. This is necessary so that you know how hard it is to travel from the start position to the current node. The cost is easy to figure out, as all you need to do is take the start cost of the parent node and add it to the current node's base cost. This gives you the total cost from the start node.

Cost from the Goal Node

The last cost component is the cost for the current node to make it to the goal node. This cost is calculated by taking the number of horizontal and vertical nodes that the current node is away from the goal and adding them together. Say, for example, the current node is one node below and ten nodes to the left of the goal node. The cost from the goal node becomes 11 since $1+10 = 11$. Simple, eh?

Total Cost

Once you have all three costs figured out, all you need to do is add them together to find the total cost of the node. I know this all sounds really confusing, so take a look at Figure 12.8 to see the costs associated with the open list nodes in the example.

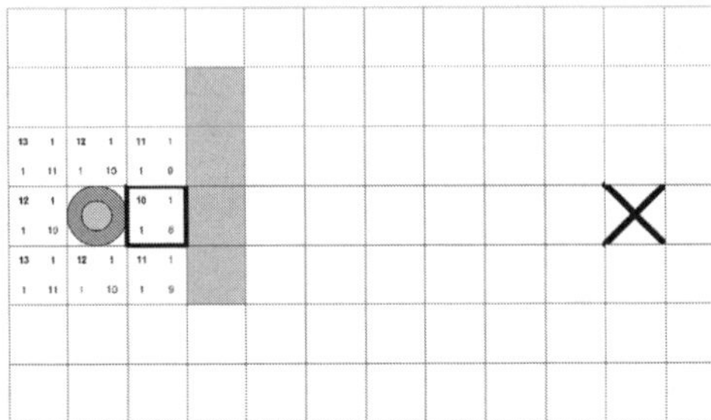

Figure 12.8: Cost of the open nodes.

In Figure 12.8 you can see the nodes on the open list along with their costs. The layout of each node resembles that in Figure 12.9.

Total Cost	Map Cost
14	1
Dist From Start	Dist From Goal
3	10

Figure 12.9: Node cost layout.

As you can see in both Figure 12.8 and 12.9, the total cost for each node is in the upper-left corner. The base cost for each node is in the upper-right corner, the cost from the start is in the lower-left corner, and the cost from the goal is in the lower-right corner.

Find the Best Node

Armed with the total cost of each node, it is easy to find the best node to add to the closed list. You sort the nodes by total cost and pick the one with the lowest total cost. In Figure 12.8, the node with the lowest cost is the node to the right of the starting position. It has a total cost of 10 and is the cheapest one in the lot. I even have the node highlighted to show you that it is the best one to pick.

Once you find the node with the lowest total cost, you need to add it to the closed list as a candidate for the final path solution. You also need to remove it from the open list so that it is not processed again. To recap, the steps so far are as follows:

1. Put the start node on the closed list.
2. Put passable nodes adjacent to the start node onto the open list.
3. Find the node with the lowest total cost and add it to the closed list.
4. Remove the node with the lowest total cost from the open list.

Continue Searching

Assuming you haven't found the goal node in the open list yet, you continue your search by opening up nodes around the one you just added to the closed list. You then check for the cheapest open node and add it to the closed list. This process repeats until you find the end goal on the open list.

Backtrack to Find the Path

Once you find the end goal on the open list, you need to create the path back home. This is done by looking at the parent of the open node that sits on the goal. You look at the parent of the parent and so forth until you get back to the start position. Eventually you end up with a path from the goal to the start. Then all you need to do is reverse the path to have one that runs from the start to the goal. The solution to the example path can be seen in Figure 12.10.

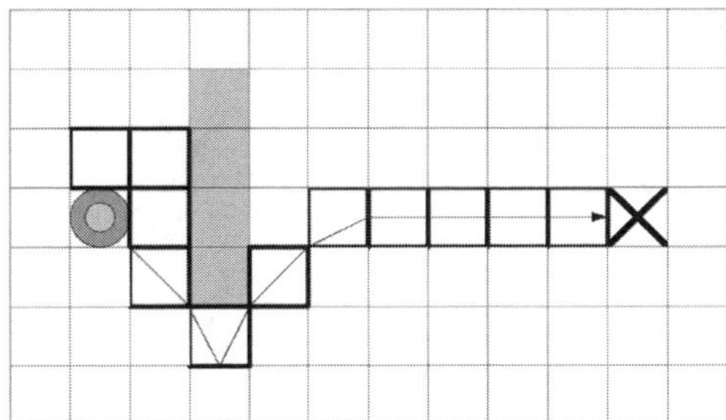

Figure 12.10: The final path solution.

In this figure you can see that the final path solution took a couple of wrong turns on the way. This is due to more than one node having the same total cost. You can't pick two nodes, so you just pick the first one in the list. This can cause some extra work, but the path system fixes itself in the end.

Code Implementation

Now that the theory is out of the way, load up the D3D_PathFinding project and follow along with me. The project consists of the following source files: main.h, main.cpp, CPathFinder.h, and CPathFinder.cpp. The two most important files are the CPathFinder files. They contain the code for the path-finding class.

There is nothing special in the program up until the actual path-finding takes place. The code does the usual work of creating the windows and setting up the graphics. Once the graphics are loaded, the program loads up a default map for the path finder to complete. The path is solved once the user selects the Go option from the command bar. The user can also load up other maps to see the path-finding algorithm in action.

The Init Path Function

Take a look at Figure 12.11 to see the flow of the path-finding code.

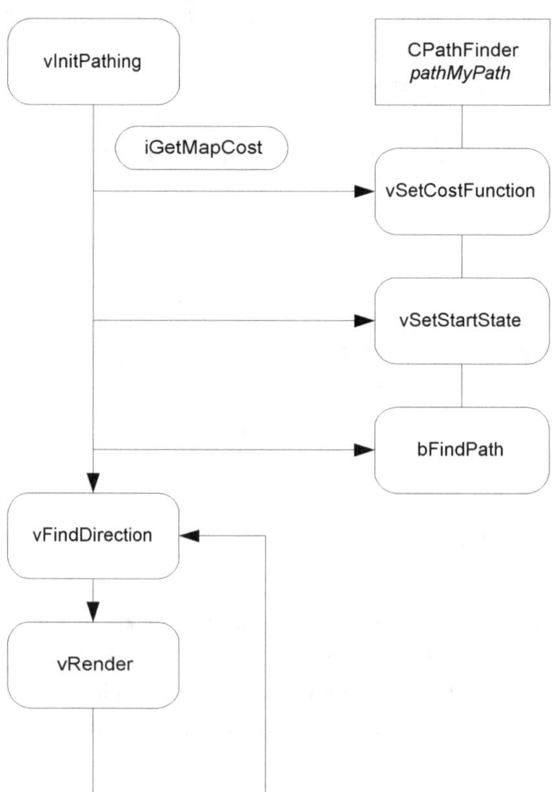

Figure 12.11: Flow of the path-finding code in main.cpp.

Notice how the `vInitPathing()` function uses a CPathFinder class object to perform the path calculations. The other function listed, `iGetMapCost()`, figures out the terrain cost on the map for a given node. Here is the code for the map cost function:

```
int iGetMapCost(int iX, int iY)
{
    // If out of horizontal bounds return impassable
    if(iX < 0 || iX >= g_iTilesWide)
        return(-1);

    // If out of vertical bounds return impassable
    if(iY < 0 || iY >= g_iTilesHigh)
        return(-1);

    // Return impassable if not the 0 tile
    if(g_iTileMap[iX+(iY*g_iMapWidth)][1] != 0) {
        return(-1);
    }
    // Return tile value for anything else
    else {
        return(g_iTileMap[iX+(iY*g_iMapWidth)][1]);
    }
}
```

The get map cost function takes in a coordinate pair and returns values based on the map value at the given coordinates. If the coordinate pair is out of bounds, the function returns a –1. If the coordinate pair points to an impassable part on the map, a –1 is returned. As long as the coordinates point to a map square that is both within bounds and passable, a valid value is returned.

As I said earlier, the `vInitPathing()` function uses the get map cost function in its calls to the path finder object. Here is the code for the init pathing function:

```
void vInitPathing(void)
{
    bool        bRet;
    int         iTempX;
    int         iTempY;
    int         iDir;
    // Start & end map positions
    int         iNodeStartX;
    int         iNodeStartY;
    int         iNodeEndX;
    int         iNodeEndY;
    // Timers
    DWORD       dwStartTime;
    DWORD       dwTotalTime;
    // Path class object
    CPathFinder pathMyPath;

    // Clear the arrow map
```

```cpp
// Use it later to show the path
for(int i = 0; i < g_iMapWidth * g_iMapHeight; i++) {
   g_iArrowMap[i] = -1;
}

// Search the map for a "start" tile
for(int y = 0; y < g_iMapHeight; y++) {
   for(int x = 0; x < g_iMapWidth; x++) {
      if(g_iTileMap[x+(y*g_iMapWidth)][0] == 19) {
         g_iRabbitXPos = x;
         g_iRabbitYPos = y;
         // Create a start state
         iNodeStartX = g_iRabbitXPos;
         iNodeStartY = g_iRabbitYPos;
         break;
      }
   }
}
// Search the map for an "end" tile
for(y = 0; y < g_iMapHeight; y++) {
   for(int x = 0; x < g_iMapWidth; x++) {
      if(g_iTileMap[x+(y*g_iMapWidth)][0] == 20) {
         iNodeEndX = x;
         iNodeEndY = y;
         break;
      }
   }
}

// Update rendered message
sprintf(g_szPathStatus, "CALCULATING PATH");
vRender();

// Set up the cost function
pathMyPath.vSetCostFunction(iGetMapCost);
// Start the timer
dwStartTime = timeGetTime();
// Set up the start and end
pathMyPath.vSetStartState(iNodeStartX, iNodeStartY,
            iNodeEndX, iNodeEndY);
// Find the path - 300 maximum nodes
bRet = pathMyPath.bFindPath(300);
// Stop the timer
dwTotalTime = timeGetTime()-dwStartTime;

// Exit on failure
if(!bRet) {
   // Update rendered message
   sprintf(g_szPathStatus,
         "FAILED, OPEN = %d, CLOSED = %d, TIME = %ld",
         pathMyPath.m_iActiveOpenNodes,
         pathMyPath.m_iActiveClosedNodes,
         dwTotalTime);
   return;
}
```

```
    else {
        // Update rendered message
        sprintf(g_szPathStatus,
                "COMPLETE, OPEN = %d, CLOSED = %d, TIME = %ld",
                pathMyPath.m_iActiveOpenNodes,
                pathMyPath.m_iActiveClosedNodes,
                dwTotalTime);
    }

    // Follow the path now
    CPathNode *GoalNode = pathMyPath.m_CompletePath->m_Path[0];
    int     iTotalNodes = 0;

    // Set temp position to figure out direction arrow
    iTempX = GoalNode->m_iX;
    iTempY = GoalNode->m_iY;

    // Start at position 1 not 0
    iTotalNodes++;
    GoalNode = pathMyPath.m_CompletePath->m_Path[iTotalNodes];

    // Loop through the path and follow it
    // Draw an arrow for each step
    while(iTotalNodes < pathMyPath.m_CompletePath->m_iNumNodes) {
        // Figure out direction
        iDir = vFindDirection(iTempX, iTempY,
                GoalNode->m_iX, GoalNode->m_iY);

        // Set arrow on arrow map
        g_iArrowMap[GoalNode->m_iX+(GoalNode->m_iY*g_iMapWidth)]
            = iDir;

        // Render the scene
        vRender();

        // Set temp position to figure out direction arrow
        iTempX = GoalNode->m_iX;
        iTempY = GoalNode->m_iY;

        // Increment node count
        iTotalNodes++;

        // Get next node
        GoalNode =
            pathMyPath.m_CompletePath->m_Path[iTotalNodes];
    };
}
```

Whew — that is a lot of code to digest. I know it seems complicated, but
the majority of it is spent on rendering the path once it is calculated. The
first part of the code figures out where the rabbit's start and end points
are on the map. Since special tiles placed on the map represent the start
and end points, the code searches the map and stores the coordinates of
the points once located.

Once the start and end points are found, the code sets up the map cost function pointer in the path-finding class. This is done so that the path-finding class knows how to calculate the best possible path based on terrain costs. As soon as the cost function is set, the code sets the start and end state of the path in the path-finding object. This tells the path-finding object which two points to find the path between.

The fireworks really begin when the program calls the `bFindPath()` function that belongs to the path-finding object. This does the work of calculating the most efficient path between the start and end positions on the map. If the path is found, the function returns a 1; otherwise, it returns a 0.

To display the path on-screen, the program starts at the first path node and traverses the path until it gets to the goal node. Along the way, arrows are rendered to show which way the rabbit moves to get from node to node. The direction is figured out based on the previous path node's position relative to the current path node. This is where the `vFindDirection()` function comes into play. It is very simple, as it just has to figure out which arrow tile to use.

The CPathFinder::bFindPath() Function

I could spend 50 pages showing you code, but in reality, there is only one very important function in the CPathFinder class. It is the `bFindPath()` function, and it does all of the work to find the most efficient path. Take a look at Figure 12.12 to see the flow of the function.

The code starts by putting the start node onto the closed path list. It then finds all of the open nodes around the current node, which is the start node. Once the open nodes are found, the code checks to see if the goal has been located. If the goal has been located, the path is inverted and the function returns a success code. If the goal has not been found yet, the function finds the cheapest node on the open list and adds it to the closed list. The whole process repeats until the path is found, there are no more open nodes, or the path exceeds its maximum search size.

The find path function is not the most complicated or largest in size, but it does coordinate the path-finding effort. The other functions it uses are really just the fluff, and you need to tailor them to your program.

Note   The path-finding code is not optimized. Do not use it directly in your code without adding optimization code first.

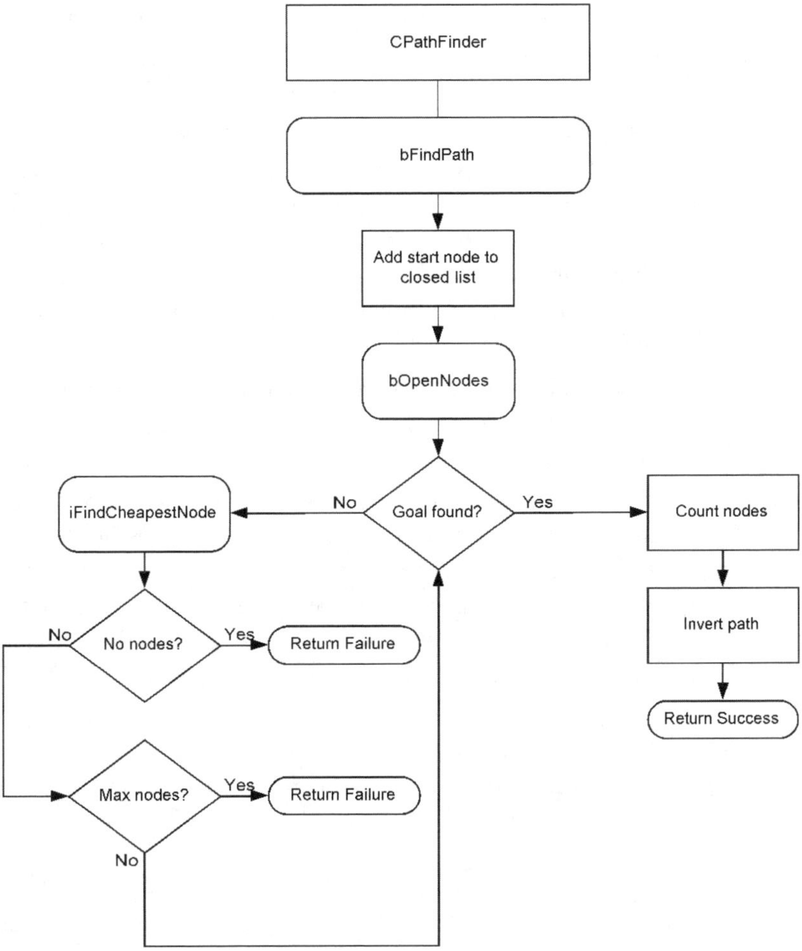

Figure 12.12: Flow of the bFindPath() function.

Recap/Optimization

There are many other things to consider in your path-finding code. Work on the following to bring your path-finding ambition to fruition:

- When searching for open nodes, start with nodes that are closest to the goal. This can reduce the number of node searches required to find the path in many cases.

- Do not put other units on your collision map. Units move and can cause problems if you do this. One solution is to calculate your paths without considering other units and recalculate if you run into another unit on the map. If units don't block one another, this isn't necessary.

- Use a path manager to manage a fixed pool of paths. If you use a fixed pool of paths, you can reduce the overhead associated with dynamically allocated paths.

- Use multiple levels of path-finding. To do this, use a large collision map of few tiles for units to maneuver around large terrain obstacles. Once units reach complicated areas, switch to smaller collision maps with more tiles. Multiple levels of path-finding can speed up your code greatly.

- Never calculate movement for many units at once. Create a path queue to get around this, and only calculate paths for x number of units per game tick.

- If it takes time for units to move in your game, add direction-change costs to the terrain calculations for new nodes on the path list. This will make units choose the most efficient path even when a lot of direction changes are necessary. You can do several neat tricks like this with terrain costs modifications. You could even make terrain cost more near enemy positions to keep your units from walking into combat inadvertently!

- The A* algorithm works for many types of maps, including non-square ones. Try it out on hex maps and even route-based maps.

Chapter 13

Particle Rendering

Most strategy games show cool explosions, smoke trails, and other pyrotechnic displays. The heart of these effects lies in a particle system. A particle system allows you to show organic-looking graphic displays without manually creating each part of the graphic. You can use algorithms to generate the effects on the fly without storing tons of image data. In this chapter I give you an introduction to particle systems and show you the following:

- Particle basics
- Particle characteristics
- Particle class structure
- Particle implementation

Particle Basics

Here you are in particle boot camp. The first question of the day is, what is a particle? Chances are, if you open up your computer case and blow some compressed air in it, you will see dust particles fly around the room. If you have ever used an electric saw, you probably have seen particles of sawdust. Set off some firecrackers, and you will see particles of sparks fly around. Basically, a particle is a very small piece of something. Since the word "something" is ambiguous, so are particles. For this reason, you can have particles of wood, sand, dust, water, etc. To give you some examples, the following particles might be used in a strategy game:

- Particles of fire for explosions
- Particles of smoke for missile trails
- Particles of dust for vehicle movement
- Particles of water for rain

- Particles of ice for snow
- Particles of energy for shock waves

Particle Characteristics

Now that you have some particle examples, you need to know the basic characteristics of particles. For game development, you need a particle system to handle your particles. I personally like to use a simple class, but you may find that a manager or more complicated system is required. The following characteristics make up basic particles:

- Image
- Motion
- Animation

Particle Image

First and foremost, you need to have a graphic or set of graphics for your particle. The nice thing about particles is that they can be as intricate or as simple as you want. You will find that simple particle graphics are usually all you need most of the time though.

Since a particle is a small piece of a larger entity, its image is small as well. So, if you were coding an explosion particle system, your particles would be small blobs of white, orange, and red. If you code a particle system for rain, you would use strips of gray.

Particle Motion

For particles to have any effect, they need to move around. Take fireworks for example; when they explode into a ton of particles, the particle movement dictates how cool the firework is. Some burst into spheres; others send out streamers. Particle systems for games work the same way. You, as the developer, must write movement algorithms for your particles to follow. See Figure 13.1 for a couple of examples.

Figure 13.1 shows two particle motion types. On the left you have rain particles moving down toward the ground. On the right you have explosion particles moving out from an epicenter. The algorithm for the rain is simpler than the explosion, but the effect is just as strong.

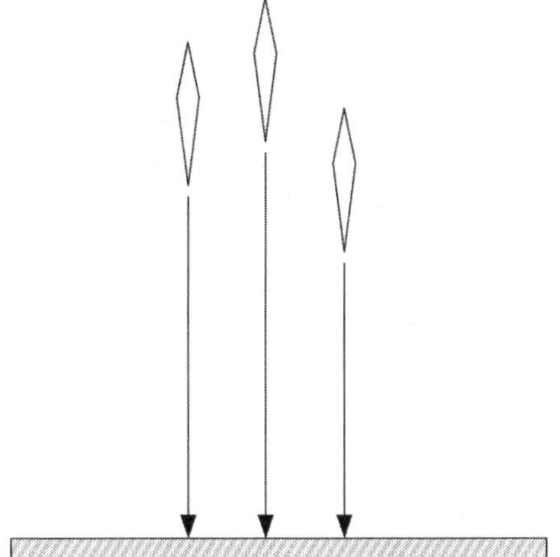

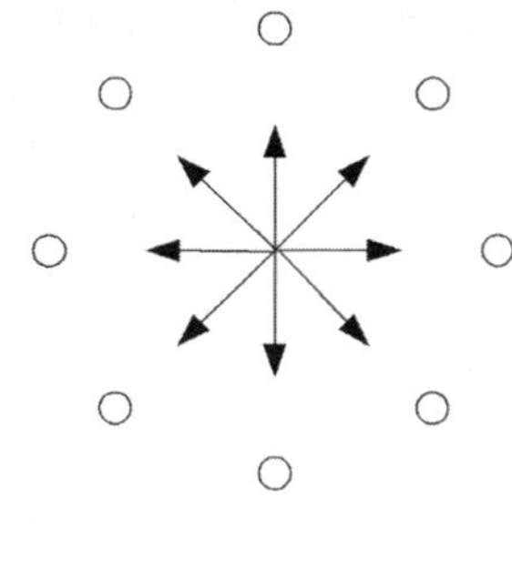

Figure 13.1: Particle motion examples.

Particle Animation

Like most things in life, particles can change over time. This is a very good feature to include in your particle system, since it allows for some really cool effects. Take Figure 13.2 for example.

Figure 13.2: Particle changes over time.

In Figure 13.2 you see a missile with smoke particles coming out the back of it. The interesting thing in the image is that the smoke particles change color from dark gray to light gray over time. Instead of using different particles for each position in the smoke trail, you use the same particle but have it animate from dark gray to light gray over time. This is the essence of particle animation. There are other options as well. You can animate the size of the particle or the actual texture if you want to. The possibilities are only limited by your imagination.

Particle Class Structure

For the particle class example I have a project in the downloadable files named D3D_Particles. Load it up now so you can follow along with my class example. The project is made up of two class files: CParticle.cpp and CParticle.h. The header file looks like the following:

```
class CVector
{
    public:
        float fX;
        float fY;
        float fZ;

        CVector() { fX=0.0f, fY=0.0f, fZ=0.0f; };
};

class CParticle
{
    public:
        CVector    m_vecPos;
        CVector    m_vecCurSpeed;
        CVector    m_vecAcceleration;
        CVector    m_vecGravity;
        int        m_iLife;
        int        m_iTextureStart;
        int        m_iTextureEnd;
        int        m_iTextureType;
        int        m_iTextureCur;
        int        m_iTextureSteps;
        int        m_iTextureCurStep;

        CParticle();
        ~CParticle();
        void vUpdate(void);
        bool bIsAlive(void);
        void vSetTextures(int iType, int iStart,
                  int iStop, int iSteps);
        void vSetPos(float x, float y, float z);
        void vSetAcceleration(float x, float y, float z);
        void vSetGravity(float x, float y, float z);
        void vSetSpeed(float x, float y, float z);
        void vSetLife(int iLife);
};
```

The CVector Class

At the top of the header file, you can see the implementation of a very simple vector class. I could have used Direct X's helper classes for vectors, but I chose to use my own to keep the code as generic as possible. I use the vector class to hold the x, y, and z values for particle elements, such as position and speed. As you can tell from the code, the class is really just a placeholder for the values and does nothing more.

The CParticle Class

The CParticle class is meant to hold all of the information necessary to maintain a single particle in a particle system. It does not manage a complete set of particles. You need to write a particle manager if you want to create systems of particles.

Member Elements

In the particle class I have several base member data elements to define the particle. They are as follows:

The m_vecPos vector defines where the particle is in 3D space. The render function uses this information to place it on the screen in the proper location.

The m_vecCurSpeed vector defines how fast the particle is moving in all three directions. Every game update, the particle takes the current speed and adds it to the current position. This makes the particle move over time at the rate set here.

The m_vecAcceleration vector defines how much to modify the current speed of the particle on every game update. This allows you to have your particle speed up or slow down over time.

The m_vecGravity vector defines how strong gravity is for the particle. On every game update, the gravity values are added to the current speed values. This allows you to have gravity affect your particle without modifying the base speed.

The m_iLife element tells how many game updates it has left before it dies off and become inactive. On every game update, the particle life loses one point. This value is very useful for particles that have a life span. Some particles, such as water, might bounce around forever, but particles of smoke and fire usually die off after a period of time.

The m_iTextureStart and m_iTextureEnd elements tell the particle the texture range to use for graphic animation. The particle class supports texture animation in the form of texture start and end positions. You can set it up where the particle cycles from the start texture to the end texture. This allows for cool animation effects, such as the smoke trail example I covered earlier.

The m_iTextureType element tells the particle how to animate its textures. You can tell it to use only one texture (i.e., no animation), or you can tell it to cycle from the start texture to the end texture and stop. Or you can tell it to cycle from the start texture to the end texture and back again. Basically, this setting gives you control over the texture animation style.

The `m_iTextureCur` element tells the particle which texture is active for the current game update.

The `m_iTextureSteps` element tells the particle how many game updates to wait for the next texture update. This allows you to have the texture animation pause over a period of game cycles.

The `m_iTextureCurStep` element tells the particle where it is in the texture animation cycle before the next texture update. This number starts at 0 and goes up to the value specified in `m_iTextureSteps`. Once it reaches the value, the `m_iTextureCur` is advanced and the `m_iTexture-CurStep` value starts back at 0.

Member Functions

The member functions use the member elements that I just covered to set up, move, and animate the particle during its life in the game. Here are the functions and their purpose:

The `CParticle()` function is the class constructor, and its main purpose is to clear out the member elements to their default values.

The `~CParticle()` function is the class destructor, and it cleans up memory when the class object is destroyed.

The `vUpdate()` function advances the game cycle and updates the particle position, speed, and texture state.

The `bIsAlive()` function tells you if the particle is still alive or not. If it returns a 0, the particle is dead. If it returns a 1, the particle is still alive. The function looks at the `m_iLife` element to make this determination.

The `vSetTextures()` function sets up the texture animation information for the particle.

The `vSetPos()` function sets the starting position of the particle.

The `vSetAcceleration()` function sets the starting acceleration of the particle.

The `vSetGravity()` function sets the gravity constant for the particle.

The `vSetSpeed()` function sets the starting speed of the particle.

The `vSetLife()` function sets the life span of the particle.

The CParticle::vUpdate() Function

In the CParticle.cpp file you can find the class function implementation code. There are many functions, but the update function is the only slightly complicated one. The purpose of the update function is to advance the particle one game state change. This means the particle updates its speed, position, and texture animation state. Here is the code to do this:

```cpp
// Update the acceleration
m_vecCurSpeed.fX += m_vecAcceleration.fX;
m_vecCurSpeed.fY += m_vecAcceleration.fY;
m_vecCurSpeed.fZ += m_vecAcceleration.fZ;
// Update with gravity
m_vecCurSpeed.fX += m_vecGravity.fX;
m_vecCurSpeed.fY += m_vecGravity.fY;
m_vecCurSpeed.fZ += m_vecGravity.fZ;
// Update the position
m_vecPos.fX += m_vecCurSpeed.fX;
m_vecPos.fY += m_vecCurSpeed.fY;
m_vecPos.fZ += m_vecCurSpeed.fZ;
//
// Update texture
//
// Static
if(m_iTextureType == 0) {
   m_iTextureCur = m_iTextureStart;
}
// Frame based
else {
   m_iTextureCurStep++;
   if(m_iTextureCurStep >= m_iTextureSteps) {
      // Linear
      if(m_iTextureType == 1) {
         if(m_iTextureCur != m_iTextureEnd) {
            m_iTextureCur++;
         }
      }
      // Looping - forward
      else if(m_iTextureType == 2) {
         m_iTextureCur++;
         if(m_iTextureCur > m_iTextureEnd) {
            m_iTextureCur = m_iTextureStart;
         }
      }
      // Looping - backward
      else if(m_iTextureType == 3) {
         m_iTextureCur--;
         if(m_iTextureCur < m_iTextureStart) {
            m_iTextureCur = m_iTextureEnd;
         }
      }
      // Reset texture counter
      m_iTextureCurStep = 0;
   }
}
// Subtract life counter
m_iLife--;
```

You can see how the code starts off by adding the current acceleration of the particle to its speed value. You have to be careful, as a large acceleration value will result in the particle flying out into no-man's-land very quickly.

The next part of the code takes into account the gravity value and adds it to the speed as well. This gives you two types of control over the speed of the particle: the acceleration and the gravity. Once the speed values are brought up to date, the speed is added to the particle position in space. This puts the particle into a new location.

The next block of code checks the texture animation style and updates the current texture accordingly.

There are four types of animation implemented in the code. The first type indicates static texture animation. This means that the start texture is the only texture in the animation cycle, and no action is taken during game updates.

The second animation type handles linear animation. This means that the texture is incremented until it reaches the end state. Once it reaches the end state, it stays there and no further updates are required.

The third animation type loops from the start of the texture range to the end of the range. Once it reaches the end, the texture loop starts back at the beginning again and continues until the particle is dead.

The fourth animation type is a reverse loop. It starts at the beginning of the texture loop and goes backward until it loops back around to the end again. The process repeats for the life of the particle.

The last thing the update function does is subtract one life point from the particle.

Particle Implementation

Load up the D3D_Particles project now if you haven't yet and compile it. Run the program, and you should see a scene similar to that in Figure 13.3.

Notice the blob particles in various positions and of different colors. The particles program demonstrates how to create a random set of particles and toss them up in the air. You may call it a popcorn demo, but I leave that choice up to you. I think I know what you are thinking now: "What does this have to do with strategy game programming?" The answer is kind of simple — the program is meant to show you how to get started with particles in a simple way. More complicated formations such as explosions and shock waves can come later once you have the basics of particles down.

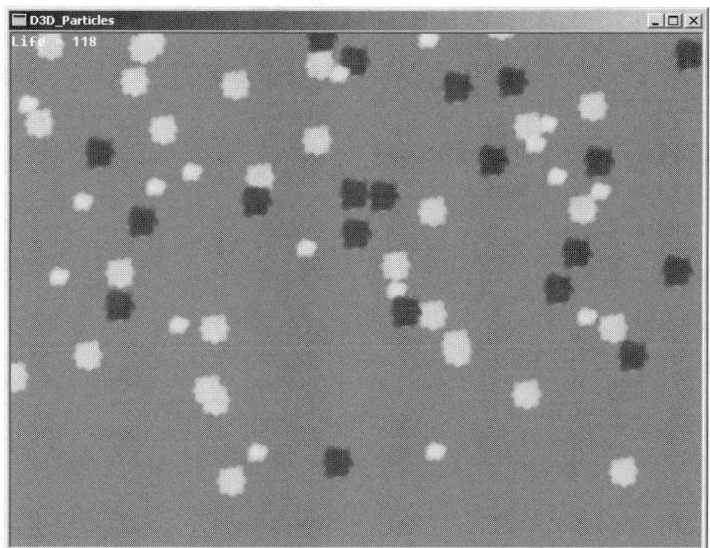

Figure 13.3: Output from the D3D_Particles program.

The project is made up of four files: main.cpp, main.h, CParticle.cpp, and CParticle.h. You also need the following libraries for the code to compile: d3d9.lib, dxguid.lib, d3dx9dt.lib, and d3dxof.lib.

D3D_Particles Layout

The particles program flow follows the same method that I have used for most of the examples in this book. Check out Figure 13.4 on the following page to see the function flow in action.

In Figure 13.4 you can see how the `WinMain()` function initializes the system with calls to `InitD3D()`, `vInitInterfaceObjects()`, and `vInit-Particles()`. The first two functions are just like previous examples, but the particle initialization function is new to this program example. Its purpose is to create the particles for the scene and set their attributes for the animation.

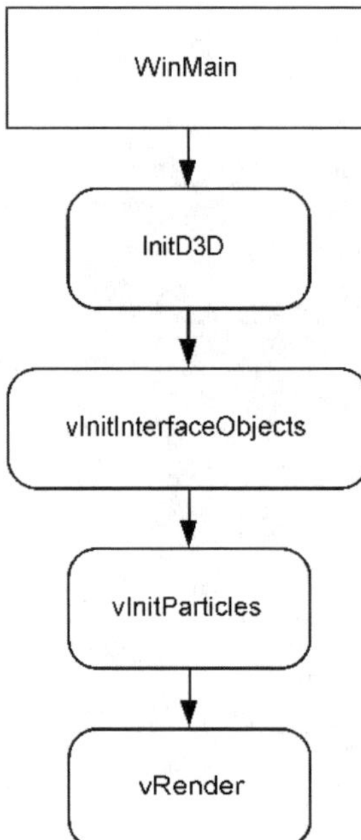

Figure 13.4: Flow of the D3D_Particles program.

Initialize the Particles

The code to initialize the particles is as follows:

```
void vInitParticles(void)
{
    // Initialize each particle
    for(int i = 0; i < TOTAL_PARTICLES; i++) {
        // Set texture animation sequence
        g_partExplosion[i].vSetTextures(
            rand()%3, // Animation type
            0,          // Start texture
            5,          // End texture
            10);        // Steps between textures
        // Set starting position
        g_partExplosion[i].vSetPos(
            0.0f+(rand()%g_iWindowWidth),     // X
            0.0f+(rand()%g_iWindowHeight),    // Y
            0.0f);                            // Z
        // Set starting speed
        g_partExplosion[i].vSetSpeed(
            -1.0f+rand()%2,                   // X
            -8.0f+rand()%4,                   // Y
            0.0f);                            // Z
        // Set gravity effect
        g_partExplosion[i].vSetGravity(
            0.0f,                             // X
```

```
        0.1f,                          // Y
        0.0f);                         // Z
    // Set how long the particle will live
    g_partExplosion[i].vSetLife(200);
  }
}
```

The function loops through the total number of particles as defined by
the TOTAL_PARTICLES constant in the header file. As it goes through each
particle, it randomly sets the position and speed of the particle. The gravity value is set next, and finally the life of the particle is set to 200. This
tells the system that the particle will live through 200 game cycles.

For the random position, I am setting the particle someplace within
the size of the screen. The random speed is generated using a small
range for horizontal movement and a more extreme range for vertical
movement. This gives the particles the effect of flying out the bottom of
the screen to the top.

The animation type is randomly set and uses textures 0 through 5 to
animate with. I put a step value of 10 in place so that the animation
frames don't animate too rapidly.

Render the Particles

Now that you have the particles initialized, it is time to render them.
This is done in the usual vRender() function. Here is the main portion of
the code that renders the particles:

```
// Loop through the particles
for(int i = 0; i < TOTAL_PARTICLES; i++) {
    // Check if alive
    if(g_partExplosion[i].bIsAlive()) {
        // Render the particle
        vDrawInterfaceObject(g_partExplosion[i].m_vecPos.fX,
                    g_partExplosion[i].m_vecPos.fY,
                    (float)g_iParticleSize,
                    (float)g_iParticleSize,
                    g_pTexture[
                    g_partExplosion[i].m_iTextureCur
                    ]);
        // Update the particle
        g_partExplosion[i].vUpdate();
    }
    else {
        // Reset the particles if they are dead
        vInitParticles();
    }
}
```


The render function loops through the total number of particles as
defined by the TOTAL_PARTICLES constant defined in the header file. The
first thing the logic does is check to see if the particle is still alive. If the

particle is still alive, it renders the particle at its current location. The current texture stored in the particle is used to tell the rendering function which texture to use for the particle. Once the particle is rendered, it is updated using the vUpdate() function.

Tip   You can change the TOTAL_PARTICLES value in the header file if you want more or fewer particles. Try setting it higher and higher until your system chokes. My system starts slowing down at around 6,000 particles.

If the render function finds out that a particle is dead, the program calls the initialization function to reset the particles. This allows the particle animation to loop endlessly until you exit the program.

Recap

I have given you a brief look at particles as used in game development. Take the foundation I have given you and try to make your own particle system. There are tons of things you can do with particles, and you are really only limited by your imagination. If you come up with any cool particle examples, send me an email and I will post them on my web site. Here are a few nuggets to take with you:

■ Particles are small pieces of larger objects.

■ Although particles are small, you can use any graphic you want in your particle animations.

■ Animating textures give your particles cool looks and a lot of flexibility.

■ Use a particle system class to manage your particles.

Chapter 14

Network Programming Primer

D on't you hate it when you read game development books and they leave out how to at least get started making your game playable over a LAN or the Internet? I don't know about you, but it really chaps my you-know-what! I don't fall into the same trap with this book. As with everything else, you may first need a primer on networks and how they work in regard to game development. In this chapter I cover the following:

- Network connections
- Network protocols
- Packets
- Latency
- Peer-to-peer networking
- Client-server networking
- Sockets and DirectPlay
- Sockets example code

Network Connections

In order to play a game against another person on a different computer, you obviously must first be connected to that person. There are many types of connections out there, but the gaming community breaks them up into two main categories: LAN and Internet.

LAN Games

LAN, or local area network, games are those you play against computers on a private network. Some games only support a couple of players simultaneously, while others support several dozen at a time. The great thing about LAN games is that they usually don't suffer from bad delays associated with network traffic. Since you play them on closed or private networks, you don't suffer from the unpredictability of the Internet.

The British Connectors Are Coming!

A long time ago in a galaxy…. You know the rest. Anyway, in the not-so-distant past there were several methods of connecting in a LAN. One older method utilized BNC (British Nut Connectors) over coaxial cable. I have seen others that used custom hardware with parallel cables. Luckily for you, most LAN connections today work over CAT-5 cable and use the same connectors. Figure 14.1 shows you an illustration of CAT-5 and coaxial cable.

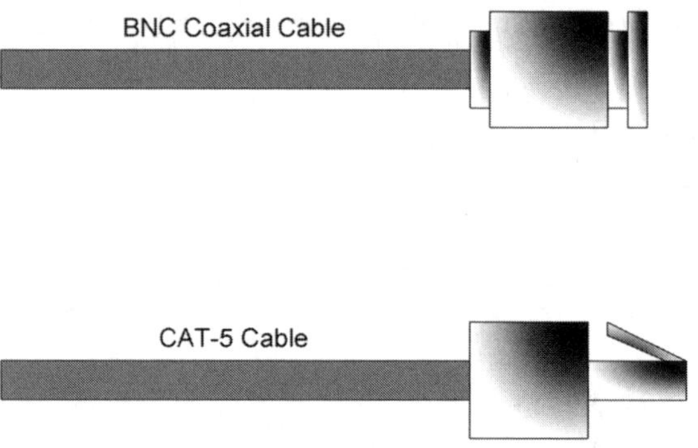

Figure 14.1: CAT-5 and BNC coaxial network cabling.

The bummer about BNC and coaxial cabling is you have to string each computer together, going from one to the other. You cannot just set up a hub for them all to connect to; you actually have to wire them in a single line and use terminators at each end to keep signals from bouncing back and forth. Figure 14.2 illustrates how BNC and coaxial cable networks are set up.

As you can see in the figure, computer A is connected to computer B. Computer B is connected to computer C, and computer C is connected to computer D. Terminators are set up on computers A and D to terminate the signal. These are very important or the network would not function properly. If you have ever used SCSI devices, you are probably

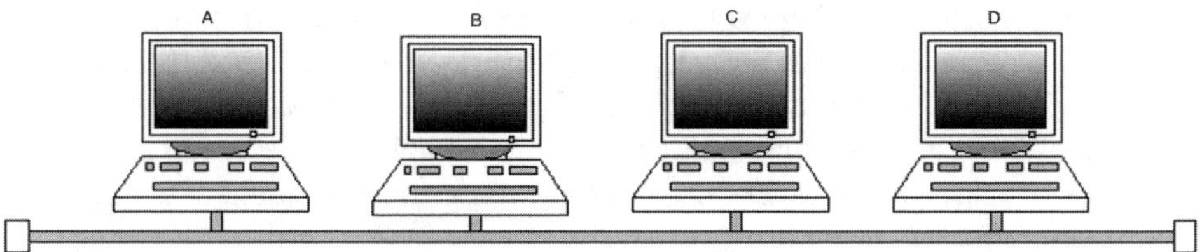

Figure 14.2: Computers connected via coaxial cabling.

familiar with line termination. The basic physics behind it is that electric signals in the network wire travel from one computer to the next until the signal hits a terminator. If there is no terminator at the end of the wire, the signal bounces back. This results in computers on the network getting the same information multiple times, once for each loop the electric signals make. You can probably imagine how problematic this is.

CAT-5 Connections

There are a few options when utilizing CAT-5 connections. The following hardware is common to gamers:

- Laplink
- Hubs
- Switches
- Routers

Laplink Connections

When you only have two computers on a LAN, you can utilize a special network cable commonly referred to as a Laplink cable. Basically, it is a normal CAT-5 cable with the wires twisted. This allows the cable to have a machine on each end without special hardware. You can buy this type of cable at CompUSA or the like for about $30 USD. Figure 14.3 illustrates how two computers connect via a Laplink cable.

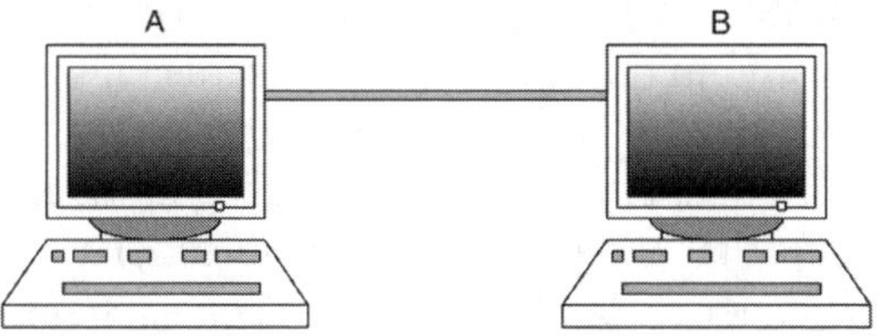

Figure 14.3: Computers connected via a Laplink cable.

As you can see in Figure 14.3, computer A is connected to computer B via a single cable. It's not very complicated, which is really the beauty of it. If you only have two computers, I recommend that you use this method. I also recommend that you have a Laplink cable handy if you own a laptop. You never know when you may need to connect to another computer to share files.

Networking with Hubs

Hubs are used to connect multiple computers on a CAT-5 network together. Some hubs are very small, while others are quite large. There are two attributes that set hubs apart: the number of ports and the speed of the hub.

Considering a hub allows multiple computers to connect through it, it must have ports for each cable connecting to it. This is why the number of ports is important. Most hubs have at least five ports that allow up to four or five computers to connect to each other. Are you wondering why I said four or five and not five connections? I said this because some hubs allow you to daisy chain them together. They utilize the last port as the chain port for attaching to other hubs or switches. Before I get into that, check out Figure 14.4 to see a basic hub connection setup.

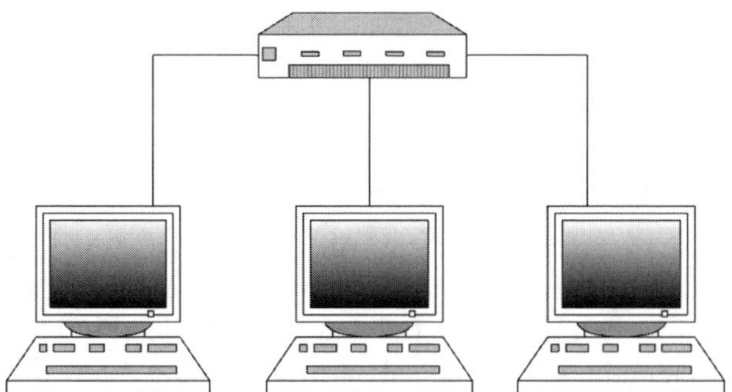

Figure 14.4: Computers connected via a single hub.

Basic hubs that allow four to five computer connections run about $30 USD. Some even come with multiple NIC, network cards, in the retail package. When you move up to hubs that connect eight computers, the price normally jumps more than twofold. They get even more expensive when you move up to hubs that allow 16 or more connections. I have usually found that it is cheaper to daisy chain several cheap hubs together than it is to buy a single hub that supports many connections. Figure 14.5 illustrates several hubs chained together.

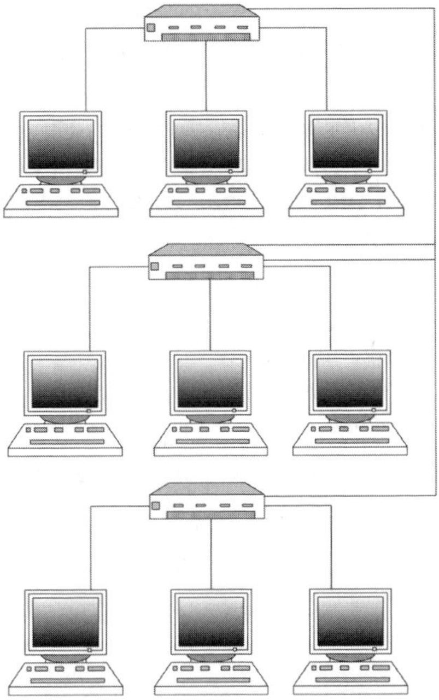

Figure 14.5: Computers connected via several hubs.

The main problem with hubs is that all of the computers connected to one share the same internal bandwidth. This means that every computer on the hub competes with the others for communication. This results in a lot of cross-traffic and packet loss when you have many computers on the hub. The best analogy I can give is that a hub is like a telephone party line. When you have five or more people on a party line, who is speaking and who is not can be quite confusing. Hubs have this same problem.

As far as hub speed goes, there are three options currently available: 10-megabit, 100-megabit, and 1-gigabit. The speed ratings indicate the total bandwidth given to each channel on the hub. If your computers have 10-megabit Ethernet cards in them, you only need a 10-megabit hub. If your computers have 100-megabit Ethernet cards in them, you need a 100-megabit hub. The same holds true for gigabit hubs and cards. The speed of the hub comes at an additional cost, of course.

Networking with Switches

The next logical step up from using a hub is using a switch. Basically, a switch operates in the same manner as a hub except that it gives each computer connected to it its own communication channel. This stops the cross talk and packet loss problems associated with hubs. The main difference between hubs and switches is the cost. A five-port switch may run about $50 to $70 USD, whereas a five-port hub may run about $20 to $30 USD. Personally, I always buy switches. They may cost more, but they perform much better than hubs.

You can find switches and hubs more cheaply than the prices mentioned above. Some brands, such as Linksys, make very inexpensive hardware. The main problem is that the old saying holds true in that you get what you pay for. I would much rather pay 50 percent more for a higher-quality networking device than save money on a cheap one. My personal favorite brand is Netgear. They don't always have a ton of features, but they get the job done well and reliably.

Routers — The Gateway to the Internet

Routers are interesting in that they come in so many configurations. There are four basic options when it comes to routers:

- Number of ports
- Speed
- Firewall support
- Wireless connectivity

Before I move on to the options of a router, check out Figure 14.6 to see how a router connects to PCs in a network.

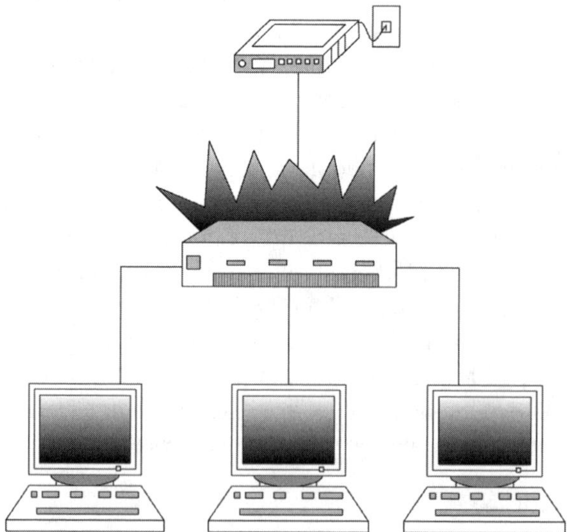

Figure 14.6: Computers connected via a router.

As you can see in Figure 14.6, the computers are all connected to each other through the router. The main difference between this illustration and the one for a hub is that the router connects to the Internet as well. This means that each computer on the network sees the Internet as other computers on the network. Cool, eh?

Most routers have a built-in hub or switch. I prefer routers with built-in switches, as they are inherently better than what I described earlier. The same holds true for routers with this type of built-in hardware for hubs and switches in that there are a number of ports available. Most routers come with at least five total ports, four for computer connections and the fifth one to connect to other switches or hubs.

Routers with a built-in hub or switch also have the same options speed-wise. You can currently buy routers that support 10-megabit, 100-megabit, or even 1-gigabit connections. A good speed to stick with for most applications is the 100-megabit variety.

Number of Ports

As I said before, the number of ports on a router tells you how many computers can connect to it. This is an important factor to consider when purchasing a router for your setup.

Speed

Most routers come in speeds of 10-megabit, 100-megabit, or 1-gigabit. Personally, I go for 100-megabit equipment most of the time since it is faster than DSL anyway.

Firewall Support

Most routers have a firewall built into them. What does a firewall do for you? It helps to protect your computer against connections from the outside world. I know this may sound strange at first considering you want other gamers to connect to you, but believe me, open connections are not a good thing. The quality and functionality of firewalls varies little from manufacturer to manufacturer. The main thing to watch out for is hardware that doesn't support port forwarding. If you can't open ports for connections, you are going to have a hard time playing games.

Basically, port forwarding allows you to have pipes opened in your firewall that allow connections to get through. You can think of this as poking a hole in an actual firewall. The hole would let some fire through but not through the entire wall.

Wireless Connectivity

Nowadays you can buy almost any network gear with wireless connectivity built in. Wireless allows you to connect your computers via high frequency radio waves. If you opt for a wireless router, as I did, make sure you buy wireless cards for your PCs that match the same specification. Some wireless specifications are downward compatible, but many are not. Also be mindful of the support you may get with wireless hardware. Last time I checked, some game companies refused to offer tech support to people with wireless connections. I won't point fingers or anything, but let's just say that the makers of the black box sitting under my TV with a big X on it don't like to support my wireless connection.

Network Protocols

When it comes to game development, there are really only two protocols that you need to concern yourself with: TCP/IP and UDP. These are the two main protocols in use today, and unless you're reading this book long after its publication date, they are the only real choices for game development.

TCP/IP Protocol

The TCP/IP protocol allows for guaranteed messaging between computers. It also does fun things for you such as packet ordering. The main benefit of TCP/IP is that it handles a lot of the work for you since it can guarantee delivery of information. What does guaranteed information mean? It means that if the system tells you that it sent a message to another computer, you can be guaranteed that it really did send the data. I know this sounds like an obvious feature, but it is not in the land of network programming.

The main detriment to the TCP/IP protocol is that it is slow. It is slow because of the guaranteed delivery system. In order to guarantee delivery, the system has to send information, check for a response, and validate the transmission. This takes valuable time, and on today's hardware, this is really unacceptable for game development.

UDP Protocol

The UDP protocol is a much simpler version of TCP/IP. For one thing, it does not guarantee delivery of information. Maybe the data gets to the target, and maybe it doesn't — who knows? In addition to not guaranteeing delivery, UDP sends data out of order. Take, for example, the following phrase:

"The quick brown fox jumped over the lazy dog"

If you transmit the phrase over UDP, it may come across as:

"dog The brown quick fox lazy over jumped the"

As you can see in the example above, this can be problematic for game development. There are technical ways to overcome this problem, but you have to develop them yourself or use someone else's API that does it for you.

The main benefit to UDP is that it is very fast and flexible. Since it doesn't worry about such things as data ordering and guaranteed delivery, it can speed along quite nicely. The other good point is that you can make guaranteed delivery systems on top of it and turn them on when needed. This allows you to send guaranteed data when necessary but maintain speedy transmissions when the data is not as critical.

TCP/IP Versus UDP

Maybe you are wondering which protocol to use and when. Let me try to help with the following scenarios:

■ **Turn-based Strategy Game**

For a turn-based strategy game, you should probably stick with TCP/IP. Since turn data is transmitted on a regular basis, you don't need the speed and problems of UDP.

■ **Real-time Strategy Game**

You definitely need UDP for RTS games. You constantly have to send data for everything ranging from chat messages to unit movements. Don't even think about using TCP/IP for this one.

■ **MMORPG (Massively Multiplayer Online Role-playing Game)**

Hey, this is a book about strategy games! (Just kidding.) The answer to this one is more vague. MMORPGs transmit a huge amount of data; therefore, they seem perfect for the UDP protocol. The problem is that UDP is not as efficient at guaranteed delivery as TCP/IP, and in MMORPGs, you end up needing a lot of guaranteed transmissions. I hate to be vague, so I suggest that you try UDP first and switch to TCP/IP if you can't make it work out.

Packets

Packets, packets, who's got the packet? Hmm, I think I used that line in another book. Anyway, packets are nothing more than blocks of information. When you send data to another player, you send it in the form of a packet. Usually the packet contains information such as the receiver's address, the sender's address, and the actual data. Check out the example packet in Figure 14.7.

Sender
Receiver
Packet Type
Unit ID
New X-Pos
New Y-Pos
New Direction

Figure 14.7: Example packet.

In Figure 14.7 you can see the layout for a sample packet. The first part of the packet, called the packet header, is shaded darker than the rest of the packet. The header contains the information about the packet, and the non-shaded area contains the data for the packet. In the header you can see slots for the sender, receiver, and packet type. The sender and receiver blocks would carry the appropriate IP addresses, and the packet type block would tell you the type of packet. In this example, the packet type is a unit movement packet. Since the packet is a unit movement packet, the data contains information about the unit ID, new x-position, new y-position, and new direction. This information tells the recipient that a unit moved, where it moved, and what direction it now faces.

You can make a mountain out of a molehill, or you can just accept that a packet contains information about the packet and data that you want to transmit. Personally, I like the molehill approach.

Latency

Ooh, the dreaded word in multiplayer game programming. Latency is the time it takes for a packet to transmit from one computer to another computer. On a LAN, latency isn't much of a problem since high-speed connections are uber cheap and reliable for the most part. Introduce the Internet into the picture, and you have a whole new problem. Packets can get delayed because of the sender's hardware, the receiver's hardware, or the hardware between the sender and the receiver. The bottom line here is that the Internet throws a wrench into any sort of predictive network gaming. Never fear though; there are ways to work around it.

To battle latency you need to make your code robust. Never base your code on guesses about latency. If you write your code to accept long delayed packet transmission, you should be safe. But, if you make your program expect packets to deliver on time, be prepared for disappointment.

Peer-to-Peer Networking

There are two networking architectures to use in game development: peer-to-peer and client-server. Peer-to-peer networking takes place when you have each player in the game send his data to the other players in the game. There is no central location to send information to. It is up to the players to send their data to one another. Look to Figure 14.8 to see this illustrated.

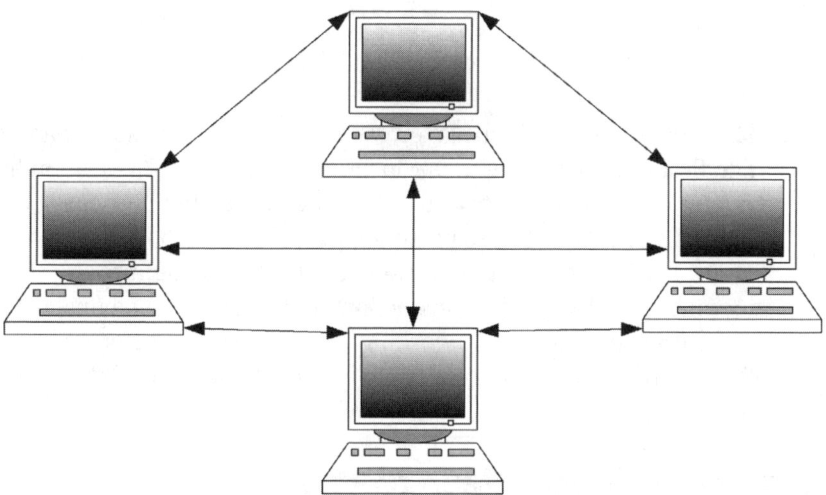

Figure 14.8: Sample peer-to-peer network.

In Figure 14.8 you can see the communication lines between the computers involved in a four-player game. Since each computer has to communicate to the other systems on the network, you see many lines of traffic. This works well as long as everyone on the network has a fast connection, but it becomes problematic when one or more people have slow connections.

Client-Server Networking

Client-server networking works by having a single computer act as the relay station for all communication. Each client on the network sends its information to the server, and the server relays it to the other clients on the network. Check out Figure 14.9 to see this illustrated.

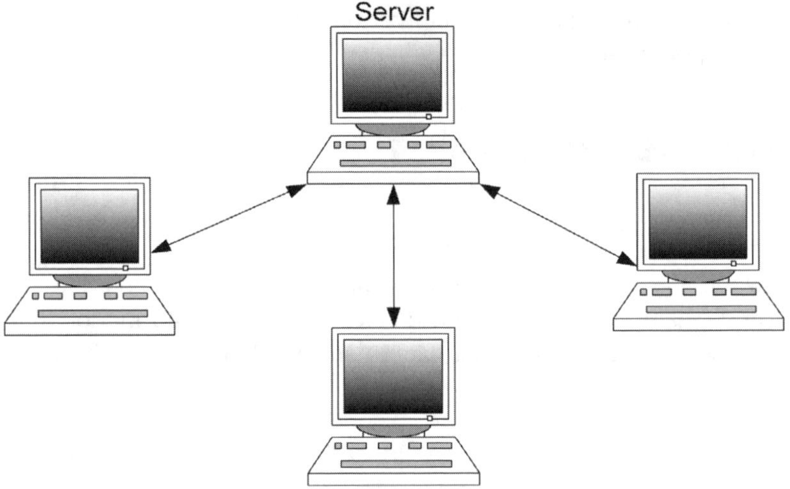

Figure 14.9: Sample client-server network.

This figure shows a four-player game based on client-server architecture. The first item of note is the reduced number of communication lines. Since the clients only have to talk to the server, the number of open lines is greatly reduced. The main benefit to this is that only the server must have a fast connection to the Internet. Another benefit to the client-server network is that it can support many players. The final benefit is that with client-server networking, the server can perform validity checks on incoming information. This is invaluable for detecting cheaters.

Client-Server Versus Peer-to-Peer

Once again, you are at an impasse. Which architecture do you use: client-server or peer-to-peer? The following scenarios should help to clear things up for you.

◼ **Turn-based Strategy Game**

Go with client-server for this. Since client-server supports tons of players, you won't find yourself limited in any way. You also get the benefit of server-side sanity checks to prevent rampant cheating.

■ **Real-time Strategy Game**

Stick with client-server programming for this type of game as well. The same reasons apply as with turn-based games.

■ **MMORPG (Massively Multiplayer Online Role-playing Game)**

You *must* use client-server architecture here. You cannot have thousands of players with peer-to-peer networking, period.

Do you see a common trend here? In my humble opinion, peer-to-peer networking is a waste of time, and you shouldn't even bother with it. Not only is it inefficient, but it also causes headaches with firewalls and many other things. You might want to try it out, but I don't suggest it.

Sockets and DirectPlay

When it comes time to actually develop your game for multiplayer communication, you have two choices in your API selection. You can go with straight sockets, or you can use DirectPlay. DirectPlay is actually based on sockets. With either one you are using sockets, but DirectPlay wraps around sockets and provides a lot of high-level functions.

What are sockets? Sockets are pipes of communication between computers that carry data back and forth. You can open up multiple sockets at once and are really not limited to the total number you can have open.

The main benefit to using straight sockets is that you have complete control over what happens on the communication channel. You also can port your code to operating systems other than Windows. The main deterrent to sockets is that you have to code everything yourself.

The main benefit to using DirectPlay is that it handles a lot of the work for you. You don't have to worry about packet ordering, guaranteed delivery, or even session management. The main detriment to DirectPlay is that you don't have complete control over it. The other problem is that you can't use it in operating systems other than Windows. To help you make the proper choice, consider the following rules:

■ If you need to port your game to multiple platforms, use sockets.

■ If you want DirectX to handle the hard work for you, use DirectPlay.

Sockets Example Code

I love to teach by example, so how about a TCP/IP program that connects to the Internet, sends an HTTP request to a web server, and then displays the main web page for the site? Before I jump into the code, check out Figure 14.10 to see how the whole thing works.

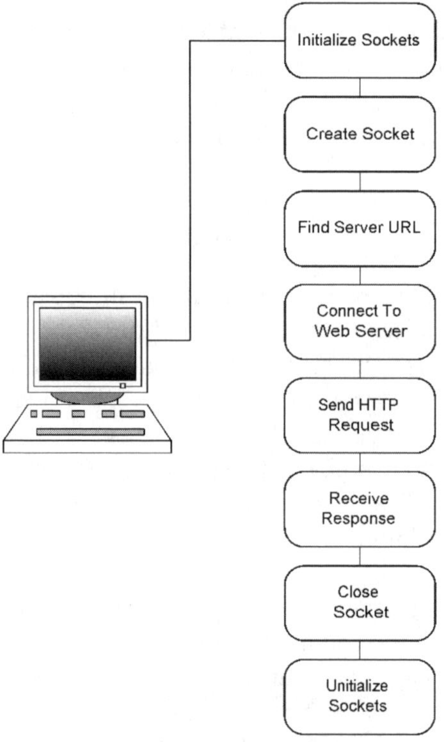

Figure 14.10: Flow of a simple sockets program.

Here you can see the steps required to connect to a web server and pull down the main page. You first have to initialize sockets to get the communication layer up and running. You then create a socket to use for the connection to the web server. Once you have the socket ready, you find the IP address of the web server and connect to it. As soon as you are connected, you send an HTTP request for the main page contents. You then sit and wait to receive the contents into a receive buffer. Once you receive the contents, you close the socket and shut down the socket's system.

The Sockets_Receive Program

I have implemented the code necessary to recreate the steps in Figure
14.10. Load up the Sockets_Receive program now, and you can follow
along with me. The project contains the main.cpp file and one library
named ws2_32.lib, which contains everything you need for Windows
socket programming. Compile the program now and execute it. You will
see a console window pop up and display the contents of the web site
that I have listed in the code. It should resemble Figure 14.11.

```
"C:\Source\RTSDX9\Sockets_Receive\Debug\Sockets_Receive.exe"
<--- SOCKET CREATED --->
<--- LOOKING UP HOST IP --->
<--- CONNECTED TO SERVER --->
<--- SENT 256 BYTES --->
<--- RECEIVED 22513 BYTES --->
HTTP/1.1 200 OK
Date: Mon, 31 Mar 2003 01:55:04 GMT
Server: Apache/1.3.27
Connection: close
Content-Type: text/html

<html>
<head>
<title>Lost Logic Home Page</title>
<meta http-equiv="Content-Type" content="text/html; charset=iso-8859-1">
<META NAME="Keywords" CONTENT="multiplayer, network, multiplayer game programmin
g, tcp/ip, directx, direct x, direct input, networking, todd barron, andre lamot
he, direct play, direct 3d, game development, game programming, graphics program
ming, OpenGL, DirectX, Direct3D, AI, artificial intelligence, game design, game,
 development, programming, c++, games, program, create, design, gouraud, shading
, tutorial, art, internet, 3dsmax, review, photoshop,multi-player,lost logic, lo
stlogic, lost, logic">
<style>
<!--
.LostLogicPages { font-family: Arial; padding: 0 }
```

Figure 14.11: Output of the Sockets_Receive program.

Open the main.cpp file now to see the following contents:

```cpp
#include <iostream.h>
#include <winsock.h>
#include <stdio.h>

void main(void)
{
    SOCKET skSocket;
    sockaddr_in saServerAddress;
    int       iPort = 80;
    int       iStatus;
    WSADATA   wsaData;
    WORD      wVersionRequested;
    LPHOSTENT lpHost;
    char      szHost[128];
    char      szSendBuffer[256];
    char      szRecvBuffer[32768];
    int       iBytesSent;
    int       iBytesReceived;

    sprintf(szHost,"www.lostlogic.com");
    // Tell WinSock we want version 2
```

```cpp
wVersionRequested = MAKEWORD(2, 0);
// Initialize the socket handle
skSocket = INVALID_SOCKET;
// Start up WinSock
iStatus = WSAStartup(wVersionRequested, &wsaData);
// Create the socket
skSocket = socket(AF_INET, SOCK_STREAM, 0);
// Check if there was an error
if(skSocket == INVALID_SOCKET) {
   cout << "**ERROR** Could Not Create Socket" << endl;
   exit(1);
}
memset(&saServerAddress,0,sizeof(sockaddr_in));
saServerAddress.sin_family = AF_INET;
saServerAddress.sin_addr.s_addr = inet_addr(szHost);

if(saServerAddress.sin_addr.s_addr == INADDR_NONE)
{
   lpHost = gethostbyname(szHost);
   if (lpHost != NULL) {
      // Load the server address with the host information
      saServerAddress.sin_addr.s_addr =
         ((LPIN_ADDR)lpHost->h_addr)->s_addr;
   }
   else {
      cout << "**ERROR** Could Not Locate Host" << endl;
      exit(1);
   }
}
// Set the server port
saServerAddress.sin_port = htons(iPort);
// Attempt to connect to the server
iStatus = connect(skSocket,
      (struct sockaddr*)&saServerAddress,
      sizeof(sockaddr));

// Check if there was an error
if(iStatus == SOCKET_ERROR) {
   cout << "**ERROR** Could Not Connect To Server" << endl;
   exit(1);
}
sprintf(szSendBuffer,"GET / HTTP/1.0\n\n");
// Send the HTTP request
iBytesSent = send(skSocket, szSendBuffer, 256, 0);
memset(szRecvBuffer, 0x00, 32768);
// Receive the data
iBytesReceived = recv(skSocket, szRecvBuffer, 32768, 0);
cout << szRecvBuffer << endl;
// Shut down
closesocket(skSocket);
WSACleanup();
}
```

Include the WinSock Header File

The winsock.h header file contains the necessary header information for the ws2_32.lib sockets library. Be sure to include it in all of your sockets-based code. The rest of the header files are used for your normal everyday programming.

Set the WinSock Version

Before you can use any type of socket, you must first initialize the Windows socket system with a call to the WSAStartup() function. This function takes in the version of sockets that you want to use and initializes the communication system. Since you want to use version 2 of sockets, you need to set the version requested to 2.

Create the Socket

In order to connect to the outside world, you need a connection pipe in the form of a socket. To create the pipe, you must call the socket() function provided by the sockets library. As long as the function is successful, it returns the ID number of the SOCKET handle.

Tip   A socket handle is really nothing more than a number. For every socket that you create, another number representing the socket is returned by the system.

Find the Server URL

If you want to connect to a server that uses a URL instead of an IP number, you must first find the IP address for the URL. This is accomplished with the gethostbyname() function. This function takes the server name and resolves its IP address for you.

Set the Port Number

Servers can accept connections on multiple lines of communication. Each of these lines is called a port. Since there are multiple ports to choose from, you must specify the connection port you want to connect to. This is accomplished by setting the sockaddr_in server address structure to use the desired port number. The sockaddr_in server address structure has a member variable named sin_port that holds the information. Set the sin_port variable to the port desired, and you are good to go.

Connect to the Server

Once the port number and IP address are set, you can connect to the server. This is done with a call to the connect() function provided by sockets. It expects the socket you want to use and the address of the server you want to connect to. If the connect function returns a SOCKET_ERROR, you failed to connect; otherwise, you are connected.

Send Data to the Server

Now that you are connected to the server, you can send the HTTP request packet. The request packet tells the server that you want to see the contents of the default web page. To send the packet, you need to use the send() function. This function takes in the socket to send on, the data to send, and the size of the data to send. In this instance I am sending the contents of the szSendBuffer buffer using the socket ID contained in skSocket.

If everything works on the send, the send function returns the number of bytes transmitted.

Receive Data from the Server

Now that you have sent your HTTP request to the server, it should send a response back to you. In order to look at the response, you need to call the recv() function to pull the data out of the socket's communication buffer. The cool part about sockets is that they automatically receive the data into the system buffer for you so you don't have to worry about missing it if your program is busy. Be careful not to wait long though, as you will lose any data that sits around in the buffer for too long.

The receive function takes in the socket ID on which you want to receive, the buffer to receive the data, and the size of the buffer. As soon as you have some data to receive, it will transmit into the receive buffer, and the program will continue. If data is never sent, the function will sit there forever until you shut it down. This is the nature of blocking sockets.

Note A blocking socket waits until each command is completed until continuing. This can be problematic, as your program can easily get locked up. The best method is to use non-blocking sockets since they continue immediately after functions are called. The main downside to non-blocking sockets is that they are harder to program.

Once the receive function returns, you can look at the contents of the
web page by outputting the szRecvBuffer buffer.

Close the Socket

Now that you are done with your socket, you need to close it down. This
is done with the closesocket() function. The close socket function takes
in the ID number of the socket to close and shuts it off.

Shut Down Sockets

When you are completely done with sockets, you need to close down the
socket's communication system with a call to WSACleanup(). This only
needs to be called once at the end of your program.

What a whirlwind tour of blocking sockets that was! I know I really
sped right through it, but I want to get the basics out of the way to make
room for the cooler stuff.

Turn-based Network Programming

As you well know, there are two types of strategy games: real-time and
turn-based. Have you ever wanted to make a turn-based game that runs
over the Internet? I mean, hot-seat games are fun to play, but they aren't
very convenient since both parties have to be in the same location. This
is where the next program I cover comes in handy. In the companion files
you will find a project named Sockets_TurnGame. The program, once
compiled, demonstrates how to run a turn-based game over a LAN or the
Internet. Go ahead and load up the project now to follow along with me.

Turn-based Program Flow

In a turn-based networked game, you have a pretty straightforward flow
to follow. Check out Figure 14.12 on the following page to see it in action.

In the illustration you can see the client and the server for a turn-
based networked game. The process starts off with the server listening
for the client to connect. Once the client connects, the server accepts the
connection and waits for the client to take its turn. Once the client is
ready, it sends the turn packet to the server and waits for the server to
take its turn. When the server player is ready, he ends his turn and sends
the turn packet to the client. The process repeats until the game is over.
Basically, what you have is a game where you take your turn, end your
turn, and then wait for the other player to do the same.

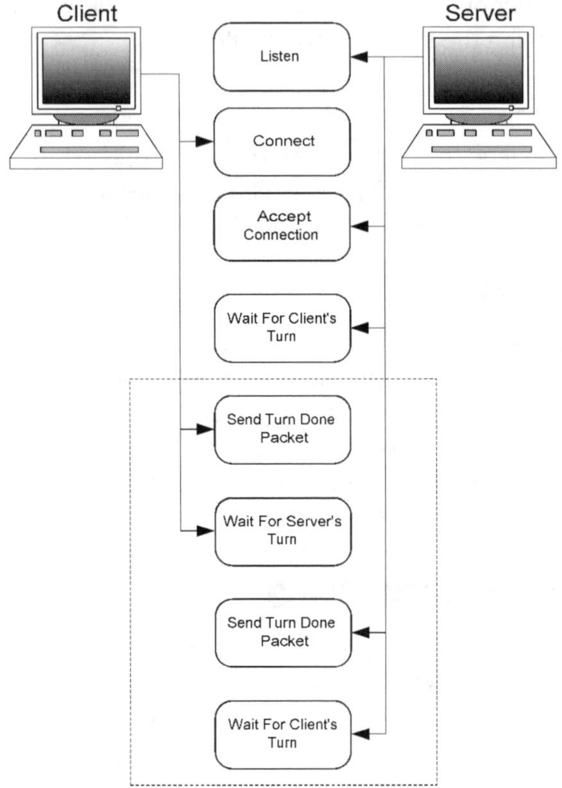

Figure 14.12: Flow of a turn-based network-enabled game.

The Sockets_TurnGame Program

The Sockets_TurnGame program gives you an example of the flow illustrated in Figure 14.12. Launch the program, and you are presented with the window shown in Figure 14.13.

In Figure 14.13 you see a small window with controls to host or connect. The Host button turns the program into the game server, and the Connect button turns the program into the game client. Since you can't have the chicken before

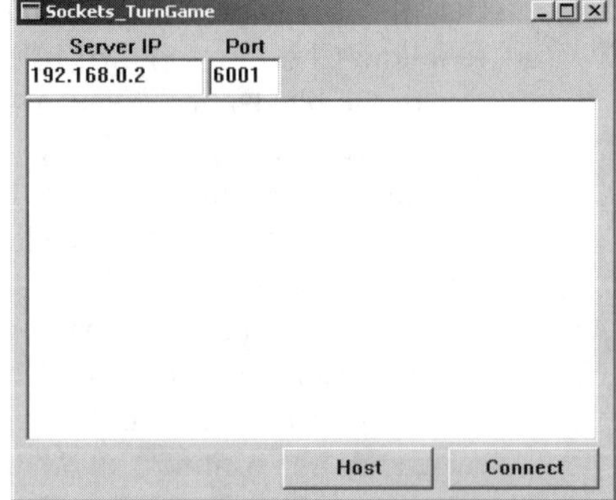

Figure 14.13: Output from the Sockets_TurnGame program.

the egg, you need to have the host set up before you can connect with the client.

If you haven't figured it out yet, you need to launch the program twice for it to work properly. This is necessary since you need both a host and a client to show turns bouncing back and forth. Launch the program twice if you haven't done so already, and select Host on one of the instances. Once that is done, select Connect on the other instance. With that done, you should see something like in Figure 14.14.

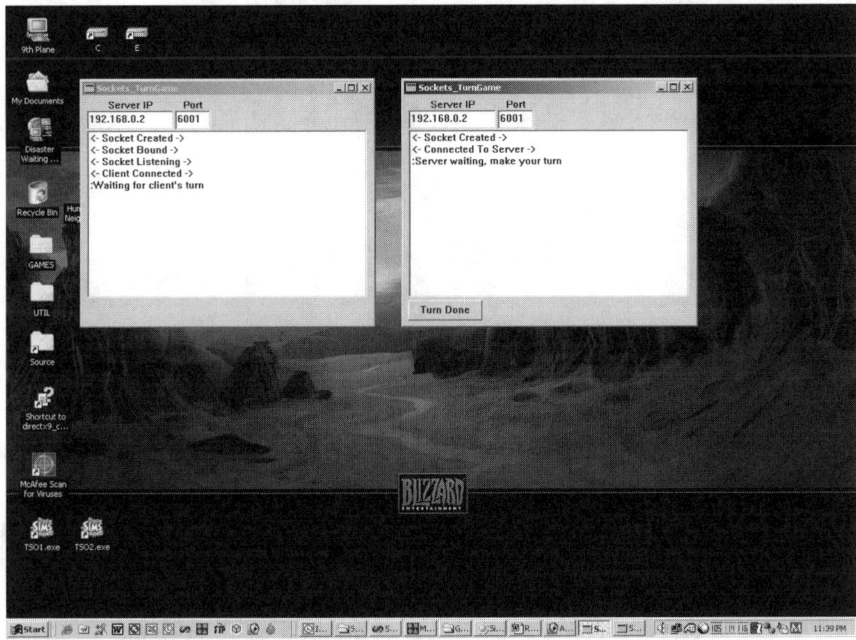

Figure 14.14: The client connected to the server.

In Figure 14.14 and on your screen, you should see two instances of the program. The host program should be waiting for the client to make its turn, and the client program should have a button named Turn Done ready for use. The player with the Turn Done button visible has control of the game and can pass control to the other player by pressing it. You can pass the turn back and forth by pressing the Turn Done button as it appears. I know it's a stretch of the imagination, but pretend you are taking a very complicated game turn between each button press.

In the sockets program, I opted to include functions for both the server and the client. Due to this, the code branches off in two different directions depending on the action that the user takes. Take a look at Figure 14.15 to see the flow of the program illustrated.

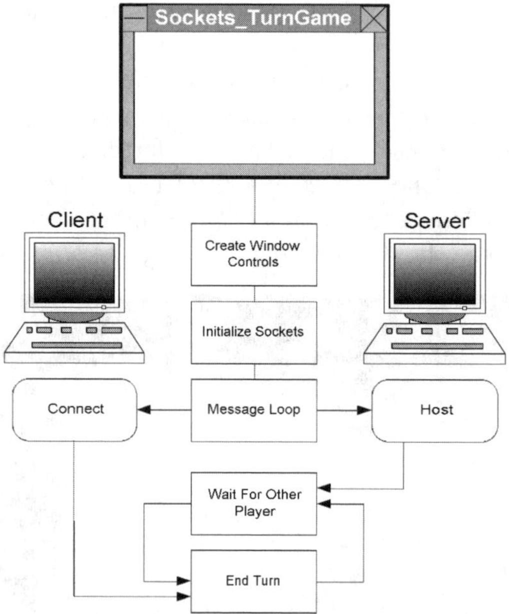

Figure 14.15: Flow of the Sockets_TurnGame program.

This figure shows how the sockets program starts out by initializing the window controls and sockets. Once the initialization is out of the way, the program sits in the message loop and waits for the user to select Host or Connect. If the user selects the Connect button, the program waits for the user to end his turn. If the user selects the Host button, the program waits for the client connection.

The code for the project is contained within the main.cpp and main.h files. There are only two libraries required: winmm.lib and ws2_32.lib. The winmm.lib isn't necessary for networking, but I use it to play a sound when the user ends his turn.

The Sockets_TurnGame Globals

Load up the main.h header file, and you can see the following code listed in it:

```
// Socket vars
SOCKET g_skListenSocket;
SOCKET g_skClientSocket;
bool      g_bIsServer  = 0;
bool      g_bMyTurn    = 0;
bool      g_bConnected = 0;
```

I have two socket handles listed in the code. The host of the game listens for new connections on the g_skListenSocket handle. The other handle, `g_skClientSocket`, is used by the client to connect to the server or by the server to assign to the connecting client. Either way, the client socket is used to manage the connection between the client and the server.

The `g_bIsServer` Boolean value tells you if the program is hosting the game. If the value is set to 1, the game is the host and must wait for a client connection. If the value is 0, the game is the client and must connect to the host game computer.

The `g_bMyTurn` Boolean value tells you if it is your turn in the game. If it is your turn, you have the option to select the Turn Done button to relinquish your control. A value of 1 means it is your turn, and a value of 0 means it is not.

The `g_bConnected` Boolean value tells you if the program is connected to the other player. A value of 1 means the connection exists, and a value of 0 means the connection does not exist.

There are quite a few other global variables, but they deal with Windows controls and the like.

The Sockets_TurnGame Functions

Further in the main.h header file, you can find the functions specific to the program. They are as follows:

```
void vHost();
void vInitializeSockets(void);
void vShutdownSockets(void);
void vConnect(void);
void vSendTurnMessage(void);
void vReceiveTurnMessage(void);
void vTurnDone(void);
```

The `vHost()` function is called when the user selects the Host button. It listens on the host port and waits for an incoming connection. Once the client connects, the host accepts the connection and communication can proceed.

The `vInitializeSockets()` function is used to set up WinSock.

The `vShutdownSockets()` function shuts down any active connections and also shuts down the WinSock system.

The `vConnect()` function is called when the user presses the Connect button. It attempts to connect to the Host IP address. Once connected, the client has control of the game and can end his turn at a time of his choosing.

The `vSendTurnMessage()` function sends the end-of-turn packet to the other player. The packet doesn't really contain anything useful; it's just meant to show you how to send data across the wire.

The vReceiveTurnMessage() function waits for the other player to send the end-of-turn packet. The function will sit and wait until the cows come home.

The vTurnDone() function calls the send turn message and receive turn message functions to complete a turn. It is called when the user presses the Turn Done button.

The other functions present in the main.h header file are standard Windows stuff and not very entertaining, so I will leave them out for now. You really don't want to see them covered for the hundredth time, do you? Now I have more time to play a round of Age of Mythology!

The vHost() Function

Pretend for a minute that you have loaded up the turn game program and hit the Host button. The following code gets executed:

```
sockaddr_in saServerAddress;
sockaddr_in saClientAddress;
int    iClientSize = sizeof(sockaddr_in);
int    iPort = 6001;
int    iStatus;

// Set global var
g_bIsServer = 1;
// Initialize the socket handle
g_skListenSocket = INVALID_SOCKET;
// Create the socket
g_skListenSocket = socket(AF_INET, SOCK_STREAM, 0);
// Check if there was an error
if(g_skListenSocket == INVALID_SOCKET) {
    vShowText("** ERROR ** Could Not Create Socket");
    return;
}
vShowText("<- Socket Created ->");
// Clear out the socket address structure
memset(&saServerAddress, 0, sizeof(sockaddr_in));
// Initialize the socket address structure
saServerAddress.sin_family = AF_INET;
saServerAddress.sin_addr.s_addr = htonl(INADDR_ANY);
saServerAddress.sin_port = htons(iPort);
// Attempt to bind
if(bind(g_skListenSocket, (sockaddr*) &saServerAddress, sizeof(sockaddr)) ==
        SOCKET_ERROR) {
    vShowText("** ERROR ** Could Not Bind Socket");
    return;
}
vShowText("<- Socket Bound ->");
// Listen for a connection
iStatus = listen(g_skListenSocket, 32);
if(iStatus == SOCKET_ERROR) {
    vShowText("** ERROR ** Could Not Listen");
    // Close the socket
```

```
    closesocket(g_skListenSocket);
    return;
}
vShowText("<- Socket Listening ->");
g_skClientSocket = accept(g_skListenSocket, (struct sockaddr*)&saClientAddress,
                        &iClientSize);
if(g_skClientSocket == INVALID_SOCKET) {
    vShowText("** ERROR ** Could Not Accept Client");
    // Close the socket
    closesocket(g_skListenSocket);
    return;
}
// Turn off buttons
DestroyWindow(hBU_Connect);
DestroyWindow(hBU_Host);
vShowText("<- Client Connected ->");
// Flag as connected
g_bConnected = 1;
// Flag that it is the other player's turn
// to end the turn
g_bMyTurn = 0;
// Wait for client's first turn
vTurnDone();
```

The first part of the code handles the client connection logic. Basically, the program listens for a connection and accepts it once one comes in. The code then removes the Host and Connect buttons so that the user cannot select them again. The program then sets the turn variable to indicate that the client has control of the game. Finally, the turn is ended with a call to the turn done function. This puts the server in receive mode so that it can receive the client's end-of-turn message. All of this is illustrated in Figure 14.16.

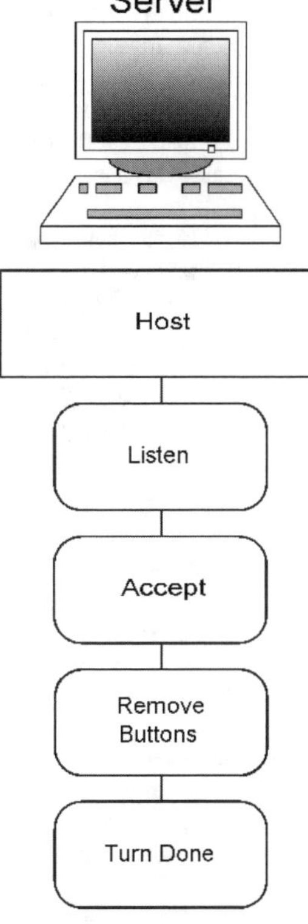

Figure 14.16: Flow of the vHost() function.

The vConnect() Function

The vConnect() function is called when the player selects the Connect button. Here is the code for it:

```c
sockaddr_in saServerAddress;
int    iPort = 6001,iStatus;
LPHOSTENT lpHost;
char   szHost[128];

// Set global var
g_bIsServer = 0;
// Init the host value, change this IP to whatever valid IP you wish
sprintf(szHost,"192.168.0.2");
// Initialize the socket handle
g_skClientSocket = INVALID_SOCKET;
// Create the socket
g_skClientSocket = socket(AF_INET, SOCK_STREAM, 0);
// Check if there was an error
if(g_skClientSocket == INVALID_SOCKET) {
   vShowText("** ERROR ** Could Not Create Socket");
   return;
}
vShowText("<- Socket Created ->");
// Initialize the server address data structure
memset(&saServerAddress,0,sizeof(sockaddr_in));
// Set this by default
saServerAddress.sin_family = AF_INET;
// Load the IP address
saServerAddress.sin_addr.s_addr = inet_addr(szHost);

// If the host specified is not an IP address we must look up the value
if(saServerAddress.sin_addr.s_addr == INADDR_NONE) {
   vShowText("<- Looking Up Host ID ->");
   // Get the host name
   lpHost = gethostbyname(szHost);
   // Check if we got something back
   if (lpHost != NULL) {
      // Load the server address with the host information
      saServerAddress.sin_addr.s_addr = ((LPIN_ADDR)lpHost->h_addr)->s_addr;
   }
   else {
      vShowText("** ERROR ** Could Not locate host");
      return;
   }
}
// Set the server port
saServerAddress.sin_port = htons(iPort);
// Attempt to connect to the server
iStatus = connect(g_skClientSocket, (struct
sockaddr*)&saServerAddress,sizeof(sockaddr));
// Check if there was an error
if(iStatus == SOCKET_ERROR) {
   vShowText("** ERROR ** Could Not Connect To Server");
   return;
```

```
}
// Turn off buttons
DestroyWindow(hBU_Connect);
DestroyWindow(hBU_Host);
vShowText("<- Connected To Server ->");
// Flag as connected
g_bConnected = 1;
// Flag that it is my turn to end the turn
g_bMyTurn = 1;
// Turn on the Turn Done window
hBU_TurnDone = CreateWindow(
    "BUTTON",
    "Turn Done",
    WS_CHILD | WS_VISIBLE | BS_PUSHBUTTON,
    5,
    280,
    100,
    28,
    g_hWnd,(HMENU)IDC_hBU_TurnDone,g_hInst,NULL);
vShowText(":Server waiting, make your turn");
```

The connect code is very similar to what I showed you in the web connection example. The client first resolves the server address and then connects to it. As long as the connection is successful, the client removes the Connect and Host buttons and adds a new one called Turn Done. At this point, the client can take its time to end the turn. The flow of the function can be seen in Figure 14.17.

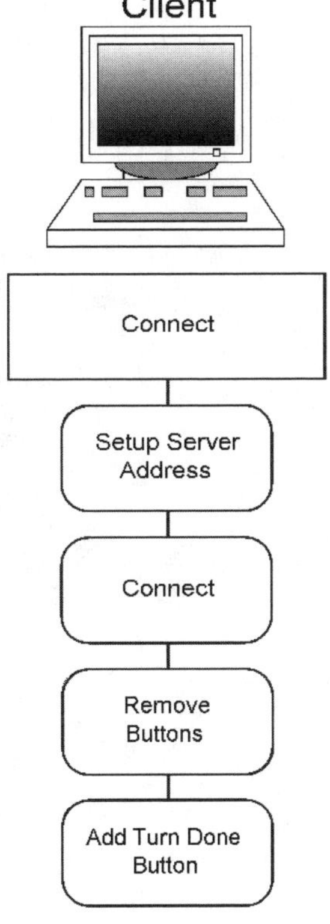

Figure 14.17: Flow of the vConnect() function.

The vTurnDone() Function

The turn done function accomplishes two different things. If it is your turn, it sends the turn done message to the other player and waits for him to finish. If it is not your turn, the function waits for the other player's turn. The flow of the function can be seen in Figure 14.18.

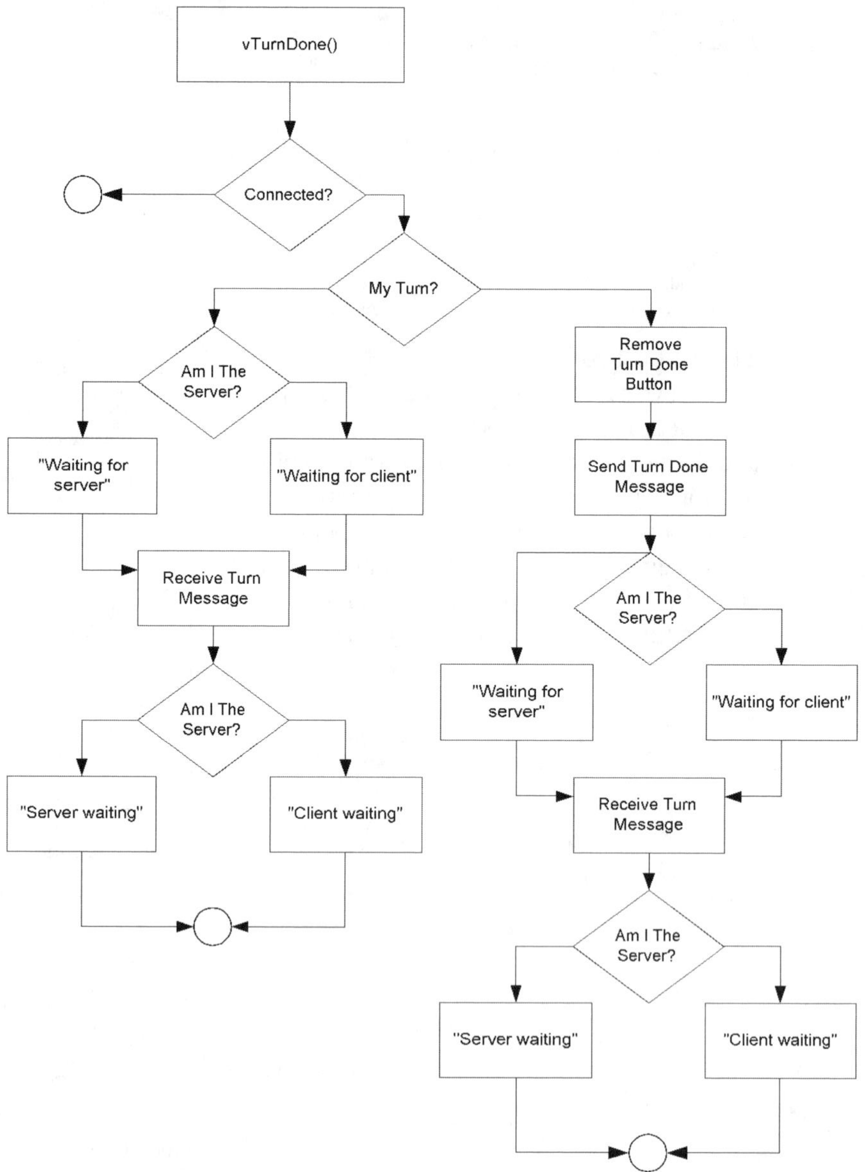

Figure 14.18: Flow of the vTurnDone() function.

Although the flowchart seems complicated, the code for the function is not. The majority of it is taken up with messages to the window. If you take out the messages, the code looks like the following:

```
// If connected, check to send or receive turn message
if(g_bConnected) {
    // My turn, send the message
    if(g_bMyTurn) {
        // Disable turn button
        DestroyWindow(hBU_TurnDone);
        // Send turn over message
        vSendTurnMessage();
        // Wait for receive message
        vReceiveTurnMessage();
    }
    else {
        // Wait for receive message
    }
}
```

If you compare the code above to what is in the main.cpp, you will notice that the code above is much shorter. I removed the text messages so that you can more easily see what is going on.

The vSendTurnMessage() Function

When it comes time to send the end-of-turn message, the send turn message function is called. The code for it is as follows:

```
void vSendTurnMessage(void)
{
    char   szTurnPacket[32];
    int iBytes = 0;

    // Create a "dummy" packet
    sprintf(szTurnPacket, "turnpacket");
    // Send the packet
    iBytes = send(g_skClientSocket, szTurnPacket, 32, 0);
    if(iBytes != SOCKET_ERROR) {
    }
    else {
        vShowText("** ERROR ** Sending");
        return;
    }
    // Set to receive mode now
    g_bMyTurn = 0;
}
```

The code starts off by creating the packet to send to the client or server. The packet contains some text for demo purposes only. Once the packet is composed, the code sends the packet to the other player. The program will block and wait until the receiver confirms the transmission. Once the confirmation is received, the turn flag is set and the function is done.

The vReceiveTurnMessage() Function

When it is your turn to wait for the other player, the receive turn message function is executed. It sits and waits for the turn packet to come across the wire. Once the packet arrives, the turn flag is set and the Turn Done button is displayed. Here is the code to perform this:

```
void vReceiveTurnMessage(void)
{
    char    szTurnPacket[32];
    int iBytes = 0;

    iBytes = recv(g_skClientSocket, szTurnPacket, 32, 0);
    // Check return code
    if(iBytes != SOCKET_ERROR) {
    }
    else {
        vShowText("** ERROR ** Receiving");
        return;
    }
    // Set to send mode now
    g_bMyTurn = 1;

    // Turn on the Turn Done button
    hBU_TurnDone = CreateWindow(
        "BUTTON",
        "Turn Done",
        WS_CHILD | WS_VISIBLE | BS_PUSHBUTTON,
        5,
        280,
        100,
        28,
        g_hWnd,(HMENU)IDC_hBU_TurnDone,g_hInst,NULL);
}
```

In the receive function I make a call to receive a packet from the other player. Once the packet comes in, the code sets the turn flag and creates the Turn Done button. That's about it for sending and receiving!

I have only scratched the surface of multiplayer game programming in this section, but hopefully you have enough information to at least start on a turn-based network-enabled game.

Recap

Remember the following about networking and sockets:

- TCP/IP gives you guaranteed packet delivery at the expense of speed.
- UDP gives you fast packet delivery but requires more development time.
- Straight sockets are great for multiplatform programming and times when you want complete control.
- DirectPlay is good for when you do not want to write everything yourself.

Photoshop — The World's Best Texture Editor

Have you ever wondered how artists and game developers create the cool textures and graphics you see in video games? Personally, I believe it is 10 percent technical skill, 40 percent persistence, and 50 percent talent. You may be wondering why I only put talent at 50 percent. The reason is because without persistence, all of the talent in the world won't bring a product to completion. The first rule of game development is you must be committed to finishing the project at all costs. Not only will you feel better about yourself, but you also will be more marketable as a person who follows through.

Enough preaching about follow-through. There are two basic building blocks to art in modern games: 2D textures and 3D models. To realize the power of textures all you have to do is render a 3D model without any. Right away you notice how the model is very boring and plastic looking. With textures added, the model looks vibrant and takes on a life of its own. Check out Figure A.1 to see a 3D model without and with textures. It doesn't take a Rembrandt to notice that the textured model looks superior.

Figure A.1: The figure on the left shows a 3D model without textures, while the picture on the right is the same model with textures.

Even if you lack the talent to create great-looking textures, you need at least a basic understanding of how the tools work. Many times in the production cycle you will end up creating placeholder textures and other artwork. You do this so that you don't have to wait on the art department to catch up to you before proceeding. In this chapter I cover the following:

■   Adobe Photoshop

■   Creating a screen shot with Adobe Photoshop

■   Using layers in Photoshop

■   Creating images with alpha channels in Photoshop

Adobe Photoshop

There are many 2D graphics packages available, but none of them are as valuable to a game developer as Adobe's Photoshop. Now in its seventh major release, Photoshop is the de facto standard in 2D editing packages. It is on the pricey side for most hobbyist developers, but it is well worth it.

I think the best way to explain the power of Photoshop is to show you. So, go grab a cold one and get ready for a primer on my favorite 2D package, Photoshop.

When you open up Photoshop, you are greeted with a screen resembling that in Figure A.2.

Figure A.2: The Adobe Photoshop 6.0 interface as displayed when the program is first launched.

There are a few key areas of interest in this figure: the floating toolbar on the left, the standard menu bar at the top, and the floating panels on the right of the image. Before I get into detail about those items I want you to capture a screen shot of your desktop and then paste it into Photoshop.

Creating Screen Shots with Photoshop

The first step to creating a screen shot with Photoshop is to capture the screen to the Windows clipboard. You do this by hitting the Print Screen key located on your keyboard. Once you hit the key, your entire desktop display is put into the clipboard for pasting into other applications.

Now that you have the display in clipboard memory, it is time to paste it into Photoshop. The first thing you need is a blank image or canvas in which to paste the picture. Luckily for you, the engineers at Adobe thought about this need and made it as simple as hitting the Ctrl+N key combination. Make sure the program is active and try this out yourself. The dialog box shown in Figure A.3 should now be on your screen.

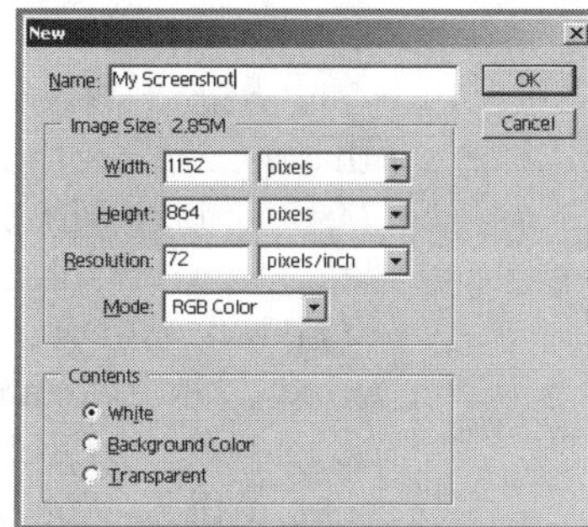

Figure A.3: The new image dialog box in Adobe Photoshop 6.0.

The New Image Dialog Box

Wow! Isn't that exciting, a new dialog box! Okay, I know, it's not too thrilling, but there is one cool thing about it. Take a look at the Width and Height fields. Do you see how they are automatically filled in with your screen resolution? Isn't that cool? All right, if you don't think that is cool, let me explain why it is.

Setting the Image Attributes

In most paint programs, when you create a new image for a screen shot, you have to fill in the size of the image you want each and every time. Adobe has removed this repetitive task by having the image dimensions match that of whatever image is in the system clipboard at the time. If there is nothing in the clipboard, the dialog merely fills in the dimensions from the image used last. So, if you have an 800 x 600 image in the clipboard and open up the new image dialog box, it automatically uses 800 x

600 for the image dimensions. If you cut out a portion of an image, say 100 x 100, and open up the new image dialog box, you see those dimensions in the box. This is a very useful feature you will come to rely on as your Photoshop skills get better.

Enough about that feature. If you want dimensions other than those presented in the dialog, all you have to do is change them. One thing you may have to do is change the units of measure for the image size. Photoshop normally defaults to inches, and you need pixels. The little drop-down boxes to the right of Width and Height let you choose pixels, inches, cm, points, picas, or columns for the unit of measure.

The next text field, Resolution, lets you set the number of units per inch stored in the image. This is really meant for printing or scanning, so you don't need to worry about it for now. I always leave it at 72 pixels/inch.

There are three radio buttons under the Contents section of the dialog that let you set the background of the new image you are creating. Feel free to play with this but for the purpose of taking a screen shot, just leave it at the default setting.

The last item of interest in the dialog box is the image name. It defaults to Untitled, and I just leave it at that for most purposes. Go ahead and hit the OK button on the dialog now. Figure A.4 should now be present in all its glory on your screen if you followed these directions.

Figure A.4: The program desktop with a new image on it ready for work.

One thing you may be wondering is why the image looks so small considering it is the size of your entire Windows desktop. This is because the program shrinks new images to fit within the Photoshop workspace. The title bar of the new image shows the name of your picture and next to it you see the current zoom settings. On my machine it defaults to 66.7% zoom rate in order to fit the image in the workspace.

Pasting the Capture Buffer

You are now at the last step to creating a screen shot. Hit the F4 key now. Ta da! If all has gone well, you should now see the screen shot pasted in the window similar to Figure A.5.

Figure A.5: The screen shot in all its glory.

Flattening the Image

You are almost ready to save your newly created screen shot. Go to the Layer menu in Photoshop and select the Flatten Image command, as shown in Figure A.6.

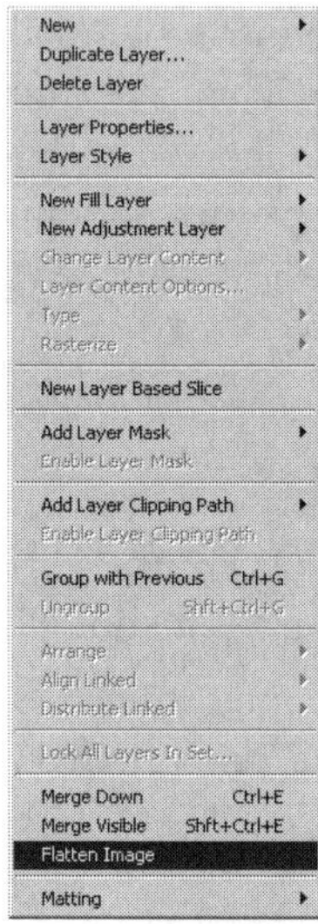

Figure A.6: The Layer menu in Photoshop.

Now that the image is flattened, you can go ahead and save it by selecting Save As from the File menu. Selecting Save As brings up the dialog in Figure A.7.

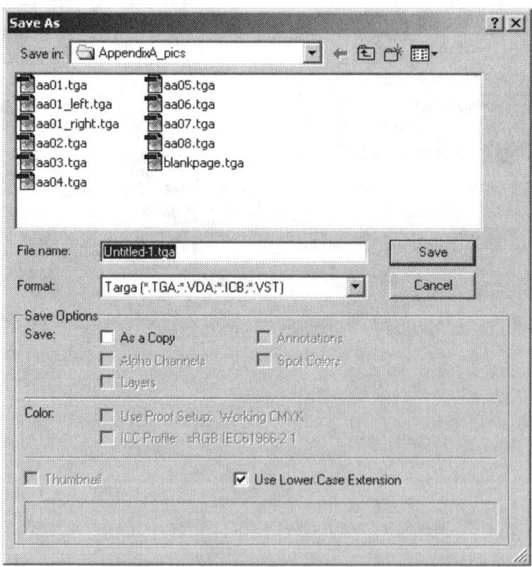

Figure A.7: The Save As dialog in Photoshop.

Saving the Image

There are many options for saving the file. First of all, there are tons of formats available to you. Some formats are appropriate for game development, while others are not. Table A.1 shows the various formats useful for game development.

Table A.1: Photoshop image formats

Extension	Description
PSD	The native format of Photoshop images. This format is useful for images in progress as it saves everything about the image including layer information. Do not use this format for the final image though, as DirectX does not support loading it directly. Files of this format also tend to be rather large, which is another reason not to use it for the final output.
BMP	The standard format of Windows images. This format is usable by game engines but it takes up a lot of storage space due to lack of compression. The upside to this though is that the format loads quickly, as no decompression is necessary. Another problem with this format is the lack of 32-bit support. If you need alpha transparency, do not use this format.
GIF	The format owned by CompuServe. This format is generally used for web pages and is not very useful for game development. The main problem with the format is the license you must purchase from CompuServe to use it legally. For this reason alone I highly suggest you stay away from it.
JPG	This is the granddaddy format of small images. JPGs are great for small file sizes, as you can compress them as little or as much as you want. The main downside to JPGs is that they do not always look very good. Of course, you can alleviate this by using a low compression method but that kind of defeats the purpose. Another problem with JPGs is that they take a long time to load, as they have to be decompressed first. The last gripe I have with the JPG format is the lack of standardization. If you ever try to write your own JPG loader code, be prepared for a nightmare.
PNG	This format has been developed openly by the development community and is free of charge to use. Basically, a lot of people got hacked off at CompuServe for charging for GIFs, so they came up with this format. It is a good image format with a small file footprint. The main disadvantage to PNGs in Photoshop is that you cannot save them in 32-bit. This makes them bad if you require transparency.
TGA	The Targa file format is one of my personal favorites since it supports 32-bit images and is easy to load. DirectX now encapsulates the loading of images but it wasn't always this way. If you plan on ever using your own image loading routines, Targa files are the way to go.

Fill out the name of your screen shot by typing it in the File name edit box. Now, pick the Targa format and hit the Save button. The dialog shown in Figure A.8 is now on your screen; it needs the depth at which you want the image saved.

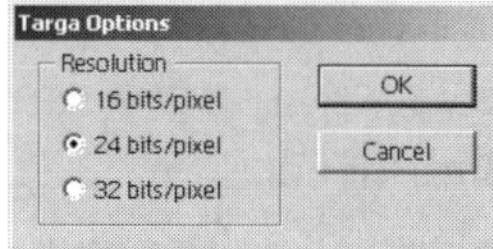

Figure A.8: The Targa Options dialog in Photoshop.

The dialog presents you with three choices: 16 bits/pixel, 24 bits/pixel, and 32 bits/pixel. In the case of the screen shot, you only need 24 bits/pixel, so select that and hit OK. If you create an image with an alpha channel, you need to select 32 bits/pixel.

There you go: The screen shot is now saved and archived on your hard drive. See, that wasn't so hard, was it?

Layers

Are you wondering why I asked you to select the Flatten Image command from the Image menu? If so, take a look at the window with three tabs in the bottom-right corner of the Photoshop interface in Figure A.5. The tabs are labeled Layers, Channels, and Paths. Inside the window you see a row named Layer 1 and a row named Background. Since you are viewing the Layers tab, these rows represent the layers of the image you are working with. Now, let me explain more about layers, as they are one of the most important aspects of Photoshop.

First you need to step back to when you create a new image. Back in Figure A.4 you have a blank image waiting to be pasted into. Take a look at the Layers tab, and notice there is one row with the label Background. The difference between Figure A.4 and Figure A.5 is that Figure A.5 contains two layers, one named Background and one named Layer 1. You see, when you first create an image it starts with a bottom layer named Background. Just like the blank canvas of a painter, the Background layer is the base of all your images.

Paste the clipboard into a blank image and it automatically creates a new layer. This is very useful as all you have to do is copy a graphic to the memory and let Photoshop do the rest as you paste it to the new image. Making composite images is a breeze because of this. Figure A.9 illustrates the layers you created with the screen shot.

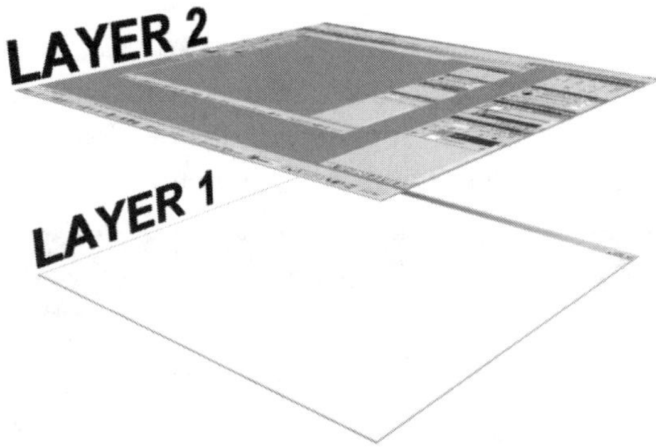

Figure A.9: The Background and Layer 1 layers illustrated.

As you can see in Figure A.9, the Background layer is Layer 1. This layer is the blank image you created. The layer above the Background layer represents the clipboard buffer you pasted into the image. By selecting the Flatten Image command, you combined the two layers into a single layer. Figure A.10 shows the final flattened image.

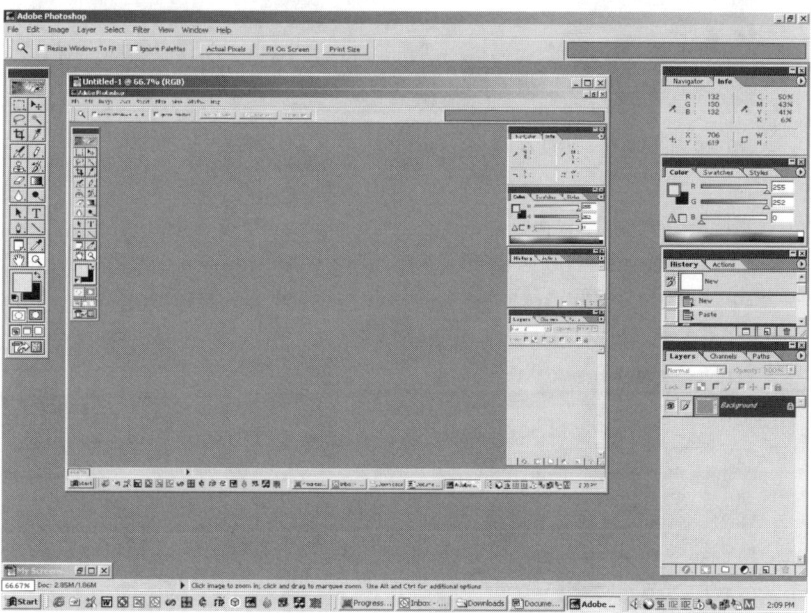

Figure A.10: The screen shot after being flattened.

Take a peek at the Layers tab again and notice that there is only one layer in Figure A.10, named Background. There is only one layer because you flattened all of the layers together with the Flatten Image command.

Playing with Layers

Close the newly created screen shot and open up the file named mylayer.psd located in the ChapterAA folder in the downloadable files. If all goes well, you should now see Figure A.11 on your screen.

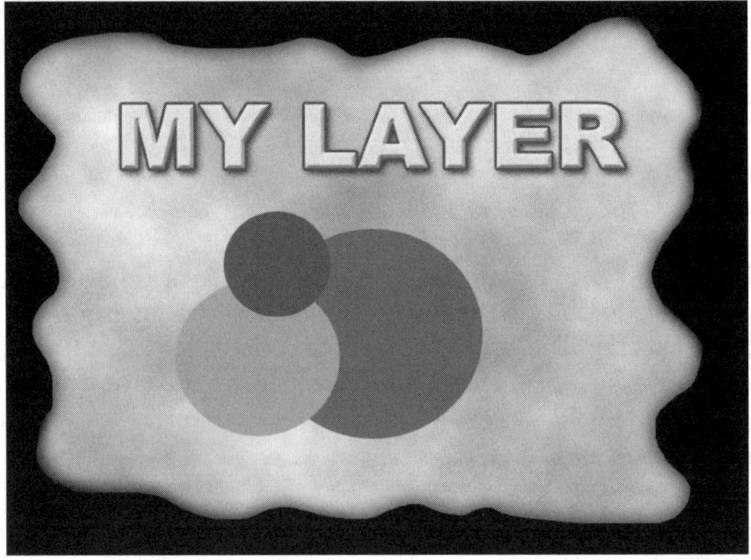

Figure A.11: The mylayer.psd image.

I'm no Picasso, but the image does the trick of demonstrating multiple layer options. The first thing I want you to look at is the Layers tab on the bottom-right area of the Photoshop workspace. Figure A.12 shows what you should see.

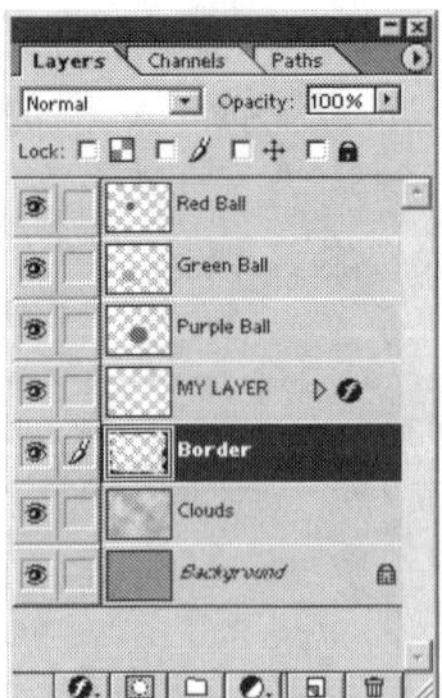

Figure A.12: The Layers tab for the mylayer.psd image.

In Figure A.12, the layers show up as individual rows named Background, Clouds, Border, MY LAYER, Purple Ball, Green Ball, and Red Ball. Hopefully you get the correlation between the layer names and the elements of the mylayer.psd image now on your screen. Basically, each layer represents an element of the picture that is now loaded. The cool part about this is that you can move the layers around without changing the other elements.

Moving Layers

The first step to moving a layer around is to select the layer you want to move. Select the Green Ball layer now by left-clicking on the Green Ball layer row. (When I refer to rows on the Layers tab I am talking about what you see in Figure A.13.)

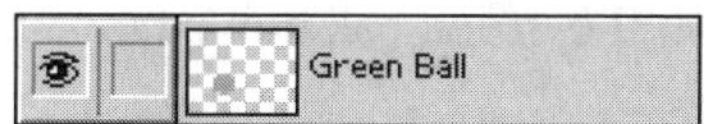

Figure A.13: The Green Ball row on the Layers tab.

There are a few elements to each row. The first little box on the left denotes whether the layer is currently visible. When the layer is visible, you see an eyeball in the box. If the box is empty, the layer is not visible. Easy enough, eh?

The box to the right of the visibility box denotes whether or not the layer is active. When the layer is active, a small paintbrush is displayed in the box. If the layer is not active, the box is empty. There is another use for this box that I discuss later on.

The next item for display is a thumbnail image of the layer in its entirety. The thumbnail is useful for telling at a glimpse what the layer contains.

The last element in the row is the name of the layer. Layers default to such interesting names as Layer 1, Layer 2, etc. I have modified the ones in the mylayer.psd image to accurately describe each layer. I show you how to do this later.

Now that you have the Green Ball layer selected, the row is blue, indicating it is active. The little paintbrush is also viewable on the left side of the row in the Layers tab. Move your eyes over to the toolbar on the left side of the Photoshop interface. It contains all of the various tools you use for editing images. Figure A.14 shows the toolbar in its entirety.

Figure A.14: The main toolbar for the Photoshop interface.

There are many tools on the bar, but I only want you to concern yourself with the one in the upper-right corner of the toolbar. It looks like what is shown in Figure A.15.

Figure A.15: The Move tool from the main toolbar.

This tool is aptly named the Move tool. Its only purpose in life is to move elements around within an image. Select it now to activate the move-ment functionality. Now that the Move tool is activated, drag and drop the green ball in the image to the bottom-left corner of the image. Notice how the ball moves without affecting the other layers? I don't know about you, but I think it is a very cool feature. Figure A.16 shows what your screen should look like now with the green ball moved in a different position.

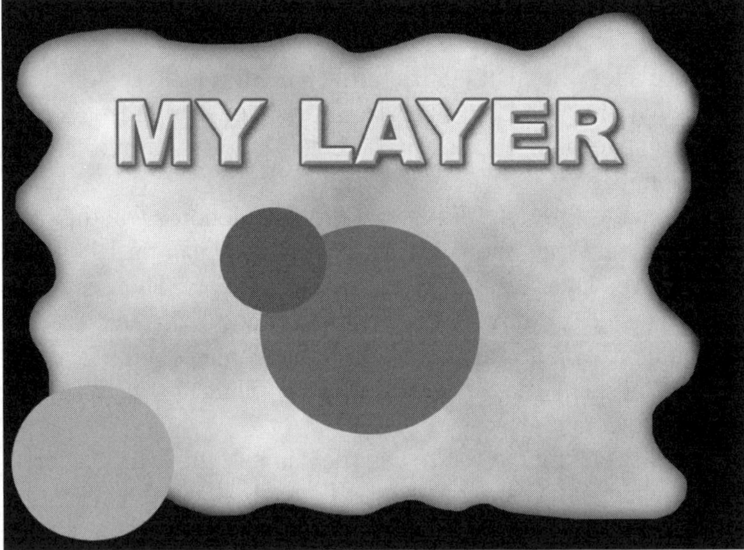

Figure A.16: The image shown with the green ball moved.

If you are picky or have an obsessive-compulsive disorder, you are proba-bly having issues with the fact that the green ball overlaps the image border. This happened because the green layer sits higher in the pecking order than the border layer does. Don't fret too much though, as this is easily remedied.

Changing Layer Ordering

Changing the order of layers is as easy as dragging and dropping a layer row from the Layers tab. Select the Border layer now and drag it onto the Red Ball layer. Ta da! The Border layer is now the topmost layer and it covers everything below it. Figure A.17 shows the results.

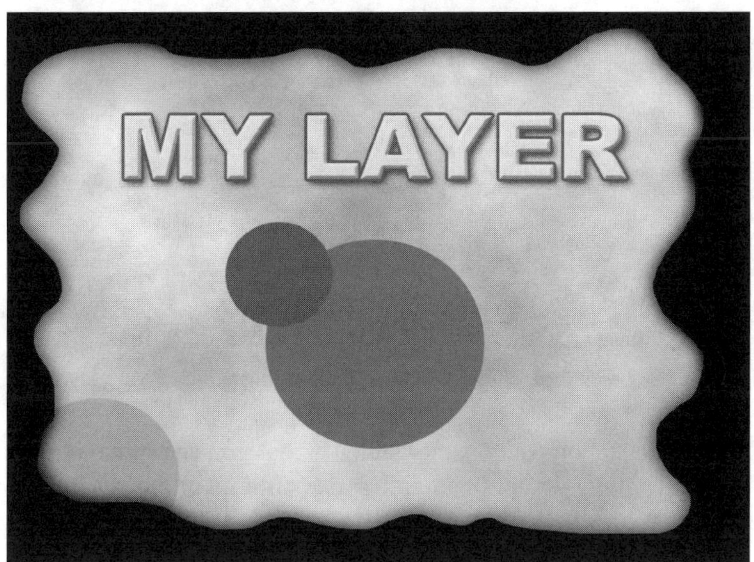

Figure A.17: The image shown with the Border layer in a new order.

Everything is right with the world now that the border covers the green ball. Play around with moving the contents of layers around as well as the order of the layers until you get the hang of it.

Changing Layer Opacity

Let's say you want to make the border of the picture less opaque. Maybe you are feeling gray or you just have it out for the border. Who knows? The easiest way to accomplish this is to change the opacity of the border with the opacity slider.

Check out Figure A.12 again and take a close look at the Opacity setting. Normally the opacity of a layer starts out at 100%. This means that nothing can be seen through it. There is an arrow to the right of the Opacity setting that activates the opacity slider. Left-click on the arrow now to see the opacity slider. Once the slider is visible, slide it to the left until the opacity reads 35%. Let go of the slider to see the image updated to reflect the change. Check out Figure A.18 to see the new, less opaque layer.

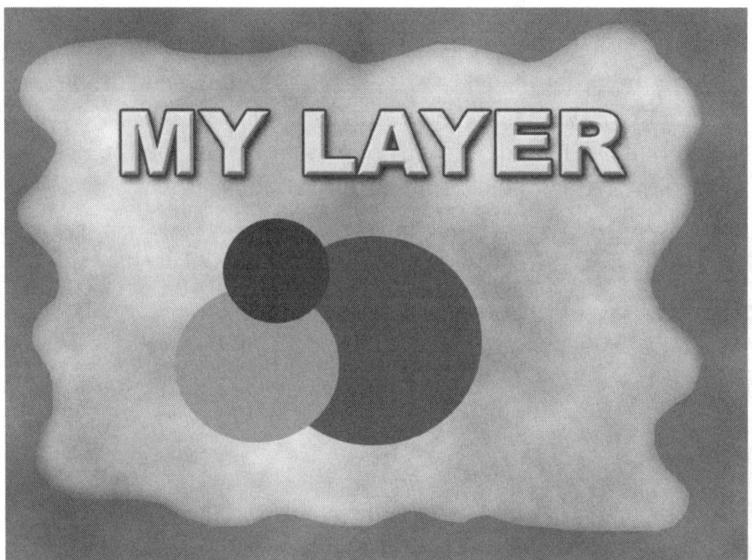

Figure A.18: The image shown with the Border layer at 35% opacity.

The cool part about the opacity slider is that you can move it back and forth all day long without damaging the contents of the layer. Play around with adjusting various layer opacity settings until you get the hang of it.

Layer Effects

Now for the interesting aspects of layers — layer effects. Go to the Layers tab and right-click on the row labeled Green Ball. This action shows you the Layer Options menu, which is illustrated in Figure A.19.

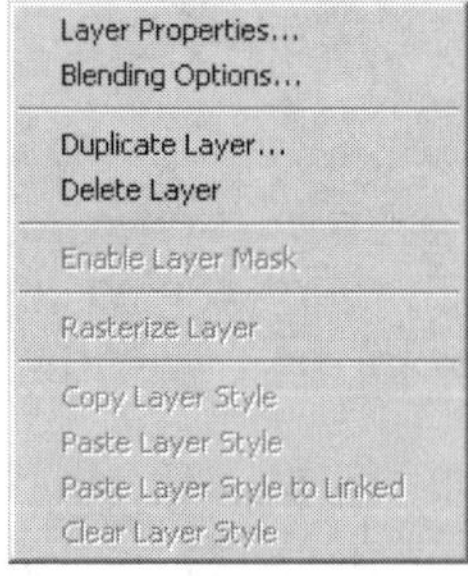

Figure A.19: The Layer Options menu.

In Figure A.19 you see four options: Layer Properties, Blending Options, Duplicate Layer, and Delete Layer.

Layer Properties

Select Layer Properties from the Layer Options menu and check out the Layer Properties dialog box. Basically you can either change the name of the layer here or change the color of the layer row. Why would you want to change the row color? Well, this is very useful when you have dozens of layers and wish to set them apart somehow. Try selecting different colors to see the effect it has on the view.

Blending Options

Buckle your seatbelt; this next one is a doozie! Back on the Layer Options menu, select Blending Options to bring up the dialog in Figure A.20.

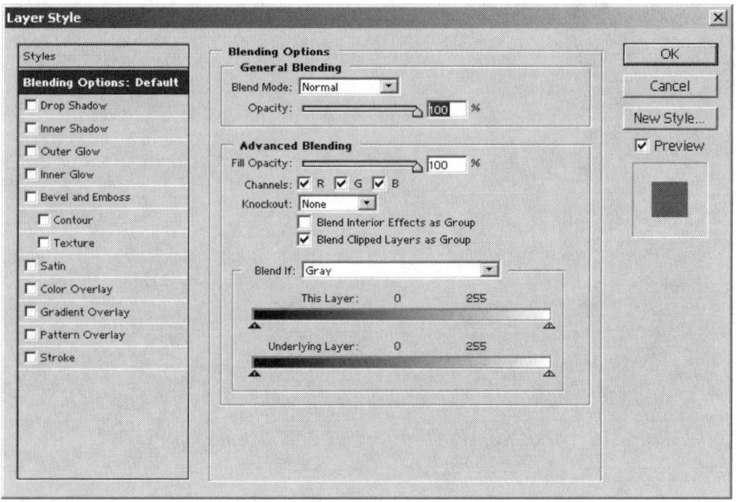

Figure A.20: The Blending Options dialog.

Check out the left side of Figure A.20 to see the myriad effects you can use with layers. The effects are as follows:

- Drop Shadow
- Inner Shadow
- Outer Glow
- Inner Glow
- Bevel and Emboss
- Satin
- Color Overlay
- Gradient Overlay

- Pattern Overlay
- Stroke

If you are familiar with versions previous to Photoshop 6.0, you know that effects such as these required costly plug-ins or lengthy steps to accomplish. Versions 6 and higher have these cool features built in.

Open up the file named Layer F_X.psd in the ChapterAA folder in the companion files. You should now see the image shown in Figure A.21 on your screen.

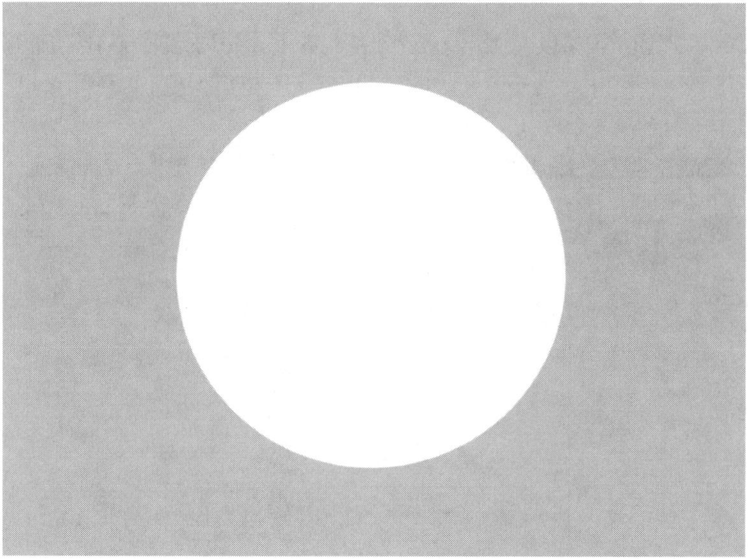

Figure A.21: The sphere image with no effects applied to it.

There is nothing special about this figure. It is just an ordinary white sphere on a gray background. I chose this image because it is suitable for demonstrating various layer effects.

Drop Shadow

Bring up the Blending Options dialog using the steps I explained earlier. Select the effect named Drop Shadow to activate the Drop Shadow effect. This brings up the Drop Shadow panel as shown in Figure A.22.

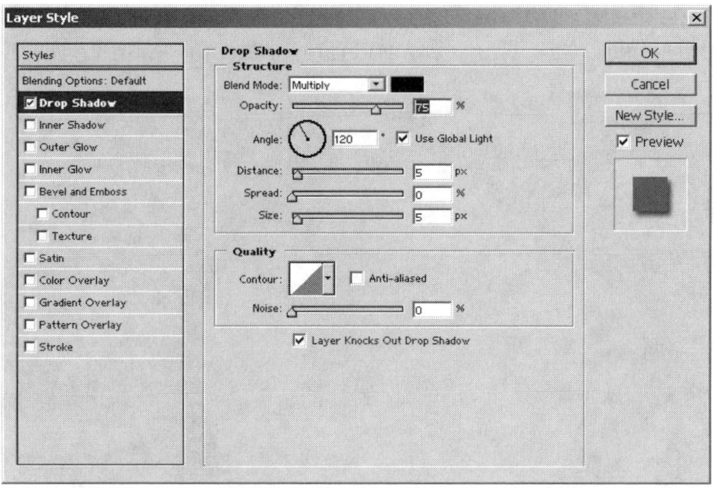

Figure A.22: The Drop Shadow blending options dialog.

Depending on the resolution of your desktop, you may or may not realize the Drop Shadow effect is already active. Move the Blending Options dialog box around so you can see the sphere with a newly formed drop shadow on it. You can always go back and turn it off by unchecking the Drop Shadow check box.

There are several drop shadow options such as Blend Mode, Opacity, Angle, Distance, Spread, Size, Contour, and Noise. I bet you can guess what the Opacity setting does! Check Table A.2 for a list of settings and their purpose.

Table A.2: Drop Shadow settings

Setting	Purpose
Blend Mode	Sets how the layer blends with other layers.
Opacity	Sets the translucency of the drop shadow. The higher the percentage, the darker the shadow.
Angle	Sets the angle at which the "sun" hits the object. This affects where the drop shadow falls.
Distance	Sets how far the object is from the shadow. Use this setting to simulate the height of the sun.
Spread	Sets the sharpness of the shadow. Use it to fine-tune the look of the shadow edge.
Size	Sets the fuzziness of the shadow. Use a large size for a diffused shadow and a small size for a tight shadow.
Contour	Sets the contour of the shadow. The best way to understand this is for you to try it out yourself.
Noise	Sets the amount of disruption in the shadow. Use it to give the shadow a television noise type look.

As a quick test, move the Distance to 61, the Spread to 37, the Size to 40, and the Noise to 20. This gives you the sphere shown in Figure A.23.

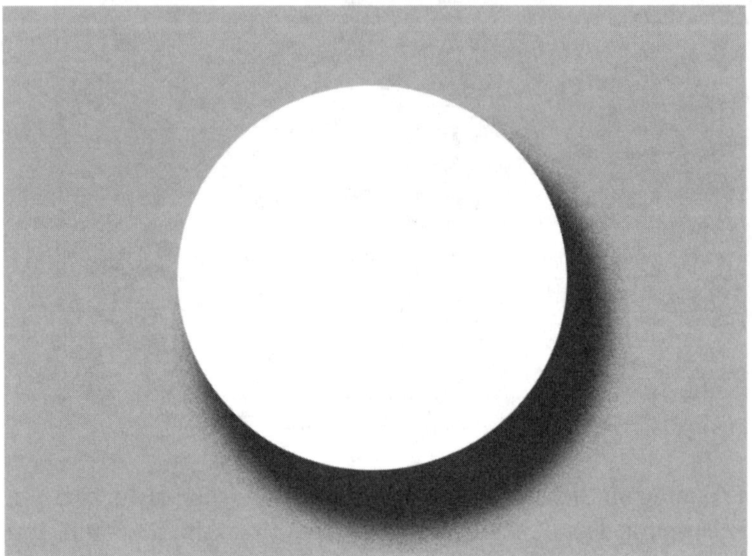

Figure A.23: The white sphere with the Drop Shadow effect applied to it.

The drop shadow in this figure is very noticeable. Normally you create more subtle shadows; I just went to the extreme to give you an idea of what is possible. Play around with the various Drop Shadow settings and see what you come up with.

I've only scratched the surface of the Blending Options dialog. It is up to you to try out different ones now to suit your needs.

Layer Filters

Not only can you create special layer effects with the Blending Options dialog, but you can also create them with Photoshop filters. The great thing about filters is Adobe supports an open format that allows developers to write their own for the software package. That means enterprising developers or artists can create their own special effects and share them with others or even sell them if they so desire.

Under the main menu of Photoshop, click the Filter menu. Once there, click on the Texture sub-menu to bring up the various texture filters. Figure A.24 illustrates the menu.

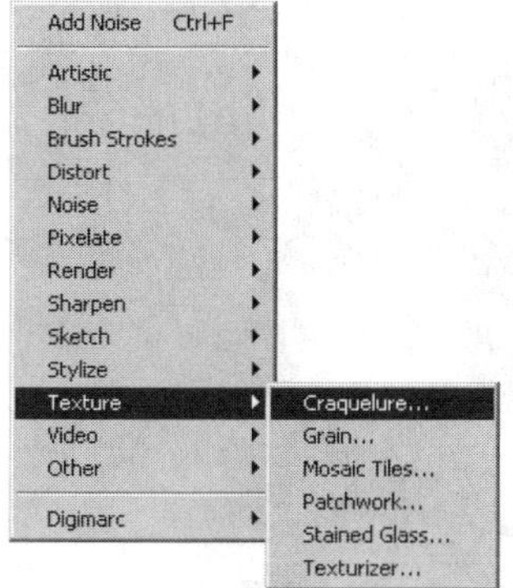

Figure A.24: The texture filter effect sub-menu.

There are six filters listed: Craquelure, Grain, Mosaic Tiles, Patchwork, Stained Glass, and Texturizer.

Try out the various filters to see what effect you get. I think you will find the Texturizer filter to be very useful in adding bump maps to your textures.

Tip I suggest you search the Internet for free filters. There are tons of them out there and many of them have truly astonishing effects. Always be wary of viruses, of course.

I have talked enough about layers for now. How about a tutorial on making alpha maps?

Alpha Maps

By now you have probably used alpha masks in game development. They allow textures to have varying degrees of translucency. Basically an alpha map is a mask for a texture. Where the mask has holes in it, the texture shows through. Where the mask is opaque, the texture is covered. It's really a basic topic when you think about it.

I have taken the liberty of creating a very simple texture in Figure A.25.

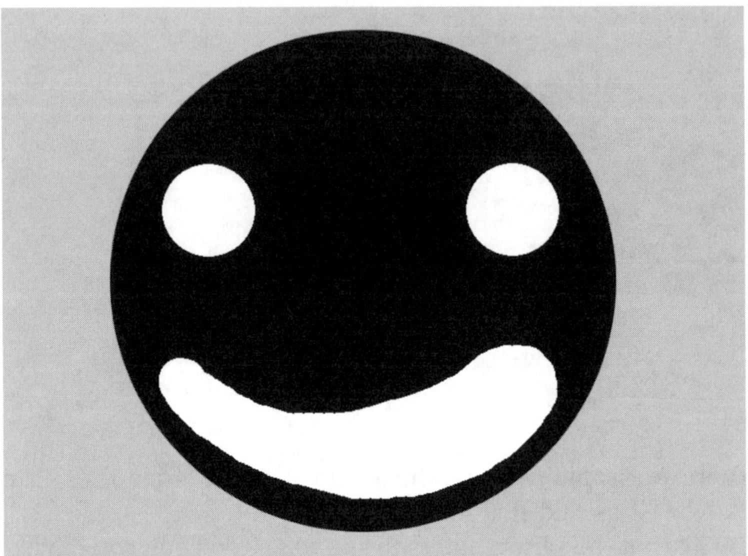

Figure A.25: A simple texture.

I know the texture isn't anything special, but it gets the point across for your needs. Now pretend the texture has no alpha channel and pretend you are blitting the texture over a background texture. Figure A.26 illustrates the effect of doing this operation.

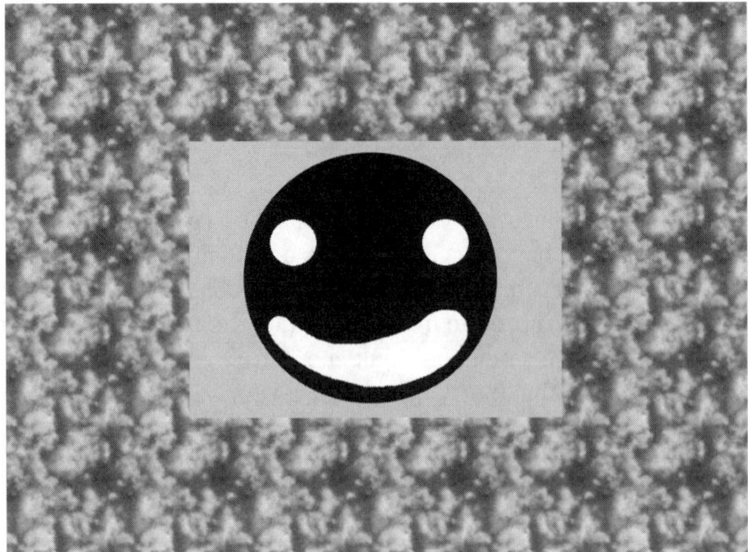

Figure A.26: The texture blitted over a background texture.

Hopefully you can see the blatant problem with the cartoon face texture. For one thing, it has an ugly square around it! This is because the texture lacks an alpha map and its entire border covers up everything below it.

Imagine taking a square piece of cardboard and cutting a hole out of it. This leaves you with a mask for the cartoon face. Put the mask over the image and pretend everything covered by cardboard is invisible. This results in Figure A.27.

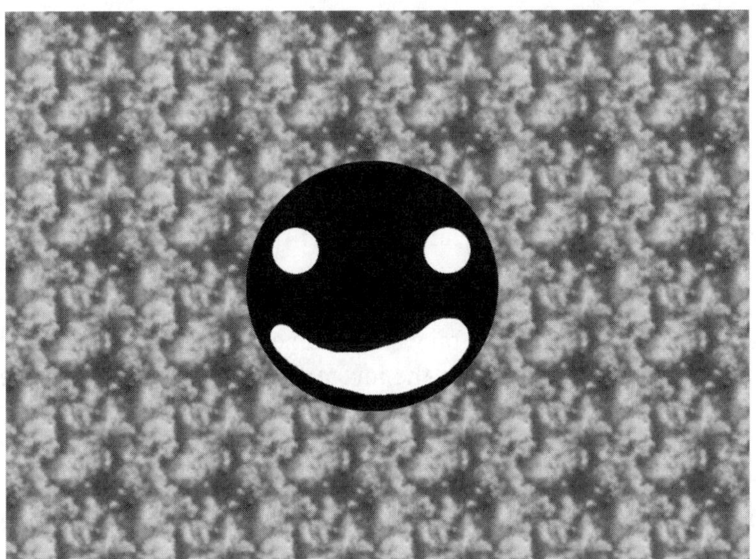

Figure A.27: The texture blitted over a background texture with an alpha mask.

Ta da! Notice how the imaginary cardboard mask renders the texture border invisible. Now the cartoon face looks good with a nice rounded edge. Enough with imaginary cardboard cutouts; it's time to make one for real!

Making an Alpha Map

Load up the cartoonface.psd file from the companion files to follow along. Once you have it loaded, the image from Figure A.25 presents itself again.

The Channels Tab

Back in the "Layers" section, you learned about the Layers tab. Now you get to learn about its neighbor, the Channels tab. It is located right next to the Layers tab. Click the Channels tab now to bring up the Channels dialog. The Channels tab in all its glory is seen in Figure A.28.

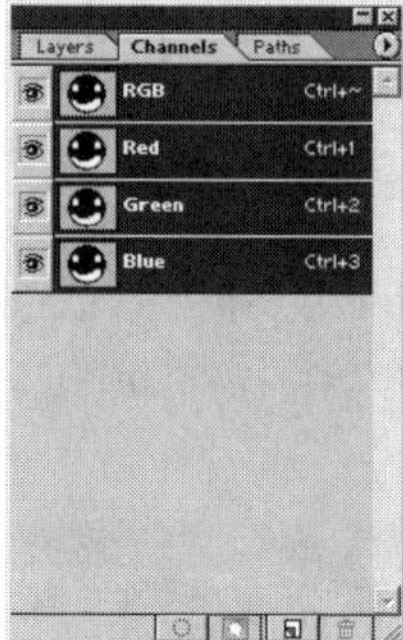

Figure A.28: The Channels tab for the cartoon face picture.

Notice how there are currently four channels in the picture: RGB, Red, Green, and Blue. There really are only three channels present. The RGB one just makes it easy to turn the other three on with a single click.

By selecting the various channels, you can alter the individual color component of the image. Say for instance you only want to alter the red component of an image. You would just select the Red channel from the Channels tab and then alter the image as normal. Most every operation can be performed on individual channels.

So, there you are, all alone in the woods with three different color channels. What do you do? You create a brand new channel! That's right; you need to create an alpha channel to make a mask for the lovely cartoon face.

The Magic Wand Tool

There is a great Photoshop tool appropriately called the Magic Wand tool. It is on the second row of icons on the main toolbar window. Select the tool now to activate it.

The Magic Wand tool lets you select regions of an image based on a single color or a range of colors. Now that you have it selected, you are presented with options at the top of the Photoshop window. You are allowed to set the tolerance amount, whether it is anti-aliased, whether it is contiguous, and whether it uses all layers.

The Tolerance setting sets the amount of deviation allowed in the color selection. If the target color is red and you want to pick up dark or light red, you set the tolerance to something around 50. This allows the Magic Wand to pick colors whose components are within 50 units of the selected color. If you only want the precise target color picked and nothing else, you set the tolerance to 0.

The Anti-aliased check box sets whether the Magic Wand selection area has anti-aliased edges. You almost always use this for creating alpha masks as it gives you nice smooth edges. If you turn off anti-aliasing, you will get very jagged-looking masks.

The Contiguous check box sets whether or not the Magic Wand picks up colors matching the criteria connected to your selection point. If you leave the box at its default checked state, the Magic Wand only picks up colors touching your selection area. If you uncheck the box and select a color, the Magic Wand picks every color in the image matching the criteria.

The Use All Layers check box sets whether or not the selection area merges the contents of every layer during selection time. This is useful if you want multiple layers of the image to contribute to the selection area but do not want to merge them permanently. For the cartoon face example, just leave this deselected.

Create the Selection

Select a point on the gray area around the cartoon face now. With that accomplished you see a crawling edge appear around the entire gray area of the picture. The crawling line gives you a visual clue as to where the selection area is.

Now that you have the mask selected, you need to save the selection to a new channel. You do this by picking the Save Selection option from the Select menu at the top of the Photoshop interface. Figure A.29 shows this menu item.

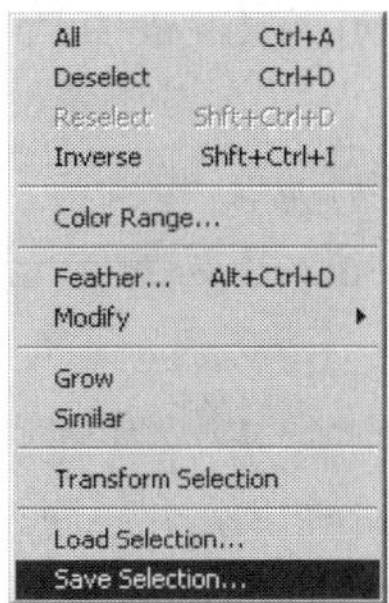

Figure A.29: The Select menu.

Select Save Selection to bring up the Save Selection dialog box. There is nothing special about the dialog; just give the new channel a name such as "Happy Alpha" and select the OK button.

Create the Mask

Go over to the Channels tab again and notice the new channel listed below the Blue channel. This shows you that the new channel has been created and is ready for editing. Activate the channel now by clicking on its row.

Did you notice the other channels turn off when you selected the new channel? This is normal and is easily remedied by selecting the RGB channel row to reactivate them. Do this now.

Wow, look at that! If you followed the instructions carefully, you now see a reddish cartoon face on your screen. The red actually represents where the mask covers or hides the texture.

Note Adobe uses the red color to denote the masked area because traditional artists use masking gel that has the same color.

If you are wondering why the face is masked out and not the border around the face, give yourself a pat on the back. The bottom line is that the mask is reversed from where you need it to be. This is easily fixed though!

Invert the Mask

As long as you didn't click on the image, you still have the crawling line effect that represents the selection area. If you don't have the selection visible, select the Magic Wand tool again and click on the gray area.

The first step is to fill in the border with a 100 percent opaque color. Alpha masks consist of only grayscale colors, so follow these three simple rules:

- Black — Fully opaque. Nothing shows through black areas.
- Gray — Translucent. The amount of translucency depends on how black or white the gray is.
- White — Full transparent. Everything shows through white areas.

From the above list you know to fill in the area around the cartoon face with the color black. Do this now by selecting the color black on the toolbar palette box and then selecting Fill from the Edit menu. If all went well you now have a completely red tinted image on your screen. This indicates that the entire image is masked out.

The next action item is to fill in the cartoon face area with the fully transparent color of white. Do this by inverting the current selection mask. Go to the Select menu now and select Inverse. This inverts the active selection area.

Do you notice how the selection area now surrounds the cartoon face instead of the area around the cartoon face? If not, you may need to go back through the previous steps. Select the color white on the palette menu and then select Fill again from the Edit menu. The Channels tab should look like the one in Figure A.30 if all goes well.

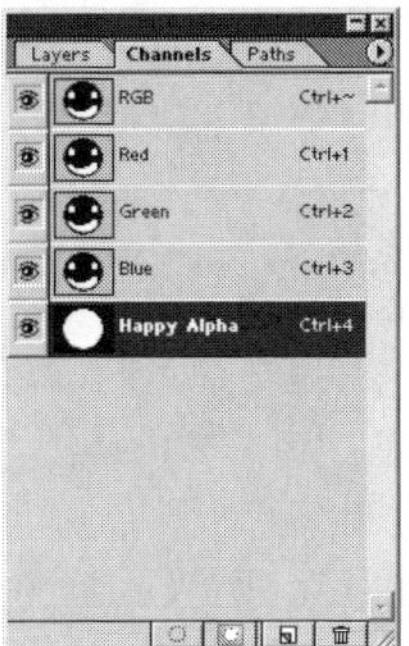

Figure A.30: The Channels tab with the new alpha channel visible.

There you have it! The cartoon face is now cleared of the red tint and the border around it is tinted. This indicates the face is visible and the area around it is masked out.

Save the Alpha Image

Your first clue in realizing the alpha channel is working comes when you save the image. When images have no alpha channel, you are not given the option to save them in 32-bit mode. When images have an alpha channel, you are allowed to save them in 32-bit mode. Save the image as a Targa file now and you should be prompted to pick 16-, 24-, or 32-bit mode. Save it as a 32-bit image, and you are finished with this lesson.

Recap

To create a screen shot with Photoshop, you perform the following steps:

1. Press Print Screen to capture the image to the clipboard.
2. Switch to the Photoshop application.
3. Create a new image by pressing Ctrl+N.
4. Paste the clipboard into the image with the F4 key.
5. Flatten the image with the Flatten Image command from the Layer menu.
6. Save the image by pressing Ctrl+S.

To create an alpha mask with Photoshop, you perform the following steps:

1. Select the area you wish to mask off.
2. Save the selection with the Save Selection command from the Select menu.
3. Select the new channel from the Channels tab.
4. Select the RGB channel from the Channels tab.
5. Fill in the selection with black by using the Fill command from the Edit menu.
6. Invert the selection by selecting the Inverse command from the Select menu.
7. Fill in the selection with white by using the Fill command again.
8. Save the image in 32-bit format.

Development Resources

There are many resources out there for developers, but here is a list of some of my favorites.

2D Art

Adobe Photoshop — This is by far the best paint package on the market. It has tons of flexibility and can accomplish just about anything you need to do in the 2D world. The URL is www.adobe.com.

3D Art

3ds max — Discreet makes this program, which is my personal favorite for 3D modeling and animation. You can use it to create in-game models, animation, and even cut-scenes. The URL is www.discreet.com.

LightWave — Newtek makes this product, which I have used for several years. It is another favorite among game developers, and I suggest you take a good look at it before buying another product. The URL is www.newtek.com.

Game Development Community

GameDev.net — This is my personal favorite of the game development web sites, as it has great forums and many articles. You can even find me there moderating the Multiplayer section. The URL is www.gamedev.net.

Flip Code — This is another one of my favorite game development web sites, as it has many great articles and a very active community. The URL is www.flipcode.com.

Hardware

ATI — ATI makes some of the best video cards around and their new Radeon series blows away the competition. If you are looking for a good card to practice shader code on, check them out at www.ati.com.

Nvidia — Nvidia makes great video cards as well. I don't personally have many of their cards, but they always receive good marks in reviews. The URL is www.nvidia.com.

Index

T

TCP/IP, 478
    program example, 484-489*
    vs. UDP, 479
technical documentation phase, 80-82
technology,
    cost of, 73-74
    types of, 72-73
technology trees, 71-74
testing phase, 87
text input, 344-354
    activating, 347-348*
    processing, 349-350*
    rendering, 351-354*
texture class, 299-301*
texture data, 294
    loading, 300-301*
    releasing, 301*
    setting, 174-175
textures, 503
    loading, 294-296*
    loading into vertex buffer, 196
    managing, 317-318*
The Seven Cities of Gold, 22
theme, 55
three-dimensional, *see* 3D
tile class,
    header, 122-124*
    implementation example, 127-128*
    implementing, 122-128*
tile picker toolbar, 371-372*
tile picker, map editor, 362
tile properties, 128-131
tile rendering, 131-154*
tiles, 93-94
    adding animated, 117
    creating, 98-100
    displaying, 100-107
    loading, 368*
    multi-layering, 107-117
    reasons for using, 95
    rendering, 368-369*
    storing, 118-128
    using, 95-97 107-117
TILEVERTEX structure, 134-135
timeGetTime() function, 143, 209
toolbar,
    creating for map editor, 371-372*
    modifying, 390*
    rendering tiles in, 372-375*

tracking,
    bug, 85-86
    source, 85-86
TranslateMessage() function, 51
translation, modifying, 426*
turn speed, 289
turn-based networked game, implementing,
    489-500*
tweening, 400
two-dimensional, *see* 2D

U

UDP, 478-479
    vs. TCP/IP, 479
unit class, 301-306*
unit templates, coding, 278-318*
unit testing, 86
unit vertex buffer, rendering, 320-322*
units,
    adding, 315-316*
    armor, 63-65
    cost, 62-63
    creating, 315-317*, 327-328*
    defensive capability, 63-65
    defining, 271-278
    firepower, 65-66
    loading, 327-328*
    naming, 271-272
    rendering, 318-327*
    setting base values for, 306*
    setting position of, 306*
    speed, 63, 275
    type of defense, 277-278
    type of offense, 276-277
    types of movement, 272-274
    updating, 324-327*
usability, interface, 168-169
Utopia, 3
    analysis of, 3-8

V

vChangeLayer() function, 389, 391-392*
vCheckInput() function, 204, 208-211*,
    224-227*, 346*, 366-368*
vCheckMouse() function, 375-376*, 394*
vCheckMusicStatus() function, 248, 254-256*
vCleanup() function, 248
vConnect() function, 496-497*
vCreateMinimap() function, 381-382*
vCreateToolbar() function, 371-372*, 390*
vDisplayTile() function, 102*

3D Graphics Programming With Direct3D

Examines the premier 3D graphics programming API on the Microsoft Windows platform. Create a complete 3D game engine with animated characters, light maps, special effects, and more.

3D Graphics Programming With OpenGL

An excellent course for newcomers to 3D graphics programming. Also includes advanced topics like shadows, curved surfaces, environment mapping, particle systems, and more.

Advanced BSP/PVS/CSG Techniques

A strong understanding of spatial partitioning algorithms is important for 3D graphics programmers. Learn how to leverage the BSP tree data structure for fast visibility processing and collision detection as well as powerful CSG algorithms.

Real-Time 3D Terrain Rendering

Take your 3D engine into the great outdoors. This course takes a serious look at popular terrain generation and rendering algorithms including ROAM, Rottger, and Lindstrom.

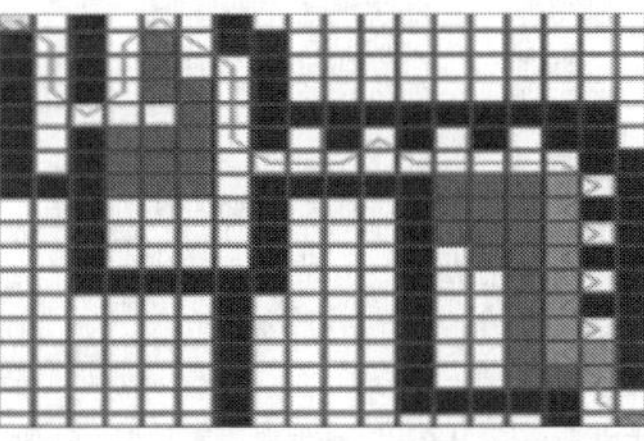

Path Finding Algorithms

Study the fundamental art of maneuver in 2D and 3D environments. Course covers the most popular academic algorithms in use today. Also includes an in-depth look at the venerable A*.

Network Game Programming With DirectPlay

Microsoft DirectPlay takes your games online quickly. Course includes coverage of basic networking, lobbies, matchmaking and session management.

MORE COURSES AVAILABLE AT

www.GameInstitute.com

ONLY 100 WILL BE CHOSEN FOR THE QUEST *of a* LIFETIME

Twice a year the challenge is raised — and **100** of the best are admitted to the Hart eCenter at SMU Digital Games Guildhall. The Guildhall is designed to train talented students to become immediately productive digital games developers. The program is just like the industry — intense, results oriented, and only for the dedicated few.

The Guildhall grants membership to those who complete the **18-month** certificate program, designed by industry professionals to train the next generation of game developers. High-profile industry leaders from top name development companies have designed the courses and take special interest in the Guildhall as teachers, mentors, and craft experts.

For more information and details on how to apply, contact David Najjab at **214-768-9903** or email **najjab@smu.edu**.

Check out the website at **guildhall.smu.edu**.

SMU will not discriminate in any employment practice, educational program, or educational activity on the basis of race, color, religion, national origin, sex, age, disability or veteran status.